Discover

Contents

France

Throughout this book, we use these icons to highlight special recommendations:

The Best…
Lists for everything from bars to wildlife – to make sure you don't miss out

Don't Miss
A must-see – don't go home until you've been there

Local experts reveal their top picks and secret highlights

Detour
Special places a little off the beaten track

If you like…
Lesser-known alternatives to world-famous attractions

These icons help you quickly identify reviews in the text and on the map:

Sights

Eating

Drinking

Sleeping

Information

This edition written and researched by

Nicola Williams

Oliver Berry, Stuart Butler, Jean-Bernard Carillet, Kerry Christiani, Gregor Clark, Emilie Filou, Catherine Le Nevez

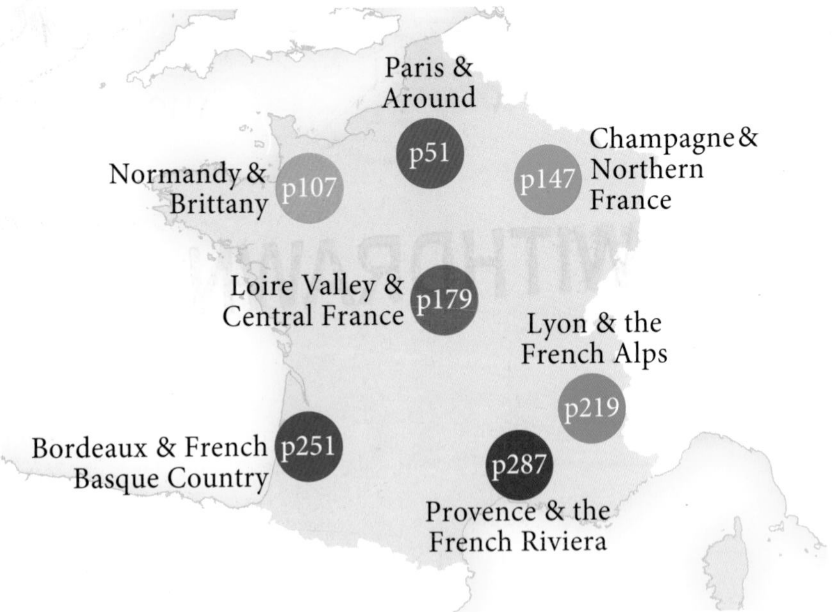

Paris & Around p51
Normandy & Brittany p107
Champagne & Northern France p147
Loire Valley & Central France p179
Lyon & the French Alps p219
Bordeaux & French Basque Country p251
Provence & the French Riviera p287

Paris & Around

- Musée du Louvre
- Versailles
- Cathédrale de Notre Dame de Paris
- Eiffel Tower
- Musée d'Orsay
- Cimetière du Père Lachaise
- The Seine

Normandy & Brittany

- Mont St-Michel
- Giverny
- Bayeux Tapestry
- Carnac Megaliths
- D-Day Sites
- St-Malo

Champagne & Northern France

- Wine Tasting in Champagne
- Louvre-Lens
- Centre Pompidou-Metz
- Reims & Amiens' Cathédrales Notre Dame
- Alsace
- WWI Sites

Lyon & the French Alps

- Action Chamonix!
- Basilique Notre Dame de Fourvière, Lyon
- Feasting in the French Gastronomic Capital
- Annecy
- Megève
- Gorges de l'Ardèche

Bordeaux & French Basque Country

- Bordeaux Wine Tasting
- Bordelaise Cuisine
- St-Émilion
- Dune du Pilat
- Cognac
- Basque Culture
- Île de Ré

Provence & the French Riviera

- Provençal Markets
- Riviera High Life
- Three Corniches
- Vieux Nice
- Pont du Gard
- Carcassonne
- Les Arènes de Nîmes

Contents

Plan Your Trip

On the Road

Contents

On the Road

Provence & the French Riviera 287

In Focus

Survival Guide

This Is France

Snooty, sexy, superior, chic, infuriating, arrogant, officious and inspired, France never fails to stir up passionate opinion. Even if you've never set foot on French soil, it's a place that already seems immediately familiar: every time you've gazed at an impressionist painting, watched a new-wave film or sipped on a glass of sparkling Champagne, you've been letting a little bit of Gallic flair seep into your soul.

France is all about art and seduction, Roman to Renaissance and beyond. Stroll the lily-clad gardens Monet painted and sip *un café* in a Parisian cafe where Sartre and Simone de Beauvoir met to philosophise. Imagine the glorious life of French kings at bourgeois Versailles or view tomorrow's art stars at new headline-grabbing museums up north. Ride magnificent mechanical elephants in an old Nantes shipyard. Listen to Marseille rap and Parisian jazz. Sense the subtle infusion of language, music and mythology in Brittany, brought by 5th-century Celtic invaders. Yes, French culture fills any stay in France with never-ending possibilities.

The country's feast of fine food and wine woos every traveller. But gastronomic France goes far deeper than Parisian bistro dining, long lunches outside, shopping for fruit and veg at the market and wolfing down croissants hot from the *boulangerie* (bakery). Taste wine with world-class sommeliers in Bordeaux; visit an Atlantic Coast oyster farm; drink sparkling Champagne in ancient cellars in Reims; tour a Provençal melon farm; harvest olives, peaches and cherries in the hot south; and realise that food is as much an *art de vivre* (art of living) for the French as an essential to survive.

Then there is the *terroir* (land) and its wonderful variety. Its rich and fabulous journey starts in northern France with chalky cliffs and sand dunes, continues south through to pea-green vineyards, and onwards to the bright blue sea of the French Riviera.

> "Sense the subtle infusion of language, music and mythology"

Gardens at Château de Versailles (p101)

France

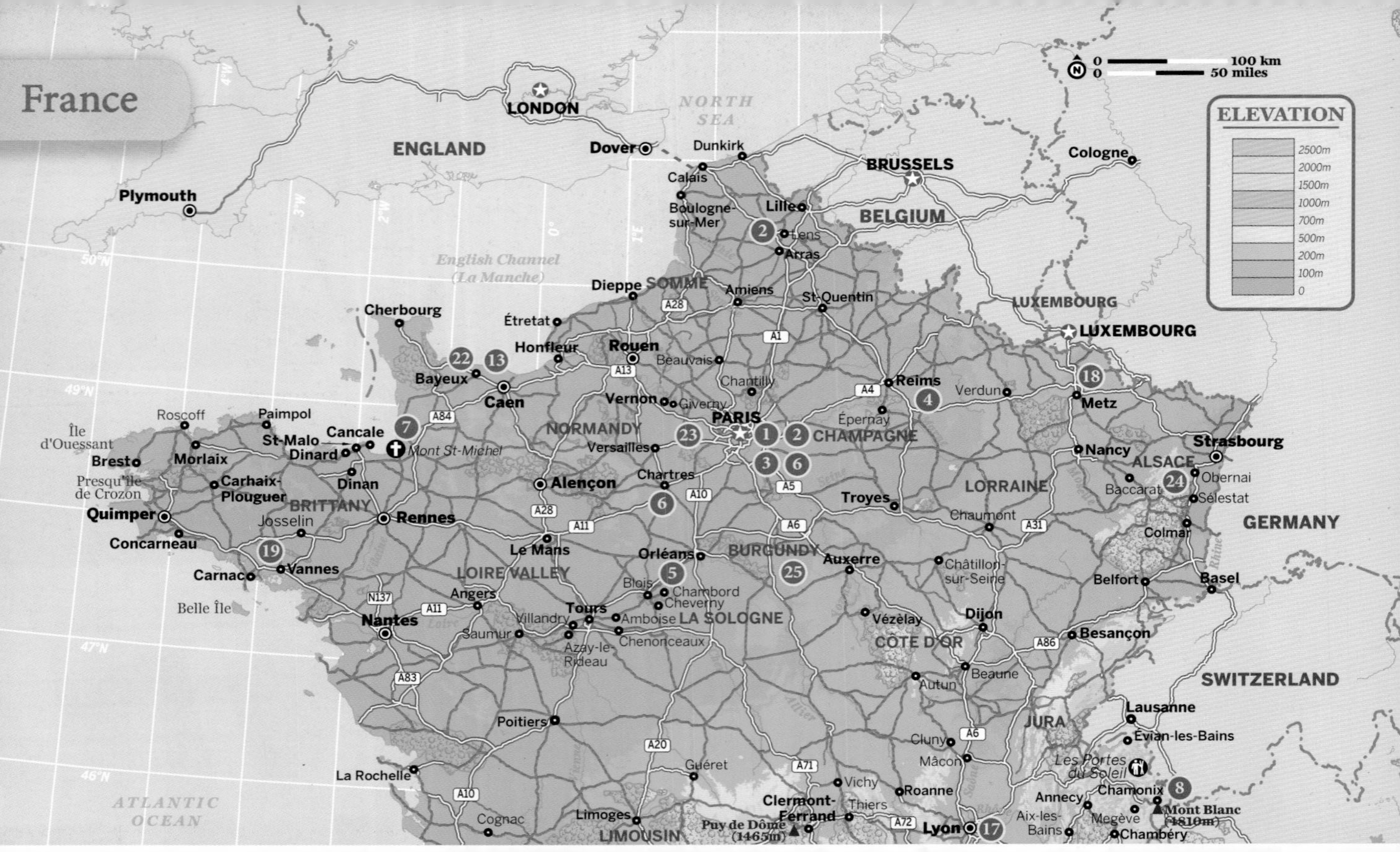
France
ELEVATION
2500m
2000m
1500m
1000m
700m
500m
200m
100m
0
0 100 km
0 50 miles
ENGLAND
LONDON
Plymouth
Dover
NORTH SEA
English Channel (La Manche)
ATLANTIC OCEAN
BELGIUM
BRUSSELS
LUXEMBOURG
GERMANY
SWITZERLAND
Cologne
Dunkirk
Calais
Boulogne-sur-Mer
Lille
Lens
Arras
Dieppe
SOMME
Amiens
St-Quentin
Cherbourg
Étretat
Honfleur
Rouen
Beauvais
Bayeux
Caen
Chantilly
Reims
Verdun
Metz
Vernon
Giverny
PARIS
Épernay
CHAMPAGNE
NORMANDY
Versailles
Roscoff
Paimpol
Île d'Ouessant
St-Malo
Cancale
Mont St-Michel
Dinard
Brest
Morlaix
Presqu'île de Crozon
Carhaix-Plouguer
Dinan
Alençon
Chartres
Troyes
LORRAINE
Nancy
ALSACE
Strasbourg
Obernai
Baccarat
Sélestat
Colmar
Quimper
BRITTANY
Rennes
Josselin
Concarneau
Le Mans
Chaumont
Orléans
BURGUNDY
Auxerre
Châtillon-sur-Seine
LOIRE VALLEY
Carnac
Vannes
Belle Île
Blois
Chambord
Cheverny
Belfort
Basel
Angers
Tours
Nantes
Villandry
Amboise
LA SOLOGNE
Vézelay
Dijon
Saumur
Chenonceaux
Azay-le-Rideau
CÔTE D'OR
Besançon
Beaune
Autun
JURA
Lausanne
Évian-les-Bains
Poitiers
Cluny
Mâcon
Les Portes du Soleil
La Rochelle
Guéret
Vichy
Roanne
Annecy
Chamonix
Clermont-Ferrand
Thiers
Mont Blanc (4810m)
Cognac
Limoges
Puy de Dôme (1465m)
Lyon
Aix-les-Bains
Megève
Chambéry
LIMOUSIN
Rhine
A1
A4
A5
A6
A10
A11
A13
A20
A28
A31
A71
A72
A83
A84
A86
N137
50°N
49°N
47°N
46°N
4°W
3°W
2°W
0°
1°E
1
2
3
4
5
6
7
8
13
17
18
19
22
23
24
25

25
Top Experiences
1 Eiffel Tower, Paris
2 Louvre & Louvre-Lens
3 Parisian Dining
4 Champagne
5 Loire Valley Châteaux
6 Ste-Chapelle & Chartres
7 Mont St-Michel
8 Skiing, Chamonix
9 Dune du Pilat
10 St-Tropez
11 Three Corniches, Nice
12 Carcassonne
13 D-Day Beaches, Normandy
14 Pont du Gard
15 Markets, Provence
16 Hilltop Villages, Provence & the Riviera
17 Bistros, Lyon
18 Centre Pompidou-Metz
19 Carnac Megaliths
20 Grotte de Lascaux
21 Wine Tasting, Bordeaux
22 Bayeux Tapestry
23 Monet's Garden, Giverny
24 Wine Route, Alsace
25 Route des Grands Crus, Burgundy
Bay of Biscay
Soulac-sur-Mer
Bordeaux
Arcachon
Dune du Pilat
DORDOGNE
Brantôme
Périgueux
Brive-la-Gaillarde
Les Eyzies-de-Tayac
Sarlat-la Canéda
Cahors
Figeac
Puy de Sancy (1885m)
Puy Mary (1787m)
Mont Lozère (1699m)
Ambert
St-Étienne
MASSIF CENTRAL
Le Puy-en-Velay
Vienne
Grenoble
Valence
FRENCH ALPS
Alpe d'Huez
Briançon
Sestriere
ITALY
Vaison-la-Romaine
Mont Ventoux (1909m)
Carpentras
Alès
Pont du Gard
Nîmes
Avignon
Fontaine de Vaucluse
Arles
Aix-en-Provence
PROVENCE
Marseille
Toulon
St-Tropez
Castellane
St-Paul de Vence
Cannes
Antibes
Nice
MONACO
See Enlargement
LIGURIAN SEA
CORSICA
MEDITERRANEAN SEA
LANGUEDOC
Montpellier
Albi
Toulouse
Carcassonne
Narbonne
ROUSILLON
Perpignan
Collioure
Puig Neulós
ANDORRA
ANDORRA LA VELLA
PYRENEES
Vignemale (3298m)
Monte Perdido (3355m)
Biarritz
Bayonne
St-Jean de Luz
St-Jean Pied de Port
Pau
Tarbes
Lourdes
Pamplona
SPAIN
Zaragoza
0 100 km
0 50 miles
Cap Corse
Bastia
Île Rousse
Calvi
Piana
Porto
Les Calanques
Cargèse
Corte
Aléria
CORSICA
Ajaccio
Propriano
Sartène
Porto-Vecchio
Bonifacio

25 France's Top Experiences

Eiffel Tower

Seven million people visit the Eiffel Tower (p66) annually but few disagree each visit is unique. From an evening ascent amid twinkling lights to lunch up the tower in the company of a staggering city panorama, there are 101 ways to 'do' it. Pedal beneath it, skip the lift and hike up, buy a crêpe from a stand here or a key ring from a street vendor, snap yourself in front of it, visit it at night or – our favourite – on the odd special occasion when all 324m of the tower glows a different colour.

1

THIERRY/GETTY IMAGES ©

2

Louvre & Louvre-Lens

Art aficionados have never had it so good. Linger over the lush collection of 35,000-odd pieces – think paintings, sculptures, artefacts, royal crown jewels, Sèvres porcelain and so forth – in Paris' palatial Musée du Louvre (p73). Then catch a TGV to Lens, a once-forgotten mining town 200km north of the capital that everyone suddenly knows about thanks to the opening of the equally magnificent Louvre-Lens (p173). Musée du Louvre (p73), Paris

Parisian Dining

Be it old-fashioned bistro, new millennium neo-bistro, Michelin-starred gastronomic meal or street-stall crêpe, dining in the City of Light is irresistible. And with innovative places hitting the scene, restless tastebuds have never been better served: try gourmet burgers at Blend (p87), tapas-style plates down a back alley at Au Passage (p89) or a cocktail and steak from the Beef Club (p85). Parisian dining is an essential part of the capital experience.

3

The Best... Boutique Sleeps

HIDDEN HOTEL
Packed with Parisian style, and tucked away just off the Champs-Élysées. (p72)

COUR DES LOGES
Four period townhouses in old Lyon; one superb boutique hotel. (p235)

L'HÔTEL PARTICULIER
Top spot in Arles, housed inside an 18th-century private mansion. (p265)

LA COLOMBE D'OR
Indulge in this former hang-out of Chagall, Matisse and Picasso. (p334)

The Best... Châteaux

VERSAILLES
France's grandest, busiest and most glorious château, just a quick skip from Paris. (p101)

CHAMBORD
François I's modest country retreat features a staircase rumoured to have been designed by Leonardo da Vinci. (p203)

CHENONCEAU
This château is the work of several aristocratic ladies, hence its nickname: the Château des Dames (Ladies' Château). (p198)

CHEVERNY
Impossibly elegant and still owned by its founding family. (p194)

BLOIS
No single castle better illustrates architectural history. (p195)

SAN ROSTRO/GETTY IMAGES ©

4 Champagne

Name-brand Champagne houses, such as Mumm (p159), Mercier (p162) and Moët & Chandon (p162) in the main towns of Reims and Épernay, are known the world over. But much of Champagne's best liquid gold is made by almost 5000 small-scale vignerons (winegrowers) in 320-odd villages. Dozens of Champagne *maisons* (houses) welcome visitors for a taste, tipple and shopping at producer prices, rendering the region's scenic driving routes the best way to taste fine bubbly amid rolling vineyards and gorgeous villages.

LOUISE HEUSINKVELD/GETTY IMAGES ©

5 Loire Valley Châteaux

If it's aristocratic pomp and architectural splendour you're after, this regal valley is the place to linger. The Loire is one of France's last *fleuves sauvages* (wild rivers) and its banks provide a 1000-year snapshot of French high society with its profusion of beautiful châteaux. If you're a romantic seeking the perfect fairy-tale castle, head for moat-ringed Azay-le-Rideau (p200) and Villandry (p210) with its dreamy gardens. Château de Chenonceau (p198)

6 Ste-Chapelle & Chartres

This is a top experience reserved strictly for sunny days. Be stunned and inspired by the stained glass in Paris' Ste-Chapelle (p67), one of Christendom's most beautiful places of worship. Then head out of town to Chartres, where you can't get bluer blue than the awesome stained-glass windows of Cathédrale Notre Dame de Chartres (p105). Ste-Chapelle (p67), Paris

COLSTRAVEL/ALAMY ©

GUY VANDERELST/GETTY IMAGES ©

7 Mont St-Michel

The dramatic play of tides on this abbey-island in Normandy is magical, mysterious and full of folklore. Said by Celtic mythology to be a sea tomb to which souls of the dead were sent, Mont St-Michel (p128) is rich in legend and history, keenly felt as you make your way barefoot across rippled sand to the stunning architectural ensemble. Hook up with a guide in nearby Genêts for a dramatic day hike across the bay.

Adrenalin Kick, Chamonix

Sure, 007 did it, but so can you: skiing the Vallée Blanche (p241) is a once-in-a-lifetime experience. You won't regret the €75-odd it costs to do the 20km off-piste descent from the spike of the Aiguille du Midi to mountaineering mecca Chamonix – every minute of the five hours it takes to get down will pump more adrenalin in your body than anything else you've ever done. Craving more? Hurl yourself down Europe's longest black run, La Sarenne, at Alpe d'Huez.

8

LUCAS KANE/GETTY IMAGES ©

The Best... Cathedrals

CATHÉDRALE DE NOTRE DAME, PARIS
The cathedral to end all cathedrals; sadly, no hunchbacks in sight when we visited. (p81)

CATHÉDRALE NOTRE DAME, CHARTRES
If stained glass is your thing, you won't find any finer than in the luminous windows of Chartres' cathedral. (p105)

CATHÉDRALE NOTRE DAME, REIMS
Climb the cathedral tower for a bird's-eye view of this Champagne city. (p163)

CATHÉDRALE NOTRE DAME, AMIENS
Marvel at the largest Gothic cathedral in France. (p174)

CATHÉDRALE ST-ÉTIENNE, METZ
This lacy beauty is famous for its intricate spire. (p171)

Dune du Pilat

The Dune du Pilat (p273) is a 'mountain' that just has to be climbed. Not only is the coastal panorama from the top of Europe's largest sand dune a stunner – it takes in the Banc d'Arguin bird reserve and Cap Ferret across the bay – but the nearby beaches have some of the Atlantic Coast's best surf. Cycle here from Arcachon and top off the heady trip with a dozen oysters, shucked before your very eyes and accompanied by *crepinettes* (local sausages).

9

ERIC ROBERT/SYGMA/CORBIS ©

The Best... Iconic Beaches

PLAGE DE L'ÉCLUSE
Old-fashioned bathing tents bring an air of the belle époque to this exclusive Breton beach in Dinard. (p135)

PROMENADE DES ANGLAIS
Join the sun-worshippers on Nice's pebbly beach. (p325)

BD DE LA CROISETTE
Private beaches full of rich and famous guests characterise Cannes' cinematic seafront. (p335)

PLAGE DE PAMPELONNE
Pout like Bardot in the classic Riviera resort at St-Tropez. (p339)

GRANDE PLAGE & PLAGE MIRIMAR
Biarritz's beaches have been in vogue since the Second Empire. (p275)

St-Tropez

No seaside town in France is more fabled than the old fishing port of St-Tropez, where millionaire yachts jostle for space at the Vieux Port with peddling street artists and tourists by the million. Arrive early to catch the best of St-Tropez' atmospheric Place des Lices (p338) market, breakfast at La Tarte Tropézienne (p340), gorge on fine art at the Musée de l'Annonciade (p339), frolic away the afternoon over lunch and hobnob-bing, or flop on the sand at achingly hip Plage de Pampelonne (p339). Brigitte Bardot, eat your heart out.

11 Three Corniches, Nice

It's impossible to drive this dramatic trio of coastal roads (p343), each one higher and with more hairpin bends than the next, without conjuring up cinematic im-ages of Grace Kelly, Hitchcock, the glitz of Monaco high life, and the glamour of the royal family – all while absorbing big view after big view of sweeping blue sea fringing Europe's most mythical coastline. To make a perfect day out of it, shop for a picnic at the cours Saleya (p331) morning market before leaving Nice. Looking towards Monaco (p345) from Moyenne Corniche (p343)

12 Carcassonne at Dusk

That first glimpse of La Cité's sturdy, stone, witch's-hat turrets above Carcassonne (p322) in the Languedoc is enough to make your hair stand on end. To properly savour this fairy-tale walled city, linger at dusk after the crowds have left, when the old town belongs to its 100 or so inhabitants and the few visitors staying at the handful of lovely hotels within its ramparts. Don't forget to look back when you leave to view the old city, beautifully illuminated, glowing in the warm night.

DENNIS K. JOHNSON/GETTY IMAGES ©

13 D-Day Beaches, Normandy

The broad stretches of sand are quiet now, but on 6 June 1944 the beaches of northern Normandy (p122) were a cacophony of gunfire and explosions, the bodies of Allied soldiers lying in the sand as their comrades charged inland. Just up the hill from Omaha Beach, rows of gravestones at the Normandy American Cemetery & Memorial (p126) bear testimony to the price paid for France's liberation from Nazi tyranny. US military cemetery (p125), Omaha Beach

Pont du Gard

This Unesco World Heritage Site (p324) near Nîmes in southern France is gargantuan: 35 arches straddle the Roman aqueduct's 275m-long upper tier, containing a watercourse that was designed to carry 20,000 cu metres of water per day. View it from afloat a canoe on the River Gard or pay extra to jig across its top tier. Oh, and don't forget your swimming gear for a spot of post-Pont daredevil diving and high jumping from the rocks nearby – a plunge that will entice the most reluctant of young historians.

14

The Best... Medieval Villages

SARLAT-LA-CANEDA
Golden and gorgeous, the Dordogne's gem boasts some of France's most beautiful medieval architecture. (p211)

CARCASSONNE
Be bewitched by the witch's-hat turrets of this Languedoc beauty. (p322)

ST ÉMILION
Combine wine tasting with medieval enchantment in this Unesco-listed village. (p270)

ST-PAUL DE VENCE
Art history sits alongside historic architecture in this hilltop village on the French Riviera. (p333)

DINAN
Wander the cobbled streets and sturdy ramparts of one of Brittany's oldest villages. (p138)

The Best... Foodie Cities

PARIS

Bursting with buzzy bars, iconic bistros, historic cafes and Michelin-starred marvels. (p51)

LYON

Famous for its pig-centric cuisine, and often touted as France's top foodie town. (p230)

MARSEILLE

Tuck into authentic bouillabaisse (fish stew) in Marseille's atmospheric old port (p305).

STRASBOURG

Savour sauerkraut, sausages and lots of beer in an Alsatian *winstub* (wine room). (p165)

DIJON

Dijon mustard and some serious Burgundy reds for wine lovers. (p202)

Provençal Markets

No region is more of a market-must than this one. Be it fresh fish by the port in seafaring Marseille (p300), early summer's strings of pink garlic, melons from Cavaillon all summer long or wintertime's earthy 'black diamond' truffles, Provence (p300) thrives on a bounty of fresh produce – grown locally and piled high each morning at the market. While you're here, stock up on dried herbs, green and black olives marinated a dozen different ways, courgette flowers and oils.

Hilltop Villages, Provence & the Riviera

16

Impossibly perched on a rocky peak above the Mediterranean, gloriously lost in back country, fortified or château-topped… southern France's portfolio of *villages perchés* (p335) is vast and impressive, and calls for go-slow touring – on foot, by bicycle or car. Most villages are medieval, built from golden stone with cobbled lanes, flower-filled alleys and hidden squares silent but for the glug of a fountain.

View of Cote d'Azur from Èze (p343)

JEAN-PIERRE LESCOURRET/CORBIS ©

17

Lyonnais Bouchons

The checked tablecloths and decades-old bistro decor could be anywhere in France. It's the local cuisine that makes *bouchons* (small bistros) in Lyon (p237) unique, plus the culinary customs, such as totting up the bill on the paper tablecloth, or serving wine in a glass bottle wrapped with an elastic band to stop drips. Various piggy parts drive Lyonnais cuisine, but have faith – this city is said to be the gastronomic capital of France. Dine and decide.

Centre Pompidou-Metz

Bright white by day, all aglow after dark, this is the star of the northern France art scene (p171). A provincial cousin to the well-known Centre Pompidou in Paris, this modern art museum was designed by a world-class, Japanese-French duo of architects and is as much an architectural gem as an exhibition powerhouse, easily on par with Bilbao's Guggenheim and London's Tate. Part of the experience is a designer lunch, aka edible art on a plate, at the museum's La Voile Blanche. Centre Pompidou-Metz, designed by Shigeru Ban & Jean de Gastines

18

The Best... Viewpoints

EIFFEL TOWER
The capital's 'metal asparagus' needs no introduction – it's just a must-visit. (p66)

BASILIQUE DU SACRÉ-CŒUR, PARIS
This Montmartre landmark gives a different perspective on the capital. (p63)

AIGUILLE DU MIDI, CHAMONIX
If you can handle the height (3842m), unforgettable summit views of the French, Swiss and Italian Alps await. (p244)

FOURVIÈRE, LYON
The essential viewpoint for admiring Lyon's architecture. (p236)

PIC DU JER, LOURDES
Panoramic views of Lourdes and the central Pyrenees. (p284)

Carnac Megaliths

Pedalling past fields dotted with the world's greatest concentration of megaliths (p143) gives a poignant reminder of Brittany's ancient human inhabitants. No one knows for sure what inspired these gigantic menhirs, dolmens, cromlechs, tumuli and cairns to be built. A sun god? A phallic fertility cult? It's a mystery worth acquainting yourself with during a visit to northern France. One kilometre north of Carnac, the Alignements du Ménec, touting a mind-boggling 1099 stones, is the area's largest menhir field.

The Best... Nature Parks

PARC NATUREL RÉGIONAL D'ARMORIQUE
One of the most beautiful coastal spots in Brittany, a paradise for hikers and bikers. (p139)

PARC NACIONAL DES ÉCRINS
Miles of high-altitude trails make this a hiker's paradise. (p248)

PARC NACIONAL DE LA VANOIS
France's oldest national park is as close as you'll get to untouched wilderness. (p248)

PARC NATIONAL DES CALANQUES
Clifftop paths wind through France's newest national park. (p310)

SUDRES JEAN DANIEL/HEMIS/ALAMY ©

20 Grotte de Lascaux

Europe's oldest prehistoric paintings are hidden deep in the limestone caves of the Vézère Valley. None are more breathtaking than those inside the Grotte de Lascaux (p216), decorated with the most sophisticated cave art ever discovered (in 1940 by four lads out looking for their dog!), including a mural of a bull measuring over 5.5m. The original cave is closed to prevent irreparable damage to the priceless paintings, but key sections have been recreated – to astonishing effect – in another cave nearby.

Bordeaux Wine Tasting

The Bordeaux region's wine is famous worldwide; a visit to its vineyards is a must for wine lovers. Quintessential wine town St-Émilion tickles palates with robust reds, while the Médoc is packed with grand names, such as Mouton Rothschild, Latour and Lafite Rothschild. Complete your wine-tasting tour with a course at École du Vin (p268) and an unforgettable meal with some AOC Bordeaux at La Tupina (p265).

Bayeux Tapestry

Stretching for a mind-boggling 68.3m, the world's most celebrated tapestry (p124) is among France's most treasured historical artefacts. The work of art illustrates William the Conqueror's invasion of England in 1066. It was thought to have been commissioned in England by the Bishop Odo of Bayeux, William's half-brother, for the opening of Bayeux cathedral in 1077, although some argue it was produced in France.

Monet's Garden, Giverny

Claude Monet purchased this idyllic Norman country house (p123) in 1883 and spent the next 30-odd years redesigning its gardens and grounds, adding trees, greenhouses, ornamental ponds and – most famously – a graceful Japanese bridge that any art lover will feel they have seen before. They have – on canvas. Giverny's grounds provided the inspiration for some of Monet's most famous works, most notably his iconic *Nymphéas* (Water Lily) series. No prizes for guessing where the lily-coated pond can be found.

23

The Best... Island Escapes

ÎLE DE LA CITÉ
This little island in the heart of Paris is a refuge from the modern metropolis. (p67)

BELLE ÎLE
Brittany's largest island is as beautiful as its name suggests. (p137)

ÎLES DE LÉRINS
These tiny islands provide the perfect getaway from Cannes' summer bustle. (p341)

ÎLES D'HYÈRES
A trio of Mediterranean islands fringed by sand, coastal paths and crystal-clear sea. (p342)

ÎLE D'OUESSANT
Explore shipwrecks on this wild, windswept island 32km off the Breton coastline. (p137)

Alsatian Wine Route

This is one of France's most popular drives – and for good reason. Motoring in this far northeast corner of France (p165) takes you through a kaleidoscope of lush green vines, perched castles and gentle mist-covered mountains. The only pit stops en route are half-timbered villages and roadside wine cellars, where fruity Alsace vintages can be swirled, tasted and bought. To be truly wooed, drive the Route des Vins d'Alsace in autumn, when vines are heavy with grapes waiting to be harvested and colours are at their vibrant best.

24

The Best... Shopping

PARIS
From flea markets to haute couture, Paris' shops have it all. (p94)

CHAMPAGNE
Épernay and Reims are stocked with cellars; pick up bottles of bubbly direct from the source. (p158)

NICE
Don't miss the Riviera's largest outdoor market, on the cours Saleya. (p325)

QUIMPER
Buy colourful *faïence* (earthenware) in Finistère's half-timbered capital. (p140)

BORDEAUX
Tour the vineyards and take home some top vintages. (p264)

STRASBOURG
Pick up handmade chocolates, sweets and gingerbread in this stately northern city. (p165)

25

Route des Grands Crus, Burgundy

No route is more sublime to saunter along at a snail's pace than this famous Burgundy wine trail (p185). Narrow lanes wend their way from main towns Beaune and Dijon to countryside villages safeguarded by steeple-topped churches and château turrets peeping down between trees. Vines cascade down the slopes to picture-postcard hamlets where generations of vintners open their century-old cellars to those keen to taste and buy. Lovers of fine wine and the slow-paced good life: this is your heaven.

France's Top Itineraries

Paris to Chartres
Capital Trips

Five days should be just enough time to delve into the delights of the City of Lights and add on a few days' sightseeing beyond the capital, including visits to Versailles, Monet's gardens at Giverny and the medieval city of Chartres.

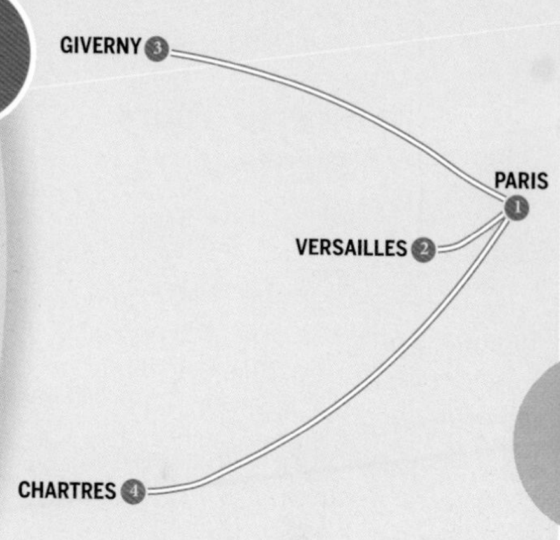

1 Paris (p51)

Every French adventure has to begin in Paris. With a couple of days you can squeeze in the **Eiffel Tower**, **Notre Dame** and the **Louvre**, plus a **river cruise** along the Seine and a stroll around **Montmartre**. Base yourself on the Left Bank to be near the main sights or the Marais on the Right Bank to be near hip dining and nightlife.

PARIS ➔ VERSAILLES

30 minutes From Pont de Sèvres in the 15e. **30 minutes** From Paris' Left Bank stations on the RER Line C5.

Versailles (p100)

Day three takes you to Louis XIV's country retreat at **Versailles**, claimed as the grandest château of them all. Guided tours take in the château's main rooms, including the **royal apartments** and the **Hall of Mirrors**.

PARIS ➔ GIVERNY

50 minutes From Paris St-Lazare, followed by a quick shuttle-bus trip. **One hour** Along A13 and N13; follow signs to Vernon.

Giverny (p123)

On day four, catch the train from Paris to **Claude Monet's house and gardens** in Giverny. It's where the artist painted some of his most famous canvases. Don't miss the photo opp on the **Japanese bridge**. At the nearby **Musée des Impressionismes**, the work of other impressionists takes centre stage.

PARIS ➔ CHARTRES

One to 1¼ hours From Paris Montparnasse. **1¼ hours** Along A10 and A11 motorways.

Chartres (p105)

On the last day, bid farewell to Paris and head to medieval Chartres. The city's ancient streets and squares are riddled with charm, but it is the **Cathédrale Notre Dame** – France's best-preserved medieval basilica – that takes your breath away. The cathedral's 172 stained-glass windows, almost all dating to the 13th century, are world-renowned.

Château de Versailles (p101)

Blois to Tours Architectural Elegance

France is synonymous with fabulous châteaux, and they don't get more French-fabulous than those lacing the Loire Valley. This trip from Blois follows the course of the Loire River via the elegant, history-rich city of Tours.

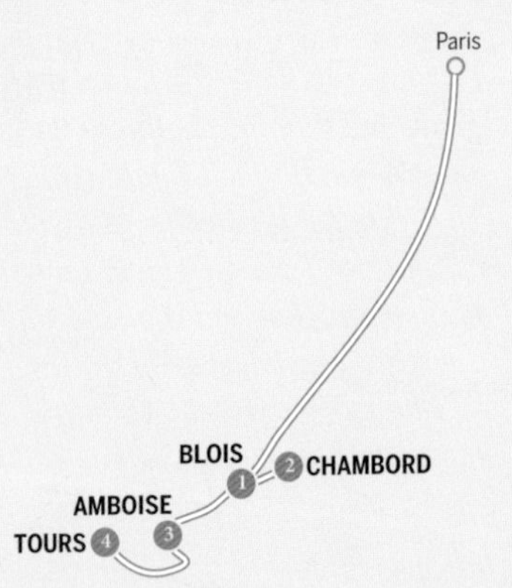

1 Blois (p191)

An easy two-hour train trip from Paris' Gare d'Austerlitz or Montparnasse (or two hours along the A10 motorway) brings you to Blois, a deeply historic town looming large on a rocky escarpment on the northern bank of the majestic Loire River. Once the seat of power for the French monarchy, the town's **château** is a glorious romp through French architectural history. Built as a showpiece rather than a defensive fortress, it showcases four different periods of architecture – from Gothic to classical – and its lavish main hall featured in Luc Besson's 1999 biopic of Joan of Arc. Don't miss a post-château meander around the warren of an old town wrapped around Blois' 17th-century cathedral, followed by a gastronomic feast – alfresco in summer – at **L'Orangerie**.

BLOIS ➔ CHAMBORD

40 minutes **20 minutes** Along the D33.

2 Chambord (p203)

Devote day two to the Loire's most magnificent **castle**, Chambord. It was built by François I as a country retreat, but he hardly ever stayed there. A famous double-helix staircase spirals up to the rooftop, which gives wonderful views over the château's landscaped park. True château fiends absolutely must squeeze in a detour to **Cheverny**, famed above all else for its late-afternoon **Soupe de Chiens** (feeding of the hunting dogs). An easy drive links the twinset and both are included in organised minibus trips from Blois.

BLOIS ➔ AMBOISE

20 minutes. **30 minutes** Along the N152.

Amboise (p199)

From Blois, head west to Amboise, another enchanting royal town where you can visit another impressive **royal château** and unexpected treat, **Clos Lucé**. It's the retirement pad where Leonardo da Vinci beavered away on wacky creations during his later years; the house museum is packed with life-size prototypes of da Vinci's inventions, and many are dotted about the particularly handsome grounds.

AMBOISE ➔ TOURS

35 minutes. **30 minutes** Along the N152 or quieter D751.

Tours (p196)

The final day takes you via the lovely **Château de Chenonceau** – an absolutely unmissable and appropriately swoonworthy address more photographed than any other château – en route to Tours, the Loire Valley's main city. Its twin-towered Gothic **cathedral** dominates the skyline, but you can also visit several museums, including the elegant, art-filled **Musée des Beaux-Arts**.

Château de Chambord (p203)
PHOTOGRAPHER: SHAUN EGAN/GETTY IMAGES ©

Mont St-Michel to Avignon
Unesco Treasures

This trip takes in France's biggest, finest, oldest and loveliest; every stop is a Unesco World Heritage Site, making the trip a must for culture vultures and history buffs. From otherworldly abbeys to iconic cathedrals and Roman ruins, this adventure has it all.

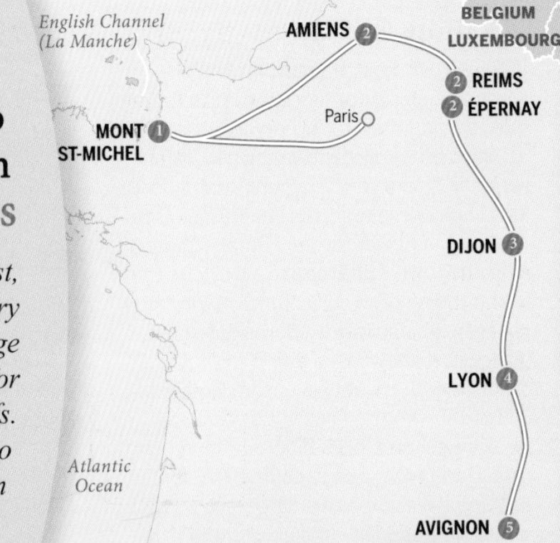

1 Mont St-Michel (p128)

France's iconic island abbey, Mont St-Michel, is a three-hour car trip from Paris (along the N13 and A84) or 3½ hours by train (TGV from Paris to Rennes, then a regional train to Pontorson and bus 6 to Mont St-Michel). Mont St-Michel is best seen at dawn, dusk or after dark when it's lit up like a Roman candle. Walk around the mount before delving in or hook up with a guide in nearby **Genêts** for a bare-footed walk across the sands. Break the journey to Champagne with a stop in **Bayeux** to admire the world's most celebrated embroidery, which vividly recounts the story of the Norman conquest of England in 1066.

MONT ST-MICHEL ➜ AMIENS

Three hours Along the A84, A132, A29 and A16 motorways. **Three hours** From Pontorson via Rennes to Paris Montparnasse, then Paris Gare du Nord to Amiens.

2 Champagne (p158)

Is there possibly any more sparkling region in France to stop in transit than Champagne in northeastern France? Tasting the bubbly tipple in name-brand Champagne houses in **Reims** and **Épernay** aside, there is also the remarkable Gothic Unesco World Heritage twinset of **Reims** and **Amiens'** cathedrals. Awe-inspiring is an understatement.

AMIENS ➜ DIJON

Five hours Along the A29, A26, A4, A5 and A31. **3-¾ hours** From Amiens to Paris Gare de Nord, then from Paris Gare de Lyon to Dijon.

3 Dijon (p202)

Burgundy has two wonderful World Heritage Sites around an hour's drive from **Dijon:** the hilltop basilica of **Vézelay** and the Cistercian abbey of **Fontenay**. The monks are long gone, but both continue to inspire quiet contemplation.

DIJON ➜ LYON

2¼ hours Along the A31 and A6. **Two hours**.

4 Lyon (p230)

Lyon's architectural heritage encompasses everything from Roman ruins to Renaissance town houses, and most of the city has been designated a World Heritage Site. The monuments and museums are a major draw, while the city's culinary reputation ensures its busy *bouchons* (small bistros) buzz round the clock.

LYON ➜ AVIGNON

2¼ hours Along the A7. **One hour** Via the TGV.

5 Avignon (p315)

The beautiful walled city of Avignon safeguards an impressive **papal palace** and a **medieval bridge**. Further afield, Provence is littered with Gallo-Roman monuments including **Pont du Gard**, the world's largest and best-preserved Roman aqueduct, easily reached by car from Avignon.

Bridge over Saône River, Lyon (p230)

Nice to Biarritz
Coast to Coast

This tour begins on the big blue Mediterranean before crossing the Pyrenees to the Atlantic Coast. En route you'll encounter ritzy cities, quaint villages and lofty mountains – not to mention a wealth of unforgettable views.

1 Nice (p325)

Start the trip in the Côte d'Azur's classic beach town, Nice. Kick back along the **Promenade des Anglais**, shop at the **cours Saleya market** and explore the backstreets of **Vieux Nice**. With an extra day, you could visit the city's **art museums**, motor out of town along a trio of jaw-dropping coastal **corniches**, or ride a train along the coast to moneyed **Monaco**.

NICE → CANNES

30 minutes. **45 minutes** Along the coastal N98.

2 Cannes (p334)

After Nice, head west to star-spangled **Cannes**. Spot famous faces along **bd de la Croisette**, cruise out to the idyllic **Îles de Lérins**, then spin along the Mediterranean coastline for a day in chi-chi **St-Tropez**.

CANNES → MARSEILLE

Two hours Along the A8 motorway, longer along the coastal N98. **Two hours**.

3 Marseille (p300)

Rough-and-ready Marseille encapsulates the fiery spirit of the French south. Sample **bouillabaisse** by the harbour, climb to the **basilica** and cruise to the island fortress of the **Château d'If**. An optional and oh-so-elegant detour might take in **Aix-en-Provence**, where Cézanne painted his most famous canvases.

MARSEILLE → CARCASSONNE

3½ hours Along the coastal N98. **Three hours**.

View over the Mediterranean towards Nice (p325)

4 Carcassonne (p322)

A three-hour cruise along the Mediterranean takes you to Carcassonne, one of the Languedoc's most beautiful medieval towns. Nearby **Narbonne** boasts a wonderful street market where you can stock up on local produce and soak up the southern atmosphere.

CARCASSONNE → LOURDES

You'll need your own wheels to explore the Pyrenees.

5 Lourdes (p282)

West of Carcassonne, the snowcapped peaks of the **Pyrenees** zig-zag along the Franco-Spanish border. Less visited than the Alps, these wild mountains offer fantastic walking and wildlife-spotting, and plunge people into the heart of one of the world's most visited pilgrimage sites, the holy city of **Lourdes**.

LOURDES → BIARRITZ

2¾ hours **1¾ hours** From Lourdes along the A68, D1 and D810.

6 Biarritz (p275)

Switch the saw-tooth peaks of the Pyrenees for glitzy beach-babe Biarritz. With its belle époque architecture and gorgeous bays, this coastal city is ideal for further forays into **French Basque Country**: the ancient pilgrims' village of **St-Jean Pied de Port** and the riverside town of **Bayonne** are on your doorstep.

Paris to Paris
The Grand Tour

This is the big one: a whistle-stop circular adventure around France, taking in as many must-see sights as possible. It's doable in two weeks if you pack things in, but we've suggested optional side-trips for each area if your timetable allows a bit more flexibility.

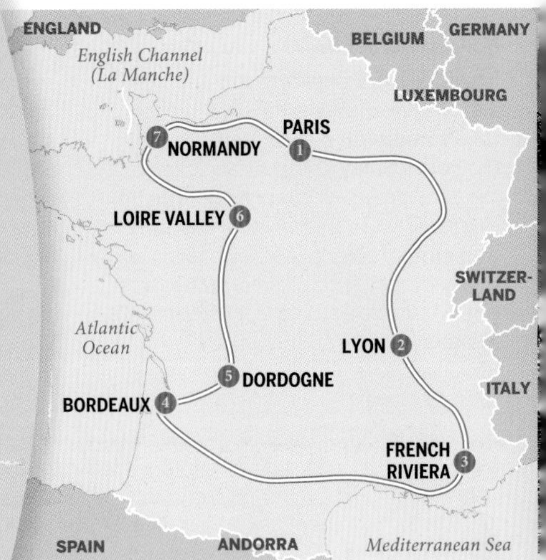

Paris (p51)

Kick off with at least two days in the French capital, ticking off as many sights, museums and restaurants as you can. Add in another couple of days for day trips to either **Château de Versailles**, the cathedral city of **Chartres**, or Champagne capital **Reims**.

PARIS ➔ LYON

Two hours From Paris Gare de Lyon aboard a TGV. **About five hours** Along the A6 motorway.

Lyon (p230)

From Paris, it's a speedy TGV trip to the lovely Roman city of Lyon. Spend a day exploring the sights, monuments and museums of this elegant cultural hub, followed by an evening meal in a traditional Lyonnais *bouchon*. Ideally, you should allow some time to explore the French Alps – base yourself in the shade of Mont Blanc in **Chamonix**, or lakeside in **Annecy** – but if you're pushed for time, skip the mountains and head directly to the French Riviera.

LYON ➔ NICE

Four to five hours On the TGV. **Less than one hour**.

French Riviera (p325)

You could soak up weeks lounging along the Côte d'Azur, but for this trip we've allowed two days: one for the lively city of **Nice**, and another for the playground principality of **Monaco**. En route you'll have the chance to experience France's most dazzling drive, along the coastal **corniches**. Big blue views aside, keep your eyes firmly on the (steep, hairpin-laced) road.

NICE ➔ BORDEAUX

Two hours. **Eight hours** Via direct TGV, longer if changes are required.

Bordeaux (p264)

Mark the start of week two with a cross-country flight to the capital of French winemaking, **Bordeaux**. It's a beautiful city in its own right, but for most people it's Bordeaux's viticultural heritage that's

Place de la Liberté, Sarlat-la-Canéda (p211)
PHOTOGRAPHER: TIBOR BOGNAR/GETTY IMAGES ©

the main draw. Tailored minibus trips are ideal if you're short on time: try to choose one that includes visits to the vineyards of the **Médoc** and the hilltop village of **St-Émilion**.

BORDEAUX ➔ SARLAT-LA-CANÉDA

2¾ hours. 2¼ hours Along regional roads.

⑤ The Dordogne (p211)

Meander inland through the rolling countryside of the **Dordogne** en route to one of France's loveliest medieval towns, **Sarlat-la-Canéda** (the Saturday market here is a real biggie). Devote at least a day to visiting the amazing prehistoric artworks of the world-renowned **Grotte de Lascaux** and the other caves of the **Vézère Valley**.

SARLAT-LA-CANÉDA ➔ TOURS

Four hours. Six hours Usually with changes at Souillac and Limoges.

⑥ The Loire Valley (p190)

From Bordeaux, it's on to the Loire Valley and its fairytale **châteaux**. Base yourself in the cafe-busy city of **Tours**, and visit da Vinci's house in **Amboise**, the graceful palace of **Chenonceau** and François I's lavish hunting lodge, **Chambord**.

TOURS ➔ BAYEUX

3¼ hours. 5 hours Change at Caen

⑦ Normandy (p118)

From the Loire, travel north via the abbey of **Mont St-Michel** en route to Bayeux, which makes an ideal base for tracing the story of two landmark invasions. William the Conqueror's raid on England in 1066 is dramatically recounted in the **Bayeux Tapestry**, while **Normandy's beaches** will be forever linked with the historic events of 6 June 1944 – known to the French as Jour-J, and to the rest of the world as D-Day. From Bayeux, it's a short hop back to the journey's end in **Paris**.

France Month by Month

Top Events

- **Festival d'Avignon,** July
- **Fête du Citron,** February
- **Fête des Lumières,** December
- **Cannes Film Festival,** May
- **Monaco Grand Prix,** May

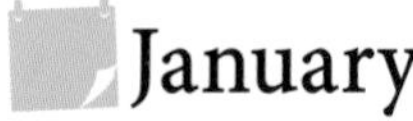

January

Vive le Ski!

Grab your skis, hit the slopes. Resorts in the Alps, Pyrenees and Jura open mid- to late December, but January is the start of the French ski season in earnest. Whether a purpose-built station or lost Alpine village, there's a resort to match every mood and moment.

Hunting Black Diamonds

No culinary product is more aromatic or decadent than black truffles. Hunt them in the Dordogne and Provence – the season runs late December to March, but January is the prime month.

February

Nice Carnival

Nice makes the most of its mild climate with this crazy Lenten carnival (www.nicecarnaval.com). As well as parade and costume shenanigans, merrymakers pelt each other with blooms during the legendary flower battles. Dunkirk in northern France is another French city to celebrate Mardi Gras with gusto.

Citrus Celebrations

It's no surprise that Menton on the French Riviera was once Europe's biggest lemon producer, given its exotic Fête du Citron (Lemon Festival, www.feteducitron.com). These days it has to ship in a zillion lemons from Spain to sculpt into gargantuan carnival characters.

Left: Tour de France

March

Féria Pascale

No fest sets passions in France's hot south blazing more than Féria de Pâques (www.feriaarles.com), held at Easter in Arles to open the bullfighting season. Four days of street dancing, music, concerts alfresco and bullfighting is what this exuberant event is all about. Not all bulls die.

April

Counting Sheep

During the Fête de la Transhumance, an ancient festival in late April or May, shepherds walk their flocks of sheep up to lush green summer pastures; St-Rémy de Provence's fest is among the best known. Or head to villages in the Pyrenees and Massif Central to witness this transit.

May

May Day

No one works on 1 May, a national holiday that incites summer buzz with its *muguets* (lilies of the valley) sold at roadside stalls and given to friends for good luck. In Arles, Camargue cowboys show off their bull-herding and equestrian skills at the Fête des Gardians.

Pèlerinage des Gitans

Roma flock to the Camargue on 24 and 25 May and again in October for a flamboyant fiesta of street music, dancing and dipping their toes in the sea (www.gitans.fr).

Starring at Cannes

In mid-May, film stars and celebrities walk the red carpet at Cannes, Europe's biggest cinema extravaganza (www.festival-cannes.com).

Monaco Grand Prix

How fitting that Formula One's most glamorous people rip around the streets of one of the world's most glam countries at the Monaco Grand Prix (www.grand-prix-monaco.com).

June

Fête de la Musique

Orchestras, crooners, buskers and bands fill streets with free music during France's vibrant nationwide celebration of music on 21 June (www.fetedelamusique.culture.fr).

Paris Jazz Festival

No festival better evokes the brilliance of Paris' interwar jazz age than this annual fest in the Parc de Floral (http://parisjazzfestival.paris.fr).

July

Tour de France

The world's most prestigious cycling race ends on av des Champs-Élysées in Paris on the third or fourth Sunday of July, but you can catch it for three weeks before all over France – the route changes each year but the French Alps are a hot spot (www.letour.fr).

Bastille Day

Join the French in celebrating the storming of the Bastille on 14 July 1789 – countrywide there are firework displays, balls, processions, parades and lots of hoo-ha all round.

Festival d'Avignon

Rouse your inner thespian with Avignon's legendary performing-arts festival (www.festival-avignon.com). Street acts in its fringe fest are as inspired as those on official stages.

 **Jazz à Juan**

Jive to jazz cats in Juan-les-Pins at this mythical Riviera music fest, which has been around for 50-odd years. Jazz à Juan (www.jazzajuan.fr) commands tickets, but the fringe 'Off' part of the music festival does not.

 **Festival de Cornouaille**

Traditional Celtic music takes over the Breton town of Quimper during this inspiring summer festival in late July (www.festival-cornouaille.com).

August

 **Celts Unite!**

Celtic culture is the focus of the Festival Interceltique de Lorient (www.festival-interceltique.com), when hundreds of thousands of Celts from Brittany and abroad flock to Lorient to celebrate just that.

 **Proud to be Breton**

The Fêtes d'Arvor is a passionate celebration of Breton culture. Think street parades, concerts and dozens of authentic *festoù-noz* (night festivals) spilling across the half-timbered, cobbled Vannes (www.fetes-arvor.org, in French).

September

 **The Rutting Season**

Nothing beats getting up at dawn to watch mating stags, boar and red deer at play. Observatory towers are hidden in woods around Château de Chambord (p203), but when a valley like the Loire is so choc-a-bloc with Renaissance hunting pads, who cares which one?

 **Braderie de Lille**

The mountains of empty mussel shells engulfing the streets after three days of mussel-munching have to be seen to be believed. Then there's the real reason for visiting Lille on the first weekend in September – its huge flea market is Europe's largest.

October

Nuit Blanche

In one last-ditch attempt to stretch out what's left of summer, Paris museums, monuments, cultural spaces, bars, clubs and so on rock around the clock during Paris' so-called 'White Night' (www.paris.fr), aka one fabulous long all-nighter!

November

Beaujolais Nouveau

At the stroke of midnight on the third Thursday in November the first bottles of cherry-red Beaujolais *nouveau* wine are cracked open – and what a party it can be in Beaujolais, Lyon and other places nearby!

December

Alsatian Christmas Markets

Visitors meander between fairy-light-covered craft stalls, mug of *vin chaud* (warm mulled wine) in gloved hand, at Alsace's traditional pre-Christmas markets.

Fête des Lumières

France's biggest and best light show, on and around 8 December, transforms the streets and squares of Lyon into an open stage (www.lumieres.lyon.fr).

Far left: Contortionist, Cannes Film Festival **Left:** Nice Carnival

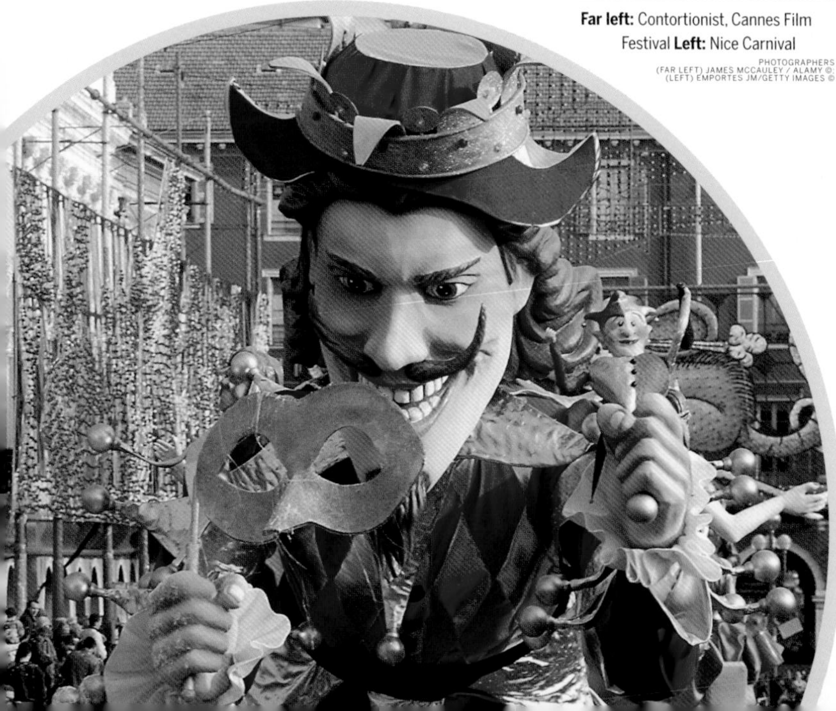

What's New

For this new edition of Discover France, our authors have hunted down the fresh, the transformed, the hot and the happening. These are some of our favourites. For up-to-the-minute recommendations, see lonelyplanet.com/france.

1 **ART IN PARIS**
New 'Flying carpet' Islamic art gallery at the Louvre, the Louis Vuitton arts centre à la Frank Gehry, the Musée Picasso. Oh, what capital openings art lovers are enjoying! (p73 and p67)

2 **GOURMET BURGERS**
The burger trend sweeping Paris is, unsurprisingly, *très gourmet ma chère*. Hot on the heels of Blend, with its hand-cut meat in brioche buns, comes the achingly cool Beef Club. (p87 and p85)

3 **LOUVRE-LENS**
It's ingenius. France's latest temple to fine art – aka the Louvre-Lens in northern France – also lets visitors peek into its restoration workshops and storerooms. (p173)

4 **AU 36**
Never has Champagne *dégustation* (tasting) been so chic. This inventive new wine bar in one of Champagne's prettiest hilltop villages has a tasting wall of fizz arranged by aroma. (p162)

5 **MUSÉOPARC ALÉSIA, BURGUNDY**
Julius Caesar's crushing of Vercingetorix at Alésia in 52 BC ended centuries of conflict between the Gauls and the Romans. This new sight is where it happened. (p209)

6 **MARSEILLE, EUROPEAN CAPITAL OF CULTURE 2013**
The makeover of this mythical Mediterranean port will climax with a new national museum on European and Mediterranean civilisations inside 13th-century Fort St-Jean. (p301)

7 **A NEW NATIONAL PARK**
It's absolutely right that Les Calanques, spectacular cliffs rising from bright turquoise waters east of Marseille, should be protected as a national park. Explore by sea kayak. (p310)

8 **MUSÉE D'ART CLASSIQUE DE MOUGINS**
Never has the French Riviera village that seduced Picasso been so top-drawer. This art creation of collector and British entrepreneur Christian Levett only adds to its natural panache. (p335)

9 **JEAN NOUVEL IN SARLAT-LA-CANÉDA**
Architect of Paris' Arab World Institute and Musée du Quai Branly strikes gold again, this time with a panoramic lift inside a village church–turned-market in the Dordogne. (p212)

10 **LE CARROUSEL DES MONDES MARINES, NANTES**
There's no doubt about it: no experience is so fantastical, so mischievously fun and frivolous, as a trip around Nantes' Les Machines de l'Ile. And the latest creation at the rejuvenated shipyard, Le Carrousel des Mondes Marines, will not disappoint. (p280)

Get Inspired

Books

- **A Year in the Merde** (Stephen Clarke) Expat Brit's rant on dog poo, bureaucracy and more.
- **More France Please, We're British** (Helena Frith Powell) Life in rural France.
- **Everybody Was So Young** (Amanda Vaill) The French Riviera in the roaring twenties.
- **Me Talk Pretty One Day** (David Sedaris) Caustic take on moving to France, and learning the lingo.
- **Paris in Color** (Nichole Robertson) No photographic title better captures the colours of the capital.

Films

- **Cyrano de Bergerac** (1990) Glossy version of the classic, with Gérard Depardieu.
- **La Môme** (La Vie en Rose; 2007) Biopic of French singer Édith Piaf.
- **Bienvenue Chez Les Ch'tis** (2008) Comedy satirising France's north–south divide.
- **Midnight in Paris** (2011) Woody Allen tale about a family in Paris, with dream scenes set in the 1920s.
- **The Artist** (2011) Most awarded French film in history; romantic comedy with charismatic actor Jean Dujardin.

Music

- **Eternelle** (Édith Piaf; 2002) Excellent intro to the sparrow chanteuse.
- **Histoire de Melody Nelson** (Serge Gainsbourg; 1971) France's most-loved crooner.
- **L'Absente** (Yann Tiersen; 2001) Raw, emotional music from a multitalented Breton.
- **Château Rouge** (Abd al Malik; 2010) Rap music by Franco-Congolese rapper and slam-poet.
- **Voilà Voilà, the Best Of** (Rachid Taha; 2011) Cross-cultural sounds from Franco-Algerian DJ and singer.

Websites

- **Météo France** (www.meteo.fr) Weather forecasts.
- **SNCF** (www.sncf.com) French national railways.
- **Paris by Mouth** (http://parisbymouth.com) Capital dining and drinking.
- **Wine Travel Guides** (www.winetravelguides.com) Practical guides to France's wine regions.
- **France 24** (www.france24.com/en/france) French news in English.

Short on time?

This list will give you an instant insight into the country.

Read *Stuff Parisians Like* (Olivier Magny) has brilliant vignettes on Parisians and the French by a Parisian sommelier.

Watch *Amélie* (2001) is a film about a gal who sets out to make her Montmartre neighbourhood a happier place.

Listen *Le Voyage dans la Lune* (2012) offers electronica from French duo AIR ('Amour, Imagination, Rêve').

Log on www.franceguide.com is the French government tourist-office website.

Lavender field, Provence (p300)
PHOTOGRAPHER: BETHUNE CARMICHAEL

Need to Know

Currency
Euro (€)

Language
French

ATMs
At airports, train stations and city street corners.

Credit Cards
Visa and MasterCard widely accepted.

Visas
Generally not required for stays of up to 90 days (or at all for EU nationals); some nationalities need a Schengen visa.

Mobile Phones
European and Australian phones work. Only American cells with 900 and 1800 MHz networks are compatible.

Wi-Fi
Free in many hotels, train stations and airports.

Internet Access
Most towns have at least one internet cafe. Costs €3 to €6 per hour.

Driving
Steering wheel is on the left, drive on the right. Be aware of the 'priority to the right' rule.

Tipping
At least 10% for good service. *Service compris* means service is included.

When to Go

High Season (Jul & Aug)
- Queues at big sights and on the road, especially August when the French holiday
- Christmas, New Year and Easter equally busy
- Late December to March is high season in French Alpine ski resorts

Shoulder (Apr–June & Sep)
- Accommodation rates drop in southern France and other hot spots
- Spring brings warm weather and plentiful local produce
- Visit in autumn for the *vendange* (grape harvest)

Low Season (Oct–Mar)
- Prices up to 50% less than high season
- Sights, attractions and restaurants open fewer days and shorter hours

Advance Planning

- **Three months before** Book flights and accommodation; book tickets for popular festivals and sporting events, such as the Festival d'Avignon and Nice Jazz Festival.
- **One month before** Book train tickets via the SNCF website (www.sncf.com) to get the cheapest fares. Arrange car hire. Reserve dinner at top tables in Paris, Nice and elsewhere.
- **Two weeks before** Choose which guided walks and tours you want to do, and book if necessary. Order euros, or charge up your pre-paid card.

Your Daily Budget

Budget up to €100

- Dorm bed: €15–35
- Double room in budget hotel €60–80
- Free admission to many attractions first Sunday of month
- Set lunches: €12–18

Midrange €100–200

- Double room in a midrange hotel: €80–180
- Lunch *menus* (set meals) in gourmet restaurants: €20–40

Top End over €200

- Double room in a top-end hotel: €180–200
- Lower weekend rates in business hotels
- Top restaurant dinner: *menu* €50, à la carte €100–150

Exchange Rates

Australia	A$1	€0.80
Canada	C$1	€0.78
Japan	¥100	€0.94
NZ	NZ$1	€0.62
UK	UK£1	€1.24
US	US$1	€0.77

For current exchange rates see www.xe.com.

What to Bring

- **Sunglasses, sunscreen and mosquito repellent** Vital for southern France.
- **Plug adaptors** France uses two-pin European plugs; UK, US and others need adaptors.
- **A corkscrew** Essential for impromptu picnics; few bottles of French wine are screwtop.
- **French phrasebook** Choose one with a good food section.
- **Travel insurance** Check the policy for coverage on snow sports, luggage loss and health care.
- **EHIC Card** Covers health care for EU citizens.
- **ID and passport** Don't forget visas if required.
- **Driving licence** Your standard home licence should be sufficient.

Arriving in France

- **Paris Charles de Gaulle**

Trains, buses and RER (*Réseau Express Régional*) – to Paris centre every 15 to 30 minutes, 5am to 11pm.

Night buses – hourly, 12.30am to 5.30am.

Taxis – €50–60; 30 minutes to Paris centre.

- **Paris Orly**

Orlyval rail, RER and buses – at least every 15 minutes, 5am to 11pm.

Taxis – €45–60; 25 minutes to Paris centre.

Getting Around

- **Train** France's railway is fast, extensive and efficient. Regular trains travel to practically every town and city.
- **Car** Having a car buys freedom and flexibility, but driving in big cities can be a nightmare.
- **Bicycle** A hip way of navigating Paris, Lyon and other big cities.

Accommodation

- **Hotels** Wide range of budget, midrange and top-end hotels.
- **Chambres d'hôte** Staying in a B&B is particularly popular in rural France.
- **Châteaux** Some châteaux have been converted into luxurious hotels or B&Bs.

Be Forewarned

- **Shops** Nearly everywhere shuts on Sunday and public holidays. Shops usually close for lunch from noon to 2pm.
- **Restaurants** Few serve all day; orders are generally taken between noon and 2pm, and 7pm to 10.30pm, six days a week. Sunday evening and all day Monday are popular times to close.
- **Driving in France** Tolls are charged on motorways *(autoroutes)*. Automatic cars are very unusual in France.
- **Crowds** Many sights are at their busiest in July and August, but this can be a good time to visit Paris, as it's when most French people go on holiday.

Paris & Around

Paris has all but exhausted the superlatives that can reasonably be applied to any city. Notre Dame, the Eiffel Tower, the Seine – at sunrise, sunset, at night – and Left Bank–Right Bank differences have been described countless times. But what writers haven't quite captured is the grandness and magic of simply strolling the city's broad avenues past impressive public buildings and exceptional museums to parks, gardens and esplanades.

With more famous landmarks than any other city, the French capital evokes all sorts of expectations: of grand vistas, of intellectuals discussing weighty matters in cafes, of Seine-side romance, of naughty nightclub revues. Look hard enough and you'll find them all. Or set aside those preconceptions of Paris and explore the city's avenues and backstreets as though the tip of the Eiffel Tower or the spire of Notre Dame weren't about to pop into view at any moment.

Gargoyle, Cathédrale de Notre Dame (p81), Paris

Paris & Around

Bd Périphérique
Bd Ney
Bd Ney
Bd Macdonald
R de la Chapelle
PANTIN
Cité des Sciences et de l'Industrie
Canal de L'Ourcq
Parc de la Villette
18E
Porte de Pantin
19E
Av Jean Jaurès
Square de la Marseillaise
Gare du Nord
R La Fayette
Porte du Pré St-Gervais
Parc des Buttes Chaumont
LES LILAS
Mairie des Lilas
Bd Périphérique
9E
Bd de Magenta
Gare de l'Est
Pl du Colonel Fabien
Bd Mortier
10E
Canal St-Martin
R de Belleville
Bd de Belleville
R des Pyrénées
Bd St-Martin
R du Faubourg du Temple
2E
BELLEVILLE
Gare Routière Internationale de Paris-Galliéni
Porte de Bagnolet
RIGHT BANK
3E
See Central Paris – South Map (p68)
Av Gambetta
Cimetière du Père Lachaise
Galliéni
1
6
20E
Bd Davout
St-Michel Notre Dame
3
11E
Bd Voltaire
4E
Nation
Jardin du Luxembourg
7
Bd Diderot
Cours de Vincennes
Gare de Lyon
R de Reuilly
St-Mandé Tourelle
Gare d'Austerlitz
Bd Soult
Luxembourg
5E
Port Royal
Av Daumesnil
Observatoire de Paris
Parc de Bercy
12E
Square René Le Gall
Seine
Cimetière de Bercy
Lac Daumesnil
Parc Zoologique
Q de Bercy
Cimetière Valmy
Île de Bercy
Parc de Choisy
13E
R de Tolbiac
Av d'Italie
Boulevard Masséna
Av de Gravelle
Bois de Vincennes
CHINATOWN
Parc Montsouris
Q de Bercy
Q Marcel Boyer
CHARENTON-LE-PONT
Cité Universitaire
Bd Masséna
Square Robert Bajac
Bd Périphérique
Gentilly
Porte de Gentilly
GENTILLY
IVRY-SUR-SEINE
Ivry-sur-Seine
LE KREMLIN-BICÊTRE
Cimetière Parisien d'Ivry
Seine

Paris & Around's Highlights

1

Musée du Louvre

I've worked at the Louvre for more than 10 years and each day I still experience many emotions; it is a magical place, charged with history and very intimate. It was a 12th-century fortress, then a royal palace; today it's one of the most famous art museums in the world. Top Right: Mona Lisa; Bottom Right: *Winged Victory of Samothrace*, Musée du Louvre

Need to Know

FACTS Six hectares of gallery space, 35,000 art works, 8 million visitors annually **BRUTAL TRUTH** One visit can't possibly cover it all **For further coverage, see p73**

Local Knowledge

Louvre Don't Miss List

BY NIKO SALVATORE MELISSANO, MUSÉE DU LOUVRE

1 WINGED VICTORY OF SAMOTHRACE

It's impossible to reduce the collections of the Louvre to a hit parade... A definite highlight is the *Winged Victory of Samothrace* atop the Daru Staircase (1st floor, Denon Wing). I adore her wings. I just cannot stop contemplating her from all angles. She is, moreover, very photogenic.

2 THE SEATED SCRIBE & MONA LISA

I could admire this statuette (Room 22, 1st floor, Sully Wing) from the ancient Egyptian empire for hours. The face of the scribe (probably that of Saqqara), like his posture (a little 'yoga') and his deep stare, say several things to me: serenity, strength of character, eternal wisdom. Then there is *La Joconde* (Mona Lisa; Room 6, 1st floor, Salle de la Joconde, Denon Wing) and that amazing fascination of why and how she intrigues spirits with her mysteries.

3 COUR KHORSABAD

With its enormous human-headed winged bulls, this courtyard on the ground floor of the Richelieu Wing is a jump in time into the cradle of one of the oldest cultures in the world: Mesopotamia. During the reign of King Sargon II in the 8th century, these bulls, carved from alabaster, guarded the Assyrian city and palace of Khorsabad (northern Iraq). Their bearded faces with bull ears and a heavy tiara of horns wore a benevolent smile. A mix of force and serenity, perfectly balanced despite their colossal size, these protective monsters with four or five paws were a measure of the power of the Assyrian Empire in its heyday.

4 GRANDE GALERIE

It's a real highlight, this gallery (1st floor, Denon Wing), with masterpieces from the greats of the Italian Renaissance: Leonardo da Vinci, Raphael, Arcimboldo, Andrea Mantegna...

Versailles

Versailles (p100), as official residence of the kings of France, is magnificent – the only place where the daily life of the monarchy before the French Revolution can be felt. My favourite moment is the evening, when I walk quietly from room to room lecturing to just a small group...extraordinary. Top Right: King Louis XVI's Library; Bottom Right: Gilded Lamps, Hall of Mirrors (p101)

Need to Know

NIGHTMARE QUEUES Avoid by buying tickets in advance and arriving first thing or after 4pm **AVOID** Tuesday and Sunday, the busiest days **For further coverage, see p100**

2

Local Knowledge

Versailles Don't Miss List

BY SYLVAIN POSTOLLE, OFFICIAL GUIDE, CHÂTEAU DE VERSAILLES

1 KING'S PRIVATE APARTMENT This is the most fascinating part of the palace as it shows the king as a man and reflects his daily life in the 18th century. Of the 10 or so rooms, the most famous is his bedroom, where he not only slept but also held ceremonies. Up to 150 courtiers and people would watch him have supper here each evening! By the 1780s, the king's life had become more private – he had an official supper just once a week on Sunday.

2 KING LOUIS XVI'S LIBRARY This is a lovely room – full of books, a place where you can really imagine the king coming to read for hours and hours. Louis XVI loved geography and his copy of *The Travels of James Cook* – in English – is still here.

3 HERCULES SALON I love one particular perspective inside the palace: from the Hercules Salon you can see all the rooms comprising the King's State Apartment, and to the right, through the gallery leading to the opera house. The salon served as a passageway for the king to go from his state apartment to the chapel to celebrate daily mass.

4 THE ROYAL CHAPEL This is an exquisite example of the work of architect Jules Hardouin-Mansart (1646–1708). The paintings, representative of art fashions at the end of the reign of Louis XIV, are also stunning: they evoke the idea that the French king was chosen by God, and as such was God's lieutenant on earth. This is the chapel where, in 1770, the future king Louis XVI wed Marie Antoinette – the beginning of the French Revolution.

5 ENCELADE GROVE Versailles' gardens are extraordinary but my favourite spot is this grove, typical of the gardens created for Louis XIV by André Le Nôtre. A gallery of trellises surround a pool with a statue of Enceladus, chief of the Titans, punished for his pride by the gods from Mount Olympus. The fountains are impressive.

Cathédrale de Notre Dame de Paris

France has its share of stunning cathedrals, but none can match the might and majesty of Notre Dame (p81), Paris' most-visited monument. Idyllically situated on an island in the middle of the Seine, the cathedral is renowned for its stained glass and soaring Gothic architecture, not to mention an unmissable panorama over the rooftops of Paris.

3

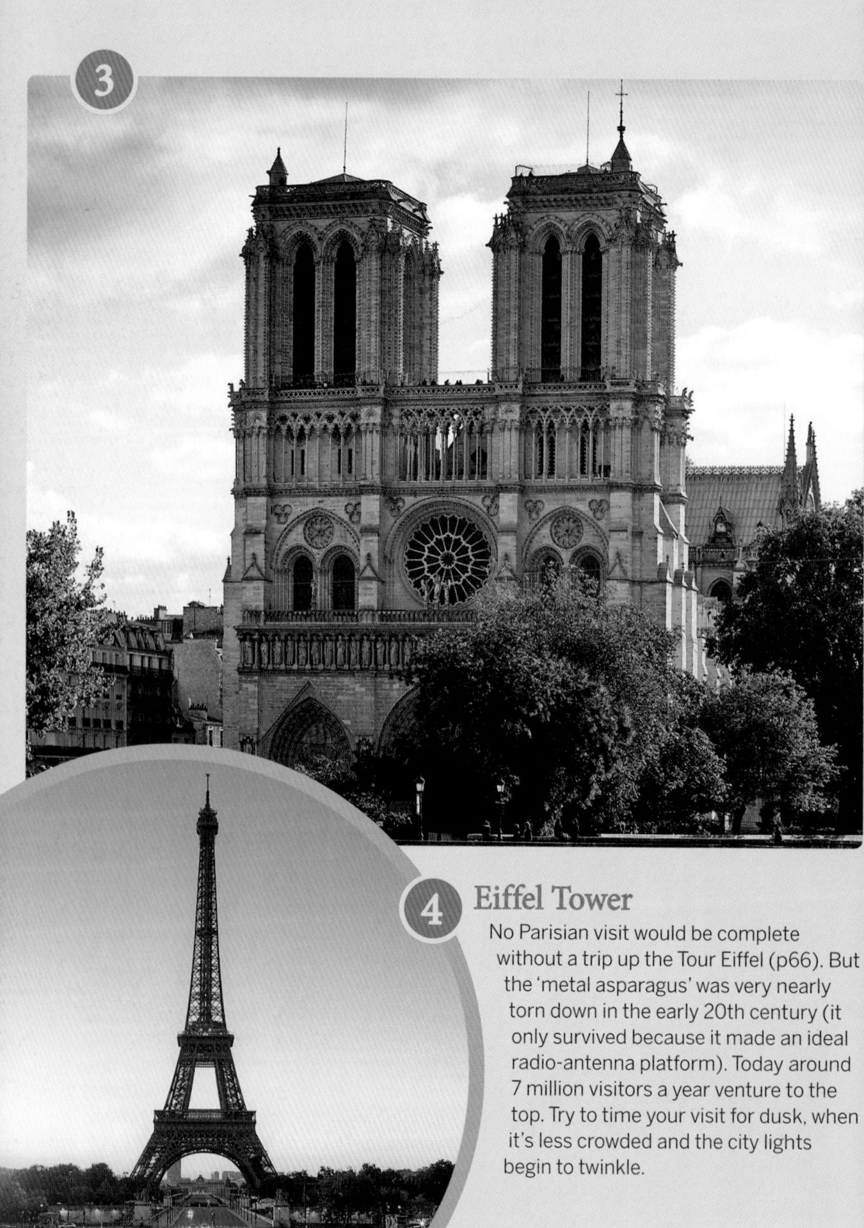

4 Eiffel Tower

No Parisian visit would be complete without a trip up the Tour Eiffel (p66). But the 'metal asparagus' was very nearly torn down in the early 20th century (it only survived because it made an ideal radio-antenna platform). Today around 7 million visitors a year venture to the top. Try to time your visit for dusk, when it's less crowded and the city lights begin to twinkle.

IZZET KERIBAR/GETTY IMAGES ©

5 Musée d'Orsay

It might not be as monumental as the Louvre, but for many people this fine-arts museum (p71) offers a more-rewarding experience. Housed in a turn-of-the-century train station overlooking the Seine, the museum contains France's national collection of art from the 1840s to 1914, including key works by Renoir, Degas, Monet, Cézanne and Vincent van Gogh. Absolutely not to be missed.

DAVID YATES/GETTY IMAGES ©

6 Cimetière du Père Lachaise

More sculpture garden than cemetery, this graveyard (p86) in northeastern Paris contains over 69,000 ornate tombs, including those belonging to Molière, Chopin, Oscar Wilde and Jim Morrison. Criss-crossed by wooded paths and winding walkways, it feels a world away from downtown Paris, and makes an ideal refuge when the hustle and bustle of the city gets too much.

7 The Seine

The stately Seine has been a part of Paris' history since Roman times, and the river still plays an integral role in the life of the city. Exploring the Seine is a key part of the Parisian experience, whether that means brunching at a waterfront brasserie, cycling along the riverbanks or strolling across the Pont Neuf – just remember to leave plenty of time for a scenic boat cruise.

Paris & Around's Best...

City Views

- **Eiffel Tower** (p66) Need we say more?
- **Cathédrale de Notre Dame** (p81) Gargoyles, flying buttresses and unforgettable views.
- **Centre Pompidou** (p67) Head to the rooftop – it's high!
- **Basilique du Sacré-Cœur** (p63) Look out from the dome of Montmartre's basilica.
- **Galeries Lafayette** (p95) Staggering – and free – views from the top floor of this grand department store.

Romantic Spots

- **Musée Rodin** (p80) Swoon over Rodin's garden-framed *The Kiss.*
- **Eiffel Tower** (p66) At the top, there are three marriage proposals every hour!
- **Jardin du Palais Royal** (p65) No urban garden is so elegant.
- **Canal St-Martin** (p85) Stroll hand-in-hand along towpaths.
- **Le Coupe-Chou** (p91) Dine by candlelight in a vine-clad, 17th-century town house.

Places to Eat

- **Septime** (p88) New beacon of modern cuisine near Bastille.
- **Au Passage** (p89) Creative bistro fare accompanied by back-alley simplicity.
- **Derrière** (p89) Cheeky apartment-style dining with sophisticated home-cookin' feel.
- **Bouillon Racine** (p92) Art nouveau 'soup kitchen' from 1906.
- **Beef Club** (p85) Chic and feisty meat-lovers' address; killer cocktails to boot.

Quintessential Cafes

- **Les Deux Magots** (p93) Too famous for its own good, but a Left Bank must.
- **Café Constant** (p84) Favourite cafe-lunch address by the Eiffel Tower.
- **Café La Palette** (p93) Fashionable, fin-de-siècle cafe; erstwhile stomping ground of Cézanne and Braque.
- **Claus** (p87) Only in Paris: a *haute couture* breakfast cafe.

Left: Entrance to metro St-Michel; **Above:** Arc de Triomphe (p65), viewed from the Eiffel Tower

(LEFT) RACHEL LEWIS/GETTY IMAGES ©; (ABOVE) CHRISTOPHER GROENHOUT/GETTY IMAGES ©

Need to Know

ADVANCE PLANNING

- **As early as possible** Book accommodation and make restaurant reservations.
- **One week before** Dodge the queues by buying tickets online for Versailles, the Louvre, Grand Palais exhibitions and Centre Pompidou.
- **Tickets** Pick up concert, musical and theatre tickets from Fnac and Virgin Megastore.

RESOURCES

- **Paris Convention & Visitors Bureau** (www.parisinfo.com) The city's central tourist office.
- **Go Go** (www.gogoparis.com) 'Fashion, food, arts, gigs, gossip'.
- **Paris.fr** (www.paris.fr) Comprehensive city information.
- **My Little Paris** (www.mylittleparis.com) Insider secrets from Parisian writers.
- **Paris by Mouth** (www.parisbymouth.com) Latest local tips.

GETTING AROUND

- **Metro & RER** Paris' subway system runs between 5.30am and 1am (up to 2am on Fridays, Saturdays and bank holidays); tickets are also valid on buses.
- **Bicycle** The capital's bike-rental scheme, Vélib', has over 1500 stations dotted across the city.
- **Boats** Scenic cruise boats run regularly along the Seine.

BE FOREWARNED

- **Arrondissements** Paris addresses are split into 20 arrondissements (districts) – 1er for *premier* (1st), 2e for *deuxième* (2nd), 3e for *troisième* (3rd) etc.
- **Museums** Most museums close on Mondays but some, including the Louvre and Centre Pompidou, close on Tuesdays instead.
- **Bars & cafes** A drink costs more sitting at a table than standing, and more on a fancy square than on a backstreet.
- **Metro stations** Avoid late at night: Châtelet–Les Halles, Château Rouge (Montmartre), Gare du Nord, Strasbourg–St-Denis, Réaumur-Sébastopol and Montparnasse Bienvenüe.

Montmartre Walking Tour

Pretty squares, cobbled streets and city views – not to mention famous cabarets and artistic connections – make Montmartre the ultimate Parisian neighbourhood. It's ideal for walking, as long as you can handle the hills.

WALK FACTS

- **Start** Ⓜ Blanche
- **Finish** Ⓜ Abbesses
- **Distance** 2.5km
- **Duration** 2½ hours

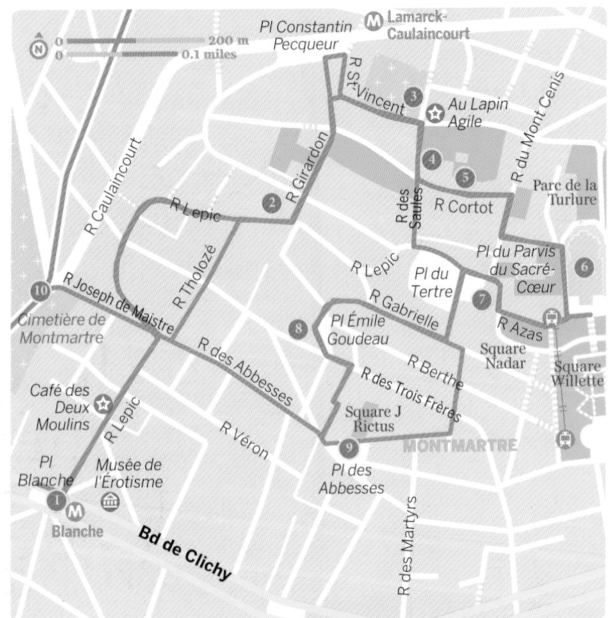

❶ Place Blanche

Begin outside Blanche metro station. To the northwest is the legendary **Moulin Rouge** beneath its red windmill. To the right is the saucy **Musée de l'Érotisme**. Halfway along rue Lepic is **Café des Deux Moulins**, where Audrey Tautou worked in the film *Amélie*. **(****Map p76****; www.musee-erotisme.com; 72 bd de Clichy, 18e; adult/student €10/6; 10am-2am; Ⓜ Blanche)**

❷ Montmartre Windmills

Further along rue Lepic are Montmartre's twin windmills: the **Moulin de la Galette**, immortalised in an 1876 painting by Renoir, and the Moulin Radet, now a restaurant. **(Map p76) (Map p76)**

❸ Cimetière St-Vincent

This cemetery on rue St-Vincent is the final resting place of Maurice Utrillo (1883–1955), the 'painter of Montmartre'. Just east is the notorious cabaret **Au Lapin Agile**, named after a mural by caricaturist André Gill, which still features on the west wall. **(****Map p76****; 01 46 06 85 87; www.au-lapin-agile.com; 22 rue des Saules, 18e; adult €24, student except Sat €17; 9pm-1am Tue-Sun; Ⓜ Lamarck–Caulaincourt)**

❹ Clos Montmartre

South along rue des Saules is Clos Montmartre, a tiny vineyard that produces around 800 bottles of wine a year, which are auctioned for charity in October. **(****Map p76****; 18 rue des Saules, 18e)**

5 Musée de Montmartre

This museum is housed in Montmartre's oldest building, a 17th-century house once occupied by Renoir, Utrillo and Raoul Dufy. **(Map p76; www.museedemontmartre.fr; 12 rue Cortot, 18e; adult/18-25yr/10-17yr €8/6/4; ⌚10am-6pm; Ⓜ Lamarck–Caulaincourt)**

6 Basilique du Sacré-Cœur

Inside this iconic landmark, 234 steps spiral up to the dome and one of Paris' most spectacular panoramas. **(Map p76; www.sacre-coeur-montmartre.com; place du Parvis du Sacré-Cœur; Basilica dome admission €5, cash only; ⌚6am-10.30pm, dome 9am-7pm Apr-Sep, to 5.30pm Oct-Mar; Ⓜ Anvers)**

7 Place du Tertre

It would be hard to miss this square, one of the most touristy and vibrant spots in Paris, packed with buskers and portrait artists.

8 Bateau Lavoir

The Bateau Lavoir is where the artists Modigliani, Picasso, Kees Van Dongen and Max Jacob lived in an old piano factory (later a laundry). The original building was at No 13; it burned down in 1970 and was rebuilt two doors away in 1978. **(Map p76; 11bis place Émile Goudeau; Ⓜ Abbesses)**

9 Abbesses Metro Station

Take the steps from place Émile Goudeau and walk to place des Abbesses to see the famous art-nouveau entrance to the Abbesses metro station, designed in 1912 by Hector Guimard.

10 Cimetière de Montmartre

At the western end of rue des Abbesses is Montmartre's largest cemetery, where you'll find the graves of Alexandre Dumas and Edgar Degas, among others. The entrance is on rue Caulaincourt. **(Map p76; admission free; ⌚8am-5.30pm Mon-Fri, from 8.30am Sat, from 9am Sun; Ⓜ Place de Clichy)**

Paris in…

TWO DAYS

Kick off with a morning cruise or tour, then concentrate on the most Parisian of sights and attractions: **Notre Dame**, the **Louvre**, the **Eiffel Tower** and the **Arc de Triomphe**. In the late afternoon have a coffee or glass of wine on **av des Champs-Élysées** before making your way to **Montmartre** for dinner. The following day take in such sights as the **Musée d'Orsay**, **Ste-Chapelle**, **Conciergerie**, **Musée National du Moyen Âge** or **Musée Rodin**. Dine in the hip area of **Le Marais**.

FOUR DAYS

With another two days to spare, follow our walking tour of Montmartre, take a cruise along the **Seine** or **Canal St-Martin**, meander further afield to **Cimetière du Père Lachaise** or the Bois de Boulogne, or squeeze in a side trip to **Versailles**. You might also visit the **Musée du Quai Branly** or do a spot of shopping along the **Champs-Élysées**. By night, choose from the many restaurants and bars in **Bastille**, **Opéra** and **Montparnasse**.

Basilique du Sacré-Cœur

Discover Paris & Around

At a Glance

- **Louvre & Les Halles** (p65) Right bank of the Seine, dominated by Paris' monumental art museum.
- **Le Marais & Bastille** (p66) Hip dining and drinking 'hoods.
- **Étoile & Champs-Élysées** (p65) Paris' famous shop-laced boulevards.
- **Montmartre** (p62) Touristed artistic quarter.
- **St-Germain & Luxembourg** (p71) Left-bank cafe life and Paris' grandest park.
- **Latin Quarter** (p68) Historic university district with the Sorbonne as centrepiece.

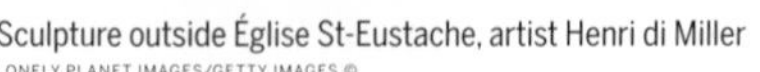

Sculpture outside Église St-Eustache, artist Henri di Miller

LONELY PLANET IMAGES/GETTY IMAGES ©

PARIS

Sights

The **Paris Museum Pass** (**www.parismuseumpass.fr; 2/4/6 days €39/54/69**) is valid for entry to over 60 museums and monuments in and around Paris – including the Louvre, Centre Pompidou, Musée d'Orsay and parts of the château at Versailles. Buy the pass online, at participating venues, Paris Convention & Visitors Bureau branches, Fnac outlets, RATP information desks and major metro stations.

Eiffel Tower Area

MUSÉE DU QUAI BRANLY Art Museum

(**Map p76; www.quaibranly.fr; 37 quai Branly, 7e; adult/child €8.50/free; 11am-7pm Tue, Wed & Sun, 11am-9pm Thu-Sat; M Alma-Marceau or RER Pont de l'Alma**) No other museum in Paris provides such inspiration for travellers, armchair anthropologists, and those who simply appreciate the beauty of traditional craftsmanship. A tribute to the incredible diversity of human culture, the Musée du Quai Branly, which opened in 2006, presents an overview of indigenous and folk art from around the world.

Divided into four main sections – Oceania, Asia, Africa and the Americas – the museum showcases an impressive array of masks, carvings, weapons, jewellery and more, all displayed in a unique interior without rooms or high walls. Be sure to check out the temporary exhibits and performances, both of which are generally excellent.

Étoile & Champs-Élysées

ARC DE TRIOMPHE Landmark

(Map p76; www.monuments-nationaux.fr; place Charles de Gaulle; adult/18-25yr €9.50/6; 10am-10.30pm, to 11pm Apr-Sep; M Charles de Gaulle–Étoile) If anything rivals the Eiffel Tower as the symbol of Paris, it's this magnificent 1836 monument to Napoléon's 1805 victory at Austerlitz, which he commissioned the following year. The intricately sculpted triumphal arch stands sentinel in the centre of the Étoile ('star') roundabout. From the viewing platform on top of the arch (50m up via 284 steps and well worth the climb) you can see the dozen avenues. Av de la Grande Armée heads northwest to the skyscraper district of La Défense, where the **Grande Arche** **(1 Parvis de la Défense; M La Défense)** marks the western end of the Axe Historique.

PLACE DE LA CONCORDE City Square

(Map p76; M Concorde) With its majestic vistas in just about every direction – the Arc de Triomphe, the Assemblée Nationale (the lower house of Parliament) and even a rare swath of open sky above – place de la Concorde is one of Paris' most impressive squares. It was first laid out in 1755 and originally named after King Louis XV, but its associations with royalty meant that it would go on to take centre stage during the Revolution.

Louvre & Les Halles

JARDIN DES TUILERIES Garden

(Map p68; 7am-7.30pm, later in summer; M Tuileries or Concorde) Filled with fountains, ponds and sculptures, the formal, 28-hectare Tuileries Garden, which begins just west of the Jardin du Carrousel, was laid out in its present form, more or less, in 1664 by André Le Nôtre, who also created the gardens at Versailles. The Tuileries soon became the most fashionable spot in Paris for parading about in one's finery. It now forms part of the Banks of the Seine World Heritage Site listed by Unesco in 1991.

PALAIS ROYAL Palace

(Map p76; place du Palais Royal; M Palais Royal–Musée du Louvre) The Royal Palace, which accommodated a young Louis XIV for a time in the 1640s, lies to the north of place du Palais Royal and the Louvre. Construction was begun in 1624 by Cardinal Richelieu, though most of the present neoclassical complex dates from the latter part of the 18th century. Today it contains the governmental **Conseil d'État** (State Council) and is closed to the public.

The colonnaded building facing place André Malraux is the Comédie Française (p94); founded in 1680, it's the world's oldest national theatre.

Just north of the palace is the **Jardin du Palais Royal** **(Map p76; 2 place Colette, 1er; 7.30am-10pm Apr & May, 7am-11pm Jun-Aug, 7am-9.30pm Sep, 7.30am-8.30pm Oct-Mar; M Palais Royal–Musée du Louvre)**, an exquisite park surrounded by two arcades. On the eastern side, **Galerie de Valois** shelters designer fashion shops, art galleries and jewellers, while **Galerie de Montpensier** on the western side still has a few old shops remaining.

At the southern end there's a controversial **sculpture** of black-and-white-striped columns of various heights by Daniel Buren.

ÉGLISE ST-EUSTACHE Church

(Map p76; www.st-eustache.org; 2 impasse St-Eustache, 1er; admission free; 9.30am-7pm Mon-Fri, 10am-7pm Sat, 9am-7pm Sun; M Les Halles) This majestic church, one of the most beautiful in Paris, is just north of the Forum des Halles. Constructed between 1532 and 1637, St-Eustache is primarily Gothic, though a neoclassical façade was added on the western side in the mid-18th century. Inside, some exceptional Flamboyant Gothic arches hold up the ceiling of the chancel, though most of the ornamentation is Renaissance and even classical. Above the western entrance, the gargantuan organ, with 101 stops and 8000 pipes dating from 1854, is used for concerts (long a tradition here) and at Sunday Mass at 11am and Sunday recitals at 5.30pm.

PAWEL LIBERA/GETTY IMAGES ©

Don't Miss Eiffel Tower

No one could imagine Paris today without its signature spire. But Gustave Eiffel only constructed this graceful tower – the world's tallest, at 320m, until it was eclipsed by Manhattan's Chrysler Building some four decades later – as a temporary exhibit for the 1889 Exposition Universelle (World Fair). Luckily, the tower's popularity assured its survival beyond the fair, and its elegant art nouveau webbed-metal design has become the defining fixture of the city's skyline.

Lifts/elevators yo-yo up and down the north, west and east pillars to the tower's three platforms (57m, 115m and 276m); change lifts on the 2nd level for the final ascent to the top, from where views extend up to 60km. (There's wheelchair access to the 1st and 2nd levels.) If you're feeling athletic, you can take the south pillar's 1665 stairs as far as the 2nd level. Pre-book tickets online to avoid monumentally long ticket queues.

Refreshment options in the tower include the 1st-level 58 Tour Eiffel (p84), the sublime 2nd-level Le Jules Verne and, at the top, the new Bar à Champagne.

NEED TO KNOW

(☎01 44 11 23 23; www.tour-eiffel.fr; lift to 3rd fl adult/12-24yr/4-12yr €14/12.50/9.50, lift to 2nd fl €8.50/7/4, stairs to 2nd fl €5/3.50/3; 🕐lifts & stairs 9am-midnight mid-Jun–Aug, lifts 9.30am-11pm, stairs 9.30am-6pm Sep–mid-June; M Bir Hakeim or RER Champ de Mars–Tour Eiffel)

Le Marais & Bastille

Paris' *marais* (marsh) was converted to farmland in the 12th century. In the early 17th century, Henri IV built the place Royale (today's place des Vosges), turning the area into Paris' most fashionable residential district and attracting wealthy aristocrats who then erected their own luxurious *hôtels particulier* (private mansions).

CENTRE POMPIDOU Art Museum

(Map p68; 01 44 78 12 33; www.centrepompidou.fr; place Georges Pompidou, 1er; museum, exhibitions & panorama adult/child €13/free; 11am-9pm Wed-Mon; M Rambuteau) Paris' premier cultural centre has amazed visitors since it was inaugurated in 1977.

On the ground floor, the **Forum du Centre Pompidou** has temporary exhibitions and information desks, while the 4th and 5th floors house the **Musée National d'Art Moderne** (adult/child €12/free; 11am-9pm Wed-Mon), France's national collection of art dating from 1905 onward. The 6th floor has two galleries for **temporary exhibitions** and a chic, hyperindustrial restaurant, **Georges**, with panoramic views of Paris, accessed by a free lift/elevator (look for the red door to the left of the main entrance).

Rooftop admission is included in museum and exhibition admission – or buy a **panorama ticket** (€3; 11am to 11pm Wednesday to Monday) for just the roof.

MUSÉE PICASSO Museum

(Map p68; 01 42 71 25 21; www.musee-picasso.fr; 5 rue de Thorigny; M St-Paul or Chemin Vert) The Picasso Museum, housed in the stunning mid-17th-century Hôtel Salé, will reopen after extensive renovations in mid-2013. Its collection includes more than 3500 drawings, engravings, paintings, ceramic works and sculptures by the *grand maître* (great master), Pablo Picasso (1881–1973), which his heirs donated to the French government in lieu of paying inheritance taxes. Also here is Picasso's personal art collection, which includes works by Braque, Cézanne, Matisse, Modigliani, Degas and Rousseau.

PLACE DES VOSGES City Square

(Map p68; place des Vosges, 4e; M St-Paul or Bastille) Inaugurated in 1612 as place Royale, Paris' oldest square is a strikingly elegant ensemble of 36 symmetrical houses with ground-floor arcades, steep slate roofs and large dormer windows.

The Islands

Paris' two inner-city islands could not be more different. The bigger Île de la Cité is full of sights, including Notre Dame, while little Île St-Louis is residential and much quieter, with a scattering of boutiques and restaurants – and legendary ice-cream maker Berthillon.

STE-CHAPELLE Chapel

(Map p68; 4 bd du Palais, Île de la Cité, 1er; adult/under 18yr €8.50/free; 9.30am-5pm Nov-Feb, to 6pm Mar-Oct; M Cité) Try to save Ste-Chapelle for a sunny day, when Paris' oldest, finest stained glass is at its dazzling best. Enshrined within the Palais de Justice (Law Courts), this gemlike Holy Chapel is Paris' most exquisite Gothic monument. Ste-Chapelle was built in just six years (compared with nearly 200 years for Notre Dame) and consecrated in 1248. The chapel was conceived by Louis IX to house his personal collection of holy relics, including the famous Holy Crown (now in Notre Dame).

A combined ticket with the Conciergerie costs €12.50.

CONCIERGERIE Monument

(Map p68; www.monuments-nationaux.fr; 2 bd du Palais, Île de la Cité, 1er; adult/under 18yr €8.50/free, 1st Sun of month Nov-Mar free; 9.30am-6pm; M Cité) The Conciergerie was built as a royal palace in the 14th century, but later lost favour with the kings of France and became a prison and torture chamber. During the Reign of Terror (1793–94), it was used to incarcerate (in various 'classes' of cells) alleged enemies of the Revolution before they were brought before the Revolutionary Tribunal, next door in the Palais de Justice.

Among the almost 2800 prisoners held in the dungeons here before being sent in tumbrils to the guillotine were Queen Marie Antoinette (see a reproduction of her cell) and, as the Revolution began to turn on its own, the radicals Danton, Robespierre and, finally, the judges of the Tribunal themselves. The 14th-century **Salle des Gens d'Armes** (Cavalrymen's Hall), a fine example of Rayonnant Gothic style, is Europe's largest surviving medieval hall.

Central Paris – South

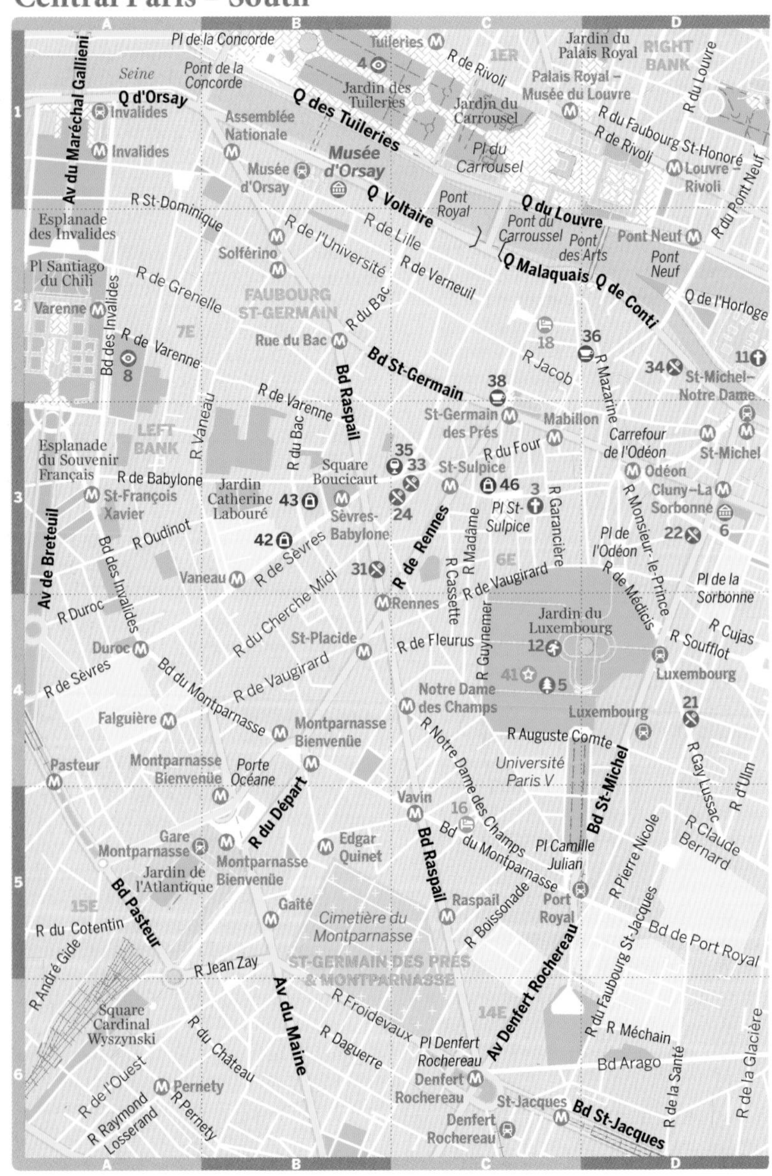

Latin Quarter

The centre of Parisian higher education since the Middle Ages, the Latin Quarter is so called because conversation between students and professors until the Revolution was in Latin. It still has a large population of students and academics affiliated with institutions that include the

world-famous Sorbonne university. To the southeast is the city's beautiful botanic gardens, the **Jardin des Plantes**.

MUSÉE NATIONAL DU MOYEN ÂGE History Museum

(Map p68; www.musee-moyenage.fr; 6 place Paul Painlevé; adult/18-25yr/under 18yr €8.50/6.50/

Central Paris – South

Top Sights

Cathédrale de Notre Dame de Paris ... E3
Musée d'Orsay ... B1

Sights

1 Centre Pompidou ... E1
2 Conciergerie ... E2
3 Église St-Sulpice ... C3
4 Jardin des Tuileries ... B1
5 Jardin du Luxembourg ... C4
Musée National d'Art Moderne ... (see 1)
6 Musée National du Moyen Âge ... D3
7 Musée Picasso ... F2
8 Musée Rodin ... A2
9 Panthéon ... E4
10 Place des Vosges ... G2
11 Ste-Chapelle ... D2

Activities, Courses & Tours

12 Shetland Ponies for Hire ... C4

Sleeping

13 Five Hotel ... E5
14 Hôtel Jeanne d'Arc ... F2
15 Hôtel Minerve ... E4
16 L'Apostrophe ... C5
17 Le Pavillon de la Reine ... G2
18 L'Hôtel ... C2

Eating

19 Au Passage ... G1
20 Berthillon ... F3
21 Bistrot Les Papilles ... D4
22 Bouillon Racine ... D3
23 Chez Marianne ... F2
24 Cuisine de Bar ... C3
25 Derrière ... F1
26 L'Agrume ... F5
27 L'AOC ... F3
28 Le Coupe-Chou ... E4
29 Marché aux Enfants Rouges ... F1
30 Marché Bastille ... G2
31 Marché Raspail ... B3
32 Nanashi ... F1
33 Poilâne ... C3
34 Ze Kitchen Galerie ... D2

Drinking

35 Au Sauvignon ... C3
36 Café La Palette ... D2
37 Le Baron Rouge ... H3
38 Les Deux Magots ... C2

Entertainment

39 Opéra Bastille ... G3
40 Opéra Bastille Box Office ... G3
41 Théâtre des Marionnettes du Jardin du Luxembourg ... C4

Shopping

42 La Grande Épicerie de Paris ... B3
43 Le Bon Marché ... B3
44 Mariage Frères ... F2
45 Merci ... G1
46 Pierre Hermé ... C3
47 Rue Mouffetard ... E4
48 Shakespeare & Company ... E3

free; 9.15am-5.45pm Wed-Mon; M Cluny–La Sorbonne) The National Museum of the Middle Ages occupies both a *frigidarium* (cooling room), which holds remains of Gallo-Roman *thermes* (baths) dating from around AD 200, and the 15th-century **Hôtel des Abbés de Cluny**, Paris' finest example of medieval civil architecture. Inside, spectacular displays include statuary, illuminated manuscripts, weapons, furnishings and *objets d'art* made of gold, ivory and enamel. But nothing compares with *La Dame à la Licorne* (The Lady with the Unicorn), a sublime series of late-15th-century tapestries from the southern Netherlands.

PANTHÉON Mausoleum

(Map p68; www.monum.fr; place du Panthéon; adult/under 18yr €8.50/free; 10am-6.30pm Apr-Sep, to 6pm Oct-Mar; M Maubert-Mutualité, Cardinal Lemoine or RER Luxembourg) The Panthéon is a rather superb example of 18th-century neoclassicism. The domed landmark was commissioned by Louis XV around 1750 as an abbey, but due to financial and structural problems it wasn't completed until 1789 – not a good year for church openings in Paris. Two years later the Constituent Assembly turned it into a secular mausoleum. The 80-odd permanent residents of the crypt include Voltaire, Victor Hugo, Émile Zola,

Jean Moulin and Nobel Prize–winner Marie Curie.

St-Germain & Les Invalides

Despite gentrification since its early-20th-century bohemian days, there remains a startling cinematic quality to this soulful part of the Left Bank, where artists, writers, actors and musicians cross paths and *la vie germanopratine* (St-Germain life) is *belle*.

MUSÉE D'ORSAY Art Museum

(Map p68; www.musee-orsay.fr; 62 rue de Lille, 7e; adult/18-25yr/under 18yr €9/6.50/free; 9.30am-6pm Tue, Wed & Fri-Sun, to 9.45pm Thu; M Assemblée Nationale or RER Musée d'Orsay) The home of France's national collection from the impressionist, postimpressionist and art nouveau movements from the 1840s to 1914 is the glorious former Gare d'Orsay railway station – itself an art nouveau showpiece – where a roll-call of masters and their world-famous works are on display.

Top of every visitor's must-see list is the museum's painting collections, centred on the world's largest collection of impressionist and post-impressionist art. Just some of its highlights are Manet's *On The Beach* and *Woman With Fans*; Monet's gardens at Giverny; Cézanne's card players and still-lifes; Renoir's *Ball at the Moulin de la Galette* and *Girls at the Piano*; Degas' ballerinas; Toulouse-Lautrec's cabaret dancers; Pissarro's *The Harvest*; Sisley's *View of the Canal St-Martin*; and Van Gogh's self-portraits, *Bedroom in Arles* and *Starry Night*.

ÉGLISE ST-SULPICE Church

(Map p68; www.paroisse-saint-sulpice-paris.org; place St-Sulpice, 6e; 7.30am-7.30pm; M St-Sulpice) Work started on the twin-towered Church of St Sulpicius in 1646 and took six architects 150 years to finish. What draws most people today is not its striking Italianate façade with two rows of superimposed columns, Counter-Reformation-influenced neoclassical decor or even the frescoes by Delacroix – but its setting for a murderous scene in Dan Brown's *The Da Vinci Code*.

JARDIN DU LUXEMBOURG Park

(Map p68; numerous entrances; hrs vary; M St-Sulpice, Rennes or Notre Dame des Champs, or RER Luxembourg) This inner-city oasis of formal terraces, chestnut groves and lush lawns has a special place in the hearts of Parisians. Napoléon dedicated the 23 gracefully laid-out hectares of the Luxembourg Gardens to the children of Paris, and many residents spent their childhood prodding 1920s **wooden sailboats** **(per 30/60min €2/3.20; Apr-Oct)** with long sticks on the octagonal **Grand Bassin** pond, watching puppets perform Punch and Judy–type shows at the **Théâtre des Marionnettes du Jardin du Luxembourg** **(01 43 26 46 47; admission €4; 3.30pm Wed, 11am & 3.30pm Sat & Sun, daily during school holidays)**, and riding the *carrousel* (merry-go-round) or **Shetland ponies**. All those activities are still here today, as are modern **playgrounds** **(adult/child €1.20/2.50; 10am-park close)** and sporting and games venues.

Tours

FAT TIRE BIKE TOURS Cycling

(Map p76; 01 56 58 10 54; www.fattirebiketours.com)

BATEAUX-MOUCHES Boat Tour

(Map p76; 01 42 25 96 10; www.bateauxmouches.com; Port de la Conférence, 8e; adult/4-12yr €11/5.50; Apr-Dec; M Alma Marceau)

L'OPEN TOUR Bus Tour

(Map p76; www.pariscityrama.com; 2-day passes adult/child €32/15) This hop-on, hop-off bus tour runs daily open-deck buses along four circuits.

PARIS WALKS Walking Tour

(www.paris-walks.com; adult/child €12/8) Thematic tours (fashion, chocolate, the French Revolution).

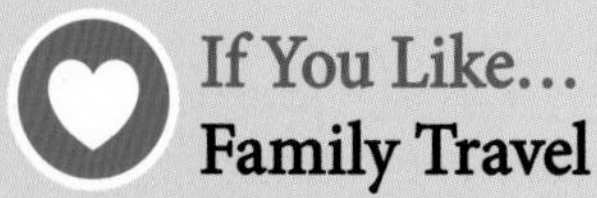

If You Like… Family Travel

If you're in town with the kids, you're gonna love these dependable family outings. For the lowdown on current exhibitions and events with kids in mind see *Pariscope* and *L'Officiel des Spectacles*.

1 **CITÉ DES SCIENCES** **(Map p52; ☎01 40 05 12 12; www.cite-sciences.fr; Parc de la Villette; adult/under 26yr €8/6; ⏰10am-6pm Tue-Sat, to 7pm Sun; M Porte de la Villette)** This is the city's top museum for kids, with three floors of hands-on exhibits for children ages two and up, plus two special-effects cinemas, a planetarium and a retired submarine. Reserve tickets in advance via the website.

2 **PALAIS DE LA DÉCOUVERTE** **(Map p76; www.palais-decouverte.fr; av Franklin D Roosevelt, 8e; adult/senior & 6-25yr/under 6yr €8/6/free; ⏰9.30am-6pm Tue-Sat, 10am-7pm Sun; M Champs-Élysées–Clemenceau)** This children's science museum has excellent temporary exhibits (eg moving lifelike dinosaurs) as well as a hands-on, interactive permanent collection focusing on astronomy, biology, physics and the like.

3 **MUSÉE DES ÉGOUTS DE PARIS** **(Map p76; place de la Résistance, 7e; adult/child €4.20/3.40; ⏰11am-5pm Sat-Wed May-Sep, 11am-4pm Sat-Wed Oct-Dec & Feb-Apr; M Alma Marceau or RER Pont de l'Alma)** Raw sewage flows beneath your feet as you walk through 480m of odoriferous tunnels in this working sewer museum. Enter via a rectangular maintenance hole topped with a kiosk across the street from 93 quai d'Orsay, 7e.

Sleeping

Étoile & Champs-Élysées

HIDDEN HOTEL Boutique Hotel €€€
(Map p76; ☎01 40 55 03 57; www.hidden-hotel.com; 28 rue de l'Arc de Triomphe, 17e; r from €376; ❄@📶; M Charles de Gaulle–Étoile) The Hidden is one of the Champs-Élysées' best secrets: an ecofriendly boutique hotel, it's serene, stylish, reasonably spacious, and it even sports green credentials. The earth-coloured tones are the result of natural pigments (there's no paint), and all rooms have handmade wooden furniture, stone basins for sinks and linen curtains surrounding the beds. The Emotion rooms are among the most popular.

Louvre & Les Halles

HÔTEL CRAYON Boutique Hotel €€
(Map p76; ☎01 42 36 54 19; www.hotelcrayon.com; 25 rue du Bouloi, 1er; s €129-249, d €149-299; ❄📶; M Les Halles or Sentier) Line drawings by French artist Julie Gauthron bedeck walls and doors at this creative boutique hotel – a work of art. The pencil *(le crayon)* is the theme, with rooms sporting a different shade of each floor's chosen colour – we love the coloured-glass shower doors and the books on the bedside table that guests can swap and take home.

HÔTEL TIQUETONNE Hotel €
(Map p76; ☎01 42 36 94 58; www.hoteltiquetonne; 6 rue Tiquetonne, 2e; d €65, with shared shower €45; 📶; M Étienne Marcel) What heart-warmingly good value this 45-room vintage cheapie is. This serious, well-tended address in the heart of party land has been in the hotel business since the 1900s and is much-loved by a loyal clientele of all ages. Rooms straddling seven floors are spick and span and sport an inoffensive mix of vintage decor – roughly 1930s to the 1980s. Recently renovated rooms have brand-new bathrooms and parquet flooring.

Ask for a room with a view of the Sacré-Cœur (Nos 701, 702 or 703) or Eiffel Tower (Nos 704 and 705). Shared shower *jeton* (tokens) are €5; ask at reception.

LE PRADEY Design Hotel €€€
(Map p76; ☎01 42 60 31 70; www.lepradey.com; 5 rue St-Roch, 1er; d from €220; ❄@📶; M Tuileries) Enviably tucked behind the Louvre and Jardin des Tuileries alongside the boutique-smart rue St-Honoré, Le Pradey boasts an exclusive new address that's the last word in luxury hotel design.

© PYRAMIDE DU LOUVRE, ARCHITECT I.M. PEI
ED FREEMAN/GETTY IMAGES ©

Don't Miss **Musée du Louvre**

The vast **Palais du Louvre** was constructed as a fortress by Philippe-Auguste in the early 12th century and rebuilt in the mid-16th century as a royal residence.

When the museum opened in the late 18th century it contained 2500 paintings and *objets d'art*; today some 35,000 are on display. Late 2012 saw the opening of the new Islamic-art galleries in the restored **Cour Visconti**, topped with an elegant, shimmering gold 'flying carpet' roof designed by Italian architects Mario Bellini and Rudy Ricciotti.

For many, the star attraction is Leonardo da Vinci's *La Joconde*, better known as Mona Lisa (Room 6, 1st floor, Denon Wing).

The main entrance and ticket windows are covered by the 21m-high **Grande Pyramide**, a glass pyramid designed by the Chinese-born American architect IM Pei. You can avoid the queues outside the pyramid or at the Porte des Lions entrance by entering the Louvre complex via the underground shopping centre, **Carrousel du Louvre**, at 99 rue de Rivoli. Buy your tickets in advance from the ticket machines in the Carrousel du Louvre, by phoning ☎0 892 684 694 or 01 41 57 32 28, or from the *billetteries* (ticket offices) of Fnac or Virgin Megastores, and walk straight in without queuing. Tickets are valid for the whole day, so you can come and go as you please. The centrepiece of the Carrousel du Louvre is the glass **Pyramide Inversée** (Inverted Pyramid), also by Pei.

NEED TO KNOW

(Map p76; ☎01 40 20 53 17; www.louvre.fr; rue de Rivoli & quai des Tuileries, 1er; permanent/temporary collection €11/12, both €15, under 18yr free; 🕒9am-6pm Mon, Thu, Sat & Sun, to 9.45pm Wed & Fri; Ⓜ Palais Royal–Musée du Louvre)

The Louvre

A Half-Day Tour

Successfully visiting the Louvre is a fine art. Its complex labyrinth of galleries and staircases spiralling three wings and four floors renders discovery a snakes-and-ladders experience. Initiate yourself with this three-hour itinerary – a playful mix of *Mona Lisa* obvious and up-to-the-minute unexpected.

Arriving by the stunning main entrance, pick up colour-coded floor plans at the lower-ground-floor **information desk** 1 beneath IM Pei's glass pyramid, ride the escalator up to the Sully Wing and swap passport for multimedia guide (there are limited descriptions in the galleries) at the wing entrance.

The Louvre is as much about spectacular architecture as masterly art. To appreciate this zip up and down Sully's Escalier Henri II to admire **Venus de Milo** 2, then up parallel Escalier Henri IV to the palatial displays in **Cour Khorsabad** 3.Cross room 1 to find the escalator up to the 1st floor and staircase-as-art **L'Esprit d'Escalier** 4. Next traverse 25 consecutive galleries (thank you, floor plan!) to flip conventional contemplation on its head with Cy Twombly's **Ceiling** 5 and the hypnotic **Winged Victory of Samothrace sculpture** 6 – just two rooms away – which brazenly insists on being admired from all angles. End with the impossibly famous **The Raft of Medusa** 7, **Mona Lisa** 8 and **Virgin & Child** 9.

TOP TIPS

Floor Plans Don't even consider entering the Louvre's maze of galleries without a Plan/Information Louvre brochure, free from the information desk in the Hall Napoléon

Crowd dodgers The Denon Wing is always packed; visit on late nights Wednesday or Friday or trade Denon in for the notably quieter Richelieu Wing

2nd floor Not for first-timers: save its more specialist works for subsequent visits

Mission Mona Lisa

If you just want to venerate the Louvre's most famous lady, use the Porte des Lions entrance (closed Tuesday and Friday), from where it's a five-minute walk. Go up one flight of stairs and through rooms 26, 14 and 13 to the Grande Galerie and adjoining room 6.

L'Esprit d'Escalier

Escalier Lefuel, Richelieu

Discover the 'Spirit of the Staircase' through François Morellet's contemporary stained glass, which casts new light on old stone. **DETOUR»** Napoleon III's gorgeous gilt apartments.

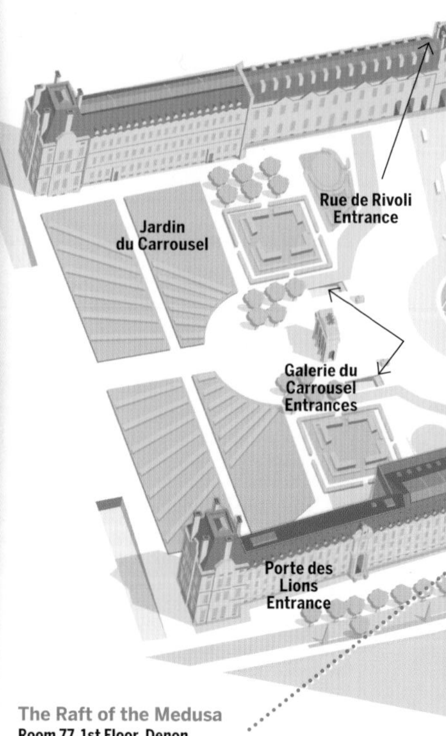

The Raft of the Medusa

Room 77, 1st Floor, Denon

Decipher the politics behind French romanticism in Théodore Géricault's *Raft of the Medusa.*

JOHN SONES SINGING BOWL MEDIA/GETTY IMAGES ©

Cour Khorsabad

Ground Floor, Richelieu

Time travel with a pair of winged human-headed bulls to view some of the world's oldest Mesopotamian art. **DETOUR»** Night-lit statues in Cour Puget.

WITOLD SKRYPCZAK/GETTY ©

Venus de Milo

Room 16, Ground Floor, Sully

No one knows who sculpted this seductively realistic goddess from Greek antiquity. Naked to the hips, she is a Hellenistic masterpiece.

The Ceiling

Room 32, 1st Floor, Sully

Admire the blue shock of Cy Twombly's 400-sq-metre contemporary ceiling fresco – the Louvre's latest, daring commission. **DETOUR»** *The Braque Ceiling*, room 33.

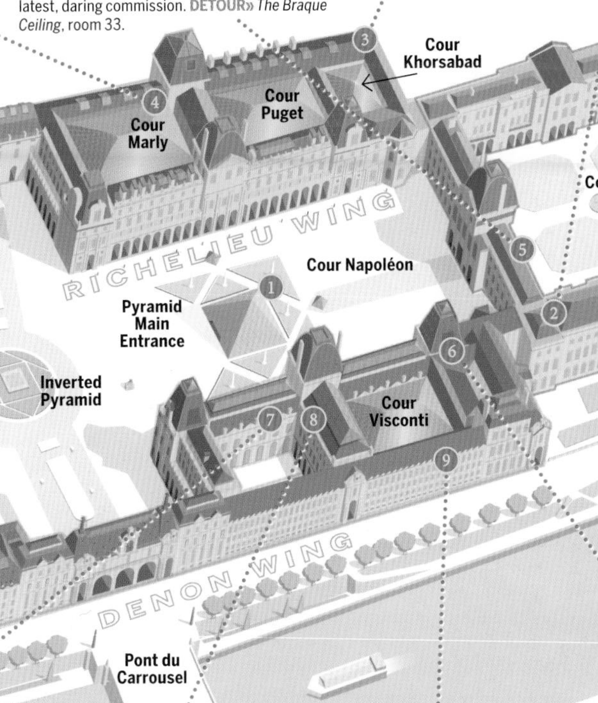

Mona Lisa

Room 6, 1st Floor, Denon

No smile is as enigmatic or bewitching as hers. Da Vinci's diminutive *La Joconde* hangs opposite the largest painting in the Louvre – sumptuous, fellow Italian Renaissance artwork *The Wedding at Cana.*

Virgin & Child

Room 5, Grande Galerie, 1st Floor, Denon

In the spirit of artistic devotion save the Louvre's most famous gallery for last: a feast of Virgin-and-child paintings by Raphael, Domenico Ghirlandaio, Giovanni Bellini and Francesco Botticini.

TERRY SMITH IMAGES/ALAMY ©

Winged Victory of Samothrace

Escalier Daru, 1st Floor, Sully

Draw breath at the aggressive dynamism of this headless, handless Hellenistic goddess. **DETOUR»** The razzle-dazzle of the Apollo Gallery's crown jewels.

Central Paris – North

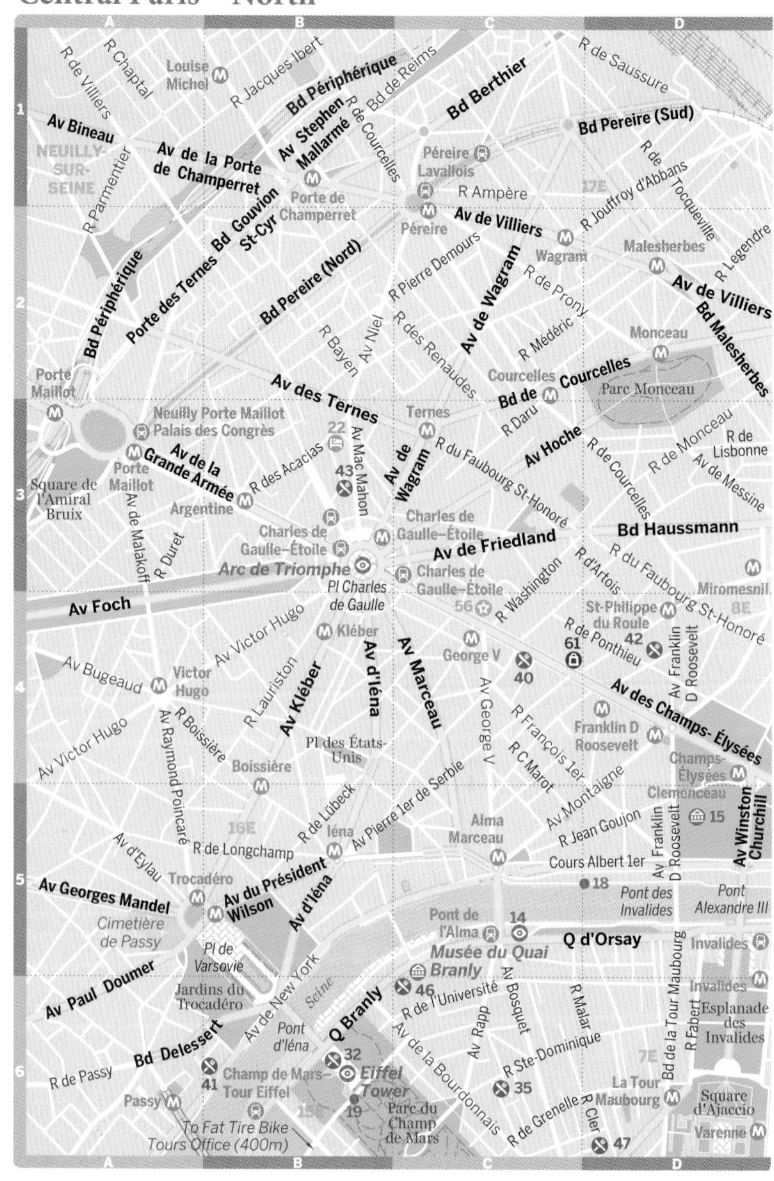

Guests linger over glossy art books in the understatedly chic, mezzanine lounge – if they can drag themselves away from whichever individually themed suite they are staying in.

Opéra & Grands Boulevards

W PARIS – OPÉRA Design Hotel **€€€**

(Map p76; ☎01 77 48 94 94; www.wparisopera.fr; 4 rue Meyerbeer, 9e; d €340-500; ❄@; MChausée d'Antin–La Fayette) Melding 1870s

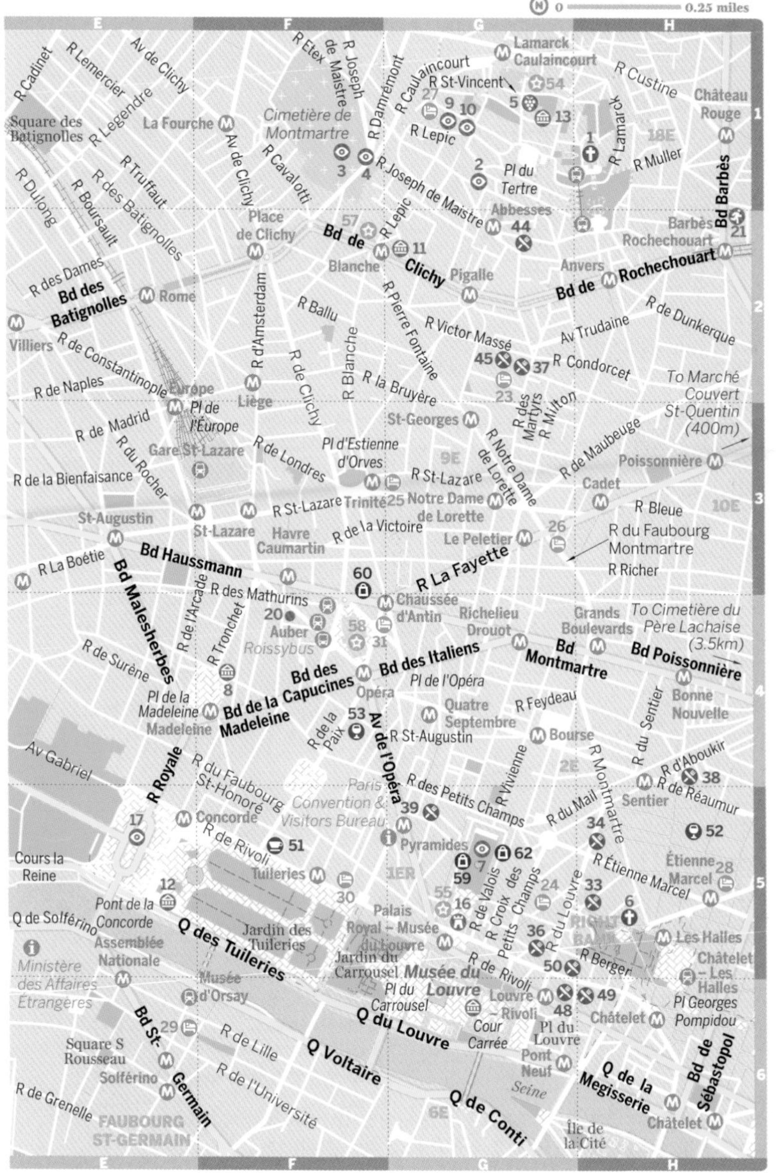

Haussmann style with modern design, this sleek new hotel has the plushest rooms on the Grands Boulevards. Don't sell yourself short with a Cozy or Wonderful room: what you want is a Spectacular room – or maybe even a Wow suite – with superlative views of the Palais Garnier next door.

HÔTEL LANGLOIS Historic Hotel **€€**

(Map p76; ☎01 48 74 78 24; www.hotel-langlois.com; 63 rue St-Lazare, 9e; s €110-120,

Central Paris – North

Top Sights
- Arc de Triomphe ... B3
- Eiffel Tower ... B6
- Musée du Louvre ... G6
- Musée du Quai Branly ... C5

Sights
- 1 Basilique du Sacré-Cœur ... H1
- 2 Bateau Lavoir ... G1
- 3 Cimetière de Montmartre ... F1
- 4 Cimetière de Montmartre Entrance & Conservation Office ... F1
- 5 Clos Montmartre ... G1
- Conseil d'État ... (see 16)
- 6 Église St-Eustache ... H5
- 7 Jardin du Palais Royal ... G5
- 8 La Pinacothèque ... F4
- 9 Moulin de la Galette ... G1
- 10 Moulin Radet ... G1
- 11 Musée de l'Érotisme ... G2
- 12 Musée de l'Orangerie ... E5
- 13 Musée de Montmartre ... G1
- 14 Musée des Égouts de Paris ... C5
- 15 Palais de la Découverte ... D5
- 16 Palais Royal ... G5
- 17 Place de la Concorde ... E5

Activities, Courses & Tours
- 18 Bateaux-Mouches ... D5
- 19 Fat Tire Bike Tours ... B6
- 20 L'Open Tour ... F4
- 21 Vélib' ... H2

Sleeping
- 22 Hidden Hotel ... B3
- 23 Hôtel Amour ... G2
- 24 Hôtel Crayon ... G5
- 25 Hôtel Langlois ... G3
- 26 Hôtel Monte Carlo ... G3
- 27 Hôtel Particulier Montmartre ... G1
- 28 Hôtel Tiquetonne ... H5
- 29 Le Bellechasse ... E6
- 30 Le Pradey ... F5
- 31 W Paris – Opéra ... F4

Eating
- 32 58 Tour Eiffel ... B6
- 33 Beef Club ... H5
- 34 Blend ... H5
- 35 Café Constant ... C6
- 36 Claus ... G5
- 37 Cul de Poule ... G2
- 38 Frenchie ... H4
- 39 Kunitoraya ... G5
- 40 Ladurée ... C4
- 41 L'Astrance ... B6
- 42 Le Boudoir ... D4
- 43 Le Hide ... B3
- 44 Le Miroir ... G2
- 45 Le Pantruche ... G2
- Les Cocottes ... (see 35)
- 46 Les Ombres ... C6
- Les Pâtes Vivantes ... (see 26)
- 47 Rue Cler ... D6
- 48 Spring ... G6
- 49 Spring Épicerie ... H6
- 50 Yam'Tcha ... G5

Drinking
- 51 Angelina ... F5
- 52 Experimental Cocktail Club ... H5
- 53 Harry's New York Bar ... F4

Entertainment
- 54 Au Lapin Agile ... G1
- 55 Comédie Française ... G5
- 56 Le Lido de Paris ... C4
- 57 Moulin Rouge ... F2
- 58 Palais Garnier ... F4

Shopping
- 59 Didier Ludot ... G5
- 60 Galeries Lafayette ... F3
- 61 Guerlain ... C4
- 62 La Petite Robe Noire ... G5

d €140-150; ; M Trinité) If you're looking for a bit of belle époque Paris, the Langlois won't let you down. Built in 1870, this 27-room hotel has kept its charm, from the tiny caged elevator to sandstone fireplaces in many rooms (sadly decommissioned) as well as original bathroom fixtures and tiles. Room 64 has wonderful views of Montmartre's rooftops.

HÔTEL MONTE CARLO Hotel €

(Map p76;) 01 47 70 36 75; www.hotelmontecarlo.fr; 44 rue du Faubourg Montmartre, 9e; s €45-120, d €59-147, tr €119-179; ; M Le Peletier) A unique budget hotel, the Monte Carlo is a steal, with colourful, personalised rooms and a great neighbourhood location. The owners go the extra mile and even provide a partly organic breakfast.

Montmartre & Pigalle

HÔTEL AMOUR Boutique Hotel €€

(Map p76; ☎01 48 78 31 80; www.hotelamourparis.fr; 8 rue Navarin, 9e; s €105, d €155-215; 📶; Ⓜ St-Georges or Pigalle) Planning a romantic escapade to Paris? Say no more. One of the 'in' hotels of the moment, the inimitable black-clad Amour (formerly a by-the-hour love hotel) features original design and artwork in each of the rooms and is very much worthy of the hype – you won't find a more original place to lay your head in Paris at these prices.

HÔTEL PARTICULIER MONTMARTRE Boutique Hotel €€€

(Map p76; ☎01 53 41 81 40; http://hotel-particulier-montmartre.com; 23 av Junot, 18e; ste €390-590; ❄📶; Ⓜ Lamarck-Caulaincourt) An 18th-century mansion hidden down a private alleyway, this VIP bijou sparkles from every angle. Much more than an exclusive hotel, it's the equivalent of staying in a modern art collector's personal residence, with rotating exhibitions, five imaginative suites designed by top French artists (Philippe Mayaux, Natacha Lesueur) and a lush garden landscaped by Louis Benech of Jardin des Tuileries fame.

Le Marais & Bastille

HÔTEL JEANNE D'ARC Hotel €

(Map p68; ☎01 48 87 62 11; www.hoteljeannedarc.com; 3 rue de Jarente, 4e; s €65, d €81-96, tr €149, q €164; 📶; Ⓜ St-Paul) About the only thing wrong with this gorgeous address is that everyone knows about it, meaning you need to book well in advance to snag one of its cosy, excellent-value rooms. Games, a painted rocking chair for tots in the bijou lounge, knick-knacks everywhere, and the most extraordinary mirror in the breakfast room create a real 'family home' air in this 35-room house.

LE PAVILLON DE LA REINE Historic Hotel €€€

(Map p68; ☎01 44 59 80 40; www.pavillondelareine.com; 28 place des Vosges, 3e; d from €330; Ⓜ Chemin Vert) Dreamily set on Paris' most beautiful and elegant square, place des Vosges, this sumptuous address loaded with history doesn't come cheap. But who cares when you can sleep like a queen?

COSMOS HÔTEL Hotel €

(☎01 43 57 25 88; www.cosmos-hotel-paris.com; 35 Jean-Pierre Timbaud, 11e; s/d/tr €55/62/78; 📶; Ⓜ République) Cheap, brilliant-value and just footsteps from the fun and happening bars, cafes and music clubs of increasingly trendy rue JPT, Cosmos is a shiny star with retro style on the budget-hotel scene. It has been around for 30-odd years, but, unlike most other hotels in the same price bracket, Cosmos

Basilique du Sacré-Cœur (p63)

If You Like... Art Museums

If the Louvre and Musée d'Orsay sent you into a wild state of ecstacy, you risk pure unadulterated delirium with this smart selection of lesser-known but equally impressive art addresses.

1 **MUSÉE RODIN**
(Map p68; www.musee-rodin.fr; 79 rue de Varenne, 7e; permanent exhibition adult/under 25yr €7/5, garden €1/free; 10am-5.45pm Tue-Sun; M Varenne) Sculptor and painter Auguste Rodin donated his entire collection to the French state in 1908 on the proviso they dedicate his workshop and showroom, the beautiful 1730 Hôtel Biron, to displaying his works. The rose-clambered garden of the Musée Rodin is one of the most peaceful places in Paris and a wonderful spot to contemplate his famous work *The Thinker*.

2 **MUSÉE DE L'ORANGERIE**
(Map p76; www.musee-orangerie.fr; quai des Tuileries & rue de Rivoli; adult/child €7.50/5.50; 9am-6pm Wed-Mon; M Tuileries or Concorde) Admire Monet's prized cycle of eight enormous water lilies, conceived specifically for this former palace greenhouse, and additional works by Sisley, Renoir, Cézanne, Picasso and Matisse at this astonishing but often-missed museum.

3 **LA PINACOTHÈQUE**
(Map p76; www.pinacotheque.com; 28 place de la Madeleine, 8e; adult/12-25yr/under 12yr €10/8/free; 10.30am-6pm daily, to 9pm Wed & Fri; M Madeleine) Paris' top private museum, La Pinacothèque organises three to four major exhibits a year. Its nonlinear approach to art history, with exhibits that range from Mayan masks to retrospectives covering the work of artists such as Edvard Munch, has shaken up the otherwise rigid Paris art world.

has been treated to a thoroughly modern makeover this century. Enjoy.

Latin Quarter

FIVE HOTEL Design Hotel €€€
(Map p68; 01 43 31 74 21; www.thefivehotel-paris.com; 3 rue Flatters, 5e; d €202-342; ; M Les Gobelins) Choose from one of five perfumes to fragrance your room at this contemporary romantic sanctum.

HÔTEL MINERVE Hotel €€
(Map p68; 01 43 26 26 04; www.parishotelminerve.com; 13 rue des Écoles, 5e; s €99, d €129-165, tr €165; @; M Cardinal Lemoine) Oriental carpets, antique books, frescoes of French monuments and reproduction 18th-century wallpaper make this family-run hotel a charming place to stay. Some rooms have small balconies with views of Notre Dame, and two have tiny courtyards that are swooningly romantic.

St-Germain & Les Invalides

L'HÔTEL Boutique Hotel €€€
(Map p68; 01 44 41 99 00; www.l-hotel.com; 13 rue des Beaux Arts, 6e; d €285-795; @; M St-Germain des Prés) In a quiet quayside street, this award-winning hostelry is the stuff of romance, Parisian myths and urban legends. Rock- and film-star patrons fight to sleep in room 16, where Oscar Wilde died in 1900.

L'APOSTROPHE Design Hotel €€
(Map p68; 01 56 54 31 31; www.apostrophe-hotel.com; 3 rue de Chevreuse, 6e; d €150-350; @; M Vavin) A street work-of-art with its stencilled façade, this art hotel's 16 dramatically different rooms pay homage to the written word. Spray-painted graffiti tags cover one wall of room U (for '*urbain*'), which has a ceiling shaped like a skateboard ramp. Room P (for 'Paris parody') sits in the clouds overlooking Paris' rooftops.

LE BELLECHASSE Design Hotel €€
(Map p76; 01 45 50 22 31; www.lebellechasse.com; 8 rue de Bellechasse, 7e; d from €161; ; M Solférino) Fashion designer (and,

ROGDY ESPINOZA PHOTOGRAPHY/GETTY IMAGES ©

Don't Miss Cathédrale de Notre Dame de Paris

Notre Dame, the most visited unticketed site in Paris, with upwards of 14 million people crossing its threshold a year, is not just a masterpiece of French Gothic architecture; it was also the focus of Catholic Paris for seven centuries.

Inside, exceptional features include three spectacular **rose windows** – the most renowned of which is the 10m-wide one over the western façade above the 7800-pipe organ – and the window on the northern side of the transept, which has remained virtually unchanged since the 13th century. The **trésor** in the southeastern transept contains artwork, liturgical objects and first-class relics. Among these is the Ste-Couronne, the 'Holy Crown', which is purportedly the wreath of thorns placed on Jesus' head before he was crucified, brought here in the mid-13th century. It's exhibited between 3pm and 4pm on the first Friday of each month, 3pm to 4pm every Friday during Lent, and 10am to 5pm on Good Friday.

The entrance to the **Tours de Notre Dame** is from the North Tower. Climb the 422 spiralling steps to the top of the western façade, where you'll find yourself face-to-face with the cathedral's most frightening gargoyles, the 13-tonne bell Emmanuel (all of the cathedral's bells are named) in the South Tower, and, last but not least, a spectacular view of Paris from the Galerie des Chimères (Dreams Gallery).

NEED TO KNOW

(Map p68; www.cathedraledeparis.com; 6 place du Parvis Notre Dame, 4e; admission free; 7.45am-7pm; M Cité)

tian Lacroix's entrancing room themes make you feel like you've stepped into a larger-than-life oil painting. Themes include 'St-Germain', with brocades, zebra with trompe l'oeil and palms, and 'Jeu de Paume', with giant playing-card motifs.

Notre Dame

Timeline

1160 Maurice de Sully becomes bishop of Paris. Mission: to grace growing Paris with a lofty new cathedral.

1182–90 The **choir with double ambulatory** (1) is finished and work starts on the nave and side chapels.

1200–50 The **west facade** (2), with rose window, three portals and two soaring towers, goes up. Everyone is stunned.

1345 Some 180 years after the foundation stone was laid, the Cathédrale de Notre Dame is complete. It is dedicated to *Notre Dame* (Our Lady), the Virgin Mary.

1789 Revolutionaries smash the original **Gallery of Kings** (3), pillage the cathedral and melt all its bells except the great bell Emmanuel. The cathedral becomes a Temple of Reason, then a warehouse.

1831 Victor Hugo's novel *The Hunchback of Notre Dame* inspires new interest in the half-ruined Gothic cathedral.

1845–50 Architect Viollet-le-Duc undertakes its restoration. Twenty-eight new kings are sculpted for the west facade. The heavily decorated **portals** (4) and **spire** (5) are reconstructed. The neo-Gothic **treasury** (6) is built.

1860 The area in front of Notre Dame is cleared to create the *parvis*, an alfresco classroom where Parisians can learn a catechism illustrated on sculpted stone portals.

1935 A rooster bearing part of the relics of the Crown of Thorns, St Denis and St Geneviève is put on top of the cathedral spire to protect those who pray inside.

1991 The architectural masterpiece of Notre Dame and its Seine-side riverbanks become a Unesco World Heritage Site.

2013 Notre Dame celebrates 850 years since construction began with a bevy of new bells and restoration works.

Virgin & Child

Spot all 37 artworks representing the Virgin Mary. Pilgrims have revered the pearly-cream sculpture of her in the sanctuary since the 14th century. Light a devotional candle and write some words to the *Livre de Vie* (Book of Life).

North Rose Window

See prophets, judges, kings and priests venerate Mary in vivid blue and violet glass, one of three beautiful rose blooms (1225–70), each almost 10m in diameter.

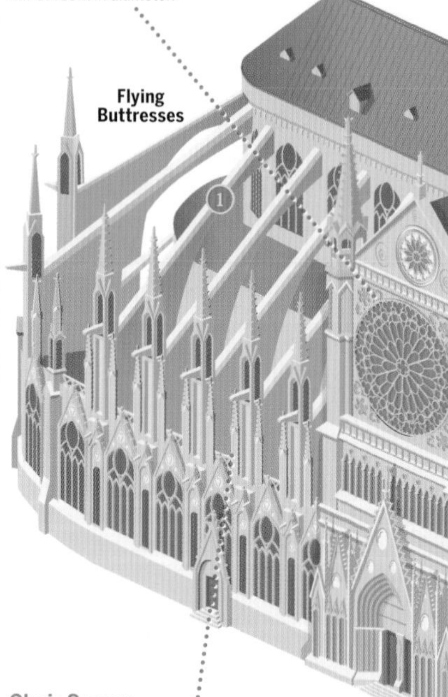

Choir Screen

No part of the cathedral weaves biblical tales more evocatively than these ornate wooden panels, carved in the 14th century after the Black Death killed half the country's population. The faintly gaudy colours were restored in the 1960s.

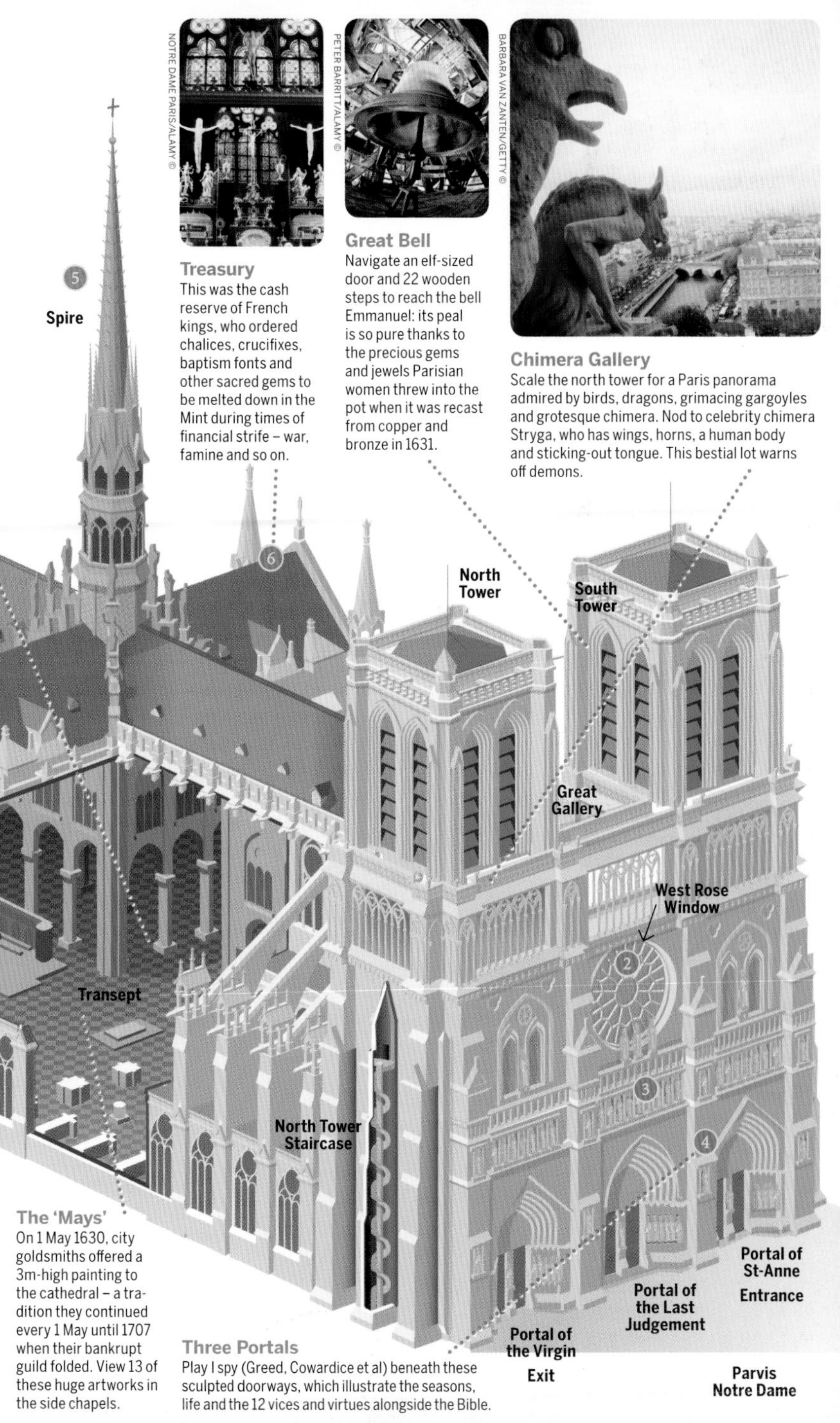
NOTRE DAME PARIS/ALAMY ©
PETER BARRITT/ALAMY ©
BARBARA VAN ZANTEN/GETTY ©
Treasury
This was the cash reserve of French kings, who ordered chalices, crucifixes, baptism fonts and other sacred gems to be melted down in the Mint during times of financial strife – war, famine and so on.
Great Bell
Navigate an elf-sized door and 22 wooden steps to reach the bell Emmanuel: its peal is so pure thanks to the precious gems and jewels Parisian women threw into the pot when it was recast from copper and bronze in 1631.
Chimera Gallery
Scale the north tower for a Paris panorama admired by birds, dragons, grimacing gargoyles and grotesque chimera. Nod to celebrity chimera Stryga, who has wings, horns, a human body and sticking-out tongue. This bestial lot warns off demons.
5
Spire
6
North Tower
South Tower
Great Gallery
West Rose Window
2
3
4
Transept
North Tower Staircase
The 'Mays'
On 1 May 1630, city goldsmiths offered a 3m-high painting to the cathedral – a tradition they continued every 1 May until 1707 when their bankrupt guild folded. View 13 of these huge artworks in the side chapels.
Three Portals
Play I spy (Greed, Cowardice et al) beneath these sculpted doorways, which illustrate the seasons, life and the 12 vices and virtues alongside the Bible.
Portal of the Virgin
Exit
Portal of the Last Judgement
Portal of St-Anne
Entrance
Parvis Notre Dame

Eiffel Tower Area & 16e

L'ASTRANCE Gastronomic **€€€**

(Map p76; ☎01 40 50 84 40; 4 rue Beethoven, 16e; lunch/dinner menus €70/210; ⏰Tue-Fri; M Passy) It's been over a decade now since Pascal Barbot's dazzling cuisine at the three-star L'Astrance made its debut, but it has shown no signs of losing its cutting edge. Look beyond the complicated descriptions on the menu – what you should expect are teasers of taste that you never even knew existed, and a presentation that is an art unto itself.

You'll need to reserve two months in advance (one month for lunch) for this culinary experience unique to Paris.

LES OMBRES Modern French **€€€**

(Map p76; ☎01 47 53 68 00; www.lesombres-restaurant.com; 27 quai Branly, 7e; lunch €26-38, dinner €65; ⏰daily; M Iéna or RER Pont de l'Alma) Paris gained not only a museum in the Musée du Quai Branly but also this glass-enclosed rooftop restaurant on the 5th floor. Named 'The Shadows' for the patterns cast by the Eiffel Tower's webbed ironwork, it has dramatic views complemented by the kitchen's creations, such as *gambas* (prawns) with black rice and fennel, or sea bream in a parmesan crust.

CAFÉ CONSTANT Neo-Bistro **€**

(Map p76; www.cafeconstant.com; 139 rue Ste-Dominique, 7e; 2-/3-course menus €16/23; ⏰lunch & dinner Tue-Sun; M École Militaire or RER Pont de l'Alma) Take a former Michelin-star chef and a dead-simple corner cafe and what do you get? This jam-packed address, with original mosaic floor, wooden tables and huge queues every mealtime. The pride and joy of Christian and Catherine Constant, it doesn't take reservations but you can enjoy a drink at the bar (or on the pavement outside) while you wait.

Nearby, **Les Cocottes (Map p76; www.leviolondingres.com; 135 rue Ste-Dominique, 7e; 2-/3-course lunch menus €9/15, mains €14-28; ⏰lunch & dinner Mon-Sat; M École Militaire or RER Pont de l'Alma)** is another Constant hit.

58 TOUR EIFFEL Brasserie **€€**

(Map p76; ☎01 45 55 20 04; www.restaurants-toureiffel.com; 1st level, Champ de Mars, 7e; lunch menus €18-23, dinner menus €67-150; ⏰11.30am-4.30pm & 6.30-11pm; M Bir Hakeim or RER Champ de Mars–Tour Eiffel) If you're intrigued by the idea of a meal in the Tower, the 58 Tour Eiffel is a pretty good choice. It may not be the caviar and black truffles of Le Jules Verne (on the 2nd level), but Alain Ducasse did sign off on the menu, ensuring that this is much more than just another tourist cafeteria.

For lunch, go first to the restaurant's outside kiosk (near the north pillar); for dinner, reserve online or by telephone.

L'Astrance restaurant

BLOOMBERG/GETTY IMAGES ©

Detour: Canal St-Martin

The shaded towpaths of the tranquil, 4.5km-long Canal St-Martin are a wonderful place for a romantic stroll or a bike ride.

Dug out in 1825, the canal was a major cargo thoroughfare by the time Marcel Carné's 1938 film *Hôtel du Nord* was set in the canalside hotel – now a **cafe/bar** (www.hoteldunord.org; 102 quai de Jemmapes, 10e; 9am-2.30am; ; Jacques Bonsergent) – of the same name. The canal's fortunes fell in the 1960s when barge transportation declined. It was slated to be concreted over and turned into a roadway until local residents rallied to save it. When the title character of *Amélie* skipped stones here in 2001, the cheap rents and quaint setting were just starting to lure artists, designers and students, who set up artists' collectives, vintage and offbeat boutiques, and a bevy of neo-retro cafes and bars.

Today Canal St-Martin is the centre of Paris' *bobo* (bohemian bourgeois) life, but maritime legacies endure, including old swing-bridges that still pivot 90 degrees when barges pass through the canal's double-locks. Take a **canal boat cruise** (01 42 39 15 00; www.canauxrama.com; adult/student & senior/4-12yr €16/12/8.50) to savour the full flavour.

Étoile & Champs-Élysées

LADURÉE Patisserie €

(Map p76; www.laduree.fr; 75 av des Champs-Élysées, 8e; pastries from €1.50; 7.30am-11pm; George V) One of the oldest patisseries in Paris, Ladurée has been around since 1862. The tea room here is the classiest spot to indulge your sweet tooth on the Champs; alternatively, pick up some pastries to go – from croissants to its trademark macarons, it's all quite heavenly.

LE BOUDOIR Traditional French €€

(Map p76; 01 43 59 25 29; www.boudoirparis.fr; 25 rue du Colisée, 8e; lunch menus €25, mains €25-29; lunch Mon-Fri, dinner Tue-Sat; St-Philippe du Roule or Franklin D Roosevelt) Spread across two floors, the quirky salons here – Marie Antoinette, Palme d'Or, le Fumoir – are individual works of art with a style that befits the name. Expect classy bistro fare (quail stuffed with dried fruit and foie gras, chateaubriand steak with chestnut purée) prepared by chef Arnaud Nicolas, a recipient of France's top culinary honour.

LE HIDE Traditional French €€

(Map p76; 01 45 74 15 81; www.lehide.fr; 10 rue du Général Lanrezac, 17e; menus from €24; lunch Mon-Fri, dinner Mon-Sat; Charles de Gaulle–Étoile) A reader favourite, Le Hide is a tiny neighbourhood bistro serving scrumptious traditional French fare: snails, baked shoulder of lamb with pumpkin purée or monkfish in lemon butter. Unsurprisingly, this place fills up faster than you can scamper down the steps at the nearby Arc de Triomphe. Reserve well in advance.

Louvre & Les Halles

BEEF CLUB Steak €€

(Map p76; 09 54 37 13 65; www.eccbeefclub.com; 58 rue Jean-Jacques Rousseau, 1er; mains €20-45; dinner daily; Les Halles) No steak house is more chic or hip than this. Packed out ever since it threw its first T-bone on the grill in spring 2012, this beefy spot is all about steak, prepared to sweet perfection by legendary Paris butcher Yves-Marie Le Bourdonnec. The vibe is hip New York and the downstairs cellar bar, the Ballroom du Beef Club, shakes a mean cocktail (€12 to €15) courtesy of the cool guys from the Experimental Cocktail Club. An address not to be missed – if you are lucky enough to score a table, that is!

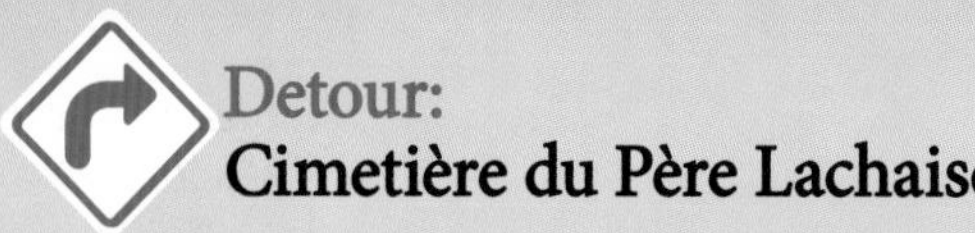

Detour: Cimetière du Père Lachaise

The world's most visited cemetery, **Cimetière du Père Lachaise** (Map p52; ☎01 43 70 70 33; www.pere-lachaise.com; 16 rue du Repos & bd de Ménilmontant, 20e; admission free; ⏰8am-6pm Mon-Fri, from 8.30am Sat, from 9am Sun; Ⓜ Père Lachaise or Philippe Auguste), opened its one-way doors in 1804. Its 69,000 ornate, even ostentatious, tombs of the rich and/or famous form a verdant, 44-hectare sculpture garden. Among those buried here are composer Chopin; playwright Molière; poet Apollinaire; writers Balzac, Proust, Gertrude Stein and Colette; actors Sarah Bernhardt and Yves Montand; painters Pissarro, Seurat, Modigliani and Delacroix; chanteuse Édith Piaf; and dancer Isadora Duncan.

Particularly visited graves are those of Oscar Wilde, interred in division 89 in 1900, and 1960s rock star Jim Morrison, who died in a flat at 17-19 rue Beautreillis (4e) in the Marais in 1971 and is buried in division 6.

Père Lachaise has five entrances, two of which are on bd de Ménilmontant. Free maps of noteworthy graves are available from the conservation office.

FRENCHIE Bistro €€

(Map p76; ☎01 40 39 96 19; www.frenchie-restaurant.com; 5-6 rue du Nil, 2e; menus €34-45; ⏰dinner Mon-Fri; Ⓜ Sentier) Tucked down an alley you wouldn't venture down otherwise, this bijou bistro with wooden tables and old stone walls is iconic. Frenchie is always packed and for good reason: excellent-value dishes are modern, market-driven (the menu changes daily, with a choice of two dishes by course) and prepared with just the right dose of unpretentious creative flair by French chef Gregory Marchand.

The only hiccup is snagging a table: reserve for one of two sittings (7pm or 9.30pm) two months in advance, arrive at 7pm and pray for a cancellation, or – failing that – share tapas-style small plates with friends across the street at Frenchie's **Bar à Vin**. No reservations: write your name on the sheet of paper strung outside, loiter in the alley and wait for your name to be called.

YAM'TCHA Fusion €€€

(Map p76; ☎01 40 26 08 07; www.yamtcha.com; 4 rue Sauval, 1er; lunch/dinner menus from €50/85; ⏰lunch Wed-Sun, dinner Wed-Sat; Ⓜ Louvre Rivoli) Adeline Grattard's ingeniously fused French and Chinese flavours recently earned the chef a Michelin star. Pair dishes on the frequently changing menu with wine or exotic teas. Book well ahead.

SPRING Modern French €€€

(Map p76; ☎01 45 96 05 72; www.springparis.fr; 6 rue Bailleul, 1er; lunch/dinner menus €44/76; ⏰lunch Wed-Fri, dinner Tue-Sat; Ⓜ Palais Royal–Musée du Louvre) A 'talk-of-the-town' address with an American in the kitchen and stunning food. Spring has no printed menu, meaning hungry gourmets put their appetites in the hands of the chef and allow the multilingual wait staff to reveal what's cooking as each course is served. Advance reservations essential.

At lunchtime, nip in to the **Spring Épicerie** (Map p76; 52 rue de l'Arbre Sec, 1er; ⏰noon-8pm Tue-Sat), a tiny wine shop that serves steaming bowls of market-inspired, 'hungry worker–style' *bouillon du poule* (chicken soup).

KUNITORAYA Japanese €

(Map p76; www.kunitoraya.com; 39 rue Ste-Anne, 1er; mains €12-14; ⏰11.30am-10pm; Ⓜ Pyramides) Some of the best-value *udon* (handmade Japanese noodles) is what this buzzing address in Paris' food-rich Japantown is all about. Grab a stool at the kitchen bar and watch the hip young chefs strut their stuff over steaming bowls of soup, *grands bols de riz* (big bowls of rice) laced with battered prawns, sweet duck or beef, and other meal-in-one dishes. No credit cards.

BLEND Burgers €

(Map p76; www.blendhamburger.com; 44 rue d'Argout, 2e; burgers €10, lunch menus €15-17; lunch & dinner Mon-Sat; M Sentier) This gourmet burger bar the size of a pocket handkerchief has been the talk of the town since its 2012 opening. Easy to spot by the hungry crowd lingering outside waiting for a table, the sharp, smart, black-and-wood space cooks up bijou-sized burgers with homemade buns and meat from celebrity butcher Yves-Marie Le Bourdonnec.

CLAUS Breakfast €

(Map p76; 01 42 33 55 10; www.clausparis.com; 14 rue Jean-Jacques Rousseau, 1er; breakfasts €13-18, lunches €19; 7.30am-6pm Mon-Fri, 9.30am-5pm Sat & Sun; M Étienne Marcel) Dubbed the 'haute-couture breakfast specialist' in Parisian foodie circles, this inspired *épicerie du petit-déjeuner* (breakfast grocery shop) has everything you could possibly desire for the ultimate gourmet breakfast and brunch – organic mueslis and cereals, fresh juices, jams, honey and so on. Breakfast or brunch on site, shop at Claus to create your own or ask for a luxury breakfast hamper to be delivered to your door. Its lunchtime salads, soups and tarts are equally tasty.

Opéra & Grands Boulevards

LES PÂTES VIVANTES Chinese €

(Map p76; 46 du Faubourg Montmartre, 9e; noodles €9.50-12; Mon-Sat; M Le Peletier) This is one of the only spots in Paris for hand-pulled noodles *(là miàn)*, made to order in the age-old northern Chinese tradition. It packs in a crowd, so arrive early to stake out a table on the ground floor and watch as the nimble noodle-maker works his magic.

Montmartre & Pigalle

CUL DE POULE Modern French €€

(Map p76; 01 53 16 13 07; 53 rue des Martyrs, 9e; 2-/3-course menus lunch €15/18, dinner €23/28; closed lunch Sun; M Pigalle) With plastic orange cafeteria seats outside, you probably wouldn't wander into the Cul de

Cimetière du Père Lachaise

Poule by accident. But the light-hearted spirit (yes, there is a mounted chicken's derrière on the wall) is deceiving; this is one of the best and most affordable kitchens in the Pigalle neighbourhood, with excellent neo-bistro fare that emphasises quality ingredients from the French countryside.

LE MIROIR Bistro €€

(Map p76; ☎01 46 06 50 73; 94 rue des Martyrs, 18e; lunch menus €18, dinner menus €25-40; ⏰lunch Tue-Sun, dinner Tue-Sat; Ⓜ Abbesses) This unassuming modern bistro is smack in the middle of the Montmartre tourist trail, yet it remains a local favourite. There are lots of delightful pâtés and rillettes to start off with – guinea hen with dates, duck with mushrooms, haddock and lemon – followed by well-prepared standards such as stuffed veal shoulder.

LE PANTRUCHE Bistro €€

(Map p76; ☎01 48 78 55 60; www.lepantruche.com; 3 rue Victor Masse, 9e; lunch/dinner menus €17/32; ⏰Mon-Fri; Ⓜ Pigalle) Named after a nearby 19th-century theatre, classy Pantruche has been making waves in the already-crowded dining hot spot of South Pigalle. No surprise, then, that it hits all the right notes: seasonal bistro fare, reasonable prices and an intimate setting. The menu runs from classics (steak with Béarnaise sauce) to more daring creations (scallops served in a parmesan broth with cauliflower mousseline). Reserve well in advance.

Le Marais & Bastille

SEPTIME Modern French €€€

(☎01 43 67 38 29; 80 rue de Charonne, 11e; lunch/5-course menus €26/55; ⏰lunch Tue-Fri, dinner Mon-Fri; Ⓜ Charonne) Reading the menu at Septime won't get you far – it looks mostly like an obscure shopping list (hanger steak/chicory/roots, chicken's egg/foie gras/*lardo*). But rest assured, the alchemists in the kitchen here, run by Bertrand Grébaut, are capable of producing some truly beautiful creations. The Northern European bistro feel (hardwood tables, blue-smocked wait staff) marries well with the modern cuisine. Reserve in advance – particularly for the unbeatable lunch deal.

LE SIFFLEUR DE BALLONS Wine Bar €

(www.lesiffleurdeballons.com; 34 rue de Citeaux, 12e; lunch menus €14, mains €7-15; ⏰10.30am-3pm & 5.30-10pm Tue-Sat; Ⓜ Faidherbe Chaligny) With Tom Waits on the stereo and a few cactuses atop the register, this contemporary wine bar clearly has a dash of California in its soul. The wines, though, are all French – and all natural – and paired with a quality selection of simple but delicious offerings: *tartines*, soups, lentil salad with truffle oil, cheeses and Iberian charcuterie plates. Look out for the weekly tastings with winemakers.

Marché Bastille

BISTROT PAUL BERT Bistro €€

(☎01 43 72 24 01; 18 rue Paul Bert, 11e; 3-course lunch/dinner menus €18/36; ⊙lunch & dinner Tue-Sat; Ⓜ Faidherbe-Chaligny) When food writers make lists of the best Paris bistros, one of the names that almost always pops up is Paul Bert. The timeless decor and perfectly executed classic dishes guarantee that you'll need to reserve well in advance, even if the service isn't always up to snuff.

AU PASSAGE Bistro €€

(Map p68; ☎01 43 55 07 52; www.facebook.com/aupassage; 1bis passage de St-Sébastien, 11e; 2-/3-course lunch menus €13.50/19.50, dinner €20-35; ⊙lunch Mon-Fri, dinner Mon-Sat; Ⓜ St-Sébastien-Froissart) Have faith in talented Australian chef James Henry at this raved-about *petit bar de quartier* (neighbourhood bar) with vegetable crates piled scruffily in the window and a fridge filling one corner of the old-fashioned dining room. The lunch menu – a good-value, uncomplicated choice of two starters and two mains – is chalked on the blackboard, while dinner sees waiting staff in jeans twirl in and out the pocket-size kitchen with tapas-style starters to share, followed by a feisty shoulder of lamb, side of beef or other meaty cut for the entire table. Advance reservations essential.

CHEZ MARIANNE Jewish €

(Map p68; 2 rue des Hospitalières St-Gervais, 4e; mains €19-24; ⊙noon-midnight; Ⓜ St-Paul) Absolutely heaving at lunchtime, Chez Marianne translates as elbow-to-elbow eating beneath age-old beams on copious portions of felafel, hummus, purées of aubergine and chickpeas, and 25-odd other *zakouski* (hors d'œuvres; €12/14/16 for plate of 4/5/6). Fare is Sephardic rather than Ashkenazi (the norm at most Pletzl eateries), not Beth Din kosher, and a hole-in-the-wall window sells felafel in pita (€6) to munch on the move.

NANASHI Fusion €

(Map p68; ☎09 60 00 25 59; www.nanashi.fr; 57 rue Charlot, 3e; bento €14-16; ⊙noon-midnight Mon-Fri, to 6pm Sat & Sun; Ⓜ Filles du Calvaire) A fabulous lunch and after-dark address wedged between boutiques in the Haut Marais, this hip industrial space with street-facing windows and concrete floor is ubercool, ultrahealthy and great value. Pick from salads, soups and bento boxes chalked on the board; don't miss out on the amazing and astonishing freshly squeezed fruit and veg cocktails. Weekend brunch €17.

DERRIÈRE Modern French €€

(Map p68; ☎01 44 61 91 95; www.derriere-resto.com; 69 rue des Gravilliers, 3e; lunch menus €25, mains €17-24; ⊙lunch Mon-Fri & Sun, dinner daily; Ⓜ Arts et Métiers) Play ping pong

Parisian Food Markets

Nowhere encapsulates Paris' village atmosphere more than its markets. No markets take place on Mondays.

Marché aux Enfants Rouges (Map p68; 39 rue de Bretagne, 3e; ⊙8.30am-1pm & 4-7.30pm Tue-Fri, 4-8pm Sat, 8.30am-2pm Sun; Ⓜ Filles du Calvaire) Paris' oldest covered market with communal tables for lunch.

Marché Bastille (Map p68; bd Richard Lenoir, 11e; ⊙7am-2.30pm Thu & Sun; Ⓜ Bastille or Richard Lenoir) Arguably the best open-air market in Paris.

Marché Raspail (Map p68; bd Raspail btwn rue de Rennes & rue du Cherche Midi, 6e; ⊙regular market 7am-2.30pm Tue & Fri, organic market 9am-3pm Sun; Ⓜ Rennes) Especially popular on Sundays, when it's filled with organic produce.

Rue Cler (Map p76; rue Cler, 7e; ⊙8am-7pm Tue-Sat, 8am-noon Sun; Ⓜ École Militaire) Fabulous commercial street that almost feels like a party on weekends, when the whole neighbourhood seemingly shops en masse.

Rue Mouffetard (Map p68; rue Mouffetard, 5e; ⊙8am-7.30pm Tue-Sat, 8am-noon Sun; Ⓜ Censier Daubenton) Paris' most photogenic commercial street.

between courses, sit on the side of the bed, glass of champers in hand, lounge between bookcases, or entertain a dinner party of 12 – such is the nature of this apartment restaurant, which has courtyard seating in summer. Its vibe might be chilled in a trendy 'shoes-off' kind of way, but Derrière (literally 'Behind') is deadly serious in the kitchen. Classic French bistro dishes and more inventive creations are excellent, as is its Sunday brunch. Advance reservations for dinner essential.

The Islands

BERTHILLON Ice Cream €

(Map p68; 31 rue St-Louis en l'Île, 4e; ice cream from €2; ⏲10am-8pm Wed-Sun; Ⓜ Pont Marie) Berthillon is to ice cream what Château Lafite Rothschild is to wine and Valhrona is to chocolate. And with nigh on to 70 flavours to choose from, you'll be spoiled for choice. While the fruit-flavoured sorbets (cassis, blackberry etc) produced by this celebrated *glacier* (ice-cream maker) are renowned, the chocolate, coffee, *marrons glacés* (candied chestnuts), Agenaise (Armagnac and prunes), *noisette* (hazelnut) and *nougat au miel* (honey nougat) are richer. Eat in or grab a cone with one/two/three/four small scoops (€2.30/3.60/4.90/6.20) to take away.

Latin Quarter

L'AOC Regional Cuisine €€

(Map p68; ☎01 43 54 22 52; www.restoaoc.com; 14 rue des Fossés St-Bernard, 5e; 2-/3-course lunch menus €21/29, mains €18-32; ⏲lunch & dinner Tue-Sat; Ⓜ Cardinal Lemoine) *'Bistrot carnivore'* is the strapline of this ingenious restaurant concocted around France's most respected culinary products. The concept here is AOC (Appellation d'Origine Contrôlée): everything has been reared or made according to strict guidelines designed to protect products that are unique to a particular village, town or area.

L'AGRUME Neo-Bistro €€

(Map p68; ☎01 43 31 86 48; 15 rue des Fossés St-Marcel, 5e; 2-/3-course lunch menus €19/24,

Left: Cheese, Rue Mouffetard (p89); **Below:** Delicatessen, Rue Cler (p89)
(LEFT) STUART DEE/GETTY IMAGES ©; (BELOW) HEMIS/ALAMY ©

mains €26-39; ⌚lunch & dinner Tue-Sat; Ⓜ Censier Daubenton) Snagging a table at L'Agrume – meaning 'Citrus Fruit' – is tough; reserve several days ahead. The reward is watching chefs work with seasonal products in the open kitchen while you dine – at a table, bar-stool or *comptoir* (counter) – at this pocket-size contemporary bistro on a little-known street on the Latin Quarter's southern fringe. Lunching is magnificent value and a real gourmet experience. Evening dining is an exquisite, no-choice *dégustation* (tasting) melody of five courses, different every day.

LE COUPE-CHOU Traditional French **€€**
(Map p68; ☎01 46 33 68 69; www.lecoupechou.com; 9 & 11 rue de Lanneau, 5e; 2-/3-course lunch menus €27, mains €18-25; ⌚Mon-Sat; Ⓜ Maubert-Mutualité) This maze of candlelit rooms inside a vine-clad, 17th-century town house is overwhelmingly romantic. Ceilings are beamed, furnishings are antique, and background classical music mingles with the intimate chatter of diners. As in the days when Marlene Dietrich et al dined here, advance reservations are essential. Timeless French dishes include Burgundy snails, steak tartare and bœuf bourguignon, finished off with fabulous cheeses sourced from *fromagerie* Quatrehomme and a silken crème brûlée.

BISTROT LES PAPILLES Bistro **€€**
(Map p68; ☎01 43 25 20 79; www.lespapillesparis.com; 30 rue Gay Lussac, 5e; lunch/dinner menus from €22/31; ⌚10.30am-midnight Mon-Sat; Ⓜ Raspail or RER Luxembourg) This hybrid bistro, wine cellar and *épicerie* with a sunflower-yellow façade is one of those fabulous dining experiences that packs out the place. Dining is at simply dressed tables wedged beneath bottle-lined walls, and fare is market-driven: each weekday cooks up a different *marmite du marché* (market casserole). But what really sets it apart is its exceptional wine list.

St-Germain & Les Invalides

BOUILLON RACINE Brasserie €€

(Map p68; ☎01 44 32 15 60; www.bouillonracine.com; 3 rue Racine, 6e; lunch menu €14.50, menus €30-41; ⏰noon-11pm; Ⓜ Cluny–La Sorbonne) Inconspicuously situated in a quiet street, this heritage-listed art nouveau 'soup kitchen', with mirrored walls, floral motifs and ceramic tiling, was built in 1906 to feed market workers. Despite the magnificent interior, the food – inspired by age-old recipes – is by no means an afterthought. Superbly executed dishes include stuffed, spit-roasted suckling pig, pork shank in Rodenbach red beer, and scallops and shrimps with lobster coulis. And why not finish off your foray in gastronomic history with an old-fashioned sherbet.

ZE KITCHEN GALERIE Gastronomic €€€

(Map p68; ☎01 44 32 00 32; www.zekitchengalerie.fr; 4 rue des Grands Augustins, 6e; lunch/dinner menus €26.50/65; ⏰lunch Mon-Fri, dinner Mon-Sat; Ⓜ St-Michel) William Ledeuil's passion for Southeast Asian travel is certainly on display in the feisty dishes he creates in his Michelin-starred glass-box kitchen. Hosting three to five art exhibitions a year, the restaurant/gallery's menu is a vibrant feast of broths loaded with Thai herbs and coconut milk, meat and fish cooked *à la plancha* (grilled on a metal plate) and inventive desserts such as white chocolate and wasabi ice cream.

CUISINE DE BAR Sandwich Bar €

(Map p68; 8 rue du Cherche Midi, 6e; dishes €7.50-13; ⏰8.30am-7pm Tue-Sat; Ⓜ Sèvres-Babylone) As next-door neighbour to one of Paris' most famous bakers, this is not any old sandwich bar. *Au contraire, mes amis.* Rather, it is an ultrachic spot to lunch between designer boutiques. Open sandwiches are cut from that celebrated **Poilâne** (Map p68; www.poilane.fr; 8 rue du Cherche Midi, 6e; ⏰7.15am-8.15pm Mon-Sat; Ⓜ Sèvres-Babylone) bread and fabulously topped with gourmet goodies such as foie gras, smoked duck, gooey St-Marcellin cheese and Bayonne ham.

Drinking

LE BARON ROUGE Wine Bar

(Map p68; 1 rue Théophile Roussel, 12e; ⏰10am-2pm & 5-10pm Mon-Fri, 10am-10pm Sat, 10am-4pm Sun; Ⓜ Ledru-Rollin) Just about the ultimate Parisian wine-bar experience, this place has a dozen barrels of the stuff stacked up against the bottle-lined walls. As unpretentious as you'll find, it's a local meeting place where everyone is welcome and is especially busy on Sundays after the Aligre Market wraps up. All the usual suspects – cheese, charcuterie and oysters – will keep your belly full. For a small deposit, you can even fill up 1L bottles straight from the barrel for under €5.

HARRY'S NEW YORK BAR Cocktail Bar

(Map p76; www.harrysbar.fr; 5 rue Daunou, 2e; Ⓜ Opéra) One of the most popular American-style bars in the prewar years, Harry's once welcomed writers such as F Scott Fitzgerald and Ernest Hemingway, who no doubt sampled the bar's unique cocktail and creation: the Bloody Mary. The Cuban mahogany interior dates from the mid-19th century and was brought over from a Manhattan bar in 1911.

EXPERIMENTAL COCKTAIL CLUB Cocktail Bar

(Map p76; www.experimentalcocktailclub.com; 37 rue St-Saveur, 2e; Ⓜ Réaumur-Sébastopol) Called ECC by trendies, this fabulous speakeasy, with grey façade and old-beamed ceiling, is effortlessly hip. Oozing spirit and soul, the cocktail bar – with retro-chic decor by American interior designer Cuoco Black – is a sophisticated flashback to those *années folles* (crazy years) of prohibition New York. DJs set the space partying until dawn at weekends.

AU SAUVIGNON Wine Bar

(Map p68; 80 rue des Saints Pères, 7e; ⏰8.30am-10pm; Ⓜ Sèvres-Babylone) There's no more authentic *bar à vin* than this. Grab a table in the evening sun or head to the quintessential bistro interior, with an original zinc bar, tightly packed tables and hand-painted ceiling celebrating French

Le Baron Rouge

HEMIS/GETTY IMAGES ©

viticultural tradition. Order a plate of *casse-croûtes au pain Poilâne* – toast with ham, pâté, terrine, smoked salmon, foie gras and so on.

ANGELINA Tearoom

(Map p76; 226 rue de Rivoli, 1er; M Tuileries) This beautiful, high-ceilinged tea room has exquisite furnishings, mirrored walls and fabulous fluffy cakes. More importantly, it serves the best and most wonderfully decadent 'African' hot chocolate (€7) in the history of time, served with a pot of whipped cream. It's a positive meal replacement. Branches include two at Versailles.

LES DEUX MAGOTS Cafe

(Map p68; www.lesdeuxmagots.fr; 170 bd St-Germain, 6e; 7.30am-1am; M St-Germain des Prés) If ever there were a cafe that summed up St-Germain des Prés' early-20th-century literary scene, it's this former hang-out of anyone who was anyone, darling. You will spend *beaucoup* to sip a coffee in a wicker chair on the terrace shaded by dark-green awnings and geraniums spilling from window boxes, but it's an undeniable piece of Parisian history. If you're feeling decadent, order the famous shop-made hot chocolate, served in porcelain jugs. And if you're curious about the name of the cafe, it actually refers to the two *magots* (grotesque figurines) of Chinese dignitaries at the entrance.

CAFÉ LA PALETTE Cafe

(Map p68; www.cafelapaletteparis.com; 43 rue de Seine, 6e; 6.30am-2am Mon-Sat; M Mabillon) In the heart of Parisian gallery land, this fin-de-siècle cafe and erstwhile stomping ground of Paul Cézanne, Pablo Picasso and Georges Braque attracts a grown-up set of fashion people and local art dealers. Its large summer terrace overlooking rue Jacques Callot is a beautiful place to relax.

Entertainment

Paris' two premier listings guides, *Pariscope* (€0.40) and *L'Officiel des Spectacles*, both in French, are available from newsstands on Wednesdays and are crammed with everything that's on in the capital.

Cabaret

Whirling lines of feather boa–clad, high-kicking dancers are a quintessential fixture on Paris' entertainment scene – for everyone but Parisians. Still, the dazzling sets, costumes and routines guarantee an entertaining evening (or matinee). Tickets to major cabaret spectacles start from around €90 (from €130 with lunch, from €150 with dinner), and usually include a half-bottle of Champagne. Reservations are essential; venues sell tickets online.

MOULIN ROUGE Cabaret

(Map p76; ☎01 53 09 82 82; www.moulinrouge.fr; 82 bd de Clichy, 18e; M Blanche) Immortalised in the posters of Toulouse-Lautrec and later on screen by Baz Luhrmann, the Moulin Rouge twinkles beneath a 1925 replica of its original red windmill.

LE LIDO DE PARIS Cabaret

(Map p76; ☎01 40 76 56 10; www.lido.fr; 116bis av des Champs-Élysées, 8e; M George V) Founded at the close of WWII, this showstopping cabaret gets top marks for its lavish costumes.

Theatre

COMÉDIE FRANÇAISE Theatre

(Map p76; www.comedie-francaise.fr; place Colette, 1er; M Palais Royal–Musée du Louvre) Founded in 1680 under Louis XIV, the 'French Comedy' theatre bases its repertoire around the works of classic French playwrights. The theatre has its roots in an earlier company directed by Molière at the Palais Royal – the French playwright and actor was seized by a convulsion on stage during the fourth performance of the *Imaginary Invalid* in 1673 and died later at his home on nearby rue de Richelieu.

Opera & Ballet

PALAIS GARNIER Opera

(Map p76; ☎08 92 89 90 90; www.operadeparis.fr; place de l'Opéra, 9e; M Opéra) The city's original opera house.

OPÉRA BASTILLE Opera, Ballet

(Map p68; ☎08 92 89 90 90; www.operadeparis.fr; 2-6 place de la Bastille, 12e; M Bastille) Tickets at this monolithic 3400-seat venue, which opened in 1989, go on sale online two weeks before they're available by telephone or at the **box office (☎01 40 01 19 70; 130 rue de Lyon, 12e; 2.30-6.30pm Mon-Sat)**. Standing-only tickets (*places débouts*; €5) are available 90 minutes before performances begin.

Shopping

DIDIER LUDOT Fashion

(Map p76; www.didierludot.fr; 19-20 & 23-24 Galerie de Montpensier, 1er; M Palais Royal–Musée du Louvre) In the rag trade since 1975, collector Didier Ludot sells the city's finest couture creations of yesteryear in his exclusive twinset of boutiques. He also hosts exhibitions and has

Moulin Rouge ©MoulinRouge®

published a book portraying the evolution of the little black dress, brilliantly brought to life in his boutique that sells just that, **La Petite Robe Noire** (125 Galerie de Valois, 1er; M Palais Royal–Musée du Louvre).

SHAKESPEARE & COMPANY Books

(Map p68; www.shakespeareandcompany.com; 37 rue de la Bûcherie, 5e; ⏲10am-11pm Mon-Fri, from 11am Sat & Sun; M St-Michel) A kind of spell descends as you enter this enchanting bookshop, where nooks and crannies overflow with new and second-hand English-language books. Fabled for nurturing writers, at night its couches turn into beds where writers stay in exchange for stacking shelves. Readings by emerging to illustrious authors take place at 7pm most Mondays.

MERCI Concept Store

(Map p68; www.merci-merci.com; 111 bd Beaumarchais, 3e; M St-Sébastien–Froissart) The landmark Fiat Cinquecento in the courtyard marks the entrance to this unique multistorey concept store whose rallying cry is one-stop shopping. Fashion, accessories, linens, lamps and various other nifty designs for the home (a kitchen brush made from recycled egg shells and coffee grounds, anyone?). A trio of inspired eating-drinking spaces complete Paris' hippest shopping experience. All proceeds go to a children's charity in Madagascar.

GALERIES LAFAYETTE Department Store

(Map p76; www.galerieslafayette.com; 40 bd Haussmann, 9e; ⏲9.30am-8pm Mon-Sat, to 9pm Thu; M Auber or Chaussée d'Antin) Probably the best known of the big Parisian department stores.

GUERLAIN Perfume

(Map p76; www.guerlain.com; 68 av des Champs-Élysées, 8e; ⏲10.30am-8pm Mon-Sat, noon-7pm Sun; M Franklin D Roosevelt) Guerlain is Paris' most famous *parfumerie*, and its shop (dating from 1912) is one of the most beautiful in the city. For total indulgence, make an appointment at its decadent **spa** (☎01 45 62 11 21).

PIERRE HERMÉ Food, Drink

(Map p68; www.pierreherme.com; 72 rue Bonaparte, 6e; ⏲10am-7pm Sun-Fri, to 8pm Sat; M Odéon or RER Luxembourg) It's the size of a chocolate box, but once you're in, your tastebuds will go wild. Pierre Hermé is one of Paris' top chocolatiers.

LE BON MARCHÉ Department Store

(Map p68; www.bonmarche.fr; 24 rue de Sèvres, 7e; ⏲10am-8pm Mon-Wed & Fri, to 9pm Thu & Sat; M Sèvres Babylone) Built by Gustave Eiffel as Paris' first department store in 1852. The icing on the cake is its glorious food hall, **La Grande Épicerie de Paris** (www.lagrandeepicerie.fr; 36 rue de Sèvres, 7e; ⏲8.30am-9pm Mon-Sat; M Sèvres Babylone).

MARIAGE FRÈRES Tea

(Map p68; www.mariagefreres.com; 30, 32 & 35 rue du Bourg Tibourg, 4e; ⏲daily; M Hôtel de Ville) Founded in 1854, this is Paris' first and arguably finest tea shop.

Information

Paris Convention & Visitors Bureau (Office de Tourisme et de Congrès de Paris; ☎08 92 68 30 00; www.parisinfo.com; 25-27 rue des Pyramides, 1er; ⏲9am-7pm Jun-Oct, shorter hrs rest of year; M Pyramides)

Getting There & Away

Air

Aéroport Roissy Charles de Gaulle (CDG; ☎01 70 36 39 50; www.aeroportsdeparis.fr) Paris' biggest airport 30km northeast of the centre in the suburb of Roissy.

Aéroport d'Orly (ORY; ☎01 70 36 39 50; www.aeroportsdeparis.fr) Aéroport d'Orly is the older, smaller of Paris' two major airports, 19km south of the city.

Aéroport Beauvais (BVA; ☎08 92 68 20 66; www.aeroportbeauvais.com) Beauvais is 75km north of Paris.

Train

Gare du Nord (rue de Dunkerque, 10e; M Gare du Nord) The terminus for the Eurostar and

Thalys trains, serving London and Amsterdam, respectively, as well as north-bound domestic trains.

Gare de l'Est (**bd de Strasbourg, 10e; M Gare de l'Est**) The terminus for east-bound trains, including services to Strasbourg, Berlin and Vienna.

Gare de Lyon (**bd Diderot, 12e; M Gare de Lyon**) The terminus for southeast-bound trains, with destinations including Provence, the Alps, the Riviera and Italy. Also serves Geneva.

Gare d'Austerlitz (**bd de l'Hôpital, 13e; M Gare d'Austerlitz**) The terminus for a handful of south-bound trains, including services to Orléans and Limoges.

Gare Montparnasse (**av du Maine & bd de Vaugirard, 15e; M Montparnasse Bienvenüe**) The terminus for southwest- and west-bound trains, including services to Brittany, the Loire, Bordeaux, Toulouse and Spain and Portugal.

Gare St-Lazare (**rue St-Lazare & rue d'Amsterdam, 8e; M St-Lazare**) The terminus for Normandy-bound trains.

Getting Around

To/From the Airports

AÉROPORT ROISSY CHARLES DE GAULLE

A **taxi** to the city centre takes approximately 40 minutes, assuming no traffic jams. During the day, expect to pay around €50; the fare increases 15% between 5pm and 10am and on Sundays. Only take taxis at a clearly marked rank. Never follow anyone who approaches you at the airport and claims to be a driver.

RER B (**32 46; www.ratp.fr; one-way €9; 5am-11pm**) Departs every 10 to 15 minutes, serving the Gare du Nord, Châtelet–Les Halles and St-Michel–Notre Dame stations in the city centre. Journey time is approximately 35 minutes.

Air France Bus 2 (**08 92 35 08 20; http://videocdn.airfrance.com/cars-airfrance; one-way €15; 6am-11pm**) To the Arc de Triomphe.

Air France Bus 4 (**08 92 35 08 20; http://videocdn.airfrance.com/cars-airfrance; adult €16.50; 6am-10pm from Roissy Charles de Gaulle, 6am-9.30pm from Paris**) Links the airport with Gare de Lyon (50 minutes) in eastern Paris and Gare Montparnasse (55 minutes) in southern Paris.

RATP Bus 350 (**32 46; www.ratp.fr; adult €5.10 or 3 metro tickets; 5.30am-11pm**) Links the airport with Gare de l'Est in northern Paris every 30 minutes. Journey time is one hour.

Roissybus (**32 46; www.ratp.fr; adult €10; 5.30am-11pm**) Direct bus every 15 minutes to/from Opéra (corner of rue Scribe and rue Auber, 9e). Journey time is 45 minutes to one hour.

AÉROPORT D'ORLY

There is no direct train to/from Orly; you'll need to change transport halfway.

The **RER B** (€11, 35 minutes, every four to 12 minutes) connects Orly with the St-Michel–Notre Dame, Châtelet–Les Halles and Gare du Nord stations in the city centre. To get from Orly to the RER station (Antony), you must first take the **Orlyval** automatic train. The service runs from 6am to 11pm; there are fewer trains on weekends. You only need one ticket.

Air France Bus 1 (**08 92 35 08 20; http://videocdn.airfrance.com/cars-airfrance; adult €11.50; 5am-10.20pm from Orly, 6am-11.20pm from Invalides**) This bus runs to/from the Gare Montparnasse (35 minutes) in southern Paris, Invalides in the 7e, and the Arc de Triomphe.

Orlybus (**32 46; www.ratp.fr; adult €6.90; 6am-11.20pm from Orly, 5.35am-11.05pm from Paris**) RATP bus every 15 to 20 minutes to/from metro Denfert Rochereau (30 minutes) in the 14e.

Bicycle

The Vélib' (**www.velib.paris.fr**) bike share scheme has revolutionised how Parisians get around. There are some 1800 stations throughout the city, each with anywhere from 20 to 70 bike stands. The bikes are accessible around-the-clock.

- To get a bike, you first need to purchase a one-/seven-day subscription (€1.70/8). There are two ways to do this: either at the terminals (which require a credit card with an embedded smartchip) at docking stations or online.
- After you authorise a deposit (€150) to pay for the bike should it go missing, you'll receive an ID number and PIN code and you're ready to go.

PARIS MARKET/ALAMY ©

Don't Miss Flea Markets

Marché aux Puces de Montreuil (av du Professeur André Lemière, 20e; ⌚8am-7.30pm Sat-Mon; Ⓜ Porte de Montreuil) Pictured above, this 19th-century *marché aux puces* (flea market) particularly known for its secondhand clothing, designer seconds, engravings, jewellery, linen, crockery, old furniture and appliances.

Marché aux Puces de St-Ouen (www.marcheauxpuces-saintouen.com; rue des Rosiers, av Michelet, rue Voltaire, rue Paul Bert & rue Jean-Henri Fabre; ⌚9am-6pm Sat, 10am-6pm Sun, 11am-5pm Mon; Ⓜ Porte de Clignancourt) Founded in the late 19th century and said to be Europe's largest.

Marché aux Puces de la Porte de Vanves (http://pucesdevanves.typepad.com; av Georges Lafenestre & av Marc Sangnier, 14e; ⌚from 7am Sat & Sun; Ⓜ Porte de Vanves) The Porte de Vanves flea market is the smallest and one of the friendliest of the lot.

- Bikes are rented in 30-minute intervals: the first half-hour is free, the second is €2, the third and each additional half-hour are €4. If you return a bike before a half-hour is up and then take a new one, you will not be charged.
- If the station you want to return your bike to is full, log in to the terminal to get 15 minutes for free to find another station.
- Bikes are geared to cyclists aged 14 and over, and are fitted with gears, an antitheft lock with key, reflective strips and front/rear lights. Bring your own helmet, though!

Public Transport

Paris' underground network, run by the RATP, consists of two separate but linked systems: the metro and the RER suburban train line.

- Each metro train is known by the name of its terminus.
- Trains usually start at around 5.30am, with the last train beginning its run between 12.35am and 1.15am (2.15am on Friday and Saturday).
- The same RATP tickets are valid on the metro, RER (for travel within the city limits), buses, trams and the Montmartre funicular. A ticket – called *Le Ticket t+* – costs €1.70 (half-price

for children aged four to nine years) if bought individually and €12.70 for adults for a *carnet* (book) of 10. Ticket windows and vending machines accept most – but not all – credit cards.

Tourist Passes

The **Mobilis** and **Paris Visite** passes are valid on the metro, RER, SNCF's suburban lines, buses, night buses, trams and Montmartre funicular railway.

The Mobilis card allows unlimited travel for one day and costs €6.40 (two zones) to €14.20 (five zones). Buy it at any metro, RER or SNCF station in the Paris region.

Paris Visite allows unlimited travel (including to/from airports) as well as discounted entry to certain museums and other discounts and bonuses. Passes are valid for either three or five zones. The zone 1 to 3 pass costs €10/16/22/31 for one/two/three/five days.

Taxi

The *prise en charge* (flag fall) is €2.40. Within the city limits, it costs €0.96 per kilometre for travel between 10am and 5pm Monday to Saturday (*Tarif A*; white light on taxi roof and meter).

To order a taxi, call or reserve online with Taxis G7 (☎01 41 27 66 99; www.taxisg7.fr), Taxis Bleus (☎01 49 36 10 10; www.taxis-bleus.com) or Alpha Taxis (☎01 45 85 85 85; www.alphataxis.com).

AROUND PARIS

Disneyland Resort Paris

It took almost €4.6 billion to turn the beet fields 32km east of Paris into Europe's first Disney theme park. What started out as Euro-Disney in 1992 today comprises three main areas: the traditional Disneyland Park, the film-oriented Walt Disney Studios Park, and hotel-, shop- and restaurant-filled Disney Village.

One-day admission fees at **Disneyland Resort Paris** (☎hotel booking 01 60 30 60 30, restaurant reservations 01 60 30 40 50; www.disneylandparis.com; 1-day adult/child €59/53; Ⓜ Marne-la-Vallée/Chessy) include unlimited

Left: Arc de Triomphe du Carrousel, Jardin des Tuileries (p65);
Below: Macarons
(LEFT) CRAIG PERSHOUSE/GETTY IMAGES ©; (BELOW) CHARITY BURGGRAAF/GETTY IMAGES ©

access to attractions in *either* Disneyland Park or Walt Disney Studios Park. The latter also includes entry to Disneyland Park three hours before it closes. A multitude of multiday passes, special offers and packages are always available. The multiday passes also allow you to enter and leave both parks as often as you like over nonconsecutive days within one year.

Sights

DISNEYLAND PARK Theme Park
(⏲10am-8pm Mon-Fri, 9am-8pm Sat & Sun Sep-May, 9am-11pm Jun-Aug, hours can vary) Disneyland Park has five themed *pays* (lands): the 1900s-styled **Main Street USA**; **Frontierland**, home of the legendary Big Thunder Mountain ride; **Adventureland**, which evokes exciting and exotic lands with popular rides such as Pirates of the Caribbean; **Fantasyland**, crowned by Sleeping Beauty's exquisite castle; and the high-tech **Discoveryland**, with massive queues for rides such as Space Mountain: Mission 2 and Buzz Lightyear Laser Blast.

WALT DISNEY STUDIOS PARK Theme Park
(⏲9am-7pm late Jun-early Sep, 10am-7pm Mon-Fri & 9am-7pm Sat & Sun early Sep-late Jun) The sound stage, production backlot and animation studios provide an up-close illustration of how films, TV programs and cartoons are produced, with behind-the-scenes tours, larger-than-life characters and spine-tingling rides such as the Twilight Zone Tower of Terror.

Getting There & Away

TRAIN Marne-la-Vallée/Chessy, Disneyland's RER station, is served by line A4; trains run frequently from central Paris (€7.10).

Around Paris

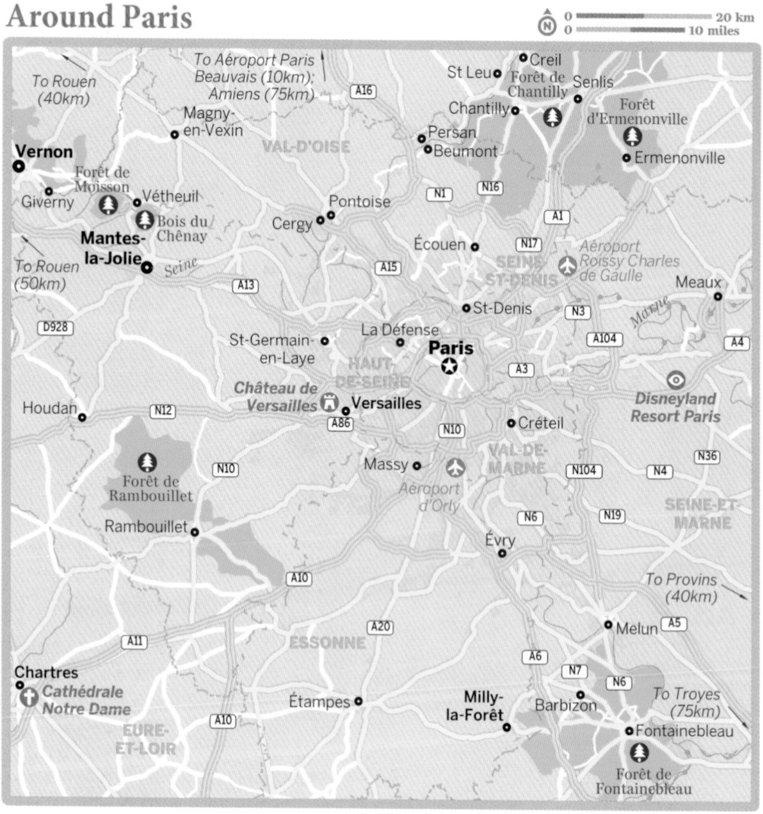

CAR Follow route A4 from Porte de Bercy (direction Metz-Nancy) and take exit 14.

Versailles

Louis XIV transformed his father's hunting lodge into the monumental Château de Versailles in the mid-17th century, and it remains France's most famous, grandest palace. Situated in the prosperous, leafy and bourgeois suburb of Versailles, 28km southwest of Paris, the Baroque château was the kingdom's political capital and the seat of the royal court from 1682 up until the fateful events of 1789 when revolutionaries massacred the palace guard and dragged Louis XVI and Marie Antoinette back to Paris, where they were ingloriously guillotined.

By noon queues for tickets and entering the château spiral out of control: arrive early morning and avoid Tuesday and Sunday, its busiest days. Save time by pre-purchasing tickets on the château's website or at Fnac branches and head straight to Entrance A.

Try to time your visit for the Grandes Eaux Musicales or the after-dark Grandes Eaux Nocturnes, truly magical 'dancing water' displays – set to music composed by Baroque- and classical-era composers – throughout the grounds in summer.

Sights

To access areas that are otherwise off limits and to learn more about Versailles' history, take a 90-minute guided tour of the Private Apartments of Louis XV and Louis

XVI and the Opera House or Royal Chapel. Tour tickets include access to the most famous parts of the palace, such as the Hall of Mirrors and the King's and Queen's State Apartments; prebook online.

CHÂTEAU DE VERSAILLES Palace

(☎01 30 83 78 00; www.chateauversailles.fr; admission passport (estate-wide access) €18, with musical events €25, palace €15; ⏰8am-6pm Tue-Sat, 9am-6pm Sun Apr-Oct, 8.30am-5.30pm Tue-Sat, 9am-5.30pm Sun Nov-Mar) This splendid and enormous palace was built in the mid-17th century during the reign of Louis XIV – the Roi Soleil (Sun King) – to project the absolute power of the French monarchy, which was then at the height of its glory. Its scale and decor reflect Louis XIV's taste for profligate luxury and his boundless appetite for grandstanding. Some 30,000 workers and soldiers toiled on the structure, the bills for which all but emptied the kingdom's coffers. The château has undergone relatively few alterations since its construction, though almost all the interior furnishings disappeared during the Revolution and many of the rooms were rebuilt by Louis-Philippe (r 1830–48). The current €400 million restoration program is the most ambitious yet and until it's completed in 2020 at least a part of the palace is likely to be clad in scaffolding when you visit.

Work began in 1661 under the guidance of architect Louis Le Vau (Jules Hardouin-Mansart took over from Le Vau in the mid-1670s); painter and interior designer Charles Le Brun; and landscape artist André Le Nôtre, whose workers flattened hills, drained marshes and relocated forests as they laid out the seemingly endless gardens, ponds and fountains.

Le Brun and his hundreds of artisans decorated every moulding, cornice, ceiling and door of the interior with the most luxurious and ostentatious of appointments: frescos, marble, gilt and woodcarvings, many with themes and symbols drawn from Greek and Roman mythology. The King's Suite of the **Grands Appartements du Roi et de la Reine** (King's and Queen's State Apartments), for example, includes rooms dedicated to Hercules, Venus, Diana, Mars and Mercury. The opulence reaches its peak in the recently restored **Galerie des Glaces** (Hall of Mirrors), a 75m-long ballroom with 17 huge mirrors on one side and, on the other, an equal number of windows looking out over the gardens and the setting sun.

CHÂTEAU DE VERSAILLES GARDENS & PARK Gardens

(admission free except during musical events; ⏰gardens 8.30am-8.30pm Apr-Oct, 8am-6pm Nov-Mar, park 7am-7pm Apr-Oct, 8am-6pm Nov-Mar) The section of the vast gardens nearest the palace, laid out between 1661 and 1700 in the formal French style, is famed for its geometrically aligned terraces,

Château de Versailles gardens
ALBERTO COTO/GETTY IMAGES ©

Versailles

A Day in Court

Visiting Versailles – even just the State Apartments – may seem overwhelming at first, but think of it as a house where people ate, drank, worked, slept and conspired and you'll be on the right path.

Some two decades into his long reign, Louis XIV began turning his father's hunting lodge into a palace large enough to house his entire court (to keep closer tabs on the 6000-strong army of courtiers). Sparing no expense, the Sun King employed the greatest artists and craftspeople of the day and by 1682 he'd created the most extravagant dormitory in history.

The royal schedule was as accurate and predictable as a Swiss watch. By following this itinerary of rooms you can recreate the king's day, starting with the **King's Bedchamber** 1 and the Queen's Bedchamber 2, where the royal couple was roused at about the same time. The royal procession then leads through the **Hall of Mirrors** 3 to the **Royal Chapel** 4 for morning Mass and returns to the **Council Chamber** 5 for late-morning meetings with ministers. After lunch the king might ride or hunt or visit the **King's Library** 6. Later he could join courtesans for an 'apartment evening' starting from the **Hercules Drawing Room** 7 or play billiards in the Diana **Drawing Room** 8 before supping at 10pm.

VERSAILLES BY NUMBERS

Rooms 700 (11 hectares of roof)
Windows 2153
Staircases 67
Gardens and parks 800 hectares
Trees 200,000
Fountains 50 (with 620 nozzles)
Paintings 6300 (measuring 11km laid end to end)
Statues and sculptures 2100
Objets d'art and furnishings 5000
Visitors 5.3 million per year

CHRISTOPHE LEHENAFF/PHOTOLIBRARY ©

Queen's Bedchamber
Chambre de la Reine
The queen's life was on constant public display and even the births of her children were watched by crowds of spectators in her own bedchamber. **DETOUR »** The Guardroom, with a dozen armed men at the ready.

Lunch Break

Diner-style food at Sister's Café, crêpes at Le Phare St-Louis or picnic in the park.

Guardroom

South Wing

King's Library
Bibliothèque du Roi
The last resident, bibliophile Louis XVI, loved geography and his copy of *The Travels of James Cook* (in English, which he read fluently) is still on the shelf here.

GIANNI DAGLI ORTI/ALAMY ©

Savvy Sightseeing

Avoid Versailles on Monday (closed), Tuesday (Paris' museums close, so visitors flock here) and Sunday, the busiest day. Also, book tickets online so you don't have to queue.

DENNIS JOHNSON/GETTY ©

Hall of Mirrors

Galerie des Glaces

The solid-silver candelabra and furnishings in this extravagant hall, devoted to Louis XIV's successes in war, were melted down in 1689 to pay for yet another conflict. **DETOUR»** The antithetical Peace Drawing Room, adjacent.

MIKE BOOTH/ALAMY ©

King's Bedchamber

Chambre du Roi

The king's daily life was anything but private and even his *lever* (rising) at 8am and *coucher* (retiring) at 11.30pm would be witnessed by up to 150 sycophantic courtiers.

Council Chamber

Cabinet du Conseil

This chamber, with carved medallions evoking the king's work, is where the monarch met his various ministers (state, finance, religion etc) depending on the days of the week.

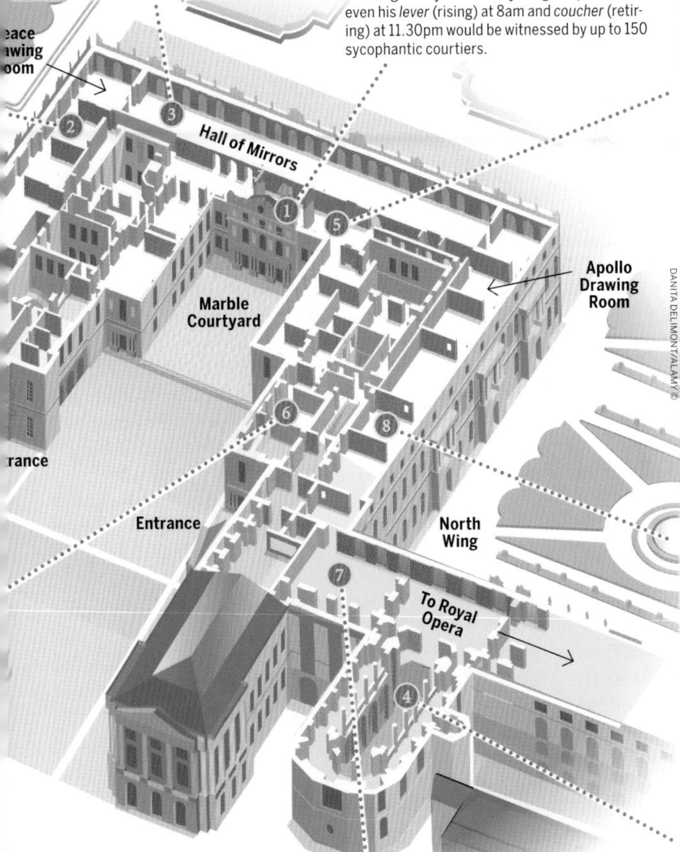

DANITA DELIMONT/ALAMY ©

Diana Drawing Room

Salon de Diane

With walls and ceiling covered in frescos devoted to the mythical huntress, this room contained a large billiard table reserved for Louis XIV, a keen player.

Royal Chapel

Chapelle Royale

This two-storey chapel (with gallery for the royals and important courtiers, and the ground floor for the B-list) was dedicated to St Louis, patron of French monarchs. **DETOUR»** The sumptuous Royal Opera.

Hercules Drawing Room

Salon d'Hercule

This salon, with its stunning ceiling fresco of the strong man, gave way to the State Apartments, which were open to courtiers three nights a week. **DETOUR»** Apollo Drawing Room, used for formal audiences and as a throne room.

Cathédrale Notre Dame, Chartres

ORICI-FLICKR/GETTY IMAGES ©

flowerbeds, tree-lined paths, ponds and fountains. The 400-odd statues of marble, bronze and lead were made by the most talented sculptors of the era. The English-style Jardins du Petit Trianon are more pastoral and have meandering, sheltered paths.

The **Grand Canal** (Chateau gardens), 1.6km long and 62m wide, is oriented to reflect the setting sun. It is traversed by the 1km-long Petit Canal, creating a cross-shaped body of water with a perimeter of more than 5.5km.

The **Orangerie**, built under the Parterre du Midi (Southern Flowerbed) on the southwestern side of the palace, shelters tropical plants in winter.

The gardens' largest fountains are the 17th-century **Bassin de Neptune**, a dazzling mirage of 99 spouting gushers 300m north of the palace, and the **Bassin d'Apollon**, built in 1688 at the eastern end of the Grand Canal. The straight side of the Bassin de Neptune abuts a small round pond graced by a winged dragon. Emerging from the water in the centre of the Bassin d'Apollon is Apollo's chariot, pulled by rearing horses.

VERSAILLES STABLES Stables

Today, Versailles' school of architecture and restoration workshops fill the **Petites Écuries** (Little Stables), while the **Grandes Écuries** (Big Stables) house the **Académie du Spectacle Équestre** (Academy of Equestrian Arts; ☎01 39 02 07 14; www.acadequestre.fr; 1 av Rockefeller). In addition to its 45-minute **Les Matinales** (morning training sessions; adult/13-18yr/under 13yr €12/10/6.50; ⏰11.15am Sat & Sun & some Thu) the academy presents spectacular **Reprises Musicales** (musical equestrian shows; adult/13-18yr/under 13yr €25/22/16; ⏰6pm Sat, 3pm Sun & some Thu), which sell out weeks in advance.

Information

Tourist office (☎01 39 24 88 88; www.versailles-tourisme.com; 2bis av de Paris; ⏰10am-6pm Mon, 9am-7pm Tue-Sun Apr-Sep, 11am-5pm Sun & Mon, 9am-6pm Tue-Sat Oct-Mar)

Getting There & Away

TRAIN RER line C5 (€3.20, 45 minutes, frequent) goes from Paris' Left Bank RER stations to Versailles–Rive Gauche station. Less convenient, RER line C8 links Paris with Versailles-Chantiers station, a 1.3km walk from the château. SNCF operates trains from Paris' Gare Montparnasse to Versailles-Chantiers (€12.10, 45 to 60 minutes), and from Paris' Gare St-Lazare to Versailles–Rive Droite, 1.2km from the château.

Chartres

Step off the train in Chartres, 91km southwest of Paris, and the two very different spires – one Gothic, the other Romanesque – of its glorious 13th-century cathedral beckon. Don't miss a stroll around Chartres' carefully preserved old town. Adjacent to the cathedral, staircases and steep streets lined with half-timbered medieval houses lead downhill to the narrow western channel of the Eure River, romantically spanned by footbridges.

Sights

CATHÉDRALE NOTRE DAME Cathedral
(www.diocese-chartres.com; place de la Cathédrale; 8.30am-7.30pm, to 10pm Tue, Fri & Sun Jun-Aug) One of the crowning architectural achievements of Western civilisation, the 130m-long Cathédrale Notre Dame de Chartres was built in the Gothic style during the first quarter of the 13th century to replace a Romanesque cathedral that had been devastated by fire – along with much of the town – in 1194.

The cathedral's west, north and south entrances have superbly ornamented triple portals, but the west entrance, known as the **Portail Royal**, is the only one that predates the fire. Carved from 1145 to 1155, its superb statues, whose features are elongated in the Romanesque style, represent the glory of Christ in the centre, and the Nativity and the Ascension to the right and left, respectively. The structure's other main Romanesque feature is the 105m-high **Clocher Vieux** (Old Bell Tower; also called the Tour Sud or 'South Tower'). Construction began in the 1140s; it remains the tallest Romanesque steeple still standing.

A visit to the 112m-high **Clocher Neuf** **(New Bell Tower; adult/child €7/free; 9.30am-12.30pm & 2-6pm Mon-Sat, 2-6pm Sun May-Aug, 9.30am-12.30pm & 2-5pm Mon-Sat, 2-5pm Sun Sep-Apr)**, also known as the Tour Nord (North Tower), is worth the ticket price and the climb up the long spiral stairway (350 steps).

The cathedral's 172 extraordinary **stained-glass windows**, almost all of which date back to the 13th century, form one of the most important ensembles of medieval stained glass in the world. The three most exquisite windows, dating from the mid-12th century, are in the wall above the west entrance and below the rose window. Survivors of the fire of 1194 (they were made some four decades before), the windows are renowned for the depth and intensity of their tones, famously known as 'Chartres blue'.

Guided **tours in English** **(02 37 28 15 58; millerchartres@aol.com; tour €10; noon & 2.45pm Mon-Sat Apr-Oct)** of the cathedral with the incomparable Malcolm Miller depart from the shop.

Getting There & Away

TRAIN Frequent SNCF trains link Paris' Gare Montparnasse (€14.40, 55 to 70 minutes) with Chartres, some of which stop at Versailles-Chantiers.

CAR If you're driving from Paris, follow the A6 from Porte d'Orléans (direction Bordeaux–Nantes), then the A10 and A11 (direction Nantes) and take the 'Chartres' exit.

Normandy & Brittany

Stretching along France's northern coastline overlooking La Manche (the English Channel), Normandy has been at the centre of French history for more than 1000 years. And so it's a region awash with historical sights, from the iconic spires of Mont St-Michel and the handwoven epic of the Bayeux Tapestry to the landmark beaches of D-Day. It's also home to three of the nation's favourite 'C's – Camembert, cider and the potent apple-flavoured spirit *calvados*.

Across the border is Brittany. Once an independent kingdom, it's still governed by its own culture, language and fiery Celtic spirit. This wild and windswept region boasts France's craggiest coastline, as well as a whole host of prehistoric monuments, medieval châteaux and timeless towns, including the corsaire city of St-Malo and the lovely half-timbered Quimper.

Étretat cliff, Normandy
LOIC LAGARDE/GETTY IMAGES

Normandy & Brittany

1. Mont St-Michel
2. Giverny
3. Bayeux Tapestry
4. Carnac Megaliths
5. D-Day Sites
6. St-Malo

0 50 km
0 25 miles
ENGLISH CHANNEL (LA MANCHE)
Côte d'Albâtre
Dieppe
SOMME
A28
D915
Étretat
SEINE-MARITIME
Cherbourg Aéroport
Cherbourg
Utah Beach
D-Day Landing Beaches
Le Havre Aéroport
A29
N15
A151
Abbaye de Jumièges
A28
N13
Pointe du Hoc Ranger Memorial
5
Longues-sur-Mer
Pont de Normandie
Honfleur
Le Marais Vernier
Rouen
N31
Trouville
Deauville
N13
D79
Juno Beach
A13
Aéroport Rouen Vallée du Seine
OISE
Parc Naturel Régional des Marais du Cotentin et du Bessin
Omaha Beach
Bayeux
3
Aéroport Caen-Carpiquet
Caen
N175
Touques
Les Andelys
CALVADOS
Seine
A13
Vire
A84
A28
Charentonne
EURE
2
Giverny
D562
N13
Granville
Collines de Normandie
Falaise
Vire
D973
D836
Orne
Avranches
D977
1
MANCHE
Risle
Iton
ORNE
Dreux
Mont St-Michel
Parc Naturel Régional Normandie-Maine
Collines du Perche
A84
Alençon
Montagne-au-Perche
Park Naturel Régional du Perche
Chartres
Eure
A11
N12
N12
EURE-ET-LOIR
A84
Sarthe
A28
Vitré
MAYENNE
SARTHE
A11
A81
Laval
ILLE-ET-VILAINE
Le Mans
LOIRET
N171
A11
BLÉSOIS
ANJOU
Blois
Angers
A11
Tours
MAINE-ET-LOIRE
INDRE-ET-LOIRE
Indre
DEUX-SÈVRES
INDRE
VENDÉE
VIENNE

Normandy & Brittany's Highlights

1

Mont St-Michel

The mount's charm is in the *marais* (salt marshes) and the immense view – so magical, so mysterious. It evokes the crossing of the Red Sea. Pilgrims have trekked across the sand since the 8th century and it's steeped in legend. Top Right: Pilgrimage to Mont St-Michel; Bottom Right: Abbaye du Mont St-Michel (p128)

Need to Know

DANGER! Take a guide to navigate the swift tides and River Couesnon **TOURS** Guided walks (www.decouvertebaie.com); canoe-kayak trips (www.seakayak-fr.com) **For more, see p128**

Local Knowledge

Mont St-Michel Don't Miss List

BY JACK LECOQ, WALKING GUIDE AND STORYTELLER EXTRAORDINAIRE

1 THE BAREFOOT WALK

You can wear plastic shoes, but walking the 13km from Bec d'Andaine in Genêts to Mont St-Michel barefoot is wonderful. We walk across pitch sand, quicksand, sand flats and endless ripple marks made by the tides. At times we're almost knee-deep in mud.

2 ÎLOT DE TOMBELAINE

After walking for about an hour (3km) this islet, occupied by the English for 35 years during the Hundred Years War, pops up. It is now a bird reserve and, from April to July, full of exceptional birdlife. November to March, once the birds have left, you can follow a tiny footpath to the top of the islet from where a stunning view of Mont St-Michel unfolds – quite astonishing.

3 ABBAYE DU MONT ST-MICHEL

We cross the River Couesnon, the medieval border between Normandy and Brittany, and there is the mount. The abbey is marvellous. It has beautiful works of art and rooms: the hall where pilgrims gathered is magnificent, as is the Salle des Chevaliers (Knights Hall), where monks spent hours illuminating manuscripts.

4 AVRANCHES

I was born here. After visiting the abbey it's worth going to Avranches to **Le Scriptorial (Musée des Manuscrits du Mont St-Michel; ☎ 02 33 79 57 00; place d'Estouteville; adult/child €7/3; ⏰10am-7pm Jul & Aug, shorter hours rest of year)**, where all the historical documents and manuscripts scribed at the abbey are preserved. It illuminates Mont St-Michel's many legends and stories.

5 MEMORABLE MOUNT VIEWS

The view from the Jardin des Plantes in Avranches is unique; as are the bay panoramas from Pointe du Grouin du Sud near the fishing village of St-Léonard, 5km southwest, and the clifftops in Carolles, 20km north. If you like oysters, enjoy the view from Cancale; if wildlife is your thing, being afloat on a tiny boat in the 365-island archipelago of Îles Chausey is out of this world.

Giverny

Discover your inner impressionist in the village of Giverny (p123), where Claude Monet lived and worked for 43 years surrounded by the gardens and lily ponds that inspired his most celebrated paintings. Also home to a museum exploring the work of impressionists in France, Giverny makes an ideal day trip from either Rouen or Paris.

2

3

Bayeux Tapestry

Travel back a thousand years with the world's oldest comic strip, the 68.3m Bayeux Tapestry (p124), which recounts the story of the Norman invasion of England in 1066. It is believed to have been commissioned by Bishop Odo of Bayeux, William the Conqueror's half-brother, to celebrate the opening of Bayeux cathedral in 1077, although opinion is divided on where it was actually made.

MAX HOMAND/GETTY IMAGES ©

4

Carnac Megaliths

If your imagination's fired by ancient history, you definitely shouldn't miss Carnac (p143). Comprising 3000 menhirs arranged in parallel lines measuring over 6km end to end, it's one of the world's most monumental prehistoric building projects. No one has managed to definitively explain exactly how – or why – the monument was built. Then again, the megalithic mystery is all part of the fun.

MEDIOIMAGES/PHOTODISC/GETTY IMAGES ©

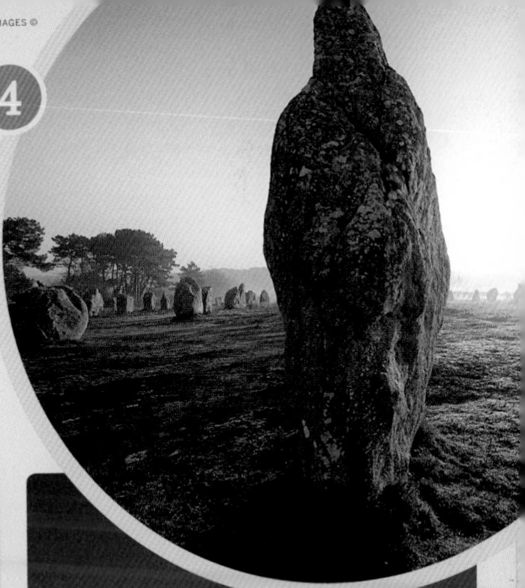

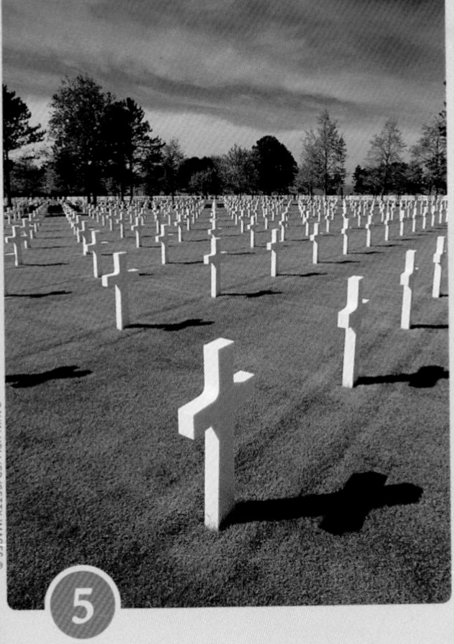

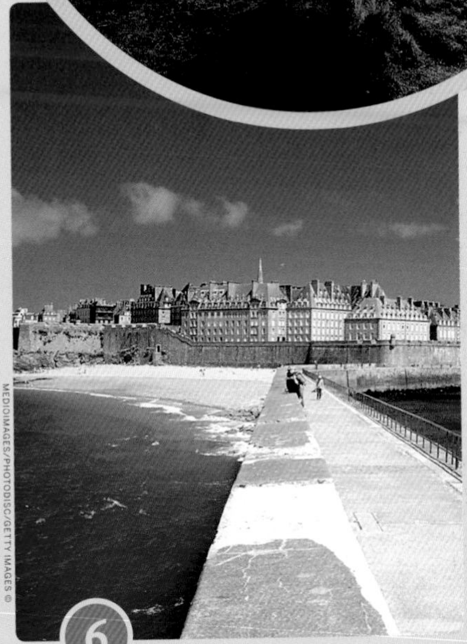

5

D-Day Sites

On 6 June 1944, six Allied divisions stormed ashore along the Norman coastline during 'Operation Overlord', otherwise known as the D-Day landings. Though ultimately successful, the human cost of the invasion was immense; the Normandy American Cemetery & Memorial (p126) above Omaha Beach is one of many memorials dotted along the coastline. For the historical background, head for the fascinating Caen Mémorial. American Cemetery (p126), Colleville-sur-Mer

6

St-Malo

Seaside cities don't come much more spectacular than St-Malo (p132), the 'corsaire city', which is ringed by defensive walls designed by the great military architect Vauban during the 18th century. Though badly damaged during WWII, St-Malo has been impeccably restored over the last half-century; don't miss a stroll along the ramparts and a cruise to nearby Dinard.

Normandy & Brittany's Best...

Museums

- **Musée des Impressionnismes Giverny** (p123) Impressionism in the Norman countryside.
- **Bayeux Tapestry** (p124) Devour the illustrated exploits of William the Conqueror.
- **Musée Eugène Boudin** (p127) Art aplenty in lovely Honfleur.
- **Caen Mémorial** (p126) Immerse yourself in WWII at this audiovisual extravaganza.
- **Musée Départemental Breton** (p141) Quimper's Breton-history museum.

Dining

- **Le Bistro de Jean** (p134) Fabulous, elbow-to-elbow bistro dining in St-Malo.
- **Le Coquillage** (p136) Dine in serious style near Cancale courtesy of celebrity chef Olivier Roellinger.
- **Les Nymphéas** (p119) Rouen address known for its imaginative take on traditional Norman dishes.
- **La Balafon** (p135) Much-loved modern and unpretentious bistro in Dinard.
- **Léon le Cochon** (p145) Feast on pork in all its guises at Rennes' Léon the Pig.

Boat Trips

- **Île de Batz** (p138) Ferries link Roscoff with this offshore escape.
- **Île d'Ouessant** (p137) Brave the waves en route to this craggy, windswept island.
- **Honfleur** (p127) Take a memorable cruise from Honfleur's historic harbour.
- **St-Malo to Dinard** (p135) Catch the water taxi between these seaside neighbours.
- **Dinan** (p138) Canal boats putter along the River Rance to St-Malo.

Culinary Must-Tries

- **Cider** (p140) Try Breton cider at Argol's Cider Museum.
- **Oysters** (p136) Eat freshly shucked oysters on Cancale's quayside.
- **Crêpes** (p142) Quimper's Crêperie du Quartier is a favourite for Breton pancakes.
- **Camembert** (p128) Sample Normandy's soft cheese at the Président Farm.

eft: Stained glass window, Cathédrale St-Corentin (p141); **Above:** Rooftops of Dinan (p138)

Need to Know

ADVANCE PLANNING

- **At least a month before** Book hotels in St-Malo, Dinard, Dinan and Rouen.
- **Two or three weeks before** Reserve your table at the big restaurants.
- **One day before** Reserve ferries to offshore islands such as the Île d'Ouessant, especially in July and August.

RESOURCES

- **Brittany Tourism** (www.brittanytourism.com) Brittany's main tourist site.
- **Normandy Tourism** (www.normandie-tourisme.fr) Normandy's main tourist site.
- **Normandie Mémoire** (www.normandiememoire.com) Multimedia D-Day site.
- **Cider Route** (www.larouteducidre.fr) Site for cider lovers.
- **Bretagne Rando** (Hiking, biking, kayaking and canoeing trails in Brittany.

GETTING AROUND

- **Budget flights** Fly from the UK to Dinard, Brest and Nantes.
- **Ferries** The main ports for cross-channel ferries are Roscoff, St-Malo and Cherbourg, although some ferries sail to Le Havre, Dieppe and Ouistreham (Caen).
- **Trains & Buses** Trains serve major towns, but you'll be stuck with buses to the smaller villages.
- **Car** Gives you maximum freedom, but be prepared for summer-time traffic jams and incomprehensible one-way systems in big cities.
- **Organised minibus tours** An excellent way to visit the D-Day beaches; book through Bayeux tourist office.

BE FOREWARNED

- **Mont St-Michel** The climb to the top involves lots of steps, many spiral and steep. Pay attention to tide times when walking to the mount. Arrive early or late in the day to avoid the worst crowds.
- **St-Malo** Accommodation books up fast in summer. If you decide to stay in the old city, you'll probably have to park outside, beyond the city walls.

Normandy & Brittany Itineraries

History seems to be etched into the landscape all over Normandy and Brittany. From medieval towns to ancient monuments, these regions offer a smorgasbord of historic sights, not to mention a truly stirring coastline.

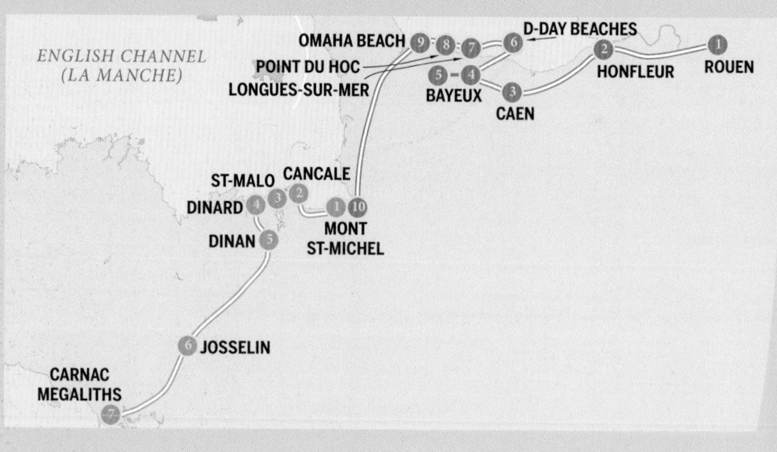

3 DAYS

ROUEN TO MONT ST-MICHEL

Norman Highlights

Start with a day exploring the old town of **(1) Rouen**, famous for its half-timbered architecture and Joan of Arc connections (the Maid of Orléans was burned at the stake here in 1431). Factor in the Musée des Beaux-Arts and the Cathédrale Notre Dame, followed by a meal to remember at Les Nymphéas and an overnight at Hôtel de Bourgtheroulde.

On day two head west to **(2) Honfleur** for lunch at one of the busy quayside bistros around the Vieux Bassin. Spend the afternoon at the **(3) Caen Mémorial**, which documents the history of WWII in impressive fashion. In the early evening, arrive in **(4) Bayeux** and check in to Les Logis du Rempart – don't leave without tasting the homemade *calvados* and cider.

Day three begins with a visit to the **(5) Bayeux Tapestry**, followed by an afternoon tour around the **(6) D-Day beaches**. Detour via the massive cannons of **(7) Longues-sur-Mer** and the **(8) Pointe du Hoc Ranger Memorial** before finishing up at **(9) Omaha Beach**, where you can pay your respects at the American military cemetery, featured in the opening shots of *Saving Private Ryan*. If time allows, continue to **(10) Mont St-Michel** for the start of our Breton tour.

MONT ST-MICHEL TO CARNAC
The Best of Brittany

This whistle-stop tour of Brittany begins just across the Norman border at **(1) Mont St-Michel**, France's famous island abbey. Summer crowds can be oppressive, so arrive early to dodge the crush or, better still, take a guided walk across the sands, followed by an atmospheric night-time visit.

Day two starts with a spin along the coast to sample fresh oysters in **(2) Cancale** before arriving at the walled city of **(3) St-Malo**, where you can take a walk around the town's ramparts and choose from plenty of excellent restaurants. On day three catch the boat across the water to the elegant resort town of **(4) Dinard**, a favourite seaside getaway for wealthy Parisians since the days of the belle époque.

On day four visit delightfully medieval **(5) Dinan** before cutting across Brittany's centre to visit **(6) Château de Josselin**. Spend your last day exploring the monumental **(7) Carnac Megaliths**, the largest prehistoric structure anywhere on earth.

St-Malo (p132)

Discover Normandy & Brittany

At a Glance

- **Normandy** (p118) A joy to visit for its soft cheese, rolling countryside, iconic abbey of Mont St-Michel and historic D-Day beaches.
- **Brittany** (p132) Privy to its own history, heritage and language (not to mention cuisine), this spectacular coastal region is unique.

Painter at Honfleur (p127)
TAI POWER STEEF/GETTY IMAGES ©

NORMANDY

Ever since the armies of William the Conqueror set sail from its shores in 1066, Normandy has played a pivotal role in European history, from the Norman invasion of England to the Hundred Years' War and the D-Day beach landings of 1944. This rich and often brutal past is what draws travellers to the region today, though the pastoral landscapes, small fishing ports, dramatic coastline and cuisine are all good reasons to include this accessible and beautiful chunk of France on any trip.

Rouen

POP 119,930

With its elegant spires, beautifully restored medieval quarter and soaring Gothic cathedral, the ancient city of Rouen is one of Normandy's highlights. Rouen has had a turbulent history – it was devastated several times during the Middle Ages by fire and plague, and was occupied by the English during the Hundred Years' War. The young French heroine Joan of Arc (Jeanne d'Arc) was tried for heresy and burned at the stake in the central square in 1431.

Sights

PLACE DU VIEUX MARCHÉ Square

The old city's main thoroughfare, rue du Gros Horloge, runs from the cathedral west to this square, where 19-year-old Joan of Arc was executed for heresy in 1431. Dedicated in 1979, the **Église Jeanne d'Arc** (place du Vieux Marché; 10am-noon & 2-6pm Apr-Oct), with its fish-scale exterior, marks the spot where Joan was burned at the stake. The church's soaring modernist interior, lit by some marvellous 16th-century stained glass, is well worth a look.

CATHÉDRALE NOTRE DAME Cathedral
(place de la Cathédrale; ⌚2-6pm Mon, 7.30am-7pm Tue-Sat, 8am-6pm Sun) Rouen's stunning Gothic cathedral, with its polished, brilliant-white facade, is the famous subject of a series of paintings by Monet. Its 75m-tall **Tour de Beurre** (Butter Tower) was financed by locals who donated to the cathedral in return for being allowed to eat butter during Lent – or so the story goes.

MUSÉE DES BEAUX-ARTS Art Museum
(☎02 35 71 28 40; www.rouen-musees.com; esplanade Marcel Duchamp; adult/child €5/free; ⌚10am-6pm Wed-Mon) Housed in a grand structure erected in 1870, Rouen's fine-arts museum features canvases by Caravaggio, Rubens, Modigliani, Pissarro, Renoir, Sisley (lots) and (of course) several works by Monet.

ABBATIALE ST-OUEN Abbey
(place du Général de Gaulle; ⌚10am-noon & 2-6pm Tue-Thu, Sat & Sun) This 14th-century abbey is a fine example of the Rayonnant Gothic style. The entrance is through a lovely garden along rue des Faulx.

FREE **AÎTRE ST-MACLOU** Historic Quarter
(186 rue Martainville; ⌚8am-8pm Apr-Oct, 8am-7pm Nov-Mar) For a macabre thrill, check out the courtyard of this curious ensemble of half-timbered buildings built between 1526 and 1533. Decorated with lurid woodcarvings of skulls, crossbones, gravediggers' tools and hourglasses, it was used as a burial ground for plague victims as recently as 1781.

Sleeping

HÔTEL DE BOURGTHEROULDE Hotel €€€
(☎02 35 14 50 50; www.hotelspa rouen.com; 15 place de la Pucelle; r €240-380; ❄📶🏊**)** This stunning conversion of an old private mansion brings a dash of glamour and luxury to Rouen's hotel scene. Rooms are large, gorgeously designed and feature beautiful bathrooms. There's a pool (you can see through the sleek lobby bar's glass floor down into it), a sauna and spa in the basement, and two restaurants.

LA BOULANGERIE B&B €
(☎06 12 94 53 15; www.laboulangerie.fr; 59 rue St-Nicaise; d €77-92, q €150; 📶**)** Tucked into a quiet side street slightly off the historic quarter, this adorable B&B occupying a former bakery offers three pleasingly decorated rooms. The largest 'Levain' room can sleep up to four people, while the smaller 'Patte d'Ours' features exposed beams. Your charming hosts are a mine of local information.

Eating

LES NYMPHÉAS Traditional French €€
(☎02 35 89 26 69; www.lesnympheas-rouen.com; 7-9 rue de la Pie; mains €29-37, menus €34-52; ⌚lunch & dinner Tue-Sat) Its formal table settings arrayed under 16th-century beams, this fine restaurant serves cuisine based on fresh ingredients. Let chef Patrick Kukurudz and his team seduce you with meat and fish dishes accompanied with inspired sauces. Even the cheaper lunch menu (€34) is exquisite.

MINUTE ET MIJOTÉ Bistro €
(58 rue de Fontenelle; mains €20, menus €13-30; ⌚lunch & dinner Mon-Sat) This smart bistro is one of our favourite finds in Rouen. The trademark here is freshness and great value for money, hence its fast-growing reputation. There's outdoor seating in summer.

DAME CAKES Pastries €
(☎02 35 07 49 31; www.damecakes.fr; 70 rue St-Romain; mains €11, menus €14-22; ⌚10.30am-7pm Mon-Sat) This gourmet emporium is a veritable feast of perfectly presented pastries, cakes and chocolates. Best of all, there's a *salon de thé* (tea room) attached, where you can tuck

Rouen

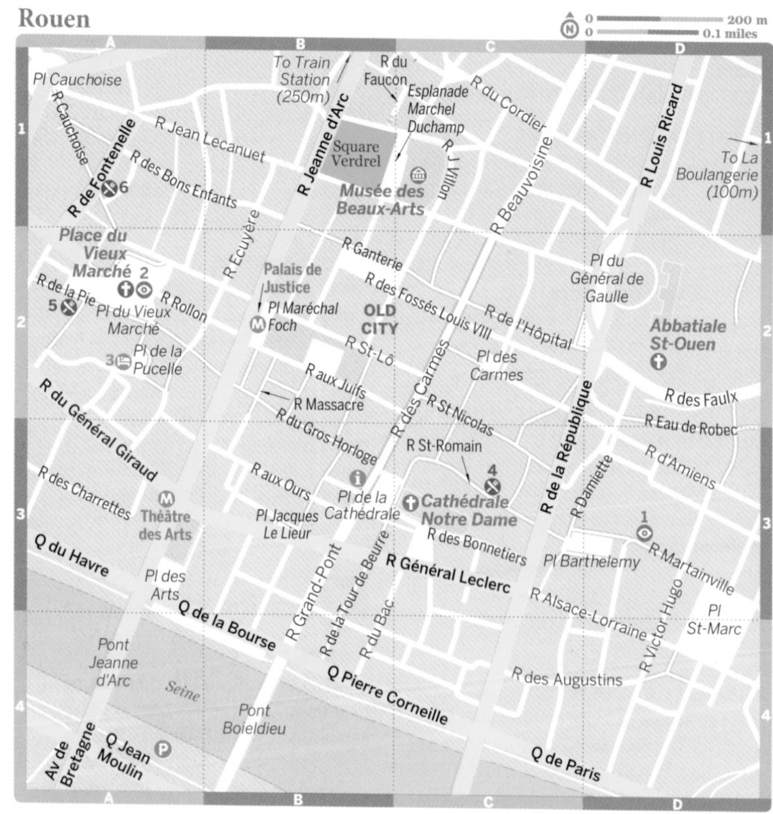

Rouen

Top Sights

Abbatiale St-Ouen	D2
Cathédrale Notre Dame	C3
Musée des Beaux-Arts	C1
Place du Vieux Marché	A2

Sights

1 Aître St-Maclou	D3
2 Église Jeanne d'Arc	A2

Sleeping

3 Hôtel de Bourgtheroulde	A2

Eating

4 Dame Cakes	C3
5 Les Nymphéas	A2
6 Minute et Mijoté	A1

into well-prepared quiches and salads at lunchtime. Save room for the exquisite *tarte tatin* (upside-down apple cake). Lovely.

Information

Tourist office (02 32 08 32 40; www.rouentourisme.com; 25 place de la Cathédrale; 9am-7pm Mon-Sat, 9.30am-12.30pm & 2-6pm Sun & holidays)

Getting There & Away

The train station is just north of the city centre. Trains from Rouen run to the following destinations:

Caen From €24.90, 1½ hours, eight to 10 daily.

Paris St-Lazare From €21.90, 1¼ hours, about 27 daily Monday to Friday, 14 to 19 Saturday and Sunday.

Bayeux

POP 14,350

Bayeux has become famous throughout the English-speaking world thanks to a 68m-long piece of painstakingly embroidered cloth: the 11th-century Bayeux Tapestry (p124), whose 58 scenes vividly tell the story of the Norman invasion of England in 1066. But there's more to Bayeux than this unparalleled piece of needlework. The first town to be liberated after D-Day (on the morning of 7 June 1944), it is one of the few in Calvados to have survived WWII practically unscathed. A great place to soak up the Norman atmosphere, Bayeux' delightful city centre is crammed with 13th- to 18th-century buildings, including lots of wood-framed Norman-style houses, and a fine Gothic cathedral. Bayeux also makes an ideal launch pad for exploring the D-Day beaches just to the north.

Sights

CATHÉDRALE NOTRE DAME Cathedral

(rue du Bienvenu; 8.30am-6pm) Most of Bayeux' spectacular Norman Gothic cathedral dates from the 13th century, though the crypt (accessible from the north side of the choir), the arches of the nave and the lower portions of the entrance towers are 11th-century Romanesque. The central tower was added in the 15th century; the copper dome dates from the 1860s. First prize for tackiness has got to go to 'Litanies de la Sainte Vierge', a 17th-century retable in the first chapel on the left as you enter the cathedral.

FREE **CONSERVATOIRE DE LA DENTELLE** Lace Workshop

(Lace Conservatory; 02 31 92 73 80; http://dentelledebayeux.free.fr; 6 rue du Bienvenu; 9.30am-12.30pm & 2.30-5pm Mon-Sat) This workshop is dedicated to the preservation of traditional Norman lacemaking, and you can watch some of France's most celebrated lacemakers create intricate designs using dozens of bobbins and hundreds of pins. At its height, the local lace industry employed 5000 lacemakers.

Detour: Abbaye de Jumièges

Following the Seine valley west of Rouen, the D982 road winds through little towns, occasionally following the banks of the Seine as it climbs and descends. About 27km west of Rouen, in Jumièges, the **Abbaye de Jumièges (02 35 37 24 02; ; adult/child €5/free; 9.30am-6.30pm Jul-Aug, 9.30am-1pm & 2.30-5.30pm Sep-Jun)** is an absolute must-see, even if you're not a history buff. With its ghostly white stone set off by a backdrop of trees, it's one of the most evocative ruins in Normandy. The church was begun in 1020, and William the Conqueror attended its consecration in 1067. It declined during the Hundred Years' War and then enjoyed a renaissance under Charles VII. It continued to flourish until the 18th-century revolutionaries booted out the monks and allowed the buildings to be mined for construction materials.

MUSÉE MÉMORIAL DE LA BATAILLE DE NORMANDIE War Museum

(Battle of Normandy Memorial Museum; bd Fabien Ware; adult/child €7/3.80; 9.30am-6.30pm May-Sep, 10am-12.30pm & 2-6pm Oct-Apr) Using well-chosen photos, personal accounts, dioramas and wartime objects, this first-rate museum offers an excellent introduction to WWII in Normandy. Don't miss the 25-minute film on the Battle of Normandy, screened in English up to five times daily.

Sleeping

LES LOGIS DU REMPART B&B €

(02 31 92 50 40; www.lecornu.fr; 4 rue Bourbesneur; d €60-80, q €130;) What a find. This *maison de famille* (family home) shelters three rooms that ooze old-fashioned cosiness. Our favourite, the Bajocasse, has parquet floor and Toile de Jouy wallpaper. Best of all, your hosts run a tasting shop downstairs – the perfect place to stock up on top-quality, homemade *calvados* and cider. Breakfast is extra (€6) and features – you guessed it – organic apple juice and apple jelly.

HÔTEL D'ARGOUGES Traditional Hotel **€€**
(**02 31 92 88 86; www.hotel-dargouges.com; 21 rue St-Patrice; d €134-149; closed Dec-Jan;**) This graceful venture, in a stately 18th-century residence, has 28 comfortable rooms with old-time touches, such as exposed beams, thick walls and old-fashioned furniture, and a deliciously lush little garden. Most bathrooms have been recently upgraded. Breakfast is served in an enchanting room complete with an 18th-century tapestry, period wood panels and parquet floors.

Eating

LA RAPIÈRE Norman **€€**
(**02 31 21 05 45; 53 rue St-Jean; menus €15-33.50; lunch & dinner Fri-Tue**) Housed in a late-1400s mansion composed of stone walls and big wooden beams, La Rapière is an atmospheric restaurant that specialises in Normandy staples such as terrines, duck and veal with Camembert. Four fixed-price menus assure a splendid meal on any budget.

LE POMMIER Norman **€€**
(**02 31 21 52 10; www.restaurantlepommier.com; 38-40 rue des Cuisiniers; menus €15-30; closed Sun Nov-Mar & mid-Dec–mid-Jan;**) A celebration of all things Norman, Le Pommier's menus include such classics as Caen-style tripe and steamed pollock. A vegetarian menu – a rarity in Normandy – is also available, with dishes such as soya-beans steak in Norman cream. The restaurant has a romantic setting, with bare stone walls, warm feature walls and hardwood floors.

Information

Tourist office (**02 31 51 28 28; www.bessin-normandie.com; pont St-Jean; 9.30am-12.30pm & 2-6pm**).

Getting There & Away

TRAIN For Paris Gare St-Lazare and Rouen, change at Caen (€6.20, 20 minutes, at least hourly).

D-Day Beaches

Code-named 'Operation Overlord', the D-Day landings were the largest military operation in history. On 6 June 1944, swarms of landing craft – part of an armada of over 6000 ships and boats – hit the northern Normandy beaches and tens of thousands of soldiers from the USA, the UK, Canada and elsewhere arrived on French soil.

The majority of the 135,000 Allied troops stormed ashore along 80km of beaches north of Bayeux code-named (from west to east) Utah, Omaha, Gold, Juno and Sword. The landings on D-Day – known as 'Jour J' in French – were followed by the 76-day Battle of Normandy, during which the Allies suffered 210,000 casualties, including 37,000 troops killed. German casualties are believed to have been around 200,000; another 200,000 German soldiers were taken prisoner. About 14,000 French civilians also died.

Caen's Mémorial (p126) and Bayeux' Musée Mémorial (p121) provide a comprehensive overview of the events of D-Day.

You can drive on the D514 along the D-Day coast or several signposted circuits around the battle sites – look for signs for 'D-Day-Le Choc' in the American sectors and 'Overlord-L'Assaut' in the British and Canadian sectors. The area is also sometimes called the Côte de Nacre (Mother-of-Pearl Coast). A free booklet called *The D-Day Landings and the Battle of Normandy*, available from tourist offices, has details on the eight major visitors' routes.

DIANA MAYFIELD/GETTY IMAGES ©

Don't Miss Giverny

The tiny country village of Giverny, 15km south of Les Andelys, is a place of pilgrimage for devotees of impressionism, and can feel swamped by the tour-bus crowd in the summer months. Monet lived here from 1883 until his death in 1926, in a rambling house surrounded by flower-filled gardens that's now the immensely popular **Maison et Jardins de Claude Monet**. Monet bought the Jardin d'Eau (Water Garden) in 1895 and set about creating his trademark lily pond, as well as the famous Japanese bridge (since rebuilt). Seasons have an enormous effect on Giverny. From early to late spring, daffodils, tulips, rhododendrons, wisteria and irises appear, followed by poppies and lilies. By June, nasturtiums, roses and sweet peas are in flower. Around September, there are dahlias, sunflowers and hollyhocks.

Giverny's other lure is the **Musée des Impressionnismes Giverny**, 100m down the road from the Maison et Jardinds de Claude Monet. Surrounded by beautiful gardens, this museum displays works by various impressionists as well as temporary exhibitions.

From Paris Gare St-Lazare there are up to 15 daily trains to Vernon (€13.30, 50 minutes), 7km west of Giverny. From Rouen (€10.80, 40 minutes), seven trains leave for Vernon before noon; to get back to Rouen, there's about one train every hour between 5pm and 8pm. Shuttle buses (€6.50 round trip, three to six daily April to October) meet most trains to and from Paris. Taxis usually wait outside the train station in Vernon and charge around €12 for a ride to Giverny, or you can rent a bicycle from Café L'Arrivée de Giverny across from Vernon train station.

NEED TO KNOW

Maison et Jardins de Claude Monet (☎02 32 51 28 21; www.fondation-monet.com; adult/child €9/5; ⏰9.30am-5.30pm Apr-Oct); **Musée des Impressionnismes Giverny** (☎02 32 51 94 65; www.mdig.fr; 99 rue Claude Monet; adult/child €6.50/3; ⏰10am-5.30pm Apr-Oct)

DANITA DELIMONT/GETTY IMAGES ©

Don't Miss Bayeux Tapestry

Undoubtedly the world's most celebrated embroidery, the misnamed Bayeux Tapestry (it's actually wool thread embroidered onto linen cloth) vividly recounts the story of the conquest of England in 1066 from an unashamedly Norman perspective. Divided into 58 scenes briefly captioned in almost-readable Latin, the main narrative fills up the centre of the canvas, while religious allegories and depictions of daily life in the 11th century unfold along the borders. The final showdown at the Battle of Hastings is depicted in truly graphic fashion, complete with severed limbs and decapitated heads (along the bottom of scene 52). Halley's Comet, which blazed across the sky in 1066, makes an appearance at the top of scene 32, while at the bottom of scene 15 there's – no, it can't be! – an 11th-century 'full Monty'. Scholars believe the 68.3m-long tapestry was commissioned by Bishop Odo of Bayeux, William the Conquerer's half-brother, for the opening of Bayeux' cathedral in 1077.

NEED TO KNOW

(☎ 02 31 51 25 50; www.tapisserie-bayeux.fr; rue de Nesmond; adult/child incl audioguide €7.80/3.80; 🕘 9am-6.30pm mid-Mar–mid-Nov, to 7pm May-Aug, 9.30am-12.30pm & 2-6pm mid-Nov–mid-Mar)

Tours

An organised minibus tour is an excellent way to get a sense of the D-Day beaches and their place in history. The Bayeux tourist office can handle reservations.

NORMANDY SIGHTSEEING TOURS D-Day Tour

(☎ 02 31 51 70 52; www.normandywebguide.com) From May to October (and on request the rest of the year), this experienced outfit offers morning (adult/child €45/25) tours of various beaches and cemeteries. These can be combined into an all-day excursion (€90/50).

NORMANDY TOURS D-Day Tour
(☎02 31 92 10 70; 26 place de la Gare, Bayeux; adult/child €48/41) This local operator offers five-hour tours of the main sites from 1pm to 6pm most days, as well as personally tailored trips. Based at Bayeux' Hotel de la Gare.

Getting There & Away

Bus Verts (www.busverts.fr) runs bus 70 (two or three daily Monday to Saturday, more frequently and on Sunday and holidays in summer), which goes northwest from Bayeux to Colleville-sur-Mer (Omaha Beach and the American Cemetery; €2.30, 35 minutes), Pointe du Hoc (€4.50) and Grandcamp-Maisy. Bus 74 (bus 75 in summer; three or four daily Monday to Saturday, more frequently and on Sunday and holidays in summer) links Bayeux with Arromanches (€2.30, 30 minutes), Gold and Juno Beaches, and Courseulles (€3.40, one hour).

Arromanches

In order to unload the vast quantities of cargo needed by the invasion forces without having to capture – intact – one of the heavily defended Channel ports (a lesson of the 1942 Dieppe Raid), the Allies set up prefabricated marinas, code-named **Mulberry Harbour**, off two of the landing beaches. These consisted of 146 massive cement caissons towed over from England and sunk to form a semicircular breakwater in which floating bridge spans were moored. In the three months after D-Day, the Mulberries facilitated the unloading of a mind-boggling 2.5 million men, four million tonnes of equipment and 500,000 vehicles.

The harbour established at Omaha was completely destroyed by a ferocious gale just two weeks after D-Day, but the remains of the second, **Port Winston** (named after Churchill), can still be seen near Arromanches, 10km northeast of Bayeux. At low tide you can walk out to one of the caissons from the beach. The best view of Port Winston and nearby **Gold Beach** is from the hill east of town, marked with a statue of the Virgin Mary.

Down in Arromanches itself and right on the beach, the **Musée du Débarquement** (Landing Museum; ☎02 31 22 34 31; www.normandy1944.com; place du 6 Juin; adult/child €7/5; ⏲9am-6pm, closed Jan), redesigned in 2004 for the 60th anniversary of D-Day, makes an informative stop before visiting the beaches. Dioramas, models and two films explain the logistics and importance of Port Winston. Written material is available in 18 languages.

Longues-sur-Mer

Part of the Nazis' Atlantic Wall, the massive casemates and 150mm German guns near Longues-sur-Mer, 6km west of Arromanches, were designed to hit targets some 20km away, including both Gold Beach (to the east) and Omaha Beach (to the west). Over six decades later, the mammoth artillery pieces are still in their colossal concrete emplacements – the only in situ large-calibre weapons in Normandy. For details on the tours in English available from April to October, contact the **Longues tourist office** (☎02 31 21 46 87; www.bessin-normandie.com).

Parts of the classic D-Day film, *The Longest Day* (1962), were filmed both here and at Pointe du Hoc. On clear days, Bayeux' cathedral, 8km away, is visible to the south.

Omaha Beach

The most brutal fighting on D-Day took place on the 7km stretch of coastline around Vierville-sur-Mer, St-Laurent-sur-Mer and Colleville-sur-Mer, 15km northwest of Bayeux, known as 'Bloody Omaha' to US veterans. Sixty years on, little evidence of the carnage unleashed here on 6 June 1944 remains except for concrete German bunkers, though at very low tide you can see a few remnants of the Mulberry Harbour.

These days Omaha is a peaceful place, a glorious stretch of fine golden sand partly lined with sand dunes and summer homes. Near the car park in St-Laurent-sur-Mer, a **memorial** marks the site of the first US military cemetery on French soil. **Circuit de la Plage d'Omaha**, trail-marked with a yellow stripe, is a self-guided tour along Omaha Beach.

On a bluff above the beach, the huge **Normandy American Cemetery & Memorial** (www.abmc.gov; Colleville-sur-Mer; 9am-5pm), 17km northwest of Bayeux, is the largest American cemetery in Europe. Featured in the opening scenes of Steven Spielberg's *Saving Private Ryan,* it contains the graves of 9387 American soldiers, including 41 pairs of brothers, and a memorial to 1557 others whose remains were never found. White marble crosses and Stars of David stretch off in seemingly endless rows, surrounded by an immaculately tended expanse of lawn.

Opened in 2007, the **visitor center**, mostly underground so as not to detract from the site, has an excellent free multimedia presentation on the D-Day landings.

Pointe du Hoc Ranger Memorial

At 7.10am on 6 June 1944, 225 US Army Rangers commanded by Lt Col James Earl Rudder scaled the 30m cliffs at Pointe du Hoc, where the Germans had a battery of huge artillery guns perfectly placed to rain shells onto the beaches of Utah and Omaha. Unbeknown to Rudder and his team, the guns had already been transferred inland, and they spent the next two days repelling fierce German counterattacks. By the time they were finally relieved on 8 June, 81 of the rangers had been killed and 58 more had been wounded.

Today the **site** (02 31 51 90 70; admission free; 9am-5pm), which France turned over to the US government in 1979, looks much as it did more than half a century ago. The ground is pockmarked with bomb craters, and the German command post (no longer open to the public because it's too close to the eroding cliff) and several of the concrete gun emplacements are still standing, scarred by bullet holes and blackened by flame-throwers.

As you face the sea, Utah Beach is 14km to the left.

Utah Beach

This beach is marked by memorials to the various divisions that landed here and the **Musée du Débarquement** (Landing Museum; 02 33 71 53 35; www.utah-beach.com; Ste-Marie du Mont; adult/child €7.50/3; 9.30am-7pm).

Caen Mémorial

Situated 3km northwest of Caen city centre, the innovative **Mémorial – Un Musée pour la Paix** (Memorial – A Museum for Peace; 02 31 06 06 45; www.memorial-caen.fr; esplanade Général Eisenhower; adult/child €18.80/16.30; 9am-6.30pm, closed Jan & Mon mid-Nov – mid-Dec) provides an insightful and vivid account of the Battle of Normandy. The visit begins with a whistle-stop overview of Europe's descent into total war, tracing events

View from inside a German WWII gun post, Normandy
JIM RICHARDSON/GETTY IMAGES ©

from the end of WWI and the Treaty of Versailles, through the rise of fascism in Europe and the German occupation of France, right up through the Battle of Normandy. It's a hugely impressive affair, using sound, lighting, film, animation and audio testimony, as well as a range of artefacts and exhibits, to graphically evoke the realities of war, the trials of occupation and the joy of liberation. A second section focuses on the Cold War. There's also an underground gallery dedicated to winners of the Nobel Peace Prize, located in bunkers used by the Germans in 1944. To get here by car, follow the signs marked 'Mémorial'.

Honfleur

POP 8350

Long a favourite with painters but now more popular with the Parisian jet set, Honfleur is arguably Normandy's most charming seaside town. Even though it can be overrun with tourists in the summer months, it's hard not to love its graceful beauty.

Sights

ÉGLISE STE-CATHERINE Church

(place Ste-Catherine; 9am-6pm) Initially intended as a temporary structure, this extraordinary church has been standing in the square for over 500 years. Across the square is the church's free-standing wooden bell tower, **Clocher Ste-Catherine**, supposedly built away from the church in order to avoid lightning strikes and damage to the clock's clanging bells.

MUSÉE EUGÈNE BOUDIN Art Museum

(02 31 89 54 00; www.musees-honfleur.fr; 50 rue de l'Homme de Bois; adult/child €5.10/3.40, Jul-Sep €5.80/4.30; 10am-noon & 2-6pm Wed-Mon mid-Mar–Sep, 2.30-5.30pm Mon & Wed-Fri, 10am-noon & 2.30-5.30pm Sat-Sun Oct–mid-Mar) Named in honour of Eugène Boudin, an early impressionist painter born here in 1824, this museum features a collection of impressionist paintings from Normandy, including works by Dubourg, Dufy and Monet.

LES MAISONS SATIE Museum

(02 31 89 11 11; 67 bd Charles V; adult/child €5.70/4.20; 10am-6pm Wed-Mon) The quirky Maisons Satie capture the spirit of the eccentric, avant-garde composer Erik Satie (1866–1925), who lived and worked in Honfleur and was born in the half-timbered house that now contains the museum.

Sleeping

LA MAISON DE LUCIE Boutique Hotel **€€€**

(02 31 14 40 40; www.lamaisondelucie.com; 44 rue des Capucins; d €150-200, ste €250-315;) This marvellous little hideaway has just 10 rooms and two suites, which ensures intimacy. Some of the bedrooms, panelled in oak, have Moroccan-tile bathrooms and boast fantastic views across the harbour to the Pont de Normandie. The shady terrace is a glorious place for a summer breakfast. There's a chic jacuzzi in the old brick-vaulted cellar. No lift.

L'ÉCOLE BUISSONNIÈRE B&B **€€**

(06 16 18 43 62; www.a-lecole-buissonniere.com; 4 rue de la Foulerie; d €100-130;) Located right in the centre of Honfleur, this old primary school, lovingly restored and decorated, is pristine and convivial, with biggish, comfortable and airy rooms overlooking a courtyard. The owner knows about nutrition and serves generous, organic breakfasts. Bikes are available for hire.

LA PETITE FOLIE B&B **€€**

(06 74 39 46 46; www.lapetitefolie-honfleur.com; 44 rue Haute; d €145-185;) Penny Vincent, born in the US, and her French husband welcome you in their elegant mansion right in the heart of Honfleur. The house is spotlessly clean, neat and cosy, and Penny willingly shares her great know ledge of all things Norman – in perfect English, of course. The garden at the rear is a plus. La Petite Folie has a two-night minimum stay.

LE GAMBETTA Modern French **€€**

(**☎02 31 87 05 01; 58 rue Haute; mains €15-20, menu €23; ⏰lunch Sat-Wed, dinner Fri-Wed**) Le Gambetta is well worth seeking out. The decor is a lovely mix of traditional and modern touches, and the food is deliberately eclectic; seafood predominates, but everything's laced with a creative twist. *Andouilles à la plancha* (grilled tripe sausage)? More please.

LE BRÉARD Gastronomic **€€€**

(**☎02 31 89 53 40; www.restaurant-lebreard.com; 7 rue du Puits; menus €29-55; ⏰lunch & dinner Wed-Sun**) *The* place to go in Honfleur for *gastronomique* specialities of the highest order, served in two chic, modern dining rooms. The cuisine is wonderfully imaginative and permeated from every region of France.

Information

Tourist office (**☎02 31 89 23 30; www.ot-honfleur.fr; quai Lepaulmier; ⏰9.30am-12.30pm & 2-6pm Mon-Sat**)

Getting There & Away

The **bus station** (**☎02 31 89 28 41**) is two blocks east of the tourist office. **Bus Verts** (**☎08 10 21 42 14; www.busverts.fr**) services include an express bus to Caen (€11, one hour). Buses go to the following destinations:

Caen €7.95, two hours, 12 daily Monday to Saturday, six Sunday.

Deauville & Trouville €2.30, 30 minutes.

Camembert

Some of the most enduring names in the world of French *fromage* (cheese) come from Normandy, including **Pont L'Évêque**, **Livarot** and, most famous of all, **Camembert**, all of which are named after towns south of Honfleur, on or near the D579.

The invention of Camembert is generally credited to Marie Harel, who was supposedly given the secret of soft cheesemaking by an abbot from Brie on the run from Revolutionary mobs in 1790. Whatever the truth of the legend, the cheese was a huge success at the local market in Vimoutiers, and production of Camembert quickly grew from a cottage industry into an international operation. The distinctive round wooden boxes, in which Camembert is placed, have been around since 1890; they were designed by a local engineer to protect the soft disc during long-distance travel.

To see how cheese is made, take a guided tour of the **Président Farm** (**☎02 33 36 06 60; www.fermepresident.com; adult/child €3/2; ⏰10am-7pm May-Aug, to 6pm Apr, 10am-5pm Mar & Sep-mid-Nov, closed mid-Nov-Feb**), an early-19th-century farm restored by Président, one of the region's largest Camembert producers. It's in the centre of the town of Camembert, which is about 60km south of Honfleur.

Mont St-Michel

POP 43

It's one of France's most iconic images: the slender towers and skyscraping turrets of the abbey of Mont St-Michel rising from stout ramparts and battlements, the whole ensemble connected to the mainland by a narrow causeway (which will be replaced by a bridge by 2014; see www.projetmontsaintmichel.fr).

The bay around Mont St-Michel is famed for having Europe's highest tidal variations; the difference between low and high tides can reach an amazing 15m. Regardless of the time of year, the waters sweep in at an astonishing clip, said to be as fast as a galloping horse. At low tide the Mont is surrounded by bare sand for kilometres around, but at high tide, barely six hours later, the whole bay can be submerged.

Be prepared for lots of steps and big crowds; come early in the morning to miss the worst of them.

Sights

ABBAYE DU MONT ST-MICHEL Abbey

(**☎02 33 89 80 00; www.monuments-nationaux.fr; adult/child incl guided tour €9/free; ⏰9am-7pm, last entry 1hr before closing**) The Mont's major attraction is the stunning architec-

BILDARCHIV MONHEIM GMBH/ALAMY ©

tural ensemble of the Abbaye du Mont St-Michel, towards which you'll be swept by a human tide ascending the Grande Rue and a steep stairway. From Monday to Saturday in July and August, there are illuminated *nocturnes* (night-time visits) with music from 7pm to 10pm.

ÉGLISE ABBATIALE Church

(Abbey Church) The Église Abbatiale was built on the rocky tip of the mountain cone. The transept rests on solid rock, while the nave, choir and transept arms are supported by the rooms below. The church is famous for its mix of architectural styles: the nave and south transept (11th and 12th centuries) are solid Norman Romanesque, while the choir (late 15th century) is Flamboyant Gothic.

LA MERVEILLE Historic Site

(The Marvel) The buildings on the northern side of the Mont are known as La Merveille. The famous **cloître** (cloister) is surrounded by a double row of delicately carved arches resting on granite pillars. The early-13th-century, barrel-roofed **réfectoire** (dining hall) is illuminated by a wall of recessed windows – remarkable, given that the sheer drop precluded the use of flying buttresses. The Gothic **Salle des Hôtes** (Guest Hall), dating from 1213, has two enormous fireplaces. Look out for the **promenoir** (ambulatory), with one of the oldest ribbed vaulted ceilings in Europe, and the **Chapelle de Notre Dame sous Terre** (Underground Chapel of Our Lady), one of the abbey's oldest rooms, rediscovered in 1903.

Information

Tourist office – Mont St-Michel (**☎02 33 60 14 30; www.ot-montsaintmichel.com; 🕘9am-12.30pm & 2-6.30pm Mon-Sat, 9am-noon & 2-6pm Sun, no midday closure Jul & Aug**)

Getting There & Away

BUS Mont St-Michel is linked to Beauvoir (€2.20, eight minutes) and Pontorson (€2.20, 13 minutes) by bus 6, operated by **Manéo** (**☎08 00 15 00 50; www.vtni50.com**), six to eight times daily (more frequently in July and August). Buses will drop you in La Caserne, from where you can take free shuttle buses to the Mont itself. Times are coordinated with the arrival in Pontorson of some trains from Caen and Rennes. **Keolis Emeraude** (**☎02 99 19 70 80; www.destination-montsaintmichel.com**) links Rennes' railway

Mont St-Michel

Timeline

708 Inspired by a vision from **St Michael** (1), Bishop Aubert is compelled to 'build here and build high'.

966 Richard I, Duke of Normandy, gives the Mont to the Benedictines. The three levels of the **abbey** (2) reflect their monastic hierarchy.

1017 Development of the abbey begins. Pilgrims arrive to honour the cult of St Michael. They walk barefoot across the mudflats and up the **Grande Rue** (3) to be received in the almonry (now the bookshop).

1203 The monastery is burnt by the troops of Philip Augustus, who later donates money for its restoration and the Gothic 'miracle', **La Merveille** (4), is constructed.

1434 The Mont's **ramparts** (5) and fortifications ensure it withstands the English assault during the Hundred Years War. It is the only place in northern France not to fall.

1789 After the Revolution, Monasticism is abolished and the Mont is turned into a prison. During this period the **treadmill** (6) is built to lift up supplies.

1878 The **causeway** (7) is created. It allows modern-day pilgrims to visit without hip-high boots, but it cuts off the flow of water and the bay silts up.

1979 The Mont is declared a Unesco World Heritage Site.

2012 The car park is set up on the mainland. The Mont is only accessed on foot or by shuttle bus.

TOP TIPS

Bring a packed lunch from Pontorson to avoid the poor lunch selection on the Mont

Leave the car – it's a pleasant walk from Beauvoir, with spectacular views

Pay attention to the tides – they are dangerous

Take the excellent audioguide – it tells some great stories

Treadmill
The giant treadmill was powered hamsterlike by half a dozen prisoners, who, marching two abreast, raised stone and supplies up the Mont.

Îlot de Tombelaine

Occupied by the English during the Hundred Years War, this islet is now a bird reserve. From April to July it teems with exceptional birdlife.

Ramparts
The Mont was also a military garrison surrounded by machicolated and turreted walls, dating from the 13th to 15th centuries. The single entrance, Porte de l'Avancée, ensured its security in the Hundred Years War. Tip: Tour du Nord (North Tower) has the best views.

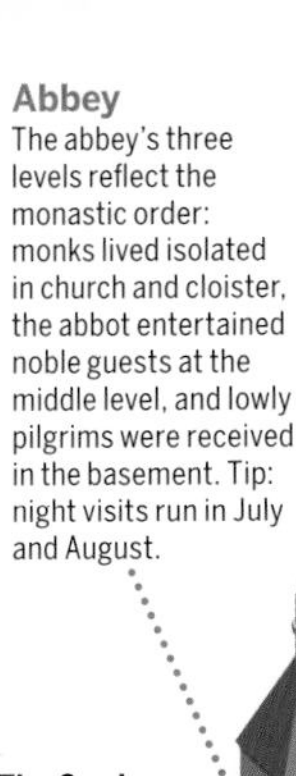

Abbey

The abbey's three levels reflect the monastic order: monks lived isolated in church and cloister, the abbot entertained noble guests at the middle level, and lowly pilgrims were received in the basement. Tip: night visits run in July and August.

SIMON GREENWOOD/GETTY ©

St Michael Statue & Bell Tower

A golden statue of the winged St Michael looks ready to leap heavenward from the bell tower. He is the patron of the Mont, having inspired St Aubert's original devotional chapel.

IZZET KERIBAR/GETTY ©

La Merveille

The highlights of La Merveille are the vast refectory hall lit through embrasured windows, the Knights Hall with its elegant ribbed vaulting, and the cloister (above), which is one of the purest examples of 13th-century architecture to survive here.

1
The Gardens
4
2
6
Église St-Pierre
Cemetery
3
Toilets
Tour de l'Arcade
Tour du Roi
Tourist Office
Porte de l'Avancée (Entrance)
7

Grande Rue

The main thoroughfare of the small village below the abbey, Grande Rue has its charm despite its rampant commercialism. Don't miss the famous Mère Poulard shop here, for souvenir cookies.

DAVID TOMLINSON/GETTY ©

Causeway

In 2014 the causeway will be replaced by a new bridge, which will allow the water to circulate and will return the Mont to an island. Tip: join a barefoot walking tour and see the Mont as pilgrims would.

JOHN ELK III/GETTY ©

Best Views

The view from the Jardin des Plantes in nearby Avranches is unique, as are the panoramas from Pointe du Grouin du Sud near the village of St-Léonard.

If You Like... Seaside Chic

If you love the see-and-be-seen vibe of hip Honfleur, you might just find yourself extending your catwalk strut along the boardwalks of these two enticing beach towns. Both are hugely popular with trendy Parisians who flock here at weekends year-round and all week long from April to September.

1 **DEAUVILLE**

Chic Deauville (population 4100), 15km southwest of Honfleur, has been a playground of the wealthy ever since it was founded by Napoléon III's half-brother, the Duke of Morny, in 1861. Exclusive, expensive and brash, it's packed with designer boutiques, deluxe hotels, renowned horse-racing tracks, and public gardens of impossible neatness. The rich and beautiful strut their stuff along the beachside Promenade des Planches, a 643m-long boardwalk lined with cabins named after famous Americans (mainly film stars).

2 **TROUVILLE**

Trouville (population 5075), another veteran beach resort with the celebrity set, is also a working fishing port and, in many ways, a more attractive place to visit. The town was frequented by painters and writers during the 19th century, including Mozin and Flaubert, and many French celebrities have holiday homes here, lured by the 2km-long sandy beach, casino and laid-back seaside ambience. The town's history is recounted in the **Musée de Trouville** (02 31 88 16 26; 64 rue du Général Leclerc; adult/child €2/1.50; 11am-1pm & 2-5.30pm Wed-Mon Easter–mid-Nov), inside the fine beach-facing Villa Montebello. Trouville is linked to Deauville by Pont des Belges, just east of Deauville's train and bus stations, and by a low-tide footpath near the river's mouth.

station with Mont St-Michel (€12.10, 1¼ hours, four to six daily); times are coordinated with the arrival in Rennes of TGVs from Paris.

TRAIN The town of Pontorson is the transport hub for travellers arriving by train.

Destinations from Pontorson include Bayeux (€22.30, 1¾ hours, three direct daily), Cherbourg (€28.10, three hours, two to three daily) and Rennes (€13.30, 50 minutes, two to four daily).

BRITTANY

Brittany is for explorers. Its wild, dramatic coastline, medieval towns and thick forests make an excursion here well worth the detour from the beaten track. This is a land of prehistoric mysticism, proud tradition and culinary wealth, where fiercely independent locals celebrate Breton culture and Paris feels a long way away indeed.

St-Malo

POP 48,800

The enthralling mast-filled port town of St-Malo has a cinematically changing landscape. With one of the world's highest tidal ranges, brewing storms under blackened skies see waves lash the top of the ramparts ringing its beautiful walled city. Hours later, the blue sky merges with the deep marine-blue sea, exposing beaches as wide and flat as the clear skies above and creating land bridges to the granite outcrop islands.

The town became a key port during the 17th and 18th centuries as a base for both merchant ships and government-sanctioned privateers (pirates, basically) against the constant threat of the English. These days English arrivals are tourists, for whom St-Malo, a short ferry hop from the Channel Islands, is a summer haven.

Sights & Activities

St-Malo's first inhabitants originally lived in St-Servan but later moved to this former island, which became linked to the mainland by the sandy isthmus of Le Sillon in the 13th century. For the best views of the walled city, either stroll along the **jetty** that pokes out to sea off the southwestern tip of intra-muros, from the end of which you'll get the wide-angle view, or, to zoom in, clamber along the top of the **ramparts**, constructed at the end of the 17th century under military architect Vauban, and measuring 1.8km.

CATHÉDRALE ST-VINCENT Cathedral
(place Jean de Châtillon; 9.30am-6pm) The city's centrepiece was constructed between the 12th and 18th centuries. The battle to liberate St-Malo destroyed around 80% of the old city during August 1944, and damage to the cathedral was particularly severe. A mosaic plaque on the floor of the nave marks the spot where Jacques Cartier received the blessing of the bishop of St-Malo before his 'voyage of discovery' to Canada in 1535.

MUSÉE DU CHÂTEAU Museum
(02 99 40 71 57; adult/child €6/3; 10am-noon & 2-6pm Apr-Sep, Tue-Sun Oct-Mar) Within Château de St-Malo, built by the dukes of Brittany in the 15th and 16th centuries, this museum looks at the life and history of the city.

ÎLE DU GRAND BÉ Island
(www.petit-be.com) At low tide, cross the beach to walk out via the Porte des Bés to this rocky islet where the great St-Malo-born 18th-century writer Chateaubriand is buried. Once the tide rushes in, the causeway remains impassable for about six hours; check tide times with the tourist office. About 100m beyond the Île du Grand Bé is the Vauban-built 17th-century **Fort du Petit Bé** (**06 08 27 51 20**), also accessible at low tide.

FORT NATIONAL Ruin
(www.fortnational.com; adult/child €5/3; Easter, school holidays & Jun–mid-Sep) The ramparts' northern stretch looks across to the remains of this former prison, built by Vauban in 1689. Standing atop a rocky outcrop, the fort can only be accessed at low tide. Ask at the tourist office for times of tours.

Sleeping

HÔTEL QUIC EN GROIGNE Boutique Hotel **€€**
(02 99 20 22 20; www.quic-en-groigne.com; 8 rue d'Estrées; s €64-72, d €79-102; closed mid-Nov–Feb;) This exceptional hotel has 15 rooms that are the epitome of clean, simple style, and many a hotel twice the price should be envious of this place. If straight-out good value for money isn't enough then consider also staff who could hardly be more accommodating, an ideal location on a quiet old town street just a few metres from a (low tide only) beach and secure lock-up parking.

LA RANCE HOTEL Boutique Hotel **€€**
(02 99 81 78 63; www.larancehotel.com; 15 quai Sébastopol; r €65-84;) This is a fabulous little hotel with searing white rooms decorated with hand-painted wooden ship communication flags and

St-Malo

smart blue-and-white tiled bathrooms. Hosts Chantal and Thierry are warm and helpful, there's a nice little garden, a charming breakfast room and it's just a few metres from the Tour Solidor and the cute Port-Solidor.

HÔTEL SAN PEDRO Hotel €
(☎02 99 40 88 57; www.sanpedro-hotel.com; 1 rue Ste-Anne; s €58-60, d €69-79;) Tucked at the back of the old city, the San Pedro has a cool, crisp, neutral-toned decor with subtle splashes of colour, friendly service and superb sea views. Private parking is €10 per day.

Eating

LE BISTRO DE JEAN Bistro €
(☎02 99 40 98 68; 6 rue de la Corne-de-Cerf; mains €15-19, menus from €12; closed Wed & Sat lunch, all day Sun) Want to know where the locals choose to eat inside the walls? Peer through the windows of this lively and authentic bistro and you'll get your answer. The place is packed at lunchtime with loyal regulars, and there's rarely a foreign tourist in sight, which is strange, because for the price you simply won't get a better proper French meal in St-Malo.

LE CHALUT Seafood €€
(☎02 99 56 71 58; 8 rue de la Corne-du-Cerf; menus €26-70; Wed-Sun) This unremarkable-looking establishment is, in fact, St-Malo's most celebrated restaurant. Its kitchen overflows with the best the Breton coastline has to offer – buttered turbot, line-caught sea bass and scallops in Champagne sauce.

Information

Tourist office (☎08 25 13 52 00; www.saint-malo-tourisme.com; esplanade St-Vincent; 9am-7.30pm Mon-Sat, 10am-6pm Sun)

Getting There & Away

Brittany Ferries (www.brittany-ferries.com) sails between St-Malo and Portsmouth, and **Condor Ferries** (www.condorferries.co.uk) runs to/from Poole via Jersey or Guernsey. Car ferries leave from the Gare Maritime du Naye.

In July and August, **Compagnie Corsaire** (☎08 25 13 80 35; www.compagniecorsaire.com; adult/child €7.70/4.90) runs a Bus de Mer shuttle

Diners overlooking beach, Dinard

SIMON GREENWOOD/GETTY IMAGES ©

service (10 minutes, at least half-hourly) between St-Malo and Dinard. Outside the July–August peak season both frequency and cost falls. Taxi de la Mer (www.taxibateau.fr; adult/child €5/free) runs a similar service.

TGV trains run from St-Malo to these destinations:

Dinan Costs €8.20-9.30, one hour, 10 daily (requiring a change in Dol de Bretagne).

Paris Montparnasse Costs €52-64, three hours, up to 10 daily.

Rennes Costs €13.60, one hour, roughly hourly.

Dinard

POP 11,230

Visiting Dinard 'in season' is a little like stepping into one of the canvases Picasso painted here in the 1920s. Belle époque mansions built into the cliffs form a timeless backdrop to the beach dotted with blue-and-white striped bathing tents and the beachside carnival. Out of season, when holidaymakers have packed up their buckets and spades, the town is decidedly dormant, but wintry walks along the coastal paths are spectacular.

Sights & Activities

SCENIC WALKS Walking

The romantically named **promenade du Clair de Lune** (moonlight promenade) has views across the Rance River estuary to St-Malo's walled city, and nightly sound-and-light spectacles in summer.

Two-hour **guided walks** (adult/child €5/3; 2.30pm) explaining the town's history, art and architecture (in English and French) depart from the tourist office. The tourist office also doles out maps and leaflets detailing self-guided walking tours taking in the best of the town's architecture.

Beautiful **seaside trails** extend along the coast in both directions. Walkers can follow the shoreline from Plage du Prieuré to Plage de St-Énogat via Pointe du Moulinet, while cyclists can shadow the coastline on the road.

BEACHES & SWIMMING Swimming

Framed by fashionable hotels, a casino and neo-Gothic villas, **Plage de l'Écluse** is the perfect place to shade yourself in style by renting one of Dinard's trademark blue-and-white-striped bathing tents; you can also hire parasols and deckchairs. Reproductions of Picasso's paintings are often planted in the sand here in high summer.

Eating

LA BALAFON Modern French €

(02 99 46 14 81; 31 rue de la Vallée; menu from €17, mains €9-15; closed dinner Sun & Thu & lunch Mon) This is a quality bistro serving meals using produce from the nearby market. The lunch menu consists of a couple of well-chosen and presented dishes, usually one fish and one meat. It's unpretentious, well priced and many locals rate it as the best place in town.

LA PASSERELLE DU CLAIR DE LUNE Modern French €€

(02 99 16 96 37; promenade du Clair de Lune, 3 Av George-V; menus €20-35, mains €19; dinner only Jul-Aug, closed Mon & Tue Sep-Jun, all Jan) Creative, modern seafood is served up at this intimate little restaurant with stunning views over the former home of the fish now sitting on your plate.

Information

Tourist office (02 99 46 94 12; www.ot-dinard.com; 2 bd Féart; 9.30am-12.15pm & 2-6pm Mon-Sat)

Getting There & Away

Compagnie Corsaire (08 25 13 81 00; www.compagniecorsaire.com) runs a Bus de Mer shuttle service (€7.70/4.90 per adult/child return; 10 minutes) between St-Malo and Dinard, operating at least half-hourly. A similar service is offered by Taxi de la Mer (www.taxibateau.fr; adult/child €5/free).

Illenoo (www.illenoo-services.fr) buses connect Dinard and the train station in St-Malo (€1.90, 30 minutes, hourly). Several buses travel to Rennes (€4.30, two hours).

Cancale oysters

OLIVIER CIRENDINI/GETTY IMAGES ©

Cancale

POP 5440

The idyllic little fishing port of Cancale, 14km east of St-Malo, is famed for its offshore *parcs à huîtres* (oyster beds).

Sights

FERME MARINE Farm

(☎02 99 89 69 99; www.ferme-marine.com; corniche de l'Aurore; adult/child €7/3.70; ⌚guided tours in French 11am, 3pm & 5pm Jul-Aug, in English 2pm, in German 4pm) Entry to this small museum and working oyster farm is by guided tour only. Tour frequency decreases out of season.

Eating

MARCHÉ AUX HUÎTRES Market

(12 oysters from €3.50, lunch platters €20; ⌚9am-6pm) Clustered by the Pointe des Crolles lighthouse, stalls at this market sell oysters from €3.50 per dozen for small *huîtres creuses*.

LE COQUILLAGE Gastronomic €€€

(☎02 99 89 64 76; www.maisons-de-bricourt.com; 1 rue Duguesclin; menus €27-135; ⌚Mar-Dec) Super chef Olivier Roellinger's latest project is his sumptuous restaurant and hotel housed in the extremely impressive Château Richeux, 4km to the south of Cancale. Roellinger's creations have earned him three Michelin stars and you won't have trouble seeing why if you're lucky enough to get a table here. The food takes in the culinary highlights of both Brittany and Normandy, all beautifully cooked and imaginatively served. Booking well ahead is essential. As well as offering rooms at Château Richeux, Roellinger offers a range of cottages and other deluxe accommodation around Cancale. See the website for details.

Information

Tourist office (☎02 99 89 63 72; www.cancale-tourisme.fr; ⌚9.30am-1pm & 2.30-7pm)

Getting There & Away

Keolis Emeraude (www.keolis-emeraude.com) has year-round services to and from St-Malo (€2, 30 minutes).

Roscoff

POP 3780

Unlike many of its industrial and less-than-beautiful sister Channel ports, Roscoff (Rosko in Breton) provides a captivating first glimpse of Brittany. Granite houses dating from the 16th century wreathe the pretty docks, which are surrounded by emerald-green fields that produce cauliflowers, onions, tomatoes, new potatoes and artichokes.

Once upon a time, Roscoff farmers were known as 'Johnnies'. Wearing distinctive horizontally striped tops, they loaded up their boats with plaited strings of locally grown small pink onions and crossed the Channel to the UK, then peddled – and pedalled – with their onions hanging from their bikes' handlebars, creating the traditional British stereotype of the French today. This trade began in the early 19th century, reaching its peak in the 1920s. Today, Johnnies have a near-mythical status in the region, with a number still continuing the trade and a new wave of younger-generation Johnnies ensuring the survival of this iconic tradition.

Sights & Activities

ÉGLISE NOTRE DAME DE KROAZ-BATZ Church

(place Lacaze-Duthiers; ⏲9am-noon & 2-6pm) The most obvious sight in Roscoff is this unusual but distinctive church at the heart of the old town. With its Renaissance belfry rising above the flat landscape, the 16th-century Flamboyant Gothic structure is one of Brittany's most impressive churches.

MAISON DES JOHNNIES Museum

(☎02 98 61 25 48; 48 rue Brizeux; adult/child over 10yr/child under 10 yr €4/2.50/free; ⏲tours 11am, 3pm & 5pm Mon-Fri) Photographs trace Roscoff's roaming onion farmers from the early 19th century at this popular museum. A visit is by guided

If You Like... Islands

Île de Batz is just one of many idyllic islands dotted around the Breton coastline. Blessed with beautiful beaches, rich wildlife and stunning coastal walks, the islands are perfect day-trip fodder.

1 ÎLE D'OUESSANT

There's a real end-of-the-world air to go-slow Île d'Ouessant, a remote paradise with little to do bar hike its 45km craggy coastal path, picnic or flop in the sun. Its black-and-white-striped **Phare de Créac'h** is the world's most powerful lighthouse; discover its history inside in the **Musée des Phares et des Balises** (Lighthouse & Beacon Museum; ☎02 98 48 80 70; adult/child €4.30/3; ⏲10.30am-6pm Jul-Aug, 11am-5pm Apr-Jun & Sep). **Penn Ar Bed** (☎02 98 80 80 80; www.pennarbed.fr) ferries depart from Brest (adult/under 26 yr/child return €32/26/19.50, 2½ hours) and Brittany's most westerly point, Le Conquet (same prices, 1½ hours).

2 ÎLE MOLÈNE

Scarcely 1km wide, Île Molène is carless, virtually treeless, home to just 270 people and its electricity supply comes from a single diesel generator. The only village is Le Bourg, a huddle of whitewashed fisher cottages clustered around a granite quay. Explore on foot, or hire a kayak or canoe at the port. Ferries to Ouessant stop here en-route.

3 BELLE ÎLE

Brittany's largest island (population 5200), with its dramatic Vauban-designed citadel and quaint Le Palais port, sees its population swell ten-fold in summer. Surfers get a kick out of **Plage de Donnant** while hikers pound the 95km coastal path; the fretted southwestern coast has spectacular rock formations and caves, including Grotte de l'Apothicairerie (Cave of the Apothecary's Shop). Sail here from Quiberon with **Compagnie Océane** (☎08 20 05 61 56; www.compagnie-oceane.fr; 45 minutes, year-round).

If You Like… Medieval Towns

If you've been smitten by the olde-worlde charms of Château de Josselin (p142), you'll love exploring the region's other medieval marvels:

1 DINAN

If you're looking for Brittany's most authentic medieval town, look no further than Dinan, still encircled by its medieval battlements and watchtowers. Set high above the fast-flowing Rance River, the narrow cobblestone streets and squares lined with crooked half-timbered houses of the old town have barely changed since the days when doublet and hose were still in fashion. Get all your info at the **tourist office** (☎02 96 87 69 76; www.dinan-tourisme.com; 9 rue du Château; ⏱9.30am-7pm Mon-Sat, 10am-12.30pm & 2-6pm Sun).

2 VANNES

Street art, sculptures and intriguing galleries pop up unexpectedly throughout the medieval city of Vannes, a town with a distinctly quirky, creative bent overlooking the Golfe du Morbihan. Duck into the **tourist office** (☎08 25 13 56 10; www.tourisme-vannes.com; quai de Tabarly; ⏱9.30am-7pm Mon-Sat, 10am-6pm Sun Jul-Aug, 9.30am-12.30pm & 1.30-6pm Mon-Sat Sep-Jun) at the newly developed marina before getting lost in the walled old town framed by a flower-filled moat.

3 VITRÉ

With its winding streets and colossal castle complete with witch-like pointy turrets, Vitré rivals Dinan as one of Brittany's prettiest medieval towns. Its **tourist office** (☎02 99 75 04 46; www.ot-vitre.fr; place Général de Gaulle; ⏱9.30am-12.30pm & 2-6.30pm Mon-Sat, 10am-12.30pm & 3-6pm Sun) is right outside the train station.

tour only and there's an extra tour at 9.30am on Thursdays. Call ahead for tour times, as they change frequently.

CENTRE DE DÉCOUVERTE DES ALGUES Museum

(☎02 98 69 77 05; www.thalado.fr; 5 rue Victor Hugo; admission free, walks per adult/child €6/3; ⏱9am-noon & 2.15-7pm Mon-Fri, 9am-noon & 2-6.30pm Sat) You can learn about local seaweed harvesting at this enthusiastically run museum, which also organises guided walks and gives regular free lectures (often in English and German).

ÎLE DE BATZ Island

(www.iledebatz.com) Bordering what is basically a 4-sq-km vegetable garden fertilised by seaweed, the beaches on the Île de Batz (pronounced 'ba, enez vaz' in Breton) are a peaceful place to bask. The mild island climate supports the luxuriant **Jardins Georges Delaselle** (☎02 98 61 75 65; www.jardin-georgesdelaselle.fr; adult/child €5/2.50; ⏱1-6.30pm Jul & Aug, 2-6pm Wed-Mon Apr-Jun & Sep-Oct), founded in the 19th century, with over 1500 plants from all five continents.

Ferries (adult/child return €8/4, bikes €8, 15 minutes each way) between Roscoff and Île de Batz run every 30 minutes between 8am and 8pm in July and August, with less-frequent sailings the rest of the year.

Bicycles can be rented on the island for around €10 per day.

Sleeping & Eating

HÔTEL LA RESIDENCE Boutique Hotel €

(☎02 98 69 74 85; www.hotelroscoff-laresidence.fr; 14 rue des Johnnies; d from €69; ⏱closed Dec-Jan; 📶) This superb new hotel ticks all the boxes for a good place to stay. Colour-coordinated, bright and modern, all the rooms here are slightly different and there's a piano in the arty reception area. The staff are helpful and it's on a central, quiet street (close to a free car park), making this place very good value for money.

HÔTEL DU CENTRE Boutique Hotel **€€**
(02 98 61 24 25; www.chezjanie.com; Le Port; s/d from €64/100, Chez Janie menu €24; mid-Feb–mid-Nov;) Minimalist, sleek rooms at this boutique hotel look like they've been lifted from a magazine, and indeed they've featured in many. For a sea-view room looking out over the postcard-pretty old port, add a further €25. It's perhaps best known for its restaurant, **Chez Janie**, serving Breton classics such as *kig ha farz* – a farmers' family meal based on the Breton cake *far,* cooked in a linen bag within a boiling bacon and vegetable stew.

L'ÉCUME DES JOURS Gourmet **€€**
(02 98 61 22 83; quai d'Auxerre; menus €15-55; closed Wed Jul & Aug, Tue Sep-Jun) Regarded as the best restaurant in town, this elegant place is housed inside a former ship-owner's house and serves magnificent and inventive local dishes that marry seafood tastes with land-lubbers' delights. There's also an excellent wine list. It's quite formal so dress smart.

Information

Tourist office (02 98 61 12 13; www.roscoff-tourisme.com; quai d'Auxerre; 9am-12.30pm & 1.30-7pm Mon-Sat, 10am-12.30pm & 2.30-7pm Sun Jul-Aug, 9.15am-noon & 2-6pm Mon-Sat Sep-Jun)

Getting There & Away

Brittany Ferries
(reservations in France 08 25 82 88 28, reservations in UK 0871 244 0744; www.brittany-ferries.com) links Roscoff to Plymouth in England (five to nine hours, one to three daily year-round) and Cork in Ireland (14 hours, once-weekly June to September). Boats leave from Port de Bloscon, about 2km east of the town centre.

There are regular trains and SNCF buses to Morlaix (€5.80, 35 minutes), where you can make connections to Brest, Quimper and St-Brieuc.

Presqu'île de Crozon

The anchor-shaped Crozon Peninsula is part of the **Parc Naturel Régional d'Armorique**, and one of the most scenic spots in Brittany. The partly forested peninsula is criss-crossed by some 145km of signed walking trails and excellent biking terrain, with crêperies in traditional stone buildings tucked in and around the hinterland.

At the western extremity of the Crozon Peninsula, **Camaret-sur-Mer** (unusually in French, the final 't' is pronounced) is a classic fishing village – or at least it was until early in the 20th century, when it was France's then-biggest crayfish port. Abandoned fishing-boat carcasses now decay in its harbour, but it remains an enchanting place that lures artists. There's an ever-increasing number of galleries dotted around town, particularly

Presqu'île de Crozon
/LONELY PLANET IMAGES ©

Below: Festival de Cornouaille (p44), Quimper;
Right: Quimper street, looking towards Cathédrale St-Corentin

along rue de la Marne and around place St-Thomas, one block north of the waterfront.

Three kilometres south of Camaret is the spectacular headland of **Pointe de Pen-Hir**, bounded by steep, sheer sea cliffs, with two WWII memorials. On a pensinsula full of breathtaking scenery this might be the most impressive lookout of them all and on a stormy day, with giant waves hurling themselves at the cliff faces, it feels like the end of the world. There are opportunities for short walks as well as a handful of little cove beaches and some ancient megalithic sites.

Argol

Argol is a quaint village in its own right, but its main draw is the **Musée du Cidre du Bretagne** (Breton Cider Museum; ☎02 98 17 21 87; www.musee-cidre-bretagne.com; adult/child €5/free; ⏲10am-noon & 2-7pm Jul-Aug, 2-7pm Apr-Jun & Sep). This former dairy's old stone buildings have been transformed into a working *cidrerie* producing over 300,000 bottles annually. A visit (allow around an hour, including time for a French-language but understandable film) takes you through the history of cider in Brittany and present-day production. And you get to taste it. In July and August, one of the barns is used as a **crêperie** (crêpes €4.50-7.50; ⏲noon-10pm).

Quimper

POP 66,911

Small enough to feel like a village, with its slanted half-timbered houses and narrow cobbled streets, and large enough to buzz as the troubadour of Breton culture and arts, Quimper (kam-pair) is Finistère's thriving capital. Derived from the Breton word *kemper,* meaning 'confluence', Quimper sits at the juncture of the small Rivers Odet and Steïr, criss-crossed by footbridges with cascading flowers. Despite being one of Brittany's most charming towns, it is often overlooked by visitors.

Sights

CATHÉDRALE ST-CORENTIN Church

(8.30am-noon & 1.30-6.30pm Mon-Sat, 8.30am-noon & 2-6.30pm Sun) At the centre of the city is its cathedral with its distinctive kink, said to symbolise Christ's inclined head as he was dying on the cross. Construction began in 1239 but the cathedral's dramatic twin spires weren't added until the 19th century. High on the west facade, look out for an equestrian statue of King Gradlon, the city's mythical 5th-century founder.

MUSÉE DÉPARTEMENTAL BRETON Museum

(02 98 95 21 60; 1 rue du Roi Gradlon; adult/child €4/free; 9am-6pm) Beside the cathedral, recessed behind a magnificent stone courtyard, this superb museum showcases Breton history, furniture, costumes, crafts and archaeology, in a former bishop's palace.

CENTRE D'ART CONTEMPORAIN DE QUIMPER Gallery

(02 98 55 55 77; www.le-quartier.net; 10 esplanade François Mitterrand; admission €2; 10am-noon & 1-6pm Tue-Sat, 2-6pm Sun) A splendid temple to modern art, with cutting-edge and sometimes-challenging temporary exhibitions on display. Note that when exhibitions are being changed over it may be closed for a few days. Entry on Sundays is free.

Tours

VEDETTES DE L'ODET Boat Tour

(02 98 57 00 58; www.vedettes-odet.com) From June to September, Vedettes de l'Odet runs boat trips (adult/child €27/16, 1¼ hours one way) from Quimper along the serene Odet estuary to Bénodet, leaving from quai Neuf. Stop for a look about Bénodet and then hop on a boat back.

Eating

CRÊPERIE DU QUARTIER Crêperie €
(**02 98 64 29 30; 16 rue du Sallé; menus from €6, galettes €5-7.10**) In a town where the crêpe is king, this cosy stone-lined place has some of the best. Its wide-ranging menu offers a *galette* of the week or you can go for the full monty, such as a crêpe stuffed with apple, caramel, ice-cream, almonds and chantilly. Choose from a range of local ciders to wash it all down.

L'AMBROISIE Gastronomic €€€
(**02 98 95 00 02; www.ambroisie-quimper.com; 49 rue Elie Fréron; menus €25-62; lunch & dinner Tue-Sat, lunch Sun**) Quimper's most celebrated gastronomic restaurant is sumptuously decorated with contemporary art and features elegant china on snow-white tablecloths. Regional produce provided by chef Gilbert Guyon's friends is used in the creation of house specials such as turbot with eschalots and there's lots of those Breton favourites, scallops. Cooking classes are available on request.

LE COSY RESTAURANT Breton Cuisine €
(**02 98 95 23 65; 2 rue du Sallé; mains €10-14.50; closed Sun, lunch Mon & dinner Tue**) Make your way through the *épicerie* (specialist grocer) crammed with locally canned sardines, ciders and other Breton specialities to this eclectic dining room, where you can tuck into top-quality gratins and *tartines* (open-faced sandwiches).

Information

Tourist office (**02 98 53 04 05; www.quimper-tourisme.com; place de la Résistance; 9am-7pm Mon-Sat, 10am-12.45pm & 3-5.45pm Sun Jul-Aug, 9.30am-12.30pm & 1.30-6.30pm Mon-Sat, 10am-12.45pm Sun Jun & Sep**)

Getting There & Away

TRAIN There are frequent services to the following destinations:

Brest Costs €16.50, 1¼ hours, up to 10 daily.

Paris Montparnasse Costs €70-86, 4¾ hours, hourly.

Rennes Costs €28-34, 2½ hours, hourly.

Vannes Costs €19.30-23, 1½ hours, hourly.

Château de Josselin

Guarded by its three round towers, the extraordinary town castle of **Château de Josselin** (**02 97 22 36 45; www.chateaujosselin.com; adult/child €8/5.20; 11am-6pm mid-Jul–Aug, 2-6pm Apr–mid-Jul, 2-5.30pm Sep**) is an incredible sight that remains the home of the Rohan family today. As such, it can only be visited by guided tour: one English-language tour departs daily (at 2.30pm) from June to September; otherwise you can ask for a leaflet in English. The château is filled with treasures, including an ornate writing desk of which only two others exist (one in Windsor Castle), a clock that has so many gadgets it must have been considered the iPhone of its time and a library containing 3000 books, some of which date back to the 17th century. Within the château is the Musée de Poupées – a museum of puppets and dolls. A combination ticket for both costs €13/8.70 per adult/child.

Rennes

POP 212,200

A crossroads since Roman times, Brittany's vibrant capital sits at the junction of highways linking northwestern France's major cities. It's a beautifully set-out city, with an elaborate and stately centre and a charming old town. At night, this student city has no end of lively places to pop in for a pint and its restaurants are also superb.

Sights

CATHÉDRALE ST-PIERRE Cathedral
(**9.30am-noon & 3-6pm**) Crowning Rennes' old town is the 17th-century cathedral, which has an impressive, if dark, neoclassical interior. Much of the surrounding old town was gutted by the great fire of 1720, started by a drunken carpenter who accidentally set alight a pile of shavings. Half-timbered houses that survived line the old city's cobbled streets, such as rue St-Michel and rue St-Georges.

DIANA HARONIS/DIANASPHOTOART.COM/GETTY IMAGES ©

Don't Miss Carnac Megaliths

Predating Stonehenge by around 100 years, Carnac (Garnag in Breton) also tops it with the sheer number of ancient sites found in the vicinity, making this the world's greatest concentration of megalithic sites. There are no fewer than 3000 of these upright stones, most around thigh-high, erected between 5000 and 3500 BC.

Carnac, some 32km west of Vannes, comprises the old stone village Carnac-Ville and the seaside resort of Carnac-Plage, 1.5km south, bordered by the 2km-long sandy beach. Its megaliths stretch 13km north from Carnac-Ville and east as far as the village of Locmariaquer.

Sign up for a one-hour guided visit at the **Maison des Mégalithes**. Tour times vary considerably depending on time of year. Opposite, the largest menhir field – with 1099 stones – is the **Alignements du Ménec**, 1km north of Carnac-Ville; the eastern section is accessible in winter. From here, the D196 heads northeast for about 1.5km to the equally impressive **Alignements de Kermario** (which is open year-round). Climb the stone observation tower midway along the site to see the alignment from above. Another 500m further on are the **Alignements de Kerlescan**, a smaller grouping also accessible in winter.

Between Kermario and Kerlescan, 500m to the south of the D196, deposit your fee in an honour box at **Tumulus de Kercado**, dating from 3800 BC and the burial site of a Neolithic chieftain. From the parking area 300m further along the D196, a 15-minute walk brings you to the **Géant du Manio**, the highest menhir in the complex.

For some background, the **Musée de Préhistoire** chronicles life in and around Carnac from the Palaeolithic and Neolithic eras to the Middle Ages.

NEED TO KNOW

Tourist office (☎02 97 52 13 52; www.ot-carnac.fr; 74 av des Druides; ⏰9am-7pm Mon-Sat & 3-7pm Sun); **Maison des Mégalithes** (☎02 97 52 29 81; rte des Alignements; tour adult/child €6/free; ⏰10am-8pm Jul & Aug, to 5.15pm Sep-Apr, to 7pm May & Jun); **Musée de Préhistoire** (☎02 97 52 22 04; www.museedecarnac.fr; 10 place de la Chapelle, Carnac-Ville; adult/child €5/2.50; ⏰10am-6pm)

Rennes

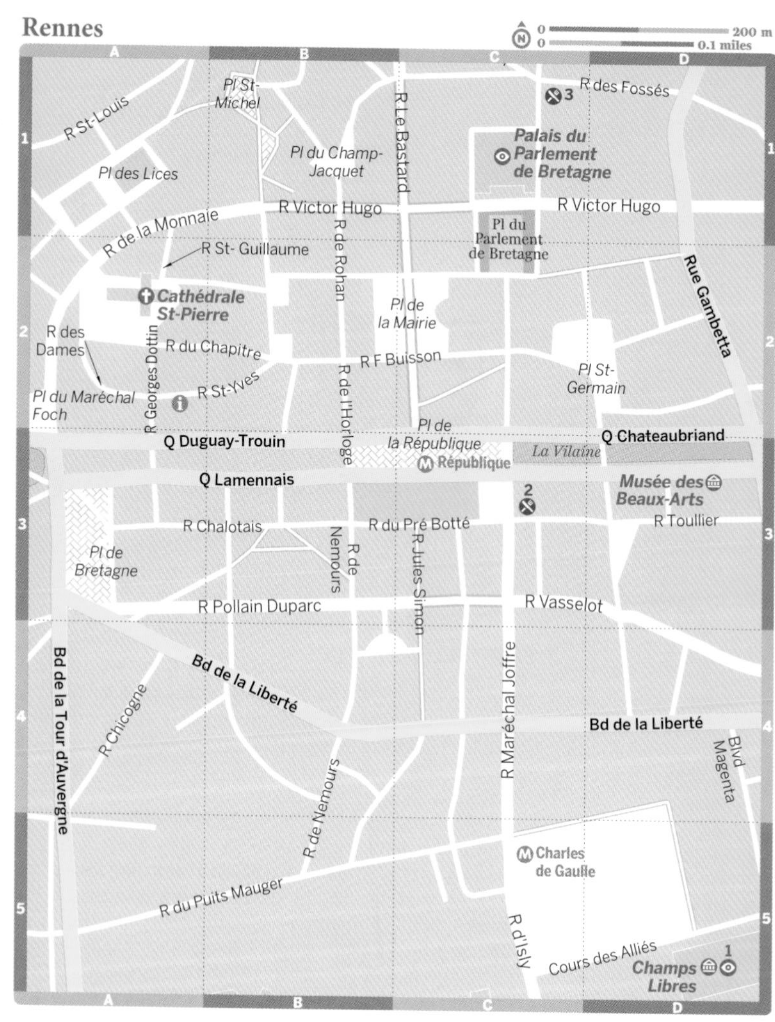

PALAIS DU PARLEMENT DE BRETAGNE Law Courts

(place du Parlement de Bretagne; adult/child €7/free) This 17th-century former seat of the rebellious Breton parliament has in more recent times been home to the Palais de Justice. In 1994 this building was destroyed by a fire started by demonstrating fishers. Now restored, it houses the Court of Appeal. Daily guided tours (request in advance for a tour in English) take you through the ostentatiously gilded rooms. Tour bookings must be made through the tourist office.

MUSÉE DES BEAUX-ARTS Gallery

(02 23 62 17 45; www.mbar.org; 20 quai Émile Zola; adult/child €5.95/free; 10am-6pm Tue, 10am-noon & 2-6pm Wed-Sun) Rooms devoted to the Pont-Aven school are the indisputable highlight of the Musée des Beaux-Arts, which also has a 'curiosity gallery' of antiques and illustrations amassed in the 18th century. It also hosts numerous

Rennes

temporary exhibitions: note that when there is no temporary exhibition, entrance fees are a little lower than those quoted here.

CHAMPS LIBRES Cultural Centre
(02 23 40 66 00; www.leschampslibres.fr; 10 cours des Alliés; noon-9pm Tue, noon-7pm Wed-Fri, 2-7pm Sat-Sun) Rennes' futuristic cultural centre is home to the **Musée de Bretagne** (02 23 40 66 00; www.musee-bretagne.fr), with displays on Breton history and culture. Conveniently located under the same roof is **Espace des Sciences** (02 23 40 66 40; www.espace-sciences.org), an interactive science museum, along with a planetarium, a temporary exhibition space and a library. If you're keen to immerse yourself in local culture and science, a combined ticket for all sections costs €10/7 per adult/under 26.

Eating

LÉON LE COCHON Pork €€
(02 99 79 37 54; 1 rue Maréchal Joffre; menu €25, mains €11-25) Basking in the plaudits of almost every French gastronomic guidebook, but still fun and informal, 'Léon the Pig' specialises not just in pork but porcine products in all their many and varied manifestations.

L'ÉPICERIE Cafe €
(02 99 38 76 70; 2 rue des Fossés; tartines €5-9; noon-midnight) This fantastic old-town eatery is riotously popular with a student-style crowd, who pile in to enjoy the generous *tartines* (including some rather unusual ones, such as one with 'vanishing pears' – *trois fromages avec ou sans poire*) and flasks of beer on the buzzing terrace outside.

Information

Tourist office (02 99 67 11 11; www.tourisme-rennes.com; 11 rue St-Yves; 9am-7pm Mon-Sat, 11am-1pm & 2-6pm Sun)

Getting There & Away

TRAIN There are frequent train services to the following destinations:

Dinan Costs €12-14.30, one hour including a change.

Paris Montparnasse Costs €58, 2¼ hours.

Quimper Costs €34-38, 2½ hours.

St-Malo Costs €13.60, one hour.

Vannes Costs €20-24, 1½ hours.

Champagne & Northern France

Nowhere sums up the effervescent French spirit better than Champagne. This region has been famous for its bubbly since the 17th century, when a monk by the name of Dom Pierre Pérignon added some fizz to his otherwise humdrum wine and discovered he'd created something altogether more exciting.

A few centuries on, you'll find famous Champagne houses dotted throughout the region, especially around the elegant towns of Reims and Épernay: a tasting tour of their musty cellars is an absolutely unforgettable experience.

Looking west, the regions of Alsace and Lorraine crackle with a unique blend of French and Germanic cultures. And to the north, the many memorials and cemeteries dotted around Picardy and the Pas-de-Calais recall the region's tragic history as one of the key battlegrounds of WWI.

Champagne vineyards
SLOW IMAGES/GETTY IMAGES ©

Champagne & Northern France

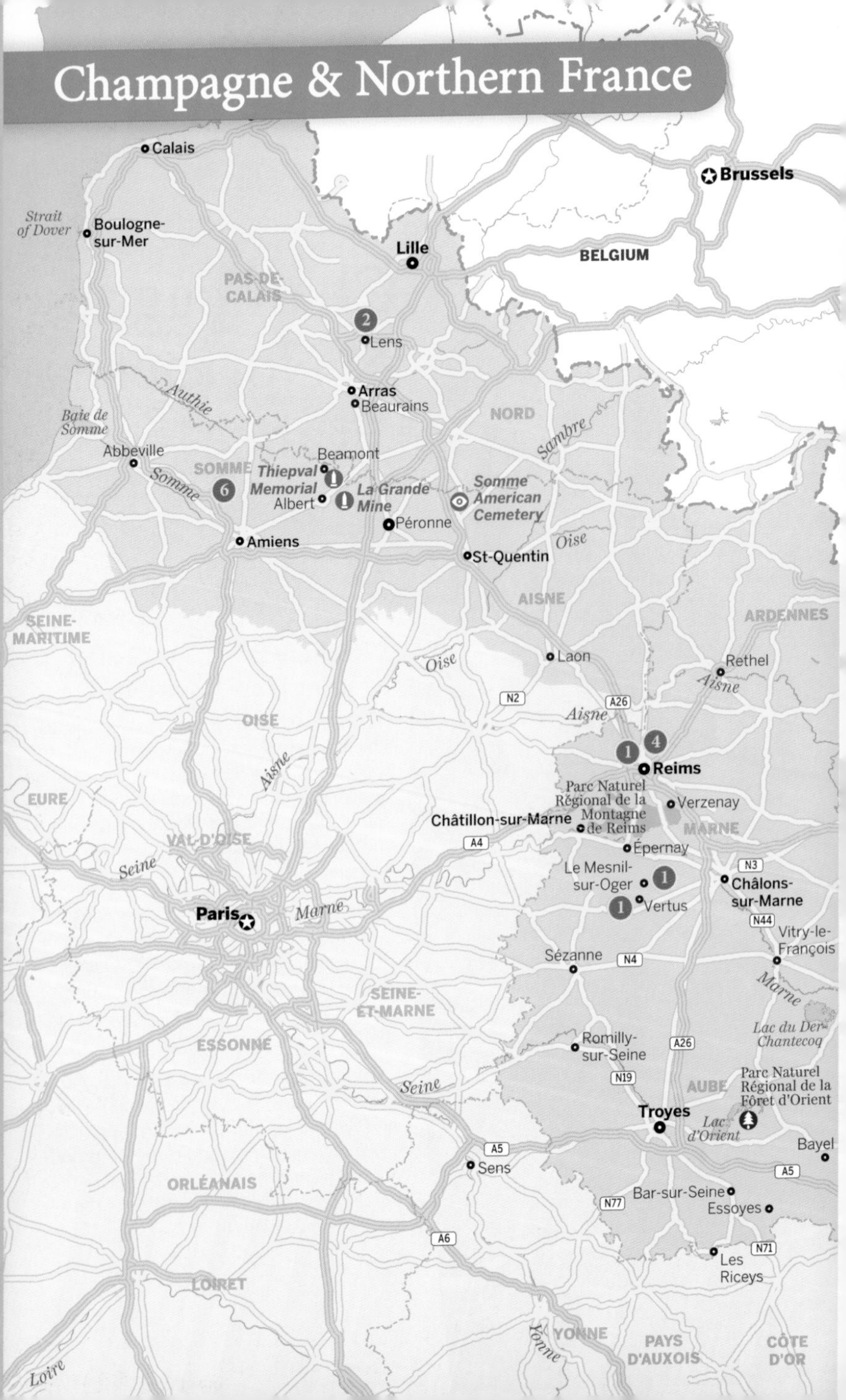

Calais
Brussels
Strait of Dover
Boulogne-sur-Mer
Lille
BELGIUM
PAS-DE-CALAIS
2
Lens
Arras
Beaurains
Authie
Baie de Somme
NORD
Sambre
Abbeville
Beamont
SOMME
Thiepval Memorial
Somme
6
Albert
La Grande Mine
Somme American Cemetery
Péronne
Amiens
St-Quentin
Oise
AISNE
SEINE-MARITIME
ARDENNES
Laon
Rethel
Oise
N2
A26
Aisne
Aisne
OISE
1
4
Reims
Aisne
EURE
Parc Naturel Régional de la Montagne de Reims
Verzenay
Châtillon-sur-Marne
MARNE
VAL-D'OISE
A4
Épernay
Seine
Le Mesnil-sur-Oger
1
N3
Châlons-sur-Marne
1
Vertus
Paris
Marne
N44
Vitry-le-François
Sézanne
N4
Marne
SEINE-ET-MARNE
Lac du Der-Chantecoq
ESSONNE
Romilly-sur-Seine
A26
N19
Parc Naturel Régional de la Fôret d'Orient
Seine
AUBE
Troyes
Lac d'Orient
Bayel
A5
Sens
A5
ORLÉANAIS
Bar-sur-Seine
N77
Essoyes
A6
N71
Les Riceys
LOIRET
YONNE
Yonne
PAYS D'AUXOIS
CÔTE D'OR
Loire

0 50 km
0 25 miles
NETHERLANDS
GERMANY
1 Wine Tasting, Champagne
2 Louvre-Lens
3 Centre Pompidou-Metz
4 Reims & Amiens' Cathédrales Notre Dame
5 Alsace
6 WWI Sites
LUXEMBOURG
Luxembourg
Romagne-sous-Montfaucon
Veckring
Saarbrücken
Douaumont
Fleury
MOSELLE
Forêt d'Argonne
Verdun
Metz
St-Avold
A4
MEUSE
Metz-Nancy-Lorraine Airport
Lac de Madine
Butte de Montsec
Karlsruhe/Baden Baden Airport
Rhine
BAS-RHIN
Bar-le-Duc
Nancy
MEURTHE-ET-MOSELLE
Strasbourg
St-Dizier
N4
Strasbourg Airport
Marne
Moselle
Dambach-la-Ville
Château du Haut Kœnigsbourg
Sélestat
GERMANY
Colombey-les-Deux-Églises
VOSGES
Ribeauvillé
Épinal
Col du Bonhomme (949m)
Riquewihr
N19
Col de la Schucht (1139m)
Kaysersberg
Colmar
Chaumont
HAUTE-MARNE
Col de la Schucht (1140m)
Petit Ballon (1267m)
A5
A31
Grand Ballon (1424m)
Ballon d'Alsace (1247m)
Saône
HAUT-RHIN
TERRITOIRE DE BELFORT
HAUTE-SAÔNE
Basel
SWITZERLAND

Champagne & Northern France's Highlights

1

Wine Tasting in Champagne

Champagne is a cold misty land, with the subtle beauty of huge skies, rolling hills and austerely attractive villages. Oh, and the wine, it has a restrained exuberance of flavour of which I never tire, and an exceptional aptitude to age well and mellow. Top Right: Cathédrale Notre Dame (p163), Reims

Need to Know

HARVEST In September – grapes must be hand-picked **BEST WINE BOUTIQUE** Reims' La Cave Salvatori on rue Flodoard: collection of 20-year-old Champagne prestige cuvées

Local Knowledge

Wine Tasting in Champagne Don't Miss List

BY MICHAEL EDWARDS, GASTRONOMIC WRITER, RESTAURANT CRITIC & CHAMPAGNE CONNOISSEUR

1 REIMS

This great city centre of culture, gastronomy and wine tourism is so easy to access: 45 minutes by TGV from Paris Gare de l'Est and just 30 minutes direct from Paris Charles de Gaulle airport to TGV station Champagne Ardennes near the city. For me, the cathedral (p163) and exquisite Basilique St-Rémi (p159) uplift the spirit before a good meal. My favourite restaurants include **Le Jardin des Crayères** (www.lescrayeres.com), 1930s-styled Café du Palais (p161; ⏲lunch Tue-Sat), **Brasserle du Boulingrin** (www.boulingrin.fr), and Le Foch (p160), one of France's finest fish restaurants.

2 GROWERS' CHAMPAGNE

The big change in the past five years is the greater availability of Champagne direct from the best grower-producers. For a real sense of place and individual flavour my top addresses include JL Vergnon and Clos Cazals in Le Mesnil-sur-Oger in the Côte des Blancs, Veuve Fourny in Vertus, Jacques Selosse and Pascal Agrapart in Avize, and Champagne Lilbert in Cramant.

3 CHAMPAGNE PRODUCER

My favourite right now is **Veuve Fourny & Fils** (☎03 26 52 16 30; www.champagne-veuve-fourny.com; rue du Mesnil, Vertus). They are masters of the bone-dry, non-dosed Champagne; theirs is called Brut Nature and is a wonderful partner for all sorts of shellfish and those great cheese pastry balls called *gougères au fromage*.

4 THE CHAMPENOIS

I love the region so much, mainly because of the people. Reserved but with great inner warmth and a deliciously dry sense of humour, the Champenois are resilient and hard working. But they also know how to play: go to any dance hall and you'll see what I mean.

Louvre-Lens

As if one top-drawer art museum is not enough, northern France now lures art lovers with t Louvre-Lens (p173), one of Europe's most exciting new museums. Its location – an unknow former coal-mining town – is incongruous with its celebrity stature, but that is precisely the point: art is for everyone. The same vision is reflected in the Louvre-Lens' open architecture and invitation to visitors to peek behind the scenes into its storerooms and restoration studios. Entrance to Louvre-Lens © SANAA, IMREY CULBERT, Catherine Mosbach

2

3

Centre Pompidou-Metz

Metz has long been known for its Gothic cathedral (p171), but it now has a thoroughly modern lure, too. A northern offshoot of the Centre Pompidou in Paris, Centre Pompidou-Metz (p171) presents major exhibitions of modern art and – like its sister in the capital – worth a visit for its outlandish architec ture; architects Shigeru Ban and Jean de Gastines are its creators.

BENOIT TESSIER/REUTERS/CORBIS ©

DEA/G.DAGLI ORTI/GETTY IMAGES ©

Reims & Amiens' Cathédrales Notre Dame

4

Cathedrals don't get much grander than this Gothic duo, both Unesco World Heritage Sites. Until the Revolution, French monarchs were crowned at Reims (p163), and it remains one of France's most regal cathedrals. Further north, highlights of Amiens' cathedral (p174) include a famous 'crying' angel and a jewel-encrusted skull of John the Baptist.

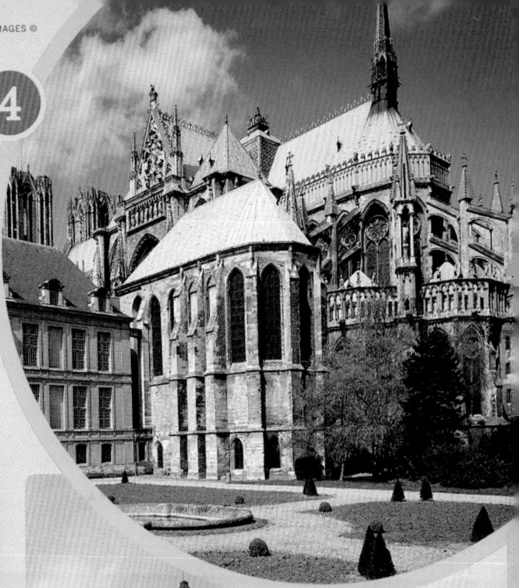

Cathédrale Notre Dame (p163), Reims

LEE ERGULEC/GETTY IMAGES ©

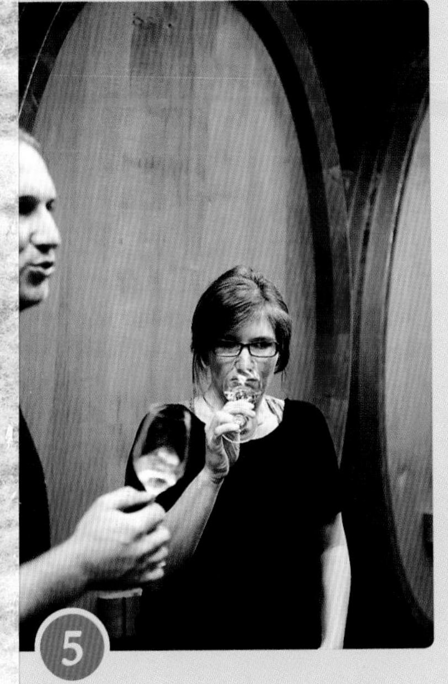

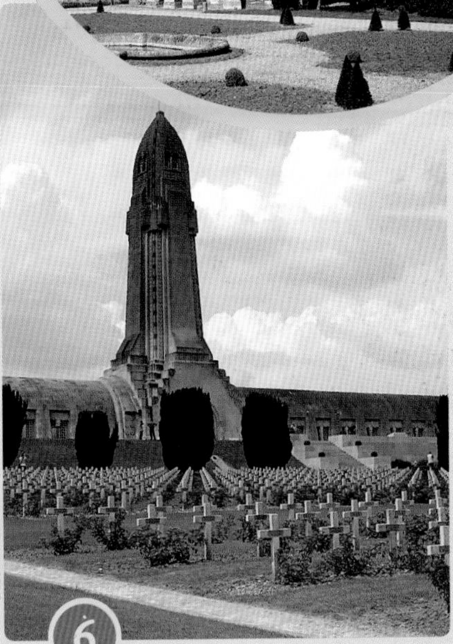

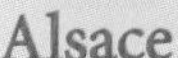

5

Alsace

Sprinkled with picturesque vineyards, hilltop villages and fortified towns, this region is chock-full of rustic charm. Start out with a few days exploring stately Strasbourg (p165), then spin south for a couple more days on the peaceful canals of Colmar (p169). Finish up with a road trip along the 170km Route des Vins d'Alsace (p175) to sample local wines and grandstand views. Wine Tasting, Alsace

6

WWI Sites

It's been nine decades since the guns of the Western Front fell silent, but the echoes of WWI can still be felt across much of northern France. Dozens of moving memorials and cemeteries commemorate the millions of men who laid down their lives during the course of the conflict, and you can visit many sites associated with the infamous battles of Verdun (p176) and the Somme (p176). Ossuaire de Douaumont (p176)

Champagne & Northern France's Best...

Culinary Experiences

- **Winstubs** (p175) Tuck into hearty fare at these cosy Alsatian restaurants.
- **Sweet treats** (p168) Pick up handmade chocolates and gingerbread in Strasbourg.
- **Biscuits roses** (p161) Try these sweet pink bites with a glass of Champagne.
- **Bergamotes de Nancy** (p175) Try Nancy's unique bergamot-flavoured bonbons.
- **Alsace Wines** (p175) Sample local vintages in Ribeauvillé.

Photogenic Views

- **Reims' cathedral** (p163) Climb the tower of Reims' Cathédrale Notre Dame for 360-degree views.
- **Petite Venise** (p169) See the sights around Colmar's prettiest neighbourhood.
- **Château du Haut Kœnigsbourg** (p175) This fairy-tale castle offers one of Alsace's best panoramas.
- **Petite France** (p167) Gaze across the water to Strasbourg's monumental Barrage Vauban.
- **Quartier Impérial** (p172) Admire the architecture in Metz' Germanic quarter.

Art Pilgrimages

- **Centre Pompidou-Metz** (p171) & **Louvre-Lens** (p173) Satellite branches of Paris' Pompidou and Louvre.
- **Musée des Beaux-Arts, Reims** (p159) Centuries of fine art in an 18th-century abbey.
- **Musée d'Art Moderne et Contemporain** (p167) Modern art in a glass cube in Strasbourg.
- **Musée Bartholdi** (p170) Visit Colmar to see where the *Statue of Liberty* was created.
- **Atelier Renoir, Essoyes** (p168) A painter's paradise, much-loved by Renoir.

Soul-Stirring Surprises

- **Place Notre Dame, Amiens** (p174) Most uplifting in summer when light shows illuminate the cathedral.

- **Place Stanislas, Nancy** (p171) This neoclassical square is a World Heritage Site.

- **Maison de Jules Verne, Amiens** (p174) Yes, this is the sci-fi pioneer's former home.

- **Café du Palais, Reims** (p161) Champagne by dozens of producers sipped amid art deco splendour.

Left: Alsace wine;
Above: Petite Venise (p169), Colmar

Need to Know

ADVANCE PLANNING

- **A month before** Book accommodation as early as possible, especially in Reims, Strasbourg, Épernay and Metz.

- **Two weeks before** Reserve a guided tour of some Champagne cellars.

- **One week before** Research money-saving city passes. Strasbourg and Reims both have passes covering sights, museums and public transport.

RESOURCES

- **Champagne-Ardenne** (www.tourisme-champagne-ardenne.com) Walks, sights and ideas for the region.

- **Northern France Tourist Office** (www.cdt-nord.fr) Offers several themed routes around the region.

- **Northern Alsace** (www.tourisme67.com) Driving tours, cultural activities and outdoor pursuits.

- **Southern Alsace** (www.tourisme68.com) Similar info for further south.

- **Lorraine** (www.tourism-lorraine.com) Main portal for the Lorraine region.

- **Somme Battlefields** (www.somme-battlefields.co.uk)

GETTING AROUND

- **Car** Useful for Champagne's more out-of-the-way spots, and pretty much essential in Alsace. Just don't overdo the bubbly.

- **Trains** The big cities can be easily reached by train. Reims, Épernay and Metz all make excellent day trips from Paris.

- **Eurostar** (www.eurostar.com) The high-speed Eurostar connects London with Lille and Strasbourg.

- **Buses** Buses are limited, making bus travel something of a no-go.

BE FOREWARNED

- **Champagne** Producers around Reims and Épernay close their doors to visitors during the *vendange* (grape harvest) in September and October.

- **Hotels** Reims and Épernay are often full at weekends Easter to September and weekdays May, June and September. Hotels in Strasbourg are often booked out during the week when European parliament is in session.

- **WWI sites** Visitor centres are often closed in January, but cemeteries are open year-round.

Champagne & Northern France Itineraries

With famous fizz houses, chic cities and elegant architecture, Champagne and northern France encapsulate France's love affair with the finer things in life. This trip is a treat from start to finish.

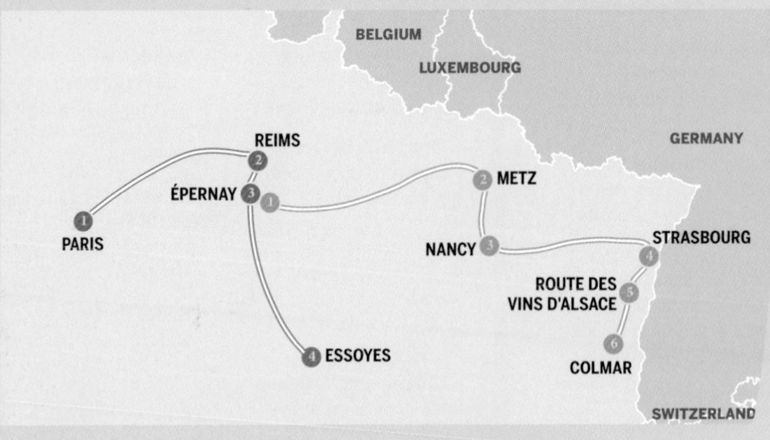

PARIS TO ESSOYES

Champagne Taster

This trip provides a perfect introduction to the Champagne region. From **(1) Paris**, it's an easy trip by train or car to **(2) Reims**, home to some of the world's biggest bubbly producers. Spend the first day tasting your way around Mumm, Taittinger and the other big-name Champagne houses. Lunch in style at Le Foch before tackling the 250 steps of the city's spectacular cathedral tower. Indulge in a spot of wine and Champagne shopping, before partaking in a champagne aperitif at Café du Palais. Overnight at Les Telliers for real 'home-away-from-home' atmosphere.

On day two, catch a train on to **(3) Épernay** and its wealth of subterranean cellars, where 200-million-plus bottles of Champers are being aged, just waiting to be popped open for some sparkling occasion. Take your pick of the city's Champagne houses before enjoying a tasty bistro lunch at La Grillade Gourmande, an afternoon's shopping and sightseeing, and an evening at C. Comme.

Spend day three on a leisurely bike ride or a guided tour of some of the region's smaller vineyards; or see what inspired Renoir in **(4) Essoyes**.

5 DAYS

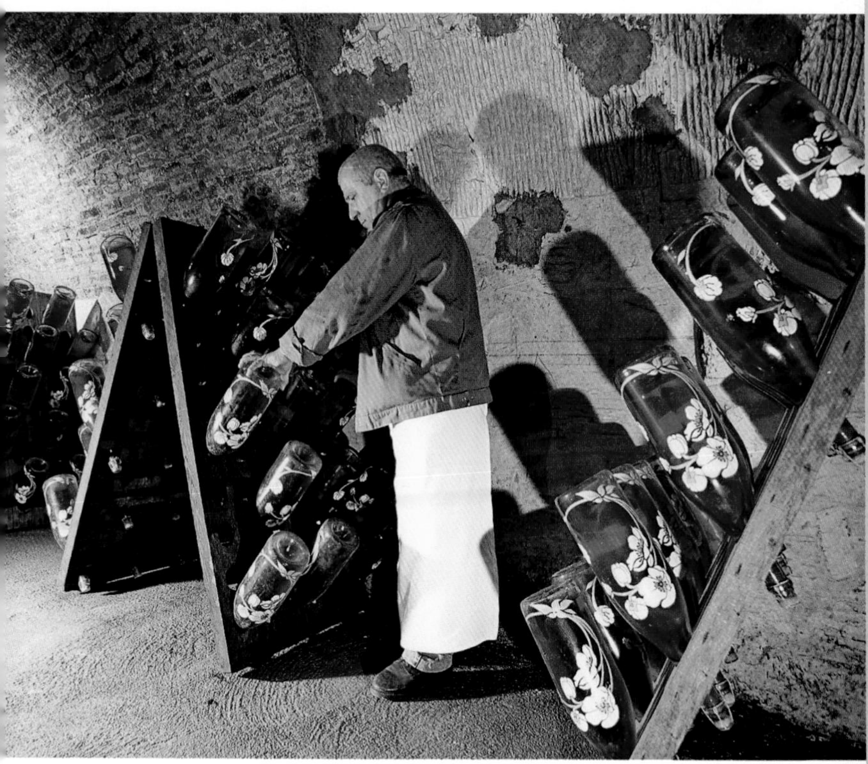

ÉPERNAY TO COLMAR
Architecture

This trip takes in some of northeast France's top architectural sights. Train is easiest between cities, but car is best along the Route des Vins d'Alsace. From **(1) Épernay** head to elegant **(2) Metz**. Visit its cathedral and celebrated modern landmark, the Centre Pompidou-Metz.

Next, move on to **(3) Nancy**. Its splendid 18th-century buildings are best seen around Unesco-listed place Stanislas.

Then head to stately **(4) Strasbourg**, the official home of the EU parliament. It's a suitably grand city, with elements from nearly all of the key periods of French architecture. Step back into the Middle Ages around Grande Île and Petite France, admire the Renaissance at the Palais Rohan, experience 19th-century splendour on the place de la République and marvel at the bold modern statement of the Musée d'Art Moderne et Contemporain.

Spend a couple of days exploring the wider Alsace region. Follow the **(5) Route des Vins d'Alsace** through picturesque vineyards and hilltop villages, before finishing up in atmospheric **(6) Colmar**.

Champagne cellar, Épernay (p162)
SYLVAIN GRANDADAM/GETTY IMAGES ©

Discover Champagne & Northern France

At a Glance

- **Champagne** (p158) Famed the world over for its bubbly, this region in northeast France seduces wine-lovers with Europe's elite fizz houses and smaller vignerons aplenty.
- **Northern France** (p165) Travellers who make it this far north won't regret it – experience some of France's most fascinating cities or emotional moments at WWI battlefields.

Palais du Tauhemis
HEMIS/ALAMY ©

CHAMPAGNE

Champagne arouses all of the senses: the eyes feast on vine-covered hillsides and vertical processions of tiny, sparkling bubbles; the nose is tantalised by the damp soil and the heavenly bouquet of fermentation; the ears rejoice at the clink of glasses and the barely audible fizz; and the palate tingles with every sip.

Reims

POP 184,984

No matter what you have read, nothing can prepare you for that first skyward glimpse of Reims' gargantuan Gothic cathedral (p163). Rising golden and imperious above the city, the cathedral is on the site where some 34 sovereigns – among them two dozen kings – began their reigns. Along with Épernay, it is the most important centre of Champagne production and a fine base for exploring the Montagne de Reims Champagne Route.

Sights

PALAIS DU TAU Museum

(http://palais-tau.monuments-nationaux.fr; 2 place du Cardinal Luçon; adult/child €7.50/free, incl cathedral tower €11/free; 9.30am-6.30pm Tue-Sun) A Unesco World Heritage Site, this former archbishop's residence, constructed in 1690, was where French princes stayed before their coronations – and where they hosted sumptuous banquets afterwards. Now a museum, it displays truly exceptional statuary, liturgical objects and tapestries from the cathedral, some in the impressive, Gothic-style Salle de Tau (Great Hall).

BASILIQUE ST-RÉMI Basilica

(place du Chanoine Ladame; ⏲8am-nightfall, to 7pm summer) This 121m-long former Benedictine abbey church, a Unesco World Heritage Site, mixes Romanesque elements from the mid-11th century (the worn but stunning nave and transept) with early Gothic features from the latter half of the 12th century (the choir, with a large triforium gallery and, way up top, tiny clerestory windows). It is named in honour of Bishop Remigius, who baptised Clovis and 3000 Frankish warriors in 498. The 12th-century-style chandelier has 96 candles, one for each year of the life of St Rémi, whose tomb (in the choir) is marked by a mausoleum from the mid-1600s. The basilica is situated about 1.5km south-southeast of the tourist office; take the Citadine 1 or 2 bus or bus A or F to the St-Rémi stop.

Next door, **Musée St-Rémi (53 rue Simon; adult/child €3/free; ⏲2-6.30pm Mon-Fri, to 7pm Sat & Sun)**, in a 17th- and 18th-century abbey, features local Gallo-Roman archaeology, tapestries and 16th- to 19th-century military history.

MUSÉE DES BEAUX-ARTS Art Museum

(8 rue Chanzy; adult/child €3/free; ⏲10am-noon & 2-6pm Wed-Mon) This institution's rich collection, housed in an 18th-century abbey, boasts one of only four versions of Jacques-Louis David's world-famous *The Death of Marat* (yes, the bloody corpse in the bathtub), 27 works by Camille Corot (only the Louvre has more), 13 portraits by German Renaissance painters Cranach the Elder and the Younger, lots of Barbizon School landscapes, some art-nouveau creations by Émile Gallé, and two works each by Monet, Gauguin and Pissarro.

Tours

MUMM Champagne House

(☎03 26 49 59 70; www.mumm.com; 34 rue du Champ de Mars; tours €11; ⏲tours begin 9-11am & 2-5pm daily, closed Sun Nov-Feb) Mumm (pronounced 'moom'), the only Champagne *maison* (house) in central Reims, was founded in 1827 and is now the world's third-largest producer (almost eight million bottles a year). Engaging and edifying one-hour tours take you through cellars filled with 25 million bottles of fine bubbly. Wheelchair accessible. Phone ahead if possible.

TAITTINGER Champagne Cellar

(☎03 26 85 84 33; www.taittinger.com; 9 place St-Niçaise; tours €16; ⏲tours begin 9.30-11.50am & 2-4.20pm, closed Sat & Sun Dec–mid-Mar) The headquarters of Taittinger is an excellent place to come for a clear, straightforward presentation on how Champagne is actually made – there's no claptrap about 'the Champagne mystique' here. Parts of the cellars occupy 4th-century Roman stone quarries; other bits were excavated by 13th-century Benedictine monks. No need to reserve. Situated 1.5km southeast of Reims centre; take the Citadine 1 or 2 bus to the St-Niçaise or Salines stops.

Sleeping

LES TELLIERS B&B €€

(☎09 53 79 80 74; http://telliers.fr; 18 rue des Telliers; s €76, d €87-110, tr €123, q €142; 📶) Enticingly positioned down a quiet alley near the cathedral, this bijou B&B extends one of Reims' warmest *bienvenues*. The high-ceilinged rooms are big on art-deco character, handsomely decorated with ornamental fireplaces, polished oak floors and the odd antique. Breakfast is a generous spread of pastries, fruit, fresh-pressed juice and coffee.

LA PARENTHÈSE B&B €€

(☎03 26 40 39 57; www.laparenthese.fr; 83 rue Clovis; 2-night stay d €170-220; 📶) Tucked away in the backstreets of old Reims, this little B&B has got everything going for it. The rooms are tastefully done out with wood floors and bursts of pastel colour, and all come with kitchenettes. The good-natured owner will squeeze in a cot if you ask.

Reims

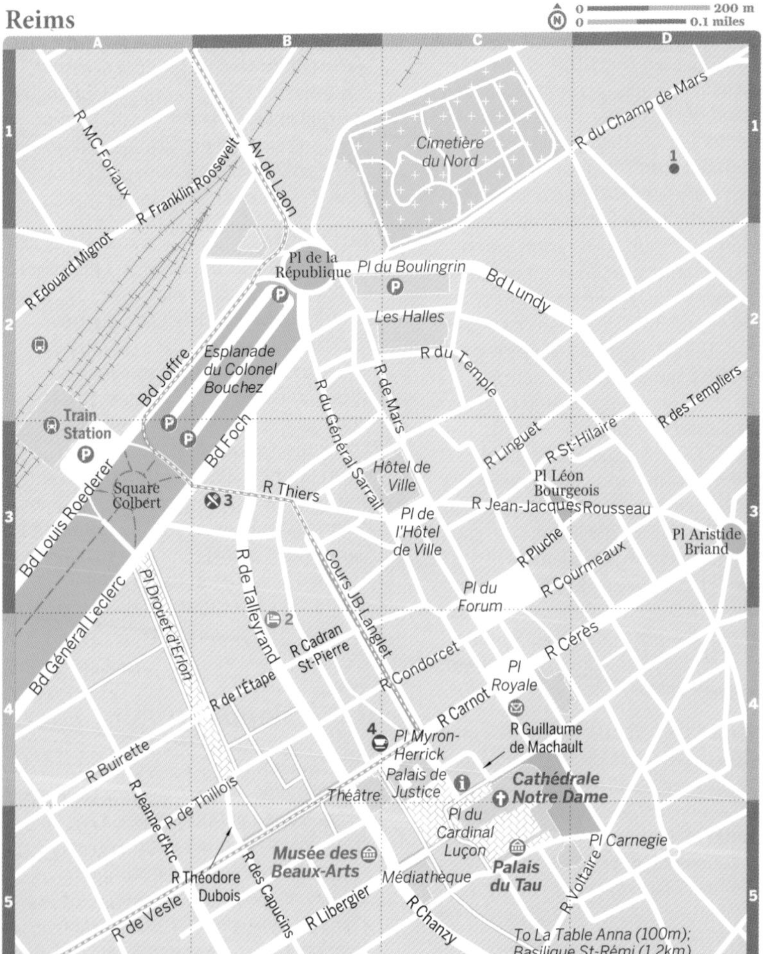

Eating

LE FOCH Gastronomic **€€€**

(**03 26 47 48 22; www.lefoch.com; 37 bd Foch; lunch menus €31, dinner menus €48-80; lunch Tue-Fri & Sun, dinner Tue-Sat**) Described as 'one of France's best fish restaurants' by the food critic Michael Edwards, Michelin-starred Le Foch serves up cuisine that is as beautiful as it is delicious. Specialities such as scallops with Jerusalem artichokes, pistachios and truffle emulsion are expertly paired with wines and presented with panache.

LA TABLE ANNA Traditional French **€€**

(**03 26 89 12 12; 6 rue Gambetta; lunch menus €17, dinner menus €25-42; lunch Tue-Sun, dinner Tue & Thu-Sun**) So what if the decor is chintzy – there is a reason why this bistro is as busy as a beehive. Friendly service and a menu packed with well-executed classics – guinea fowl cooked with herbs, fillet of veal in a rich, earthy morel sauce – hit the mark every time. The three-course, €17 lunch is a steal.

Reims

Top Sights

CAFÉ DU PALAIS Cafe
(www.cafedupalais.fr; 14 place Myron-Herrick; Tue-Sat) Run by the same family since 1930, this art deco cafe is *the* place to nibble divine *biscuits roses* (a speciality of the region), sip a glass of Champagne and see and be seen, at least if you're a *bon bourgeois* or a theatre type.

Information

Tourist office (08 92 70 13 51; www.reims-tourisme.com; 2 rue Guillaume de Machault; @per minute €0.34; 9am-7pm Mon-Sat, 10am-6pm Sun)

Getting There & Away

TRAIN Reims train station, 1km northwest of the cathedral, was renovated in 2010; the bullet marks on the facade date from both world wars. Frequent services run to Paris Gare de l'Est (€26 to €34, 45 minutes to 3¾ hours, 12 to 17 daily). Direct services also go to Épernay (€6.50, 21 to 50 minutes, seven to 18 daily) and Laon (€9.50, 35 to 50 minutes, three to nine daily).

Champagne Routes of the Marne

The **Champagne Routes** (www.tourisme-en-champagne.com) of the Marne département wend their way among neat rows of hillside vines, through hilltop forests and across lowland crop fields. Along the way, they call on winemaking villages and hamlets. At almost every turn, beautiful panoramas unfold and small-scale, family-run Champagne wineries welcome travellers in search of bubbly.

Montagne de Reims Champagne Route

Linking Reims with Épernay by skirting the Parc Natural Régional de la Montagne de Reims, a regional park covering the forested Reims Mountain plateau, this meandering, 70km route passes through vineyards planted mainly with pinot noir vines.

For the region's best introduction to the art of growing grapes and the cycles of the seasons, head to the **Phare de Verzenay** (Verzenay Lighthouse; www.lepharedeverzenay.com; D26; lighthouse adult/child €3/2, incl museum €7/4; 10am-5pm Tue-Fri, to 5.30pm Sat & Sun, closed Jan-Mar), on a hilltop at the eastern edge of the village. Exactly 101 spiral stairs lead to the top of the lighthouse (constructed as a publicity stunt in 1909), which rewards visitors with unsurpassed 360-degree views of vine, field and forest – and, if you're lucky, a tiny TGV zipping by in the distance. The Sillery sugar mill, visible on the horizon, turns an astounding 16,000 tonnes of beets (a major regional crop) into 2600 tonnes of sugar each day! Stop by the **Jardin Panoramique** (admission free) to get a look at the four authorised techniques for tying grape vines to horizontal wires (can you make out the differences?).

Vallée de la Marne Champagne Route

A stronghold of pinot meunier vines, this 90km itinerary winds from Épernay to Dormans, heading more or less west along the hillsides north of the River Marne; it then circles back to the east along the river's south bank.

Perching above a sea of emerald vines and ablaze with forsythia and tulips in spring, **Hautvillers** (population 790), 6km north of Épernay, is where Dom

Pierre Pérignon is popularly believed to have created Champagne. The good Dom's tomb is located in front of the altar of the Église Abbatiale, adorned with 17th-century woodwork. The village is one of Champagne's prettiest, with ubiquitous medieval-style wrought-iron signs providing pictorial clues to the activities taking place on the other side of the wall.

Steps away from the attractive main square, place de la République, is **Au 36** (www.au36.net; 36 rue Dom Pérignon; 10.30am-1pm & 3-7pm Thu-Tue), a slinky wine boutique with a 'wall' of Champagne, innovatively arranged by aroma, and a laid-back upstairs tasting room. A two-/three glass tasting costs €10/15.

Épernay

POP 25,000

Prosperous Épernay, the self-proclaimed *capitale du champagne* and home to many of the world's most celebrated Champagne houses, is the best place for touring cellars and sampling bubbly. The town also makes an excellent base for exploring the Champagne Routes.

Beneath the streets in 110km of subterranean cellars, more than 200 million bottles of Champagne, just waiting to be popped open on some sparkling occasion, are being aged. In 1950 one such cellar – owned by the irrepressible Mercier family – hosted a car rally without the loss of a single bottle!

Épernay is 25km south of Reims and can be visited by train or car as a day trip from Reims.

Sights

Épernay's handsome and eminently strollable avenue de Champagne fizzes with *maisons de champagne* (Champagne houses).

COMTESSE LAFOND Champagne House
(03 86 39 18 33; www.deladoucette.net; 79 av de Champagne; 3-glass tasting €9, incl cellar tour €14; 10am-noon & 2-5.30pm) Owned by wine magnate Baron Patrick de Ladoucette, the whimsically turreted Comtesse Lafond is the most intimate and charming of all the *maisons* on the avenue de Champagne. Tastings of three Champagnes, including the excellent Blanc des Blancs, take place in the elegant salon or in manicured gardens overlooking vine-streaked hills.

MOËT & CHANDON Champagne House
(03 26 51 20 20; www.moet.com; 20 av de Champagne; adult incl 1/2 glasses €16.50/23, 10-18yr €9.50; tours 9.30-11.30am & 2-4.30pm, closed Sat & Sun mid-Nov–mid-Mar) Proudly flying the Moët, French, European and Russian flags, this prestigious *maison* offers frequent one-hour tours that are among the region's most impressive.

MERCIER Champagne House
(03 26 51 22 22; www.champagnemercier.fr; 68-70 av de Champagne; adult incl 1/2/3 glasses €11/16/19, 12-17yr €5.50; tours 9.30-11.30am & 2-4.30pm, closed mid-Dec–mid-Feb) France's most popular brand was founded in 1847 by Eugène Mercier, a trailblazer in the field of eye-catching publicity stunts and the virtual creator of the cellar tour. Everything here is flashy, including the 160,000L barrel that took two decades to build (for the Universal Exposition of 1889), the lift that transports you 30m underground and the laser-guided touring train.

DE CASTELLANE Champagne House
(03 26 51 19 11; www.castellane.com; 64 av de Champagne; adult incl 1 glass €10, under 12yr free; tours 10am-noon & 2-6pm, closed Christmas–mid-Mar) The 45-minute tours, in French and English, take in an informative Champagne museum dedicated to elucidating the *méthode champenoise* and its diverse technologies. The reward for painstakingly climbing the 237 steps up the 66m-high tower (built 1905) is a fine panoramic view.

Tours

CHAMPAGNE DOMI MOREAU Vineyard Tour
(06 30 35 51 07, after 7pm 03 26 59 45 85; www.champagne-domimoreau.com; tours €20;

SONNET SYLVAIN/GETTY IMAGES ©

Don't Miss Cathédrale Notre Dame

Imagine the egos, extravagance and the over-the-top costumes of a French royal coronation... The focal point of all the bejewelled pomposity was Reims' cathedral, a Gothic edifice begun in 1211 – and mostly completed 100 years later – on a site occupied by churches since the 5th century. The single most famous event to take place here was the coronation of Charles VII, with Joan of Arc at his side, on 17 July 1429.

Seriously damaged by artillery and fire during WWI, the 139m-long cathedral is more interesting for its dramatic history than its heavily restored architectural features.

The finest stained-glass windows are the western facade's 12-petalled great rose window; its cobalt-blue neighbour below; and the rose window in the north transept (to the left as you walk from the entrance to the high altar), above the Flamboyant Gothic organ case (15th and 18th centuries) topped with a figure of Christ. Nearby is a 15th-century wooden astronomical clock. There are windows by Chagall (1974; a sign explains each panel) in the central axial chapel (directly behind the high altar) and, two chapels to the left, you'll find a statue of Joan of Arc in full body armour (1901); there's a second statue of her outside on the square, to the right as you exit the cathedral. The tourist office rents audioguides (€6) with self-paced tours of the cathedral. The cathedral is closed during Sunday morning Mass.

Feeling as strong as Goliath? (Look for his worn figure up on the west facade, held in place with metal straps.) Then consider climbing 250 steps up the cathedral tower on a one-hour tour. Book at the Palais du Tau.

NEED TO KNOW

(www.cathedrale-reims.culture.fr; place du Cardinal Luçon; tower adult/child €7.50/free, incl Palais du Tau €11/free; ⌚7.30am-7.30pm, tower tours hourly 10am-5pm Tue-Sat, 2-5pm Sun Apr-Sep)

tours 9.30am & 2.30pm except Wed & 2nd half of Aug) This company runs scenic and insightful three-hour minibus tours, in French and English, of nearby vineyards. Pick-up is across the street from the tourist office. It also organises two-hour vineyard tours by bicycle (€15). Call ahead for reservations.

Eating & Drinking

LA GRILLADE GOURMANDE Regional Cuisine **€€**
(03 26 55 44 22; www.lagrilladegourmande.com; 16 rue de Reims; menus €19-55; lunch & dinner Tue-Sat) This chic, red-walled bistro is an inviting spot to try char-grilled meats and dishes rich in texture and flavour, such as crayfish pan-fried in Champagne and lamb cooked until meltingly tender in rosemary and honey. Diners spill out onto the covered terrace in the warm months.

C. COMME Champagne Bar
(8 rue Gambetta; light meals €7.50-12, 6-glass Champagne tasting €33; 10am-8.30pm Sun-Wed, 10am-11pm Thu, 10am-midnight Fri-Sat) The downstairs cellar has a stash of 300 different varieties of Champagne; sample them (from €5.50 a glass) in the softly lit bar-bistro upstairs. And why not accompany, indeed enhance, your bubbly experience with a tasting plate of regional cheese, charcuterie and *rillettes* (pork pâté).

Information

Tourist office (03 26 53 33 00; www.ot-epernay.fr; 7 av de Champagne; 9.30am-12.30pm & 1.30-7pm Mon-Sat, 11am-4pm Sun)

Getting There & Away

The **train station (place Mendès-France)** has direct services to Reims (€6.40, 20 to 90 minutes, seven to 18 daily) and Paris Gare de l'Est (€22, 1¼ hours, five to 10 daily).

Left: Christmas market, Strasbourg; **Below:** Astronomical clock (p167), Strasbourg

NORTHERN FRANCE

When it comes to culture, cuisine, beer, shopping and dramatic views – not to mention good old-fashioned friendliness – the Ch'tis (residents of France's northern tip) and their region compete with the best France has to offer. In Lille and French Flanders, the down-to-earth Flemish vibe mixes easily with French sophistication and savoir-faire. And in the Somme WWI memorials and cemeteries marking the front lines of 1916 remain places of pilgrimage and reflection.

Alsace is a one-off cultural hybrid, with its Germanic dialect and French sense of fashion, love of foie gras and *choucroute* (sauerkraut), fine wine and beer. Next door Lorraine's historic roll call of dukes and art-nouveau pioneers, blessedly underrated cities, cathedrals and art collections leave visitors spellbound, while its WWI battlefields render visitors speechless time and again with their painful beauty.

Strasbourg

POP 276,136

Strasbourg is the perfect overture to all that is idiosyncratic about Alsace – walking a fine tightrope between France and Germany and between a medieval past and a progressive future, it pulls off its act in inimitable Alsatian style.

Sights

CATHÉDRALE NOTRE-DAME Cathedral
(place de la Cathédrale; astronomical clock adult/child €2/1.50, platform adult/child €5/2.50; 7am-7pm; astronomical clock tickets sold from 11.45am, platform 9am-7.15pm; Langstross)
At once immense and intricate, this red-sandstone cathedral is a riot of filigree stonework and flying buttresses, leering gargoyles and lacy spires. On a sunny day, the 12th- to 14th-century **stained-glass windows** – especially the rose

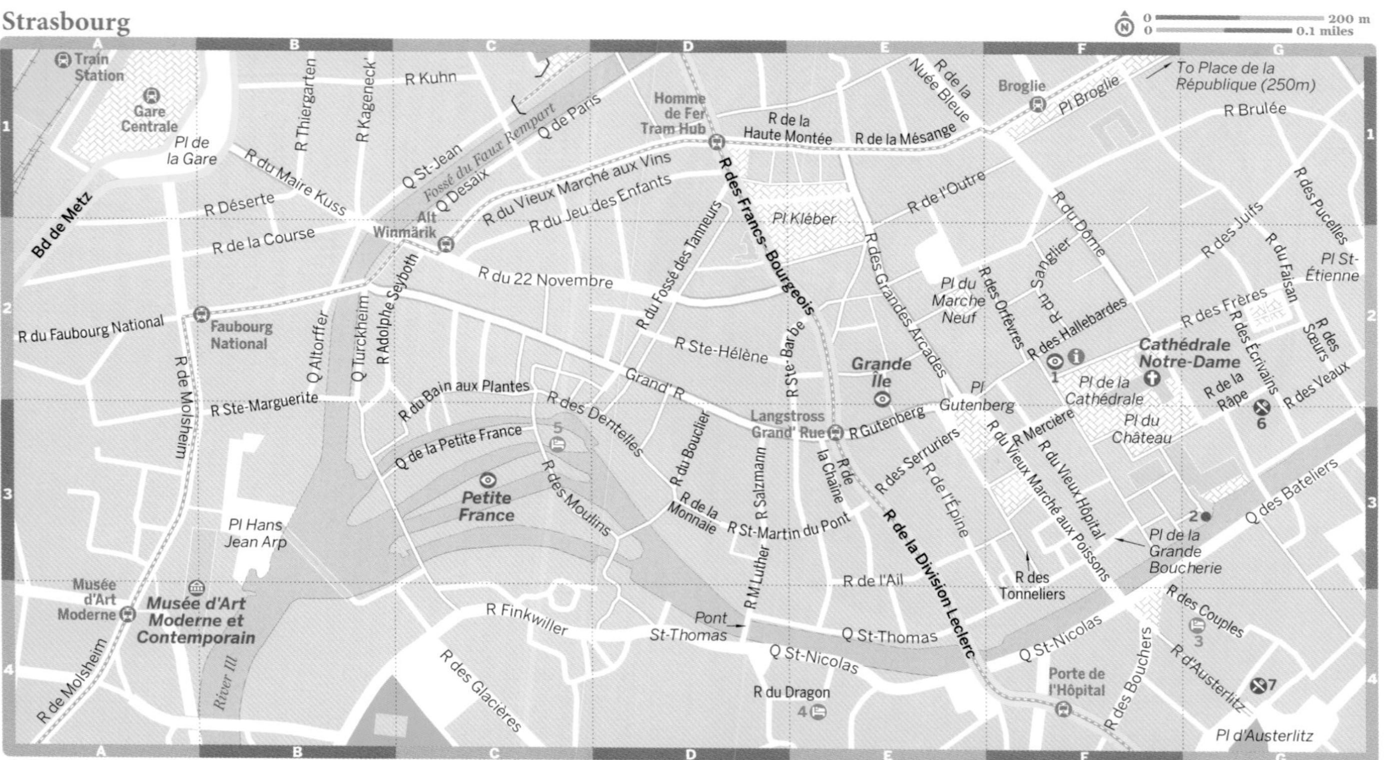
Strasbourg
0 200 m
0 0.1 miles
To Place de la République (250m)
Train Station
Gare Centrale
Pl de la Gare
Bd de Metz
R du Faubourg National
Faubourg National
R de Molsheim
Musée d'Art Moderne
Musée d'Art Moderne et Contemporain
Pl Hans Jean Arp
River Ill
R Ste-Marguerite
R de la Course
R Déserte
R du Maire Kuss
R Thiergarten
R Kageneck
R Kuhn
Q Altorffer
Q Turckheim
R Adolphe Seyboth
Alt Winmärik
Q St-Jean
Q Desaix
Fossé du Faux Rempart
Q de Paris
R du Vieux Marché aux Vins
R du Jeu des Enfants
R du 22 Novembre
R du Bain aux Plantes
Q de la Petite France
Petite France
R des Moulins
R des Dentelles
R Finkwiller
R des Glacières
Grand' R
R du Fossé des Tanneurs
Homme de Fer Tram Hub
R des Francs- Bourgeois
R Ste-Hélène
R Ste-Barbe
Pl Kléber
R de la Haute Montée
R de la Mésange
R de la Nuée Bleue
Broglie
Pl Broglie
R Brulée
R des Grandes Arcades
Grande Île
R Gutenberg
Langstross Grand' Rue
R de la Chaîne
R du Bouclier
R de la Monnaie
R St-Martin du Pont
R Salzmann
R M Luther
Pont St-Thomas
Q St-Thomas
Q St-Nicolas
R du Dragon
R de l'Ail
R de la Division Leclerc
R des Serruriers
R de l'Épine
Pl Gutenberg
Pl du Marché Neuf
R de l'Outre
R du Dôme
R des Orfèvres
R des Hallebardes
R du Sanglier
R Mercière
Pl de la Cathédrale
Cathédrale Notre-Dame
Pl du Château
R du Vieux Hôpital
R du Vieux Marché aux Poissons
R des Tonneliers
Porte de l'Hôpital
Pl de la Grande Boucherie
R des Bouchers
R des Couples
R d'Austerlitz
Pl d'Austerlitz
Q des Bateliers
R de la Râpe
R des Écrivains
R des Frères
R des Juifs
R du Faisan
R des Pucelles
Pl St-Étienne
R des Sœurs
R des Veaux

Strasbourg

Top Sights

Cathédrale Notre-Dame F2
Grande Île E2
Musée d'Art Moderne et Contemporain A4
Petite France C3

Sights

1 Maison Kammerzell F2

Activities, Courses & Tours

2 Batorama G3

Sleeping

3 Cour du Corbeau G4
4 Hôtel du Dragon E4
5 Hôtel Régent Petite France C3

Eating

6 Bistrot et Chocolat G3
7 Le Gavroche G4

window over the western portal – shine like jewels. To appreciate the cathedral in peace, visit in the early evening when the crowds have thinned and stay to see its facade glow gold at dusk.

The 30m-high Gothic-meets-Renaissance **astronomical clock** strikes solar noon at 12.30pm with a parade of carved wooden figures portraying the different stages of life and Jesus with his apostles.

A spiral staircase twists up to the 66m-high **platform** above the facade, from which the tower and its Gothic openwork spire soar another 76m.

GRANDE ÎLE Historic Quarter

(**Langstross**) History seeps through the twisting lanes and cafe-rimmed plazas of Grande Île, Strasbourg's Unesco World Heritage listed island bordered by the River Ill. These streets – with their photogenic line-up of wonky, timber-framed houses in sherbet colours – are made for aimless ambling. They cower beneath the soaring magnificence of the cathedral and its sidekick, the gingerbready 15th-century **Maison Kammerzell** (**rue des Hallebardes**), with its ornate carvings and leaded windows. The alleys are at their most atmospheric when lantern-lit at night.

PETITE FRANCE Historic Quarter

Criss-crossed by narrow lanes, canals and locks, Petite France is where craftsmen plied their trades in the Middle Ages. The half-timbered houses, sprouting veritable thickets of scarlet geraniums in summer, and the riverside parks attract the masses, but the area still manages to retain its Alsatian atmosphere and charm, especially in the early morning and late evening.

MUSÉE D'ART MODERNE ET CONTEMPORAIN Art Museum

(**www.musees.strasbourg.org; place Hans Jean Arp; adult/child €7/free; noon-7pm Tue, Wed & Fri, noon-9pm Thu, 10am-6pm Sat & Sun, Art Café Tue-Sun; Musée d'Art Moderne**) This striking glass-and-steel cube showcases an outstanding collection of fine art, graphic art and photography. Kandinsky, Picasso, Magritte and Monet canvases hang out alongside curvaceous works by Strasbourg-born abstract artist Hans Jean Arp.

Tours

BATORAMA Boat Tour

(**www.batorama.fr; rue de Rohan; adult/child €9.20/4.80; tours half-hourly 9.30am-7pm, hourly 8-10pm; Langstross**) This outfit runs scenic 70-minute boat trips, which glide along the storybook canals of Petite France, taking in the Vauban Dam and the glinting EU institutions. Tours depart on rue de Rohan, the quay behind Palais Rohan.

Sleeping

COUR DU CORBEAU Boutique Hotel €€€

(**03 90 00 26 26; www.cour-corbeau.com; 6-8 rue des Couples; r €190-330; ; Porte de l'Hôpital**) A 16th-century inn lovingly converted into a boutique hotel, Cour du Corbeau wins you over with its half-timbered charm and location, just steps from the river. Gathered around a courtyard, rooms blend original touches such

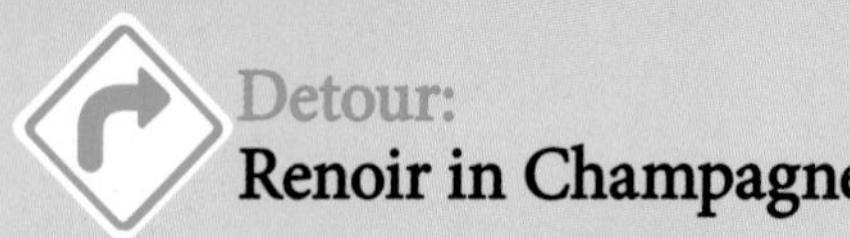

Detour: Renoir in Champagne

It's easy to see why Renoir loved **Essoyes** so much that he spent his last 25 summers here. The village, a two-hour drive from Épernay in the Aube *département* (www.aube-champagne.com), has neat stone houses, a riverfront that glows golden in the late afternoon sun and landscapes of vineyards and flower-flecked meadows that unfold in a gentle, almost artistic way.

Essoyes' *circuit découverte* is a marked trail that loops around the village, taking in viewpoints that inspired the artist, as well as the family home and the cemetery where he lies buried, his grave marked by a contemplative bronze bust. The trail begins at the **Espace des Renoir** (www.renoir-essoyes.fr; place de la Mairie, Renoir Centre; adult/child €8/4; 10am-12.30pm & 1.30-6.30pm, closed Tue Oct-Mar), which also houses the **tourist office** (03 25 29 21 27; www.essoyes.fr; place de la Mairie, Renoir Centre; same hrs). Opened in 2011, the centre screens a 15-minute film about Renoir and displays temporary exhibitions of mostly contemporary art. Marking the end of the tour and covered by the same ticket is the **Atelier Renoir** (Renoir's Studio; 10am-12.30pm & 1.30-6.30pm, closed Tue Oct-Mar), with displays zooming in on the hallmarks of Renoir's work (the female form, the vibrant use of colour and light), alongside original pieces such as his antiquated wheelchair and the box he used to carry his paintings to Paris. Perhaps loveliest of all is the studio **garden**, particularly in spring to early summer when it bursts forth with tulips, anemones and roses.

as oak parquet and Louis XV furnishings with mod cons such as flat-screen TVs.

HÔTEL DU DRAGON Hotel €€
(03 88 35 79 80; www.dragon.fr; 12 rue du Dragon; s €84-159, d €92-159; ; Porte de l'Hôpital) Step through a tree-shaded courtyard and into the, ahhh...blissful calm of this bijou hotel. The Dragon receives glowing reviews for its crisp interiors, attentive service and prime location near Petite France.

HÔTEL RÉGENT PETITE FRANCE Design Hotel €€
(03 88 76 43 43; www.regent-hotels.com; 5 rue des Moulins; r €159-460; ; Alt Winmärik) Once an ice factory and now Strasbourg's hottest design hotel, this waterfront pile is quaint on the outside and ubercool on the inside. The sleek rooms dressed in muted colours and plush fabrics sport shiny marble bathrooms. Work your relaxed look in the sauna, chic restaurant and Champagne bar with dreamy River Ill views.

Eating

LE GAVROCHE Mediterranean €€
(03 88 36 82 89; www.restaurant-gavroche.com; 4 rue Klein; menu €38; Mon-Fri; ; Porte de l'Hôpital) Bistro food is given a pinch of creativity and southern sunshine at intimate, softly lit Le Gavroche. Mains such as veal in a mint crust with crispy polenta and coriander-infused artichoke tagine are followed by zingy desserts such as lime tart with lemon-thyme sorbet. There's a menu for *les petits*.

BISTROT ET CHOCOLAT Cafe €
(www.bistrotetchocolat.net; 8 rue de la Râpe; snacks €5-8, brunch €10-26; 11am-7pm Tue-Fri, 10am-7pm Sat & Sun; ; Langstross) This boho-flavoured bistro is hailed for its solid and liquid organic chocolate (ginger is

superb). The terrace is a local hangout for light bites such as tofu tapas, wok dishes and weekend brunches. The website has details on children's cooking classes.

Information

Main tourist office (☎03 88 52 28 28; www.otstrasbourg.fr; 17 place de la Cathédrale; ⊙9am-7pm; 🚊Langstross)

Getting There & Away

Air

Strasbourg's international **airport** (www.strasbourg.aeroport.fr) is 17km southwest of the city centre (towards Molsheim), near the village of Entzheim. Ryanair links London Stansted with **Karlsruhe/Baden-Baden airport** (www.badenairpark.de), across the Rhine in Germany, 58km northeast of Strasbourg.

Train

Built in 1883, the Gare Centrale was given a 120m-long, 23m-high glass facade and underground galleries in order to welcome the new TGV Est Européen in grand style. On the Grande Île, tickets are available at the **SNCF Boutique** (www.voyages-sncf.com; 5 rue des Francs-Bourgeois; 🚊Langstross).

Destinations within France:

Lille €115, four hours, 17 daily.

Lyon €71, 4½ hours, 14 daily.

Marseille €161, 6¾ hours, 16 daily.

Metz €24.50, two hours, 20 daily.

Nancy €24, 1½ hours, 25 daily.

Paris Gare de l'Est; €71, 2¼ hours, 19 daily.

Colmar

POP 68,843

Alsace wine region capital, Colmar looks for all the world as though it has been plucked from the pages of a medieval folk tale. At times the Route des Vins d'Alsace fools you into thinking it's 1454, but here, in the alley-woven heart of the old town, the illusion is complete. Half-timbered houses in chalk-box colours crowd dark, cobblestone lanes and bridge-laced canals, which have most day-trippers wondering around in a permanent daze of neck-craning, photo-snapping, gasp-eliciting wonder.

Sights

PETITE VENISE Historic Quarter

If you see just one thing in Colmar, make it the Little Venice quarter. Canal connection aside, it doesn't resemble the Italian city in the slightest, but it is truly lovely in its own right. Its winding backstreets are punctuated by impeccably restored half-timbered houses in sugared-almond shades, many ablaze with geraniums in summer. Take a medieval mosey around **rue des Tanneurs**, with its rooftop verandas for drying

Colmar

ARPAD BENEDEK/GETTY IMAGES ©

hides, and **quai de la Poissonnerie**, the former fishers' quarter.

Rowboats (30min €6) depart next to **rue de Turenne bridge** and are a relaxed way to see Petite Venise from the water.

MUSÉE D'UNTERLINDEN Art Museum
(www.musee-unterlinden.com; 1 rue d'Unterlinden; adult/child incl audioguide €8/5; 9am-6pm) Gathered around a Gothic-style Dominican cloister, this museum hides a prized collection of medieval stone statues, late-15th-century prints by Martin Schongauer as well as an ensemble of Upper Rhine Primitives. The star attraction, though, is the late-Gothic **Rétable d'Issenheim** (Issenheim Altarpiece).

MUSÉE BARTHOLDI Museum
(www.musee-bartholdi.com; 30 rue des Marchands; adult/child €5/3; 10am-noon & 2-6pm Wed-Mon Mar-Dec) In the house where Frédéric Auguste Bartholdi was born, this museum pays homage to the sculptor who captured the spirit of a nation with his *Statue of Liberty*. Look out for the full-size plaster model of Lady Liberty's left ear (the lobe is watermelon-sized!) and the Bartholdi family's sparklingly bourgeois apartment.

Eating

L'ATELIER DU PEINTRE Gastronomic €€
(03 89 29 51 57; 1 rue Schongauer; lunch menus €20-25, dinner menus €37-72; Tue-Sat) With its art-slung walls and carefully composed cuisine, this Michelin-starred bistro lives up to its 'painter's studio' name. Seasonal masterpieces such as roast lamb with creamed artichokes and chanterelles, and mussel soup with black olives, sage and aioli, are cooked with verve and served with panache.

LA COCOTTE DE GRANDMÈRE Traditional French €
(03 89 23 32 49; 14 place de l'École; menus €12-14; Mon-Fri) Good honest food and a warm ambience attract hungry locals to this sweet bistro. The three-course €14 *menu* hits the mark every time, with deeply satisfying home cooking, from hearty casseroles to roast duck leg with creamy mash.

Cathédrale St-Étienne, Metz

RICHARD FAIRLESS/GETTY IMAGES ©

Information

Tourist office (03 89 20 68 92; www.ot-colmar.fr; 32 cours Sainte-Anne; 9am-7pm Mon-Sat, 10am-1pm Sun)

Getting There & Away

Colmar train connections:

Paris Gare de l'Est; €75 to €94, three hours, 17 daily

Strasbourg €11.50, 32 minutes, 30 daily

Metz

POP 124,024

Sitting astride the confluence of the Moselle and Seille rivers, Lorraine's graceful capital Metz (pronounced 'mess') is ready to be fêted. Though the city's Gothic marvel of a cathedral, superlative art collections and Michelin star–studded dining scene long managed to sidestep the world spotlight, all that changed with the show-stopping arrival of Centre Pompidou-Metz in 2010.

Sights

FREE CATHÉDRALE ST-ÉTIENNE Cathedral

(place St-Étienne; audioguide €7, treasury & crypt adult/child €4/2; 8am-6pm, treasury & crypt 9.30am-12.30pm & 1.30-5.30pm Mon-Sat, 1.30-5.30pm Sun) As delicate as Chantilly lace, the golden spires of this Gothic cathedral crown Metz' skyline. Exquisitely lit by kaleidoscopic curtains of 13th- to 20th-century stained glass, the cathedral is nicknamed 'God's lantern' and its sense of height and light is indeed spiritually uplifting.

CENTRE POMPIDOU-METZ Gallery

(www.centrepompidou-metz.fr; 1 parvis des Droits de l'Homme; adult/child €7/free; 11am-6pm Mon & Wed-Fri, 10am-8pm Sat, 10am-6pm Sun) The architecturally innovative Centre Pompidou-Metz is the satellite branch of Paris' Centre Pompidou and the star of the city's art scene. The gallery draws on Europe's largest collection of modern art to stage ambitious temporary exhibitions, such as the bold graphic works of

If You Like... Art & Architecture

If you swoon over the sublimity of Reims or Amiens' cathedrals, or your heart misses a beat inside Strasbourg's modern-art cube museum, there are bags more addresses to appease the art 'n' architecture lover in you:

1 LILLE

If the seduction of its Flemish-knitted old town is not sufficient, Lille woos with a trio of first-class art museums: savour 15th- to 20th-century art in the **Palais des Beaux-Arts** (Fine Arts Museum; www.pba-lille.fr; place de la République; adult/student/child €6.50/4/free; 2-6pm Mon, 10am-6pm Wed-Sun; M République Beaux Arts), modern and contemporary works in the **Musée d'Art Moderne Lille-Métropole** (03 20 19 68 68; www.musee-lam.fr; 1 allée du Musée; adult/student/child €7/5/free; 10am-6pm Tue-Sun), and applied arts and sculpture in **La Piscine Musée d'Art et d'Industrie** (www.roubaix-lapiscine.com; 23 rue de l'Espérance, Roubaix; adult/child €4.50/free; 11am-6pm Tue-Thu, 11am-8pm Fri, 1-6pm Sat & Sun; M Gare Jean Lebas), superbly at home in an art deco swimming pool.

2 ARRAS

Arras' Flemish-inspired architecture is plain to see on its market-square twinset, place des Héros and Grand'Place. For a panoramic perspective, climb the Unesco-listed bell tower. For more info, visit the tourist office (03 21 51 26 95; www.ot-arras.fr; place des Héros; 9am-noon & 2-6pm Mon-Sat, 10am-12.30pm & 2.30-6.30pm Sun & holidays)

3 NANCY

Let this former capital of the Dukes of Lorraine catapult you into 18th-century splendour; Nancy's heart-soaring Unesco-listed place Stanislas was laid out in the 1750s. Enjoy the region's bergamot-flavoured bonbons while you're here. Visit the tourist office (03 83 35 22 41; www.ot-nancy.fr; place Stanislas; 9am-7pm Mon-Sat, 10am-5pm Sun) formore info.

American conceptual artist Sol LeWitt. The dynamic space also hosts top-drawer cultural events.

QUARTIER IMPÉRIAL Historic Quarter
The stately boulevards and bourgeois villas of the German Imperial Quarter, including rue Gambetta and av Foch, are the brainchild of Kaiser Wilhelm II. Built to trumpet the triumph of Metz' post-1871 status as part of the Second Reich, the architecture is a whimsical mix of art deco, neo-Romanesque and neo-Renaissance influences. The area's unique ensemble of Wilhelmian architecture has made it a candidate for Unesco World Heritage status.

Sleeping

HÔTEL DE LA CATHÉDRALE Historic Hotel €€
(☎03 87 75 00 02; www.hotelcathedrale-metz.fr; 25 place de Chambre; d €75-110;) You can expect a friendly welcome at this classy little hotel, occupying a 17th-century town house in a prime spot right opposite the cathedral. Climb the wrought-iron staircase to your classically elegant room, with high ceilings, hardwood floors and antique trappings. Book well ahead for a cathedral view.

PÉNICHE ALCLAIR Houseboat €
(☎06 37 67 16 18; www.chambrespenichemetz.com; allée St-Symphorien; r incl breakfast €70;) What a clever idea: this old barge has been revamped into a stylish blue houseboat, with two cheerful wood-floored rooms and watery views. Breakfast is served in your room or on the sundeck. It's a 15-minute stroll south of the centre along the river.

Eating

LE BISTRO DES SOMMELIERS Bistro €€
(☎03 87 63 40 20; 10 rue Pasteur; mains €16-20; closed lunch Sat, Sun) This no-nonsense bistro near the station prides itself on its warm ambience and consistently good French cooking – a recipe that never fails. *Entrecôtes* (rib-eye steaks) are succulent, *frites* (chips) crisp, salads well dressed and wines perfectly matched to mains. The three-course *prix fixe* menu is a bargain at €15.

RESTAURANT THIERRY Fusion €€
(☎03 87 74 01 23; www.restaurant-thierry.fr; 5 rue des Piques; menus €19.50-36.50; closed Wed & Sun) Combining the historic backdrop of a 16th-century town house with the subtly spiced cuisine, lighting and bohemian flair of Morocco, this is one of Metz' most coveted tables. An aperitif in the candlelit salon works up an appetite for dishes such as sweet duck *pastilla* (pie) and seafood and dried-fruit tagine. Often full, so call ahead.

Information

Tourist office (☎03 87 55 53 76; http://tourisme.mairie-metz.fr; 2 place d'Armes; 9am-7pm Mon-Sat, 10am-5pm Sun)

Getting There & Away

Metz' ornate early-20th-century **train station** (pl du Général de Gaulle) has a supersleek TGV linking Paris with Luxembourg. Direct trains go to the following destinations:

Nancy €10, 37 minutes, 48 daily.

Paris Gare de l'Est; €61, 80 minutes, 13 daily.

Strasbourg €24.50, 1½ hours, 14 daily.

Verdun €14, 1½ hours, three daily.

Amiens

POP 137,030

One of France's most awe-inspiring Gothic cathedrals is reason enough to spend time in Amiens, the comfy, if reserved, former capital of Picardy, where Jules Verne spent the last two decades of his life. The mostly pedestrianised city centre, rebuilt after the war, is complemented by lovely green spaces along the Somme river. Some 25,000 students give the town a youthful feel.

Amiens is an excellent base for visits to the Battle of the Somme Memorials.

© SANAA, IMREY CULBERT, CATHERINE MOSBACH AFP/GETTY IMAGES ©

Don't Miss **Louvre-Lens**

After years of anticipation, Europe's most ballyhooed new art museum has opened its doors in Lens, 18km north of Arras and a 1½-hour drive north of Amiens. The Louvre-Lens showcases hundreds of treasures from Paris' venerable Musée du Louvre in a purpose-built, state-of-the-art new exhibition space.

Designed to give museum-goers a completely different experience than its Parisian cousin, the Louvre-Lens is all about making art accessible to new audiences, while showing off the Louvre's remarkable holdings in exciting new ways. There's no permanent collection here. Instead, the museum's centrepiece, a 120m-long exhibition space called the **Galerie du Temps**, displays a limited but significant, ever-rotating collection of over 200 pieces from the original Louvre, spanning that museum's full breadth and diversity of cultures and historical periods.

The museum's grand opening featured European masterpieces such as Delacroix's *Liberty Leading the People* and Raphael's *Portrait of Baldassare Castiglione* displayed alongside works as diverse as ancient Mesopotamian tablets, Persian glazed tiles, Greek statues, Pompeiian frescoes, Roman bronzes, Islamic art from Spain to Syria and 11th-century Italian mosaics.

A second building, the glass-walled **Pavillon de Verre**, displays annually changing themed exhibits – 2013's theme is the Renaissance, including Leonardo's *Saint Anne* among other works.

Lens is accessible by regular TGV trains from Paris' Gare du Nord (€28 to €46, 65 to 70 minutes), as well as regional trains from Lille (€7.60, 40 minutes) and Arras (€4.20, 15 minutes).

NEED TO KNOW

(www.louvrelens.fr; 6 rue Charles Lecocq, Lens; Galerie du Temps & Pavillon de Verre free through 2013; 10am-6pm Wed-Mon)

Sights & Activities

CATHÉDRALE NOTRE DAME Cathedral
(place Notre Dame; audioguide 1st/2nd person €4/3, north tower adult/child €5.50/free; cathedral 8.30am-6.15pm daily, north tower afternoon only Wed-Mon) The largest Gothic cathedral in France (it's 145m long) and a Unesco World Heritage Site, this magnificent structure was begun in 1220 to house the **skull of St John the Baptist**, shown – framed in gold and jewels – in the northern outer wall of the ambulatory. Connoisseurs rave about the soaring Gothic arches (42.3m high over the transept), unity of style and immense interior, but for locals, the 17th-century statue known as the **Ange Pleureur** (Crying Angel), in the ambulatory directly behind the over-the-top Baroque (18th-century) high altar, remains a favourite.

A free 45-minute **light show** bathes the cathedral's facade in vivid medieval colours nightly from mid-June to mid-September and December to 1 January; the photons start flying at 7pm in winter and sometime between 9.45pm (September) and 10.45pm (June) in summer.

HORTILLONNAGES Boat Tour
(03 22 92 12 18; 54 bd Beauvillé; adult/child €5.90/5.20; 1.30-4.30pm) Amiens' market gardens – some 3 sq km in extent – have supplied the city with vegetables and flowers since the Middle Ages. Today, their peaceful *rieux* (waterways), home to seven working farms, over 1000 private gardens and countless water birds, can be visited on 12-person boats whose raised prows make them look a bit like gondolas.

MAISON DE JULES VERNE House Museum
(Home of Jules Verne; 03 22 45 45 75; www.jules-verne.net; 2 rue Charles Dubois; adult/child €7/3.50, audioguide €2; 10am-12.30pm & 2-6.30pm Mon & Wed-Fri, 2-6.30pm Tue, 11am-6.30pm Sat & Sun) Jules Verne (1828–1905) wrote many of his best-known works of science fiction under the eaves of this turreted Amiens home. The models, prints, posters and other items inspired by Verne's imagination afford a fascinating opportunity to check out the future as he envisioned it over a century ago, when going around the world in 80 days sounded fantastic – and before WWI dashed Europeans' belief in a world destined to improve thanks to 'progress'.

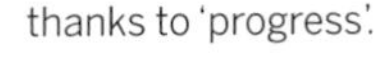

Sleeping

GRAND HÔTEL DE L'UNIVERS Hotel €€
(03 22 91 52 51; www.hotel-univers-amiens.com; 2 rue de Noyon; s €67-89, d €88-156; @) This venerable, Best Western–affiliated hostelry has an enviable parkside location in the city's pedestrianised heart,

Cathédrale Notre Dame, Amiens
DANITA DELIMONT/GETTY IMAGES ©

one block from the train station. The 41 rooms, set around a four-storey atrium, are immaculate and very comfortable; some on the 4th floor even come with views of the cathedral.

HÔTEL VICTOR HUGO Hotel €
(☎03 22 91 57 91; www.hotel-a-amiens.com; 2 rue de l'Oratoire; r €46-70; wifi) Just a block from the cathedral, this friendly, family-run two-star hotel has 10 simple but comfortable rooms. Best value, if you don't mind a long stair climb, are the welcoming top-floor units (rooms 7 and 8) with rooftop views and lots of natural light.

Eating

LE T'CHIOT ZINC Bistro €
(☎03 22 91 43 79; 18 rue de Noyon; menus €13-27; ⏲closed Sun, & Mon Jul & Aug) Inviting, bistro-style decor reminiscent of the belle époque provides a fine backdrop for the tasty French and Picard cuisine, including fish dishes and *caqhuse* (pork in a cream, wine vinegar and onion sauce). The proper, Picard pronunciation of the restaurant's name is 'shtyoh-zang'.

Information

Tourist office (☎03 22 71 60 50; www.amiens-tourisme.com; 40 place Notre Dame; ⏲9.30am-6pm Mon-Sat, 10am-noon & 2-5pm Sun)

Getting There & Away

Amiens is an important rail hub. Accessed through a dramatic modern entrance, the downtown train station offers direct services to the cities listed below. SNCF buses (€10, 45 minutes, 15 to 20 daily) also go to the Haute Picardie TGV station, 42km east of the city.

Arras €12, 45 minutes, six to 12 daily.

Calais-Ville €25, two to 2½ hours, six or seven daily.

Compiègne €13, 1¼ hours, eight to 12 daily.

If You Like… Alsatian Villages

The 170km-long **Route des Vins d'Alsace** (Alsace Wine Route) is one of France's most evocative drives, featuring castle-topped crags and the mist-enshrouded Vosges. And every mile or so there's a roadside *cave* (wine cellar) inviting you to stop, raise a glass and revel in some of France's loveliest wines.

1 KAYSERSBERG

Kaysersberg, 10km northwest of Colmar, is an instant heart-stealer with its backdrop of gently sloping vines, hilltop castle and 16th-century fortified bridge across the River Weiss.

2 RIQUEWIHR

Some 14km northwest of Colmar, this might just be *the* most enchanting town on this viticultural driving route.

3 RIBEAUVILLÉ

Sample Alsation wines at **Cave de Ribeauvillé** (2 rte de Colmar; ⏲8am-noon & 2-6pm Mon-Fri, 10am-12.30pm & 2.30-7pm Sat & Sun), France's oldest wine growers' cooperative (1895), 3km from Riquewihr.

4 OBERNAI

This wine-producing village features flower-bedecked alleyways and 13th-century ramparts. Find the **tourist office** (☎03 88 95 64 13; www.obernai.fr; place du Beffroi; ⏲9am-noon & 2-6pm Mon-Sun) behind centuries-old **Place du Marché**, and feast on traditionally earthy dishes at **Winstub La Dîme** (☎03 88 95 54 02; 5 rue des Pélerins; menus €12-22; ⏲closed Wed; family-friendly).

5 DAMBACH-LA-VILLE

Ringed by renowned Frankstein *grand cru* vineyards and sturdy pink-granite ramparts, Dambach is built from half-timbered houses painted in ice-cream colours.

6 CHÂTEAU DU HAUT KŒNIGSBOURG

Turreted red-sandstone **Château du Haut Kœnigsbourg** (www.haut-koenigsbourg.fr; adult/child €8/free; ⏲9.15am-5.15pm) is worth the detour for the panorama from its ramparts.

If You Like… WWI History

Pay your respects to those who fought in the Battle of Verdun, the longest WWI battle. The forested landscape around the town of Verdun has cemeteries, artillery craters and battlefields still pocked by trenches. By car, take the D913 and D112 and follow signs to 'Douaumont', 'Vaux' or the 'Champ de Bataille 14-18'. Alternatively, **Verdun tourist office** (www.tourisme-verdun.fr) arranges one-hour battlefield tours (adult/child €9/7; hourly 2pm to 6pm early April to mid-November).

1 **MÉMORIAL DE VERDUN**
(www.memorial-de-verdun.fr; adult/child €7/3.50; 9am-6pm, closed mid-Dec–Jan) The village of Fleury, wiped off the face of the earth in the course of being captured and recaptured 16 times, is now the site of this moving memorial.

2 **OSSUAIRE DE DOUAUMONT**
(www.verdun-douaumont.com; audiovisual presentation adult/child €5/3; 9am-6pm Mon-Fri, 10am-6pm Sat & Sun) Rising like a gigantic artillery shell above 15,000 crosses that bleed into the distance, this 137m-long Verdun Battlefields ossuary is one of France's most important WWI memorials.

3 **FORT DE DOUAUMONT**
(adult/child €4/2; 10am-6pm) Sitting high on a hill, Fort de Douaumont was the strongest of the 38 fortresses and bastions built along a 45km front to protect Verdun.

4 **MEUSE-ARGONNE AMERICAN CEMETERY**
The largest US military cemetery in Europe, Meuse-Argonne American Cemetery in Romagne-sous-Montfaucon, 41km northwest of Verdun, is the resting place of 14,246 soldiers.

5 **ROMAGNE '14-'18**
(03 29 85 10 14; www.romagne14-18.com; 2 rue de l'Andon; guided walks €12.50, donations welcome; guided walks 9am-noon, museum noon-6pm, closed Tue & Wed) Don't leave Romagne-sous-Montfaucon without visiting this war museum packed with original memorabilia.

Lille-Flandres €20, 1½ hours, six to 12 daily.

Paris' Gare du Nord €21, 1¼ to 1¾ hours, 14 to 30 daily.

Rouen €19.50, 1¼ hours, five daily.

Battle of the Somme Memorials

Almost 750,000 soldiers, airmen and sailors from Great Britain, Australia, Canada, the Indian subcontinent, Ireland, New Zealand, South Africa, the West Indies and other parts of the British Empire died during WWI on the Western Front, two-thirds of them in France. They were buried where they fell, in more than 1000 military cemeteries and 2000 civilian cemeteries that dot the landscape along a wide swath of territory – 'Flanders Fields' – running roughly from Amiens and Cambrai north via Arras and Béthune to Armentières and Ypres (Ieper) in Belgium.

Tours

Tourist offices (including those in Amiens, Arras and Péronne) can help book tours of battlefield sites and memorials. Respected tour companies include **The Battlefields Experience** (03 22 76 29 60; www.thebattleofthesomme.co.uk), **Western Front Tours** (www.westernfronttours.com.au; mid-Mar–mid-Nov), **Terres de Mémoire** (03 22 84 23 05; www.terresdememoire.com), **Chemins d'Histoire** (06 31 31 85 02; www.cheminsdhistoire.com) and **True Blue Digger Tours** (03 22 51 56 21; www.trueblue-diggertours.com).

Péronne

The best place to begin a visit to the Somme battlefields – especially if you're interested in WWI's historical and cultural context – is the outstanding **Historial de la Grande Guerre** (Museum of the Great War; 03 22 83 14 18; www.historial.org; Château de Péronne; adult/child incl audioguide €7.50/3.80; 10am-6pm, closed

mid-Dec–mid-Jan). Tucked inside Péronne's massively fortified château, this award-winning museum tells the story of the war chronologically, with equal space given to the German, French and British perspectives on what happened, how and why. The **lake** behind the museum is a fine place for a stroll or picnic.

Excellent English brochures on the battlefields can be picked up at Péronne's **tourist office (☎03 22 84 42 38; www.hautesomme-tourisme.com; 16 place André Audinot; ⏰10am-noon & 2-6pm Mon-Sat)**, 100m from the museum entrance.

Péronne (population 8450) is about 60km east of Amiens; from the D1029 or A29, follow the D1017 the last few kilometres into town.

La Grande Mine

Just outside the hamlet of La Boisselle, this enormous crater looks like the site of a meteor impact. Some 100m across and 30m deep, the **Lochnagar Crater Memorial** (as it's officially known) was created on the morning of the first day of the First Battle of the Somme (1 July 1916) by about 25 tonnes of ammonal laid by British sappers in order to create a breach in the German lines – and is a testament to the boundless ingenuity human beings can muster when determined to kill their fellow creatures.

La Grande Mine is 4km northeast of Albert along the D929.

Somme American Cemetery

In late September 1918, just six weeks before the end of WWI, American units – together with their British, Canadian and Australian allies – launched an assault on the Germans' heavily fortified Hindenburg Line. One regiment of the 27th Infantry Division, a National Guard unit from New York, suffered 337 dead and 658 wounded on a single day.

Some of the fiercest fighting took place near the village of Bony, on the sloping site now occupied by the 1844 Latin Crosses and Stars of David of the **Somme American Cemetery (www.abmc.gov; ⏰9am-5pm)**. The names of 333 men whose remains were never recovered are inscribed on the walls of the **Memorial Chapel**, reached through massive bronze doors. The small **Visitors' Building** (turn left at the flagpole) has information on the battle.

The cemetery is 24km northeast of Péronne, mostly along the D6, and 18km north of St-Quentin along the D1044. From A26, take exit 9 and follow the signs for 17km.

Thiepval Memorial

Dedicated to 'the Missing of the Somme', this Commonwealth memorial – its distinctive outline visible for many kilometres in all directions – is the region's most visited place of pilgrimage. Situated on the site of a German stronghold that was stormed on 1 July 1916 with unimaginable casualties, it was designed by Sir Edwin Lutyens and dedicated in 1932. The columns of the arches are inscribed with the names of 73,367 British and South African soldiers whose remains were never recovered or identified. The glass-walled **visitors centre (☎03 22 74 60 47; admission free; ⏰10am-6pm, closed 2 weeks around New Year)** is discreetly below ground level.

Thiepval is 7.5km northeast of Albert along the D151.

Loire Valley & Central France

In terms of architectural splendour, nowhere tops the Loire Valley. For over a thousand years, this has been the favourite weekend retreat for the cream of French society, and it's littered with lavish châteaux left behind by generations of kings, queens and courtly nobles.

Southeast along the River Loire is Burgundy (Bourgogne in French), France's second-most-famous wine region after Bordeaux. Unsurprisingly, it makes a fantastic place to try and buy wine. The region's elegant capital, Dijon, is also well worth a detour for its historic art and architecture.

Further west, across the mountains of the Massif Central, lies the Dordogne (known to the French as Périgord), known for its rich cuisine and idyllic countryside. It was once home to France's most-ancient settlers, who left behind many stunning prehistoric artworks in the murky caves of the Vézère Valley.

St-Cirq Lapopie (p217) above the River Lot

Loire Valley & Central France

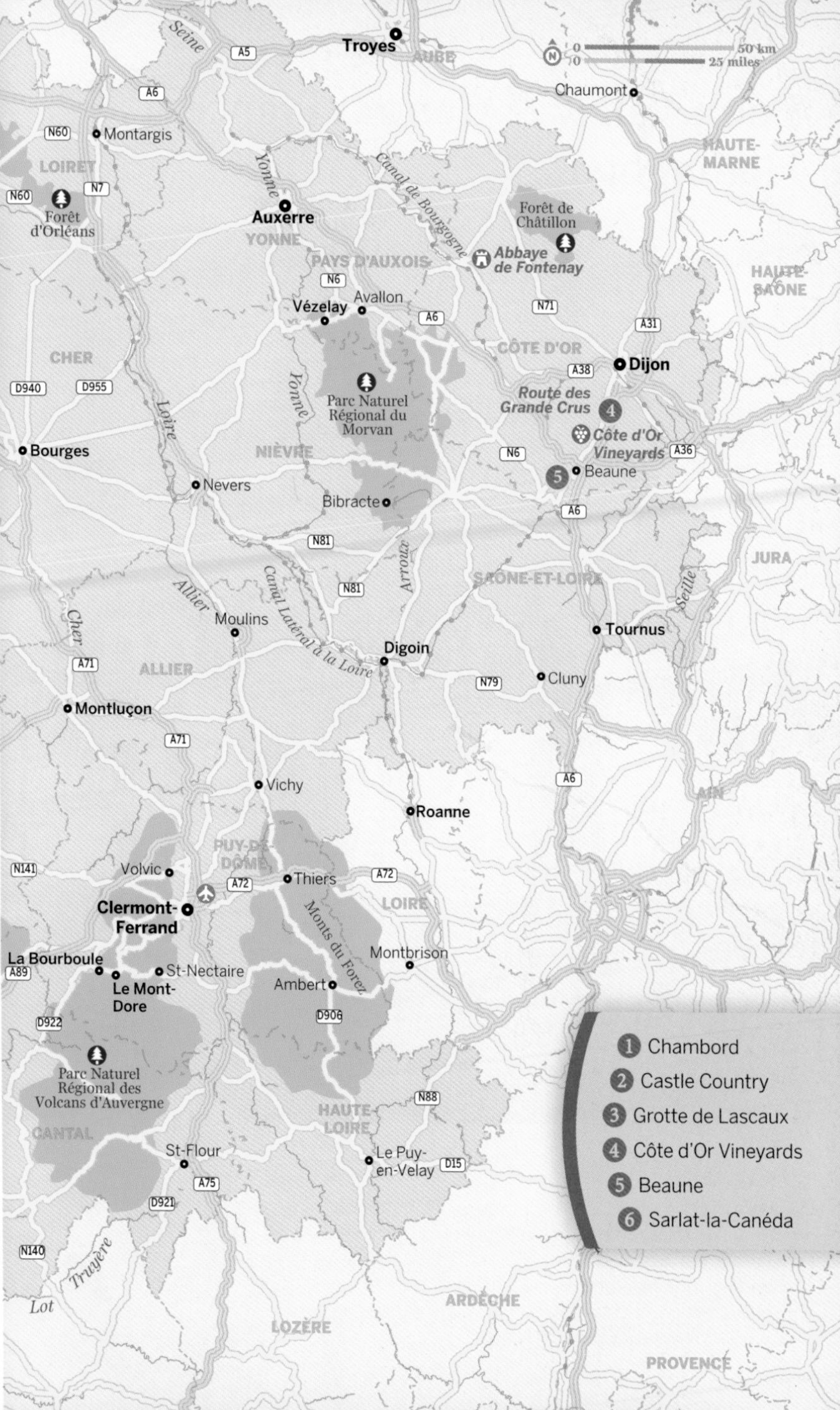

Troyes
Auxerre
Chaumont
Montargis
Forêt d'Orléans
Forêt de Châtillon
Abbaye de Fontenay
Vézelay
Avallon
Dijon
Parc Naturel Régional du Morvan
Route des Grande Crus
Côte d'Or Vineyards
Bourges
Nevers
Bibracte
Beaune
Moulins
Digoin
Tournus
Cluny
Montluçon
Vichy
Roanne
Volvic
Thiers
Clermont-Ferrand
La Bourboule
Le Mont-Dore
St-Nectaire
Montbrison
Ambert
Parc Naturel Régional des Volcans d'Auvergne
St-Flour
Le Puy-en-Velay
1 Chambord
2 Castle Country
3 Grotte de Lascaux
4 Côte d'Or Vineyards
5 Beaune
6 Sarlat-la-Canéda

Loire Valley & Central France Highlights

1

Chambord

Chambord is a vast château of complete disproportion that appears unexpectedly in the middle of a forest. An emblem of Renaissance architecture in France, it was built purely for King François I's hunting pleasure at the height of his imperial ambition. Top Right: King Louis XIV's bedroom; Bottom Right: Chambord Skylight

Need to Know

VISIT May–early July and end August–September: weather is warm and crowds smaller **BEST HOUR** 9am: the light is often magical **AUDIOGUIDE** adult/child €5/2.50 **For more, see p203**

Local Knowledge

Chambord Don't Miss List

BY ELSA BARBOU, CHÂTEAU DE CHAMBORD

1 DOUBLE-HELIX STAIRCASE & ROOFTOP

The double-helix staircase that whisks visitors from the ground floor to the rooftop keep is *the* highlight. This theatrical and majestic staircase is composed of two open parallel flights wrapped around a hollow core, the magic being that two people can see each other go up and down it without their paths ever crossing. A magnificent view of the estate unfolds from the rooftop terrace, an unforgettable place with its sculpted chimney and turrets, really a place of contemplation and daydream.

2 THE 1ST FLOOR

Take time to explore the *premier étage* (1st floor), a historical panorama of the inhabitants of Chambord from François I to Louis XIV and beyond into the 19th century. In the apartments you can really see how château lifestyle evolved over the centuries: all the furniture from François I's era was made to be dismantled and transported with him from château to château.

3 CLASSICAL MUSIC FESTIVAL

The castle hosts two weeks of classical music concerts by great artists in July: the public can attend concerts in the courtyard after the château's closed or in the closed part of the forest. You can buy a ticket on the spot – and it provides free access to the monument! Art exhibitions, included in the entrance fee, are also worth looking out for in high season.

4 THE RUTTING SEASON

Chambord is unique in that it is a monument in the middle of a vast forested park. This gives Chambord an additional magic, a place to discover the natural environment as well as culture and history. The park is a wildlife reserve with stags and wild boars. Observatories allow visitors to observe the animals during *le brame,* the rutting or mating season that falls from mid-September to mid-October. The best time to see the animals in action is at sunrise or sunset – bring binoculars.

Castle Country

For sheer architectural splendour Chambord is tough to beat, but it's certainly not the only château worthy of your time in the Loire Valley. From sturdy medieval fortresses to grand Renaissance showpieces, the Loire has enough castles to fill a lifetime of visits. Top honours go to elegant, Renaissance, river-spanning Chenonceau (p198); the supremely graceful Cheverny (p194); and history-packed, regal Blois (p195), but there are many more to discover.

Château de Chenonceau (p198)

Grotte de Lascaux

In 1940 four teenage boys out searching for their lost dog discovered the Grotte de Lascaux (p216), a vast network of subterranean chambers adorned with the most extraordinary prehistoric paintings ever found. Though the original cave is now off-limits to avoid damaging these priceless ancient artworks, they have been meticulously recreated in another cave nearby. If you're going to visit only one cave in the prehistoric-precious Vézère Valley, make sure it's this one.

ANDREW BAIN/GETTY IMAGES ©

Côte d'Or Vineyards

4

Cruising along peaceful country lanes laced with the vine-carpeted slopes of one of France's most prestigious wine-producing regions: this is reason enough to visit Burgundy's Côte d'Or (p207). Scenic motoring along the Route des Grands Crus, intimate cellar visits with local vignerons (winemakers), tasting, drinking and buying are all part and parcel of exploring this world-class 'Golden Hillside' wine region.

CHAD EHLERS/GETTY IMAGES ©

5

Beaune

Burgundy is not only about fine wine. The region is heir to a glorious architectural heritage, and there is no better place to marvel at the glories of the late Middle Ages than in elegant Côte d'Or capital, Beaune. Jewel of the crown is Hôtel-Dieu (p208), France's splendid medieval charity hospital in the heart of Beaune's picture-perfect old town. Hôtel-Dieu des Hospices de Beaune

6

Sarlat-la-Canéda

Few places in France feel as convincingly medieval as quaint Sarlat (p211). With its jumble of alleyways, culs-de-sac and honey-coloured stone houses, it makes a sublime base for exploring the caves of the Vézère Valley. Don't miss the wonderful Saturday food market (p213), where local producers from all over the Dordogne set up shop on the cobbles of the main square.

Loire Valley & Central France's Best...

Historic Architecture

- **Château Royal de Blois** (p195) A whistle-stop tour through French architecture.
- **Abbaye de Fontenay** (p213) Inner peace in a Cistercian abbey.
- **Palais des Ducs et des États de Bourgogne** (p202) Dijon's ducal palace is now a superb arts museum.
- **Château Royal d'Amboise** (p199) Climb this regal château's spiralling towers.
- **Hôtel-Dieu des Hospices de Beaune** (p208) Marvel at this medieval hospital.

Gardens

- **Château de Chaumont-sur-Loire** (p194) English-style park and host to an international garden fest.
- **Château de Chenonceau** (p198) Exquisite formal gardens with a yew-tree labyrinth.
- **Le Clos Lucé** (p199) Amboise gardens dotted with Leonardo da Vinci miniatures.
- **Château de Villandry** (p210) Water gardens, maze, green love and the poshest veg patch ever.

Photo Opps

- **Chambord's rooftop** (p203) Get a bird's-eye perspective of the Loire's grandest château.
- **St-Cirq-Lapopie** (p217) Unparalleled Lot Valley panorama atop this tiny clifftop village.
- **Sarlat-la-Canéda** (p211) Ride a panoramic lift inside Église Ste-Marie for a 360-degree view.
- **Brantôme** (p214) Scale an 11th-century belltower to peep down on Brantôme's waterways.
- **La Roque Gageac** (p214) Snap away afloat a *gabarre* (barge).

Curiosities

- **Chantier Médiéval de Guédelon** (p211) See a 13th-century château being built.
- **Gouffre de Padirac** (p212) Sail a subterranean river through a breathtaking cave.
- **Maison de la Magie** (p193) Be befuddled by optical illusions and magic tricks in Blois.
- **Soupe des Chiens** (p194) Join the dogs' dinner at Cheverny.
- **École Nationale d'Équitation** (p201) Watch the amazing dressage displays of the Cadre Noir.

Left: Château de Chambord (p203); **Above:** Garden at Château de Villandry (p210)

Need to Know

ADVANCE PLANNING

- **As early as possible** Book accommodation, particularly in hot spots such as Amboise, Dijon and Sarlat-la-Canéda.
- **Two weeks before** Book tours for Saumur's École Nationale d'Équitation (p201), Grotte de Lascaux (p216) and Grotte de Font de Gaume (p215).
- **One week before** Choose your châteaux, research ticket combinations (p192) and try to buy online.

RESOURCES

- **Châteaux Tourisme** (www.chateauxtourisme.com) Info on the Loire Valley.
- **Val de Loire** (www.valdeloire.org) Heritage site.
- **Randonnée en Val de Loire** (www.randonnee-en-val-de-loire.com) Loire Valley walks and cycling routes.
- **Burgundy Tourism** s(www.burgundy-tourism.com) Burgundy tourist board.
- **Wines of Burgundy** (www.bourgogne-wines.com) Burgundy wine.
- **Route des Grands Crus** (www.road-of-the-fine-burgundy-wines.com) Burgundy wine route.

GETTING AROUND

- **Trains** Regular trains travel from Paris to major cities; for regional route planners see www.mobigo-bourgogne.com and www.destineo.fr.
- **Car** Having a car means more flexibility and freedom – essential for the Vézère Valley.
- **Organised bus tours** An excellent way of exploring Loire châteaux (p193) and Burgundy vineyards (p202).
- **Bicycle** See **Les Châteaux à Vélo** (www.chateauxavelo.com) and **Loire à Vélo** (www.loireavelo.fr) for routes, maps and MP3 guides. For bike rental see **Détours de Loire** (www.locationdevelos.com) or contact local tourist offices. To bike Burgundy see www.burgundy-by-bike.com.

BE FOREWARNED

- **Vézère Valley** Most caves are closed in winter; visitor numbers are limited in summer. Book ahead.
- **Grotte de Lascaux** From April to October, tickets can *only* be bought next to the tourist office in Montignac.
- **Crowds** Can be a problem, especially in the Loire and the Dordogne and in July and August.

Loire Valley & Central France Itineraries

What a variety of experiences this part of France has to offer: with its Renaissance châteaux, tranquil rivers and renowned cave paintings, there's so much to see that you might well find it takes up your entire trip.

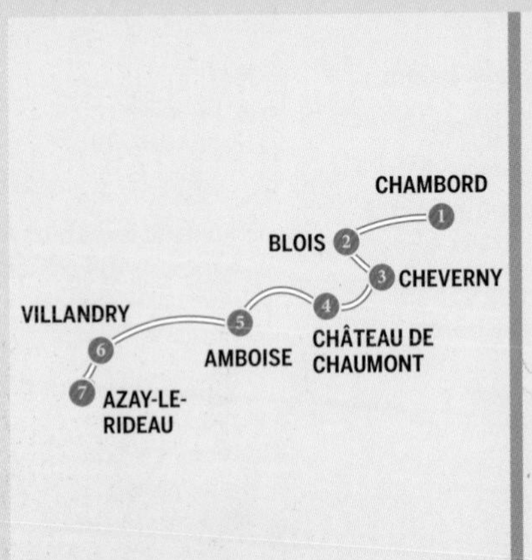

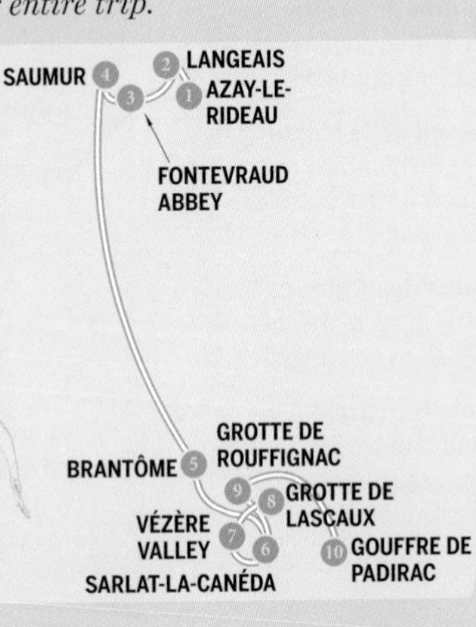

CHAMBORD TO AZAY-LE-RIDEAU
Château Classics

3 DAYS

For maximum freedom you'll want your own car in the Loire, although organised minibus trips can be good if time is short. This tour of the Loire's top châteaux begins with the biggest, boldest and best, **(1) Château de Chambord**. Tour the interior with an audioguide before scaling the double-helix staircase to the rooftop for sweeping views of the grounds, surrounded by a Tolkien-esque jumble of cupolas, domes, chimneys and lightning rods. Overnight in **(2) Blois**.

You should have time to squeeze in at least two châteaux on day two, starting with classical elegance at **(3) Château de Cheverny**, followed by medieval heritage at **(4) Château de Chaumont**. An ideal place to end the day, **(5) Amboise** has lots of luxurious sleeps to choose from: one of our favourites is Le Clos d'Amboise.

On day three, visit Château Royal d'Amboise and get to know original Renaissance man Leonardo da Vinci at Le Clos Lucé. In the afternoon, head west to see the remarkable ornamental gardens of **(6) Château de Villandry**. Wrap up with a night-time viewing of the Loire's oldest and best *son-et-lumière* (sound-and-light show), projected directly onto the walls of moat-encircled **(7) Château d'Azay-le-Rideau**.

AZAY-LE-RIDEAU TO SARLAT-LA-CANÉDA

Castles to Cave Art

Head west from **(1) Azay-le-Rideau** along the Loire. You'll find a quintessential medieval castle at **(2) Langeais**, ramparts, drawbridge and all. Spend the afternoon at **(3) Fontevraud Abbey** and overnight in **(4) Saumur**.

On day two, head south towards the Dordogne. You'll reach the riverside village of **(5) Brantôme** by afternoon, where you could stop for a late lunch or a canal cruise before heading on to **(6) Sarlat-la-Canéda**. Sarlat makes an ideal base for exploring the Dordogne region, but it deserves a day in its own right – don't miss its buzzy morning market and medieval architecture.

On day four, head off to view the amazing Stone Age art in the **(7) Vézère Valley**. Book guided visits to the Grotte de Font de Gaume and the Grotte des Combarelles before heading over to the famous **(8) Grotte de Lascaux** in the afternoon.

On the last day, you should be able to fit in two unforgettable underground adventures: a trip aboard the rattling train deep into the **(9) Grotte de Rouffignac** and a punt along the spooky subterranean river at the **(10) Gouffre de Padirac**.

Place de la Liberté, Sarlat-la-Canéda (p211)

Discover the Loire Valley & Central France

At a Glance

- **Loire Valley** (p190) A fairy-tale mirage of châteaux, all shapes, sizes and historical designs, lace the banks of France's most regal river.
- **Burgundy** (p202) Vineyards here produce France's finest wine.
- **The Dordogne** (p211) Medieval villages, clifftop castles and prehistoric works of art enhance this rural region in the pretty heart of France.
- **The Lot** (p217) Picturesque limestone cliffs, hilltop towns and canyons.

Joan of Arc statue, Orléans

THE LOIRE VALLEY

In centuries past, the River Loire was a key strategic area, one step removed from the French capital and poised on the crucial frontier between northern and southern France. Kings, queens, dukes and nobles established their feudal strongholds and country seats along the Loire, and the valley is sprinkled with many of the most extravagant castles and fortresses in France. The hundreds of châteaux dotted around the Loire Valley – now a Unesco World Heritage Site – comprise 1000 years of astonishingly rich architectural and artistic treasures.

Orléans

POP 116,830

There's a big-city buzz around the boulevards, flashy boutiques and elegant buildings of Orléans, 100km south of Paris. It's a city with enduring heritage: already an important settlement by the time of the Romans' arrival, Orléans sealed its place in history in 1429 when a young peasant girl by the name of Jeanne d'Arc (Joan of Arc) rallied the armies of Charles VII and staged a spectacular rout against the besieging English forces, a key turning point in the Hundred Years' War.

Sights

CATHÉDRALE STE-CROIX Cathedral

(place Ste-Croix; 9.15am-noon & 2.15-5.45pm)
In a country of jaw-dropping churches, the Cathédrale Ste-Croix still raises a gasp. Towering above place Ste-Croix, Orléans' Flamboyant Gothic cathedral was originally

built in the 13th century and then underwent collective tinkering by successive monarchs, including Henri IV, who started reconstruction in 1601.

MUSÉE DES BEAUX-ARTS Art Museum
(**☎02 38 79 21 55; 1 rue Fernand Rabier; adult/child incl audioguide €4/free; ⏰10am-6pm Tue-Sun)** Orléans' five-storeyed fine-arts museum is a treat, with an excellent selection of Italian, Flemish and Dutch paintings (including works by Correggio, Velázquez and Bruegel), as well as a huge collection by French artists such as Léon Cogniet (1794–1880) and Orléans-born Alexandre Antigna (1817–78).

MAISON DE JEANNE D'ARC History Museum
(**☎02 38 68 32 63; www.jeannedarc.com.fr; 3 place du Général de Gaulle; adult/child €4/free; ⏰10am-6pm Tue-Sun Apr-Sep, 2-6pm Tue-Sun Oct-Mar)** The best place to get an overview of Joan of Arc's life story is this reconstruction of the 15th-century house that hosted her between April and May 1429 (the original was destroyed by British bombing in 1940).

Sleeping

HÔTEL DE L'ABEILLE Historic Hotel €€
(**☎02 38 53 54 87; www.hoteldelabeille.com; 64 rue Alsace-Lorraine; s €52, d €69-130, ste €135-180;** ) Vintage posters adorn the walls at this turn-of-the-century house, run by the same family for four generations. It's deliciously old-fashioned, from the scuffed pine floors and wildly floral wallpapers to the hefty dressers and bee-print curtains. For breakfast (€11) there's a choice of coffees, teas, juices and exotic jams.

HÔTEL D'ARC Hotel €€
(**☎02 38 53 10 94; www.hoteldarc.fr; 37ter rue de la République; s €103-141, d €117-181;** ) Ride the vintage-style lift to swank guestrooms at this Best Western–affiliated hotel, conveniently placed between the train station and the pedestrianised centre. Rooms vary in size and the Prestige and Deluxe come with plush robes, but all are done up comfortably. Double-glazed windows help with daytime tram noise.

Eating

LA PARENTHÈSE Modern French €€
(**☎02 38 62 07 50; www.restaurant-la-parenthese.com; 26 place du Châtelet; lunch menus €13.50-16.50, dinner menus €24-28; ⏰lunch & dinner Tue-Sat)** Book ahead for this very popular restaurant, a labour of love for youthful local chef David Sterne. Produce from the Halles marketplace across the street forms the basis for ever-changing, bargain-priced *plats du jour* (dishes of the day; €9.50), plus creative lunch and dinner *menus*. Choose from relaxed sidewalk seating or two more-refined indoor dining rooms.

LES FAGOTS Traditional French €
(**☎02 38 62 22 79; 32 rue du Poirier; menus €12.50-15.60)** Delightful smoky smells lure you in from rue du Poirier at this unpretentious eatery whose menu revolves around roasted meat. The Auvergnat owner cooks everything over an open fire.

Information

Tourist office (**☎02 38 24 05 05; www.tourisme-orleans.com; 2 place de l'Étape; ⏰9.30am-1pm & 2-6pm Mon-Sat)**

Getting There & Away

The city's two stations, Gare d'Orléans and Gare des Aubrais-Orléans (the latter is 2km to the north), are linked by tram and frequent shuttle trains. Trains usually stop at both stations from the following destinations:

Blois €10.50, 35 minutes, hourly.

Paris Gare d'Austerlitz €19.40, 65 minutes, hourly.

Tours €18.80, 1¼ hours, hourly.

Blois

POP 48,110

Looming on a rocky escarpment on the northern bank of the Loire, Blois' historic château (formerly the feudal seat of the powerful counts of Blois) provides a

Orléans

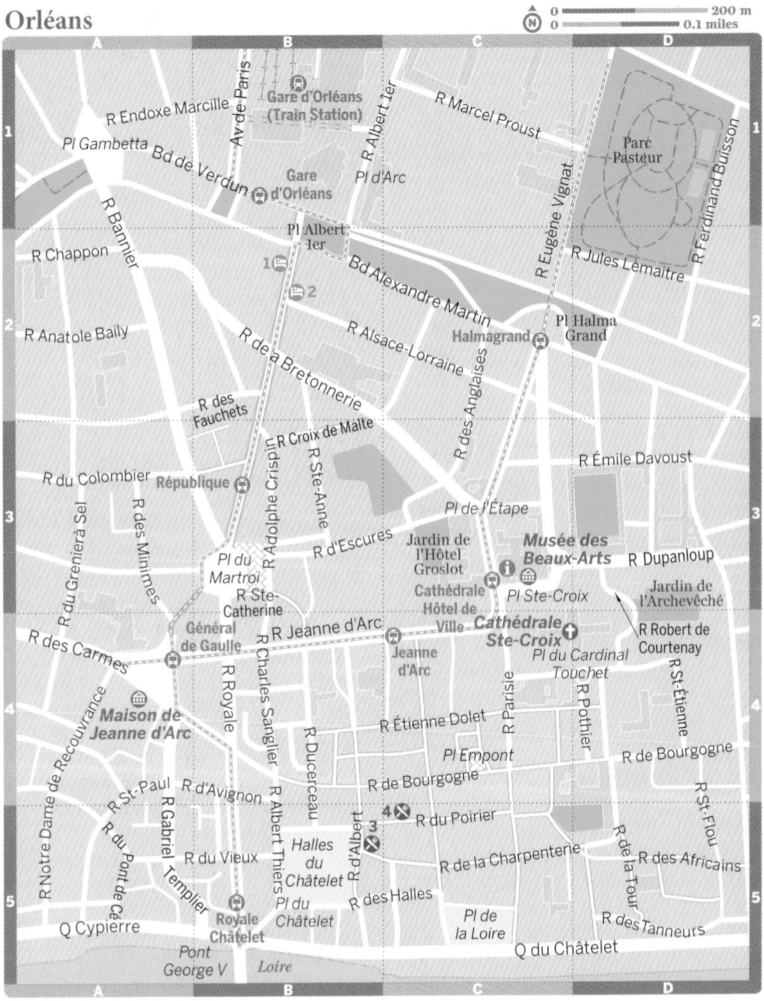

Orléans

Top Sights

- Cathédrale Ste-Croix C4
- Maison de Jeanne d'Arc A4
- Musée des Beaux-Arts C3

Sleeping

1. Hôtel d'Arc B2
2. Hôtel de l'Abeille B2

Eating

3. La Parenthèse B5
4. Les Fagots C5

whistle-stop tour through the key periods of French history and architecture.

Sights

If you're visiting Blois' château, want to experience the *son-et-lumière* show and/) or the Maison de la Magie, combination tickets (two attractions adult/child €14.50/6.50, three attractions adult/child €19/10) save a bit of cash. Kids under six are free.

OLD CITY Historic Quarter

Despite serious damage by German attacks in 1940, Blois' old city is worth exploring, especially around the 17th-century **Cathédrale St-Louis** (place St-Louis; ⌚9am-6pm), with its lovely multistoried bell tower, dramatically floodlit after dark. Most of the stained glass inside was installed by Dutch artist Jan Dibberts in 2000.

Across the square, the facade of **Maison des Acrobates** (3bis place St-Louis) – one of the few 15th-century houses to survive – is decorated with wooden sculptures taken from medieval farces.

MAISON DE LA MAGIE Museum

(www.maisondelamagie.fr; 1 place du Château; adult/child €8/5; ⌚10am-12.30pm & 2-6.30pm Apr-Aug, 2-6.30pm Sep) Opposite the château you can't miss the former home of watchmaker, inventor and conjurer Jean Eugène Robert-Houdin (1805–71), whose name was later adopted by American magician Harry Houdini. Dragons emerge roaring from the windows on the hour, while the museum inside hosts daily magic shows, exhibits on the history of magic, displays of optical trickery and a short historical film about Houdini.

Sleeping

LA MAISON DE THOMAS B&B €€

(☎02 54 46 12 10; www.lamaisondethomas.fr; 12 rue Beauvoir; s/d €75/85) Four spacious rooms and a friendly welcome await travellers at this homey bed and breakfast on a pedestrianised street halfway between the château and the cathedral. There's safe bike storage in the interior courtyard and a wine cellar where you can sample local vintages.

CÔTÉ LOIRE Hotel €

(☎02 54 78 07 86; www.coteloire.com; 2 place de la Grève; d €57-89; 📶) If it's charm and colours you want, head for the Loire Coast. Its rooms come in cheery checks, bright pastels and the odd bit of exposed brick; breakfast is served on a wooden deck.

Châteaux Tours

Indie travellers might balk at the idea of a minibus tour of the châteaux, but don't dismiss it out of hand, especially if you don't have your own transport.

From April through August, the Blois tourist office and **TLC** (☎02 54 58 55 44; www.tlcinfo.net) offer a twice-daily shuttle (€6) from Blois to the châteaux at Chambord, Cheverny and Beauregard.

Many private companies offer a choice of well-organised itineraries, taking in various combinations of Azay-le-Rideau, Villandry, Cheverny, Chambord and Chenonceau (plus wine-tasting tours). Half-day trips cost between €20 and €35; full-day trips range from €45 to €52. Entry to the châteaux isn't included, although you'll likely get a discount on tickets. Reserve via the tourist offices in Tours or Amboise, from where most tours depart.

Prefer to soar over châteaux rooftops in a balloon? Contact **Art Montgolfières** (☎02 54 32 08 11; www.art-montgolfieres.fr; solo/duo €205/390).

Eating

L'ORANGERIE Gastronomic €€€

(☎02 54 78 05 36; www.orangerie-du-chateau.fr; 1 av du Dr Jean Laigret; menus €35-80; ⌚lunch & dinner Tue-Sat) This acclaimed eatery is cloud nine for connoisseurs of *haute cuisine*. Plates are artfully stacked (duck liver, langoustine, foie gras) and the sparkling *salon* would make Louis XIV envious. On summer nights, dine in the courtyard.

LES BANQUETTES ROUGES Traditional French €€

(☎02 54 78 74 92; www.lesbanquettesrouges.com; 16 rue des Trois Marchands; menus €17-32; ⌚lunch & dinner Tue-Sat) Handwritten slate menus and wholesome food distinguish the Red Benches: rabbit with marmalade, duck with lentils, and salmon with apple vinaigrette, all done with a spicy twist.

Information

Tourist office (☎ **02 54 90 41 41; www.bloischambord.com; 23 place du Château; ⏰9am-7pm)**

Getting There & Away

BUS From April through August, **TLC** (☎ **02 54 58 55 44; www.tlcinfo.net)** runs a château shuttle (line 18), charging a flat fare of €6 for as many stops as you like on the Blois–Chambord–Bracieux–Cheverny–Beauregard–Blois circuit.

TLC also operates regular buses to and from Blois' train station (tickets €2 on board), Chambord (line 3; 25 to 40 minutes, two Monday to Saturday) and Cheverny (line 4; 45 minutes, six to eight Monday to Friday, two Saturday, one Sunday).

TRAIN The train station is 600m uphill from the château, on av Jean Laigret and services the following destinations:

Amboise €6.60, 20 minutes, 10 daily.

Orléans €10.50, 45 minutes, hourly.

Paris Gares d'Austerlitz and Montparnasse from €26.70, 1½ to two hours, 26 daily.

Tours €10.20, 40 minutes, 13 daily.

Château de Cheverny

Thought by many to be the most perfectly proportioned château of all, **Cheverny** (☎ **02 54 79 96 29; www.chateau-cheverny.fr; adult/child €8.70/5.70; ⏰9.15am-6.45pm Jul & Aug, 9.15am-6.15pm Apr-Jun & Sep, 9.45am-5.30pm Oct, 9.45am-5pm Nov-Mar)** represents the zenith of French classical architecture, the perfect blend of symmetry, geometry and aesthetic order.

Built from gleaming stone from the nearby Bourré quarries and surrounded by lush parkland, Cheverny is one of the few châteaux whose original architectural vision has survived the centuries practically unscathed. Since its construction between 1625 and 1634 by Jacques Hurault, an intendant to Louis XII, the castle has hardly been altered, and its interior decoration includes some of the most sumptuous furnishings, tapestries and *objets d'art* anywhere in the Loire Valley. The Hurault family has owned (and inhabited) the castle for the last six centuries and its fabulous **art collection** includes a portrait of Jeanne of Aragon by Raphael's studio, an 18th-century De la Tour pastel, and a who's who of court painters.

Behind the main château, the 18th-century **Orangerie**, where many priceless artworks, including the *Mona Lisa*, were stashed during WWII, is now a tea room.

Near the château's gateway, the **kennels** house pedigreed French pointer/English foxhound hunting dogs still used by the owners of Cheverny: feeding time, known as the **Soupe des Chiens**, takes place daily at 5pm April to September and 3pm October to March.

Getting There & Away

Cheverny is on the D102, 16km southeast of Blois and 17km southwest of Chambord.

Château de Chaumont

Set on a defensible bluff behind the Loire, **Chaumont-sur-Loire (www.domaine-chaumont.fr; adult/child €10/6, with gardens €15.50/11; ⏰10am-6.30pm Apr-Sep, to 5pm or 6pm Oct-Mar)** presents a resolutely medieval face, with its cylindrical corner turrets and sturdy drawbridge, but the interior mostly dates from the 19th century.

At least two earlier fortresses occupied the site (whose name derives from Chauve Mont, 'Bald Hill'), but the main phase of construction for the present château began sometime around 1465 under Pierre d'Amboise. Originally a strictly defensive fortress, the castle became a short-lived residence for Catherine de Médicis following the death of Henry II in 1560, and later passed into the hands of Diane de Poitiers (Henry II's mistress), who was forced to swap the altogether grander surroundings of Chenonceau for Chaumont by the ruthless Catherine.

The château was thoroughly renovated by Princess de Broglie, heiress to the Say sugar fortune, who bought it in 1875

ANDREA MAGUGLIANI/ALAMY ©

Don't Miss Château Royal de Blois

Intended more as an architectural showpiece than a military stronghold, Blois' Royal Château bears the creative mark of several successive French kings. It makes an excellent introduction to the châteaux of the Loire Valley, with elements of Gothic (13th century), Flamboyant Gothic (1498–1503), early Renaissance (1515–24) and classical (1630s) architecture in its four grand wings.

The most famous feature of the Renaissance wing, the royal apartments of François I and Queen Claude, is the loggia staircase, decorated with salamanders and curly 'F's (heraldic symbols of François I). Highlights include the bedchamber in which Catherine de Médicis (Henri II's machiavellian wife) died in 1589. According to Alexandre Dumas, the queen stashed her poisons in secret cupboards behind the elaborately panelled walls of the studiolo, one of the few rooms in the castle with its original decor.

The 2nd-floor king's apartments were the setting for one of the bloodiest episodes in the château's history: in 1588 Henri III had his arch-rival, Duke Henri I de Guise, murdered by royal bodyguards (the king hid behind a tapestry). He had the Duke's brother, the Cardinal de Guise, killed the next day. Henri III was himself murdered just eight months later by a vengeful monk. Period paintings chronicle the gruesome events.

In spring and summer, don't miss the nightly **son et lumière**, which brings the château's history and architecture to life with dramatic lighting and narration.

NEED TO KNOW

Château Royal de Blois (www.chateaudeblois.fr; place du Château; adult/child €9.50/4; 9am-6.30pm Apr-Sep, reduced hours rest of year); **Son et lumière** (sound & light show; 02 54 55 26 31; adult/child €7.50/4; 10pm Apr, May & Sep, 10.30pm Jun-Aug)

(and knocked down one entire wing to provide a better view of the river). The most impressive room is the **Council Chamber**, with its original maiolica-tiled floor, plundered from a palace in Palermo, but the château's finest architecture is arguably reserved for the **Écuries** (stables), built in 1877 to house the Broglies' horses in truly sumptuous style (the thoroughbreds all had their own personal padded stalls). A collection of vintage carriages is now displayed inside.

Chaumont's English-style gardens can be visited independently or together with the château. They're at their finest during the annual **Festival International des Jardins** (International Garden Festival; adult/child €11/7.50; 9.30am-sunset late Apr–mid-Oct).

Getting There & Away

Chaumont-sur-Loire is 17km southwest of Blois. Onzain, a 2.5km walk from Chaumont across the Loire, has trains to Blois (€3.40, 10 minutes, 13 daily) and Tours (€8, 30 minutes, 10 daily).

Tours

POP 138,590

Bustling Tours has a life of its own despite being one of the hubs of castle country. It's a smart, vivacious kind of place, filled with wide 18th-century boulevards, parks and imposing public buildings, as well as a busy university of some 25,000 students.

Sights

MUSÉE DES BEAUX-ARTS Art Museum
(18 place François Sicard; adult/child €4/2; 9am-12.45pm & 2-6pm Wed-Mon) Arranged around the courtyard of the archbishop's gorgeous palace, this wheelchair-accessible fine-arts museum flaunts grand rooms with works spanning several centuries, including paintings by Delacroix, Degas and Monet, as well as a rare Rembrandt miniature and a Rubens *Madonna and Child*. The stately 1804 Lebanese cedar in the courtyard measures a whopping 7.5m around the base.

Left: Château de Chaumont (p194); **Below:** Dining Room, Château de Cheverny (p194)
(LEFT) HANS GEORG EIBEN/GETTY IMAGES ©; (BELOW) DEA/G.DAGLI ORTI /GETTY IMAGES ©

CATHÉDRALE ST-GATIEN Cathedral
(place de la Cathédrale; 9am-7pm) With its twin towers, flying buttresses, stained glass and gargoyles, this cathedral is a show-stopper. The interior dates from the 13th to 16th centuries, and the domed tops of the two 70m-high towers are Renaissance. On the north side is the **Cloître de la Psallette (adult/child €3/free; 9.30am-12.30pm & 2-6pm Mon-Sat, 2-6pm Sun, closed Mon & Tue Oct-Mar)**, built from 1442 to 1524.

Eating

CAP SUD Bistro **€€**
(02 47 05 24 81; capsudrestaurant.fr; 88 rue Colbert; lunch menus €15.50-19, dinner menus €24-36; lunch & dinner Tue-Sat) The hot red interior combines nicely with genial service and refined culinary creations made from the freshest ingredients. Expect stylishly presented dishes such as warm St-Maure cheese with a pistachio-herb crumble and baby vegetables, or mullet fillet with sweet peppers, squid risotto and a ginger-tomato emulsion. Reserve in advance.

L'ATELIER GOURMAND Bistro **€€**
(02 47 38 59 87; www.lateliergourmand.fr; 37 rue Étienne Marcel; lunch/dinner menus €12/23; lunch Tue-Fri, dinner Mon-Sat) Another foodie address, but bring dark glasses: the puce-and-silver colour scheme is straight out of a Brett Easton Ellis novel. Everything's delivered with a modern spin, and many dishes feature intriguing blends of the sweet and savoury.

Information

Tourist office (02 47 70 37 37; www.tours-tourisme.fr; 78-82 rue Bernard Palissy; 8.30am-7pm Mon-Sat, 10am-12.30pm & 2.30-5pm Sun)

Getting There & Away

BUS The information desk for Touraine Fil Vert (02 47 31 14 00; www.tourainefilvert.com) is at the bus station next to the train station. Destinations in the Indre-et-Loire département include Amboise (40 minutes, 10 daily Monday to Saturday) and Chenonceau (1¼ hours, one daily), both served by line C.

TRAIN Tours is the Loire Valley's main rail hub. Trains from Tours Centre station go to the following destinations:

Amboise €5, 20 minutes, 13 daily.

Blois €10, 40 minutes, 13 daily.

Chenonceaux €6.50, 25 minutes, eight daily.

Orléans €19, 1¼ hours, hourly.

Paris Gare d'Austerlitz €33, two to 2¾ hours, five daily (slow trains).

Paris Gare Montparnasse €44 to €82, 1¼ hours, eight daily (high-speed TGVs).

Saumur €11, 45 minutes, hourly.

TGV trains from St-Pierre-des-Corps (Tours' TGV station, 4km east and linked to Tours by frequent shuttle trains) regularly serve Bordeaux (€50, 2¾ hours) and Paris Gare Montparnasse (€44 to €59, one hour).

Château de Chenonceau

Spanning the languid Cher River via a series of supremely graceful arches, the castle of **Chenonceau** (02 47 23 90 07; www.chenonceau.com; adult/child €11/8.50, with audioguide €15/12; 9am-7pm Apr-Sep, reduced hours rest of year) is one of the most elegant and unusual in the Loire Valley.

This architectural fantasy land is largely the work of several remarkable women (hence its alternative name, Le Château des Dames: 'Ladies' Château'). The initial phase of construction started in 1515 for Thomas Bohier, a court minister of King Charles VIII, although much of the work and design was actually overseen by his wife, Katherine Briçonnet. The château's distinctive arches and one of the formal gardens were added by Diane de Poitiers, mistress of King Henri II. Following Henri's death, Diane was forced to exchange Chenonceau for the rather less grand château of Chaumont by the king's scheming widow, Catherine de Médicis, who completed the construction and added the huge yew-tree **labyrinth** and the western rose garden. Louise of

Gallerie, Château de Chenonceau

Lorraine's most interesting contribution was her **mourning room**, on the top floor, all in black, to which she retreated when her husband, Henri III, was assassinated.

The château's interior is crammed with wonderful furniture and tapestries, several stunning original tiled floors and a fabulous **art collection** including works by Tintoretto, Correggio, Rubens, Murillo, Van Dyck and Ribera.

The *pièce de résistance* is the 60m-long window-lined **Grande Gallerie** spanning the Cher, scene of many a wild party hosted by Catherine de Médicis or Madame Dupin. During WWII the Cher also marked the boundary between free and occupied France; local legend has it that the Grande Gallerie was used as the escape route for many refugees fleeing the Nazi occupation.

Skip the drab wax museum (€2) and instead visit the **gardens**: it seems as if there's one of every kind of garden imaginable (maze, English, vegetable, playground, flower...). In July and August the illuminated château and grounds are open for the **Promenade Nocturne** (adult/child €5/free).

Getting There & Away

The château is 34km east of Tours, 10km southeast of Amboise and 40km southwest of Blois. From Chenonceaux, the town just outside the château grounds (spelled with an 'x', unlike the château!), seven daily trains run to Tours (€6.50, 25 minutes). Touraine Fil Vert's bus line C (€1.80) also runs once daily from Chenonceaux to Amboise (25 minutes). **Croisières Fluivales La Bélandre** (02 47 23 98 64; www.labelandre.com; adult/child €8.50/5.50; Apr-Oct) offers 50-minute boat trips along the Cher River in summer, passing directly beneath the château's arches.

Amboise

POP 12,860

The childhood home of Charles VIII and the final resting place of the great Leonardo da Vinci, elegant Amboise is pleasantly perched on the southern bank of the Loire and overlooked by its fortified 15th-century château. With some seriously posh hotels and a wonderful weekend market, Amboise has become a very popular base for exploring nearby châteaux, and coach tours arrive en masse to visit da Vinci's Clos Lucé.

Sights

LE CLOS LUCÉ Historic Manor
(www.vinci-closluce.com; 2 rue du Clos Lucé; adult/child €13.50/8.50; 9am-7pm Feb-Oct, 10am-6pm Nov-Jan;) Leonardo da Vinci took up residence at this grand manor house in 1516 on the invitation of François I, who was greatly enamoured of the Italian Renaissance. Already 64 by the time he arrived, da Vinci spent his time sketching, tinkering and dreaming up new contraptions, scale models of which are now abundantly displayed throughout the home and its expansive gardens. Visitors can see the rooms where da Vinci worked and the bedroom where he drew his last breath on 2 May 1519.

CHÂTEAU ROYAL D'AMBOISE Castle
(www.chateau-amboise.com; place Michel Debré; adult/child €10.20/7, with audioguide €14.20/10; 9am-6pm Apr-Oct, earlier closing Nov-Mar) Sprawling across a rocky escarpment above town, this easily defendable castle presented a formidable prospect to would-be attackers – but saw little military action. It was more often used as a weekend getaway from the official royal seat at nearby Blois. Charles VIII (r 1483–98), born and bred here, was responsible for the château's Italianate remodelling in 1492. Today, just a few of the original 15th- and 16th-century structures survive, notably the **Flamboyant Gothic wing** and **Chapelle St-Hubert**, believed to be the final resting place of da Vinci.

Sleeping

LE CLOS D'AMBOISE Historic Hotel €€
(02 47 30 10 20; www.leclosamboise.com; 27 rue Rabelais; r €110-180, ste €210-310;) Backed by a vast grassy lawn,

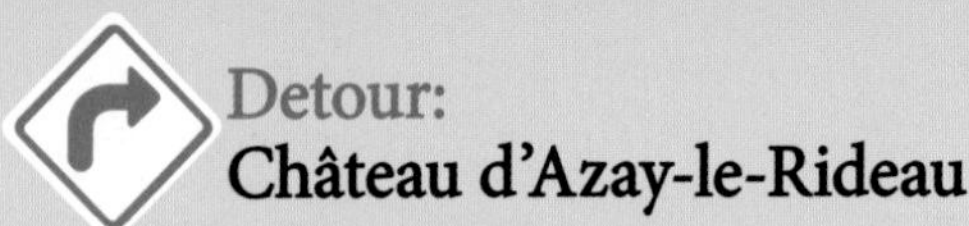

Detour: Château d'Azay-le-Rideau

Romantic, moat-ringed **Azay-le-Rideau** (02 47 45 42 04; azay-le-rideau.monuments-nationaux.fr/en; adult/child €8.50/free; 9.30am-6pm Apr-Jun & Sep, to 7pm Jul & Aug, 10am-5.15pm Oct-Mar) is adorned with slender turrets, geometric windows and decorative stonework, wrapped up within a shady, landscaped park. Built in the 1500s on a natural island in the middle of the River Indre, the château is one of the Loire's loveliest.

Its most famous feature is its open **loggia staircase**, in the Italian style, overlooking the central courtyard and decorated with the salamanders and ermines of François I and Queen Claude. The interior is mostly 19th century, remodelled by the Marquis de Biencourt from the original 16th-century château built by Gilles Berthelot, chief treasurer for François I. In July and August, a **son-et-lumière** (sound-and-light show, adult/teen/child €11/8/3) is projected onto the castle walls nightly. Audioguides (adult/child €4.50/3) are available in five languages, and 45-minute guided tours in French are free.

Château d'Azay-le-Rideau is 26km southwest of Tours. The D84 and D17, on either side of the Indre, are a delight to cycle. Touraine Fil Vert's bus V travels from Tours to Azay-le-Rideau (€1.80, 50 minutes) twice daily June to August. An SNCF bus stops near the château. Azay-le-Rideau's train station is 2.5km west of the château and services run three to eight times daily to Tours (€5.50, 25 to 30 minutes).

complete with 200-year-old trees, a heated pool and private parking for cars and bikes, this posh pad offers a taste of country living in the heart of town. Stylish features abound, from luxurious fabrics to wood-panelling to antique beds; the best rooms have separate sitting areas, original fireplaces and/or big windows overlooking the garden. Common spaces include a sauna, gym and multiple *salons*.

VILLA MARY B&B €€

(02 47 23 03 31; www.villa-mary.fr; 14 rue de la Concorde; d €90-120, apt per week €1180) Sandwiched between the river and the château walls, this spacious 18th-century town house includes four lovingly restored, old-fashioned rooms plus a 200-sq-metre top-floor apartment. The owner, a former economics professor and inveterate world traveller with a passion for history, lives on site. Pricier rooms have direct views of the Loire, while others gaze up at the château.

Eating

AUBERG DE LAUNAY Traditional French €€

(02 47 30 16 82; www.aubergedelaunay.com; Le Haut Chantier, Limeray; menus €19.50-38; lunch Tue-Fri, dinner Mon-Sat) Renowned for its cosy atmosphere and superb food, this country inn 8km east of Amboise merits the detour for anyone with their own wheels. Herbs and vegetables from the garden out back find their way into classic French meat, fish and poultry dishes, accompanied by a superb wine list and finished off with a divine artisanal cheese platter or desserts like wine-poached pears and homemade macaroons.

LA FOURCHETTE Traditional French €

(06 11 78 16 98; 9 rue Malebranche; lunch/dinner menus €15/24; lunch Tue-Sat, dinner Fri & Sat) Tucked into a back alley behind the tourist office, this is Amboise's favourite address for home cooking. Chef Christine makes you feel like you've been invited to

her house for lunch, with daily specials including *travers de porc* (spare ribs), *poulet rôti* (roast chicken) and *blanquette de veau* (veal stew).

BIGOT Patisserie €

(www.bigot-amboise.com; place du Château; ⏲noon-7.30pm Mon, 9am-7.30pm Tue-Fri, 8.30am-7.30pm Sat & Sun) Since 1913 this award-winning chocolaterie and patisserie has been whipping up some of the Loire's creamiest cakes and gooiest treats: multicoloured macarons, buttery biscuits, handmade chocolates and petits fours, alongside speciality coffees and teas and savoury lunchtime treats, including omelettes, salads and excellent quiches.

Information

Tourist office (☎02 47 57 09 28; www.amboise-valdeloire.com; quai du General de Gaulle; ⏲9.30am-6pm Mon-Sat, 10am-1pm & 2-5pm Sun)

Getting There & Away

Amboise is 34km southwest of Blois and 23km northeast of Tours. From the train station, 1.5km north of the château and across the Loire, local trains run 12 to 20 times daily to Tours (€5.20, 20 minutes) and Blois (€6.60, 20 minutes). Four daily express trains also serve Paris Gare d'Austerlitz (€30.10, 1¾ hours).

Saumur

POP 29,650

There's an air of Parisian sophistication around Saumur, but also a sense of laid-back contentment. The food is good, the wine is good, the spot is good – and the Saumurites know it. The town is renowned for its École Nationale d'Équitation, a national cavalry school that's been home to the crack riders of the Cadre Noir since 1828.

Sights

ÉCOLE NATIONALE D'ÉQUITATION Riding School

(National Equestrian School; ☎02 41 53 50 60; www.cadrenoir.fr; rte de Marson; adult/child €7/5, Cadre Noir presentations adult/child €16/9; ⏲mornings Tue-Sat & afternoons Mon-Fri Apr–mid-Nov) Three kilometres west of town, outside of sleepy St-Hilaire-St-Florent, the École Nationale d'Équitation is one of France's foremost riding academies, responsible for training the country's Olympic teams and members of the elite Cadre Noir, distinguished by their special black jackets, caps, gold spurs and three golden wings on their whips. Advance reservations are essential for the one-hour guided visits (four to 10 per day; enquire about the availability of English-language tours). If you happen to be in town for one of the semi-monthly **Cadre Noir presentations** do not miss it: they are like astonishing horse ballets.

CHÂTEAU DE SAUMUR Castle

(☎02 41 40 24 40; adult/child €9/5; ⏲10am-1pm & 2-5.30pm Tue-Sun Apr-Oct) Soaring above the town's rooftops, Saumur's fairy-tale château was largely built during the 13th century by Louis XI, and has variously served as a dungeon, fortress and country residence. After a decade-long restoration project, the castle's decorative arts collection reopened in July 2012 on the 1st floor; the 2nd floor, with its impressive collection of vintage equestrian gear, is scheduled to reopen in 2013.

Sleeping

CHÂTEAU DE VERRIÈRES Castle Hotel €€€

(☎02 41 38 05 15; www.chateau-verrieres.com; 53 rue d'Alsace; r €170-240, ste €280-310; 📶🏊) Every one of the 10 rooms in this impeccably wonderful 1890 château, ensconced within the woods and ponds of a 1.6-hectare English park, is different. But the feel is universally plush and kingly: antique writing desks, original artwork, wood panelling and fantastic bathrooms. Some, like the top-of-the-line Rising Sun suite (with a dash of modish Japanese minimalism), have views of the sun rising over the Saumur château. Regal with a capital R. Parking free.

CHÂTEAU BEAULIEU B&B **€€**
(☎02 41 50 83 52; www.chateaudebeaulieu.fr; 98 rte de Montsoreau; d €85-120, ste €140-200;) Irish expats Mary and Conor welcome you to their sprawling home with a glass of bubbling *crémant*, delicious homemade breakfasts and a wealth of friendly advice on surrounding attractions. Rooms are imaginatively and comfortably done up and the mood among the generally gregarious clientele is one of extended family. Sun yourself by the pool or play billiards in the grand salon. Parking free.

Eating

LE GAMBETTA Gastronomic **€€**
(☎02 41 67 66 66; www.restaurantlegambetta.com; 12 rue Gambetta; lunch menus €23.50-28.50, other menus €30-96; lunch Tue & Thu-Sun, dinner Tue & Thu-Sat) OK, take a deep breath and prepare yourself. This is one to write home about: a fantastic regional restaurant combining refined elegance and knock-your-socks-off creative food. The parade of exquisitely presented dishes ranges from rosemary-and-thyme roasted pork with an asparagus-lemon-parmesan *maki* to surprisingly delicious wasabi *crème brûlée*. Some menus include wine pairings, and all are punctuated by surprise treats from the kitchen.

LE POT DE LAPIN Modern French **€€**
(☎02 41 67 12 86; 35 rue Rabelais; tapas €1-7, mains €11-24; lunch & dinner Tue-Sat) Jazzy music wafts from the cheery dining room through the wine bar and onto the streetside terrace as Chef Olivier works the tables, proposing perfect wine pairings and serving up tempting platefuls of tapas and French classics. Why not begin your sensory experience with a *soupe saumuroise* – the iconic local aperitif made with triple sec, lemon juice and sparkling wine, then move on to perfectly seasoned shrimp brochettes, coulis-drizzled foie gras or pollock cooked in parchment paper.

Information

Tourist office (☎02 41 40 20 60; www.saumur-tourisme.com; 8bis quai Carnot; 9.15am-7pm Mon-Sat, 10.30am-5.30pm Sun)

Getting There & Away

SNCF offers frequent train services to Tours (€11.20, 30 to 50 minutes, 12 daily) and Angers (€8.30, 20 to 35 minutes, 16 daily).

BURGUNDY

Burgundy (Bourgogne in French) offers some of France's most gorgeous countryside: rolling green hills dotted with medieval villages, and mustard fields blooming in bright contrast. Two great French passions, wine and food, come together here in a particularly rich and enticing form.

Dijon

POP 250,000

Dijon is one of France's most appealing cities. Filled with elegant medieval and Renaissance buildings, the lively centre is wonderful for strolling, especially if you like to leaven your cultural enrichment with excellent food, fine wine and shopping.

Sights

PALAIS DES DUCS ET DES ÉTATS DE BOURGOGNE Palace
(Palace of the Dukes & States of Burgundy; place de la Libération) Once home to Burgundy's powerful dukes, this monumental palace with neoclassical façade overlooks **place de la Libération**, Old Dijon's magnificent central square dating from 1686. The palace's eastern wing houses the outstanding Musée des Beaux-Arts, whose entrance is next to the **Tour de Bar**, a squat 14th-century tower that once served as a prison.

Just off the **Cour d'Honneur**, the 46m-high, mid-15th-century **Tour Philippe le Bon** (adult/child €2.30/free;

SHAUN EGAN/GETTY IMAGES ©

Don't Miss Château de Chambord

For full-blown château splendour, you can't top Chambord, one of the crowning examples of French Renaissance architecture, and by far the largest, grandest and most visited château in the Loire Valley.

Begun in 1519 as a weekend hunting lodge by François I, it quickly snowballed into one of the most ambitious (and expensive) architectural projects ever attempted by any French monarch. Though construction was repeatedly halted by financial problems, design setbacks and military commitments (not to mention the kidnapping of the king's two sons in Spain), by the time Chambord was finally finished 30-odd years later, the castle boasted some 440 rooms, 282 fireplaces and 84 staircases, not to mention a cityscape of turrets, chimneys and lanterns crowning its rooftop, and a famous **double-helix staircase**, reputedly designed by the king's chum, Leonardo da Vinci. Ironically, François ultimately found his elaborate palace too draughty, preferring the royal apartments in Amboise and Blois; he only stayed here for 42 days during his entire reign from 1515 to 1547.

Chambord is 16km east of Blois, 45km southwest of Orléans and 17km northeast of Cheverny.

NEED TO KNOW

Château de Chambord (☎02 54 50 40 00; www.chambord.org; adult/child €11/free, parking €3; ⏰9am-6pm Apr-Sep, 10am-5pm Oct-Mar); **Château de Chambord Guided Tours** (adult/child 1hr tour €5/3, 2hr tour €7/5)

guided tours every 45min 9am-noon & 1.45-5.30pm Easter-late Nov, 1.30-3.30pm Wed, 9am-3.30pm Sat-Sun late Nov-Easter) affords fantastic views over the city. Spot Mont Blanc on a clear day.

MUSÉE DES BEAUX-ARTS Art Museum
(03 80 74 52 70; http://mba.dijon.fr; audio guide €4, tours adult/child €6/3; 9.30am-6pm Wed-Mon May-Oct, 10am-5pm Nov-Apr) Housed in the eastern wing of the Palais des Ducs, these sprawling galleries make up one of the most outstanding museums in France. The star room is the wood-panelled **Salle des Gardes** (Guards' Room), once warmed by a gargantuan Gothic fireplace. It houses the ornate, carved late-medieval sepulchres of dukes John the Fearless and Philip the Bold, as well as three impossibly intricate gilded Gothic retables from the 1300s.

ÉGLISE NOTRE DAME Church
(place Notre-Dame) A block north of the Palais des Ducs, this church was built between 1220 and 1240. Its extraordinary façade's three tiers are lined with leering gargoyles separated by two rows of pencil-thin columns.

CATHÉDRALE ST-BÉNIGNE Cathedral
(place St-Philibert) Built over the tomb of St Benignus (believed to have brought Christianity to Burgundy in the 2nd century), Dijon's Burgundian Gothic-style cathedral was built around 1300 as an abbey church. Some of Burgundy's great figures are buried in its crypt.

FREE **MUSÉE DE LA VIE BOURGUIGNONNE** Museum
(03 80 48 80 90; 17 rue Ste-Anne; 9am-noon & 2-6pm Wed-Mon) Housed in a 17th-century Cistercian convent, this museum explores village and town life in Burgundy in centuries past with evocative tableaux illustrating dress and traditional crafts. On the 1st floor, a whole street has been recreated.

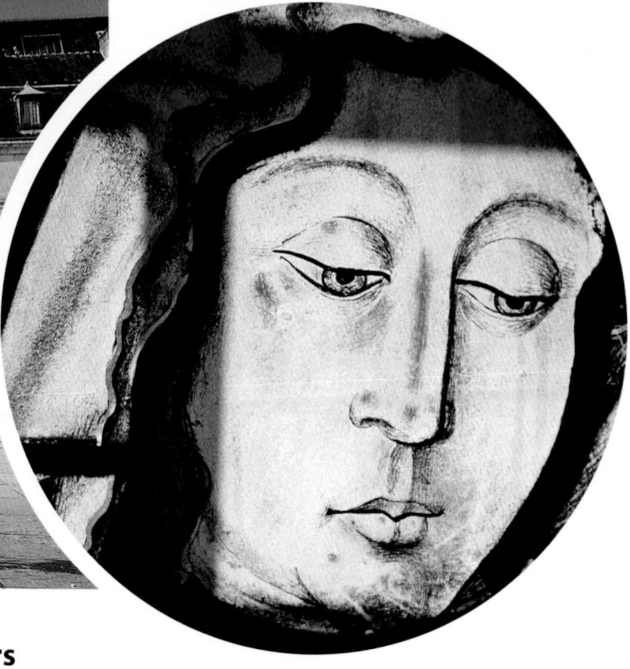

Left: Palais des Ducs et des États de Bourgogne (p202); **Below:** Church stained glass window, Dijon (p202)
(LEFT)ANDREW BAIN /GETTY IMAGES ©; (BELOW) GREG ELMS/GETTY IMAGES ©

Tours

WALKING TOURS History Tour
(adult/child €6/1) A slew of different tours depart from the main tourist office. Times vary throughout the year.

SEGWAY TOUR History Tour
(adult/child €19/9; 2.30pm & 4pm Mon-Sat) Run by the tourist office, this 1½-hour tour zips around the city centre.

VINEYARD TOURS Wine Tour
Minibus tours in English introduce the Côte d'Or vineyards. Reserve by phone, internet or via the tourist office. Operators include: **Alter & Go (06 23 37 92 04; www.alterandgo.fr; tours from €70)** with an emphasis on history and winemaking methods, **Authentica Tour (06 87 01 43 78; www.authentica-tour.com; tours €55-125)** and **Wine & Voyages (03 80 61 15 15; www.wineandvoyages.com; tours from €53).**

Sleeping

HÔTEL LE JACQUEMART Hotel €
(03 80 60 09 60; www.hotel-lejacquemart.fr; 32 rue Verrerie; s €52-58, d €60-70;) In the heart of old Dijon, this hotel is one of our favourites, with tidy, comfy rooms and friendly staff. All rooms are different; the best (Nos 5 and 6) are in a 17th-century annexe just across the street; they're larger and better equipped than those within the hotel's original core, and combine vintage touches (stone walls, beamed ceiling) and modern conveniences.

HÔTEL LE SAUVAGE Hotel €
(03 80 41 31 21; www.hotellesauvage.com; 64 rue Monge; s €48-59, d €53-64, tr €85;) Set in a 15th-century *relais de poste* (coaching inn) that ranges around a cobbled, vine-shaded courtyard, this little hotel is definitely good value. Rooms 10, 12,

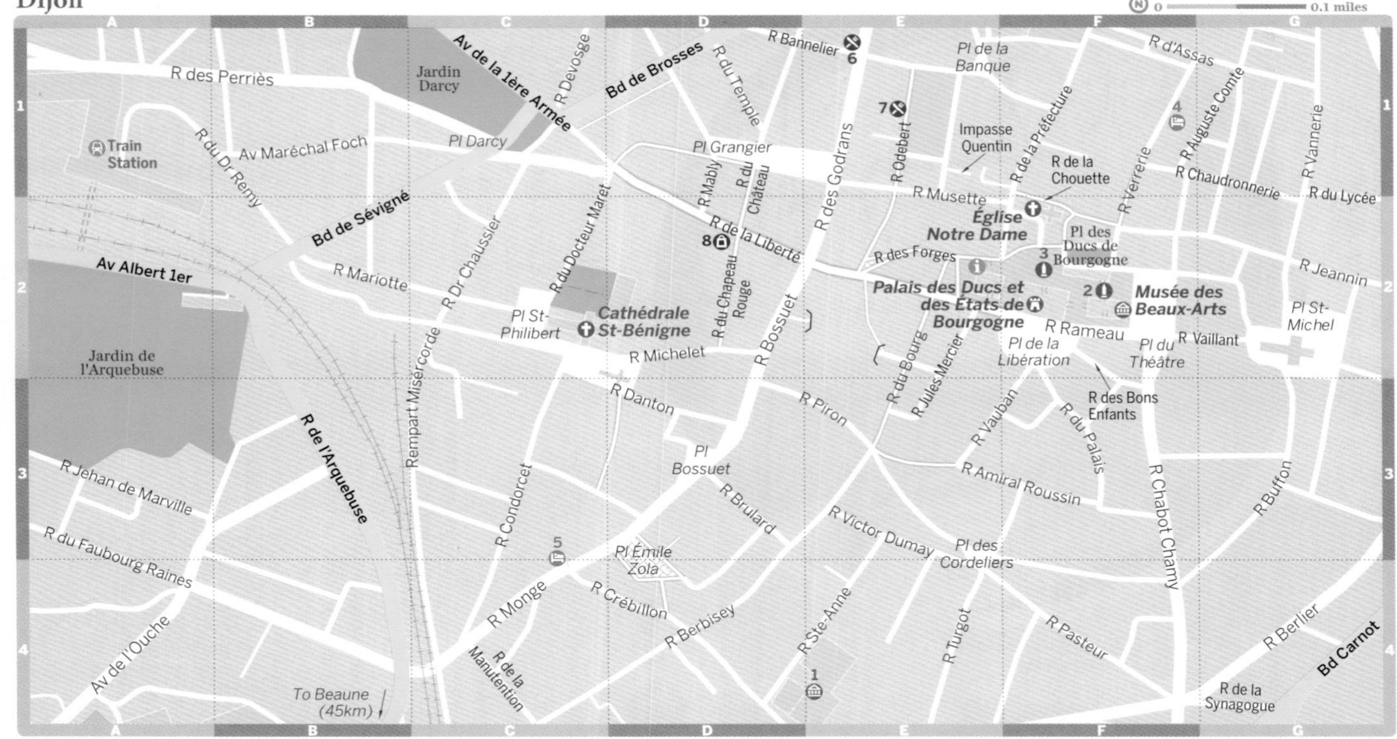
Dijon
0 200 m
0 0.1 miles
Musée des Beaux-Arts
Palais des Ducs et des États de Bourgogne
Église Notre Dame
Cathédrale St-Bénigne
Train Station
Jardin Darcy
Jardin de l'Arquebuse
To Beaune (45km)
R des Perrières
Av de la 1ère Armée
R Devosge
Bd de Brosses
R du Temple
R Bannelier
Pl de la Banque
R d'Assas
R Auguste Comte
R Vannerie
R du Lycée
R Chaudronnerie
R Verrerie
R de la Chouette
R de la Préfecture
Impasse Quentin
R Odebert
R des Godrans
Pl Grangier
R Mably
R du Château
R de la Liberté
R Musette
R des Forges
Pl des Ducs de Bourgogne
R Jeannin
Pl St-Michel
R Vaillant
Pl du Théâtre
R Rameau
Pl de la Libération
R des Bons Enfants
R du Palais
R Vauban
R Jules Mercier
R du Bourg
R Piron
R Amiral Roussin
R Chabot Chamy
R Buffon
R Berlier
Bd Carnot
R de la Synagogue
R Pasteur
R Turgot
Pl des Cordeliers
R Victor Dumay
R Ste-Anne
R Berbisey
R Crébillon
Pl Émile Zola
R Brulard
Pl Bossuet
R Bossuet
R Michelet
R Danton
R du Chapeau Rouge
Pl St-Philibert
R du Docteur Maret
R Dr Chaussier
R Mariotte
Rempart Miséricorde
R Condorcet
R Monge
R de la Manutention
R de l'Arquebuse
Av Albert 1er
Bd de Sévigné
R du Dr Remy
Av Maréchal Foch
Pl Darcy
R Jehan de Marville
R du Faubourg Raines
Av de l'Ouche
A
B
C
D
E
F
G
1
2
3
4
5
6
7
8

Dijon

Top Sights

Sights

Sleeping

Eating

Shopping

14 and 17, with exposed beams, are the cosiest. It's in a lively area but the hotel is pleasingly quiet. Parking €5.

DZ'ENVIES Modern Burgundian **€€**
(**03 80 50 09 26; www.dzenvies.com; 12 rue Odebert; mains €16-20, lunch menus €13-20, dinner menus €29-36; Mon-Sat**) This zinging restaurant with cheery decorative touches is a good choice if you're tired of heavy Burgundian classics. The menu always involves seasonal, fresh ingredients, and dishes are imaginatively prepared and beautifully presented. At €18, the lunchtime *I love Dijon* (yes) menu is a steal.

CHEZ LÉON Burgundian **€€**
(**03 80 50 01 07; www.restaurantchezleon.fr; 20 rue des Godrans; mains €11-29, lunch menus €15-21, dinner menus €22-27; Tue-Sat**) From bœuf bourguignon (beef marinated in young red wine) to *andouillettes* (chitterling sausages), this is the perfect primer course in hearty regional fare celebrated in a cosy and joyful atmosphere. The dining room is cluttered but there's outdoor seating in warm months.

MOUTARDE MAILLE Mustard
(**03 80 30 41 02; www.maille.com; 32 rue de la Liberté; 10am-7pm Mon-Sat**) When you enter the factory boutique of this mustard company, tangy odours assault your nostrils. Thirty-six kinds of mustard, such as cassis or truffle and celery, include three on tap that you can sample.

Information

Tourist office (**08 92 70 05 58; www.visitdijon.com; 11 rue des Forges; 9am-6.30pm Mon-Sat, 10am-6pm Sun**)

Getting There & Away

Services leave the **train station** (**www.voyages-sncf.com; rue du Dr Remy**) for the following destinations:

Lyon-Part Dieu From €22, 1½ hours, 25 daily.

Marseille From €54, 3½ hours by TGV, six direct daily.

Paris Gare de Lyon €42 to €49, 1¾ hours by TGV, three hours non-TGV, 25 daily.

Côte d'Or

Burgundy's most renowned vintages come from the vine-covered Côte d'Or (literally Golden Hillside, but it is actually an abbreviation of Côte d'Orient or Eastern Hillside), the narrow, eastern slopes of a range of hills made of limestone, flint and clay that runs south from Dijon for about 60km.

Noted for its powerful reds, the **Côte de Nuits** winegrowing area extends from Marsannay-la-Côte, just south of Dijon, to Corgoloin, a few kilometres north of Beaune. **Château du Clos de Vougeot** (**03 80 62 86 09; www.closdevougeot.fr; Vougeot; adult/child €4/3.10; 9am-5.30pm**), 20km south of Dijon in **Vougeot**, provides a wonderful introduction to Burgundy's winemaking techniques. Originally the property of the Abbaye de Cîteaux, the 16th-century country castle served as a getaway for the abbots. Almost 5km south in **Nuits St-Georges**, gleaming modern museum **L'Imaginarium** (☎03 80 62 61 40; www.imaginarium-bourgogne.com; av du Jura, Nuits-St-Georges; adult/child €8/5; ⏰2-7pm Mon, 10am-7pm Tue-Sun) is the place to learn about Burgundy wines and winemaking technique through movies, exhibits and interactive displays.

Known for top-quality dry whites and delicate reds, the **Côte de Beaune** area extends from Ladoix-Serrigny, just a few kilometres north of Beaune, to Santenay, about 18km south of Beaune. The delightful village of **Chassagne-Montrachet** boasts Burgundy's most fabled vineyards, while **Château de Meursault** (☎03 80 26 22 75; www.chateau-meursault.com; Meursault; admission incl tasting €15; ⏰9.30am-noon & 2.30-6pm, no midday closure Jul-Aug) – among the prettiest Côte de Beaune châteaux – has beautiful grounds and produces some of the most prestigious white wines in the world. For red-wine lovers, a visit to **Château de Pommard** (☎03 80 22 12 59; www.chateaudepommard.com; 15 rue Marey-Monge, Pommard; guided tour incl tasting adult/child €21/free; ⏰ 9.30am-6pm Apr-Nov), 3km south of Beaune, is the ultimate Burgundian pilgrimage.

Beaune

POP 22,720

Beaune (pronounced similarly to 'bone'), 44km south of Dijon, is the unofficial capital of the Côte d'Or. This thriving town's *raison d'être* and the source of its *joie de vivre* is wine: making it, tasting it, selling it, but most of all, drinking it. Consequently, Beaune is one of the best places in all of France for wine tasting.

The jewel of Beaune's old city is the magnificent Hôtel-Dieu, France's most splendiferous medieval charity hospital.

Sights & Activities

HÔTEL-DIEU DES HOSPICES DE BEAUNE Historic Building

(www.hospices-de-beaune.com; rue de l'Hôtel-Dieu; adult/child €7/3; ⏰9am-5.30pm) Built in 1443, this magnificent Gothic hospital (until 1971) is famously topped by stunning turrets and pitched rooftops covered in multicoloured tiles. Interior highlights include the barrel-vaulted **Grande Salle** (look for the dragons and peasant heads up on the roof beams); the mural-covered **St-Hughes Room**; an 18th-century **pharmacy** lined with flasks

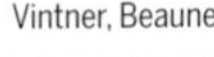

Vintner, Beaune

once filled with elixirs and powders; and the multipanelled masterpiece **Polyptych of the Last Judgement** by 15th-century Flemish painter Rogier van der Weyden, depicting Judgment Day in glorious technicolour.

MARCHÉ AUX VINS Wine Tasting
(www.marcheauxvins.com; 2 rue Nicolas Rolin; admission €10; 9.30-11.30am & 2-5.30pm, no midday closure Jul-Aug) Using a *tastevin* (wine cup), sample an impressive 15 wines in the candlelit former Église des Cordeliers and its cellars. Wandering among the vintages takes about an hour. The finest wines are at the end; look for the *premier crus* and the *grand cru*.

PATRIARCHE PÈRE ET FILS Wine Tasting
(www.patriarche.com; 5 rue du Collège; audio guide tour €13; 9.30-11.30am & 2-5.30pm) The largest cellars in Burgundy, they are lined with about five million bottles of wine. The oldest is a Beaune Villages AOC from 1904. Visitors sample 13 wines and take the *tastevin* home.

MOUTARDERIE FALLOT Mustard Factory
(Mustard Mill; www.fallot.com; 31 rue du Faubourg Bretonnière; adult/child €10/8; tours 10am & 11.30am Mon-Sat, also afternoons summer, closed Nov-Mar 15) Maison Fallot, Burgundy's last family-run stone-ground mustard company, offers tours of its facilities, which include a museum about mustard. Demonstrations include hand-milling mustard seeds – young kids love it! Reserve ahead at the tourist office.

Eating

LOISEAU DES VIGNES Gastronomic **€€€**
(03 80 24 12 06; www.bernard-loiseau.com; 31 rue Maufoux; lunch menus €20-28, dinner menus €59-95; Tue-Sat) For that special meal with your significant other, this culinary shrine is the place to go. Expect stunning concoctions ranging from caramelised pigeon to *quenelles de sandre* (dumplings made from pike fish), all exquisitely presented. And even the most budget-conscious can indulge – lunch menus are a bargain. Wines are served only by the glass (from €3). In summer, the verdant garden is a plus.

LE COMPTOIR DES TONTONS
Modern Burgundian **€€**
(03 80 24 19 64; www.lecomptoirdestontons.com; 22 rue du Faubourg Madeleine; menus €25-36; Tue-Sat) Stylishly decorated in a hip bistro style, this local treasure entices with the passionate Burgundian cooking of chef Pepita. Most ingredients are organic and locally sourced. Does the beef with paprika taste better than the fat duck in aniseed sauce? You be the judge. Service is prompt and friendly.

Detour: MuséoParc Alésia

Opened in 2012, the sensational **MuséoParc Alésia (www.alesia.fr; 1 rte des Trois Ormeaux, Alise-Ste-Reine; 9am-9pm Jul-Aug, 9am-6pm Apr-Jun & Sep, 10am-5pm Oct-Dec & Feb-Mar, closed Jan)**, near the village of Alise-Ste-Reine in the Pays d'Auxois, is well worth the drive from Dijon (67km). This was the site of what was once Alésia, the camp where Vercingétorix, the chief of the Gaulish coalitions, was defeated by Julius Caesar after a long siege. The defeat marked the end of the Gallic/Celtic heritage in France. You can visit the well-organised interpretative centre as well as the vestiges of the Gallo-Roman city that developed after the battle. The MuséoParc Alésia also offers entertaining programs and workshops for kids.

If You Like... Châteaux

Once you've done the big three – Chambord, Chenonceau and Cheverny – it's worth taking the time to discover this trio of lesser-known, equally dreamy châteaux.

1 CHÂTEAU DE VILLANDRY

(☎02 47 50 02 09; www.chateauvillandry.com; château & gardens adult/child €9.50/5.50, gardens only €6.50/4; 9am-6pm Apr-Oct, earlier rest of year, closed mid-Nov–Dec) Villandry is famous for its **landscaped gardens**, a glorious mirage of manicured lime trees, ornamental vines, razor-sharp box hedges and tinkling fountains. The **Jardin d'Ornement** depicts various aspects of love (fickle, passionate, tender and tragic). Visit between April and October when the gardens are in bloom; midsummer is spectacular. Villandry is 17km southwest of Tours and 11km northeast of Azay-le-Rideau.

2 CHÂTEAU DE BEAUREGARD

(☎02 54 70 41 65; www.beauregard-loire.com; adult/child €12.50/5; 10.30am-6.30pm, closed mid-Nov–mid-Feb) The highlight of peaceful Beauregard, a hunting lodge by François I, is an amazing portrait gallery depicting 327 notables of European royalty, clergy and intelligentsia. Spot Christopher Columbus, Sir Francis Drake, Cardinal Richelieu, Catherine de Médicis, Anne de Bretagne, Henry VIII of England and his doomed wife Anne Boleyn.

3 CHÂTEAU D'USSÉ

(www.chateaudusse.fr; adult/child €14/4; 10am-6pm, closed early Nov–mid-Feb) The main claim to fame of elaborate Château d'Ussé, 14km west of Azay-le-Rideau, is as the inspiration for Charles Perrault's classic fairy tale, *La Belle au Bois Dormant* (Sleeping Beauty). Its creamy white towers and slate roofs revel in sweeping views across wonderful formal gardens and flat Loire countryside beyond.

Information

Tourist office **(☎03 80 26 21 30; www.beaune-tourisme.fr; 6 bd Perpreuil; 9am-7pm Mon-Sat, 9am-6pm Sun)**

Getting There & Away

BUS The Transco **(☎03 80 11 29 29; www.mobigo-bourgogne.com)** bus 44 links Beaune with Dijon (€1.50, 1½ hours, two to seven daily), stopping at Côte d'Or villages such as Vougeot, Nuits-St-Georges and Aloxe-Corton. Services reduced in July and August. In Beaune, buses stop along the boulevards around the old city. Timetables at the tourist office.

TRAIN Services connect the following places:

Lyon-Part Dieu From €30, 1¾ hours, 16 daily.

Dijon €7.30, 25 minutes, 40 daily.

Nuits-St-Georges From €4.50, 10 minutes, 40 daily.

Paris Gare de Lyon From €41, 2¼ hours by TGV (non-TGV 3½ hours), 20 daily, two direct TGVs daily.

Noyers-sur-Serein

A must-see on any Burgundy itinerary, the absolutely picturesque medieval village of Noyers (pronounced 'nwa-yair'), 30km southeast of Auxerre, is surrounded by rolling pastureland, wooded hills and a sharp bend in the River Serein. Stone ramparts and fortified battlements enclose much of the village and, between the two imposing stone gateways, cobbled streets lead past 15th- and 16th-century gabled houses, wood and stone archways and several art galleries.

Noyers is a superb base for walking. Just outside the clock-topped southern gate, Chemin des Fossés leads eastwards to the River Serein and a streamside walk around the village's 13th-century fortifications, 19 of whose original 23 towers are extant. Lunch afterwards at **Les Millésimes (☎03 86 82 82 16; www.maison-paillot.com; place de l'Hôtel de Ville; menus €23-42; lunch & dinner Tue-Sun, closed Jan-Mar)**, a meticulously restored medieval house complete with large fireplace and sturdy wooden tables, which specialises in *terroir* creations ranging from *jambon au chablis* (ham flavoured with Chablis wine) to *tourte à l'Époisses* (Époisses cheese pie). It's also renowned for its respectable wine list. Or try **Ô Marquis Perché** (☎ 03 86 75 16 70; 34 place du Grenier à Sel; mains €13-16, menu €12; ⏰ lunch & dinner Wed-Mon May-Sep, lunch Wed-Mon, dinner Fri-Sun Oct-Apr), a low-key, old-town bistro with inventive house specialities and homemade desserts not to be missed.

Chantier Médiéval de Guédelon

About 45km southwest of Auxerre and 7km southwest of St-Sauveur-en-Puisaye, a team of skilled artisans, aided by archaeologists, has been hard at work building a fortified castle at the **Chantier Médiéval de Guédelon** (☎ 03 86 45 66 66; www.guedelon.fr; D955 near Treigny; adult/child €10/8.50; ⏰ 10am-6pm Jul-Aug, 10am-4.30pm or 5pm Thu-Tue mid-Mar-Jun & Sep-Oct, closed mid-Nov–mid-Mar) since 1997 using only 13th-century techniques. No electricity or power tools here: stone is quarried on site using iron hand tools forged by a team of blacksmiths, who also produce vital items like door hinges. Clay for tiles is fired for three days using locally cut wood and the mortar, made on site with lime, is transported in freshly woven wicker baskets. A very worthwhile guided tour, sometimes in English, costs €2 per person. Wear closed shoes, as the site is often a sea of muck. Child-oriented activities include stone carving (using especially soft stone).

THE DORDOGNE

This is the heart and soul of *la belle France,* a land of dense oak forests, emerald-green fields and famously rich country cooking. It's the stuff of which French dreams are made: turreted châteaux and medieval villages line the riverbanks, wooden-hulled *gabarres* (barges) wander the waterways, and market stalls overflow with foie gras, truffles, walnuts and fine wines.

The Dordogne, known to the French as the Périgord, has long been a favourite getaway for Brits looking for a second home and French families on *les grandes vacances*. It's also famous for having some of France's finest prehistoric cave art, which is abundant in the caverns and rock shelters of the Vézère Valley. After a holiday here, you may find yourself pining for a second home in the region, too.

Sarlat-la-Canéda

POP 9943

A picturesque tangle of honey-coloured buildings, alleyways and secret squares make up the beautiful town of Sarlat-la-Canéda, which boasts some of the region's best-preserved medieval architecture and makes the perfect base for exploring the Vézère Valley.

Dordogne River
SLOW IMAGES/GETTY IMAGES ©

Sights

CATHÉDRALE ST-SACERDOS Cathedral

(place du Peyrou) Whichever street you take, sooner or later you'll end up at the cathedral on place du Peyrou, once part of Sarlat's Cluniac abbey. The original abbey church was built in the 1100s, redeveloped in the early 1500s and remodelled again in the 1700s, so it's a real mix of styles. The belfry and western façade are the oldest parts of the building, while the nave, organ and interior chapels are later additions.

CHAPELLE DES PÉNITENTS BLEUS Church

Two medieval courtyards, the **Cour des Fontaines** and the **Cour des Chanoines**, can be reached via an alleyway off rue Tourny. Duck down the passage from Cour des Chanoines to the Chapelle des Pénitents Bleus, a Romanesque chapel.

ÉGLISE STE-MARIE Church

(place de la Liberté) A few steps south of place du Marché aux Oies is the Église Ste-Marie, ingeniously converted by acclaimed architect Jean Nouvel, whose parents still live in Sarlat. It now houses Sarlat's mouth-watering **Marché Couvert** (covered market; 8.30am-2pm daily mid-Apr–mid-Nov, 8.30am-1pm Fri-Wed mid-Nov–mid-Apr), as well as a spanking new **panoramic lift** affording 360-degree views across Sarlat's countryside.

PLACE DU MARCHÉ AUX OIES Square

A life-size statue of three bronze geese stands in the centre of place du Marché aux Oies (Geese Market Sq), providing a reminder of one of Sarlat's best-known gastronomic goodies. The town's markets sell a smorgasbord of goose-based products, and the town even hosts its own annual goose festival, the **Fest'Oie** (3rd Sun in Feb), when live birds and food stalls fill the square and Sarlat's top chefs prepare an outdoor banquet.

Sleeping

VILLA DE CONSULS B&B **€€**

(05 53 31 90 05; www.villaconsuls.fr; 3 rue Jean-Jacques Rousseau; d €82-103, apt €124-184;

Place de la Liberté, Sarlat-la-Canéda (p211)

@) Despite its Renaissance exterior, the enormous rooms here are modern through and through, with shiny wood floors, sofas and original roof trusses. A selection of delightful self-contained apartments are dotted round several buildings in town, all offering the same mix of period plushness – some even have private terraces overlooking the town's rooftops.

LA MAISON DES PEYRAT Hotel €€
(**☎05 53 59 00 32; www.maisondespeyrat.com; Le Lac de la Plane; r €56-103)** This beautifully renovated 17th-century house, formerly a nun's hospital and later an aristocratic hunting lodge, is set on a hill about 1.5km from the town centre. The 11 generously sized rooms are fairly plain, but ooze country charisma; the best have views over the lovingly tended gardens and the countryside beyond. The restaurant's very good, too.

Eating

LE GRAND BLEU Gastronomic €€€
(**☎05 53 29 82 14; www.legrandbleu.eu; 43 av de la Gare; menus €36-65; lunch Thu-Sun, dinner Tue-Sat)** For a proper supper in Sarlat, this Michelin-starred restaurant is unquestionably the choice. Run by head chef Maxime Lebrun, it's known for typically creative cuisine that makes maximum use of luxury produce: truffles, lobster, turbot and St-Jacques scallops all feature, and every menu starts with a *mise-en-bouche* treat. Cooking courses are also available. The only downside is the rather out-of-the-way location near the station.

SATURDAY MARKET Market €
(place de la Liberté & rue de la République; 8.30am-6pm Sat) For the full-blown French market experience, you mustn't miss Sarlat's chaotic Saturday market, which takes over the streets around Cathédrale St-Sacerdos. Depending on

If You Like... Old Abbeys

For hardcore history buffs who've already devoured the region's châteaux collection, a trio of abbeys beautifully evoke the medieval glory of monastic life in the Middle Ages.

1 **ABBAYE ROYALE DE FONTEVRAUD**
(☎02 41 51 73 52; www.abbaye-fontevraud.com; adult/child €9/6, tour or audioguide €4; 9.30am-6.30pm Apr-Oct, 10am-5.30pm Tue-Sun Nov-Mar, closed Jan) Until its closure in 1793, 12th-century Abbaye Royale de Fontevraud, 15km southeast of Saumur, was among Europe's largest. Its massive, yet movingly simple, **abbey church** is notable for its soaring pillars, Romanesque domes and the polychrome tombs of four illustrious Plantagenets. The extensive grounds include a **chapter room** with murals of the *Passion of Christ* by Thomas Pot, a spooky underground **sewer system** and a barrel-vaulted **refectory**.

2 **ABBAYE DE FONTENAY**
(Fontenay Abbey; ☎03 80 92 15 00; www.abbayedefontenay.com; adult/child €9.50/5.50; 10am-6pm Apr-11 Nov, 10am-noon & 2-5pm 12 Nov-Mar) Founded in 1118, Unesco World Heritage Site Abbaye de Fontenay, 25km north of Semur-en-Auxois, includes an unadorned Romanesque church, a barrel-vaulted monks' dormitory, landscaped gardens and the first metallurgical factory in Europe, with a forge from 1220.

3 **CLUNY**
Deep in the heart of Burgundy, Cluny, 80km south of Beaune, was home to Christendom's largest church until the construction of St Peter's Basilica in the Vatican. What remains is fragmentary and scattered, but it's still possible to imagine Cluny's Benedictine abbey in the 12th century when it held sway over 1100 priories and monasteries stretching from Poland to Portugal. Buy tickets to visit the **Église Abbatiale** (Abbey Church; ☎03 85 59 15 93; www.cluny.monuments-nationaux.fr; adult/child €9.50/free; 9.30am-6.30pm May-Aug, 9.30am-noon & 1.30-5pm Sep-Apr) inside the **Palais Jean de Bourbon**.

If You Like... Picture-Perfect Villages

Swoon over Sarlat, grab the smelling salts, then swoon again over these other drop-dead gorgeous Dordogne villages.

1 **LA ROQUE GAGEAC**
La Roque Gageac's jumble of amber buildings crammed into the cliff-face above the Dordogne have earned it recognition as another of France's *plus beaux villages (beautiful villages)*. It's an idyllic launch pad for a canoe trip or cruise, while a trio of the region's most famous castles are within a few minutes' drive. Get more info at the tourist office (**☎05 53 29 17 01; www.cc-perigord-noir.fr**).

2 **BRANTÔME**
With its five medieval bridges and romantic riverfront architecture, Brantôme, 27km north of Périgueux, befits its moniker 'Venice of the Périgord'. Set along the banks of the River Dronne, it's an enchanting spot to while away an afternoon or embark on a boat ride or paddle in a kayak. See the tourist office (**☎05 53 05 80 63; www.ville-brantome.fr**) for further information.

3 **GIMEL-LES-CASCADES**
A mixture of flower-clad cottages and slate roofs, gorgeous Gimel-les-Cascades is a place to wander the lanes, drink in the atmosphere, and stroll along the banks of the river. The three crashing **cascades**, after which the village is named, are reached via a riverside path at the foot of the village. See the tourist office (**☎05 55 21 44 32; www.gimellescascades.fr; ⏲2-4.30pm Mon-Fri, 10am-noon & 3-6.30pm Sat, 3-6.30pm Sun**) for more information.

4 **COLLONGES-LA-ROUGE**
Red sandstone houses and an 11th-century church huddle in the lanes of Collonges-la-Rouge, one of France's official *beaux villages*. Its skyline is cut from conical turrets, rickety rooftops and historic buildings built from rust-red sandstone (hence its name). Visit the tourist office (**☎05 55 25 47 57; www.ot-collonges.fr; ⏲10am-noon & 2-6pm**) for more.

the season, delicacies on offer include local mushrooms, duck- and goose-based products such as foie gras, and even the holy *truffe noir* (black truffle). There's also an atmospheric **night market** (**⏲6-10pm**) on Thursdays from mid-June to September.

LE BISTROT Regional Cuisine **€€**
(**☎05 53 28 28 40; place du Peyrou; menus €18.50-28.50; ⏲Mon-Sat**) This dinky diner is the best of the bunch on cafe-clad place du Peyrou. Gingham cloths and tiny tables create a cosy bistro feel, and the menu's heavy on Sarlat classics, especially walnuts, *magret de canard* (duck breast) and *pommes sarlardaises* (potatoes cooked in duck fat).

Information

Tourist office (**☎05 53 31 45 45; www.sarlat-tourisme.com; rue Tourny; ⏲9am-7pm Mon-Sat, 10am-1pm & 2-6pm Sun Jul & Aug, shorter hours Sep-Jun**)

Getting There & Away

Sarlat's train station is 1.3km south of the old city along av de la Gare. Many destinations require a change at Le Buisson or Libourne. Trains travel to the following destinations:

Bordeaux €25.60, 2¾ hours, six to eight daily.

Les Eyzies €9.80, 50 minutes to 2½ hours depending on connections, three daily.

The Vézère Valley

Flanked by limestone cliffs, subterranean caverns and ancient woodland, the Vézère Valley is world famous for its prehistoric sites, notably its incredible collection of cave paintings – the highest concentration of Stone Age art found in Europe. The many underground caves around the Vézère provided shelter for Cro-Magnon people, and the area is littered with tangible reminders of their time here. The otherworldly atmosphere is pretty much shattered by the summer crowds and most of the valley's sites are closed in winter, so spring and autumn are definitely the best times to visit.

Sarlat-la-Canéda, between the Vézère and Dordogne valleys to the west, is a convenient base for exploring this part of the Dordogne.

Sights

MUSÉE NATIONAL DE PRÉHISTOIRE Prehistory Museum

(☎05 53 06 45 45; www.musee-prehistoire-eyzies.fr; 1 rue du Musée; adult/child €5/3, 1st Sun of month free; ⌚9.30am-6pm Wed-Mon) Inside a marvellous modern building underneath the cliffs, this museum – 24km west of Sarlat-la-Canéda in Les-Eyzies-de-Tayac – provides a fine prehistory primer (providing your French is good), housing the most comprehensive collection of prehistoric finds in France. Highlights include a huge gallery of Stone Age tools, weapons and jewellery, and skeletons of some of the animals that once roamed the Vézère (including bison, woolly rhinoceros, giant deer and cave bears), as well as a collection of carved reliefs on the 1st floor – look out for the famous frieze of horses and a bison licking its flank. Much of the jewellery is fashioned from bone, antlers and seashells, and intricately marked with chevrons, dots, dashes and other designs.

GROTTE DE FONT DE GAUME Prehistoric Site

(☎05 53 06 86 00; http://eyzies.monuments-nationaux.fr/; adult/child €7.50/free; ⌚9.30am-5.30pm Sun-Fri mid-May–mid-Sep, 9.30am-12.30pm & 2-5.30pm Sun-Fri mid-Sep–mid-May) This extraordinary cave 1km northeast of Les Eyzies on the D47 contains the only original polychrome (as opposed to single colour) paintings that are still open to the public. About 14,000 years ago, the prehistoric artists created the gallery of over 230 figures, including bison, reindeer, horses, mammoths, bears and wolves, although only about 25 are included in the tour. Look out for the famous **Chapelle des Bisons**, a scene of courting reindeer and stunningly realised horses, several caught in mid-movement. Font de Gaume is such a rare and valuable site that there is ongoing talk of the cave being closed for its own protection. Visitor numbers are already limited to 200 per day: it's worth reserving by phone or through the tourist office a few days ahead, and a week or two in advance from July to September.

GROTTE DES COMBARELLES Prehistoric Site

(☎05 53 06 86 00; http://eyzies.monuments-nationaux.fr/; adult/child €7.50/free; ⌚9.30am-5.30pm Sun-Fri mid-May–mid-Sep, 9.30am-12.30pm & 2-5.30pm Sun-Fri mid-Sep–mid-May) Rediscovered in 1901, this narrow cave 1.5km east of Font de Gaume is renowned

The Vézère Valley

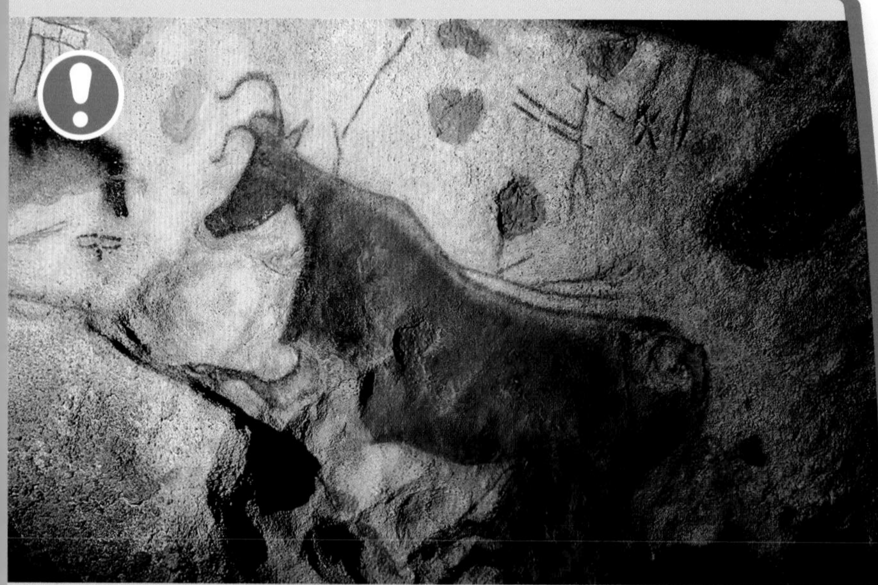

DOZIER MARC/GETTY IMAGES ©

Don't Miss Grotte de Lascaux & Lascaux II

France's most famous prehistoric cave paintings are at the Grotte de Lascaux, 2km southeast of Montignac. The site was discovered in 1940 by four teenage boys who were out searching for their lost dog. Lascaux contains an enormous network of chambers and galleries adorned with the most complex prehistoric paintings ever found. Far from the comparatively crude etchings of some of the Vézère's other caves, Lascaux' paintings are renowned for their artistry: the 600-strong menagerie of animal figures are depicted in Technicolor shades of red, black, yellow and brown, ranging from reindeer, aurochs, mammoths and horses to a monumental 5.5m-long bull, which is the largest cave drawing ever found.

Carbon dating has shown that the paintings are between 15,000 and 17,000 years old, but to this day it still remains a mystery as to why the prehistoric painters devoted such a massive amount of time and effort to their creation, and why this particular site seems to have been so important.

The original cave was opened to visitors in 1948, but within a few years it became apparent that human breath and body heat was causing irreparable damage to the paintings, and the cave was closed just 15 years later in 1963. A replica (known as Lascaux II, pictured above) of the most famous sections of the original cave was subsequently re-created a few hundred metres away, meticulously copying the same paintings and the same techniques. The original cave remains under close surveillance to preserve it.

From April to October, tickets to Grotte de Lascaux and Lascaux II are sold only in Montignac at the ticket office, next to the tourist office. There are several guided tours every hour, including several in English.

NEED TO KNOW

(☎05 53 51 95 03; www.semitour.com; adult/child €9.50/6; ⏰9am-8pm Jul & Aug, 9.30am-6pm Apr-Jun & Sep-early Nov, 10am-12.30pm & 2-5.30pm early Nov-Dec, Feb & Mar)

for its animal engravings, many of which cleverly use the natural contours of the rock to sculpt the animals' forms: look out for mammoths, horses and reindeer, as well as a fantastic mountain lion that seems to leap from the rock face. One wall seems to have been used as a kind of prehistoric sketch pad, with many animals and geometric symbols superimposed on one another. Six- to eight-person group tours last about an hour and can be reserved through the Font de Gaume ticket office.

GROTTE DE ROUFFIGNAC Prehistoric Site

(☎05 53 05 41 71; www.grottederouffignac.fr; adult/child €6.50/4.20; ⌚9-11.30am & 2-6pm Jul & Aug, 10-11.30am & 2-5pm Sep-Jun) Hidden in woodland 15km north of Les Eyzies, this cave is one of the most complex and rewarding to see in the Dordogne. The massive cavern plunges 10km into the earth through a maze of tunnels and shafts. Luckily, you visit aboard a ramshackle **electric train**, so there's no chance of getting lost.

Rouffignac is sometimes known as the 'Cave of 100 Mammoths' and you'll see many painted pachyderms on your trip into the underworld, including a frieze of 10 mammoths in procession, one of the largest cave paintings ever discovered.

Tickets are sold at the cave entrance but can't be reserved in advance so arrive early – and wrap up warmly as it's chilly below ground.

THE LOT

Southeast of the Dordogne stretches the Lot Valley, a picturesque landscape of limestone cliffs, hilltop towns and canyons carved out by the serpentine River Lot. The main town is **Cahors**, another area that's celebrated for its vineyards.

Teetering at the crest of a sheer cliff high above the River Lot 26km east is miniscule **St-Cirq Lapopie**, a village whose terracotta-roofed houses and ramshackle streets tumble down the steep hillside, affording incredible valley views. It's one of the most magical settings in the Lot.

Sights

GOUFFRE DE PADIRAC Cave

(☎05 65 33 64 56; www.gouffre-de-padirac.com; adult/child €9.80/6.80; ⌚10am-7pm Apr-Nov) Gouffre de Padirac has glittering caverns that are among the most breathtaking in France. Discovered in 1889, the cave's navigable river, 103m below ground level, is reached through a 75m-deep, 33m-wide chasm. Boat pilots ferry visitors along 1km of the subterranean waterway, visiting a series of glorious floodlit caverns en route, including the soaring **Salle de Grand Dôme** and the **Lac des Grands Gours**, a 27m-wide subterranean lake. From Rocamadour, the caverns are 15km to the northeast.

Lyon & the French Alps

The French Alps is a place of boundless natural beauty.

Whether it's virgin snow in Chamonix, the rhythm of boots on a lonely mountain pass, or the silence of a summer's morning as the first rays illuminate Mont Blanc, these colossal mountains offer a symphony of unforgettable experiences. Needless to say, the Alps are a paradise for hikers, bikers and wildlife spotters, but it's the epic pistes and après-ski that keep people coming back year after year.

At the foothills of the Alps lies grand old Lyon, France's third-largest metropolis and arguably its gastronomic capital. It's a place to savour, with Roman amphitheatres, romantic parks and a delightful old town, but for many people nothing beats tucking into some hearty Lyonnais dishes in a traditional city *bouchon* (small bistro) – old-world atmosphere, checked tablecloths, clattering pans and all.

View of Lyon from Vieux Lyon (p230)

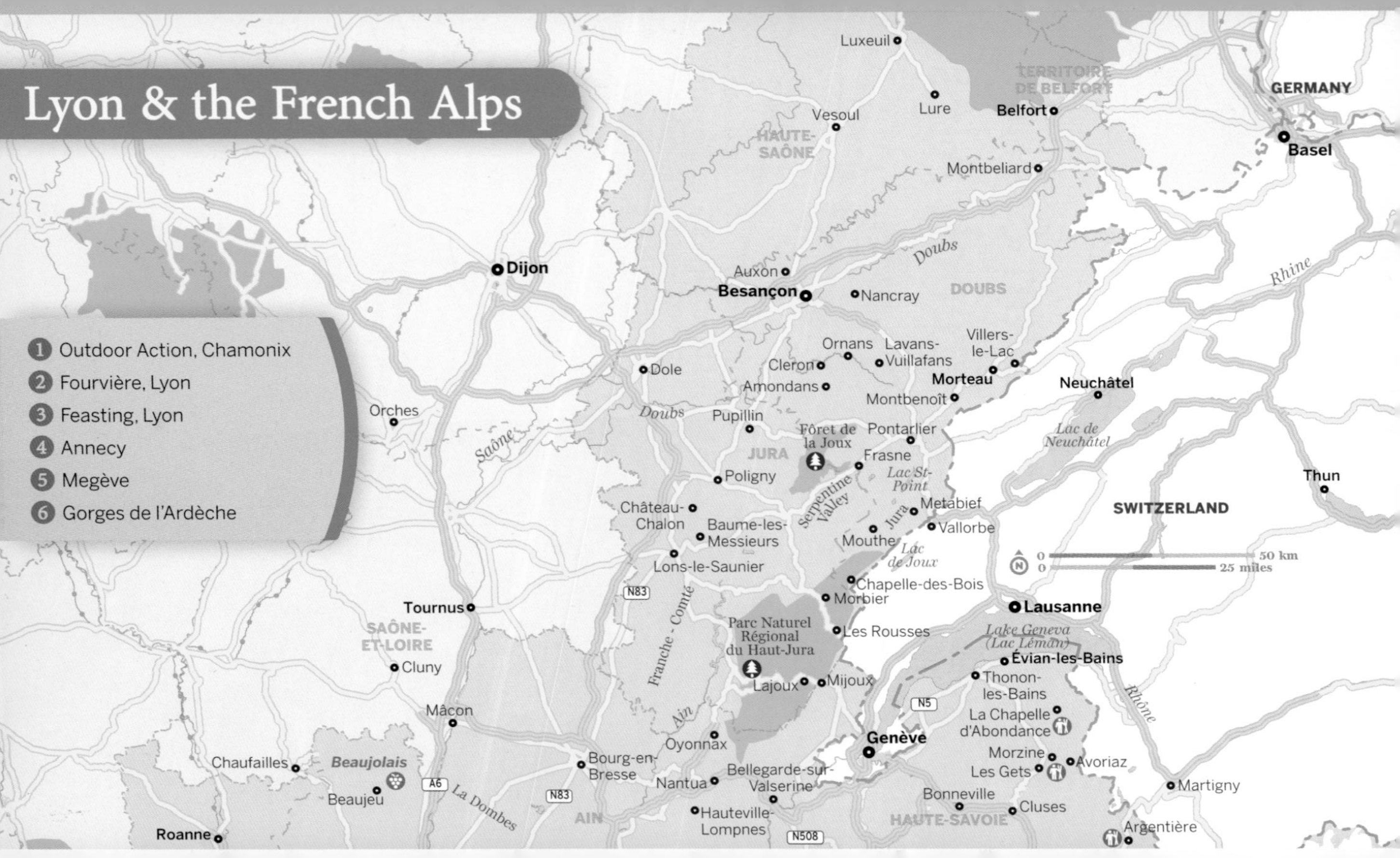
Lyon & the French Alps
1 Outdoor Action, Chamonix
2 Fourvière, Lyon
3 Feasting, Lyon
4 Annecy
5 Megève
6 Gorges de l'Ardèche
GERMANY
Basel
TERRITOIRE DE BELFORT
Belfort
Luxeuil
Lure
Vesoul
HAUTE-SAÔNE
Montbeliard
Doubs
DOUBS
Rhine
Dijon
Auxon
Besançon
Nancray
Ornans
Lavans-Vuillafans
Villers-le-Lac
Cleron
Dole
Morteau
Neuchâtel
Amondans
Montbenoît
Orches
Doubs
Pupillin
Fôret de la Joux
Pontarlier
Lac de Neuchâtel
Saône
JURA
Frasne
Lac St-Point
Poligny
Serpentine Valley
Thun
Château-Chalon
Jura
Metabief
SWITZERLAND
Baume-les-Messieurs
Vallorbe
Mouthe
Lac de Joux
Lons-le-Saunier
0 50 km
0 25 miles
Chapelle-des-Bois
N83
Morbier
Tournus
Lausanne
Parc Naturel Régional du Haut-Jura
Les Rousses
SAÔNE-ET-LOIRE
Franche - Comté
Lake Geneva (Lac Léman)
Évian-les-Bains
Cluny
Lajoux
Mijoux
Thonon-les-Bains
Rhône
N5
Mâcon
La Chapelle d'Abondance
Ain
Oyonnax
Genève
Chaufailles
Beaujolais
Bourg-en-Bresse
Morzine
Avoriaz
Bellegarde-sur-Valserine
Les Gets
Nantua
Martigny
A6
N83
Bonneville
Beaujeu
La Dombes
Cluses
AIN
Hauteville-Lompnes
HAUTE-SAVOIE
Argentière
Roanne
N508

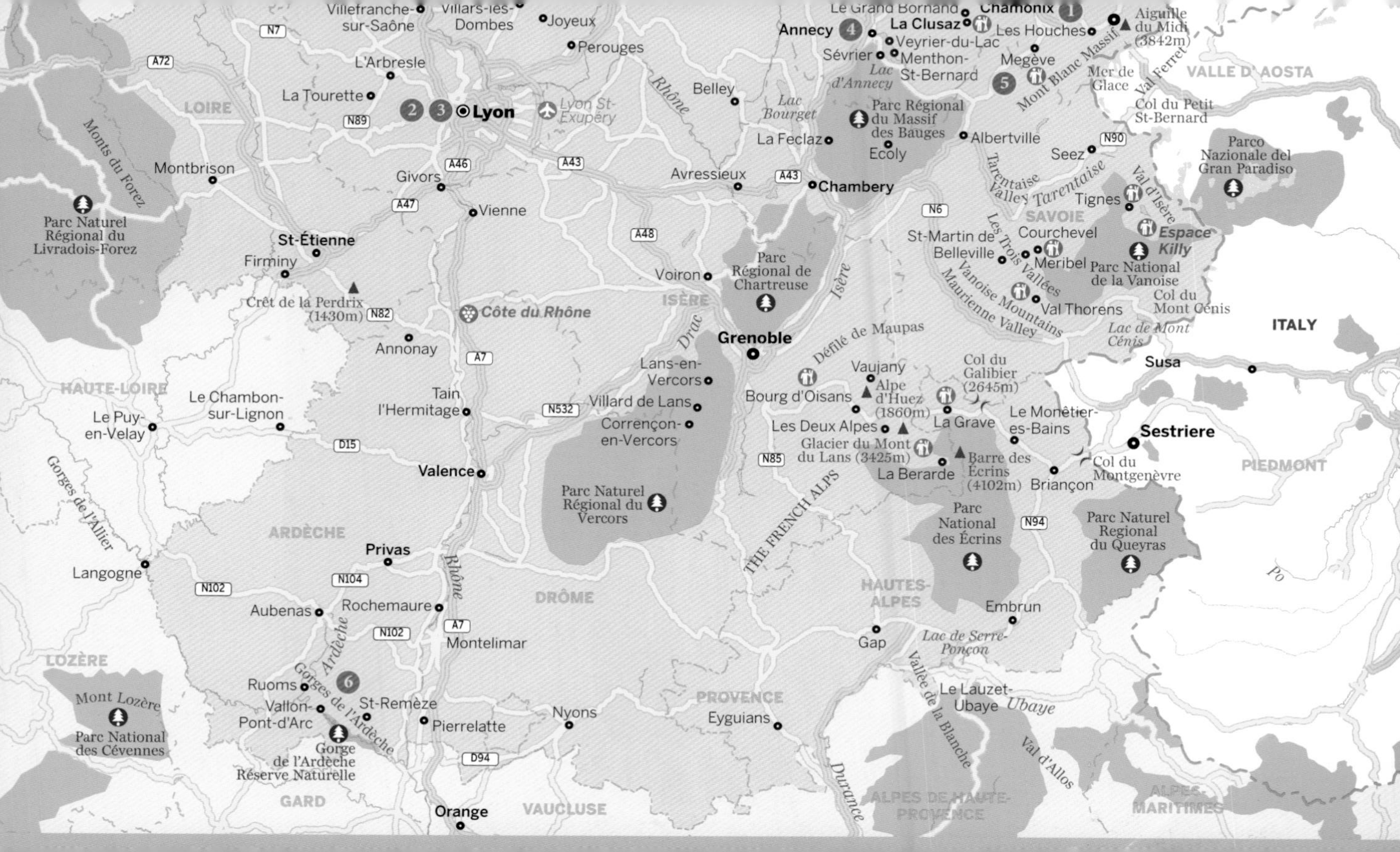

Villefranche-sur-Saône
Villars-les-Dombes
Joyeux
Perouges
N7
A72
L'Arbresle
La Tourette
LOIRE
Lyon
Lyon St-Exupéry
N89
Monts du Forez
Montbrison
Parc Naturel Régional du Livradois-Forez
Givors
A46
A43
A47
Vienne
St-Étienne
Firminy
Crêt de la Perdrix (1430m)
N82
Côte du Rhône
Annonay
A7
HAUTE-LOIRE
Le Chambon-sur-Lignon
Le Puy-en-Velay
Tain l'Hermitage
N532
D15
Valence
Gorges de l'Allier
ARDÈCHE
Privas
Langogne
N104
N102
Rhône
Aubenas
Rochemaure
Ardèche
A7
Montelimar
LOZÈRE
Ruoms
Vallon-Pont-d'Arc
St-Remèze
Gorges de l'Ardèche
Pierrelatte
Mont Lozère
Parc National des Cévennes
Gorge de l'Ardèche Réserve Naturelle
D94
GARD
Orange
VAUCLUSE
Nyons
DRÔME
Belley
Rhône
Avressieux
A48
Voiron
ISÈRE
Drac
Lans-en-Vercors
Villard de Lans
Corrençon-en-Vercors
Parc Naturel Régional du Vercors
Grenoble
Lac Bourget
La Feclaz
Annecy
Lac d'Annecy
Sévrier
Veyrier-du-Lac
Menthon-St-Bernard
Le Grand Bornand
La Clusaz
Chamonix
Les Houches
Megève
Mont Blanc Massif
Aiguille du Midi (3842m)
Mer de Glace
Val Ferret
VALLE D'AOSTA
Col du Petit St-Bernard
Parc Régional du Massif des Bauges
Ecoly
Albertville
Seez
N90
Chambery
Parc Régional de Chartreuse
Isère
Parco Nazionale del Gran Paradiso
Tarentaise Valley
Tarentaise
Val d'Isère
Tignes
N6
SAVOIE
St-Martin de Belleville
Courchevel
Les Trois Vallées
Meribel
Espace Killy
Parc National de la Vanoise
Vanoise Mountains
Maurienne Valley
Val Thorens
Col du Mont Cénis
Lac de Mont Cénis
ITALY
Susa
Défilé de Maupas
Vaujany
Alpe d'Huez (1860m)
Bourg d'Oisans
Col du Galibier (2645m)
Le Monêtier-es-Bains
La Grave
Les Deux Alpes
Glacier du Mont du Lans (3425m)
N85
La Berarde
Barre des Écrins (4102m)
Briançon
Col du Montgenèvre
Sestriere
PIEDMONT
THE FRENCH ALPS
Parc National des Écrins
N94
Parc Naturel Regional du Queyras
Po
HAUTES-ALPES
Embrun
Gap
Lac de Serre-Ponçon
PROVENCE
Eyguians
Le Lauzet-Ubaye
Ubaye
Vallée de la Blanche
Val d'Allos
Durance
ALPES DE HAUTE-PROVENCE
ALPES-MARITIMES

Lyon & the French Alps' Highlights

1

Action Chamonix!

Ever since Mont Blanc, the highest peak in the Alps, was first climbed in 1786, Chamonix (p240) has attracted travellers worldwide. Not only does it sit amid extremely condensed mountaineering potential, it is also a perfectly balanced combination of pure landscape alignment and dramatic mountain views. Top Right: Skier, Le Brévent (p240); Bottom Right: Cable car station, Aiguille du Midi (p244)

Need to Know

OFF-PISTE Hire a local certified mountain guide **ESSENTIAL STOP** Maison de la Montagne: weather office, ski school and mountain guides **For further coverage, see p240**

Local Knowledge

Chamonix Don't Miss List

BY ERIC FAVRET, MOUNTAIN GUIDE, COMPAGNIE DES GUIDES DE CHAMONIX

1 SKIING IN GRANDS MONTET

Chamonix (p240) has six main ski areas. Grands Montet is particularly heavenly, with long off-piste glacial runs, easily accessible from lifts and offering over 6000ft of vertical drop! Its north-facing aspect combined with altitude, moreover, keeps the snow really good all winter long.

2 AIGUILLE DU MIDI

The Aiguille du Midi (p244), with one of the highest cable cars in the world, cannot be missed. Beyond the summit ridge is a world of snow and ice offering some of the greatest intermediate off-piste terrain in the Alps.

3 OFF-PISTE THRILLS

The Vallée Blanche (p241) has to be seen. But the Aiguille du Midi also has amazing off-piste runs, such as Envers du Plan, a slightly steeper and more advanced version of Vallée Blanche, offering dramatic views in the heart of the Mont Blanc range. There is also the less frequented run of the 'Virgin' or 'Black Needle': a striking glacial run, offering different views and a close-up look at the Giant's seracs.

4 SUMMER HIKES ON MONT BUET

Mont Buet is a favourite. It is a summit in itself and offers outstanding 360-degree panoramas over the Mont Blanc massif and its surrounding range. It requires a good level of fitness to do in a day, but there is a hut to split the trip into two days, which also takes you into a wildlife sanctuary.

5 BEST-EVER MONT BLANC VIEW

No hesitation: the Traverse from Col des Montets to Lac Blanc. It's as popular as the Eiffel Tower for hikers in summer. I love swimming in mountain lakes, so I like to stop at Lac des Chéserys, just below, where it is quieter: what's better than a swim in pure mountain water, looking at Mont Blanc, the Grandes Jorasses and Aiguille Verte? This is what I call mountain landscape perfection!

Basilique Notre Dame de Fourvière, Lyon

Set high on a hilltop above Lyon, this late-19th-century basilica (p236) commands a panoramic position overlooking the city's rooftops. Fourvière was once the site of the Roman settlement of Lugdunum, and an intriguing museum near the basilica explores the city's Roman connections. If you don't fancy the uphill climb, catch the creaky funicular from Vieux Lyon instead.

2

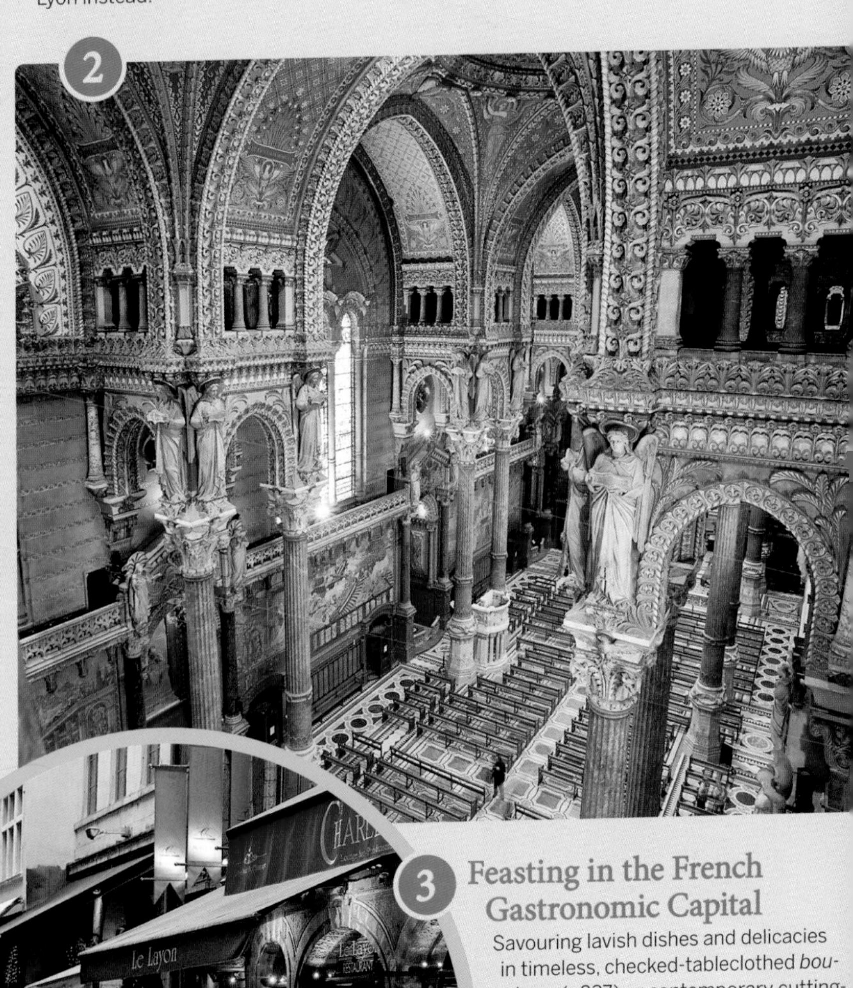

3

Feasting in the French Gastronomic Capital

Savouring lavish dishes and delicacies in timeless, checked-tableclothed *bouchons* (p237) or contemporary cutting-edge spaces is an essential part of the Lyon experience. Honour your feast with a respected red from a local Brouilly, Beaujolais, Côtes du Rhône or Mâcon vineyard. Rue Mercière on the Presqu'île, Lyon

4 Annecy

Criss-crossed by canals and set around the shores of a sparkling Alpine lake, Annecy (p246) is blessed with one of the loveliest settings in the Alps. The town is tailor-made for unwinding: wander peaceful backstreets, picnic by the water's edge, snap your picture by the famous Lovers' Bridge or just soak up the brilliant Alpine atmosphere.

5 Megève

Step into a picture-postcard with this winter wonderland village (p245) of cobbled lanes and quaint squares, with chic boutiques, horse-drawn sleighs and well-wrapped children spinning on the local ice rink. Complete the fairy-tale experience with a gastronomic dinner to remember at Michelin-starred Flocons de Sel (p245); end sweetly with sugar snowflakes for dessert.

6 Gorges de l'Ardèche

These fabulous river canyons (p242) make a fantastic day trip from Lyon. The best way to explore them is by kayak or canoe – you'll find outdoors operators all along the course of the River Ardèche. The best views are from the lookout points dotted along the Haute Corniche (D290) – but be prepared for traffic jams in summer.

Lyon & the French Alps' Best...

High-Altitude Thrills

- **Mer de Glace** (p240) Catch the rack-and-pinion train to Chamonix' 'Sea of Ice'.
- **Télécabine Panoramic Mont Blanc** (p244) Dangle above glacial crevasses in this dizzying cable-car ride from Aiguille du Midi to Pointe Helbronner.
- **La Vallée Blanche** (p241) Ski 20km of mind-blowing off-piste with this legendary Chamonix trail.

Hiking

- **Parc Nacional de la Vanois** (p248) Hit the trails in France's oldest national park between June and September.
- **Le Brévent** (p240) A multitude of routes cover this 2525m peak, offering breathtaking views of Mont Blanc.
- **Annecy** (p246) Walk or rollerblade around the shores of Lac d'Annecy.
- **Parc Nacional des Écrins** (p248) Escape the crowds in France's second-largest national park.

Cultural Sights

- **Musée des Beaux-Arts** (p231) Lyon's art museum is a showstopper.
- **Musée Lumière** (p234) Visit the boyhood Lyonnais home of cinematic pioneers Auguste and Louis Lumière.
- **Maison des Canuts** (p234) The story of Lyon's silkweavers in a 19th-century workshop.
- **Musée des Tissus** (p231) Discover Lyon's extraordinary silk heritage.
- **Château d'Annecy** (p246) Savoyard history in a château setting.

Dining

- **Le Bouchon des Filles** (p237) Contemporary take on traditional Lyonnais *bouchon* dining.
- **Mère Brazier** (p237) Mythical gastronomic temple in Lyon.
- **Les Vieilles Luges** (p243) Alpine dining in a 250-year-old farmhouse on the Chamonix slopes.
- **L'Esquisse** (p248) *The* address in Annecy, with just six tables.

.eft: Wild ibex near Mont Blanc, Chamonix (p240); .bove: Lac Blanc (p242) with Mont Blanc reflection

Need to Know

ADVANCE PLANNING

- **As early as possible** Book accommodation and ski packages.
- **Two weeks before** Arrange hiking, cycling, skiing and activity tours with local guides.
- **One week before** Book for big-name restaurants. Buy *forfaits* (ski passes) online, and ensure you have mountain-rescue insurance.

RESOURCES

- **Lyon** (www.lyon.fr) Official city website.
- **Rhône-Alpes Tourisme** (www.rhonealpes-tourisme.com) Regional tourist information.
- **France Montagnes** (www.ski-resort-france.co.uk) Guides, maps, snow reports and more.
- **Bulles de Gones** (www.bullesdegones.com) What to do with kids (up to 12 years) in and around Lyon.

GETTING AROUND

- **Airports** Major airports: **Lyon St-Exupéry** (www.lyon.aeroport.fr), **Grenoble** (www.grenoble-airport.com), **Geneva** (www.gva.ch).
- **Car & Motorcycle** Traffic on mountain roads can be hellish at weekends. Road signs indicate if mountain passes are blocked. Fit snow tyres in winter and carry snow chains.
- **Trains** Lyon has excellent rail connections to anywhere in France.
- **Satobus Alpes** (http://satobus-alpes.altibus.com) Bus shuttle between Lyon St-Exupéry airport and major ski resorts.
- **Aeroski-Bus** (www.alpski-bus.com) Buses to/from Geneva airport.

BE FOREWARNED

- **Opening times** *Bouchons* shut on weekends; many restaurants close on Mondays.
- **High-season prices** Over Christmas, New Year and during French school holidays in late February/early March.
- **Ski season** Snow covers most ski stations from mid-December to late April or early May. Summer alpine skiing on glaciers in high-altitude resorts runs for two weeks to two months, June to August.
- **Avalanches** Ski resorts announce the daily risk through signs and coloured flags. Know the golden rule: never ski, hike or climb alone.

Lyon & the French Alps Itineraries

For sheer natural drama, nowhere in France tops the Alps. Its snowy peaks and icy glaciers are essential terrain for skiers, hikers, boarders and bikers, as well as anyone who likes their views big and wild.

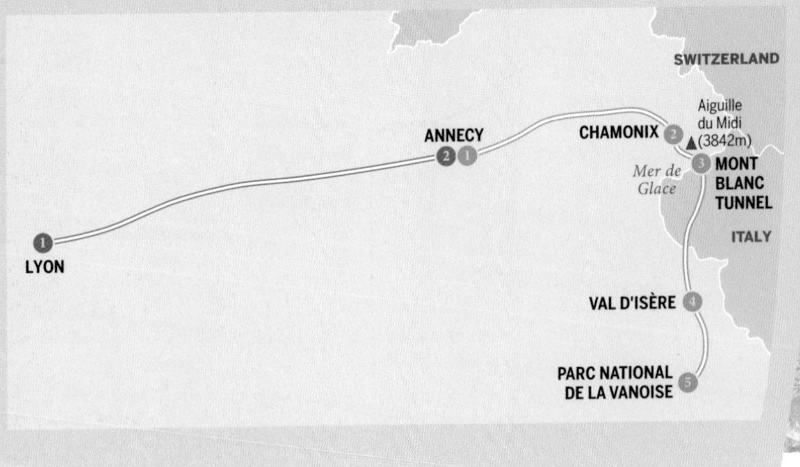

3 DAYS

LYON TO ANNECY

Big City, Little City

No city demands a weekend getaway more than **(1) Lyon**, a place most travellers arrive in unexpectedly, are pleasantly surprised by and yearn to return to.

You'll need at least a couple of days to do it justice. Devote the first to exploring the Presqu'île and Vieux Lyon, and allow a leisurely couple of hours for that quintessential long French lunch in a homely Lyonnais *bouchon* such as Les Adrets.

With downtown Lyon under your belt, day two's for exploring further afield. Delve into the city's insider heart in Croix Rousse, with its lush morning market, mysterious maze of *traboules* (secret passages) and vibrant cafe life. In the afternoon catch the funicular to Fourvière for a peek at the Roman ruins and the basilica, before descending back to the old town for an alfresco drink on one of the city's grand squares. Reward yourself with dinner at Mère Brazier.

On day three, quit the big city for the altogether more-tranquil setting of **(2) Annecy**, a chic lakeside town with a sparkling lake to swim in and another beautiful old town to get lost in.

ANNECY TO PARC NACIONAL DE LA VANOIS

Alpine Adventures

(1) Annecy makes the ideal springboard for venturing into the spectacular peaks and valleys of the French Alps. In winter it's France's main playground for skiers and snowboarders, come summer it's a paradise for hikers and mountain-bikers. The following trip traverses some high Alpine passes, so it's a summer-only adventure.

From Annecy, head straight for the source – **(2) Chamonix**, one of Europe's top spots for mountain sports. Don't miss the *télécabine* up to the Aiguille du Midi, where you can enjoy a high-altitude lunch with views over Mont Blanc. Another key Chamonix sight is the Mer de Glace (the 'Sea of Ice'), where you can step inside an ice cave that has to be recarved every year due to the movement of the glacier.

After a couple of days of activities in Chamonix, head out of town via the **(3) Mont Blanc tunnel**. Detour briefly into Italy before crossing back into France en route to **(4) Val d'Isère**, another of the Alps' classic mountain resorts. To the south sprawls **(5) Parc Nacional de la Vanois**, where you can spend the remainder of your trip strolling wildflower-laced trails and spotting wildlife.

Skiers on Val d'Isère (p247)

Lyon & the French Alps

At a Glance

- **Lyon** (p230) Grand old Roman city, France's third-largest, with Unesco-listed old town, majestic monuments and a gastronomy to die for.
- **French Alps** (p240) High in altitude and attitude, this is France's world-class outdoor playground where skiers, hikers, summer strollers and nature lovers flock like bees to a honeypot.

Canal du Thiou, Annecy (p246)

LYON

POP 487,980

Commercial, industrial and banking powerhouse for the past 500 years, today Lyon is France's third-largest city.

Outstanding museums, a dynamic cultural life, busy clubbing and drinking scene, thriving university and fantastic shopping lend the city a distinctly sophisticated air, while adventurous gourmets can indulge in their wildest gastronomic fantasies.

Sights

The **Lyon City Card** covers admission to every Lyon museum and the roof of Basilique Notre Dame de Fourvière, as well as guided city tours, a river excursion (April to October) and discounts on other selected attractions, exhibitions and shops. The card also includes unlimited travel on buses, trams, the funicular and metro. Buy it online (www.en.lyon-france.com/Lyon-City-Card), from the tourist office, or at some hotels.

Vieux Lyon

Lyon's Unesco-listed old town, with its narrow streets and medieval and Renaissance houses, is divided into three quarters: St-Paul (north), St-Jean (middle) and St-Georges (south).

CATHÉDRALE ST-JEAN Cathedral

(place St-Jean, 5e; 8am-noon & 2-7pm; M Vieux Lyon) This partly Romanesque cathedral, seat of Lyon's 133rd bishop, was built between the late 11th and early 16th centuries. The portals of its Flamboyant

Gothic façade, completed in 1480, are decorated with 280 square stone medallions. Don't miss the **astronomical clock** in the north transept chiming at noon, 2pm, 3pm and 4pm daily.

MEDIEVAL & RENAISSANCE ARCHITECTURE Architecture

(M Vieux Lyon) Lovely old buildings line rue du Bœuf, rue St-Jean and rue des Trois Maries. Crane your neck upwards to see gargoyles and other cheeky stone characters carved on window ledges along rue Juiverie, home to Lyon's Jewish community in the Middle Ages.

MUSÉES GADAGNE Museums

(www.museegadagne.com; 1 place du Petit Collège, 5e; single museum adult/child €6/free, both museums €8/free; 11am-6.30pm Wed-Sun; M Vieux Lyon) Housed in a 16th-century mansion built for two rich Florentine bankers, this twin-themed exhibition space incorporates an excellent local history museum (Musée d'Histoire de Lyon) chronicling the city's layout as its silk-weaving, cinema and transportation evolved, and an international puppet museum (Musée des Marionettes du Monde) paying homage to Lyon's iconic puppet, Guignol. On the 4th floor, a cafe adjoins tranquil, terraced gardens, here since the 14th century and laid out two centuries later.

Presqu'île

Lyon's city centre lies on this 500m- to 800m-wide peninsula bounded by the rivers Rhône and Saône.

MUSÉE DES BEAUX-ARTS Art Museum

(www.mba-lyon.fr; 20 place des Terreaux, 1er; adult/child incl audioguide €7/free; 10am-6pm Wed, Thu & Sat-Mon, 10.30am-6pm Fri; M Hôtel de Ville) This stunning and eminently manageable museum showcases France's finest collection of sculptures and paintings outside Paris from antiquity on. Highlights include works by Rodin, Rubens, Rembrandt, Monet, Matisse and Picasso. Pick up a free audioguide and be sure to stop for a drink or meal on the delightful stone terrace off its **cafe-restaurant** or take time out in its tranquil **cloister garden**.

PLACE DES TERREAUX City Square

(M Hôtel de Ville) The centrepiece of the Presqu'île's beautiful central square is a 19th-century **fountain** made of 21 tonnes of lead and sculpted by Frédéric-Auguste Bartholdi (of *Statue of Liberty* fame). The four horses pulling the chariot symbolise rivers galloping seawards. The **Hôtel de Ville** (Town Hall; M Hôtel de Ville) fronting the square was built in 1655 but given its present ornate façade in 1702. When Daniel Buren's polka-dot 'forest' of 69 **granite fountains** (embedded in the ground across much of the square) are on, join the kids in a mad dash as the water dances up, down, disappears for a second and gushes back again.

OPÉRA DE LYON Opera House

(M Hôtel de Ville) Lyon's neoclassical 1831-built opera house was modernised in 1993 by renowned French architect Jean Nouvel, who added the striking semi-cylindrical glass-domed roof. On its northern side, boarders and bladers buzz around the fountains of **place Louis Pradel**, surveyed by the **Homme de la Liberté** (Man of Freedom) on roller skates, sculpted from scrap metal by Marseille-born César.

MUSÉE DES TISSUS Silk Museum

(www.musee-des-tissus.com; 34 rue de la Charité, 2e; adult/child €10/7.50, after 4pm €8/5.50; 10am-5.30pm Tue-Sun; M Ampère) Extraordinary Lyonnais and international silks are showcased here. Ticket includes admission to the adjoining **Musée des Arts Décoratifs** (10am-noon & 2-5.30pm Tue-Sun), which displays 18th-century furniture, tapestries, wallpaper, ceramics and silver.

Croix Rousse

Independent until it became part of Lyon in 1852, and retaining its own distinct character with its bohemian inhabitants and lush outdoor food market, the hilltop quarter of Croix Rousse slinks north up the steep *pentes* (slopes).

Following the introduction of the mechanical Jacquard loom in 1805, Lyonnais *canuts* (silk weavers) built tens

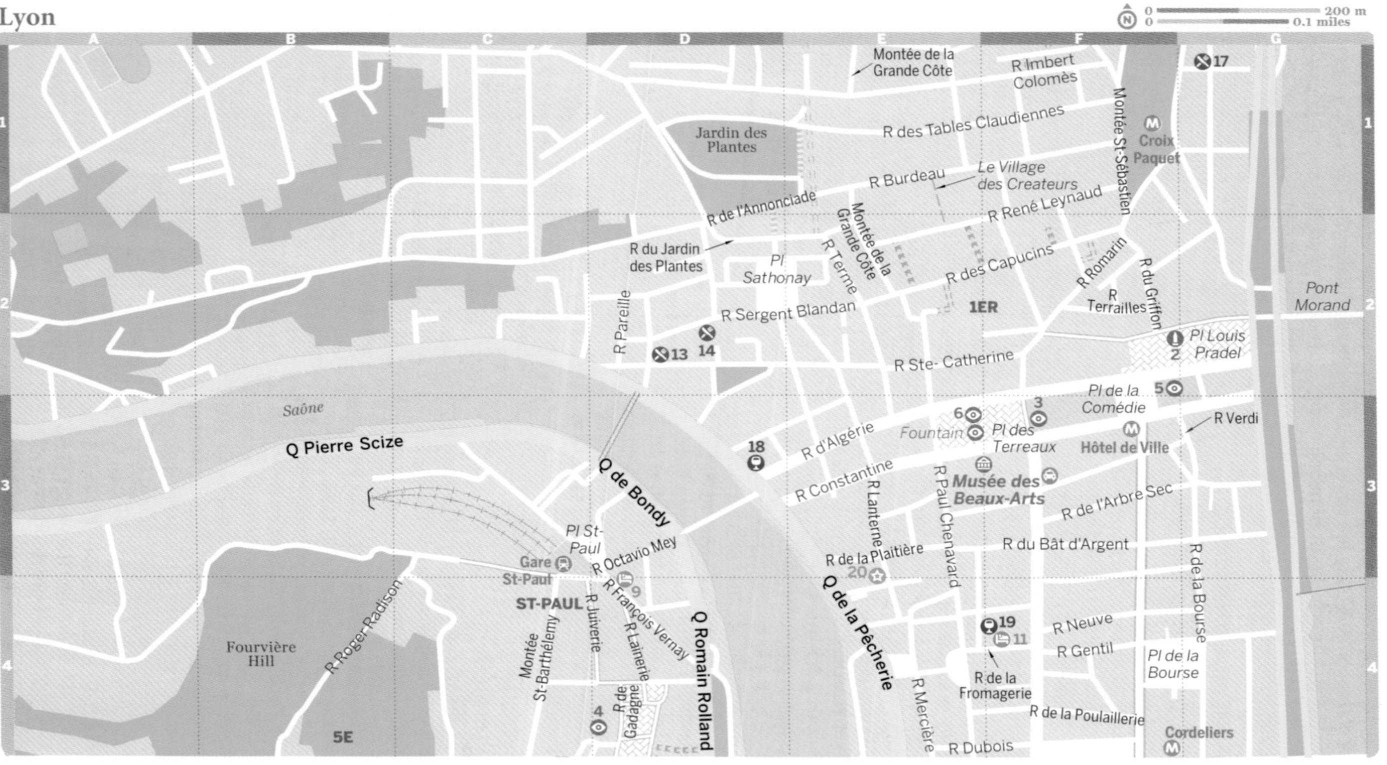
Lyon
0 200 m
0 0.1 miles
A
B
C
D
E
F
G
1
2
3
4
Montée de la Grande Côte
R Imbert Colomès
17
R des Tables Claudiennes
Montée St-Sébastien
Croix Paquet
Jardin des Plantes
R Burdeau
Le Village des Createurs
R de l'Annonciade
R René Leynaud
Montée de la Grande Côte
R du Jardin des Plantes
Pl Sathonay
R Terme
R des Capucins
R Romarin
R du Griffon
Pont Morand
R Terrailles
1ER
R Pareille
R Sergent Blandan
13
14
Pl Louis Pradel
2
R Ste- Catherine
Pl de la Comédie
5
3
6
R Verdi
Saône
Fountain
Pl des Terreaux
Hôtel de Ville
Q Pierre Scize
18
R d'Algérie
Q de Bondy
R Constantine
Musée des Beaux-Arts
R Lanterne
R Paul Chenavard
R de l'Arbre Sec
Pl St-Paul
R Octavio Mey
R du Bât d'Argent
Gare St-Paul
9
R de la Plaitière
20
R de la Bourse
ST-PAUL
R François Vernay
Q de la Pêcherie
R Juiverie
R Lainerie
Q Romain Rolland
19
R Neuve
11
Fourvière Hill
R Roger Radisson
R Gentil
Montée St-Barthélemy
Pl de la Bourse
R de la Fromagerie
R de Gadagne
R Mercière
R de la Poulaillerie
4
5E
Cordeliers
R Dubois

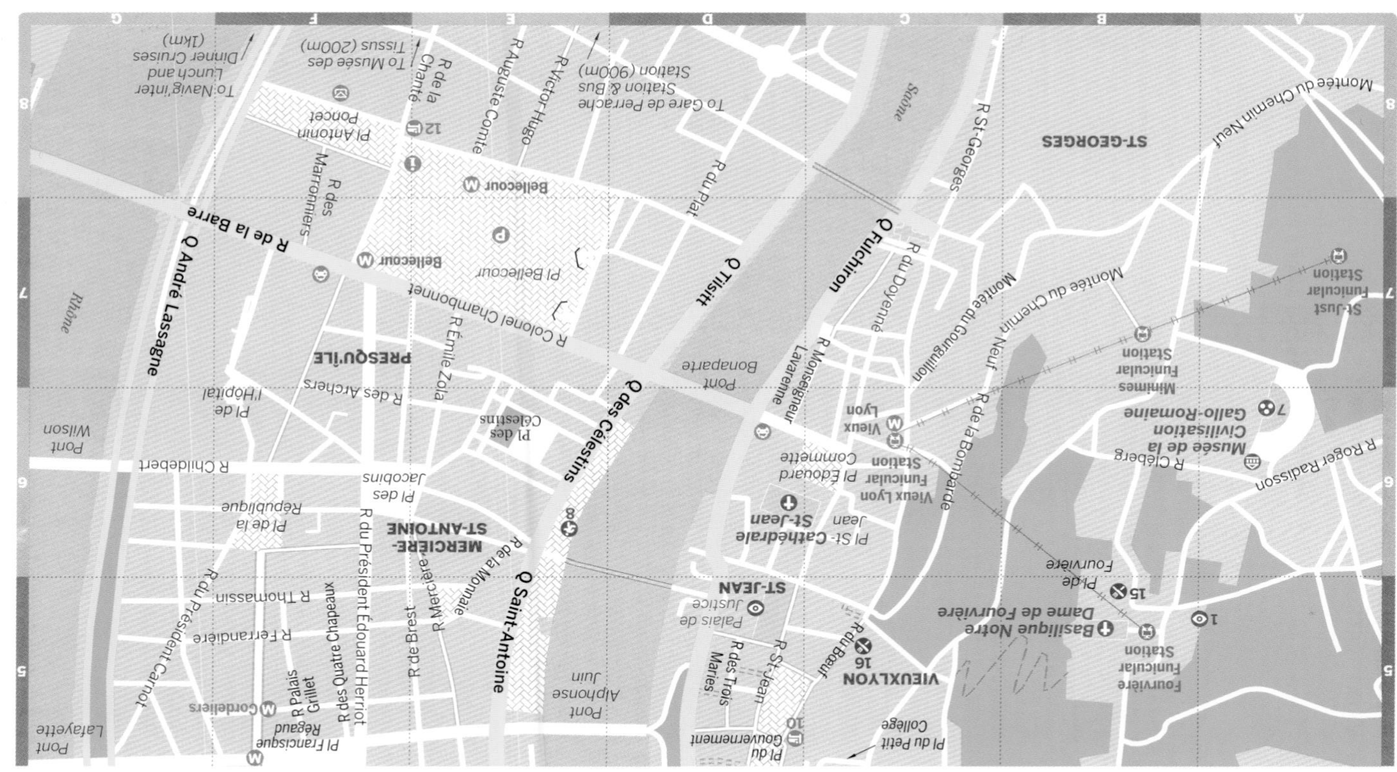
Pont Lafayette
Pont Wilson
Rhône
Saône
Q André Lassagne
R de la Barre
R du Président Carnot
Pl Francisque Régaud
Cordeliers
R Palais Grillet
R des Quatre Chapeaux
R du Président Édouard Herriot
R Ferrandière
R Thomassin
Pl de la République
R Childebert
Pl de l'Hôpital
R des Archers
PRESQU'ÎLE
R des Marronniers
Pl Antonin Poncet
To Navig'inter Lunch and Dinner Cruises (1km)
To Musée des Tissus (200m)
R de la Charité
12
R Auguste Comte
R Victor Hugo
To Gare de Perrache Station & Bus Station (900m)
Bellecour
Pl Bellecour
R Colonel Chambonnet
R Émile Zola
Pl des Jacobins
Pl des Célestins
R de Brest
R Mercière
MERCIÈRE-ST-ANTOINE
R de la Monnaie
Q Saint-Antoine
8
Q des Célestins
Pont Alphonse Juin
Pont Bonaparte
Q Tilsitt
R du Plat
Q Fulchiron
R du Doyenné
R Monseigneur Lavarenne
R St-Georges
ST-GEORGES
Pl du Gouvernement
10
R St-Jean
R des Trois Maries
Palais de Justice
ST-JEAN
Pl St-Jean
Cathédrale St-Jean
Pl Édouard Commette
Vieux Lyon Funicular Station
Vieux Lyon
Pl du Petit Collège
VIEUXLYON
R du Bœuf
16
Basilique Notre Dame de Fourvière
Pl de Fourvière
15
R de la Bombarde
Montée du Gourguillon
Montée du Chemin Neuf
Fourvière Funicular Station
1
R Cléberg
Musée de la Civilisation Gallo-Romaine
7
Minimes Funicular Station
R Roger Radisson
St-Just Funicular Station
A
B
C
D
E
F
G
5
6
7
8

Lyon

Top Sights

Sights

Activities, Courses & Tours

Sleeping

Eating

Drinking

Entertainment

of thousands of workshops in the area, with large windows to let in light and hefty wood-beamed ceilings more than 4m high to accommodate the huge new machines. Most workshops are chic loft apartments today.

MAISON DES CANUTS Silk Workshop

(www.maisondescanuts.com; 10-12 rue d'Ivry, 4e; adult/child €6.50/3.50; 10am-6pm Mon-Sat, guided tours 11am & 3.30pm; M Croix Rousse) On a guided tour, learn about weavers' labour-intensive life and the industry's evolution and see manual looms in use. You can also browse its silk boutique.

ATELIER DE PASSEMENTERIE Silk Workshop

(04 78 27 17 13; www.soierie-vivante.asso.fr; 21 rue Richan, 4e; guided tour adult/child €5/3; boutique 2-6.30pm Tue, 9am-noon & 2-6.30pm Wed-Sat, guided tours & demonstrations 2pm & 4pm Tue-Sat; M Croix Rousse) Trimmings workshop that functioned until 1979, weaving braids and intricate pictures. You can browse fabrics in the attached boutique (admission free), but to learn the history of the looms and see them at work it's well worth signing up for one of the half-hour afternoon tours.

Rive Gauche

MUSÉE LUMIÈRE Film Museum

(www.institut-lumiere.org; 25 rue du Premier Film, 8e; adult/child €6.50/5.50; 10am-6.30pm Tue-Sun; M Monplaisir-Lumière) Cinema's glorious beginnings are showcased at the art nouveau home of Antoine Lumière, who moved to Lyon with sons Auguste and Louis in 1870. The brothers shot the first reels of the world's first motion picture, *La Sortie des Usines Lumières* (Exit of the Lumières Factories) here in one of their father's photographic factories in the grounds on 19 March 1895. The former factory is the Hangar du Premier Film cinema today.

PARC DE LA TÊTE D'OR Park

(www.loisirs-parcdelatetedor.com; blvd des Belges, 6e; 6am-11pm Apr-Sep, to 9pm Oct-Mar; 41, 47, M Masséna) Spanning 117 hectares, France's largest urban park was landscaped in the 1860s. It's graced by a lake (rent a rowing boat), botanic garden with greenhouses, rose garden, zoo and **puppet theatre** (**04 78 93 71 75; www.theatre-guignol.com**).

Buses 41 and 47 link the park with metro Part-Dieu.

MUSÉE D'ART CONTEMPORAIN Art Museum

(www.mac-lyon.com; 81 quai Charles de Gaulle, 6e; adult/child €8/free; 11am-6pm Wed-Fri, 10am-7pm Sat & Sun) Lyon's contemporary art museum mounts edgy temporary exhibitions and a rotating permanent collection of post-1960 art. It closes for up to a couple of months between exhibitions, so check to make sure something's on.

Tours

NAVIG'INTER Boat Tour

(04 78 42 96 81; www.naviginter.fr; 13bis quai Rambaud, 2e; M Bellecour or Vieux Lyon) From April to October, runs river excursions from its **dock** (3 quai des Célestins, 2e; adult/child €9.50/6.50; M Bellecour or Vieux Lyon) along the Saône. One free excursion is included with the Lyon City Card. Advance bookings are essential for its **lunch and dinner cruises** (23 quai Claude Bernard, 7e; transport €20-26 plus menus €27-35; M Ampère or Guillotière, T1), which leave from a separate dock on the Rhône.

LE GRAND TOUR Bus Tour

(04 78 56 32 39; www.lyonlegrandtour.com; adult 1-/2-day ticket €18/20, child 1 or 2 days €5, Lyon by Night adult/child €15/5; 10am-6.15pm Apr-Oct, to 5.15pm Nov-Mar) Hop-on, hop-off double-decker bus tours. On Saturday evenings in July and August, a Lyon by Night tour is also offered at 10pm.

Sleeping

The tourist-office-run **reservation office** (04 72 77 72 50; resa@lyon-france.com) offers a free booking service and good-value package deals. Slowly but stylishly, *chambres d'hôte* (B&Bs) are making headway; umbrella organisations include **B&B Lyon** (04 72 32 02 74; www.bb-lyon.com), **Chambres Lyon** (04 72 13 99 35; www.chambreslyon.com) and **Gîtes de France** (04 72 77 17 50; www.gites-de-france-rhone.com). Many hotels offer cheaper rates at weekends.

COUR DES LOGES Hotel €€€

(04 72 77 44 44; www.courdesloges.com; 2-8 rue du Bœuf, 5e; d/ste from €250/530; M Vieux Lyon) Four 14th- to 17th-century houses wrapped around a *traboule* with preserved features like Italianate loggias make this an exquisite place to stay. Individually designed rooms woo with Philippe Starck bathroom fittings and a bounty of antiques, while decadent facilities include a spa, an elegant restaurant (menus €75 to €95), swish cafe (mains €17 to €25) and cross-vaulted bar.

COLLÈGE HOTEL Hotel €€

(04 72 10 05 05; www.college-hotel.com; 5 place St-Paul, 5e; d €125-155; M Vieux Lyon or Hôtel de Ville) The ultrastark white-on-white minimalism of this hotel's guestrooms is quite startling (which is to

Fountain, Place des Terreaux (p231)
JEAN-PIERRE LESCOURRET/GETTY IMAGES ©

PICTURES COLOUR LIBRARY/ALAMY ©

Don't Miss Fourvière

Over two millennia ago, the Romans built the city of Lugdunum on the slopes of Fourvière. Today it's topped by the **Tour Métallique**, an Eiffel Tower–like structure (minus its bottom two-thirds) built in 1893 and used as a TV transmitter. Crowning the hill – with stunning city panoramas from its terrace – is the 66m-long, 19m-wide and 27m-high **Basilica Notre Dame de Fourvière**, lined with intricate mosaics and a superb example of late-19th-century French ecclesiastical architecture. One-hour discovery visits take in the main features of the basilica and crypt; rooftop tours climax on the stone-sculpted roof.

The **Théâtre Romain**, built around 15 BC and enlarged in AD 120, sat an audience of 10,000. Romans held poetry readings and musical recitals in the smaller, adjacent odéon. Admire ancient artefacts found in Lugdunum and elsewhere in the Rhône Valley inside the city's nearby **Museé de la Civilisation Gallo-Romaine**.

Footpaths wind uphill but the funicular is the least taxing way up.

NEED TO KNOW

Basilica Notre Dame de Fourvière (www.fourviere.org; place de Fourvière, 5e; 8am-7pm; Fourvière funicular station); **Musée de la Civilisation Gallo-Romaine** (www.musees-gallo-romains.com; 17 rue Cléberg, 5e; adult/child €4/free, Thu free; 10am-6pm Tue-Sun; Fourvière funicular station); **Théâtre Romain** (rue Cléberg, 5e; Fourvière funicular station or Minimes funicular station); **Funicular** (place Édouard Commette, 5e; return €2.40)

say, not everyone will appreciate it). Enjoy breakfast on your balcony, on the rooftop garden terrace, or in the *salle de classe petit dejeuner*, bedecked like a classroom of yesteryear.

PÉNICHE BARNUM B&B **€€**
(06 63 64 37 39; www.peniche-barnum.com; 3 quai du Général Sarrail, 6e; d €120-150; ; **M** Foch) Moored on the Rhône between Pont Morand and the Passerelle du Collège footbridge, Lyon's most unique B&B

is this navy-and-timber barge with two smart en suite guestrooms, a book-filled lounge, and a shaded terrace up on deck. Organic breakfasts cost €10.

LE ROYAL Hotel **€€€**

(**☎04 78 37 57 31; www.lyonhotel-leroyal.com; 20 place Bellecour, 2e; d €200-390; ❄@📶; Ⓜ Bellecour)** In business since 1895, this timeless visiting card offers Lyon's ultimate in luxury, enveloping you in its stylish *salons* (lounges) and exquisite fabrics and furnishings. Rates vary wildly depending on dates and availability.

HÔTEL LE BOULEVARDIER Hotel **€**

(**☎04 78 28 48 22; www.leboulevardier.fr; 5 rue de la Fromagerie, 1er; s €47-56, d €49-59; 📶; Ⓜ Hôtel de Ville or Cordeliers)** Newly refurbished and sporting quirky touches like old skis and tennis racquets adorning the hallways, Le Boulevardier is a bargain 11-room hotel with snug, spotless rooms. It's up a steep spiral staircase above a cool little bistro and jazz club of the same name, which doubles as reception.

Eating

Cobbled rue Mercière, rue des Marronniers and the northern side of place Antonin Poncet – in the 2e – are chock-a-block with eating options (of widely varying quality), overflowing with pavement terraces in summer. Near the opera house, rue Verdi (1er) is likewise table filled.

LES ADRETS Lyonnais **€€**

(**☎04 78 38 24 30; 30 rue du Bœuf, 5e; lunch menu €15.50, dinner menus €23-45; ⏲lunch & dinner Mon-Fri; Ⓜ Vieux Lyon)** This atmospheric spot on a popular pedestrian thoroughfare serves some of Vieux Lyon's best food any time of day; the lunch *menus* (including wine and coffee) are especially good value at €15.50. The mix is half classic *bouchon* fare, half alternative choices like Parma ham and truffle risotto, or duck breast with roasted pears.

LE BOUCHON DES FILLES Lyonnais **€€**

(**☎04 78 30 40 44; 20 rue Sergent Blandan, 1er; menus €25; ⏲dinner daily, lunch Sun; Ⓜ Hôtel de Ville)** This contemporary ode to Lyon's legendary culinary *mères* (mothers) is run by an enterprising crew of young women with deep roots in the local *bouchon* scene. The light and fluffy quenelles are among the best you'll find in Lyon, and the rustic atmosphere is warm and welcoming, especially on Sundays when families flock in for lunch.

LE BISTROT DU POTAGER Tapas **€**

(**☎04 78 29 61 59; www.lebistrotdupotager.com; 3 rue de la Martinière, 1er; tapas €5-12; ⏲lunch & dinner Tue-Sat; Ⓜ Hôtel de Ville)** A newly hatched offshoot of the renowned Potager des Halles restaurant next door, this corner tapas bar is a dreamy place to while away a warm spring or summer evening. Throngs of happy diners linger over glasses of wine, sampling Provençal duck carpaccio, grilled vegetables with pistou, stuffed artichokes, octopus salad, Tunisian-style chickpeas and platters of cheeses and charcuterie.

LE RESTAURANT DE FOURVIÈRE Lyonnais **€€**

(**☎04 78 25 21 15; www.latassee.fr; 9 place de Fourvière, 5e; lunch menus €16, dinner menus €26-36; ⏲lunch & dinner daily; funicular station Fourvière)** The views are so incredible that it'd be easy for this superbly located restaurant to be a tourist trap, so it's all the more impressive because it's not. It concentrates on local specialities including a superb *salade lyonnaise* (lettuce, bacon, poached egg and croutons).

MÈRE BRAZIER Lyonnais **€€€**

(**☎04 78 23 17 20; www.lamerebrazier.fr; 12 rue Royale, 1er; lunch menus €41-45, dinner menus €67-130; ⏲lunch & dinner Mon-Fri, closed 3 weeks Aug & 1 week Feb; Ⓜ Croix Paquet or Hôtel de Ville)** Chef Mathieu Vianney has reinvented the mythical early-20th-century restaurant that earned Mère (Eugénie) Brazier Lyon's first trio of Michelin stars in 1933 (a copy of the original guidebook takes pride of place). Brazier was also the first chef to earn two sets of three Michelin stars, a feat only equalled decades later by Alain Ducasse. Vianney is doing admirable justice to Brazier's legacy, claiming two Michelin stars himself for his assured cuisine accompanied by an impressive wine list.

Drinking & Entertainment

Along the Rhône's left bank, a string of *péniches* (barges) with onboard bars rock until around 3am. Depending on the season you'll find upwards of a dozen moored along quai Victor Augagneur between Pont Lafayette in the north and Pont de la Guillotière in the south. Many have DJs and/or live bands.

LE WINE BAR D'À CÔTÉ Wine Bar
(www.cave-vin-lyon.com; 7 rue Pleney, 1er; Mon-Sat; M Cordeliers) Hidden in a tiny alleyway, this cultured wine bar feels like a rustic English gentlemen's club with leather sofa seating and library. It also doubles as a wine shop, selling local vintages in every bottle size imaginable.

LE VOXX Bar
(1 rue d'Algérie, 1er; 10am-3am daily; M Hôtel de Ville) Minimalist but lively riverside bar packed with a real mix of people, from students to city slickers.

HOT CLUB DE LYON Live Music
(www.hotclubjazz.com; 26 rue Lanterne, 1er; Tue-Sat; M Hôtel de Ville) Lyon's leading jazz club, around since 1948.

OPÉRA DE LYON Opera House
(www.opera-lyon.com; place de la Comédie, 1er; M Hôtel de Ville) Premier venue for opera, ballet and classical music.

Information

Tourist office (04 72 77 69 69; www.lyon-france.com; place Bellecour, 2e; 9am-6pm; M Bellecour)

Getting There & Away

Air

Lyon St-Exupéry Airport (www.lyon.aeroport.fr) is located 25km east of the city, serving 120 direct destinations across Europe and beyond.

Train

Lyon has two main-line train stations: Gare de la Part-Dieu (M Part-Dieu), 1.5km east of the Rhône, and Gare de Perrache (M Perrache).

Destinations by direct TGV include the following:

Dijon From €29, two hours, at least seven daily.

Lille-Europe From €90, three hours, at least 11 daily.

Marseille From €45, 1¾ hours, every 30 to 60 minutes.

Paris Gare de Lyon From €69, two hours, every 30 to 60 minutes.

Paris Charles de Gaulle Airport From €69, two hours, at least 11 daily.

Strasbourg €88, 3¾ hours, five daily

Getting Around

To/From the Airport

The Rhonexpress (www.rhonexpress.net) tramway links the airport with the Part-Dieu train station in under 30 minutes. It's a five- to 10-minute walk from the arrivals hall – follow the red signs with the Rhonexpress train logo. Trams depart approximately every 15 minutes between 6am and 9.30pm, and every 30 minutes from 5am to 6am and 9.30pm to midnight. One-way tickets cost €14 per adult, €11.50 for youths aged 12 to 25; kids under 12 are free.

By taxi, the 30- to 45-minute trip between the airport and the city centre costs around €45 during the day and €60 between 7pm and 7am.

Public Transport

Buses, trams, a four-line metro and two funiculars linking Vieux Lyon to Fourvière and St-Just are operated by TCL (www.tcl.fr), which has information offices dispensing transport maps adjacent to several metro stations throughout Lyon, including Bellecour, Croix Rousse, Hôtel de Ville, Part-Dieu, Perrache and Vieux Lyon. Public transport runs from around 5am to midnight.

Tickets valid for all forms of public transport cost a reasonable €1.60 (€14.30 for a *carnet* of 10) and are available from bus and tram drivers and also from machines at metro entrances. Tickets allowing unlimited travel for two hours after 9am cost €2.60, for all-day travel €4.90, and

MATZ SJÃ¶BERG/GETTY IMAGES ©

Don't Miss Lyon's Traboules

Deep within Vieux Lyon and Croix Rousse, dark, dingy *traboules* (secret passages) wind their way through apartment blocks, under streets and into courtyards. In all, 315 passages link 230 streets, with a combined length of 50km.

A couple of Vieux Lyon's *traboules* date from Roman times, but most were constructed by *canuts* (silk weavers) in the 19th century to transport silk in inclement weather. Resistance fighters found them equally handy during WWII.

Genuine *traboules* (derived from the Latin trans *ambulare*, meaning 'to pass through') cut from one street to another, often wending their way up fabulous spiral staircases en route. Passages that fan out into a courtyard or cul-de-sac aren't *traboules* but *miraboules* (two of the finest examples are at 16 du rue Bœuf and 8 rue Juiverie, both in Vieux Lyon).

Vieux Lyon's most celebrated *traboules* include those connecting 27 rue St-Jean with 6 rue des Trois Maries; 54 rue St-Jean with 27 rue du Bœuf (push the intercom button to buzz open the door); 10 quai Romain Rolland with 2 place du Gouvernement; 17 quai Romain Rolland with 9 rue des Trois Maries; and 31 rue du Bœuf with 14 rue de la Bombarde.

Step into Croix Rousse's underworld at 9 place Colbert, crossing cours des Voraces – renowned for its monumental staircase that zigzags up seven floors – and emerging at 29 rue Imbert Colomès. Others include those linking 1 place Colbert with 10 montée St-Sébastien and 9 place Colbert with 14bis montée St-Sébastien, and the plethora of passages on rue des Capucins – at Nos 3, 6, 13, 22 and 23.

Lyon's tourist office has more information and maps, and includes *traboules* on many of its guided walking tours.

NEED TO KNOW

Traboules – Guided Tour (begin at 27 rue du Bœuf, tours adult/student & child €9/€5)

a Ticket Liberté Soirée allowing unlimited travel after 7pm is €2.60. When purchasing tickets, make sure you bring coins as the machines don't accept notes (or some international credit cards). Remember to time-stamp your tickets on all forms of public transport or otherwise risk a fine from ticket inspectors.

THE FRENCH ALPS

The French Alps are a place of boundless natural beauty. We could rhapsodise about colossal peaks, wondrous white glaciers and sapphire lakes, but seeing really is believing when it comes to Europe's Alpine heartland. Schussing down slopes with Mont Blanc hogging the horizon, driving roller-coaster roads up to middle-of-nowhere Alpine passes, hiking to summits where mountain huts perch like eyries: this region will elevate you, make your heart pound and leave you crying 'encore!' like few other places on earth.

Chamonix

POP 9378 / ELEV 1037M

With the pearly white peaks of the Mont Blanc massif as its sensational backdrop, being an icon comes naturally to Chamonix. First 'discovered' by Brits William Windham and Richard Pococke in 1741, this is the mecca of mountaineering, its birthplace, its flag-bearer. It is also a wintertime playground of epic proportions that entices Olympic champions and hard-core skiers to its pistes, and party-mad boarders to its boot-stompin' bars.

Sights

LE BRÉVENT Viewpoint

The highest peak on the western side of the valley, Le Brévent (2525m) has tremendous views of the Mont Blanc massif, myriad hiking trails, ledges to paraglide from and summit restaurant Le Panoramic. Reach it with the **Télécabine du Brévent** (29 rte Henriette d'Angeville; adult/child return €26/22; 8.50am-4.45pm), from the end of rue de la Mollard, via midstation **Planpraz** (2000m).

MER DE GLACE Glacier

France's largest glacier, the glistening 200m-deep Mer de Glace (Sea of Ice) snakes 7km through mighty rock spires and turrets; it was named by Englishman

Mer de Glace

JASON'S TRAVEL PHOTOGRAPHY/GETTY IMAGES ©

Detour: Pérouges

French-film buffs will recognise photogenic Pérouges. Situated on a hill 30km northeast of Lyon, this enchanting yellow-stone medieval village has long been used as a set for films such as *Les Trois Mousquetaires* (The Three Musketeers). Brave the summertime crowds and stroll Pérouges' uneven cobbled alleys, admire its half-timbered stone houses and 1792-planted **liberty tree** on place de la Halle, then wolf down some *galettes de Pérouges* (warm, thin-pizza-crust-style, sugar-crusted tarts) with cider.

To appreciate Pérouges' charm after the day-trippers have left, book a romantic room (try for one with a canopied bed) at the historic **Hostellerie de Pérouges** (04 74 61 00 88; www.hostelleriedeperouges.com; place du Tilleul; s €92-139, d €128-246), which also operates a respected **restaurant** (menus €38-65).

Pérouges' tiny **tourist office** (04 74 46 70 84; www.perouges.org; 10am-noon & 2-5pm Mon-Fri, 2-5pm Sat & Sun) is on the main road opposite the village entrance.

Cars Philibert (04 78 98 56 00; www.philibert-transport.fr) bus 132 (€2, one hour) runs two to eight times daily from central Lyon to the Pérouges turnoff on route D4 (a 15-minute walk from the village).

William Windham, the first foreigner to set eyes on the glacier in 1741. The glacier moves up to 90m a year, and has become a popular attraction thanks to the rack-and-pinion railway line opened in 1908.

Wrap up warm to experience the **Grotte de la Mer de Glace** (late Dec-May & mid-Jun–Sep) ice cave, where frozen tunnels and ice sculptures change colour like mood rings.

A quaint red mountain train trundles up from **Gare du Montenvers** (35 place de la Mer de Glace; adult/child/family €26/22/79; 10am-4.30pm) in Chamonix to Montenvers (1913m), from where a cable car takes you down to the glacier and cave. Besides covering the 20-minute journey, the cable car and the ice cave, your ticket gets you entry into the **Galerie des Cristaux**, glittering with crystals from the Mont Blanc massif, and the new **Glaciorium**, spotlighting the birth, life and future of glaciers.

The Mer de Glace can be reached on foot via the Grand Balcon Nord trail from Plan de l'Aiguille. The two-hour uphill trail from Chamonix starts near the summer luge track. Traversing the crevassed glacier requires proper equipment and an experienced guide.

Activities

MAISON DE LA MONTAGNE Outdoor Activities

(190 place de l'Église; 8.30am-noon & 3-7pm) Get the Mont Blanc lowdown here, opposite the tourist office. Inside is the highly regarded **Compagnie des Guides de Chamonix** (04 50 53 00 88; www.chamonix-guides.com); the **École de Ski Français** (ESF; 04 50 53 22 57; www.esfchamonix.com); and the **Office de Haute Montagne** (OHM; 04 50 53 22 08; www.ohm-chamonix.com), which has information on trails, hiking conditions, weather forecasts and *refuges*, and topoguides and maps that are free to consult.

Winter

LA VALLÉE BLANCHE Skiing

(guided trips per person/group of 4 €75/290) This mythical descent is *the* off-piste ride of a lifetime. A veritable obstacle course of a route, La Vallée Blanche takes four to five hours, leading from Aiguille du Midi

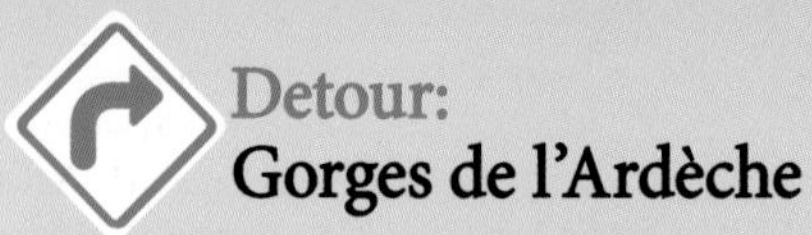

Detour: Gorges de l'Ardèche

The Ardèche River slithers between mauve, yellow and grey limestone cliffs from near **Vallon Pont d'Arc** (population 2420) to **St-Martin de l'Ardèche** (population 910), a few kilometres west of the Rhône. En route, it passes beneath the **Pont d'Arc**, a natural stone bridge created by the river's torrents. The river forms the centrepiece of the 1575-hectare **Réserve Naturelle des Gorges de l'Ardèche** (www.gorgesdelardeche.fr/reserve-naturelle.php). Eagles nest in the cliffs and there are numerous caves to explore.

Souvenir-shop-filled Vallon Pont d'Arc is the area's main hub; its **tourist office** (04 75 88 04 01; www.vallon-pont-darc.com; 1 place de l'Ancienne Gare; 9am-12.15pm & 1.30-6pm Mon-Fri, to 5pm Sat) is in the village centre. The scenic D579 out along the gorges is lined by campgrounds and canoeing rental outlets, including the **Base Nautique du Pont d'Arc** (04 75 37 17 79; www.canoe-ardeche.com; rte des Gorges de l'Ardèche; Apr-Nov). A half-day descent (8km) starts from €16/11 per adult/child (minimum age is seven).

About 300m above the gorge's waters, the **Haute Corniche** (D290) has a dizzying series of *belvédères* (panoramic viewpoints). About halfway between St-Martin and Vallon Pont d'Arc, the **Maison de la Réserve** (04 75 98 77 31; www.gorgesdelardeche.fr; D290) provides information on local flora, fauna and recreational opportunities. A further 2km west along the D290 is the trailhead for the **Sentier Aval des Gorges**, which descends 2km to the river, then follows the gorge for another 10km.

over the crevasse-riddled Mer de Glace glacier and back through forest to Chamonix, covering 2800m of jaw-dropping vertical. Because of the obvious risks, it must *only* be tackled with a guide (guides can take a maximum of eight people in a group – add an extra €20 per additional person to the price above). Snowboarders require an even better level than skiers. Snow coverage is generally best in February and March.

Summer

LAC BLANC Walking

From the top of **Les Praz l'Index Télépherique** (cable car; one-way/return €20/24) or **La Flégère** (one-way/return €12/14), the line's midway point, gentle 1¼- to two-hour trails lead to 2352m Lac Blanc (literally 'White Lake'), a turquoise-coloured lake surrounded by mountains. Stargazers can overnight at the **Refuge du Lac Blanc** (04 50 47 24 49; dm incl half board €49; mid-Jun–Sep), a wooden chalet favoured by photographers for its top-of-Europe Mont Blanc views.

CHAM' AVENTURE Water Sports

(04 50 53 55 70; www.cham-aventure.com; Maison de la Montagne, 190 place de l'Église) Thrill-seekers go in for canyoning (half/full day €68/100 per person), rafting (€38/135 for two hours/day) and hydrospeeding (€48/135 for two hours/day) on Chamonix' River Arve and the Dora Baltea in neighbouring Italy.

CYCLING TRAILS Cycling

Lower-altitude trails like the Petit Balcon Sud (250m) from Argentière to Servoz are perfect for biking. Most outdoor-activity specialists arrange guided mountain-biking expeditions.

PARAGLIDING Paragliding

Come summer, the sky above Chamonix is dotted with paragliders wheeling down from the heights. Tandem flights from Planpraz (2000m) cost €100 per person

(€225 from the Aiguille du Midi). Paragliding schools include **Summits** (☎04 50 53 50 14; www.summits.fr; 81 rue Joseph Vallot) and **AirSports Chamonix** (☎06 76 90 03 70; www.airsportschamonix.fr; 24 ave de la Plage).

Sleeping

AUBERGE DU MANOIR Hotel **€€**
(☎04 50 53 10 77; http://aubergedumanoir.com; 8 rte du Bouchet; s €109-122, d €126-176, q €178;) This beautifully converted farmhouse is ablaze with geraniums in summer. Auberge du Manoir ticks all the perfect Alpine chalet boxes: pristine mountain views, pine-panelled rooms that are quaint but never cloying, an outdoor hot tub for unwinding tired muscles and a bar where an open fire keeps things cosy. Breakfast is a treat, with fresh fruit, homemade yoghurt, cakes and tarts.

HOTEL L'OUSTALET Hotel **€€**
(☎04 50 55 54 99; www.hotel-oustalet.com; 330 rue du Lyret; d/q €148/190;) You'll pray for snow at this Alpine chalet near the Aiguille du Midi cable car, just so you can curl up by the fire with a *chocolat chaud* and unwind in the sauna and whirlpool. The rooms, including family ones, are snugly decorated in solid pine and open onto balconies with Mont Blanc views. There's a pool in the garden for chilling out during the summertime.

HÔTEL FAUCIGNY Boutique Hotel **€€**
(☎04 50 53 01 17; www.hotelfaucigny-chamonix.com; 118 place de l'Église; s/d/q €90/120/170;) This bijou hotel is a slice of minimalist Alpine cool, with its charcoal-white rooms and slate-walled spa. Your hosts bend over backwards to please: free bike rental and afternoon tea, a summer terrace with Mont Blanc views, an open fire in winter – they've thought of everything. A whirlpool, sauna and an array of luscious treatments invite post-ski relaxation.

GRAND HÔTEL DES ALPES Historic Hotel **€€€**
(☎04 50 55 37 80; www.grandhoteldesalpes.com; 75 rue du Docteur Paccard; r €335-390, ste €585-755;) This grand old dame goes down in the chronicles of Chamonix history as one of the resort's first (built in 1840) and finest. The wood-panelled rooms exude timeless elegance. What distinguishes this hotel, however, is its friendliness: in winter a scrumptious cake buffet greets hungry skiers back from the slopes.

Eating

LES VIEILLES LUGES Traditional French **€€**
(☎06 84 42 37 00; www.lesvieillesluges.com; Les Houches; menus €20-35; lunch daily,

Lac Blanc

CHRISTIAN ASLUND/GETTY IMAGES ©

Don't Miss Aiguille du Midi

A jagged needle of rock rearing above glaciers, snowfields and rocky crags, 8km from the hump of Mont Blanc, the Aiguille du Midi (3842m) is one of Chamonix' most distinctive landmarks. If you can handle the height, the 360-degree views of the French, Swiss and Italian Alps from the summit are (quite literally) breathtaking.

Year-round the vertiginous **Télépherique de l'Aiguille du Midi** cable car links Chamonix with the Aiguille du Midi. Halfway up, Plan de l'Aiguille (2317m) is a terrific place to start hikes or paraglide. In summer you'll need to obtain a boarding card (marked with the number of your departing and returning cable car) in addition to a ticket. Bring warm clothes, as even in summer the temperature rarely rises above -10°C at the top.

From the Aiguille du Midi, between late June and early September, you can continue for a further 30 minutes of mind-blowing scenery – think suspended glaciers and spurs, seracs and shimmering ice fields – in the smaller bubbles of the **Télécabine Panoramic Mont Blanc** to Pointe Helbronner (3466m) on the French-Italian border. From here another cable car descends to the Italian ski resort of Courmayeur.

NEED TO KNOW

Télépherique de l'Aiguille du Midi (place de l'Aiguille du Midi; adult/child return to Aiguille du Midi €46/39, Plan de l'Aiguille €26/22; 🕗8.30am-4.30pm); **Télécabine Panoramic Mont Blanc** (adult/child return from Chamonix €70/59; 🕗8.30am-3.30pm)

dinner by reservation) Like a scene from a snow globe in winter, this childhood dream of a 250-year-old farmhouse can only be reached by slipping on skis or taking a scenic 20-minute hike from the Maison Neuve chairlift. Under low wood beams, Julie and Claude spoil you with their home cooking – dishes such as *grand-mère*'s bœuf bourguignon and creamy *farçon* (a potato bake prepared with prunes, bacon and cream), all washed down with *vin chaud* (mulled wine) warmed over a wood fire. Magic.

LA PETITE KITCHEN International €
(80 place du Poilu; 2-course lunch menus €12.50, mains €18-28; ⏱lunch & dinner Wed-Mon) The little kitchen is just that: a handful of tables for the lucky few who get to indulge in its locally sourced food. English breakfasts, steaks with homemade *frites* (hot chips) and the stickiest of toffee puddings will send you rolling happily out the door.

LE BISTROT Gastronomic €€€
(☎04 50 53 57 64; www.lebistrotchamonix.com; 151 av de l'Aiguille du Midi; lunch menus €17-28, dinner menus €50-85; ⏱lunch & dinner) Sleek and monochromatic, this is a real foodie's place. Michelin-starred chef Mickey creates taste sensations such as pan-seared Arctic char with chestnuts, and warm chocolate macaroon with raspberry and red pepper coulis.

Drinking & Entertainment

CHAMBRE NEUF Bar
(272 av Michel Croz; ⏱daily; 📶) Cover bands, raucous après-ski drinking and dancing on the tables make Chambre Neuf one of Chamonix' liveliest party haunts. Conversations about epic off-pistes and monster jumps that are, like, totally mental, man, dominate.

MBC Microbrewery
(www.mbchx.com; 350 rte du Bouchet; ⏱4pm-2am) This trendy microbrewery run by four Canadians is fab. Be it with its burgers, cheesecake of the week, live music or amazing locally brewed and named beers (Blonde de Chamonix, Stout des Drus, Blanche des Guides etc), MBC delivers.

Information

Tourist office **(☎04 50 53 00 24; www.chamonix.com; 85 place du Triangle de l'Amitié; ⏱8.30am-7pm)**

Getting There & Away

BUS From the **Chamonix bus station** **(www.sat-montblanc.com; place de la Gare)**, located next to the train station, five buses run daily to/from Geneva airport and bus station (one-way/return €33/55, 1½ to two hours) and Courmayeur (one-way/return €13/20, 45 minutes). Advanced booking is required for both. See the website for timetables and reservations.

TRAIN The Mont Blanc Express narrow-gauge train trundles from St-Gervais-Le Fayet station, 23km west of Chamonix, to Martigny in Switzerland, stopping en route in Les Houches, Chamonix and Argentière. There are nine to 12 return trips daily between Chamonix and St-Gervais (€10, 45 minutes).

From St-Gervais-Le Fayet, there are trains to most major French cities.

Megève & St-Gervais

A Mont Blanc massif backdrop makes for fabulously scenic skiing and summertime hiking in très chic **Megève** (population 4076, elevation 1113m), a super-stylish and moneyed ski village for beginners and cruisy intermediates that was developed in the 1920s for Baroness de Rothschild (of the famous banking family) who, quite frankly darling, found Switzerland's overcrowded St-Moritz really rather tiresome. Almost too perfect to be true, the place is akin to a 3-D postcard of horse-drawn sleighs and exquisitely arranged boutique windows spilling into cobbled, medieval-style streets. For a gastronomic experience to remember, triple Michelin-starred **Flocons de Sel** **(☎04 50 21 49 99; www.floconsdesel.com; 1775 rte de Leutaz; lunch menus €39-77, dinner menus €147; ⏱lunch & dinner Thu-Mon)**, in a stylishly converted farmhouse, is the address.

Sitting snug below Mont Blanc, 24km west of Chamonix, neighbouring **St-Gervais-les-Bains** (population 5813, elevation 850m) is another picture-perfect Savoyard village with a baroque church and old-fashioned carousel. For spirit-soaring mountain views with zero effort, arrive here aboard the legendary **Mont Blanc Express** from Chamonix; or hop aboard France's highest train, the **Tramway du Mont Blanc** **(rue de la Gare, St-Gervais; return to Bellevue/Mont Lachat €28/31; ⏱9am-4.50pm)**, in St-Gervais-Le Fayet.

Information

Megève tourist office (04 50 21 27 28; www.megeve.com; 70 rue de Monseigneur Conseil; 9am-12.30pm & 2-6.30pm Mon-Sat)

St-Gervais tourist office (04 50 47 76 08; www.saintgervais.com; 43 rue du Mont-Blanc; 9am-12.30pm & 2-7pm Mon-Fri, 9am-7pm Sat & Sun

Getting There & Away

From Megève bus station, there are seven daily buses to/from St-Gervais-Le Fayet train station, the main train station for Chamonix: towns are linked by the Mont Blanc Express. Other services include several day trains to Paris (€97, 5½ hours) , Lyon (€34, 3½ hours), Annecy (€14.50, 1½ hours) and Geneva (€13, 1½ hours).

Annecy

POP 52,161

Even Savoyards spoilt rotten with Alpine views every day of their lives grow wistful at the mention of Annecy. Why? Just look around you: the mountains rise steep, wooded and snow-capped above Lac d'Annecy, so startlingly turquoise it looks unreal; the Vieille Ville (Old Town) is a ludicrously pretty ensemble of pastel-daubed, geranium-strewn houses; the turreted castle – wait, even the old prison – ticks all the medieval-fantasy boxes.

Sights

PALAIS DE L'ISLE Museum

(3 passage de l'Île; adult/child €3.50/1.50; 10.30am-6pm) Sitting on a triangular islet in the Canal du Thiou, the whimsically turreted, 12th-century Palais de l'Isle has been a lordly residence, courthouse, mint and prison (lucky inmates!) over the centuries. Today Annecy's most visible landmark hosts local-history displays.

VIEILLE VILLE & LAKEFRONT Historic Quarter

It's a pleasure simply to wander aimlessly around Annecy's medieval old town, a photogenic jumble of narrow streets, turquoise canals and colonnaded passageways. Continue down to the tree-fringed lakefront and the flowery **Jardins de l'Europe**, linked to the popular picnic spot **Champ de Mars** by the poetic iron arch of the **Pont des Amours** (Lovers' Bridge).

CHÂTEAU D'ANNECY Castle

(rampe du Château; adult/child €5/2.50; 10.30am-6pm) Rising dramatically above the old town, this perkily turreted castle was once home to the Counts of Geneva. The oldest part is the 12th-century Tour de la Reine (Queen's Tower). Its museum takes a romp through traditional Savoyard art, crafts and Alpine natural history.

Palais de L'Isle

MALCOLM PARK/GETTY IMAGES ©

Tours

TOWN TOURS Walking Tour
(per person €6; 4pm Tue & Thu) The tourist office organises guided tours of the old town; they are in French but some guides speak a little English. If you would prefer to go it alone, pick up the free *Annecy Town Walks* leaflet.

COMPAGNIE DES BATEAUX Boat Tour
(www.annecy-croisieres.com; 2 place aux Bois; 30min lake cruises €13-17; Feb–mid-Dec) Runs cruises departing from quai Bayreuth. Tickets are sold 15 minutes before departure. From May to September boats also sail across the lake to Menthon-St-Bernard (€5.50), Talloires (€7), Sévrier (€12) and other villages.

Sleeping

ANNECY HOSTEL Hostel €
(09 53 12 02 90; www.annecyhostel.fr; 32 av de Loverchy; dm/d €22/55;) Run by two well-travelled brothers, this newcomer makes backpackers' hearts sing with its bright and funky four-bed dorms, shared kitchen, chilled TV lounge and cheap bike rental. Best of all is the garden, perfect for summer games and barbecues. It's a five-minute walk southwest of the old town.

HÔTEL ALEXANDRA Hotel €
(04 50 52 84 33; www.hotelannecy-alexandra.fr; 19 rue Vaugelas; s/d/tr/q €55/75/95/110;) Nice surprise: Annecy's most charming hotel is also one of its most affordable. The welcome is five-star, rooms are fresh and spotless – the best have balconies and canal views – and breakfast (€8) is a generous spread with fresh pastries.

If You Like... Epic Skiing

Lift-pass expense and airport distance be damned, the French Alps is a land of infinite world-class pistes, of top-of-Europe elation. If you've caught the downhill bug in Chamonix, here's where else to go.

1 **TROIS VALLÉES**
Carve legendary slopes and party in the après-ski bars in the Three Valleys (elevation 1450m to 2300m; www.les3vallees.com), the world's largest ski area comprising **Val Thorens** (2300m), Europe's highest ski area; wealthy and ever-so-British **Méribel** (1450m); and ritzy **Courchevel** (1550m to 1850m).

2 **VAL D'ISÈRE**
(1850m; www.valdisere.com) It's not just roller-coaster Olympic runs at Val d'Isère. Equally known for its community spirit, this resort inspires everlasting love and loyalty. Along with nearby **Tignes** (2100m), it forms part of the **Espace Killy** skiing area.

3 **ALPE D'HUEZ**
Purpose-built Alpe d'Huez **(1860m; www.alpedhuez.com)** has 245km of groomed pistes, dead-easy to death-defying: 16km **La Sarenne** is Europe's longest black run.

4 **LES DEUX ALPES**
Year-round skiing on the **Glacier du Mont de Lans**, glorious powder, and a party atmosphere make Les Deux Alpes **(1600m; www.les2alps.com)** a resort with big air and big altitude. For the truly hardcore, there's the near-vertical **Vallons de la Meije** descent in La Grave, 21km east.

5 **LES PORTES DU SOLEIL**
'The Gates of the Sun' **(1000-2466m; www.portesdusoleil.com)** covers 12 villages along the French–Swiss border, including **Morzine** (1000m), with one of the most charming eat andsleep options in the Alps in the form of **The Farmhouse** **(04 50 79 08 26; www.thefarmhouse.fr; Le Mas de la Coutettaz, Morzine; d incl half board €208-400, dinner menus €40;)**; trendy and chic, car-free **Avoriaz** (1800m); and family-friendly, Brit-busy **Les Gets** (1172m).

If You Like... Hiking in Alpine Heaven

Have those tantalising glimpses in Lyon of a snow-glittering Mont Blanc far on the horizon left you craving glaciated grandeur close-up? Then dip into one of these spectacular national parks:

1 **PARC NACIONAL DE LA VANOIS** (www.parcnational-vanoise.fr) Rugged snowcapped peaks, mirrorlike lakes and vast glaciers are the tip of the iceberg in the 530-sq-km Parc Nacional de la Vanois, home to France's largest colony of Alpine ibexes.

2 **PARC NATUREL RÉGIONAL DU VERCORS** The gently rolling pastures, plateaux and chiselled limestone peaks of this 1750-sq-km park are perfect for soft adventure, making it a real family favourite. You can cross-country ski, snowshoe, cave and hike. From **Lans-en-Vercors** (1020m), 28km southwest of Grenoble, buses shuttle downhill skiers to the **Montagnes de Lans** ski area, with 30km of pistes.

3 **PARC NACIONAL DES ÉCRINS** (www.les-ecrins-parc-national.fr) No amount of hyperbole about towering peaks, shimmering cirque lakes and wispy falls does justice to France's second-largest national park, wedged between **Bourg d'Oisans**, 53km southeast of Grenoble, and **Briançon**, another 67km in the same direction. Age-old footpaths used by shepherds and smugglers centuries before – 700km in all – criss-cross the park and several vertiginous mountain passes make it a mountain-biking mecca. For further information visit **Maison du Parc** (rue Gambetta, Bourg d'Oisans; 9am-1pm & 2-5pm Mon-Thu, 9am-1pm Fri) in Bourg d'Oisans.

SPLENDID HÔTEL Boutique Hotel €€

(04 50 45 20 00; www.hotel-annecy-lac.fr; 4 quai Eustache Chappuis; s/d €109/121;) 'Splendid' certainly sums up the lakefront position of this hotel, with breezy views from its boutique-chic, parquet-floor rooms. It's geared up for families: whether you need an extra bed or a baby-sitter, the friendly staff will oblige.

Eating

The quays along Canal du Thiou are jam-packed with touristy cafes and pizzerias. Crêpes, kebabs, ice cream, pastries and classic French cuisine – you'll find it all along pedestrianised rue Carnot, rue Pâquier and rue Faubourg Ste-Claire.

L'ESQUISSE Regional Cuisine €€

(04 50 44 80 59; www.esquisse-annecy.fr; 21 rue Royale; lunch menus €19-22, dinner menus €29-60; lunch & dinner Mon-Tue & Thu-Sat) A talented husband-and-wife team run the show at this intimate bistro, with just six tables that fill predictably quickly. Their passion shines through in the service, wine list and, *bien sûr*, the food. The carefully composed menus sing with natural, integral flavours, from wild mushrooms to spider crab, and are presented with an eye for detail.

LE DENTI Bistro €€

(04 50 64 21 17; 25bis av de Loverchy; menus €18-31; lunch Thu-Tue, dinner Mon, Thu-Sat) Slightly off the beaten track but worth seeking out, this bistro has got a lot going for it: a loyal clientele, a midday buzz and a succinct menu of ingredient-focused dishes, from asparagus risotto to Atlantic cod with chorizo. The three-course lunch is a bargain at €18.

LA CIBOULETTE Gastronomic €€€

(04 50 45 74 57; www.laciboulette-annecy.com; 10 rue Vaugelas, cour du Pré Carré; menus €35-63; lunch & dinner Tue-Sat) Such class! Crisp white linen and gold-kissed walls set the scene at this Michelin-starred place, where chef Georges Paccard cooks fresh seasonal specialities, such as fillet of veal in a nut crust with cream of *vin jaune*, asparagus and potato-parmesan gnocchi. Reservations are essential.

Parc Nacional de la Vanois

JACQUES PIERRE/HEMIS.FR/GETTY IMAGES ©

LA NOUVELLE MAISON DE MARC VEYRAT Gastronomic **€€€**
(☎04 50 09 97 49; www.yoann-conte.com; 13 vieille rte des Pensières, Veyrier-du-Lac; menus €77-189, cooking classes with/without lunch €200/145; ⏰closed Mon, Tue, dinner Sun) At this Michelin-starred lakeside legend, French celebrity chef Marc Veyrat has handed over his stove, culinary flamboyance and signature use of wild herbs and flowers to his capable successor Yoann Conte. In Veyrier-du-Lac, 5km southeast of Annecy, the baby-blue house by the lake also has a handful of wonderful rooms (doubles €350-450). If you want to get behind the stove yourself, sign up for one of the morning cooking classes.

Information

Tourist office (☎04 50 45 00 33; www.lac-annecy.com; 1 rue Jean Jaurès, Centre Bonlieu; ⏰9am-6.30pm Mon-Sat, 9am-12.30pm & 1.45-6pm Sun)

Getting There & Away

Frequent services from Annecy's train station (place de la Gare):

Aix-les-Bains €7.50, 40 minutes

Chambéry €9.50, 50 minutes

St-Gervais €14.50, 1½ hours

Lyon €25, two hours

Paris Gare de Lyon €76, four hours

Bordeaux & French Basque Country

For wine aficionados, nowhere lights up the imagination quite like Bordeaux. For centuries this has been the undisputed heartland of French viticulture (winemaking), and the region is littered with some of the most illustrious names from the world of wine. But while the fruits of the vine are undoubtedly the main reason for a visit to the Bordeaux region, they're far from the only one.

South of Bordeaux, France's Atlantic Coast unfurls through a string of sandy beaches, sparkling bays and beautiful towns, all of which are worth a visit in their own right. There's Arcachon – famous for producing some of France's finest oysters – and Biarritz, a seaside getaway since the belle époque, now the centre of a thriving surf culture. And then there's the French Basque Country, a fiery and independent region that fizzes with a passion, energy and culture all of its own.

Cathédrale St-André (p264), Bordeaux
OLIVER STREWE/GETTY IMAGES ©

Bordeaux & French Basque Country

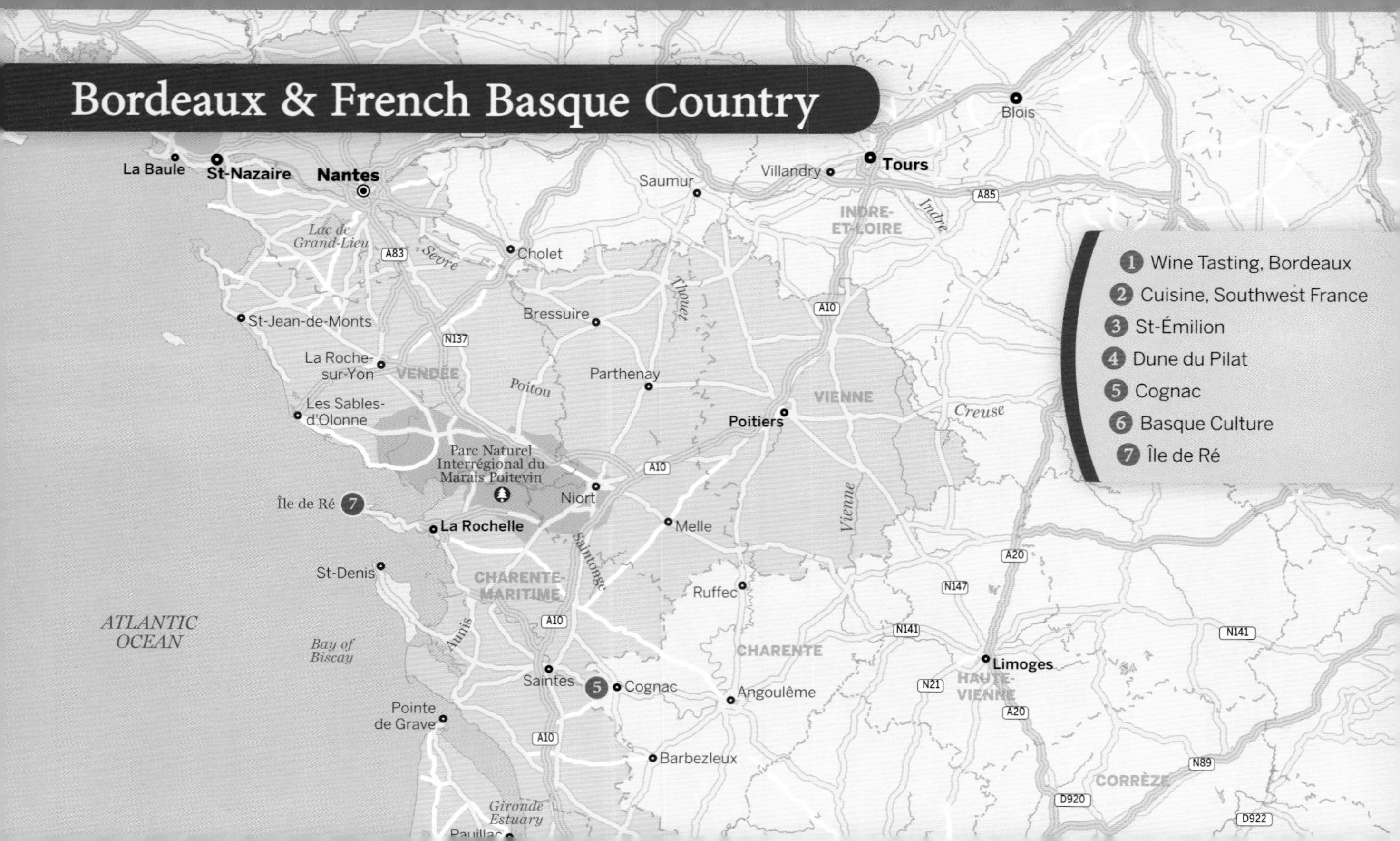

1. Wine Tasting, Bordeaux
2. Cuisine, Southwest France
3. St-Émilion
4. Dune du Pilat
5. Cognac
6. Basque Culture
7. Île de Ré

La Baule
St-Nazaire
Nantes
Saumur
Villandry
Tours
Blois
A85
INDRE-ET-LOIRE
Indre
Lac de Grand-Lieu
A83
Sèvre
Cholet
Thouet
A10
St-Jean-de-Monts
Bressuire
N137
La Roche-sur-Yon
VENDÉE
Poitou
Parthenay
VIENNE
Creuse
Les Sables-d'Olonne
Poitiers
Parc Naturel Interrégional du Marais Poitevin
A10
Niort
Île de Ré
La Rochelle
Melle
Vienne
Saintonge
St-Denis
CHARENTE-MARITIME
Ruffec
A20
N147
ATLANTIC OCEAN
Aunis
A10
N141
N141
Bay of Biscay
CHARENTE
Limoges
HAUTE-VIENNE
Saintes
Cognac
Angoulême
N21
A20
Pointe de Grave
A10
Barbezieux
N89
CORRÈZE
D920
Gironde Estuary
D922
Pauillac

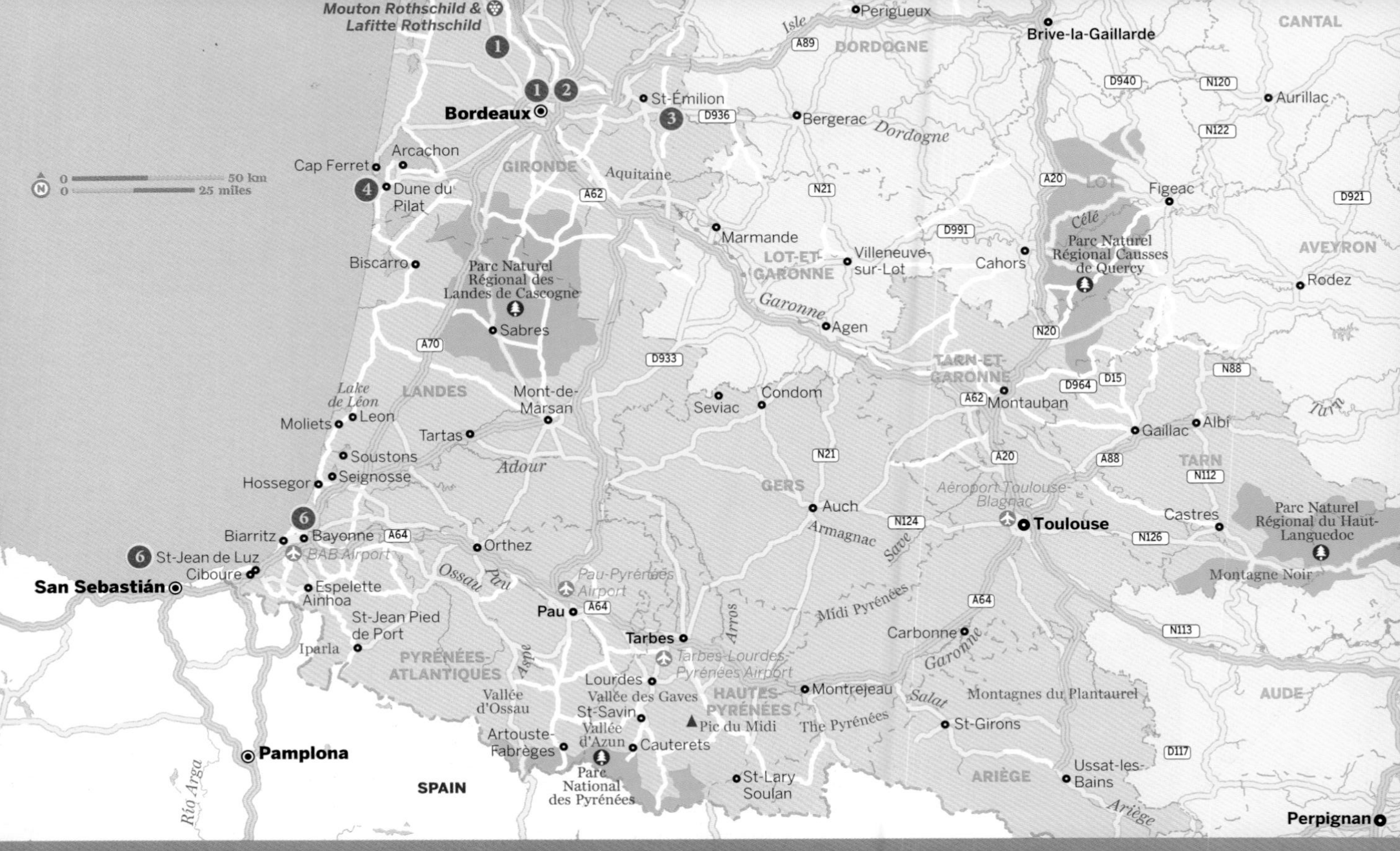
Mouton Rothschild &
Lafitte Rothschild
Perigueux
Brive-la-Gaillarde
CANTAL
Isle
DORDOGNE
Bordeaux
St-Émilion
Bergerac
Dordogne
Aurillac
Arcachon
Cap Ferret
GIRONDE
Aquitaine
Dune du
Pilat
LOT
Figeac
0 50 km
0 25 miles
Marmande
Céle
Parc Naturel
Régional Causses
de Quercy
Biscarro
LOT-ET-
GARONNE
Villeneuve-
sur-Lot
Cahors
AVEYRON
Rodez
Parc Naturel
Régional des
Landes de Cascogne
Garonne
Agen
Sabres
TARN-ET-
GARONNE
Lake
de Léon
LANDES
Mont-de-
Marsan
Seviac
Condom
Montauban
Tarn
Moliets
Leon
Tartas
Gaillac
Albi
Soustons
Adour
TARN
Hossegor
Seignosse
GERS
Aéroport Toulouse-
Blagnac
Auch
Armagnac
Save
Toulouse
Castres
Parc Naturel
Régional du Haut-
Languedoc
Biarritz
Bayonne
Orthez
St-Jean de Luz
BAB Airport
Ciboure
Ossau
Pau
Pau-Pyrénées
Airport
Montagne Noir
San Sebastián
Espelette
Ainhoa
Pau
Midi Pyrénées
St-Jean Pied
de Port
Tarbes
Arros
Carbonne
Iparla
PYRÉNÉES-
ATLANTIQUES
Aspe
Tarbes-Lourdes-
Pyrénées Airport
Garonne
Lourdes
Vallée des Gaves
HAUTES-
PYRÉNÉES
Montrejeau
Salat
Montagnes du Plantaurel
AUDE
Vallée
d'Ossau
St-Savin
Vallée
d'Azun
Pic du Midi
The Pyrénées
St-Girons
Artouste-
Fabrèges
Cauterets
Pamplona
Parc
National
des Pyrénées
St-Lary
Soulan
ARIÈGE
Ussat-les-
Bains
SPAIN
Río Arga
Ariège
Perpignan
A89
D940
N120
N122
D936
A20
D921
A62
N21
D991
N20
A70
D933
N88
D964
D15
A62
N21
A20
A88
N112
N124
N126
A64
A64
A64
N113
D117

Bordeaux & French Basque Country's Highlights

1 Bordeaux Wine Tasting

Every time I visit an estate I learn something different. As a writer and drinker I like the fact that Bordeaux is a combination of politics, history, geography and lots of big personalities who make the wine. As for taste, we are by the sea and the maritime influence gives the wine freshness, elegance.

Need to Know

RISING STARS Bordeaux whites, dry and brilliant **LEARN MORE** École du Vin (p268) **READ** New Bordeaux (www.newbordeaux.com) **For further coverage, see p268**

Local Knowledge

Bordeaux Wine Tasting Don't Miss List

BY JANE ANSON, RESIDENT WINE WRITER AND AUTHOR

1 WINE VILLAGES

Not to be missed: St-Émilion (p270), one of the most beautiful places on the Right Bank of the Dordogne River; and **Bages village**, just outside Pauillac (p267), on the Left Bank.

2 BOTH SIDES OF THE RIVER

Right Bank and Left Bank – such different personalities! Right-Bank properties tend to be smaller, more family-run, the type of place where the owner ends up showing you around. Wines are usually merlot-based, fruity, easy to drink. The Left Bank is more the dream châteaux you imagine: big properties with turrets and moats. Cabernet sauvignon is the main grape and wines are big, powerful.

3 GOING OFF THE BEATEN TRACK

Two Right-Bank places: **Fronsac**, only 10 minutes from St-Émilion but much quieter, is beautiful with plenty of lesser known châteaux to visit. Also on the Right Bank, the **Côtes de Bordeaux** (Castillon, Cadillac, Blaye and Francs) are beautiful, with lots of young winemakers to get to know.

4 CHÂTEAUX TASTINGS

Château Lynch-Bages (www.lynchbages.com) is one of the most famous Bordeaux châteaux, with an excellent tour. Further north, **Château Mouton Rothschild** (p267) is among the world's most famous châteaux and in 2013 it reopens its art gallery, which will be amazing. South of Bordeaux, **Château Smith Haut Lafitte** (www.smith-haut-lafitte.com) has a red-wine jacuzzi...

5 FAVOURITE PRODUCERS

So difficult! Right now, for red it is **Château Haut Bailly** (www.chateau-haut-bailly.com) and for white, **Château Olivier** (www.chateau-olivier.com) and **Domaine de Chevalier** (www.domainedechevalier.com), all in the Pessac–Léognan wine-growing area – one of the few parts of Bordeaux where you can get genuinely outstanding wines, capable of ageing, elegant and complex. And it's close to Bordeaux city centre, an easy day trip.

Bordelaise Cuisine

The best moment is when I catch the *bonheur* (happiness) in people's eyes as they are eating a particular dish. I was born in Blaye, 50km from Bordeaux, and my cuisine is *paysanne* (a country cuisine), using only the best products and traditional recipes from the southwest.

Need to Know

MARKETS Every village has a morning market weekly **COOKING LESSONS** With Nicolas Frion at' École de Cuisine au Chapon Fin (www.chapon-fin.com) **For further coverage see p265**

2

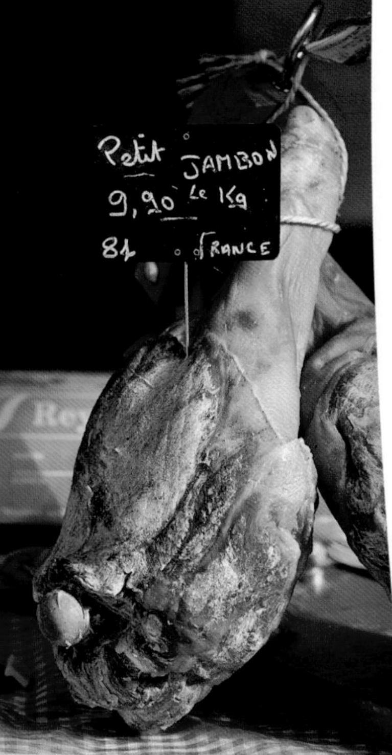

Local Knowledge

Bordelaise Cuisine Don't Miss List

BY JEAN-PIERRE XIRADAKI, CULINARY WRITER AND CELEBRITY RESTAURANT OWNER SINCE 1968

1 MARCHÉ DES CAPUCINS

Cuisine bordelaise (Bordeaux cuisine) originates from the south, from Basque-country women who came to work in the great Bordelaise houses. And the diversity of produce is enormous. We have river and sea fish, shellfish, oysters, fowl (duck and geese), lamb, beef, mushrooms, vegetables, poultry, truffles... We really have everything, although we miss cheese. I buy my produce from local producers and markets: Marché des Capucins (p267) and the twice-weekly market in Blaye (Wednesday and Saturday mornings).

2 CASSOULET, MACARONADE & EELS

I love *cassoulet*, typical to the rural southwest and traditionally eaten to celebrate; it's a heart-warming haricot bean stew with a few giblets, and a bit of sausage and pork thrown in. Then there's *macaronade aux cèpes et au foi gras*, fresh macaroni with local *cèpes* (boletus mushrooms), foie gras and cream. It is very rich, very delicious and demands a healthy appetite! *Lamproie à la Bordelaise* (eel-like lamprey), a migratory river fish cooked with wine and leeks, is very typical of our local cuisine.

3 LA SOUPE

In winter at La Tupina (p265) we always have a cauldron of soup cooking in the fireplace; the fire burns all day, just as it did at my grandparents'. We throw in cabbage, carrots, beans, a bit of duck or pork to give it taste and so on, just as peasants did centuries ago. For them it provided all the daily nutrition they needed – water, vegetables and a little meat.

4 WINE & OYSTERS

L'Essentiel (www.essentielthunevin.com) in St-Émilion is *the* place to taste wine and La Boîte à Huîtres (p267) in Bordeaux is the *dégustation* (tasting) address for oysters. Favourite wine producers include **Château Mayne Lalande** (www.lescinqsens-bordeaux.com) and **Château Lestage** (www.chateau-lestage.com), both 35km north of Bordeaux in Listrac.

St-Émilion

Perched on a limestone ridge 40km east of Bordeaux, the honey-hued town of St-Émilion (p270) is a must for wine connoisseurs. Surrounded by vines as far as the eye can see, it's also home to some of France's most hallowed châteaux – so it's a fantastic place to try and buy wines. But don't forget to leave time for a tour into the murky catacombs beneath the town's cathedral.

3

4 Dune du Pilat

This colossal sand dune (p273) stretches for almost 3km to the south of Arcachon and is still spreading eastwards at up to 4.5m a year (swallowing trees, roads and even a hotel in the process). Hum the theme tune from *Lawrence of Arabia* as you scale it for a memorable panorama over the Bassin d'Arcachon – it's the closest you'll get to the Sahara without leaving Europe.

PABLO NEGRI/GETTY IMAGES ©

5 Cognac

While Bordeaux is mainly known for its fine wines, it's not the region's only alcoholic tipple. The double-distilled spirit Cognac (p271) is produced according to a strict set of rules that have remained largely unchanged for the last three centuries. You can quaff it in musty cellars all around town, but at a minimum of 40% proof, you'll definitely need to name a designated driver...

MARTIN CHILD/GETTY ©

6 Basque Culture

A passion for bullfighting, *pelota* (ball games), peppers and spicy ham makes the French Basque Country (p272) feel closer to Spain than to the rest of France. Governed by its own culture, costumes and language, it's very much a region in its own right. The lively towns of Bayonne and St-Jean de Luz both make great bases for further exploration, situated within easy reach of the sparkling beaches of Biarritz.

7 Île de Ré

A delicious mix of island living, market meandering and salty-air cycling, Île de Ré (p274) is a west coast highlight. A secret no more, this little island (no more than 5km wide) is hugely popular for its quaint villages, fishing ports and beautiful beaches.

Bordeaux & French Basque Country's Best...

Cultural Highs

- **Musée des Beaux-Arts, Bordeaux** (p265) Enjoy one of France's finest fine-art museums.
- **St-Émilion rooftops** (p270) Slog up the bell tower for views of this hilltop hamlet.
- **St-Jean Pied de Port** (p280) Mingle with pilgrims following the way of St James through France to Spain.
- **Musée Basque et de l'Histoire de Bayonne** (p272) Devour Basque history and culture.
- **Lourdes** (p282) Take an icy dip in a sacred bath.

Culinary Shopping

- **La Winery** (p268) Groundbreaking winery with 1000 different Bordeaux wines.
- **St-Émilion** (p270) With one wine shop for every eight residents, wine shopping in St-Émilion is a breeze.
- **Bayonne** (p272) Shop for Bayonne's famous ham.
- **Cognac** (p271) Superb brandy to take home.

Beach Retreats

- **Biarritz** (p275) A classic beach resort since the belle époque, now the top surfer choice.
- **Arcachon** (p268) Sandy beaches pepper the beautiful Bassin d'Arcachon.
- **Île de Ré** (p274) Beautiful beaches lace the southern coast of this irresistible island.
- **St-Jean de Luz & Ciboure** (p278) Kick back on the golden sands of these twin Basque towns.

Seafood Dining

- **Marché des Capucins** (p267) Oysters and white wine equal a classic Bordeaux market experience.
- **La Boîte à Huîtres** (p267) Best place in Bordeaux for fresh Arcachon oysters and sausages.
- **Casa Juan Pedro** (p277) The Biarritz locals' tip for seafood, located in a fishing shack.
- **Grillerie du Port** (p280) Grilled sardines or tuna caught that morning in St-Jean de Luz.
- **Bistrot de Claude** (p271) Heady mix of oysters, seafood and Cognac.

Left: Vineyards around St Émilion (p270); **Above:** Biarritz (p275)

Need to Know

ADVANCE PLANNING

- **As early as possible** Book accommodation, particularly for Bayonne and Biarritz in July and August.
- **Two weeks before** Ask at the Bordeaux tourist office (p267) about the Découverte hotel package, which includes accommodation, admissions, a city tour, a vineyard tour and a bottle of wine.
- **One week before** Book visits at Cognac houses (p271), Bordeaux vineyards (p268) and big-name restaurants.

RESOURCES

- **Loire Atlantique** (www.ohlaloireatlantique.com) General traveller info for the Loire Atlantique region.
- **Bordeaux** (www.bordeaux.com) Become a wine expert.
- **Cognac World** (www.cognac-world.com) For Cognac aficionados.
- **Tourisme Gironde** (www.tourisme-gironde.fr) Bordeaux, its vineyards and elsewhere in Gironde.

GETTING AROUND

- **Air** The region's main airports are in Bordeaux, Nantes, Biarritz-Anglet-Bayonne and Pau, all served by low-cost operators among others.
- **Trains** Speedy TGVs serve Bordeaux, Biarritz and several other cities. Most smaller towns and villages can be reached via regional trains.
- **Car** Allows maximum freedom, but be careful not to overtipple if you're tasting wine or Cognac.

BE FOREWARNED

- **St-Émilion** Wear flat, comfy shoes: the village's steep, uneven streets are hard going.
- **Bassin d'Arcachon** Take care swimming in this area: powerful currents swirl out to sea from the deceptively tranquil *baïnes* (little bays).
- **Bordeaux wine châteaux** Generally close their doors during October's grape harvest.
- **Finding a hotel bed** Bayonne is tough from mid-July to mid-August and near impossible during the Fêtes de Bayonne.
- **Lourdes** So quiet in winter that most hotels shut down.

Bordeaux & French Basque Country Itineraries

The southwest is one of France's most popular regions. There's lots to pack in, but don't rush – life here cruises along at its own laid-back pace.

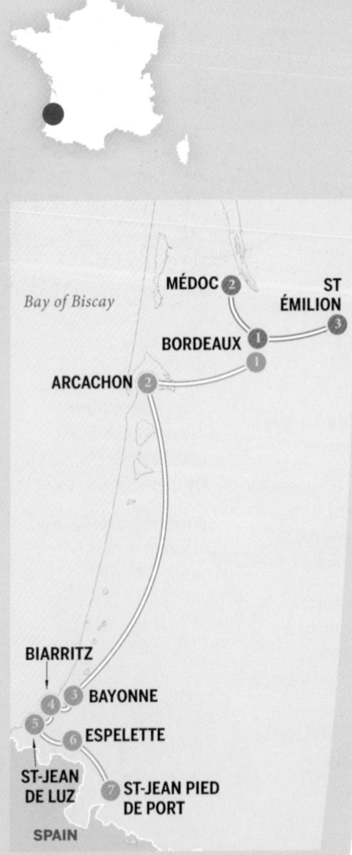

3 DAYS

BORDEAUX TO ST-ÉMILION

A Vintage Trip

If you're going to get to grips with Bordeaux wine, there's only one place to start. **(1) Bordeaux** is one of France's most impressive cities – so impressive, in fact, that Unesco has planted most of it on the World Heritage list. You should devote at least a day to sightseeing – don't miss the Cathédrale St-André and a climb up the Tour Pey-Berland, a visit to CAPC Musée d'Art Contemporain and a river cruise, followed by supper at Le Cheverus Café or La Tupina.

On day two take a guided tour of some of the region's celebrated vineyards, including the illustrious names of the **(2) Médoc**. There will be plenty of opportunities to buy some bottles en route, or treat yourself to some serious wine and cheese over lunch at Bordeaux's Baud et Millet.

On day three travel east to beautiful **(3) St-Émilion**. Perched on a limestone ridge surrounded by seemingly endless green vines, the town has umpteen wine shops and châteaux to visit. Don't miss a guided tour into the musty caverns hollowed out beneath the 11th-century Église Monolithe.

Top Left: Bordeaux vineyard; **Top Right:** Biarritz (p275)

BORDEAUX TO ST-JEAN PIED DE PORT

Into the Basque Country

After **(1) Bordeaux**, it's time to head south into the fiery heartland of the French Basques. First stop is **(2) Arcachon**, a popular seaside town that's famous for its oysters and the nearby, enormous sand dune, Dune du Pilat. If you have time, you won't regret a boat trip across the bay to the pretty peninsula of Cap Ferret.

Further south, the Basque Country begins in earnest at **(3) Bayonne**, where you can watch a game of *pelote*, buy some delicious Basque ham, dine at a delightful riverside restaurant or gorge on *pintxo* (tapas).

On day three head to hip **(4) Biarritz**, a quick trip from Bayonne, where you'll find fantastic beaches, a thriving surf culture and invigorating views of the coast from the Rocher de la Vierge. It's also a great place to try some classic Basque cuisine – for seafood by the water, ramshackle beach shack Casa Juan Pedro is the address.

On days four and five, make time for some beach-lounging in **(5) St-Jean de Luz**, chilli-eating in **(6) Espelette** and village-wandering in **(7) St-Jean Pied de Port**. Got the Basque bug? Don't fret – the Spanish border's just 8km away...

Discover Bordeaux & French Basque Country

At a Glance

- **Atlantic Coast** (p264) From fine wine in Bordeaux to ritzy beaches in Biarritz.
- **French Basque Country** (p272) Straddling the Franco-Spanish border, this fiery region feels like another country.

Biarritz (p275)
LAURENCE DELDERFIELD/GETTY IMAGES ©

ATLANTIC COAST

With quiet country roads winding through vine-striped hills and wild stretches of coastal sands interspersed with misty islands, the Atlantic Coast is where France gets back to nature. Much more laid-back than the Med (but with almost as much sunshine), this is the place to slow the pace right down.

The one thing that unites the people of this area is a love of the finer things in life. The region's exceptional wine is famous worldwide, and to accompany it you'll find fresh-from-the-ocean seafood wherever you go and plenty of regional delicacies, including crêpes in the north, snails in the centre and foie gras in the south.

Bordeaux

POP 240,500

The new millennium was a major turning point for the city long known as La Belle au Bois Dormant (Sleeping Beauty). The mayor, former prime minister Alain Juppé, roused Bordeaux, pedestrianising its boulevards, restoring its neoclassical architecture and implementing a high-tech public transport system. His efforts paid off: in mid-2007 half of the entire city (18 sq km, from the outer boulevards to the banks of the Garonne) was Unesco-listed, making it the largest urban World Heritage Site.

Sights

CATHÉDRALE ST-ANDRÉ Cathedral

Lording over the city, and a Unesco World Heritage Site prior to the city's classification, the cathedral's oldest section dates from 1096; most of what you see today was built in the 13th and 14th centuries. Exceptional masonry carvings can be seen in the north portal. Even more imposing than the cathedral itself is the gargoyled, 50m-high Gothic belfry, **Tour Pey-Berland** (adult/child €5.50/free; ⌚10am-1.15pm & 2-6pm Jun-Sep, shorter hrs rest of year), erected between 1440 and 1466. Its spire was added in the 19th century, and in 1863 it was topped off with the statue of Notre Dame de l'Aquitaine (Our Lady of Aquitaine). Scaling the tower's 231 narrow steps rewards you with a spectacular panorama of the city.

MUSEUMS & GALLERIES Museums
Bordeaux has a healthy collection of museums and galleries. Gallo-Roman statues and relics dating back 25,000 years are among the highlights at the impressive **Musée d'Aquitaine** (20 cours Pasteur). Upstairs is a small collection of statues and masks from the ex-French African and Oceania colonies. Ask to borrow an English-language catalogue.

Built in 1824 as a warehouse for French colonial produce such as coffee, cocoa, peanuts and vanilla, the cavernous Entrepôts Lainé creates a dramatic backdrop for cutting-edge modern art at the **CAPC Musée d'Art Contemporain** (rue Ferrére, Entrepôt 7; ⌚11am-6pm Tue & Thu-Sun, to 8pm Wed).

The evolution of Occidental art from the Renaissance to the mid-20th century is on view at Bordeaux's **Musée des Beaux-Arts** (20 cours d'Albret; ⌚11am-6pm daily mid-July–mid-Aug).

Sleeping

ECOLODGE DES CHARTRONS B&B €€
(☎05 56 81 49 13; www.ecolodgedeschartrons.com; 23 rue Raze; s €96-118, d €98-134; 📶) Hidden away in a little side street off the quays in Bordeaux's Chartrons wine merchant district, this *chambre d'hôte* is blazing a trail for ecofriendly sleeping in the city. Owner-hosts Veronique and Yann have added a solar-powered hot-water system, energy-efficient gas heating and hemp-based soundproofing, while preserving the 'soul' of this old wine merchant's house.

L'HÔTEL PARTICULIER Boutique Hotel €€
(☎05 57 88 28 80; www.lhotel-particulier.com; 44 rue Vital-Carles; apt from €97, d from €168; 📶) When you step into this fabulous boutique hotel with its secret courtyard garden, and find a thousand eyes staring at you from the reception walls and lampshades made only of feathers, you realise you've stumbled upon somewhere special. The rooms don't disappoint and are highly extravagant affairs with huge fireplaces, carved ceilings, free-standing bath tubs and quality furnishings throughout. It also has cheaper, but still very nice, fully equipped apartments ideal for a longer stay.

LES CHAMBRES AU COEUR DE BORDEAUX B&B €€
(☎05 56 52 43 58; www.aucoeurdebordeaux.fr; 28 rue Boulan; s/d from €85/95; 📶) This recently renovated town house is now a swish B&B run very much along the lines of a small boutique hotel. Its five charming rooms are a very Bordeaux-appropriate mix of the old and the new and each evening there is a free *apéro* (predinner drink) at 7pm.

Eating

LE CHEVERUS CAFÉ Bistro €
(☎05 56 48 29 73; 81-83 rue du Loup; menus from €11.40; ⌚Mon-Sat) In a city full of neighbourhood bistros, this one, smack in the city centre, is one of the most impressive. It's friendly, cosy and chaotically busy (be prepared to wait for a table at lunchtime). The food tastes fresh and home-cooked and it dares to veer slightly away from the bistro standards of steak and chips. The lunch *menus*, which include wine, are an all-out bargain. In the early evening it morphs into something of a tapas bar.

LA TUPINA Regional Cuisine €€€
(☎05 56 91 56 37; www.latupina.com; 6 rue Porte de la Monnaie; menus €18-65, mains €27-45)

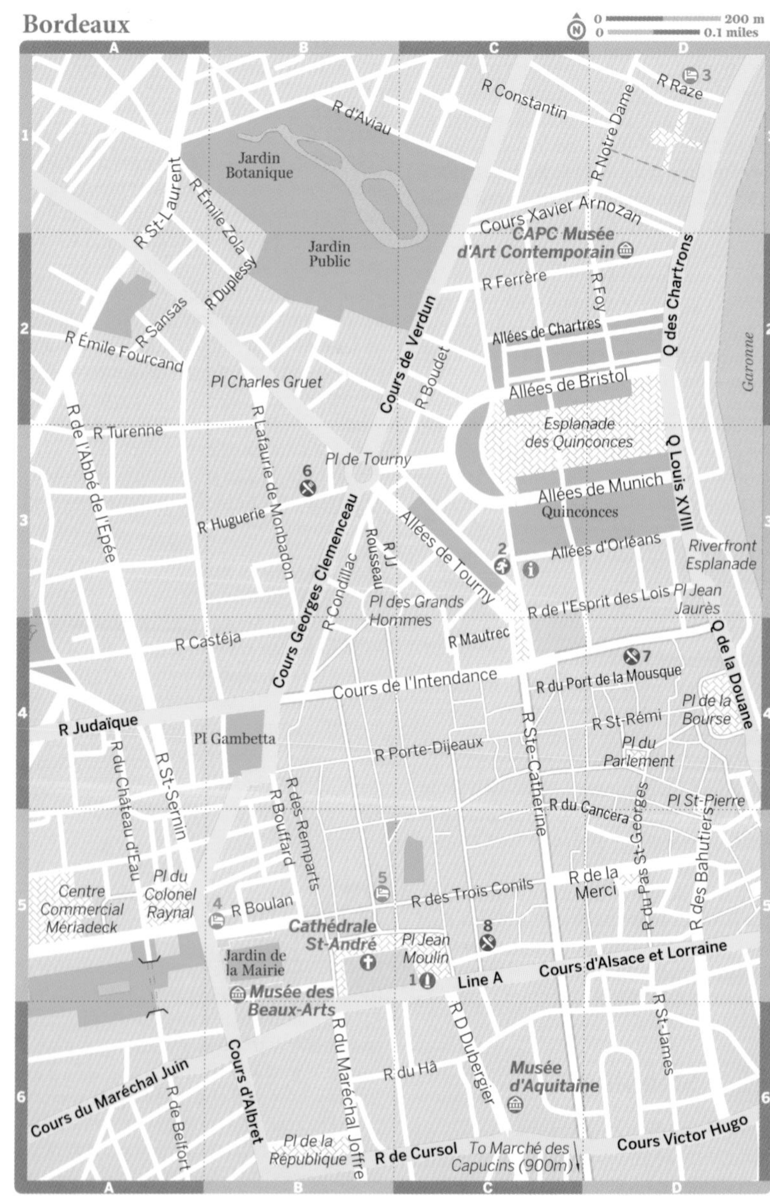

Filled with the aroma of soup simmering inside an old *tupina* ('kettle' in Basque) over an open fire, this white-tableclothed place is feted far and wide for its seasonal southwestern French specialities such as a minicasserole of foie gras and eggs, milk-fed lamb or goose wings with potatoes and parsley. An €18 lunch *menu* is available on weekdays. La Tupina is a 10-minute walk upriver from the city centre and on a small side street. Any local can point you in the right direction.

Bordeaux

Top Sights

Sights

Activities, Courses & Tours

Sleeping

Eating

LA BOÎTE À HUÎTRES Oysters €
(☎05 56 81 64 97; 36 cours du Chapeau Rouge; lunch menu €19, 6 oysters from €10) This rickety, wood-panelled little place feels like an Arcachon fisherman's hut. It's a sensation that's quite appropriate because this is by far the best place in Bordeaux to munch on fresh Arcachon oysters. Traditionally they're served with sausage but you can have them in a number of different forms, including with that other southwest delicacy, foie gras. This place will also pack up the oysters so you can take them away for a riverfront picnic.

BAUD ET MILLET Cheese, Wine €€
(☎05 56 79 05 77; 19 rue Huguerie; mains €23-25) If you like cheese or wine, or both of them, then this cute neighbourhood place with over 140 different cheeses served in myriad forms and almost as many wines is unmissable. Serious *fromage* fans should go for the *dégustation* of nine different cheese-based dishes (€45).

MARCHÉ DES CAPUCINS Market €
(6 oysters & glass of wine €6; ⏲7am-noon) If you're after a classic Bordeaux experience, then a Saturday morning spent slurping oysters and white wine from one of the seafood stands at Marché des Capucins ticks all the must-do boxes. Afterwards you can peruse the market stalls while shopping for the freshest ingredients to take on a picnic to one of the city's parks. To get to Marché des Capucins, head south down cours Pasteur and once at place de la Victoire turn left onto rue Élie Gintrec.

Information

Main tourist office (☎05 56 00 66 00; www.bordeaux-tourisme.com; 12 cours du 30 Juillet; ⏲9am-7.30pm Mon-Sat, 9.30am-6.30pm Sun)

Getting There & Away

The train station, Gare St-Jean, is about 3km from the city centre at the southern terminus of cours de la Marne. Destinations include the following:

Paris Gare Montparnasse €73, three hours, at least 16 daily.

Bayonne €29, two hours.

La Rochelle €29, 2¼ hours.

Nantes €48, four hours.

The Médoc

Northwest of Bordeaux, along the western shore of the Gironde Estuary, lie some of Bordeaux's most celebrated vineyards. On the banks of the Gironde, the port town of **Pauillac** (population 1300) is at the heart of the wine country, surrounded by the distinguished Haut-Médoc, Margaux and St-Julien appellations. The Pauillac wine appellation encompasses 18 *crus classés*, including the world-renowned Mouton Rothschild, Latour and Lafite Rothschild. The town's tourist office houses the **Maison du Tourisme et du Vin** (☎05 56 59 03 08; www.pauillac-medoc.com; ⏲9.30am-7pm Mon-Sat, 10am-1pm & 2-6pm Sun), which has information on châteaux and how to visit them.

Bordeaux' tourist office runs a day-long **Médoc 1855 tour** (including lunch €93; ⏲tours 9.15am), which takes in three of the best known châteaux; reservations are essential. **Bordeaux Excursions** (www.bordeaux-excursions.com) customises private wine-country tours, starting from €190

On the Wine Trail

Thirsty? The 1000-sq-km winegrowing area around the city of Bordeaux is, along with Burgundy, France's most important producer of top-quality wines. The Bordeaux region is divided into 57 appellations (production areas whose soil and microclimate impart distinctive characteristics to the wine produced there). The majority of the Bordeaux region's reds, rosés, sweet and dry whites and sparkling wines have earned the right to include the abbreviation AOC (Appellation d'Origine Contrôlée) on their labels, indicating that the contents have been grown, fermented and aged according to strict regulations that govern such viticultural matters as the number of vines permitted per hectare and acceptable pruning methods.

Bordeaux has over 5000 châteaux (also known as domaines, crus or *clos*), referring not to palatial residences but rather to the properties where grapes are raised, picked, fermented and then matured as wine. The smaller châteaux sometimes accept walk-in visitors, but at many places you have to make advance reservations. Many close during the *vendange* (grape harvest) in October.

Whet your palate with the tourist office's informal introduction to wine and cheese courses (adult €25), held every Thursday (and Saturdays mid-July–mid-August).

Serious students of the grape can enrol at the **École du Vin** (Wine School; ☎05 56 00 22 66; www.bordeaux.com), within the **Maison du Vin de Bordeaux** (3 cours du 30 Juillet), across the street from the tourist office.

for one to five people (excluding châteaux fees) for a half-day trip.

Don't miss Philippe Raoux' **La Winery** (☎05 56 39 04 90; www.lawinery.fr; Rond-point des Vendangeurs, D1). A first for France, this vast glass-and-steel wine centre mounts concerts and contemporary-art exhibits alongside various fee-based tastings, including innovative tastings that determine your *signe œnologique* ('wine sign') costing from €16 (booking required), and stocks over 1000 different wines.

Arcachon

POP 11,750

A long-time oyster-harvesting area on the southern side of the tranquil, triangular Bassin d'Arcachon (Arcachon Bay), this seaside town lured bourgeois Bordelaise at the end of the 19th century. Its four little quarters are romantically named for each of the seasons, with villas that evoke the town's golden past amid a scattering of 1950s architecture.

Sights

VILLE D'ÉTE & VILLE D'HIVER Town, Beach

In the **Ville d'Été** (Summer Quarter), Arcachon's sandy beach, **Plage d'Arcachon**, is flanked by two piers. Lively **Jetée Thiers** is at the western end. In front of the eastern pier, **Jetée d'Eyrac**, stands the town's turreted **Casino de la Plage**, built by Adalbert Deganne in 1953 as an exact replica of Château de Boursault in the Marne. On the tree-covered hillside south of the Ville d'Été, the century-old **Ville d'Hiver** (Winter Quarter) has over 300 villas, many decorated with delicate wood tracery, ranging in style from neo-Gothic through to colonial. It's an easy stroll or a short ride up the **art deco public lift** (free) in Parc Mauresque.

Tours

LES BATELIERS ARCACHONNAIS Boat Tours

(☎05 57 72 28 28; www.bateliers-arcachon.com; Île aux Oiseaux adult/child/under 5yr €15/10/5, Banc d'Arguin adult/child/under 3yrs €20/14/8; 👪) Daily, year-round cruises sail around the **Île aux Oiseaux**, the uninhabited 'bird island' in the middle of the bay. It's a haven for tern, curlew and redshank, so bring your binoculars. In summer there are regular all-day excursions (11am to 5.30pm) to the **Banc d'Arguin**, the sand bank off the Dune du Pilat.

Eating

The bay's oysters (served raw and accompanied by the local small, flat sausages, *crepinettes*) appear on *menus* everywhere.

AUX MILLE SAVEURS Traditional French **€€**

(☎05 56 83 40 28; 25 bd du Général Leclerc; menus €19-50; ⏰closed Wed & dinner Sun & Tue) In a light-filled space of flowing white tablecloths, this genteel restaurant is renowned for its traditional French fare artistically presented on fine china.

CHEZ PIERRE Seafood **€€**

(Cafe de la Plage; ☎05 56 22 52 94; 1 bd Veyrier Montagnères; menus from €30, seafood platters €24-42) This see-and-be-seen restaurant serves up an ocean of seafood.

Information

Tourist office (☎05 57 52 97 97; www.arcachon.com; Esplanade Georges Pompidou; ⏰9am-7pm)

Getting There & Away

There are frequent trains between Bordeaux and Arcachon (€10.50, 50 minutes).

Cognac

POP 19,500

On the banks of the River Charente amid vine-covered countryside, Cognac, 120km north of Bordeaux, is known worldwide for the double-distilled spirit that bears its name.

Oysters, Cap Ferret

SALLY DILLON/GETTY IMAGES ©

Don't Miss St-Émilion

The medieval village of St-Émilion perches above vineyards renowned for producing full-bodied, deeply coloured red wines. Named after Émilion, a miracle-working Benedictine monk who lived in a cave here between AD 750 and 767, the village and its vineyards are now Unesco-listed. Today, despite masses of tourists descending onto the town, it's well worth venturing 40km east from Bordeaux to experience St-Émilion's magic, particularly when the sun sets over the valley and the limestone buildings glow with halo-like golden hues.

For captivating views of the hilltop hamlet, climb the church **clocher** (bell tower) – collect the key from the tourist office – or the 118 steps of 13th-century **La Tour du Roi** (King's Tower). Or dig deep beneath the pretty streets into a fascinating labyrinth of catacombs with a subterranean **guided tour** organised by the tourist office.

Blind tastings and games (available in English) are a fun and informative introduction to wine tasting at **L'École du Vin de St-Émilion**; adjacent Maison du Vin also offers bilingual 1½-hour classes starting at 11am. Eight hiking circuits, from 4km to 14km, loop through the greater World Heritage jurisdiction; the tourist office has maps.

Hungry for lunch in the company of fine wine? Reserve in advance at double-Michelin-starred restaurant **Hostellerie de Plaisance**.

NEED TO KNOW

Tourist office (☎05 57 55 28 28; www.saint-emilion-tourisme.com; place des Créneaux; ⏲9.30am-8pm); **Clocher** (Bell Tower; admission €1.25); **L'École du Vin de St-Émilion** (www.vignobleschateaux.fr; 4 rue du Clocher; tasting courses €29; ⏲3pm Apr-Oct, by reservation Nov-Mar); **Hostellerie de Plaisance** (☎05 57 55 07 55; www.hostellerie-plaisance.com; place du Clocher; menus €105-150; ⏲lunch Tue-Sat, dinner Sat)

Sights & Activities

Half-timbered 15th- to 17th-century houses line the narrow streets of the **Vieille Ville** (old city), which sits snugly between the partly Romanesque **Église St-Léger** (rue Aristide Briand) and the river.

MUSEUMS Museums
(joint entry adult/child €4.80/3.50; 10am-6.30pm) At the southern corner of the leafy Jardin Public is the **Musée d'Art et d'Histoire** (05 45 32 07 25; www.musees-cognac.fr; 48 bd Denfert-Rochereau), showcasing the town's history. The **Musée des Arts du Cognac** (05 45 36 21 10; place de la Salle Verte) takes you step by step through the production of Cognac – from vine to bottle.

LA DAME JEANNE River Cruise
(05 45 82 10 71; adult/child €7/4; May-Sep;) You can float with the sticklebacks down the River Charente on *La Dame Jeanne*, a recreation of one of the flat-bottomed cargo boats known as *gabarres* that were once the lifeblood of trade along the river. The trip lasts 90 minutes and reservations should be made through the tourist office.

Cognac Houses

According to local lore, divine intervention plays a role in the production of Cognac. Made of grape *eaux-de-vie* (brandies) of various vintages, Cognac is aged in oak barrels and blended by an experienced *maître de chai* (cellar master). Each year some 2% of the casks' volume – *la part des anges* (the angels' share) – evaporates through the pores in the wood, nourishing the tiny black mushrooms that thrive on the walls of Cognac warehouses. That 2% might not sound like much, but it amounts to around 20 million bottles a year – if the angels really are up there knocking back 20 million bottles of Cognac a year, then all we can say is roll on our time behind the pearly gates!

The best-known Cognac houses are open to the public, running tours of their cellars and production facilities, and ending with a tasting session. Opening times vary annually; it's a good idea to reserve in advance.

Camus (05 45 32 72 96; www.camus.fr; 29 rue Marguerite de Navarre; adult/child from €7/free) Located 250m northeast of the Jardin Public. **Hennessey** (05 45 35 72 68; www.hennessey.com; 8 rue Richonne; adult/12-18yr/under 12 €9/7/free; closed Jan & Feb) Situated 100m uphill from quai des Flamands; tours include a film (shown in English) and a boat trip across the Charente to visit the cellars. **Martell** (05 45 36 33 33; www.martell.com; place Édouard Martell; adult/child €7.50/3) Found 250m northwest of the tourist office. **Otard** (05 45 36 88 86; www.otard.com; 127 bd Denfert-Rochereau; adult/child €9.20/4.10) Housed in the 1494 birthplace of King François I, the Château de Cognac, 650m north of place François 1er. **Rémy Martin** (05 45 35 76 66; www.visitesremymartin.com) Two locations: the **estate** (adult/child €15/7; closed Oct-Apr), 4km southwest of town towards Pons; and, in town, the **house** (adult/12-18yr/under 12yr €25/14/7; by appointment), for intimate tastings in groups of up to eight.

The **tourist office** (www.tourism-cognac.com) has a list of smaller Cognac houses near town; most close between October and mid-March.

Sleeping & Eating

HÔTEL LE CHEVAL BLANC Hotel €
(05 45 82 09 55; www.hotel-chevalblanc.fr; 6 place Bayard; d from €60;) Miniature bottles of Cognac in the vending machine satiate midnight cravings at this hotel, where rooms are set around a courtyard. Although not vast, the rooms are immaculate, and there's good wheelchair access.

BISTROT DE CLAUDE Bistro €€
(05 45 82 60 32; 35 rue Grande; menus €18-29, mains €12-29; Mon-Fri) Set in a lovely old timber building in the heart of the old

town, this character-infused restaurant specialises in oysters and both river and sea fish.

Getting There & Away

Cognac's **train station** (av du Maréchal Leclerc), 1km south of the town centre, has regular trains to/from La Rochelle (from €16, from 1¼ hours).

FRENCH BASQUE COUNTRY

Gently sloping from the foothills of the Pyrenees into the deep-sapphire-blue Bay of Biscay, the Basque Country straddles France and Spain. Yet this feisty, independent land remains profoundly different from either of the nation states that have adopted it.

Bayonne

POP 46,200

Surrounded by sturdy fortifications and splashed in red and white paint, Bayonne (Baiona in Basque), capital of the French Basque Country, is one of the most attractive towns in southwest France. Its perfectly preserved old town (until 1907 it was actually forbidden to build outside the town's fortifications) and shoals of riverside restaurants are an absolute delight to explore.

Sights

MUSÉE BASQUE ET DE L'HISTOIRE DE BAYONNE Museum

(☎05 59 59 08 98; www.musee-basque.com; 37 quai des Corsaires; adult/child €6.50/free; ⏰10am-6.30pm) The seafaring history, traditions and cultural identity of the Basque people are all explored at this superb museum through exhibits including a reconstructed farm and the interior of a typical *etxe* (home). Labelling is in French, Spanish and Basque only but English information sheets are available. In July and August free 'nocturnal' visits are possible on Thursday evenings from 6.30pm to 8.30pm.

CATHÉDRALE STE-MARIE Cathedral

(⏰10-11.45am & 3-6.15pm Mon-Sat, 3.30-6.15pm Sun, cloister 9am-12.30pm & 2-6pm) The twin towers of Bayonne's Gothic cathedral soar above the city. Construction began in the 13th century, and was completed in 1451; the mismatched materials in some ways resemble Lego blocks. Above the north aisle are three lovely stained-glass windows; the oldest, in the Chapelle Saint Jérôme, dates from 1531. The entrance to the stately 13th-century **cloister** is on place Louis Pasteur.

River Charente, Cognac (p269)

Don't Miss Dune du Pilat

This colossal sand dune (sometimes referred to as the Dune de Pyla because of its location in the resort town of Pyla-sur-Mer), 8km south of Arcachon, stretches from the mouth of the Bassin d'Arcachon southwards for almost 3km. Already the largest in Europe, it's spreading eastwards at 4.5m a year – it has swallowed trees, a road junction and even a hotel.

The view from the top – approximately 114m above sea level – is magnificent. To the west you can see the sandy shoals at the mouth of the Bassin d'Arcachon, including the **Banc d'Arguin bird reserve** and Cap Ferret. Dense dark-green pine forests stretch from the base of the dune eastwards almost as far as the eye can see.

Take care swimming in this area: powerful currents swirl out to sea from the deceptively tranquil *baïnes* (little bays).

NEED TO KNOW

(www.bassin-arcachon.com)

Tours

CITY TOURS Tour

(adult €6-10) The tourist office organises a range of different city tours (some in English), from a historical tour of old Bayonne to a chocolate-fiend tour or a museum tour. Departure times and tour type vary by the day.

Sleeping

PÉNICHE DJÉBELLE Houseboat **€€**

(☎05 59 25 77 18; www.djebelle.com; face au 17 Quai de Lesseps; d incl breakfast €145; closed Oct-Apr; wifi) Now here's something really different! If you stay here you'll have the best river view in the city (and there's a chance your fellow guests will be mermaids or pirates). Yes, this unique *chambre*

Detour: Île de Ré

Bathed in the southern sun, drenched in a languid atmosphere and scattered with villages of green-shuttered, whitewashed buildings with red Spanish-tile roofs, Île de Ré is one of the most delightful places on the west coast of France. The island spans just 30km from its most easterly and westerly points, and just 5km at its widest section. But take note, the secret's out and in the high season it can be almost impossible to move around and even harder to find a place to stay.

On the northern coast, about 12km from the toll bridge that links the island to **La Rochelle**, is the quaint fishing port of **St-Martin-de-Ré** (population 2600), the island's main town. Surrounded by 17th-century fortifications (you can stroll along most of the ramparts), the port town is a mesh of streets filled with craft shops, art galleries and salty sea views. St-Martin's **tourist office** (05 46 09 00 05; www.iledere.com; av Victor Bouthillier; 10am-6pm Mon-Sat, to noon Sun) can provide information for the entire island. For an overview of the island, climb to the **Phare des Baleines** (adult/child €3/1.50; 9.30am-9pm Jul-Aug), a lighthouse on the island's northern tip.

The island's best **beaches** are along the southern edge and around the western tip (northeast and southeast of Phare des Baleines).

Criss-crossed by well-maintained bicycle paths, the pancake-flat island is ideal for cycling. A biking map is available at tourist offices.

The one-way automobile toll (paid on your way to the island) is €8 (€16 from mid-June to mid-September).

d'hôte is in fact a houseboat floating in the River Ardour. And don't make the mistake of thinking that because it's a boat it will be uncomfortable; it's quite the opposite.

HÔTEL DES ARCEAUX Boutique Hotel €
(05 59 59 15 53; www.hotel-arceaux.com; 26 rue Port Neuf; d €42-76;) If this hotel, which is located on one of the prettiest streets in the old town, were a pop star it would surely have to be Lady Gaga or some other flamboyant and over-the-top personality. Its rooms and communal areas are a cacophony of noisy colours and stately antiques, and it's very well run.

HÔTEL CÔTE BASQUE Hotel €
(05 59 55 10 21; www.hotel-cotebasque.fr; 2 rue Maubec; r from €75;) Ride the clanky, old-fashioned lift up to your modern room with low-slung beds and colourful art on the walls. Sitting opposite the train station, this recently renovated place offers sizzling value for money.

Eating

LA FEUILLANTINE Gastronomic €€
(05 59 46 14 94; www.lafeuillantine-bayonne.com; 21 quai Amiral Dubourdieu; menus €25-67, mains €25) This riverside place might be quite small, but it's garnered a huge reputation for its spectacular Basque gastronomic fare, which is served with flair and style in its colourful dining room. The culinary skills of chef Nicolas Bertegui have received virtually universal praise in the mainstream French media.

BAR-RESTAURANT DU MARCHÉ Basque €
(05 59 59 22 66; 39 rue des Basques; menus/mains €13/8.70; lunch Mon-Sat) Run by a welcoming Basque-speaking family, this

unpretentious place is an absolute institution where everyone knows everyone (which some people may find slightly intimidating, but don't worry, just dive right in – nobody cares!). Simple but ample home-cooked dishes full of the flavours of the neighbouring market are dished up to all comers.

Information

Tourist office (☎08 20 42 64 64; www.bayonne-tourisme.com; place des Basques; ⏰9am-7pm Mon-Sat, 10am-1pm Sun)

Getting There & Away

TGVs run between Bayonne and Paris Gare Montparnasse (€88 to €129, five to six hours, eight daily).

There are five trains daily to St-Jean Pied de Port (€9.20, 1¼ hours) and fairly frequent services to St-Jean de Luz (€4.80, 25 minutes) via Biarritz (€2.40 to €2.60, nine minutes).

There are also services from Bordeaux (from €29, two hours, at least 10 daily).

Biarritz

POP 26,067

As ritzy as its name suggests, this stylish coastal town, 8km west of Bayonne, made a name for itself as a resort in the mid-19th century when Napoléon III and his Spanish-born wife, Eugénie, visited regularly. Along its rocky coastline are architectural hallmarks of this golden age, and the belle-époque and art-deco eras that followed. Although Biarritz retains a high glamour quotient (and skyrocketing prices to match), it's also a magnet for vanloads of surfers, with some of Europe's best waves.

Sights & Activities

Biarritz' raison d'être is its fashionable beaches, particularly the two central **Grande Plage** and **Plage Miramar**, which are lined end to end with sunbathing bodies on hot and balmy summer days. Stripy 1920s-style beach tents can be hired for €9.50 per day. The other central Biarritz beach is the tiny cove of **Plage**

Cathédrale Ste-Marie (p272), Bayonne

du Port Vieux which, thanks to its lack of swell, is the most favourable for young children to splash about in. North of Pointe St-Martin, the adrenaline-pumping surfing beaches of **Anglet** (the final 't' is pronounced) continue northwards for more than 4km. Take bus 10 or 13 from the bottom of av Verdun (just near av Édouard VII).

Climbing the 258 twisting steps inside the 73m-high **Phare de Biarritz**, the town's 1834 lighthouse, rewards you with sweeping views of the Basque coast.

CITÉ DE L'OCÉAN Museum

(**☎05 59 22 75 40; www.citedelocean.com; 1 Av de la Plage; adult/child €10.50/7; ⌚10am-10pm)** This is entertainment, cutting-edge technology, theme park and science museum all rolled into one attraction. Located inside a wave-shaped building south of town, this place will teach you everything about the ocean; from how it was born to the secrets of Gilgamesh, and in between you get to ride to the depths of the ocean in a submarine and watch giant squid and sperm whales do battle. It's all very child friendly but it's equally fascinating and fun for adults.

MUSÉE DE LA MER Museum

(**☎05 59 22 75 40; www.museedelamer.com; Esplanade du Rocher de la Vierge; adult/child €13/9.50; ⌚9.30am-midnight Jul-Aug, shorter hr rest of year)** Housed in a wonderful art-deco building, Biarritz' Musée de la Mer is teeming with underwater life from the Bay of Biscay and beyond, as well as exhibits on fishing recalling Biarritz' whaling past.

Sleeping

HÔTEL MIRANO Boutique Hotel €€

(**☎05 59 23 11 63; www.hotelmirano.fr; 11 av Pasteur; d €68-130;** 📶) Squiggly purple, orange and black wallpaper and oversize orange perspex light fittings are some of the rad '70s touches at this boutique retro hotel. Oh, and there's a flirty Betty Boop in the bar. The staff go above and beyond the call of duty in order to please. All up, this eccentrically funky place offers one of the best deals in town. To get there take the D910 southeast out of town, turn left onto av de Grammont and right onto av Pasteur. It's a good 10-minute walk from the centre.

Plage du Port Vieux (p275), Biarritz

JOHN HARPER/GETTY IMAGES ©

HÔTEL DE SILHOUETTE Designer Hotel €€€
(☎05 59 24 93 82; www.hotel-silhouette-biarritz.com; 30 rue Gambetta; d from €220; ❄ 📶) This fabulous new addition to the Biarritz hotel scene has designer rooms with big-city attitude that would feel quite at home in an upmarket Manhattan apartment. In order to remind you that the countryside is close at hand there are a couple of 'sheep' in the garden – as well as frequently changing outdoor art and sculpture exhibitions. The furnishings in the rooms are very high class and the shower heads as big as a rain cloud.

Eating

CASA JUAN PEDRO Seafood €
(☎05 59 24 00 86; Port des Pêcheurs; mains €7-10) Down by the old port – something of a hidden little village of wooden fishing cottages and old-timers – is this cute fishing-shack restaurant. The gregarious atmosphere ensures that you can wash down your tuna, sardines or squid with plenty of friendly banter from both the staff and other customers. There are several similar neighbouring places.

LE CRABE-TAMBOUR Seafood €
(☎05 59 23 24 53; 49 rue d'Espagne; menus €13-18) Named after the famous 1977 film of the same name (the owner was the cook for the film set), this friendly local place, a little way south of the centre, offers great seafood for a price that is hard to fault. The prawns in garlic are particularly good.

BISTROT DES HALLES Basque €€
(☎05 59 24 21 22; 1 rue du Centre; mains €15-17) One of a cluster of restaurants along rue du Centre that get their produce directly from the nearby covered market, this bustling place stands out from the pack for serving excellent fish and other fresh modern French market fare from the blackboard menu in an interior

If You Like... Basque Culture

Visit Bayonne's Musée Basque, then deepen your understanding of the region's unique culture with these quintessentially Basque experiences.

1 **FÊTES DE BAYONNE CULTURAL FESTIVAL**
(www.fetes.bayonne.fr) This Basque festival in early August attracts up to a million people to Bayonne for a five-day orgy of drinking, dancing, processions and fireworks, culminating in the town's own version of Pamplona's 'Running of the Bulls' ceremony (only here, the bulls are replaced by heifers). Wear white with a red sash and neck-scarf.

2 **FOIRE AU JAMBON**
(Ham Fair) Bayonne has honoured its esteemed local ham, jambon de Bayonne, with an Easter ham fair since 1462. To buy the famous ham, shop at Bayonne's covered market or **Pierre Ibaïalde** (41 rue des Cordeliers), a deli where you can taste before you buy.

3 **PINTXO**
Bayonne has an increasing number of *pintxo* (tapas in Basque) bars, and two of the best are **Xurasko** (16 rue Poissonnerie; pintxos from €2.50) and **Ibaia** (45 quai Amiral Jauréguiberry; pintxos from €8; ⏲closed Sun & Mon Oct-Mar). Tapas start to decorate the bar like flowers from 7pm as everyone clocks off work and stops by for a glass of wine and choice titbits.

4 **PIMENTS D'ESPELETTE**
This spicy red chilli pepper is an essential accompaniment to Basque meals (it even has its own AOC, just like fine wine). The village of **Espelette** (www.espelette.fr) hosts its own chilli festival on the last weekend in October, culminating in the crowning of the *chevalier du piment* (knight of the chilli).

5 **PELOTA**
This national Basque sport encompasses 16 different games, all played with a hard ball (the *pelote*) using bare hands and a wooden paddle or scooplike racket. Catch matches in Biarritz, Bayonne and St-Jean de Luz between June and September.

Biarritz

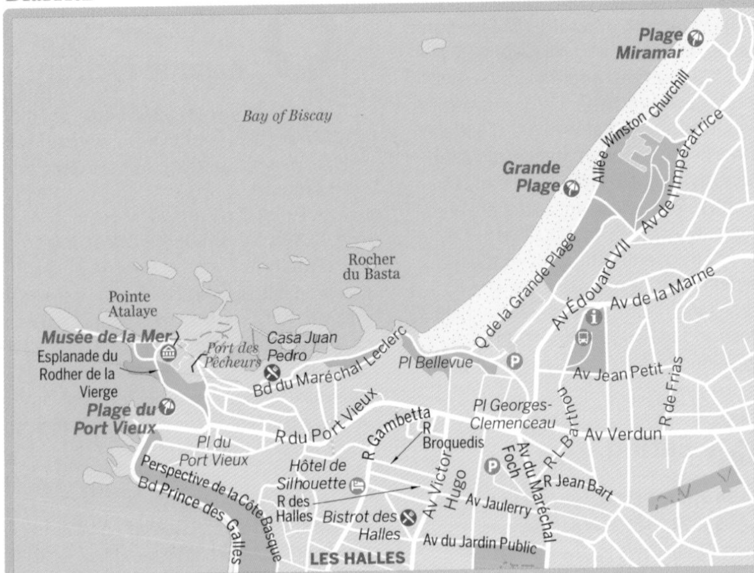

adorned with old metallic advertising posters.

Information

Tourist office (☎05 59 22 37 10; www.biarritz.fr; square d'Ixelles; ⏰9am-7pm)

Getting There & Away

BUS Buses run frequently between Bayonne and Biarritz; they work out much cheaper than taking the train as you'll pay the same to get from Biarritz' train station to its town centre as you will to get from Bayonne to Biarritz directly on the bus.

Ten daily **ATCRB** (www.transdev-atcrb.com) buses travel down the coast to St-Jean de Luz (€2) from the stop just near the tourist office beside square d'Ixelles. Buses to Spain also pick up passengers here.

TRAIN Biarritz-La Négresse train station is about 3km south of the town centre; walking to the centre isn't advised due to busy roads without footpaths, so catch bus A1. **SNCF** (13 av du Maréchal Foch; ⏰Mon-Fri) has a town-centre office. Times, fares and destinations are much the same as Bayonne's, a nine-minute train journey away.

St-Jean de Luz & Ciboure

POP 14,200

If you're searching for the quintessential Basque seaside town – with atmospheric narrow streets and a lively fishing port pulling in large catches of sardines and anchovies that are cooked up at authentic restaurants – you've found it. St-Jean de Luz, 24km southwest of Bayonne, sits at the mouth of the River Nivelle and is overlooked by the lush Pyrenean foothills. Its sleepy, smaller alter ego, Ciboure, is on the western curve of the bay, separated from St-Jean de Luz by the fishing harbour.

Sights

St-Jean de Luz' beautiful banana-shaped sandy **beach** sprouts stripy bathing tents from June to September. Ciboure has its own modest beach, **Plage de Socoa**, 2km west of Socoa on the corniche (the D912); it's served in high season by boats. Both beaches are protected from the wrath of the Atlantic by breakwaters and jetties, and are among the few child-friendly beaches in the Basque Country.

ÉGLISE ST-JEAN BAPTISTE Church

(rue Gambetta, St-Jean de Luz; 8.30am-noon & 2-7pm) The plain façade of France's largest and finest Basque church conceals a splendid interior with a magnificent Baroque altarpiece. It was in front of this very altarpiece that Louis XIV and María Teresa, daughter of King Philip IV of Spain, were married in 1660. After exchanging rings, the couple walked down the aisle and out of the south door, which was then sealed to commemorate peace between the two nations after 24 years of hostilities. You can still see its outline, opposite 20 rue Gambetta.

MAISON LOUIS XIV Historic Building

(05 59 26 27 58; www.maison-louis-xiv.fr; 6 place Louis XIV, St-Jean de Luz; adult/student & child €5.50/3.50; 10.30am-12.30pm & 2.30-6.30pm Wed-Mon, closed Nov-Easter) Sitting on a pretty, pedestrianised square is the so-called Maison Louis XIV. Built in 1643 by a wealthy shipowner and furnished in period style, this is where Louis XIV lived out his last days of bachelorhood before marrying María Teresa. Half-hour guided tours (with English text) depart several times daily in July and August.

SOCOA Old Town

The heart of Socoa is about 2.5km west of Ciboure along the continuation of quai Maurice Ravel (named for the *Boléro* composer, who was born in Ciboure in 1875). Its prominent **fort** was built in 1627 and later improved by Vauban. You can walk out to the Digue de Socoa breakwater or climb to the **lighthouse** via rue du Phare, then out along rue du Sémaphore for fabulous coastal views.

Sleeping

LA DEVINIÈRE Boutique Hotel €€

(05 59 26 05 51; www.hotel-la-deviniere.com; 5 rue Loquin, St-Jean de Luz; d €120-180;) You have to love a place that forsakes TVs for antiquarian books (room 11 even has its own mini-library). Beyond the living room, with its piano and comfy armchairs, there's a delightful small patio equipped with lounges. It's a truly charming place that feels like a little old country cottage that has somehow been sucked into the town centre.

ZAZPI Design Hotel €€€

(05 59 26 07 77; www.zazpihotel.com; 21 bd Thiers, St-Jean de Luz; r/ste from €224/400;) Seriously hip, this wonderful old mansion-turned–designer hotel is one of the most stylish hotels in southwest France. Staying here is like living in a very glam modern art gallery. There's a rooftop terrace complete with pool and sensational views over an ocean of terracotta roof tiles to the fairy-tale green Basque hills.

St-Jean de Luz

If You Like... Family Fun

When the sun fades or you start to tire of the sand and sea, try this trio of Atlantic Coast entertainers, enthralling whatever the weather.

1 **LES MACHINES DE L'ÎLE DE NANTES** (www.lesmachines-nantes.fr; Parc des Chantiers, Blvd Léon Bureau; adult/child €7/5.50; 10am-7pm Jul-Aug, hours vary rest of year) Discover a fantasy world in the city of Nantes where you can prance around like a Maharajah on the back of a 45-tonne **mechanical elephant**, sail through dangerous oceans, and fly through the sky aboard the 25m-high **Carrousel des Mondes Marines**. Gallery tickets are good for the workshop, where you can watch these fantastical contraptions being built.

2 **AQUARIUM LA ROCHELLE** (www.aquarium-larochelle.com; quai Louis Prunier; adult/child €14.50/11, audioguide €3.50; 9am-11pm) Descend in a clunky old 'submarine' to the ocean floor and step out into a tunnel of fluoro jellyfish. Other highlights include a vast open-ocean aquarium full of UFO-like rays and fearsome sharks, a jungle area with tree-level walkways above teeth-gnashing piranhas, and elegantly dancing seahorses.

3 **FUTUROSCOPE** (05 49 49 59 06; www.futuroscope.com; adult/child €38/28; 9am-11.30pm, closed Jan–mid-Feb) This futuristic theme park, 10km north of Poitiers, whizzes visitors through space via cinematic experience into deep-blue ocean depths, around city streets and so on. To keep things cutting edge, one-third of the attractions change annually. Many are motion-seat set-ups requiring a minimum height of 120cm, but there's a play area for smaller kids too. Allow at least five hours to enjoy the major attractions; two days for everything.

Eating

BUVETTE DES HALLES Seafood €
(05 59 26 73 59; bd Victor Hugo, St-Jean de Luz; dishes €7-14; 6am-2pm & dinner, closed Tue Sep-Jun) Tucked into a corner of the covered market, this minuscule restaurant serves goat's cheese, Bayonne ham, grilled sardines, fish soup, mussels and much more. Between June and September you can eat outside beneath the plane trees on the small square; the rest of the year you can eat tucked up inside, but go early for the best pickings.

GRILLERIE DU PORT Seafood €
(05 59 51 18 29; quai du Maréchal Leclerc, St-Jean de Luz; mains €7.50-9.50; mid-Jun–mid-Sep) It won't take long to peruse the menu at this old port-side classic. It's essentially a choice of grilled sardines or grilled tuna – all freshly caught that morning and utterly delicious.

LE PEITA Seafood €€
(05 59 26 86 66; 21 rue Tourasse, St-Jean de Luz; mains €14.50-20, menus from €26; Wed-Sun) Dried Espelette chillies and hams hang from the ceiling at this authentic place, which has crushed-silk tablecloths and friendly owners. For a taste of the local produce on display, order one of the combination plates accompanied by fresh local cheese.

Information

Tourist office (05 59 26 03 16; www.saint-jean-de-luz.com; 20 bd Victor Hugo, St-Jean de Luz; 9am-12.30pm & 2.30-6.30pm Mon-Sat, 10am-1pm Sun, extended hours Jul & Aug)

Getting There & Away

There are frequent trains to Bayonne (€4.80, 25 minutes) via Biarritz (€3 to €4.10, 15 minutes) and to Hendaye (€3, 15 minutes), with connections to Spain.

St-Jean Pied de Port

POP 1700

At the foot of the Pyrenees, the walled town of St-Jean Pied de Port, 53km southeast of Bayonne, was for centuries the last stop in France for pilgrims heading south over the Spanish border, a mere 8km away, and on to Santiago de

Compostela, in Galicia in western Spain. Today it remains a popular departure point for hikers attempting the pilgrim trail, but there are plenty of shorter hikes and opportunities for mountain-biking in the area.

St-Jean Pied de Port makes an ideal day trip from Bayonne, particularly on Monday when the atmospheric market is in full swing.

Sights

OLD TOWN Old Town

The walled old quarter is an attractive place of cobbled streets, geranium-covered balconies and lots of quirky boutiques. Specific sights worth seeking out include the **Église Notre Dame du Bout du Pont**, with foundations as old as the town itself but thoroughly rebuilt in the 17th century. Beyond Porte de Notre Dame is the photogenic **Vieux Pont** (Old Bridge), the town's best-known landmark, from where there's a fine view of white-washed houses with balconies leaning out above the water. A pleasant 500m riverbank stroll upstream leads to the steeply arched **Pont Romain** (meaning Roman Bridge, but in fact dating from the 17th century).

Rue de la Citadelle is edged by substantial, pink-granite 16th- to 18th-century houses. A common motif is the scallop shell, symbol of St Jacques (St James or Santiago) and of the Santiago de Compostela pilgrims. Pilgrims would enter the town through the **Porte de St-Jacques** on the northern side of town, then, refreshed and probably a little poorer, head for Spain through the **Porte d'Espagne**, south of the river.

LA CITADELLE Fortress

From the top of rue de la Citadelle, a rough cobblestone path ascends to the massive citadel itself, from where there's a spectacular panorama of the town and the surrounding hills. Constructed in 1628, the fort was rebuilt around 1680 by military engineers of the Vauban school. Nowadays it serves as a secondary school and is closed to the public.

If you've got a head for heights, descend by the steps signed *escalier*

Rue de la Citadelle, St-Jean Pied de Port

poterne (rear stairway). Steep and slippery after rain, they plunge beside the moss-covered ramparts to **Porte de l'Échauguette** (Watchtower Gate).

Eating

CHEZ ARRAMBIDE Gastronomic **€€€**
(menus €42-110, mains €30-52; ⏲closed Tue Sep-Jun) This twin-Michelin-starred restaurant, inside the (overpriced) Hôtel Les Pyrénées, is where chef Firmin Arrambide does wonders with seasonal market produce, such as truffle and foie-gras lasagne.

Information

Tourist office (☎05 59 37 03 57; www.pyrenees-basque.com; place Charles de Gaulle; ⏲9am-7pm Mon-Sat, 10am-4pm Sun Jul & Aug, 9am-noon & 2-6pm Mon-Sat Sep-Jun)

Getting There & Away

Train is the only option to travel to or from Bayonne (€9.20, 1¼ hours, up to five daily).

Lourdes

If you've ever wondered what a Catholic version of Las Vegas might look like, chances are it'd turn out pretty close to Lourdes. This sprawling town, 43km southeast of Pau, has been one of the world's most important pilgrimage sites since 1858, when 14-year-old Bernadette Soubirous (1844)79) saw the Virgin Mary in a series of 18 visions in a rocky grotto. The visions were subsequently confirmed by the Vatican, and Bernadette was beatified in 1933.

Now known as the Sanctuaires Notre Dame de Lourdes, the grotto is considered to be one of the holiest sites in Christendom. Over six million people arrive in Lourdes every year, to pray, pay homage and be doused in the supposedly miraculous waters, but in contrast to its

Left: Rue Ausonne, Bordeaux (p264); **Below:** Piments d'Espelette (p277) and cider
(LEFT) OLIVER STREWE/GETTY IMAGES ©; (BELOW)OLIVER STREWE/GETTY IMAGES ©

spiritual importance, the modern town of Lourdes itself is a pretty dispiriting experience, with a tatty tangle of neon-signed hotels and souvenir shops selling everything from plastic crucifixes to Madonna-shaped bottles (just add holy water at the shrine).

Sights

SANCTUAIRES NOTRE DAME DE LOURDES Cave

(**Porte St-Michel & Porte St-Joseph 5am-midnight, baths 9-11am & 2.30-4pm Mon-Sat, 2-4pm Sun & holy days**) The development of the Sanctuaries of Our Lady of Lourdes began within a decade of Ste Bernadette's apparitions in 1858. The most dramatic approach is via **Porte St-Joseph**, from where a broad boulevard sweeps west towards the Byzantine **Basilique du Rosaire**, and the **Basilique Supérieure**, topped by gilded turrets and tiled frescos depicting Bernadette's visions. Beneath the basilica is Lourdes' most revered site, the **Grotte de Massabielle** (sometimes known as the Grotte Miraculeuse or the Grotte des Apparitions), where Bernadette experienced her famous visions.

The **Esplanade des Processions**, lined with enormous flickering candles left by previous pilgrims, leads along the river to the grotto's entrance, where people line up to enter the cave itself, or take an icy dip in one of the sacred **baths**.

CHÂTEAU FORT Castle, Museum

(**Fortified Castle; adult/child €5/3; 9am-noon & 1.30-6.30pm, open all day in Jul & Aug**) Lourdes' imposing castle stands on a sheer hill just behind the town. There's been some kind of stronghold on this site since Roman times, but the present building is largely medieval, including the stout walls and the central keep. The castle was fortified again in the 17th and 18th centuries, and served as a state prison following the Revolution.

Since the 1920s, the castle has housed the **Musée Pyrénéen**, which owns one of the region's largest collections of folk art, rural artefacts, tools and other exhibits.

Take the free **lift** (elevator) from rue Baron Duprat or walk up the ramp at the northern end of rue du Bourg.

PIC DU JER Viewpoint

(bd d'Espagne; funicular adult/child return €9.80/7.30; 9.30am-6pm or 7pm Mar-Nov) When the crowds of pilgrims get too much, you can take refuge on the rocky 94m-high pinnacle of the Pic du Jer, which offers panoramic views of Lourdes and the central Pyrenees.

There are two routes to the top: a punishing three-hour slog along a signed trail (ideal for penitents and gluttons for punishment) or a speedy six-minute ride on the century-old **funicular** (ideal for everyone else). Either way, the summit makes a superb spot for a picnic.

Take bus 2 from place Monseigneur Laurence.

Sleeping & Eating

CITEA ST JEAN Hotel **€€**

(05 62 46 30 07; lourdes@citea.com; 1 av du Paradis; s €48-60, d €68-90;) If you're determined to stay in Lourdes, this town hotel is just about the best bet, offering plain, modern rooms with nary a Madonna or crucifix in sight. It's part of the Citea chain, so it's businesslike, but even in summer the rates stay reasonable.

HÔTEL CAZAUX Boutique Hotel **€**

(05 62 94 22 65; www.hotel-cazaux-lourdes.federal-hotel.com; 2 chemin des Rochers; s €42, d €48 Easter–mid-Oct) This small 20-room hotel is a converted private house. It's friendly, a true bargain and sparkling clean, from the immaculate white and salmon-pink exterior with its boxes of fresh flowers to the deepest bedroom corner.

LE LUMA Bistro **€**

(05 62 94 27 25; 23 av du Général Leclerc; Mon-Fri) This great little neighbourhood place with barely half a dozen tables is well worth the short walk away from the tourist eating emporiums. The three-

Basilica, Lourdes (p282)

ALAN SMITH/GETTY IMAGES ©

course set menu is a bargain and includes buffet hors d'oeuvres.

Information

Forum Information Office (☎05 62 42 78 78; www.lourdes-france.com; Esplanade des Processions; ⌚8.30am-6.30pm) For information on the Sanctuaires.

Tourist ffice (☎05 62 42 77 40; www.lourdes-infotourisme.com; place Peyramale; ⌚9am-6.30pm)

Getting There & Away

Lourdes has regular train connections, including TGVs to Pau and Paris Montparnasse.

Bayonne €19 to €22.50, 1¾ hours.

Paris Montparnasse €75 to €107, 6½ hours.

pullmantur

Provence & the French Riviera

There is no more sunny and celebrity-rich part of France than the south. So get set for heart and soul seduction. Travelling here means sensual sauntering through scented lavender fields and vineyards, around vibrant morning markets groaning with fresh produce, and along paradisaical shores lapped by clear turquoise waters.

Roughly speaking, this region splits into three: east is the iconic French Riviera, wedged between glitzy star-spangled Cannes and megalomaniacal Monte Carlo in the millionaire principality of Monaco. In the middle is Provence, hinged on the coast by the wildly contrasting fishing ports of St-Tropez and Marseille, and tethered inland by a stash of Roman vestiges, hilltop villages and exceptional natural landscapes. Languedoc lies west, an upcoming region that travellers tramp to first and foremost for the walled city of Carcassonne and its bewitching witch's-hat turrets.

St-Jean-Cap Ferrat (p343)

Provence & the French Riviera

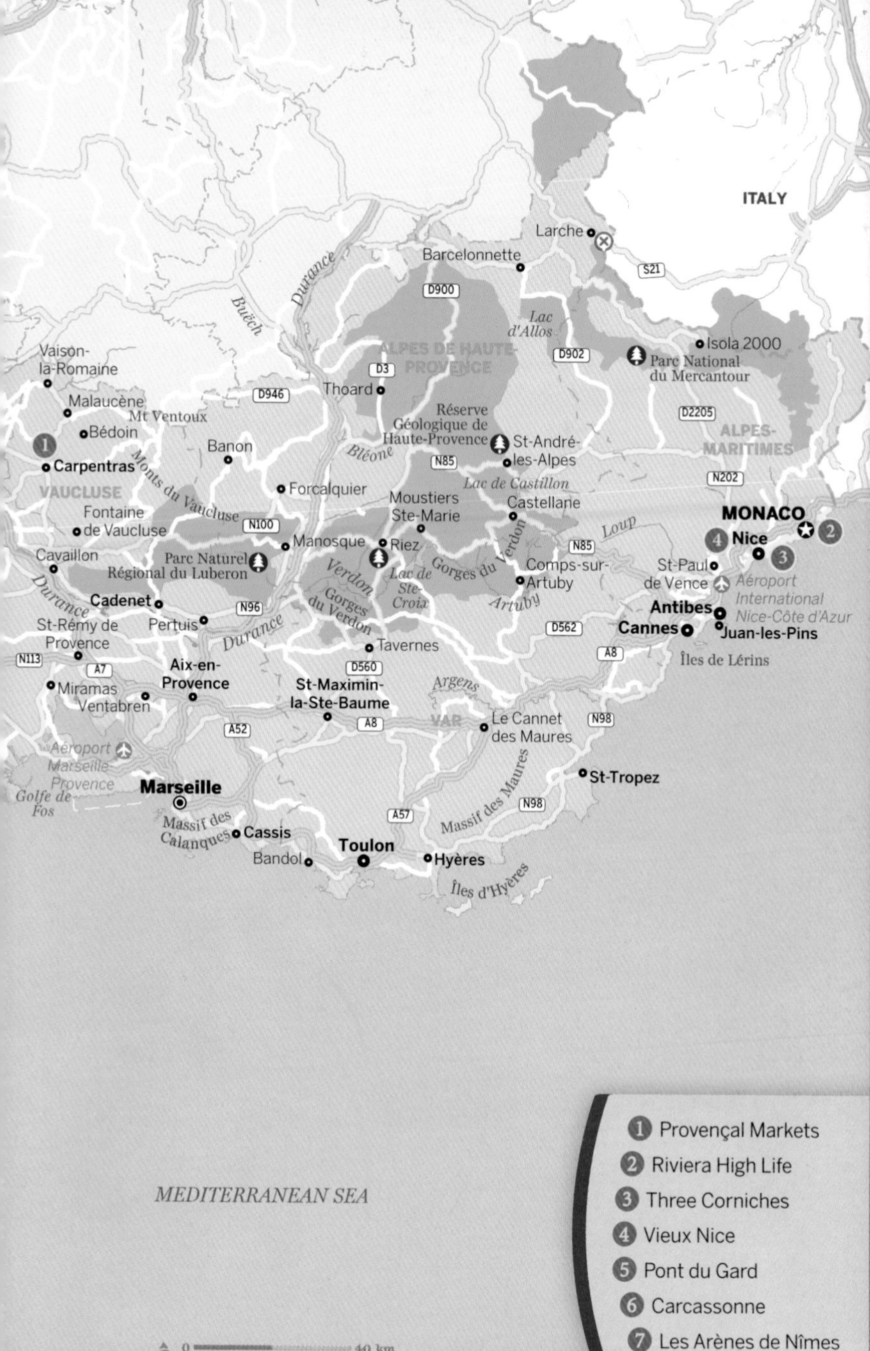
ITALY
Larche
Barcelonnette
S21
D900
Durance
Buëch
Lac d'Allos
ALPES DE HAUTE-PROVENCE
D3
D902
Isola 2000
Parc National du Mercantour
Vaison-la-Romaine
D946
Thoard
Malaucène
Mt Ventoux
Réserve Géologique de Haute-Provence
D2205
Bédoin
ALPES-MARITIMES
Banon
St-André-les-Alpes
Bléone
Carpentras
Monts du Vaucluse
N85
Lac de Castillon
N202
VAUCLUSE
Forcalquier
Moustiers Ste-Marie
Castellane
Fontaine de Vaucluse
MONACO
N100
Loup
Nice
Manosque
Riez
N85
Cavaillon
Parc Naturel Régional du Luberon
Verdon
Lac de Ste-Croix
Gorges du Verdon
Comps-sur-Artuby
St-Paul de Vence
Aéroport International Nice-Côte d'Azur
Cadenet
Gorges du Verdon
Artuby
Antibes
Durance
N96
St-Rémy de Provence
Pertuis
Durance
D562
Cannes
Juan-les-Pins
Tavernes
N113
A7
A8
Îles de Lérins
Aix-en-Provence
D560
Miramas
Ventabren
St-Maximin-la-Ste-Baume
Argens
A52
A8
VAR
Le Cannet des Maures
N98
Aéroport Marseille-Provence
St-Tropez
Marseille
Massif des Maures
Golfe de Fos
N98
A57
Massif des Calanques
Cassis
Toulon
Bandol
Hyères
Îles d'Hyères
MEDITERRANEAN SEA
0 40 km
0 20 miles
1 Provençal Markets
2 Riviera High Life
3 Three Corniches
4 Vieux Nice
5 Pont du Gard
6 Carcassonne
7 Les Arènes de Nîmes

Provence & the French Riviera's Highlights

1

Provençal Markets

Provence is the source of so many good, fresh ingredients, from black truffles to artichokes and asparagus, strawberries, melons, heirloom tomatoes, baby Delicatesse potatoes, and superb lamb, poultry and sausages. Not to mention truly bargain-priced wines and outstanding cheeses. What more does one need in life?

Need to Know

GET UP EARLY Markets run around 7am to noon **READ** *At Home in Provence* (Patricia Wells) for ideas on cooking your purchases **For further coverage, see p331**

Local Knowledge

Provençal Markets Don't Miss List

BY PATRICIA WELLS, COOKBOOK AUTHOR AND COOKING TEACHER

1 VAISON-LA-ROMAINE

The Tuesday market in Vaison-la-Romaine might be 'my' market but it is truly one of Provence's greats. It has the freshest local produce around, especially asparagus, strawberries, melons and heirloom tomatoes. Go to Lou Canesteou for cheese and Peyrerol for chocolate.

2 ST-RÉMY DE PROVENCE

My other favourite is St-Rémy on Wednesday: I love the town, the ambience. Perhaps it is more a market to buy trinkets than food, but whatever you are there for, you just always feel as though you are in the right place at the right time.

3 UZÈS

The third in my top three is also on Wednesday, in Uzès, west of Nîmes. The organic market on place aux Herbes, one of the prettiest little squares in all of France, is stunning – great goat's cheeses, *confitures* (jams) from the nuns and wonderful local olives and olive oil.

4 RICHERENCHES

My favourite speciality market is on Saturday in Richerenches, November through February. It is a fresh black-truffle market – *very* mysterious and you can't figure out what is going on, with lots of people selling pillow cases bulging with black truffles from the trunks of their cars. Stay until lunchtime and have a truffle omelette at one of the two cafes in the village.

5 THE BEST PRODUCE

Tip 1: When looking for the best meat, look for a line of elderly French women. They know how to shop! Tip 2: Look at the vendors: just as people often resemble their dogs, produce vendors resemble their produce. If the vendors are neat, trim, clean, so will their produce be neat, trim, clean. Dirty fingernails usually mean ugly produce! Tip 3: Take time to tour the entire market before you buy. Nothing is worse than a quick, rash purchase at the beginning of the market, only to find better, better-priced produce later on.

Riviera High Life

Monaco and the Riviera *are* glam and glitzy; it's simply impossible to tire of their exceptional beauty. I wander around and I'm constantly noticing it, the architecture, the beaches... To me it is very important to live in a beautiful place, which is why I've spent the best part of 20 years here. Below: Red carpet on bd de la Croisette (p335); Top Right: French Riviera; Bottom Right: Casino de Monte Carlo (p349)

Need to Know

GLAMOUR TIP Most Riviera bars aren't glam; they're just full of glam people **DRESS CODE** Smart **For further coverage, see p325**

2

Local Knowledge

Riviera High Life Don't Miss List

BY ELIZABETH LEWIS, RADIO PRESENTER AT 106.5 RIVIERA RADIO

1 LIVE JAZZ

My favourite summer event is Juan-les-Pins Jazz Festival (p44). I do some translation work when the artists need an interpreter for interviews, so it was a thrill to hang out with legends such as Sonny Rollins in 2012 and Marcus Miller in 2011. In Nice, there's the **Shapko** (www.shapko.com) music venue in the old town, where all the best local and visiting jazz musicians play all year round.

2 CELEBRITY SPOTTING

At Monte Carlo Sporting Club's **Salle des Étoiles** (www.sportingmontecarlo.com) I've chatted to Shirley Bassey (she lives next door to it) at a Liza Minnelli concert, stood behind Elton John (another Riviera resident) at a Grace Jones concert and spotted Julian Lennon at the next table when seeing Steely Dan live. Rumour has it that Lewis Hamilton is Shirley Bassey's new neighbour and John Cleese is another famous addition to the Monaco scene.

3 ROOFTOP SPAS & BARS

Rooftops are prime Riviera real estate and many of the big hotels have rooftop spas and bars open to non-guests. Nice's **Hôtel Grand Aston** (www.hotel-aston.com) has a fabulous rooftop pool where you can spend the day lounging (admission even includes a sandwich and drink!).

4 GLAMOUR

For pure glamour it has to be Monaco's **Monte Carlo Bay Hôtel** (www.montecarlobay.com). It's all majestic, art deco–style colonnades and has a fab spa with a circular pool and a bridge that you swim under to get outside.

5 PRICELESS GEMS

Cave Romagnan (http://caveromagnan.free.fr) in Nice is a tiny, unpretentious wine bar and cellar with an excellent selection of wine. In Biot village, the picturesque hotel and restaurant **Les Arcades** (www.hotel-restaurant-les-arcades.com) serves good-value, proper local food, is really convivial, and you are in one of the most beautiful 15th-century squares in the south of France.

Three Corniches

This trio of clifftop roads (p343) between Nice and Menton provides one of France's most iconic drives. Hitchcock memorably used the corniches as a backdrop in *To Catch a Thief* (1956) starring Cary Grant and Grace Kelly (who, ironically, died in a car crash along the same road in 1982). Don your shades, roll down the windows and navigate jaw-dropping hairpin bends en route to the millionaires' playground of Monaco.

3

4

Vieux Nice

Losing yourself well and truly in the labyrinthine lanes, church-blessed alleys and secret squares of Vieux Nice (Old Nice; p331) is an essential pilgrimage for anyone Riviera-bound. Oozing atmosphere, ambience and a healthy dose of cafes, bars and pavement terraces, Vieux Nice begs go-slow exploration. Break for a lavender or black olive ice-cream at Fenocchio (p330) and an end-of-day drink at Les Distilleries Idéales (p330).

Cours Saleya market (p330), Vieux Nice

5 Pont du Gard

The scale of this Unesco World Heritage Site (p324) near Nîmes is gargantuan: the 35 arches straddling the Roman aqueduct's 275m-long upper tier contain a watercourse designed to carry 20,000 cu metres of water per day. View it from afloat a canoe on the River Gard or pay extra to take a guided walk across its top tier.

6 Carcassonne

The first glimpse of La Cité's sturdy stone witch's-hat turrets above Carcassonne (p322) in the Languedoc is enough to make your hair stand on end. To savour this fairy-tale walled city in its true glory, linger at dusk after the crowds have left, when the old town belongs once again to its 100-odd inhabitants and the few visitors staying at the few lovely hotels within its ramparts.

7 Les Arènes de Nîmes

Long before the rich and famous arrived, the Romans recognised the seductive charms of southern France. The region is studded with many well-preserved Roman monuments, including this almost-intact amphitheatre (p320) in Nîmes. Built to seat over 24,000 spectators, it served as the stage for gladiatorial contests and bloodthirsty shows, and is – controversially – still used for bullfights to this day.

Provence & the French Riviera's Best...

Beaches

- **Plage de Pampelonne** (p339) Play and lunch Brigitte Bardot–style on St-Tropez's finest golden sand.
- **Promenade des Anglais** (p325) Beach-lounge on a sky-blue chair beside Nice's mythical seaside prom.
- **Z Plage** (p337) Glamour and creature comforts on La Croisette, Cannes.
- **Îles de Lérins** (p341) Flee Cannes madness for a perfect castaway cove.
- **Île de Port-Cros** (p342) and **Île de Porquerolles** (p342) Catch a ferry to a bevy of beautiful island beaches.

Modern Art

- **Chapelle du Rosaire** (p333) This bijou chapel was Matisse's pride and joy.
- **Fondation Maeght** (p334) World-class art in St-Paul de Vence.
- **Musée Picasso** (p332) View Picassos in Antibes' former studio turned museum.
- **Mamac** (p325) Nice's modern-art museum is as interesting for the architecture as the art.
- **Aix-en-Provence** (p314) Follow in the footsteps of Paul Cézanne.

Dining

- **L'Atelier** (p315) Not a meal, but an artistic (organic) experience in Arles.
- **Restaurant Pierre Reboul** (p311) Playful, gorgeous creations by Aix' newest culinary star.
- **Le Marmiton** (p317) Learn to cook in a 16th-century palace hotel in Avignon.
- **L'Epuisette** (p305) The address to savour Marseille's famously fishy bouillabaisse.
- **Sea Sens** (p337) French gastronomy and Asian elegance in Cannes.

Shopping

- **St-Tropez** (p341) Seek out *Tarte Tropézienne*, the orange-blossom-flavoured double sponge cake, at its namesake bakery.
- **La Botte Camarguaise** (p315) Camargue cowboy boots, cut, stitched and sold in Arles.
- **Cours Saleya Market** (p331) The place to buy silken olive oil from Provence, pressed from olives that are harvested from November to January.
- **Atelier Rondini** (p341) Iconic, beach-chic sandals cobbled in St-Tropez since 1927.

Left: Cathédrale de Monaco (p348); **Above:** French Riviera (p325)

Need to Know

ADVANCE PLANNING

- **As early as possible** Book accommodation, especially for July, August and during the Cannes Film Festival and Monaco Grand Prix (both in May). Reserve tickets for Avignon's theatre festival (p43).
- **Two weeks before** Book tables for big-name restaurants, especially in Marseille, Nice and St-Tropez.
- **Two days before** Order bouillabaisse at Marseille's bistros (p305).

RESOURCES

- **Provence-Alpes-Côte d'Azur** (www.decouverte-paca.fr) Pan-regional information.
- **Nice Tourisme** (www.nicetourisme.com) Nice's tourist office.
- **PACA** (www.tourismepaca.fr) Umbrella site for Provence and the Riviera.
- **Côte d'Azur Tourisme** (www.cotedazur-tourisme.com) Comprehensive Riviera resource.

GETTING AROUND

- **Trains** An ideal way to explore the Riviera coastline. Base yourself in Nice and take day trips to Monaco and Cannes.
- **Car** Essential in Provence. On the coast, July and August means hellish road traffic, especially on Saturdays and all summer around St-Tropez. Take extra care when driving along the corniches.
- **Boats** Scenic cruises depart from Marseille, Cannes and St-Tropez; don't miss a trip to the Îles de Lérins (p341) or the Îles d'Hyères (p342).

BE FOREWARNED

- **Petty theft** Stealing from backpacks, pockets and bags is rife in Marseille and on the Riviera; be extra vigilant at train stations and on the beach.
- **Cannes hotels** Prices soar to astronomical levels during May's film festival.
- **Dress code** Pack smart clothes for top-end Riviera restaurants, clubs and casinos.
- **Motoring in Monaco** You can't drive into Monaco Ville unless you have a Monaco or local 06 number plate.
- **Mosquitos** Bring repellent for a buzz-free night.

Provence & the French Riviera Itineraries

No trip to France would be complete without a few days spent exploring the French Riviera. With its swaying palm trees, hilltop towns and sparkling beaches, this is the essence of southern France.

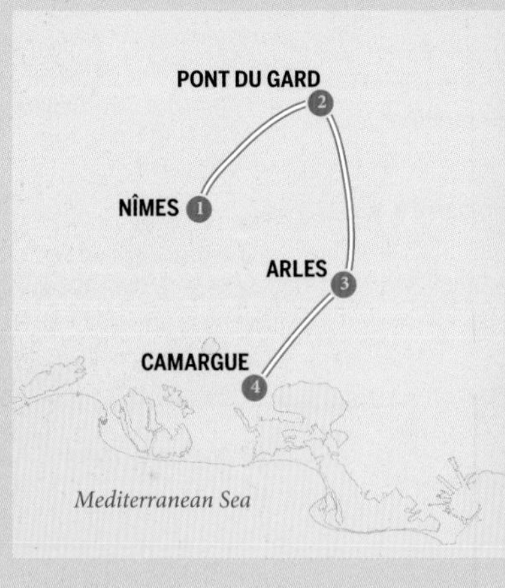

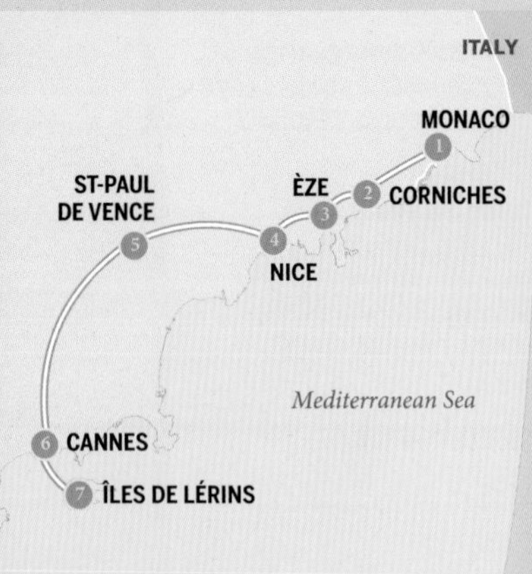

NÎMES TO THE CAMARGUE
Roman Provence

Gloriously intact amphitheatres, triumphal arches and other public buildings transport travellers back to Provence's heyday as a Gallo-Roman province.

Devote day one to **(1) Nîmes**, with its resplendent amphitheatre and theatre, still occasionally used for *férias* and concerts. Just outside Nîmes is one of the great achievements of the Gallo-Roman world – the incredible **(2) Pont du Gard**, the world's highest aqueduct. It's particularly awe inspiring when seen up close – via either a guided walk across the top tier or a self-paddled canoe trip beneath its great arches.

Spend day two in **(3) Arles**, with its duo of impressive Roman theatres. Day three, flee the hustle and bustle of town life for the idyllic wetland of the **(4) Camargue**. Spot candy-pink flamingos, wild white horses and rare bird species (over 500 species in all) in the peaceful setting of one of France's largest natural wetlands – don't forget binoculars and a telephoto lens for your camera.

MONACO TO CANNES
Riviera Highlights

This trip takes in the key sights of the Côte d'Azur. Begin in the millionaires' playground of **(1) Monaco**, where you can ogle the yachts, have a flutter at the casino and lunch fusion-style at La Montgolfière.

On day two, tackle the **(2) the corniches**, a trio of white-knuckle roads snaking across the clifftops west of Monaco. Stop for a wander around the clifftop gardens of **(3) Èze**. By late afternoon you'll reach the classic Riviera city of **(4) Nice**; check into Hôtel La Pérouse and have an authentic Niçois meal in the atmospheric old town.

Day three's for more Nice exploration: don't miss the cours Saleya street market, the promenade des Anglais, the Musée Matisse and Musée d'Art Moderne et d'Art Contemporain (Mamac).

On day four, head inland to hilltop **(5) St-Paul de Vence**, where everyone from Matisse to Picasso once went to paint and party. View the art collection at the Fondation Maeght, and dine and overnight at the legendary Colombe d'Or.

Your last day takes you to cinematic **(6) Cannes**, home of France's starriest film festival. If you can spare an extra day, catch a boat to the lovely **(7) Îles de Lérins**.

Nice (p325)

MEDIOIMAGES/PHOTODISC/GETTY IMAGES ©

Discover Provence & the French Riviera

At a Glance

- **Provence** (p300) France's hot, seductive south: sunbaked towns, lavender fields and tempting alfresco food markets.
- **Languedoc** (p320) Roman remains and rich red wines.
- **French Riviera** (p325) France's most glam coastline: mythical beaches, sparkling water and scenic but hair-raising coastal roads.

Basilique Notre Dame de la Garde, Marseille
STEVE ALLEN/GETTY IMAGES ©

PROVENCE

Marseille

POP 858,902

Marseillais will tell you that the city's rough-and-tumble edginess is part of its charm and that, for all its flaws, it is a very endearing place. They're right: Marseille grows on you with its history, fusion of cultures, souk-like markets, millennia-old port and *corniches* (coastal roads) along rocky inlets and sun-baked beaches. Their ultimate vindication came with Marseille's selection as European Capital of Culture for 2013.

Sights

Buy a **Marseille City Pass** (one-/two-day pass €22/29) at the tourist office (p308). It covers admission to 15 museums, a city tour, unlimited public-transport travel, boat trips and more.

VIEUX PORT Historic Quarter
(**M** Vieux Port) Ships have docked for more than 26 centuries at the city's birthplace, the colourful old port. The main commercial docks were transferred to the Joliette area north of here in the 1840s, but the old port remains a thriving harbour for fishing boats, pleasure yachts and tourists. The free **Cross-Port Ferry** (8am-12.30pm & 1-5pm) in front of the town hall is a fun way to get out on the water, however briefly.

Guarding the harbour are **Bas Fort St-Nicolas** on the south side and, across the water, **Fort St-Jean**, founded in the 13th century by the Knights Hospitaller of

St John of Jerusalem. Here, the national **Musée des Civilisations de l'Europe et de la Méditerranée** (MuCEM; Museum of European & Mediterranean Civilisations; ☎04 96 13 80 90; www.mucem.org; ⏰1-7pm Wed, Thu & Sat) will open a brand-new 40,000-sq-metre state-of-the-art museum in spring 2013.

The port's southern quay is dotted with theatres and bars, and restaurants and cafes buzz until the wee hours a block east on **place Thiars** and **cours Honoré d'Estienne d'Orves**.

LE PANIER Historic Quarter

(Ⓜ Vieux Port) From the Vieux Port, hike north up to this fantastic history-woven quarter, dubbed 'Marseille's Montmartre', as much for its sloping streets as its artsy ambience. In Greek Massilia, it was the site of the *agora* (marketplace), hence its name, which means 'the basket'. During WWII, the quarter was dynamited and afterwards rebuilt. Today it's a mishmash of lanes hiding artisan shops, ateliers (workshops) and terraced houses strung with drying washing.

Its centrepiece is **Centre de la Vieille Charité** (2 rue de la Charité, 2e; both museums adult/student €5/2.50; Ⓜ Joliette), and nearby **Cathédrale de la Major** stands guard between the old and new ports with a stripy façade made of local Cassis stone and green Florentine marble.

BASILIQUE NOTRE DAME DE LA GARDE Church

(Montée de la Bonne Mère; ⏰7am-8pm Apr-Sep, to 7pm Oct-Mar) Everywhere you go in Marseille, you see the opulent, domed 19th-century Romano-Byzantine basilica occupying Marseille's highest point, La Garde (162m). Built between 1853 and 1864, it is ornamented with coloured marble, murals depicting the safe passage of sailing vessels and superbly restored mosaics. The hilltop gives 360-degree panoramas of the city's sea of terracotta roofs below.

CHÂTEAU D'IF Island, Castle

(www.if.monuments-nationaux.fr; adult/child €5/free; ⏰9.30am-6.30pm May-Sep, to 4.45pm Tue-Sun Oct-Apr) Immortalised in Alexandre Dumas' classic 1844 novel *Le Comte de Monte Cristo* (The Count of Monte Cristo), 16th-century fortress-turned-prison Château d'If sits on the 30-sq-km **Île d'If**, 3.5km west of the Vieux Port. Political prisoners were incarcerated here, along with hundreds of Protestants, the Revolutionary hero Mirabeau, and the Communards of 1871.

Frioul If Express (www.frioul-if-express.com; 1 quai des Belges) boats leave for Château d'If (€10 return, 20 minutes) from the Vieux Port. There are over 15 daily departures in summer, fewer in winter.

Tours

LE GRAND TOUR Bus Tour

(☎04 91 91 05 82; www.marseillelegrandtour.com; adult/child €18/9; ⏰10am-7pm) Feel the wind in your hair as you travel between key sights and museums aboard a hop-on, hop-off open-topped bus. Tickets are sold at the tourist office or on board, and include a five-language audioguide.

GUIDED TOUR Walking Tour

(www.resamarseille.com; tours €7; ⏰2pm Sat; Ⓜ Vieux Port) Leaves from the tourist office (p308).

FREE **MARSEILLE PROVENCE GREETERS** Walking Tour

(www.marseilleprovencegreeters.com) Free walking tours by locals; advance website registration required.

CROISIÈRES MARSEILLE CALANQUES Boat Tour

(www.croisieres-marseille-calanques.com; 74 quai du Port) Runs two-hour return trips from the Vieux Port taking in six *calanques* (steep-walled inlets) (adult/child/family costs €22/7/68); three-hour return trips past 12 *calanques* to Cassis (adult/child/family €28/21/85); and 1½-hour trips around the Baie de Marseille (adult €10).

Central Marseille

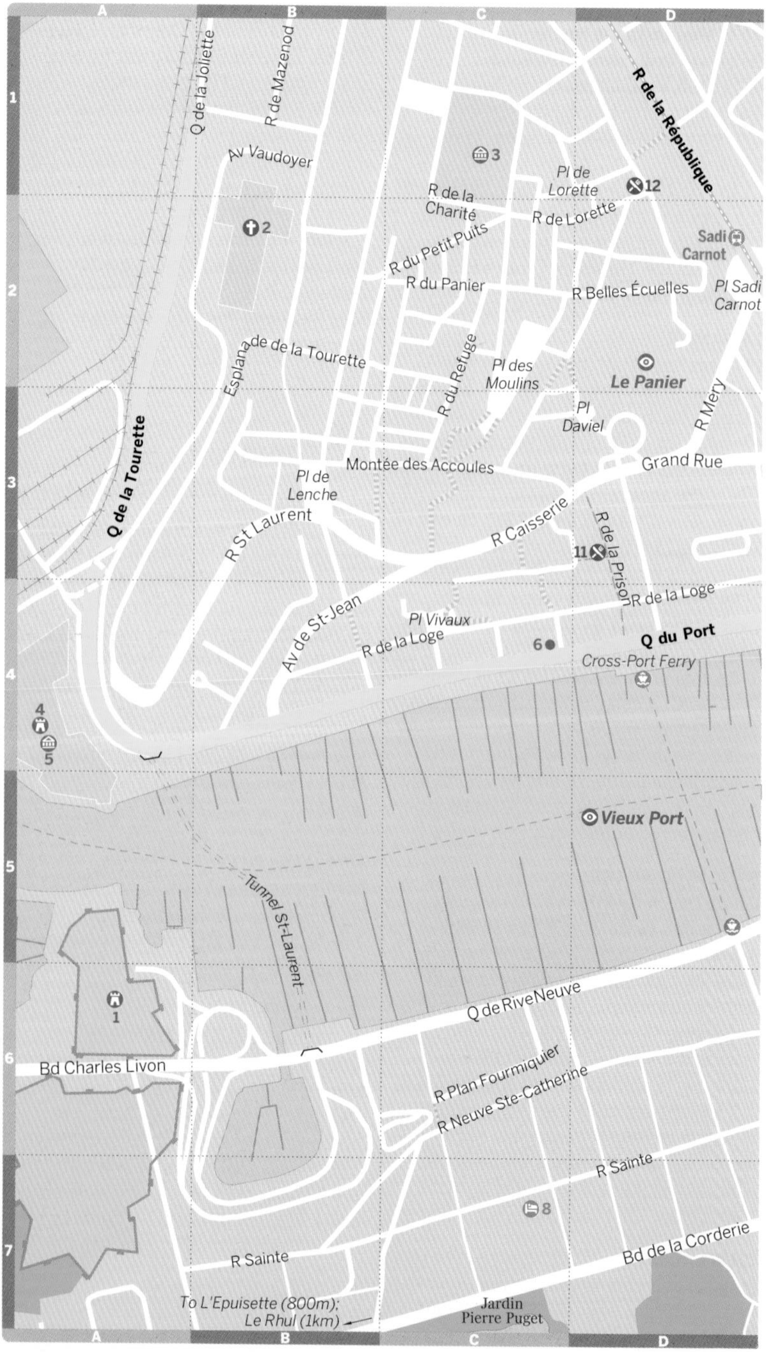

A B C D
1 2 3 4 5 6 7

Q de la Joliette
R de Mazenod
Av Vaudoyer
3
2
R de la République
Pl de Lorette
12
R de la Charité
R de Lorette
R du Petit Puits
Sadi Carnot
R du Panier
R Belles Écuelles
Pl Sadi Carnot
Esplanade de la Tourette
R du Refuge
Pl des Moulins
Le Panier
R Méry
Pl Daviel
Q de la Tourette
Montée des Accoules
Grand Rue
Pl de Lenche
R Caisserie
R St Laurent
R de la Prison
11
R de la Loge
Av de St-Jean
Pl Vivaux
R de la Loge
6
Q du Port
Cross-Port Ferry
4
5
Vieux Port
Tunnel St-Laurent
1
Q de Rive Neuve
Bd Charles Livon
R Plan Fourmiquier
R Neuve Ste-Catherine
R Sainte
8
Bd de la Corderie
R Sainte
To L'Epuisette (800m); Le Rhul (1km)
Jardin Pierre Puget

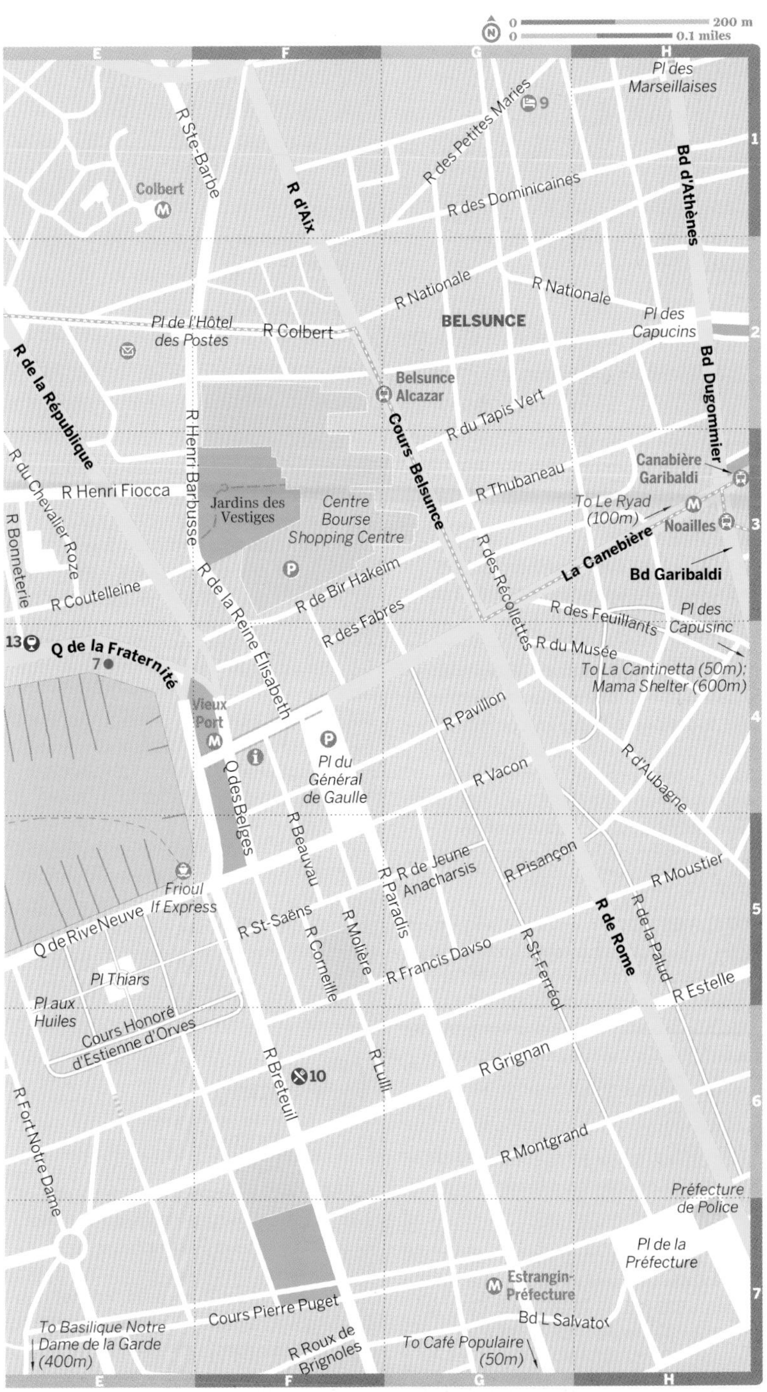
0 200 m
0 0.1 miles
Pl des Marseillaises
R des Petites Maries
9
R Ste-Barbe
R d'Aix
Bd d'Athènes
R des Dominicaines
Colbert
R Nationale
R Nationale
Pl de l'Hôtel des Postes
R Colbert
BELSUNCE
Pl des Capucins
R de la République
Belsunce Alcazar
Bd Dugommier
R du Tapis Vert
Cours Belsunce
R Henri Barbusse
Canabière Garibaldi
R Thubaneau
R du Chevalier Roze
R Henri Fiocca
Jardins des Vestiges
Centre Bourse Shopping Centre
To Le Ryad (100m)
Noailles
R Bonneterie
La Canebière
Bd Garibaldi
R de Bir Hakeim
R des Récollettes
R Coutelleine
R des Fabres
R des Feuillants
Pl des Capusinc
R de la Reine Élisabeth
13
Q de la Fraternité
7
R du Musée
To La Cantinetta (50m); Mama Shelter (600m)
Vieux Port
R Pavillon
Pl du Général de Gaulle
R d'Aubagne
Q des Belges
R Vacon
R Beauvau
R de Jeune Anacharsis
R Pisançon
Frioul If Express
R Paradis
R Moustier
R de Rome
R de la Palud
Q de Rive Neuve
R St-Saëns
R Molière
R Corneille
R Francis Davso
R St-Ferréol
R Estelle
Pl Thiars
Pl aux Huiles
Cours Honoré d'Estienne d'Orves
R Breteuil
10
R Lulli
R Grignan
R Fort Notre Dame
R Montgrand
Préfecture de Police
Pl de la Préfecture
Estrangin-Préfecture
Cours Pierre Puget
Bd L Salvator
To Basilique Notre Dame de la Garde (400m)
R Roux de Brignoles
To Café Populaire (50m)
E
F
G
H
1
2
3
4
5
6
7

Central Marseille

Top Sights
- Le Panier ... D2
- Vieux Port ... D5

Sights
- 1 Bas Fort St-Nicolas ... A6
- 2 Cathédrale de la Major ... B2
- 3 Centre de la Vieille Charité ... C1
- 4 Fort St-Jean ... A4
- 5 Musée des Civilisations de l'Europe et de la Méditerranée ... A4

Activities, Courses & Tours
- 6 Croisières Marseille Calanques ... C4
- 7 Le Grand Tour ... E4

Sleeping
- 8 Casa Honoré ... C7
- 9 Hôtel Vertigo ... G1

Eating
- 10 La Part des Anges ... F6
- 11 Le Café des Épices ... D3
- 12 Pizzaria Chez Étienne ... D1

Drinking
- 13 La Caravelle ... E4

Sleeping

CASA HONORÉ B&B €€€

(**04 96 11 01 62; www.casahonore.com; 123 rue Sainte; d incl breakfast €150-200; ; Vieux Port**) Los Angeles meets Marseille at this four-room *maison d'hôte*, built around a central courtyard with a lap pool shaded by banana trees. The fashion-forward style reflects the owner's love for contemporary interior design (she has a shop down the block), using disparate elements such as black wicker and the occasional cow skull, which come together in one sexy package. One complaint: some bathrooms are partitioned by curtains, not doors.

HÔTEL VERTIGO Hostel €

(**04 91 91 07 11; www.hotelvertigo.fr; 42 rue des Petites Maries; dm/d €25/60; ; Gare St-Charles**) This snappy boutique hostel kisses goodbye to dodgy bunks and hospital-like decor. Here it's 'hello' to vintage posters, designer chrome kitchen, groovy communal spaces and polite multilingual staff. Double rooms are particularly good, some with a private terrace. No curfew (or lift, alas). A second, all-dorm facility is closer to the Vieux Port.

LE RYAD Boutique Hotel €€

(**04 91 47 74 54; www.leryad.fr; 16 rue Sénac de Meilhan; s €80-105, d €95-125, family €170; ; Noailles, Canebière Garibaldi**) With high ceilings, arched alcoves, warm colours and minimalist decor, super-stylish Le Ryad draws sumptuous influence from Morocco. Beautiful bathrooms, garden-view rooms and great service make up for the sometimes-sketchy neighbourhood. Despite the four-storey walk up, it's worth booking the top-floor room for its tiny rooftop terrace.

MAMA SHELTER Design Hotel €€

(**01 43 48 48 48; www.mamashelter.com; 64 rue de la Loubière; d €99-139, q €159, ste €209; ; Notre Dame du Mont–Cours Julien**) The brainchild of Serge Trigano, son of Gilbert (Club Med creator), this affordable-chic new kid on the block opened with a bang in 2012. It sports design by Philippe Starck, nifty extras like Kiehl's bathroom products, and free in-room movies. The rooms are wheelchair accessible and parking costs €17 per day.

Eating

LE CAFÉ DES ÉPICES

Modern French €€

(**04 91 91 22 69; www.cafedesepices.com; 4 rue du Lacydon; 3-course lunch/dinner menu €25/40; lunch Tue-Sat, dinner Thu-Fri; ; Vieux Port**) One of Marseille's best young chefs, Arnaud de Grammont, infuses his cooking with a panoply of flavours...think squid ink spaghetti with sesame and perfectly cooked scallops, or tender roasted potatoes with hints of coriander and citrus, topped by the catch of the day.

Saturday lunch is particularly family-friendly on the sunny terrace leading onto an olive-tree-lined pedestrianised square. Reservations essential.

LA CANTINETTA Italian €
(☎04 91 48 10 48; 24 cours Julien; mains €9-19; ⏰lunch & dinner Tue-Sat; Ⓜ Notre Dame du Mont–Cours Julien) The top table at cours Julien serves perfectly al-dente house-made pasta, paper-thin prosciutto, marinated vegetables, *bresaola* (air-dried beef) and risotto. Tables in the convivial dining room are cheek by jowl, and everyone seems to know each other, or escape to the sun-dappled, tiled-patio garden.

LA PART DES ANGES Bistro €
(33 rue Sainte; mains €15; ⏰lunch Mon-Sat, dinner daily; Ⓜ Estrangin Préfecture) No address buzzes with Marseille's hip, buoyant crowd more than this fabulous all-rounder wine bistro, named after the amount of alcohol that evaporates through a barrel during wine or whisky fermentation: the angels' share.

CAFÉ POPULAIRE Neo-Bistro €
(☎04 91 02 53 96; 10 rue Paradis; mains €14-16; ⏰lunch & dinner Tue-Sat; Ⓜ Estrangin-Préfecture) Vintage tables and chairs, old books on the shelves and a fine collection of glass soda bottles all add to the retro air of this 1950s-styled jazz *comptoir* (counter). Plump for a stool at the zinc bar or lounge at a table with a view of the fabulous open kitchen, where simple daily specials like *gambas à la plancha* (fried prawns served on a hot plate) or beetroot and coriander salad are cooked up for a chic crowd.

PIZZARIA CHEZ ÉTIENNE Marseillais €
(43 rue de Lorette; mains €12-15; ⏰lunch & dinner Mon-Sat; Ⓜ Colbert) This old Marseillais haunt has the best pizza in town, as well as succulent *pavé de boeuf* (beef steak) and scrumptious *supions frits* (pan-fried squid with garlic and parsley). Since it's a convivial meeting point for the entire neighbourhood, definitely pop in well beforehand to reserve (there's no phone). Make sure you have some euros in your pocket before you dine; credit cards are not accepted.

Bouillabaisse

Originally cooked by fishermen from the scraps of their catch, bouillabaisse is Marseille's classic signature dish. True bouillabaisse includes at least four different kinds of fish, sometimes shellfish. It's served in two parts: the broth *(soupe de poisson)*, rich with tomato, saffron and fennel; and the cooked fish, deboned tableside and presented on a platter. On the side are croutons and *rouille* (a bread-thickened garlic, chilli and pepper mayonnaise) and grated cheese.

The most reliably consistent spots for real bouillabaisse include the following:

Le Rhul (☎04 91 52 01 77; www.lerhul.fr; 269 corniche Président John F Kennedy; mains €50; 🚌83) This long-standing classic has atmosphere (however kitschy): a 1940s seaside hotel with Mediterranean views.

L'Epuisette (☎04 91 52 17 82; www.l-epuisette.com; Vallon des Auffes; mains €60; ⏰Tue-Sat; 🚌83) The swankest address by far, with a Michelin star and knockout water-level views from an elegantly austere dining room. First courses cost €34 to €45 and desserts €20, though you'll likely not have room.

Vieux Port

An Itinerary

Bold and busy and open-armed to the sea, Marseille is France's oldest city. Standing on the quai des Belges it's hard to get a sense of the extent of the old port, a kilometre long on either side, running down to the great bastions of St-Jean and St-Nicolas, which once had their guns trained on the rebellious population rather than out to sea. Immerse yourself in the city's history with this full-day itinerary.

Go early to experience the **fish market** 1, where you'll swap tall tales with the gregarious vendors. Hungry? Grab a balcony seat at La Caravelle, where views of the Basilique Notre Dame de la Garde accompany your morning coffee. Afterwards, take a **boat trip** 2 to Château d'If, made famous by the Dumas novel *The Count of Monte Cristo*. Alternatively, stay landside and explore the apricot-coloured alleys of **Le Panier** 3, browsing the exhibits at the **Centre de la Vieille Charité** 4.

In the afternoon, hop on the free cross-port ferry to the port's south side and wander into the **Abbaye St-Victor** 5 to see the bones of martyrs enshrined in gold. You can then catch the sunset from the stone benches in the **Jardin du Pharo** 6. As the warm southern evening sets in, join the throngs on cours **Honoré d'Estienne d'Orves**, where you can drink pastis beneath a giant statue of a lion devouring a man – the **Milo de Croton** 7.

CAPITAL OF CULTURE 2013

The largest urban renewal project in Europe, the Euroméditerranée project aims to rehabilitate the commercial Joliette docks along the same lines as London's Docklands. The city's green-and-white striped Cathédrale de la Major, for years abandoned in an area of urban wasteland, will form its centrepiece.

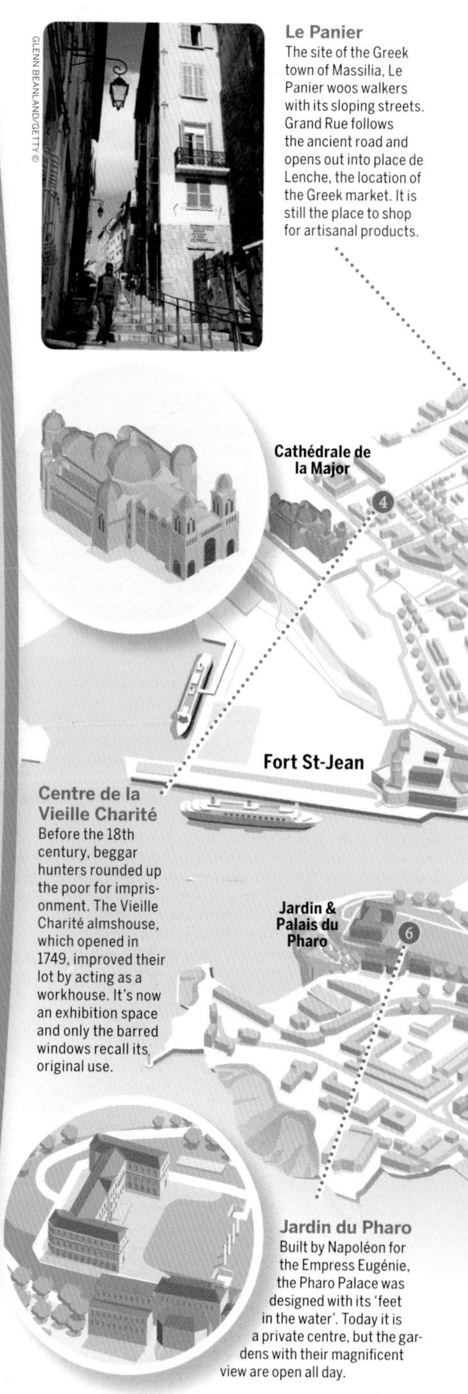

TOR EIGELAND/ALAMY

Fish Market

Marseille's small fish market still sets up each morning to hawk the daily catch. Take a lesson in local seafood, spotting sea squirts, scorpion fish, sea urchins and conger eels. Get there before 9am if you're buying.

Milo de Croton

Subversive local artist Pierre Puget carved the savage *Milo de Croton* for Louis XIV. The statue, whose original is in the Louvre, is a meditation on man's pride and shows the Greek Olympian being devoured by a lion, his Olympic cup cast down.

Frioul If Express

Catch the Frioul If Express to Château d'If, France's equivalent to Alcatraz. Prisoners were housed according to class: the poorest at the bottom in windowless dungeons, the wealthiest in paid-for private cells, with windows and a fireplace.

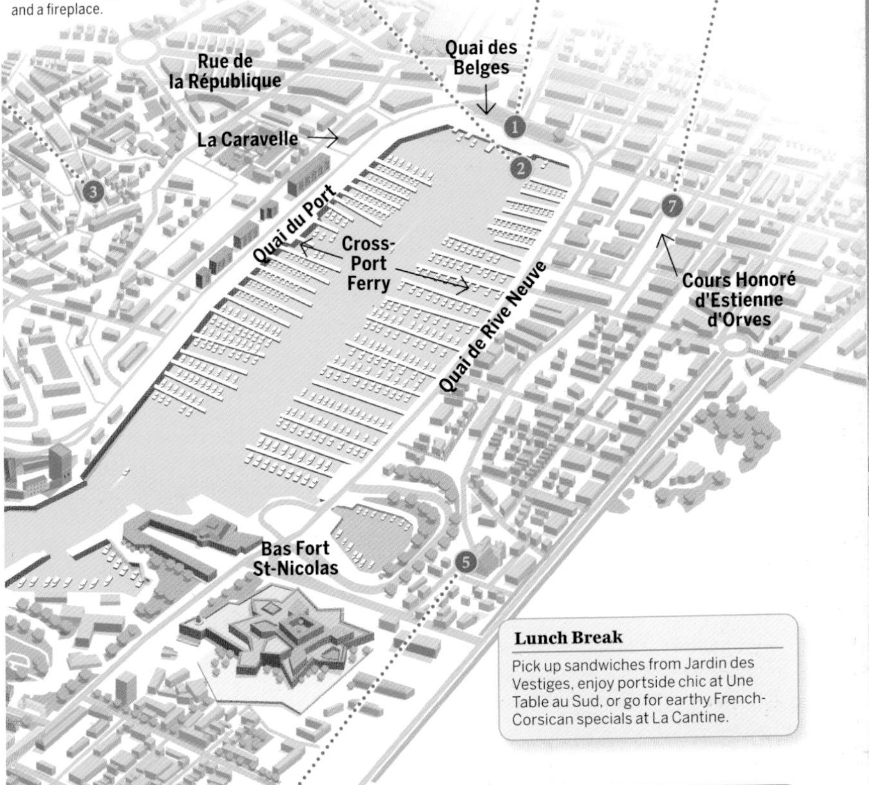

Rue de la République

Quai des Belges

1

La Caravelle

2

3

Quai du Port

Cross-Port Ferry

Quai de Rive Neuve

7

Cours Honoré d'Estienne d'Orves

Bas Fort St-Nicolas

5

Lunch Break

Pick up sandwiches from Jardin des Vestiges, enjoy portside chic at Une Table au Sud, or go for earthy French-Corsican specials at La Cantine.

Abbaye St-Victor

St-Victor was built (420–30) to house the remains of tortured Christian martyrs. On Candlemas (2 February) the black Madonna is brought up from the crypt and the archbishop blesses the city and the sea.

DAN HERRICK

A selection of bread at the market

GRANT FAINT/GETTY IMAGES ©

Drinking

LA CARAVELLE Bar
(34 quai du Port; ⌚7am-2am; Ⓜ Vieux Port)
Look up or miss this standout upstairs hideaway, styled with rich wood and leather, a zinc bar and yellowing murals. If it's sunny, snag a coveted spot on the port-side terrace. On Fridays, there's live jazz from 9pm to midnight.

Information

Tourist office (☎04 91 13 89 00; www.marseille-tourisme.com; 4 La Canebière; ⌚9am-7pm Mon-Sat, 10am-5pm Sun; Ⓜ Vieux Port)

Getting There & Away

AIR Aéroport Marseille-Provence (www.marseille.aeroport.fr), also called Aéroport Marseille-Marignane, is located 25km northwest of Marseille in Marignane.

TRAIN From Marseille, trains, including TGVs, go to destinations all over France and Europe, including the following, which all run at least half a dozen times a day:

Avignon €24, 35 minutes

Lyon €50, 1¾ hours

Nice €35, 2½ hours

Paris Gare de Lyon €103, three hours

Aix-en-Provence

POP 141,895

Aix-en-Provence is to Provence what the Left Bank is to Paris: an enclave of bourgeois-bohemian chic just 25km from chaotic, exotic Marseille. Some 30,000 students from the Université de Provence Aix-Marseille, many from overseas, set the mood on the street: there's plenty of bars,

Aix-en-Provence

Top Sights
- Cours Mirabeau B4
- Musée Granet D4

Sleeping
1. Hôtel des Augustins B3
2. Hôtel les Quatre Dauphins C4
3. L'Épicerie A2

Eating
4. Charlotte A3
5. Le Petit Verdot A3
6. Restaurant Pierre Reboul C3

Drinking
7. Les Deux Garçons C3

cafes and affordable restaurants. The city is rich in culture (two of Aix' most famous sons are Paul Cézanne and Émile Zola) and oh-so respectable, with plane-tree-shaded boulevards and fashionable boutiques.

Sights

The **Aix City Pass (€15)**, valid five days, includes a guided walking tour, admission to the Atelier Paul Cézanne, Jas de Bouffan and Musée Granet, and a trip on the mini-tram; the **Cézanne Pass (€12)** covers his three main sights. Buy them at the tourist office.

COURS MIRABEAU Historic Quarter

No avenue better epitomises Provence's most graceful city than fountain-studded **cours Mirabeau**, sprinkled with elegant Renaissance *hôtels particuliers* (private mansions) and crowned with a summer-time roof of leafy plane trees. Named after the revolutionary hero Comte de Mirabeau, it was laid out in the 1640s. Cézanne and Zola famously hung out at **Les Deux**

Aix-en-Provence

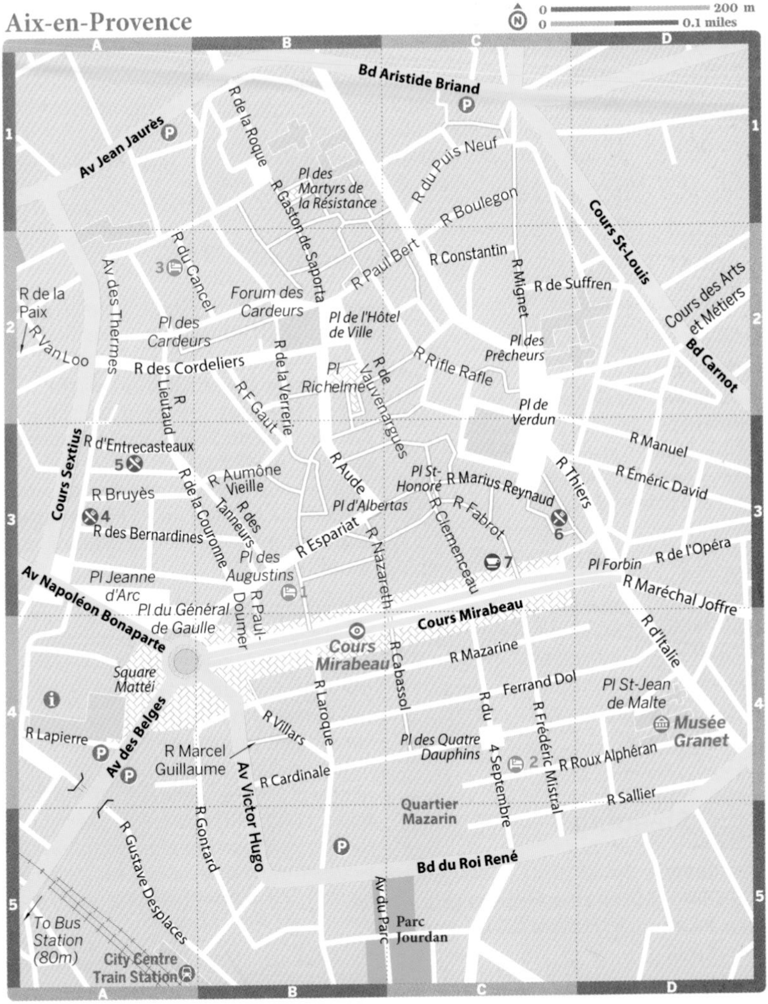

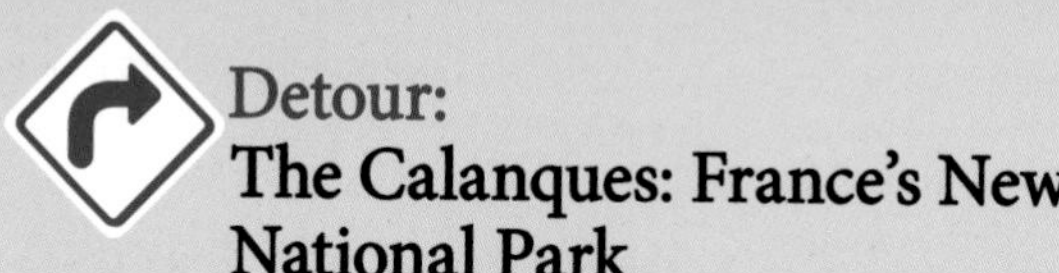

Detour: The Calanques: France's Newest National Park

Marseille abuts the wild and spectacular **Parc National des Calanques** (www.parcsnationaux.fr), a 20km stretch of high, rocky promontories, rising from brilliant-turquoise Mediterranean waters. The sheer cliffs are occasionally interrupted by small idyllic beaches, some impossible to reach without a kayak.

The best way to see the *calanques*, October to June, is to hike the many maquis-lined trails. During summer, trails close because of fire danger: take a boat tour either from Marseille or Cassis, but be forewarned, they don't stop to let you swim; alternatively, go sea kayaking with **Raskas Kayak** (www.raskas-kayak.com), drive or take public transport.

Calanque de Sormiou is the largest rocky inlet. Two seasonal restaurants serve lunch with fabulous views, and require reservations. **Le Château** (04 91 25 08 69; mains €18-24; Apr–mid-Oct) has the best food and **Le Lunch** (04 91 25 05 37, 04 91 25 05 39; http://wp.resto.fr/lelunch; mains €16-28; Apr–mid-Oct) the better view. Diners with reservations are allowed to drive through; otherwise, the road is open to cars weekdays only, September to June.

Marseille's tourist office (p308) leads guided walks (no kids under eight) of the *calanques*, and has information on walks and trail closures.

Garçons (53 cours Mirabeau; 7am-2am), one of a clutch of pavement cafes.

MUSÉE GRANET Art Museum
(www.museegranet-aixenprovence.fr; place St-Jean de Malte; adult/child €4/free; 11am-7pm Tue-Sun) Housed in a 17th-century priory of the Knights of Malta, this exceptional museum is named after the Provençal painter François Marius Granet (1775–1849), who donated a large number of works. Its collections include 16th- to 20th-century Italian, Flemish and French works. Modern art reads like a who's who: Picasso, Léger, Matisse, Monet, Klee, Van Gogh and Giacometti, among others, including the museum's pride and joy: nine Cézanne works.

Sleeping

L'ÉPICERIE B&B €€
(06 08 85 38 68; www.unechambreenville.eu; 12 rue du Cancel; s incl breakfast €80-120, d incl breakfast €100-130;) This wonderfully intimate B&B is the fabulous creation of born-and-bred Aixois lad Luc. His breakfast room and *salon de thé* (tea room) recreates a 1950s grocery store, and the beautiful flowery garden out back is perfect for evening dining (just make sure you book ahead to avoid disappointment). Morning meals are veritable feasts, so bring an appetite. Two rooms accommodate families of four.

HÔTEL DES AUGUSTINS Hotel €€
(04 42 27 28 59; www.hotel-augustins.com; 3 rue de la Masse; r €99-250;) A mere heartbeat from the hub of Aixois life, this former 15th-century convent with a stained-glass foyer has volumes of history: for example, Martin Luther stayed here after his excommunication from Rome. Filled with hand-painted furniture, the largest, most luxurious rooms have jacuzzis; two rooms have private terraces beneath the filigreed bell tower.

HÔTEL LES QUATRE DAUPHINS Boutique Hotel **€**
(☎04 42 38 16 39; www.lesquatredauphins.fr; 54 rue Roux Alphéran; s €55-60, d €70-85; ❄📶) This sweet 13-room hotel, a former private mansion, was redone in 2010 and is fresh and clean, with excellent new bathrooms.

Eating

RESTAURANT PIERRE REBOUL Gastronomic **€€€**
(☎04 42 20 58 26; www.restaurant-pierre-reboul.com; 11 Petite Rue St-Jean; 3-/7-/12-course menus €42/85/142; ⏲lunch Tue-Sat, dinner Wed-Sat, closed late Aug) Aix' newest culinary star invents playful, gorgeous creations that are homages to eating. With a minimalist sensibility, in both the relaxed dining room and on the exquisitely presented plates, Reboul crafts original juxtapositions using fresh but timeless ingredients. Think perfectly seared duck with a savoury, unexpectedly Asian-influenced broth, sea foam and tender pasta. The lunch special (€50), includes mineral water, coffee and a glass of perfectly paired wine.

LE PETIT VERDOT French **€€**
(☎04 42 27 30 12; www.lepetitverdot.fr; 7 rue d'Entrecasteaux; mains €15-25; ⏲dinner Mon-Sat, lunch Sat) Delicious menus are designed around what's in season and paired with excellent wines. Meats are often braised all day, vegetables are tender, stewed in delicious broths. Save room for an incandescent dessert. Lively dining occurs around tabletops made of wine crates (expect to talk to your neighbour), and the gregarious owner speaks multiple languages.

CHARLOTTE Bistro **€**
(☎04 42 26 77 56; 32 rue des Bernardines; 2-/3-course menus €15.50/19; ⏲lunch & dinner Tue-Sat; 👪) It's all very cosy at Charlotte, where everyone knows everyone. French classics such as veal escalope and beef steak fill the handwritten menu, and there are always a couple of imaginative *plats du jour* (dishes of the day). In summer everything moves into the garden.

Information

Tourist office (☎04 42 16 11 61; www.aixenprovencetourism.com; 37 av Giuseppi Verdi; ⏲8.30am-7pm Mon-Sat, 10am-1pm & 2-6pm Sun Oct-Jun, to 8pm Jul-Sep)

Getting There & Away

Tiny city centre train station, at the southern end of av Victor Hugo, serves Marseille (€8, 45 minutes). Aix' TGV station, 15km from the city centre and accessible by shuttle bus (€3.70

Calanque de Sormiou
HEINZ WOHNER/GETTY IMAGES ©

Left: Woman in costume, Arles festival; Right: Les Arènes, Arles

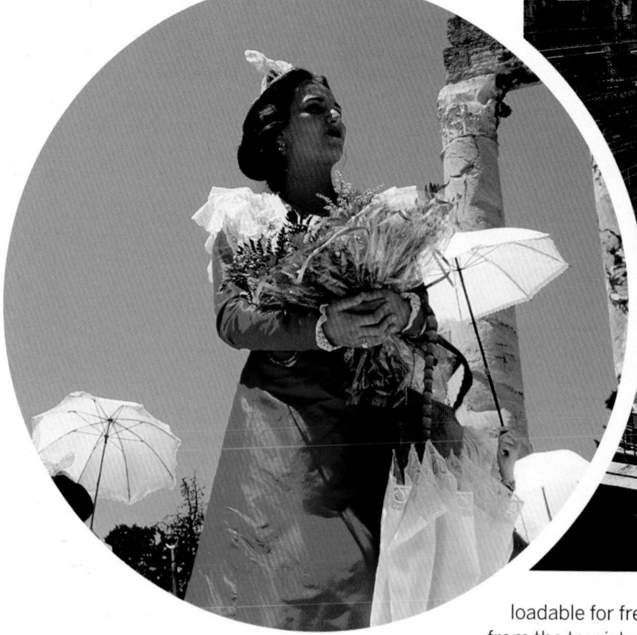

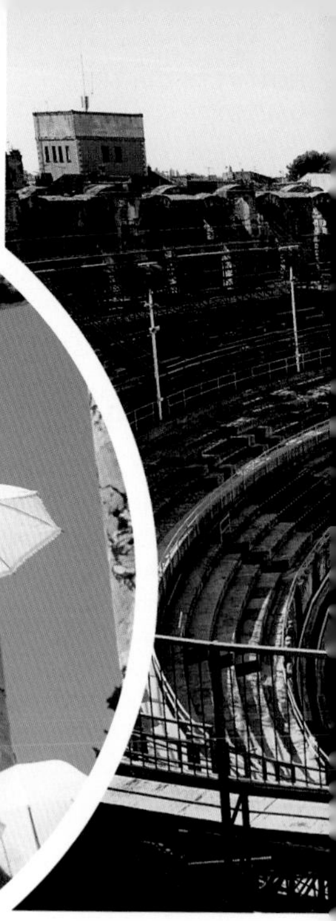

from the bus station), serves most of France; to Marseille it's 12 minutes (€8, 20 daily).

Arles

POP 54,088

Arles' poster boy is the celebrated impressionist painter Vincent van Gogh. If you're familiar with his work, you'll be familiar with Arles: the light, the colours, the landmarks and the atmosphere, all faithfully captured.

Sights & Activities

Though he painted 200-odd canvases in Arles, there are no Van Gogh artworks here today, and Van Gogh's little 'yellow house' on place Lamartine, which he painted in 1888, was destroyed during WWII. Nevertheless, there are several ways to pay homage to the master. Mapped out in a brochure (€1 or downloadable for free online) from the tourist office (p315), the evocative Van Gogh walking circuit of the city takes in scenes painted by the artist.

LES ARÈNES Roman Sites

(Amphithéâtre; adult/child incl Théâtre Antique €6.50/free; 9am-7pm) Slaves, criminals and wild animals (including giraffes) met their dramatic demise before a jubilant 20,000-strong crowd during Roman gladiatorial displays at Les Arènes, built around the late 1st or early 2nd century AD. During the early medieval Arab invasions the arch-laced circular structure, which is 136m long, 107m wide and 21m tall, was topped with four defensive towers to become a fortress. Indeed, by the 1820s, when the amphitheatre was returned to its original use, there were 212 houses and two churches that had to be razed on the site.

Buy tickets for theatre and concerts at the **Bureau de Location** (**08 91 70 03 70; www.arenes-arles.com; 9.30am-noon**

& 2-6pm Mon-Fri, 10am-1pm Sat) near the entrance.

MUSÉE RÉATTU Art Museum

(**04 90 49 37 58; www.museereattu.arles.fr; 10 rue du Grand Prieuré; adult/child €7/free; 10am-12.30pm & 2-6.30pm Tue-Sun)** This splendid modern-art museum is housed in the exquisitely renovated 15th-century Grand Priory of the Knights of Malta. Among its collections are works by 18th- and 19th-century Provençal artists and two paintings and 57 sketches by Picasso. It hosts wonderfully curated cutting-edge exhibitions.

MUSÉE DÉPARTEMENTAL ARLES ANTIQUE Antiquities Museum

(**04 13 31 51 03; www.arles-antique.cg13.fr; av de la Première Division Française Libre; adult/child €6/free; 10am-6pm Wed-Mon)** This striking, state-of-the-art cobalt-blue museum perches on the edge of what used to be the Roman chariot racing track (circus), 1.5km southwest of the tourist office. The rich collection of pagan and Christian art includes stunning mosaics. A leading mosaic restoration centre; watch work in progress.

THÉÂTRE ANTIQUE Roman Sites

(**04 90 96 93 30; bd des Lices; admission €4.50, or free with Les Arènes ticket; 9am-7pm)** Still regularly used for alfresco concerts and plays, the Théâtre Antique dates from the end of the 1st century BC. For hundreds of years it was a source of construction materials, with workers chipping away at the 102m-diameter structure (the column on the right-hand side near the entrance indicates the height of the original arcade). Enter on rue de la Calade.

Sleeping

HÔTEL DE L'AMPHITHÉÂTRE Historic Hotel **€**

(**04 90 96 10 30; www.hotelamphitheatre.fr; 5-7 rue Diderot; s/d/tr/q from €57/67/117/137;** **)** Crimson, chocolate, terracotta

CATHERINE HANSEN/GETTY IMAGES ©

Don't Miss Cézanne's Aix

The life of local lad Paul Cézanne (1839–1906) is treasured in Aix. To see where he ate, drank, studied and painted, follow the **Circuit de Cézanne** (Cézanne Trail), marked by footpath-embedded bronze plaques. The informative English-language guide to the plaques, *Cézanne's Footsteps*, is free at the tourist office. A mobile app, City of Cézanne in Aix-en-Provence (€2), is available online.

Cézanne's last studio, **Atelier Paul Cézanne**, 1.5km north of the tourist office, was preserved (and recreated: not all the tools and still-life models strewn around the single room were his) as it was at the time of his death. Though the studio is inspiring, none of his works hang here. Take bus 1 or 20 to the Atelier Cézanne stop, or walk 1.5km from the centre.

Visits to the other two sights must be reserved at the tourist office. In 1859 Cézanne's father bought **Le Jas de Bouffan**, a country manor west of Aix centre, where Cézanne painted: 36 oils and 17 watercolours in the decades that followed depicting the house, farm and chestnut-lined alley.

In 1895 Cézanne rented a cabin at **Les Carrières de Bibémus**, where he did most of his Montagne Ste-Victoire paintings. One-hour tours of the ochre quarry take visitors on foot through the burnt-orange rocks Cézanne captured so vividly.

NEED TO KNOW

Atelier Paul Cézanne (www.atelier-cezanne.com; 9 av Paul Cézanne; adult/child €5.50/2; 10am-noon & 2-6pm, closed Sun winter); **Le Jas de Bouffan** (04 42 16 10 91; adult/child €5.50/2; guided tours 10.30am-5.30pm daily summer, less frequent other times; 6 stop Corsy); **Les Carrières de Bibémus** (Bibémus Quarries; 04 42 16 10 91; adult/child €6.60/3.10; tours 9.45am daily Jun-Sep, 10.30am & 5pm Mon, Wed, Fri & Sun Apr, May & Oct, 3pm Wed & Sat Jan-Mar)

and other rich earthy colours dress the exquisite 17th-century stone structure of this stylish hotel, with narrow staircases, a roaring fire and alfresco courtyard breakfasts. The romantic suite (€157) has a dreamy lilac-walled terrace overlooking rooftops. Wheelchair access.

HÔTEL ARLATAN Historic Hotel €€
(☎04 90 93 56 66; www.hotel-arlatan.fr; 26 rue du Sauvage; d €85-157, apt €177-247; ⏰mid-Mar–mid-Nov; ❄@📶🏊) The heated swimming pool, pretty garden and plush rooms decorated with antique furniture are just some of the things going for this hotel. Add to that a setting steeped in history, with Roman foundations visible through a glass floor in the lobby and 15th-century paintings on one of the lounges' ceilings. Wheelchair access.

Eating

L'ATELIER Gastronomic €€€
(☎04 90 91 07 69; www.rabanel.com; 7 rue des Carmes; lunch/dinner menus from €55/95; ⏰lunch & dinner Wed-Sun) If you dine here, consider it not a meal, but an artistic experience. Every one of the seven or 13 edible works of art is a wondrous composition of flavours, colours and textures, and no two bites are the same. Sit back and revel in Jean-Luc Rabanel's superbly crafted symphony of fresh organic tastes. No wonder this charismatic chef with his own veggie patch has two Michelin stars. Wine pairings are an adventure in themselves.

L'AUTRUCHE Modern French €€
(☎04 90 49 73 63; 5 rue Dulau; lunch menus €18, mains €29; ⏰lunch & dinner Tue-Sat) This modern, inviting restaurant run by husband and wife team Fabien and Ouria assembles market-fresh dishes to perfection. For example, their Michelin-experienced chef layers thin strips of green-apple chutney with a superbly prepared foie gras. Extravagant desserts are a treat.

COMPTOIR DU SUD Cafe €
(☎04 90 96 22 17; 2 rue Jean Jaurès; ⏰10am-5pm Tue-Fri) Gourmet sandwiches (tasty chutneys, succulent meats, foie gras) and divine little salads, all at rock-bottom prices, are served at the counter.

Shopping

LA BOTTE CAMARGUAISE Shoes
(☎04 90 96 20 87; 22 rue Jean Granaud) Fashionistas, this is the place to purchase the ultimate trendsetting souvenir: a pair of handmade Camargue-style cowboy boots.

Information

Tourist office (www.arlestourisme.com) Main office (☎04 90 18 41 20; bd des Lices; ⏰9am-6.45pm); train station (☎04 90 43 33 57; ⏰9am-12.30pm & 2.30-5pm Mon-Fri)

Getting There & Away

There are train services to Nîmes (€7.50, 30 minutes), Marseille (€13, 45 minutes) and Avignon (€7, 20 minutes). The closest TGV stations are in Avignon and Nîmes.

Avignon

POP 92,454

Hooped by 4.3km of superbly preserved stone ramparts, this graceful city is the belle of Provence's ball. Its turn as the papal seat of power has bestowed Avignon with a treasury of magnificent art and architecture. Famed for its annual performing arts festival, these days Avignon is also an animated student city and an ideal spot from which to step out into the surrounding region.

Sights

To truly get value for money in Avignon, sightseers should get their hands on the must-have discount card, *Avignon Passion*. The card provides signficant discounts on museums, tours and monuments in Avignon and Villeneuve-lès-Avignon. The first attraction visited costs full price, but each subsequent site discounts admission by 10% to 50%. The free pass covers five sites, and is valid for 15 days. It's available from the tourist office (p319) and tourist sites.

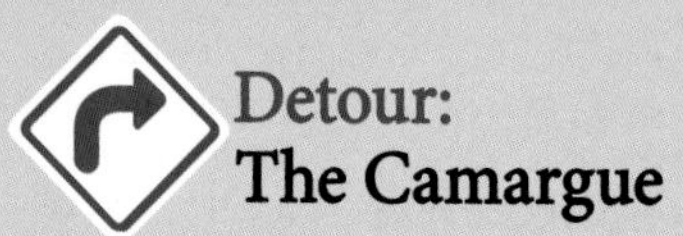

Detour: The Camargue

Just south of Arles, Provence's rolling landscapes yield to the flat, marshy wilds of the Camargue, famous for its teeming bird life, roughly 500 species. King of all is the pink flamingo, which enjoys the expansive wetlands' mild winters. Equally famous are the Camargue's small white horses; their mellow disposition makes horse riding the ideal way to explore the region's patchwork of salt pans and rice fields, and meadows dotted with grazing bulls. Bring binoculars – and mosquito repellent.

The Camargue's two largest towns are the seaside pilgrims' outpost **Stes-Maries-de-la-Mer** and, to the northwest, the walled town of **Aigues-Mortes**.

Inside an 1812-built sheep shed 10km southwest of Arles on the D570, the **Musée de la Camargue** (Musée Camarguais; 04 90 97 10 82; www.parc-camargue.fr; Mas du Pont de Rousty; adult/child €4.50/free; 9am-12.30pm & 1-6pm Wed-Mon Feb-Dec) paints an exhaustive portrait of traditional life, its exhibitions covering local history, ecosystems, farming techniques, flora and fauna. A 3.5km trail leads to an observation tower with bird's-eye views of the *mas* (farmhouse) and its protected natural surrounds.

Pink flamingos pirouette overhead and stalk the watery landscape at **Le Parc Ornithologique du Pont du Gau** (04 90 97 82 62; www.parcornithologique.com; Pont du Gau; adult/child €7/4; 9am-sunset), on the D570 in Pont du Gau, 4km north of Stes-Maries-de-la-Mer.

You will need a car to visit the area, an easy day trip from Arles.

PALAIS DES PAPES Palace

(Papal Palace; www.palais-des-papes.com; place du Palais; adult/child €6/3; 9am-8pm Jul, 9am-9pm Aug, shorter hours Sep-Jun) The immense Palais des Papes is the world's largest Gothic palace and a Unesco World Heritage Site. Built when Pope Clement V abandoned Rome in 1309 to settle in Avignon, it was the seat of papal power for 70-odd years. The immense scale, cavernous stone halls and vast courtyards testify to the papacy's wealth; the 3m-thick walls, portcullises and watchtowers emphasise their insecurity.

Today, it takes imagination to picture the former luxury of these vast, bare rooms, but PDA-style audio-video guides show 2-D and 3-D imagery of the once-sumptuous furnishings.

PONT ST-BÉNÉZET Bridge

(adult/child €4.50/3.50; 9am-8pm Jul, 9am-9pm Aug, shorter hours Sep-Jun) According to legend, Pastor Bénézet had three saintly visions urging him to build a bridge across the Rhône. Completed in 1185, the bridge linked Avignon with Villeneuve-lès-Avignon, controlling trade at this vital crossroads. It was rebuilt several times before all but four of its spans were washed away in the mid-1600s.

MUSÉE DU PETIT PALAIS Art Museum

(www.petit-palais.org; place du Palais; adult/child €6/free; 10am-1pm & 2-6pm Wed-Mon) The bishops' palace during the 14th and 15th centuries houses outstanding collections of primitive, pre-Renaissance, 13th- to 16th-century Italian religious paintings, by artists including Botticelli, Carpaccio and Giovanni di Paolo – the most famous is Botticelli's *La Vierge et l'Enfant* (1470).

MUSÉE ANGLADON Gallery

(www.angladon.com; 5 rue Laboureur; adult/child €6/4; 1-6pm Tue-Sun Apr-Nov, 1-6pm Wed-Sun Jan-Mar) Tiny Musée Angladon harbours impressionist treasures, including *Railway Wagons*, the only Van Gogh in Provence (look closely and notice the 'earth' isn't paint, but bare canvas).

Sleeping

HÔTEL LA MIRANDE Luxury Hotel **€€€**
(**04 90 14 20 20; www.la-mirande.fr; 4 place de la Mirande; d €425-610;**) Avignon's top hotel occupies a converted 16th-century palace, with dramatic interiors decked in oriental rugs, gold-threaded tapestries, marble staircases and over-the-top Gallic style. Low-end rooms are small, but still conjure the feeling of staying overnight in someone's private château. On-site formal restaurant **Le Marmiton** (mains from €35) offers cooking classes (from €80) and a twice-weekly chef's table (an informal evening akin to a dinner party when the chef cooks in front of guests; €96, reservations essential); afternoon tea is served (albeit slowly) in the glittering lobby or garden.

LE LIMAS B&B **€€**
(**04 90 14 67 19; www.le-limas-avignon.com; 51 rue du Limas; d/tr incl breakfast from €120/200;**) This chic B&B in an 18th-century town house, like something out of *Vogue Living*, is everything designers strive for when mixing old and new: state-of-the-art kitchen and minimalist white decor complementing antique fireplaces and 18th-century spiral stairs. Breakfast on the sun-drenched terrace is a treat – as is bubbly owner Marion.

LUMANI B&B **€€**
(**04 90 82 94 11; www.avignon-lumani.com; 37 rue du Rempart St-Lazare; d incl breakfast €100-170;**) Art fills this fabulous *maison d'hôte*, a wealth of inspiration for painters. Rooms include two suites and there's a fountained garden.

Eating

CUISINE DU DIMANCHE Provençal **€€**
(**04 90 82 99 10; www.lacuisinedudimanche.com; 31 rue Bonneterie; mains €15-25; daily Jun-Sep, Tue-Sat Oct-May**) Spitfire chef Marie shops every morning at Les Halles to find the freshest ingredients for her earthy flavour-packed cooking, and takes no culinary shortcuts. Market-driven menu

Pink flamingos, the Camargue

Avignon

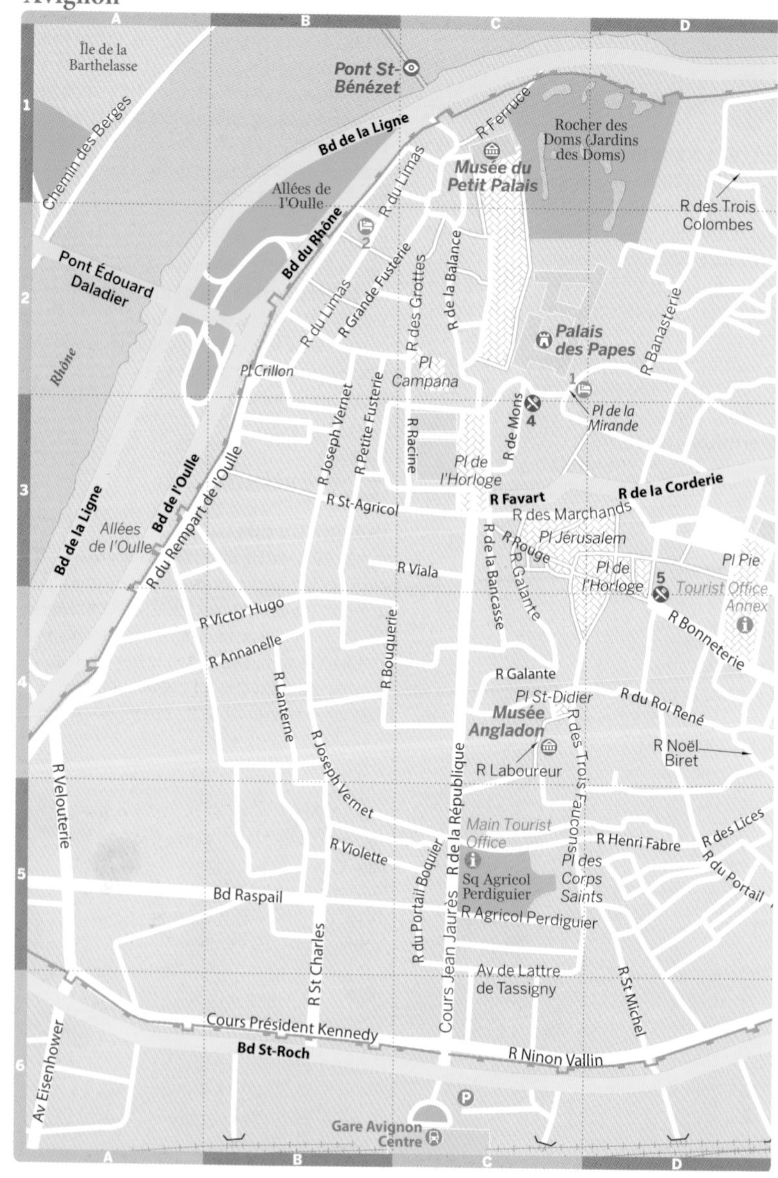

changes daily, but specialities include scallops and simple roast chicken with pan gravy. The narrow stone-walled dining room is a mishmash of textures – contemporary resin chairs to antique crystal goblets – befitting the chef's eclecticism. Reserve.

CHRISTIAN ETIENNE Provençal €€€
(☎04 90 86 16 50; www.christian-etienne.fr; 10 rue de Mons; lunch menus €31-150, dinner menus

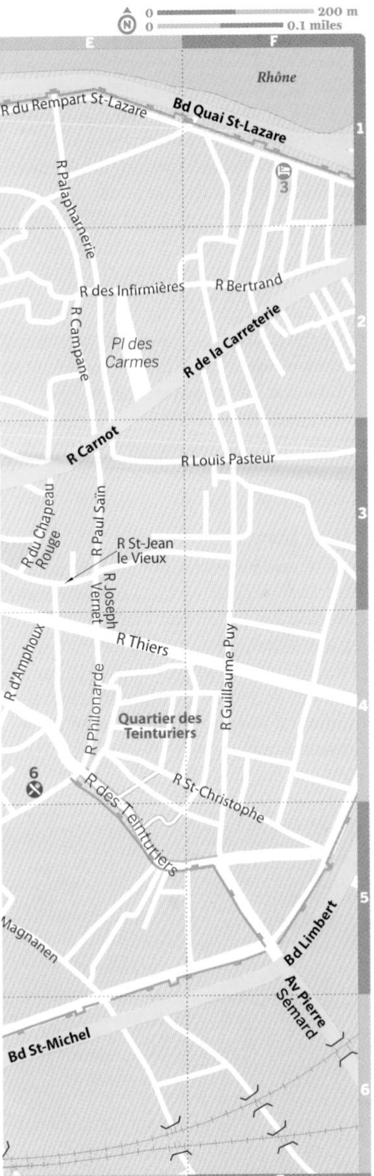

€75-150; **lunch & dinner Tue-Sat)** One of Avignon's top tables, this much vaunted restaurant occupies a 12th-century palace, with a leafy outdoor terrace, adjacent to Palais des Papes. Interiors feel slightly dated, but the refined Provençal cuisine remains exceptional, notably the summertime-only starter-to-dessert tomato menu. Book ahead.

Avignon

Top Sights

Musée Angladon C4
Musée du Petit Palais C1
Palais des Papes C2
Pont St-Bénézet C1

Sleeping

1 Hôtel La Mirande C2
2 Le Limas B2
3 Lumani F1

Eating

4 Christian Etienne C3
5 Cuisine du Dimanche D3
6 L'Epice and Love E4

L'EPICE AND LOVE French €

(**04 90 82 45 96; 30 rue des Lices; mains €11-12; dinner Mon-Sat)** Tables are cheek by jowl at this tiny bohemian restaurant – our favourite for budget dining – with nothing fancy, just straightforward bistro fare, stews, roasts and other reliably good, homestyle French dishes. Cash only.

Information

Tourist office (**04 32 74 32 74; www.avignon-tourisme.com)** Main branch (**41 cours Jean Jaurès; 9am-6pm Mon-Fri, 9am-5pm Sat, 10am-noon Sun Nov-Mar, 9am-6pm Mon-Sat, 10am-5pm Sun Apr-Oct**); annex (**Les Halles; 10am-1pm Fri-Sun**)

Getting There & Away

Avignon has two train stations: Gare Avignon TGV, 4km southwest in Courtine; and **Gare Avignon Centre** (**42 bd St-Roch**), with service to the following destinations:

Arles €6.50, 20 minutes, half-hourly

Marseille Airport (Vitrolles Station) €16, 1½ hours, half-hourly

Nîmes €8.50, 30 minutes, half-hourly

Some TGVs to Paris (€75, 3½ hours) stop at Gare Avignon Centre, but TGVs to Marseille (€29, 35 minutes) and Nice (€52.50, 3¼ hours) only use Gare Avignon TGV.

LANGUEDOC

Bordered to the east by sun-baked Provence, the broad, flat plains of Bas-Languedoc (lower Languedoc) boast all of the Languedoc's main towns, as well as its best beaches, richest Roman remains and (arguably) its finest wines.

Nîmes

POP 146,500

Nîmes' traffic-clogged, concrete-heavy outskirts provide a pretty uninspiring introduction to this ancient southern city, but persevere because the rewards are worthwhile: you'll discover some of southern France's best-preserved Roman buildings – including a 2000-year-old temple and a magnificent amphitheatre, where bullfights and gladiatorial battles are still staged.

Sights

LES ARÈNES Roman Sites

(www.arenes-nimes.com; place des Arènes; adult/child €7.90/6; ⌚9am-8pm Jul-Aug, earlier closing at other times) Nîmes' twin-tiered amphitheatre is one of southwest France's most impressive Roman structures. Built around AD 100, the amphitheatre would have held around 24,000 spectators across four seating tiers; the posher you were, the closer you would have sat to the centre. The arena would have staged gladiatorial contests and public executions, and it's still regularly used for public events – mostly of a less gory nature than in Roman times, although bullfights remain a regular fixture.

MAISON CARRÉE Roman Sites

(place de la Maison Carrée; adult/child €4.60/3.80; ⌚10am-8pm Jul-Aug, earlier closing at other times) Constructed in gleaming limestone around AD 5, this impressive temple was built to honour Emperor Augustus' two adopted sons.

CARRÉ D'ART Museum

(www.carreartmusee.com; place de la Maison Carrée; permanent collection free, exhibitions adult/child €5/3.70; ⌚10am-6pm Tue-Sun) The striking glass-and-steel building facing the Maison Carrée was designed by British architect Sir Norman Foster. Inside is the **municipal library** and the **Musée d'Art Contemporain**, with permanent and tem-

Maison Carrée, Nîmes

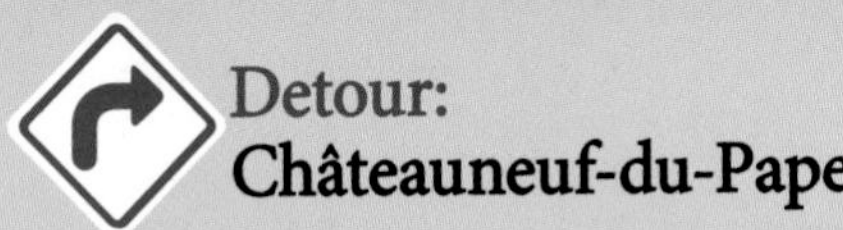

Detour: Châteauneuf-du-Pape

Carpets of vineyards unfurl around the medieval village of **Châteauneuf-du-Pape**, epicentre of one of the world's great winegrowing regions. Only a ruin remains of the château – a lone wall, high on a hilltop – once the summer residence of Avignon's popes, later bombed by Germans in WWII. Now it belongs to picnickers and day hikers who ascend the hill to scout their lines with a 360-degree panorama.

Thank geology for the luscious wines: when glaciers receded, they left *galets* scattered atop the red-clay soil; these large pebbles trap the Provençal sun, releasing heat after sunset and helping grapes ripen with steady warmth. Most Châteauneuf-du-Pape wines are red; only 6% are white. Reds come from 13 different grape varieties – grenache is the biggie – and should age at least five years. The full-bodied whites drink well young (except for all-rousanne varieties) and make an excellent, mineral aperitif wine, hard to find anywhere else.

Sample them at wine shops with free tastings *(dégustations gratuites)*, or book a two-hour wine-tasting class at **École de Dégustation** (Tasting School; 04 90 83 56 15; www.oenologie-mouriesse.com; 2 rue des Papes; 2hr courses from €40). The **tourist office** (04 90 83 71 08; www.pays-provence.fr; place du Portail; 9.30am-6pm Mon-Sat, closed lunch & Wed Oct-May) has a brochure of estates, showing which ones allow cellar visits, have English tours, allow drop-in visitors and offer free tastings.

porary exhibitions covering art from the 1960s onwards. The rooftop restaurant makes a lovely spot for lunch.

Sleeping

LE CHEVAL BLANC Hotel €€

(04 66 76 05 22; www.lechevalblanc-nimes.com; 1 place des Arènes; d €115, family €180-210;) A prime position overlooking Les Arènes and a spare, stripped-back style make this the swishest place to stay in central Nîmes. Bare wood, plaster and stone define the design, and there are several split-level apartments with galley kitchens that are ideal for families or self-caterers.

HÔTEL AMPHITHÉÂTRE Hotel €

(04 66 67 28 51; www.hoteldelamphitheatre.com; 4 rue des Arènes; s/d €65/85) Secretly tucked away along a narrow backstreet just steps from Les Arènes, this tall townhouse hotel has been stylishly renovated in a sleek palette of greys, whites and taupes. It's run by an expat Cornishman and his wife.

Eating

L'IMPRÉVU Modern French €€

(04 66 38 99 59; www.l-imprevu.com; 6 place d'Assas; mains €19.50-27.50; lunch & dinner) Enjoy fine-dining in this French bistro located in the corner of place d'Assas. The simple, amber-stoned façade looks homey, but the interior is light and contemporary, with swirly modern art, an open-plan kitchen and a cute interior courtyard. There's a sophisticated mix of *terre-et-mer* (surf-and-turf) dishes, mainly served à la carte, although there's usually a limited *menu du jour* chalked on the blackboard outside.

Left: Bullfighter, Nîmes; **Below:** Market square, Nîmes (p320)
(LEFT) FRILET PATRICK/GETTY IMAGES ©; (BELOW) PICAVET/GETTY IMAGES ©

LE MARCHÉ SUR LA TABLE Modern French **€€**
(**☎04 66 67 22 50; 10 rue Littré; mains €18-22; ⏰Wed-Sun)** Warm and welcoming bistro run by husband-and-wife team Éric and Caroline Vidal, with a focus on organic ingredients picked up daily from the nearby market. The interior feels homespun, with plain wooden furniture and stripy tablemats, and there's a quiet courtyard for alfresco dining.

CARRÉ D'ART Gastronomic **€€**
(**☎04 66 67 52 40; www.restaurant-lecarredart.fr; 2 rue Gaston Boissier; 2-/3-course menu €24/29; ⏰Mon-Sat)** Nîmes' top address for gourmet gastronomic dining. Shiny mirrors and moody lighting set the tone in the swish dining room, providing the perfect setting for artfully arranged plates of cod in pepper coulis, or veal in voilet 'essence'.

Information

Tourist office (**☎04 66 58 38 00; www.ot-nimes.fr; 6 rue Auguste; ⏰8.30am-8pm Mon-Fri, 9am-7pm Sat, 10am-6pm Sun Jul & Aug, shorter hours rest of year)**

Getting There & Away

The bus station (**☎04 66 38 59 43; rue Ste-Félicité)** is next to the train station. Destinations include Pont du Gard (30 minutes, five to seven daily in summer).

More than 12 TGVs daily run to/from Paris Gare de Lyon (€52 to €99.70, three hours). Local destinations include the following:

Arles €8 to €14, 30 minutes

Avignon €9, 30 minutes

Carcassonne

POP 49,100

Perched on a rocky hilltop and bristling with zig-zag battlements, stout walls and spiky turrets, from afar the fortified city of

Carcassonne looks like something out of a children's storybook.

Sights

LA CITÉ Walled City

The hill on which La Cité stands has been fortified countless times across the centuries – by Gauls, Romans, Visigoths, Moors, Franks and Cathars, to name a few. Following the annexation of Roussillon in 1659, the castle's usefulness as a frontier fortress declined and it slowly crumbled into disrepair, but was saved from destruction by the 19th-century architect Viollet-le-Duc, who left his inimitable mark on many of France's medieval landmarks, including Notre Dame in Paris and Vézelay in Burgundy.

The fortified town is ringed by two rampart walls and punctuated by 52 stone towers. The distinctive 'witch's-hat' roofs actually aren't original: they were added by Viollet-le-Duc during La Cité's 19th-century remodelling. The originals would have been much flatter and wouldn't have been topped by slate.

The main entrance to the fortress is beneath the **Porte Narbonnaise**, a great bastion accessed via a cobbled bridge, now home to the Cité's tourist office. From here, the souvenir-strewn street of rue Cros Mayrevieille leads uphill to place du Château, the heart of the old city, and the imposing **Château Comtal** (adult/child €8.50/free; 10am-6.30pm Apr-Sep).

Sleeping

HÔTEL DU CHÂTEAU Hotel **€€€**

(04 68 11 38 38; www.hotelduchateau.net; 2 rue Camille Saint-Saëns; d €120-280;)

You get the best of both worlds at this flashy hotel: knockout night-time views of La Cité's amber ramparts, coupled with the convenience of staying outside the walled city. The 16 rooms are snazzily finished with wood, exposed stone

MARCO MACCARINI/GETTY IMAGES ©

Don't Miss Pont du Gard

Nothing can top the Pont du Gard, 21km northeast of Nîmes. This three-tiered aqueduct was once part of a 50km-long system of water channels, built around 19 BC to transport water from Uzès to Nîmes. The scale is huge: 50m high, 275m long and graced with 35 precision-built arches, the bridge was sturdy enough to carry up to 20,000 cu metres of water per day. Each block was carved by hand and transported here from nearby quarries – no mean feat, considering the largest blocks weighed over 5 tonnes.

To put the site in context, the **Musée de la Romanité** provides background on the bridge's construction, while kids can try out educational activities in the **Ludo** play area. Nearby, the 1.4km **Mémoires de Garrigue** walking trail winds upstream through typically Mediterranean scrubland, and offers some of the best bridge views.

There are large car parks on both banks of the river, about 400m walk from the bridge. Parking costs a flat-rate €5.

NEED TO KNOW

(☎04 66 37 50 99; www.pontdugard.fr; car & up to 5 passengers €18, after 8pm €10, cyclists & walkers free; ⏰visitors centre & museum 9am-6pm Mar-May & Oct, to 7pm Jun & Sep, to 8pm Jul & Aug, to 5pm Nov-Feb, parking lots 9am-1am)

and boutique-style furnishings, and you can admire wonderful castle views from the heated pool and jacuzzi.

LA MAISON VIEILLE B&B **€€**
(☎04 68 25 77 24; www.la-maison-vieille.com; 8 rue Trivalle; d €85; 📶) Charm oozes out of every nook and cranny at this amber-stone B&B. The rooms are enormous, and decorated with supremely good taste: Barbecane in soothing blues, Cité with exposed brick, Prince Noir with a white sofa and in-room rolltop bath. Breakfast is served in the courtyard garden when the sun shines.

BLOC G B&B €€
(☎04 68 47 58 20; www.bloc-g.com; 112 rue Barbacane; d incl breakfast €90-120;) Not what you'd expect in Carcassonne – a trendy, minimalist B&B that wouldn't look out of place in Paris' fashionable quarters. It's part bistro, part design gallery, part *chambres urbaines*.

Eating

LA CANTINE DE ROBERT Traditional French €€
(☎04 68 47 37 80; www.restaurantrobertrodriguez.com; 39 rue Coste Reboulh; mains €14.50-26; closed dinner Wed & Sun;) Robert Rodriguez's ramshackle restaurant is just about as French as it gets. It's a retro treat – marble floors, net curtains and Édith Piaf warbling on the stereo – but the organic, locally sourced, pesticide-free ethos is bang on trend. The mustachioed chef loves his Languedocien cuisine, so expect a menu that's heavy on meat, river fish and gamebirds, served with a dash of Michelin flair.

AU COMTE ROGER Modern French €€
(☎04 68 11 93 40; www.comteroger.com; 14 rue St-Louis; lunch menu €19-27, dinner menu €38; lunch & dinner) Inside: starched white tablecloths, cool grey furniture and sparkling cutlery. Outside: a teeny pergola-covered patio set around an old well. On the table: nouvelle cuisine–style dishes presented with flair by chef Pierre Mesa. The result: just about the best option in La Cité for sit-down dining – just don't expect the portions to be large.

Information

La Cité tourist office (Porte Narbonnaise; 9am-6pm or 7pm Apr-Sep, Sat & Sun only Oct-Mar)

Getting There & Away

Carcassonne is on the busy main train line linking Toulouse (€15, 50 minutes) with Narbonne (€10.50, 30 minutes) and Montpellier (€23.70, 1½ hours). For Perpignan (€19.30, 1½ hours), change in Narbonne.

THE FRENCH RIVIERA

With its glistening seas, idyllic beaches and fabulous weather, the Riviera (known as Côte d'Azur to the French) encapsulates many people's idea of the good life. The beauty is that there is so much more to do than just going to the beach – although the Riviera does take beach-going *very* seriously: from nudist beach to secluded cove or exclusive club, there is something for everyone.

Nice

POP 344,460

Nice is magical. The city offers exceptional quality of life: shimmering Mediterranean shores, the very best of Mediterranean food, a unique historical heritage and Alpine wilderness within an hour's drive.

Sights & Activities

PROMENADEDES ANGLAIS Architecture
Palm-lined promenade des Anglais, paid for by Nice's English colony in 1822, is a fine stage for a stroll. It's particularly atmospheric in the evening, with Niçois milling about and epic sunsets over the sea. Don't miss the magnificent facade of **Hôtel Negresco**, built in 1912 for Romanian innkeeper Henri Negresco, or art deco **Palais de la Méditerranée**, saved from demolition in the 1980s and now part of a four-star palace.

FREE **MUSÉE D'ART MODERNE ET D'ART CONTEMPORAIN** Art Museum
(Mamac; www.mamac-nice.org; Promenade des Arts; 10am-6pm Tue-Sun) European and American avant-garde works from the 1950s to the present are the focus of this museum. Highlights include many works by Nice's New Realists Christo, César, Arman, Yves Klein and Niki de Saint-Phalle. The building's rooftop too works as an exhibition space (with panoramas of Nice to boot).

Nice

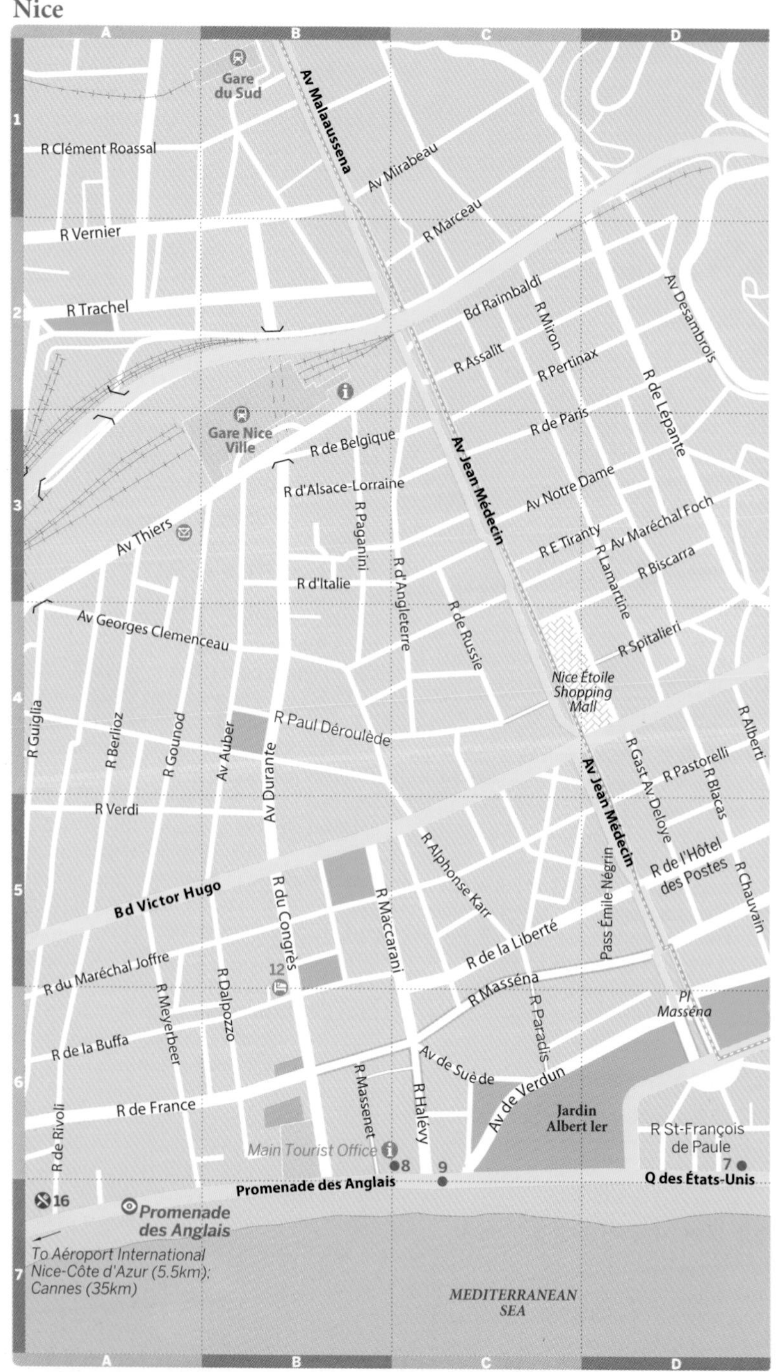

A
B
C
D
1
2
3
4
5
6
7
Gare du Sud
Av Malaussena
R Clément Roassal
Av Mirabeau
R Vernier
R Marceau
R Trachel
Bd Raimbaldi
R Miron
Av Desambrois
R Assalit
R Pertinax
Gare Nice Ville
R de Paris
R de Lépante
R de Belgique
Av Jean Médecin
R d'Alsace-Lorraine
Av Notre Dame
R Paganini
Av Thiers
R E Tiranty
Av Maréchal Foch
R d'Angleterre
R Lamartine
R Biscarra
R d'Italie
R de Russie
Av Georges Clemenceau
R Spitalieri
Nice Étoile Shopping Mall
R Guiglia
R Berlioz
R Gounod
Av Auber
R Paul Déroulède
R Alberti
Av Durante
R Gast Av Deloye
R Pastorelli
R Blacas
R Verdi
R Alphonse Karr
R de l'Hôtel des Postes
R Chauvain
Bd Victor Hugo
R du Congrès
R Maccarani
Pass Émile Négrin
R de la Liberté
R du Maréchal Joffre
12
R Dalpozzo
R Masséna
R Meyerbeer
R Paradis
Pl Masséna
R de la Buffa
Av de Suède
R Massenet
R Halévy
Av de Verdun
R de France
Jardin Albert ler
R St-François de Paule
R de Rivoli
Main Tourist Office
8
9
7
Promenade des Anglais
Q des États-Unis
16
Promenade des Anglais
To Aéroport International Nice-Côte d'Azur (5.5km); Cannes (35km)
MEDITERRANEAN SEA

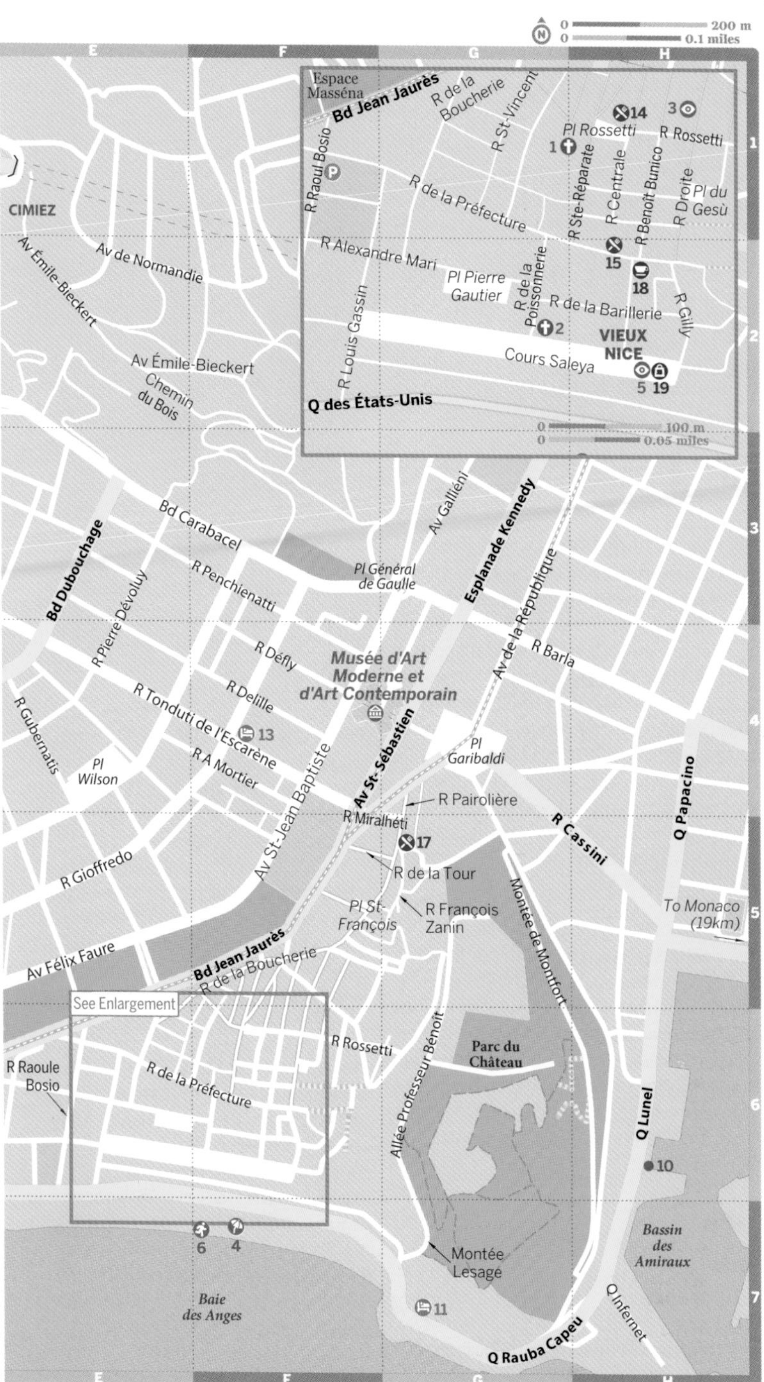

0 200 m
0 0.1 miles
Espace Masséna
Bd Jean Jaurès
R de la Boucherie
R St-Vincent
Pl Rossetti
R Rossetti
R Raoul Bosio
R de la Préfecture
R Ste-Réparate
R Centrale
R Benoît Bunico
R Droite
Pl du Gesù
R Alexandre Mari
Pl Pierre Gautier
R de la Poissonnerie
R de la Barillerie
R Gilly
R Louis Gassin
VIEUX NICE
Cours Saleya
Q des États-Unis
0 100 m
0 0.05 miles
CIMIEZ
Av Émile-Bieckert
Av de Normandie
Chemin du Bois
Bd Carabacel
Av Galliéni
Esplanade Kennedy
Pl Général de Gaulle
Av de la République
Bd Dubouchage
R Pierre Dévoluy
R Penchienatti
R Barla
R Défly
Musée d'Art Moderne et d'Art Contemporain
R Delille
R Tonduti de l'Escarène
R Gubernatis
R A Mortier
Av St-Sébastien
Pl Garibaldi
Pl Wilson
Av St-Jean Baptiste
R Pairolière
R Miralhéti
R Cassini
Q Papacino
R de la Tour
R Gioffredo
Pl St-François
R François Zanin
Montée de Montfort
To Monaco (19km)
Av Félix Faure
Bd Jean Jaurès
R de la Boucherie
See Enlargement
R Rossetti
R Raoule Bosio
R de la Préfecture
Parc du Château
Allée Professeur Bénoît
Q Lunel
Bassin des Amiraux
Montée Lesage
Baie des Anges
Q Infernet
Q Rauba Capeu

Nice

FREE **MUSÉE MATISSE** Art Museum

(www.musee-matisse-nice.org; 164 av des Arènes de Cimiez; 10am-6pm Wed-Mon) Located about 2km north of the centre in the leafy quarter of Cimiez, the Musée Matisse houses a fascinating assortment of works by Matisse documenting the artist's stylistic evolution. Its permanent collection is displayed in a red-ochre 17th-century Genoese villa overlooking an olive-tree-studded park. Temporary exhibitions are hosted in the futuristic basement building. Sadly, all explanations are in French only.

BEACHES Beaches

Nice's beaches are all pebbly; sensitive behinds should therefore opt for a comfy mattress at one of its 14 private beaches (€15 to €20 per day). Out of the free **public sections of beach** (with lifeguards, first-aid posts and cold showers), **Plage Publique des Ponchettes**, opposite Vieux Nice, is the most popular (and don't worry about your bottom, many hotels lend you mats!).

Tours

NICE GUIDED WALKING TOURS Walking Tour

The **Centre du Patrimoine (75 Quai des Etats-Unis; 8.30am-1pm & 2-5pm Mon-Thu)** runs a two-hour Vieux Nice Baroque tour (Tuesday afternoon), as well as themed tours including art deco, neoclassical and belle époque Nice. The tourist office (p330) runs a 2½-hour Vieux Nice tour in English (adult/child €12/6), at 9.30am on Saturday.

ART WITH THE TRAM Tram Tour

(www.tramway-nice.org) As well as Jaume Plensa's glow-in-the-dark *Conversation* on place Masséna, there are 13 more works of art to discover along Nice's tram route, including original sound bites at each stop, the calligraphy of the tram's stops and more visual works. The best way to appreciate this artistic input is to take the tourist office's two-hour **Art dans la Ville (adult/child €8/3, plus €2 for transport; tours 7pm Fri)** guided tour.

TRANS CÔTE D'AZUR Boat Tour

(www.trans-cote-azur.com; quai Lunel; Apr-Oct) To escape the crowds, take a scenic cruise along the coast. Trans Côte d'Azur runs one-hour trips along the Baie des Anges and the Rade de Villefranche (adult/child €16/10) from April to October. From mid-June to mid-September it also runs regular excursions to Île Ste-Marguerite (€35/25, crossing one hour), St-Tropez (€58/44, crossing 2½ hours) and Monaco (€34/25, crossing 45 minutes). Reservations are essential.

NICE LE GRAND TOUR Bus Tour

(www.nicelegrandtour.com; 1-day pass adult/child €20/5) With headphone commentary in several languages, the open-topped Le Grand Tour buses (1½ hours) give you a good overview of Nice. You can hop on or off at any one of 14 stops.

Sleeping

HÔTEL LA PÉROUSE Boutique Hotel €€€

(☎04 93 62 34 63; www.hotel-la-perouse.com; 11 quai Rauba Capeu; d from €195; ❄ @ 📶 🏊**)** Built into the rock cliff next to Tour Bellanda, La Pérouse captures the vibe of a genteel villa. Lower-floor rooms face the lemon-tree-shaded courtyard and infinity pool; upper-floor rooms have magnificent vistas of the promenade and sea, many with balconies or terraces to make the best of the panorama. Smart accent colours add flair to the traditional decor.

NICE GARDEN HÔTEL Boutique Hotel €€

(☎04 93 87 35 63; www.nicegardenhotel.com; 11 rue du Congrès; s/d €75/100; ❄ 📶**)** Behind heavy iron gates hides this little gem of a hotel: the nine beautifully appointed rooms, the work of the exquisite Marion, are a subtle blend of old and new and overlook a delightful garden with a glorious orange tree. Amazingly, all this charm and peacefulness is just two blocks from the promenade.

NICE PEBBLES Self-Contained €€

(☎04 97 20 27 30; www.nicepebbles.com; 23 rue Gioffredo; 1-/3-bedroom apt from €105/320; 📶 🏊**)** Have you ever dreamt of feeling like a real Niçois? Coming back to your designer pad in Vieux Nice, opening a bottle of ice-cold rosé and cooking up a storm with the treats you bought at the market? Nice Pebbles' concept is simple: offering the quality of a four-star boutique hotel in holiday flats.

VILLA SAINT-EXUPÉRY Hostel €

(☎04 93 84 42 83; www.villahostels.com; 22 av Gravier; dm €25-30, s/d €45/90; @ 📶**)** Why can't all hostels be like this? Set in a lovely converted monastery in the north of the city, this is a great place to put down your bags for a few days. Chill out in the 24-hour common room housed in the old stained-glass chapel, sip a €1 beer on the barbecue terrace and stock up on travel tips.

Nice

S.TAUQUEUR/GETTY IMAGES ©

Eating

LE BISTROT D'ANTOINE Modern French €€
(☎04 93 85 29 57; 27 rue de la Préfecture; mains €13-18; ⏰lunch & dinner Tue-Sat) What's so surprising about this super brasserie is how unfazed it is by its incredible success: it is full every night (booking essential), yet the 'bistro chic' cuisine never wavers, the staff are cool as cucumbers, the atmosphere is reliably jovial and the prices incredibly good-value for the area.

LE CHANTECLER Gastronomic €€€
(☎04 93 16 64 00; www.hotel-negresco-nice.com; Le Negresco, 37 promenade des Anglais; menu €90, mains €55-68; ⏰dinner Wed-Sun, lunch Sun) In a sumptuous, pink Regency dining room, Le Negresco's two-Michelin-starred restaurant is no ordinary restaurant. Make sure you're in an extravagant mood if you're going to splash out: every dish is the most exquisite creation, both in cuisine and presentation, and there is a seemingly endless succession of apetisers, palate cleansers and petits fours.

FENOCCHIO Ice Cream €
(2 place Rossetti; ice cream from €2; ⏰9am-midnight Feb-Oct) If you dither too long trying to decide over the 70-plus flavours of ice cream and sorbet at this unforgettable *glacier* (ice-cream shop), you'll never make it to the front of the queue. Admittedly, the decision is a tough one and there are worse ways to spend the time than deliberating over which luscious flavour to indulge in. Why not eschew predictable favourites and indulge in a new taste sensation: black olive, rosemary or lavender.

L'ESCALINADA Niçois €€
(☎04 93 62 11 71; www.escalinada.fr; 22 rue Pairolière; menu €24, mains €15-23; ⏰lunch & dinner daily) This enchanting old-town *auberge* (inn) has been one of the best places in town for Niçois cuisine for the last half-century: melt-in-your-mouth homemade gnocchi with tasty *daube* (Provençal beef stew), grilled prawns with garlic and herbs, Marsala veal stew. The staff are delightful and the welcome *kir* is on the house. No credit cards.

Drinking

LES DISTILLERIES IDÉALES Cafe
(24 rue de la Préfecture; ⏰9am-12.30am) Whether you're after an espresso on your way to the **cours Saleya market** (cours Saleya; ⏰6am-5.30pm Tue-Sat, to 1.30pm Sun) or an *apéritif* (complete with cheese and charcuterie platters, €5.20) before trying out one of Nice's fabulous restaurants, Les Distilleries is one of the most atmospheric bars in town. Tables on the small street terrace are ideal for watching the world go by.

Information

Tourist office (☎08 92 70 74 07; www.nicetourisme.com; 5 promenade des Anglais; ⏰9am-6pm Mon-Sat) There's also a branch at the **train station** (av Thiers; ⏰8am-7pm Mon-Sat).

Getting There & Away

France's second largest airport is **Nice Côte d'Azur Airport** (NCE; ☎08 20 42 33 33; www.nice.aeroport.fr; 📶). It has international flights to Europe, North Africa and even the US, with regular as well as low-cost companies.

Nice is the main port for ferries to Corsica. **SNCM** (www.sncm.fr; quai du Commerce, ferry terminal) and **Corsica Ferries** (www.corsicaferries.com; quai Lunel) are the two main companies.

From Nice, there are train services to the following destinations:

Cannes (€6.50, 40 minutes, hourly)

Marseille (€35, 2½ hours, hourly)

Monaco (€3.50, 25 minutes, half-hourly)

Antibes & Juan-les-Pins

POP 76,580

With its boat-bedecked port, 16th-century ramparts and narrow cobblestone streets festooned with flowers, lovely Antibes is the quintessential Mediterranean town.

Greater Antibes embraces Cap d'Antibes, an exclusive green cape studded

GÃ©RARD LABRIET/GETTY IMAGES ©

Don't Miss Vieux Nice

Nice's old town, a mellow-hued rabbit warren, has scarcely changed since the 1700s. Retracing its history – and therefore that of the city – is a highlight, although you don't need to be a history buff to enjoy a stroll in this atmospheric quarter. Vieux Nice is as alive and prominent today as it ever was. Cue **cours Saleya** (pictured above): this joyous, thriving market square hosts a well-known flower market and a thriving fruit and vegetable market, a staple of local life.

Much of Vieux Nice has a similar atmosphere, with delis, food shops, boutiques and bars crammed in its tiny lanes. Rue de la Boucherie and rue Pairolière are excellent for food shopping. You'll also find a fish market at place St-François.

Much harder to spot because of the narrow lane it sits on is the baroque **Palais Lascaris**, a 17th-century mansion housing a frescoed orgy of Flemish tapestries, *faïence* (tin-glazed earthenware) and gloomy religious paintings. On the ground floor is an 18th-century pharmacy.

Baroque aficionados shouldn't miss Nice's other architectural gems, such as **Cathédrale Ste-Réparate**, honouring the city's patron saint, or the exuberant **Chapelle de la Miséricorde**.

NEED TO KNOW

Food Markets (6am-1.30pm Tue-Sun); **Palais Lascaris** (15 rue Droite; guided tour €3; 10am-6pm Wed-Mon, guided tour 3pm Fri); **Cathédrale Ste-Réparate** (place Rossetti); **Chapelle de la Miséricorde** (cours Saleya)

with luxurious mansions, and the modern beach resort of Juan-les-Pins.

The latter is known for its 2km-long sandy beach and its exuberant nightlife, a legacy of the sizzling 1920s when Americans swung into town with their jazz music and oh-so-brief swimsuits.

Below: Cathédrale Ste-Réparate (p331), Vieux Nice; **Right:** Bassin des Amiraux, Nice (p325)

Sights

MUSÉE PICASSO Art Museum

(www.antibes-juanlespins.com; Château Grimaldi, 4 rue des Cordiers; adult/student/child €6/3/free; 10am-noon & 2-6pm Tue-Sun) Spectacularly positioned overlooking the sea, 14th-century Château Grimaldi served as Picasso's studio from July to December 1946. The museum now houses an excellent collection of the master's paintings, lithographs, drawings and ceramics, as well as a photographic record of the artist at work.

Eating

LE BROC EN BOUCHE Modern French €€

(04 93 34 75 60; 8 rue des Palmiers; mains €15-30; lunch Thu-Tue, dinner Thu-Mon) The delightful quirk about Le Broc en Bouche is that no two chairs, tables or lights are the same at this enchanting bistro: instead, every item has been lovingly sourced from antique shops and car boot sales, giving the place a sophisticated but cosy vintage feel. The charming Flo and Fred have put the same level of care and imagination into their cuisine, artfully combining Provençal and oriental flavours.

LA FERME AU FOIE GRAS Delicatessen €

(www.vente-foie-gras.net; 35 rue Aubernon; sandwiches €3.50-7; 8am-6pm Tue-Sun) Now, this place fulfils our fantasy of what a good sandwich should be like: filled with foie gras or smoked duck breast, onion chutney or fig jam, truffle cheese and fresh salad. It's difficult to keep such discoveries a secret for long. Unsurprisingly, many people share our opinion: a queue snakes down from the tiny counter of La Ferme Au Foie Gras every lunchtime.

Information

Tourist office (☎04 97 23 11 11; www.antibesjuanlespins.com; 55 bd Charles Guillaumont; 9am-noon & 2-6pm Mon-Sat, 10am-12.30pm & 2.30-5pm Sun)

Getting There & Away

Antibes' train station is on the main line between Nice (€4.20, 30 minutes, five per hour) and Cannes (€2.70, 10 minutes, five per hour).

St-Paul de Vence

POP 3540

Once upon a time, St-Paul de Vence was a small medieval village atop a hill looking out to sea. Then came the likes of Chagall and Picasso in postwar years, followed by showbiz stars such as Yves Montand and Roger Moore, and St-Paul shot to fame. The village is now home to dozens of art galleries as well as the exceptional Fondation Maeght.

Sights

CHAPELLE DU ROSAIRE Architecture

(Rosary Chapel; www.vence.fr/the-rosaire-chapel.html; 466 av Henri Matisse; adult/child €4/2; 2-5.30pm Mon, Wed & Sat, 10-11.30am & 2-5.30pm Tue & Thu) An ailing Henri Matisse moved to Vence in 1943, where he fell under the care of his former nurse and model Monique Bourgeois, who had since become a Dominican nun. She persuaded him to design this extraordinary chapel for her community. 'This work required four years of exclusive and relentless attention, and it is the fruit of my whole working life. Despite all its imperfections, I consider it my masterpiece,' he said.

From the road, all you can see are the blue-and-white ceramic roof tiles and a wrought-iron cross and bell tower. Inside, light floods through the glorious **stained-glass windows**, painting stark white walls with glowing blues, greens and yellows (symbolising respectively water/the sky, plants/life, the sun/God's presence).

FONDATION MAEGHT Art Museum
(www.fondation-maeght.com; 623 chemin des Gardettes; adult/student/child €14/9/free; 10am-6pm) The region's finest art museum, Fondation Maeght was created in 1964 by art collectors Aimé and Marguerite Maeght. Its collection of 20th-century works is one of the largest in Europe. It is exhibited on a rotating basis, which, along with the excellent temporary exhibitions, guarantees you'll rarely see the same thing twice. Find the *fondation* 500m downhill from the village.

The building was designed by Catalan architect Josep Lluís Sert and is a masterpiece in itself, integrating the works of the very best: a Giacometti courtyard, Miró sculptures dotted across the terraced gardens, coloured-glass windows by Braque and mosaics by Chagall and Tal-Coat.

There's also an on-site cafe, which is open every day except Monday.

Eating

LA COLOMBE D'OR Traditional French **€€**
(04 93 32 80 02; www.la-colombe-dor.com; place de Gaulle; mains €30-55; lunch & dinner mid-Dec–Oct; **)** A Léger mosaic here, a Picasso painting there: these are just some of the original modern artworks at the Golden Dove, the legendary restaurant where impoverished artists paid for meals with their creations. Dining is beneath fig trees in summer or in the art-filled dining room in winter, and the cuisine is surprisingly uncomplicated (terrines, rabbit stew, beef carpaccio). Book well ahead.

The restaurant is also a hotel, which blends rustic charm and modern artworks in every room (doubles €310). Hotel guests get access to the lovely pool, which is heated year-round and crowned by a Calder mobile.

Getting There & Away

St-Paul is served by bus 400 running between Nice (€1, one hour, at least hourly) and Vence (€1, 15 minutes).

Cannes

POP 74,445

Most people have heard of Cannes and its eponymous film festival. The latter only lasts for two weeks in May, but the buzz and glitz are there year-round – unlike neighbouring St-Tropez, which shuts down in winter – mostly thanks to regular visits from celebrities enjoying the creature comforts of bd de la Croisette's palaces.

Harbour, Cannes
STEVE ALLEN/GETTY IMAGES ©

Sights

LA CROISETTE Architecture

The multi-starred hotels and couture shops that line the famous **bd de la Croisette** (aka La Croisette) may be the preserve of the rich and famous, but anyone can enjoy the palm-shaded promenade and take in the atmosphere. In fact, it's a favourite amongst Cannois (natives of Cannes), particularly at night when it is lit with bright colours.

There are great views of the bay and nearby Estérel mountains, and stunning art-deco architecture from the seafront palaces, such as the **Martinez** or the legendary **Carlton InterContinental**; its twin cupolas were modelled on the breasts of the courtesan La Belle Otéro, infamous for her string of lovers – Tsar Nicholas II and Britain's King Edward VII among them.

Not so elegant but imposing nonetheless is the **Palais des Festivals** (Festival Palace; bd de la Croisette) at the western end of the prom, host of the world's most glamorous film festival. Climb the red carpet, walk down the auditorium, tread the stage and learn about cinema's most glamorous event and its numerous anecdotes on a 1½ hr **guided tour** (adult/child €3/free; guided tours 2.30pm Jun-Apr)). Tickets can only be booked in person at the tourist office.

LE VIEUX PORT & LE SUQUET Historic Quarter

On the western side of the Palais des Festivals lies the real Cannes. The yachts that frame Le Vieux Port (Old Port) are the only reminder that this is where celebrities holiday, but they don't seem to impress the pensioners playing *pétanque* on **sq Lord Brougham**. Follow **rue St-Antoine** and snake your way up Le Suquet, Cannes' oldest district, for great views of the bay.

If You Like… Gorgeous Hilltop Villages

This iconic part of France would simply not be the same without its boutique collection of enviably photogenic, hilltop villages.

1 **LES BAUX DE PROVENCE**
Clinging precariously to a limestone spur, this fortified hilltop village is among France's most visited. Cobbled lanes wend up to the ruins of **Château des Baux**. Lunch afterwards at **L'Oustau de Baumanière** (04 90 54 33 07; www.oustaudebaumaniere.com; menus €95-150;).

2 **MOUGINS**
Mougins, 9km north of Cannes, looks too perfect to be real. Picasso discovered the medieval village in 1935 and lived here with his final love, Jacqueline Roque, from 1961 until his death. Highlights include an **art museum** (www.mouginsmusee.com; 32 rue Commandeur, Mougins; adult/student/child €15/8/5; 9.30am-8.30pm daily Apr-Oct, to 7pm Tue-Sun Nov-Mar) spanning 5000 years of history and **Les Jardins du MIP** (www.museesdegrasse.com; 979 chemin des Gourettes, Mouans-Sartoux; adult/child €3/free; 10am-6pm Apr-Oct), gardens where visitors can pick and smell their way around plants used in perfumery.

3 **GORDES**
The tiered village of Gordes sits on the white rock face of the Vaucluse plateau; 4km northwest is **Abbaye Notre-Dame de Sénanque** (04 90 72 05 72; www.abbayedesenanque.com; guided tour in French adult/student/child/family €7/5/3/20; tours by reservation), famously framed by lavender in early summer.

4 **MENERBES, LACOSTE & BONNIEUX**
This trio of golden-hued, *villages perchés* (hilltop villages) in the **Luberon** commands a quintessentially bucolic Provençal landscape.

5 **ROUSSILLON**
Famed for its distinctive red-ochre colour, beautifully offset by the vegetation tumbling down its promontory, this hilltop village 11km west of Luberon capital Apt, is a dazzling red show-stopper.

Cannes

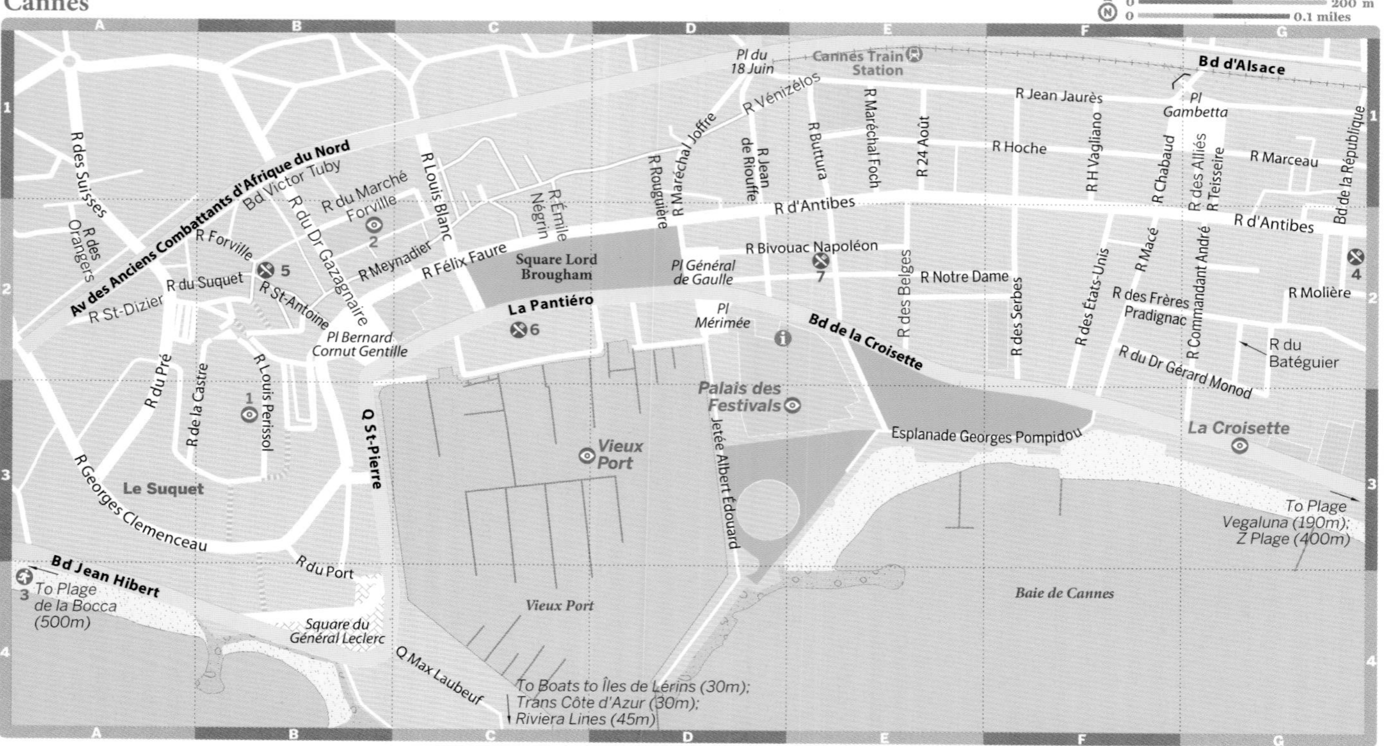
0 200 m
0 0.1 miles
Cannes Train Station
Pl du 18 Juin
Bd d'Alsace
R Jean Jaurès
Pl Gambetta
R Vénizélos
R Maréchal Joffre
R Rouguière
R Jean de Riouffe
R Buttura
R Maréchal Foch
R 24 Août
R Hoche
R H Vagliano
R Chabaud
R des Alliés
R Teisseire
R Marceau
Bd de la République
R d'Antibes
R Bivouac Napoléon
R Notre Dame
R des Belges
R des Serbes
R des États-Unis
R Macé
R Commandant André
R des Frères Pradignac
R Molière
R du Batéguier
R du Dr Gérard Monod
Pl Général de Gaulle
Pl Mérimée
Bd de la Croisette
Palais des Festivals
Esplanade Georges Pompidou
La Croisette
Jetée Albert Édouard
To Plage Vegaluna (190m); Z Plage (400m)
Baie de Cannes
Square Lord Brougham
La Pantiéro
R Félix Faure
R Émile Négrin
R Louis Blanc
Av des Anciens Combattants d'Afrique du Nord
Bd Victor Tuby
R du Marché Forville
R du Dr Gazagnaire
R Meynadier
R Forville
R du Suquet
R St-Antoine
R St-Dizier
R des Suisses
R des Orangers
Pl Bernard Cornut Gentille
Q St-Pierre
Vieux Port
R du Pré
R de la Castre
R Louis Perissol
Le Suquet
R Georges Clemenceau
R du Port
Bd Jean Hibert
To Plage de la Bocca (500m)
Square du Général Leclerc
Q Max Laubeuf
To Boats to Îles de Lérins (30m); Trans Côte d'Azur (30m); Riviera Lines (45m)
A
B
C
D
E
F
G
1
2
3
4
5
6
7

Cannes

Top Sights

Sights

Activities, Courses & Tours

Eating

For local folklore, head to **Marché Forville** (7am-1pm Tue-Sun), a couple of blocks back from the port. It is one of the most important markets in the region and the supplier of choice for restaurants (so it goes without saying it has excellent selections for your picnic!).

BEACHES Beaches

Cannes is undoubtedly blessed with sandy beaches, although much of the stretch along bd de la Croisette is taken up by private beaches (don't be perturbed by the word private; it means that these beaches are available to all for a fee). This arrangement leaves only a small strip of free sand near the Palais des Festivals for the bathing hoi polloi; the much bigger **Plage du Midi** (bd Jean Hibert) and **Plage de la Bocca**, west from Vieux Port, are also free.

If you don't want to battle it out for space on the strip of free beach, rates for private beaches range from €15 to €25 at the relaxed and family-friendly **Plage Vegaluna** (04 93 43 67 05; www.vegaluna.com; La Croisette; 9.30am-7pm), which has watersports available, to €34/30/38 for the blue loungers on the front row/other rows/pier of the super-stylish **Z Plage** (9.30am-6pm May-Sep), the beach of Hôtel Martinez.

Eating

SEA SENS Fusion €€€

(04 63 36 05 06; www.five-hotel-cannes.com; Five Hotel & Spa, 1 rue Notre Dame; 2-/3-course lunch menu €29/39, mains €26-55;) Perched on the 5th floor of the Five Hotel, the Sea Sens is Cannes' latest food sensation. Run by the brilliant Pourcel brothers, with pastry chef Jérôme de Oliveira in charge of desserts, it serves divine food blending French gastronomy and Asian elegance with panoramic views of Le Suquet and Cannes' rooftops on the side.

L'AFFABLE Modern French €€

(04 93 68 02 09; www.restaurant-laffable.fr; 5 rue Lafontaine; lunch/dinner menu €26/40, mains €34-38) Modern French cuisine has never tasted so good than at L'Affable. Everything from the ingredients, the cooking and the presentation is done to perfection, whether it be the roasted veal with its vegetable medley, the seared seabream with white butter and asparagus or the house speciality, the Grand Marnier soufflé, which arrives practically ballooning at your table. Booking essential.

MANTEL Modern European €€

(04 93 39 13 10; www.restaurantmantel.com; 22 rue St-Antoine; menus €25-38; lunch Fri-Mon, dinner Tue & Thu) Discover why Noël Mantel is the hotshot of the Cannois gastronomic scene at his refined old-town restaurant. Service is stellar and the seasonal cuisine divine: try the wonderfully tender glazed veal shank in balsamic vinegar or the original poached octopus *bourride*-style.

PHILCAT Delicatessen €

(La Pantiéro; sandwiches & salads €4-6.50; 8.30am-5pm) Don't be put off by Phillipe and Catherine's unassuming prefab cabin on the Pantiéro: this is Cannes' best lunch house. Huge salads, made to order, are piled high with delicious fresh ingredients. Or if you're *really* hungry, try one of their phenomenal *pan bagna* (a moist sandwich bursting with Provençal flavours).

Below: Purple artichokes, cours Saleya market (p331), Vieux Nice;
Right: St-Tropez

Information

Tourist office (☎04 92 99 84 22; www.cannes.travel; Palais des Festivals, bd de la Croisette; ⌚9am-7pm)

Getting There & Away

Cannes is well connected to Nice (€6.40, 40 minutes), Antibes (€2.70, 12 minutes), Monaco (€8.70, one hour) and St-Raphaël (€6.70, 30 minutes), with services every 20 minutes or so. There are trains to Marseille (€28.40, two hours) half-hourly.

St-Tropez

POP 4986

In the soft autumn or winter light, it's hard to believe that the pretty terracotta fishing village of St-Tropez is yet another stop on the Riviera celebrity circuit. It seems far removed from its glitzy siblings further up the coast, but come spring or summer, it's a different world: the town's population increases tenfold, prices triple and fun-seekers come in droves to party till dawn, strut their stuff and enjoy the creature comforts of an exclusive beach.

Sights & Activities

PLACE DES LICES Village Square
St-Tropez' legendary and very charming central square is studded with plane trees, cafes and *pétanque* players. Simply sitting on a cafe terrace watching the world go by or jostling with the crowds at its extravaganza of a twice-weekly **market** (place des Lices; ⌚8am-1pm Tue & Sat), jam-packed with everything from fruit and veg to antique mirrors and flip-flops (thongs), is an integral part of the St-Tropez experience.

MUSÉE DE L'ANNONCIADE Art Museum
(place Grammont; adult/child €6/4; 10am-noon & 2-6pm Wed-Mon Oct & Dec-May, 10am-noon & 3-7pm Wed-Mon Jun-Sep) In a gracefully converted 16th-century chapel, this small but famous art museum showcases an impressive collection of modern art infused with that legendary Côte d'Azur light. Pointillist Paul Signac bought a house in St-Tropez in 1892 and introduced others to the area. The museum's collection includes his *St-Tropez, Le Quai* (1899) and *St-Tropez, Coucher de Soleil au Bois de Pins* (1896), which hangs juxtaposed with a window-view of contemporary St-Tropez.

CITADELLE DE ST-TROPEZ Historic Site
(admission €2.50; 10am-6.30pm) Built in 1602 to defend the coast against Spain, the citadel dominates the hillside overlooking St-Tropez to the east. The views (and peacocks!) are fantastic. Its dungeons shelter **Musée Naval**, dedicated to the town's maritime history and the Allied landings in August 1944.

BEACHES Beach
About 4km southeast of town is the start of **Plage de Tahiti** and its continuation, the famous **Plage de Pampelonne**, studded with St-Tropez' most legendary drinking and dining haunts. Just east of St-Tropez, **Plage des Salins (rte des Salins)** is a long, wide sandy beach at the southern foot of **Cap des Salins**.

Sleeping

HÔTEL LOU CAGNARD Pension €€
(04 94 97 04 24; www.hotel-lou-cagnard.com; 18 av Paul Roussel; d €75-156; Jan-Oct;) Book well ahead for this great-value courtyard charmer, shaded by lemon and fig trees, and owned by schooled hoteliers. This pretty Provençal house with lavender shutters has its very own

jasmine-scented garden, strung with fairy lights at night. Bright and beautifully clean rooms are decorated with painted Provençal furniture. Five have ground-floor garden terraces. The cheapest rooms have private washbasin and standup-bathtub but share a toilet; 15 of the 19 rooms have air-con.

PASTIS Hotel €€€
(04 98 12 56 50; www.pastis-st-tropez.com; 61 av du Général Leclerc; d from €200;) This stunning townhouse-turned-hotel is the brainchild of an English couple besotted with Provence and passionate about modern art. You'll die for the pop-art-inspired interior, and long for a swim in the emerald-green pool. Every room is beautiful.

HÔTEL LE COLOMBIER Hotel €€
(04 94 97 05 31; http://lecolombierhotel.free.fr; impasse des Conquettes; r €84-158, without bath €76;) An immaculately clean converted house, five minutes' walk from place des Lices, the Colombier's fresh, summery decor is feminine and uncluttered, with pale pink bedrooms and vintage furniture. Not all rooms have air-con. Rooms without baths share a toilet, but have bidet, sink and shower, open to the bedroom; rooms with baths may only have a partial wall separating them from the bedroom.

Eating

Don't leave town without sampling St Tropez' signature cake, the *Tarte Tropézienne*. An orange-blossom-flavoured double sponge cake filled with thick cream, it was created by a Polish baker and christened by Brigitte Bardot in the 1950s.

LA TARTE TROPÉZIENNE Cafe, Bistro €
(04 94 97 04 69; www.tarte-tropezienne.com; place des Lices; mains €12-17; 7.30am-6.30pm) This cafe and its associated bakery (36 rue Georges Clémenceau), the original creator of the eponymous cake, are the best places to buy St-Tropez' delicacy. Upstairs in the lively, elegant bistro, pick from delicious daily specials, and downstairs salad/sandwich formulas (€6 to €7).

AUBERGE DE L'OUMÈDE Provençal €€€
(04 94 44 11 11; www.aubergedeloumede.com; Chemin de l'Oumède; mains €39-59, d from €225; dinner Tue-Sat May–mid-Sep, dinner daily Jul & Aug;) Epicureans come from far and wide to sample Jean-Pierre Frezia's Provençal cuisine served in a sea of vineyards: red mullet and spinach cannelloni, grilled catch of the day *aux ceps de vigne* (fired with wood from the vines, which gives grilled food a distinctive flavour) and sensational desserts, all accompanied by some very fine wines. Dining at this iso-

St-Tropez
JUERGEN RICHTER/GETTY IMAGES ©

Detour: Îles de Lérins

Although just 20 minutes away from Cannes by boat, the tranquil Îles de Lérins feel far from the madding crowd.

The closest of these two tiny islands is the 3.25km by 1km **Île Ste-Marguerite**, where the mysterious Man in the Iron Mask was incarcerated during the late 17th century. Its shores are an endless succession of perfect beaches and fishing spots, and its eucalyptus and pine forest makes for a refuge from the Riviera heat.

As you get off the boat, a map indicates a handful of rustic restaurants as well as trails and paths across the island. It also directs you to **Fort Royal** (adult/child €6/3; 10.30am-1.15pm & 2.15-5.45pm Tue-Sun), built in the 17th century, and now harbouring the **Musée de la Mer**. Exhibits interpret the fort's history, with displays on shipwrecks found off the island's coast.

Smaller still, at just 1.5km long by 400m wide, **Île St-Honorat** has been a monastery since the 5th century. Its Cistercian monks welcome visitors year-round: you can visit the church and small chapels and stroll among the vineyards and forests. Camping and cycling are forbidden.

Boats for the islands leave Cannes from quai des Îles (along from quai Max Laubeuf) on the western side of the harbour. **Riviera Lines** (www.riviera-lines.com) runs ferries to Île Ste-Marguerite (return adult/child €12/7.50), while **Compagnie Planaria** (www.cannes-ilesdelerins.com) operates boats to Île St-Honorat (return adult/child €13/6).

lated *bastide* (Provençal mansion) down a single-lane track is indeed a rare treat. It has seven rooms and a pool, handy should you really not want to leave.

LE SPORTING Brasserie €€

(04 94 97 00 65; place des Lices; mains €14-24; 8am-1am) There's a bit of everything on the menu at always-packed Le Sporting, but the speciality is the hamburger topped with foie gras and morel cream sauce. The Brittany-born owner also serves perfect buckwheat crêpes, honest lunch deals (€13), and a simple salad and *croque monsieur*.

AUBERGE DES MAURES Provençal €€

(04 94 97 01 50; 4 rue du Docteur Boutin; mains €31-39; dinner) The town's oldest restaurant remains the locals' choice for always-good, copious portions of earthy Provençal cooking, like *daube* or tapenade-stuffed lamb shoulder. Book a table (essential) on the leafy courtyard.

Shopping

ATELIER RONDINI Shoes

(04 94 97 19 55; www.rondini.fr; 16 rue Georges Clémenceau) Colette brought a pair of sandals from Greece to Atelier Rondini (open since 1927) to be replicated. They're still making the iconic sandals for about €120.

Information

Tourist office (04 94 97 45 21; www.ot-saint-tropez.com; quai Jean Jaurès; 9.30am-8pm Jul & Aug, 9.30am-12.30pm & 2-7pm Apr-Jun & Sep–mid-Oct, 9.30am-12.30pm & 2-6pm mid-Oct–Mar)

Getting There & Away

BOAT Many shuttle boats are run by **Les Bateaux Verts** (04 94 49 29 39; www.bateauxverts.com; quai Jean Jaurès). **Les Bateaux de St-Raphaël** (www.bateauxsaintraphael.com) connects

If You Like... Lunching on the Sand

If you like beaches, then you'll quiver with excitement over St-Tropez' seaside, a scene well defined by its chic collection of restaurants – all wildly different – that blanket its mythical golden sands. Mattresses (€15 to €20) and parking (€5) are extra. Most establishments are open May to September (but make sure you call ahead); all are marked on the tourist office map. Book lunch (well ahead) at one of the following.

1 **CLUB 55** **(www.leclub55.fr; 43 bd Patch, Pampelonne)** St-Tropez' oldest-running club on Plage de Pampelonne, Club 55 dates to the 1950s and was originally the crew canteen during the Brigitte Bardot–studded filming of *And God Created Woman*. Now it caters to celebs who do not want to be seen. The food is not particularly special.

2 **LA PLAGE DES JUMEAUX** **(☎04 94 58 21 80; www.plagedesjumeaux.com; rte de l'Epi, Pampelonne; mains €22-29; ⏰lunch Thu-Mon year-round, lunch & dinner daily Jul & Aug; 👪)** With its playground equipment and beach toys, Plage des Jumeaux is first choice for families. The fact that this place is also tops for seafood is just another bonus.

3 **NIKKI BEACH** **(www.nikkibeach.com/sttropez; rte de l'Epi, Epi Plage)** Favoured by dance-on-the-bar celebs (ie the likes of Paris Hilton) who want to be seen, Nikki Beach goes till midnight. See who you can spot.

4 **LIBERTY PLAGE** **(☎04 94 79 80 62; www.plageleliberty.com; chemin des Tamaris, Pampelonne; mains €17-19; ⏰year-round)** Clothing optional – yes, you can even eat naked – is the cool vibe at Liberty Plage. One for the exhibitionists or the loose and liberated.

St-Tropez (Nouveau Port) and St-Raphaël (adult/child €14/9).

BUS Tickets for **VarLib** **(www.varlib.fr)** cost €2 from the **bus station** **(☎04 94 56 25 74; av du Général de Gaulle)** for anywhere within the Var département (except Toulon-Hyères airport), including Ramatuelle (35 minutes), St-Raphaël (1¼ hours) via Grimaud and Port Grimaud, and Fréjus (one hour). Buses to Toulon (two hours, seven daily, less in summer) stop at Le Lavandou (one hour) and Hyères (1½ hours). Four buses daily serve Toulon-Hyères airport (€15, 1½ hours).

Îles d'Hyères

For some inexplicable reason, these paradisiacal islands (also known as Îles d'Or – Golden Islands – for their shimmering mica rock) have remained mostly unknown to foreign crowds.

The easternmost of this trio of islands is the little-visited **Île du Levant**, split into an odd combination of army land and nudist colony. **Île de Port-Cros**, the middle and smallest island, is the jewel in the islands' crown. France's first **marine national park** **(www.portcrosparcnational.fr)**, it boasts exceptional marine fauna and flora, which makes it a snorkelling paradise. The island is also covered with 30km of marked trails through thick forest, ragged clifftops and deserted beaches.

The largest and westernmost island is **Île de Porquerolles** **(www.porquerolles.com)**. Run as a hacienda in the early 20th century, it has kept many of its sprawling plantation features. There are plenty of walking trails, but the best way to get around is by cycling. There are several bicycle-rental places, as well as a few restaurants and hotels.

Getting There & Away

Boats to the Îles d'Hyères leave from various towns along the coast. **Vedettes Îles d'Or et Le Corsaire** **(☎04 94 71 01 02; www.vedettesilesdor.fr; 15 quai Gabriel Péri)** operates boats to all three islands from Le Lavandou, and between Port-Cros and Porquerolles in summer.

The Three Corniches

Some of the Riviera's most spectacular scenery stretches between Nice and Menton. A trio of corniches (coastal roads) hugs the cliffs between Nice and Monaco, each higher up the hill than the last. The middle corniche ends in Monaco; the upper and lower continue to Menton.

Corniche Inférieure

Skimming the villa-lined waterfront, the Corniche Inférieure (also known as the Basse Corniche, the Lower Corniche or the N98) sticks pretty close to the train line, passing (west to east) through Villefranche-sur-Mer, Beaulieu-sur-Mer, Èze-sur-Mer) and Cap d'Ail.

VILLEFRANCHE-SUR-MER

This picturesque, pastel-coloured, terracotta-roofed fishing port overlooking the Cap Ferrat peninsula was a favourite with Jean Cocteau, who painted the frescoes in the 17th-century **Chapelle St-Pierre** (admission €2.50; ⏲10am-noon & 2-6pm Wed-Mon). Steps split the steep cobblestone streets that weave through the old town, including the oldest, rue Obscure, an eerie vaulted passageway built in 1295. Looking down on the township is the 16th-century citadel. Beyond the port is a sandy beach offering picture-perfect views of the town.

ST-JEAN-CAP FERRAT

On the Cap Ferrat peninsula, this fishing-village-turned-playground-for-the-wealthy conceals an enclave of millionaires' villas, with illustrious residents both present and past. On the narrow isthmus of the town, the extravagant **Villa Ephrussi de Rothschild** (www.villa-ephrussi.com; adult/child €12/9; ⏲10am-6pm Mar-Oct, 2-6pm Nov-Feb) gives you an appreciation of the area's wealth. Housed in a 1912 Tuscan-style villa built for the Baroness de Rothschild, it's full of 18th-century furniture, paintings, tapestries and porcelain.

BEAULIEU-SUR-MER

Some of the best-preserved belle époque architecture along the coast is in the seaside holiday town of Beaulieu-sur-Mer, including its elaborate 1904 **rotunda** with Corinthian columns capped by a cupola. Another belle époque beauty is the **Villa Grecque Kérylos** (www.villa-kerylos.com; av Gustave Eiffel; adult/child €10/7.50; ⏲10am-6pm Mar-Oct, 2-6pm Nov-Feb), a reproduction of an Athenian villa built by archaeologist Théodore Reinach in 1902.

Moyenne Corniche

Cut through rock in the 1920s, the Moyenne Corniche – the middle coastal road (N7) – takes drivers from Nice to Èze and Beausoleil (the French town bordering Monaco's Monte Carlo).

ÈZE

On the pinnacle of a 427m peak is the medieval stone village of Èze (population 2865). Once occupied by Ligurians and Phoenicians, today it's home to one-off galleries and artisan boutiques within its enclosed walls (there's only one doorway in or out of the village). The high point is the **Jardin d'Èze** (adult/child €4/free; ⏲9am-sunset), a cliff-side garden of exotic cacti with views of the Med all the way to Corsica.

You can walk down from the village to Èze-sur-Mer on the coast via the steep **chemin de Nietzsche** (45 minutes); the German philosopher started writing *Thus Spoke Zarathustra* while staying in Èze and enjoyed this path.

Grande Corniche

The Grande Corniche, whose panoramas are the most dramatic of all, leaves Nice as the D2564. Stop at **Fort de la Revère** in the **Parc Natural Départemental de la Grande Corniche** for a picnic with stupendous views or a walk in the *garrigue* (Mediterranean scrubs).

Further on, the town of **La Turbie**, which sits on a promontory directly above Monaco, offers vertigo-inducing views of the principality. The best views are from the town's **Trophée des Alpes** (18 av Albert Ier; adult/student/child €5.50/4/free; ⏲10am-1pm & 2.30-5pm Tue-Sun), one of only two Roman trophy monuments in the world (the other's in Romania), built by Augustus in 6 BC.

Monaco

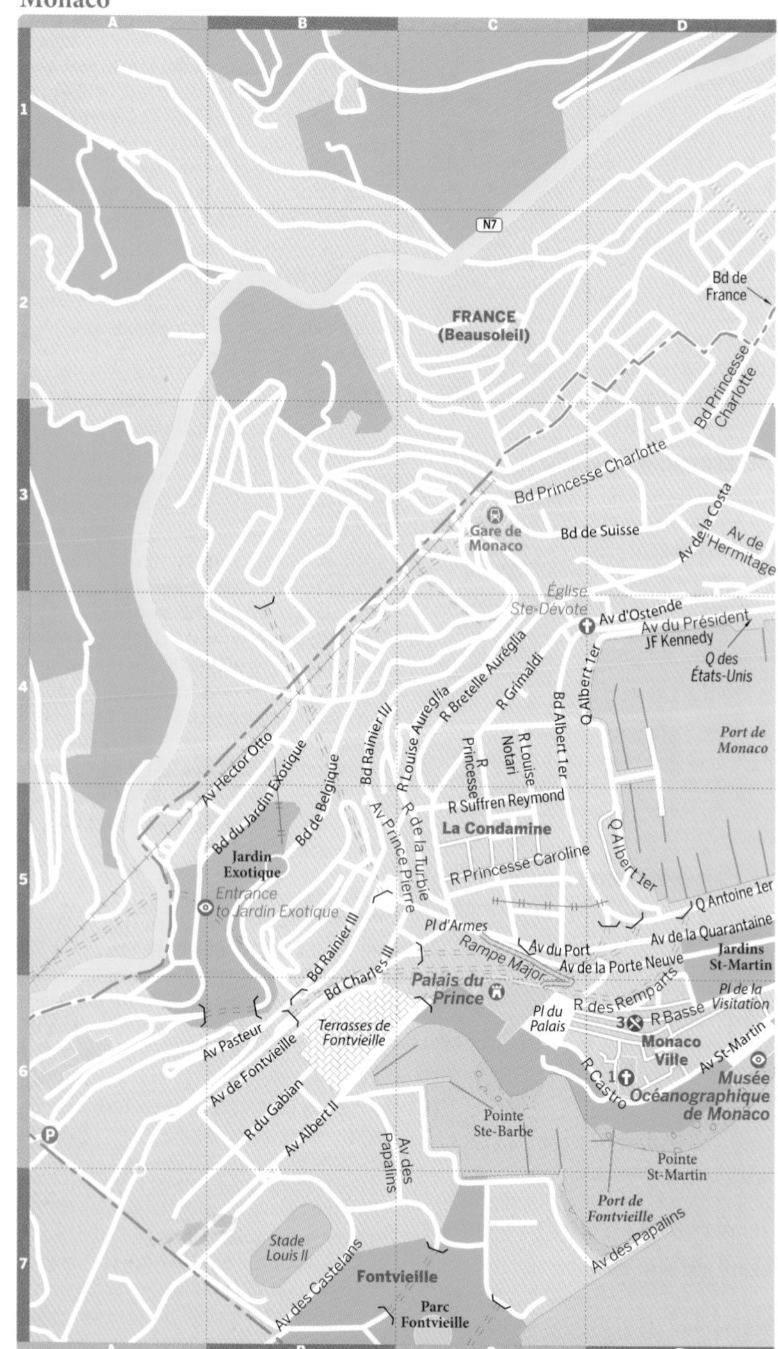
N7
FRANCE
(Beausoleil)
Bd de France
Bd Princesse Charlotte
Bd Princesse Charlotte
Gare de Monaco
Bd de Suisse
Av de la Costa
Av de l'Hermitage
Église Ste-Dévote
Av d'Ostende
Av du Président JF Kennedy
Q des États-Unis
Port de Monaco
R Bretelle Auréglia
R Grimaldi
Q Albert 1er
Bd Albert 1er
R Louise Auréglia
Bd Rainier III
R Princesse
R Louise Notari
Av Hector Otto
Bd du Jardin Exotique
Bd de Belgique
Av Prince Pierre
R de la Turbie
R Suffren Reymond
La Condamine
Q Albert 1er
R Princesse Caroline
Jardin Exotique
Entrance to Jardin Exotique
Q Antoine 1er
Pl d'Armes
Av de la Quarantaine
Rampe Major
Av du Port
Jardins St-Martin
Av de la Porte Neuve
Bd Rainier III
Bd Charles III
Palais du Prince
R des Remparts
Pl de la Visitation
Pl du Palais
R Basse
Av Pasteur
Terrasses de Fontvieille
Monaco Ville
Av de Fontvieille
R Castro
Av St-Martin
Musée Océanographique de Monaco
R du Gabian
Av Albert II
Pointe Ste-Barbe
Av des Papalins
Av des Papalins
Pointe St-Martin
Port de Fontvieille
Av des Papalins
Stade Louis II
Av des Castelans
Fontvieille
Parc Fontvieille

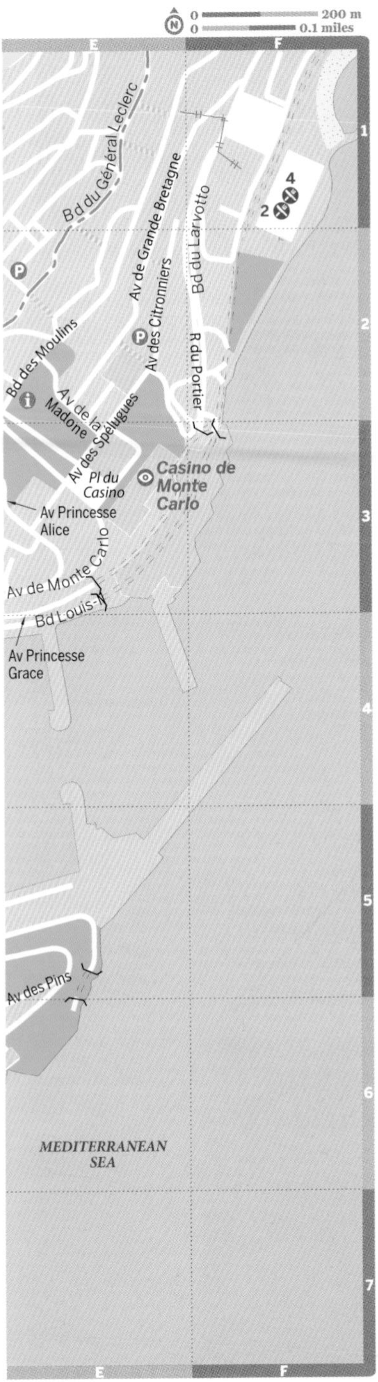

Monaco (Principauté de Monaco)

POP 32,350 / ☎377

Squeezed into just 200 hectares, this confetti principality might be the world's second-smallest country (the Vatican is smaller), but what it lacks in size it makes up for in attitude. Glitzy, glam and screaming hedonism, Monaco is truly beguiling.

Although a sovereign state, the principality's status is unusual. It is not a member of the European Union, yet it participates in the EU customs territory (meaning no border formalities crossing from France into Monaco) and uses the euro as its currency.

Sights

MUSÉE OCÉANOGRAPHIQUE DE MONACO Aquarium

(www.oceano.org; av St-Martin; adult/child €13/6.50; 9.30am-7pm) The Musée Océanographique de Monaco, founded by Prince Albert I (1848–1922), is a stunner. Its centrepiece is its **aquarium**, with a 6m-deep **lagoon** where sharks and marine predators are separated from colourful tropical fishes by a coral reef. Visit the rooftop terrace for sweeping views of Monaco and the Med.

PALAIS DU PRINCE Royal Palace

(www.palais.mc; adult/child €8/3.50; 10am-6pm Apr-Sep) You can tour the state

Monaco

Top Sights

Casino de Monte Carlo........................E3
Musée Océanographique de Monaco........................D6
Palais du Prince........................C6

Sights

1 Cathédrale de Monaco........................D6

Eating

2 Café Llorca........................F1
3 La Montgolfière........................D6
4 Zelos........................F1

Monte Carlo Casino

A Timeline

1863 Charles III inaugurates the first Casino on the Plateau des Spélugues. The atrium 1 is a small room with a wooden platform from which an orchestra 'enlivens' the gambling.

1864 Hôtel de Paris opens and the area becomes known as the 'Golden Square'.

1865 Construction of Salon Europe 2. Cathedral-like, it is lined with onyx columns and lit by eight Bohemian crystal chandeliers weighing 150kg each.

1868 The steam train arrives in Monaco and Café de Paris 3 is completed.

1878–79 Gambling moves to Hôtel de Paris while Charles Garnier is charged with building a new casino with a miniature replica of the Paris Opera House, Salle Garnier 4.

1890 The advent of electricity casts a glow on architect Jules Touzet's newly added gaming rooms 5 for high rollers.

1903 Inspired by female gamblers, Henri Schmit decorates Salle Blanche 6 with caryatids and the painting *Les Grâces Florentines*.

1904 Smoking is banned in the gaming rooms and Salon Rose 7, a new smoking room, is added.

1910 Salle Médecin 8, immense and grand, hosts the high-spending Private Circle.

1966 Celebrations mark 100 years of uninterrupted gambling despite two World Wars.

TOP TIPS

Bring photo ID

Jackets are required in the private gaming rooms, and after 8pm

The cashier will exchange any currency

In the main room, the minimum bet is €10, the maximum €2000

In the Salons Privés, the minimum bet is €500, with no maximum

JOHN VLAHIDES

Salle Blanche
Look up, away from the jarring wall-to-wall slot machines, to admire Schmit's caryatids, wings spread for flight. They illustrate the emerging emancipation of women, modelled on fashionable courtesans like La Belle Otero, who placed her first bet here age 18.

Salon Rose
Smoking was banned in the gaming rooms after a fraud involving a croupier letting his ash fall on the floor. The gaze of Gallelli's famous cigarillo-smoking nudes are said to follow you around the room.

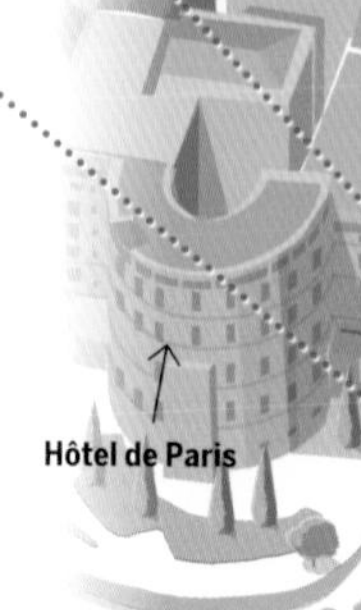

Hôtel de Paris

Notice the horse's shiny nose (and testicles) on the lobby's statue of Louis XIV on horseback. Legend has it, rubbing them brings good luck in the casino.

Salle Garnier
Taking eight months to build and two years to restore (2004–06), the opera's original statuary is rehabilitated using original moulds saved by the creator's grandson. Individual air-con and heating vents are installed beneath each of the 525 seats.

JOHN VLAHIDES

GIANNI DAGLI ORTI/ALAMY

Atrium

The casino's 'lobby', so to speak, is paved in marble and lined with 28 Ionic columns, which support a balustraded gallery canopied with an engraved glass ceiling.

BONNEMAISON JOACHIM

Salon Europe

The oldest part of the casino, where they continue to play *trente-et-quarante* and European roulette, which have been played here since 1863. Tip: the bull's-eye windows around the room originally served as security observation points.

COTE D'AZUR/ALAMY

Café de Paris

With the arrival of Diaghilev as director of the Monte Carlo Opera in 1911, Café de Paris becomes the go-to address for artists and gamblers. It retains the same high-glamour ambience today. Tip: snag a seat on the terrace and people-watch.

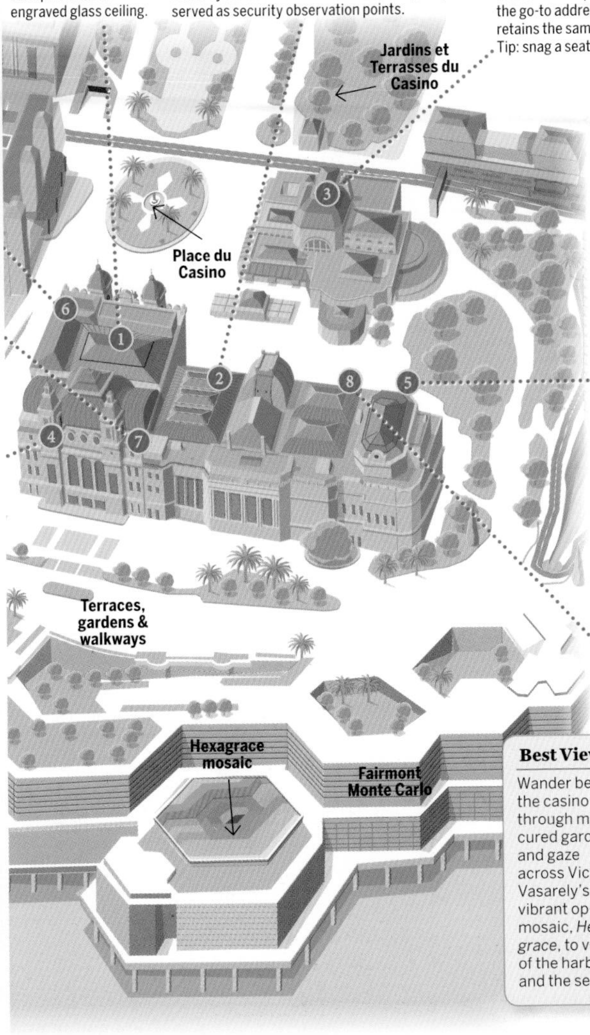

Jardins et Terrasses du Casino

Place du Casino

3

6

1

2

8

5

4

7

Terraces, gardens & walkways

Hexagrace mosaic

Fairmont Monte Carlo

Salles Touzet

This vast partitioned hall, 21m by 24m, is decorated in the most lavish style: oak, Tonkin mahogany and oriental jasper panelling are offset by vast canvases, Marseille bronzes, Italian mosaics, sculptural reliefs and stained-glass windows.

Salle Médecin

Also known as Salle Empire because of its extravagant Empire-style decor, Monégasque architect François Médecin's gaming room was originally intended for the casino's biggest gamblers. Nowadays, three adjoining Super Privés rooms keep them hidden from prying eyes.

Best Views

Wander behind the casino through manicured gardens and gaze across Victor Vasarely's vibrant op-art mosaic, *Hexagrace*, to views of the harbour and the sea.

Below: Red Ferrari, Casino de Monte Carlo; **Right:** Casino de Monte Carlo

(BELOW) HOLGER LEUE/GETTY IMAGES ©; (RIGHT) DOUG PEARSON/GETTY IMAGES ©

apartments with an 11-language audioguide.

The palace is what you would expect of any aristocratic abode: lavish furnishings and expensive 18th- and 19th-century art. It is protected by the Carabiniers du Prince; changing of the guard takes place daily at 11.55am.

CATHÉDRALE DE MONACO Cathedral

(4 rue Colonel) An adoring crowd continually shuffles past Prince Rainier's and Princess Grace's graves, located inside the cathedral choir of the 1875 Romanesque-Byzantine Cathédrale de Monaco.

Eating

LA MONTGOLFIÈRE Fusion **€€**

(97 98 61 59; www.lamontgolfiere.mc; 16 rue Basse; mains €21-30; lunch & dinner Mon, Tue, Thu, Fri, Sun, dinner Sat) This tiny fusion wonder is an unlikely find amid the touristy jumble of Monaco's historic quarter. Henri and Fabienne Geraci have spent a lot of time in Malaysia, and Henri's fusion cuisine is outstanding, as is Fabienne's welcome in their pocket-sized dining room. In winter, Henri cooks *bourride* every day, a salted cod stew typical of Monaco and Nice.

ZELOS Fusion **€€€**

(99 99 25 50; 10 av Princesse Grace, Grimaldi Forum; mains €25-30; dinner) With enormous chandeliers, intensely blue walls, a ceiling fitted with hundreds of star-like lights and uninterrupted sea views, it's hard to say which makes more of an impression, the setting or the food. The restaurant also has a huge terrace for magical summer dining.

CAFÉ LLORCA Modern French **€€**

(99 99 29 29; www.cafellorca.mc; 10 av Princesse Grace, Grimaldi Forum; mains €15-26; lunch) This new restaurant is Michelin-starred chef Alain Llorca's version of a traditional cafe: the menu is classic French fare but elevated to new heights in taste and presentation. In summer, tables are set out on the terrace overlooking the sea.

Entertainment

CASINO DE MONTE CARLO Casino

(www.montecarlocasinos.com; place du Casino; Salon Europe/Salons Privés admission €10/20; ⌚Salon Europe noon-late daily, Salons Privés from 4pm Thu-Sun) The drama of watching the poker-faced gamble in Monte Carlo's grand marble-and-gold casino makes the stiff admission fees, stakes and obligatory cloakroom 'tips' almost bearable. To enter the casino, you must be at least 18.

The **Salon Europe** has English and European roulette and 30/40; the **Salons Privés** offer European roulette, black jack and *chemin de fer*. A jacket and tie are required to enter the Salons Privés and the Salon Ordinaire in the evening.

Information

Tourist office (www.visitmonaco.com; 2a bd des Moulins; ⌚9am-7pm Mon-Sat, 11am-1pm Sun)

Getting There & Away

Train services run about every 20 minutes east to Menton (€2, 15 minutes) and west to Nice (€3.60, 25 minutes). Access to the station is through pedestrian tunnels and escalators from 6 av Prince Pierre de Monaco, pont Ste-Dévote, place Ste-Dévote and bd de la Belgique. The last trains leave around 11pm.

France In Focus

View of Eiffel Tower (p66) from Cathédrale de Notre Dame de Paris (p81)
PHOTOGRAPHER: AG PHOTOGRAPHE

France Today

> *“Within the cultural arena, France is savouring something of a high”*

Place du Tertre (p63), Montmartre

A New French President

Presidential elections in spring 2012 ushered in France's first socialist president since François Mitterrand left office in 1995. The presidential campaign saw incumbent right-wing president Nicolas Sarkozy vie for a second term in office against left-wing candidate François Hollande (b 1954) of the Socialist party. Sarkozy promised to modernise the French economy, dramatically reduce (by half) the number of immigrants to France, and lower France's budget deficit; but with the electorate tired of the austerity policies of the Conservatives, it was Hollande's ambitious talk of reducing unemployment (at a 12-year high), clearing the country's debts by 2017, upping tax on corporations and salaries over €1 million per annum and increasing the minimum salary that proved the more appealing. In the first round of voting in April 2012, Hollande pipped Sarkozy at the post with 28.6% of the vote against 27.2%. In run-off elections a fortnight later, he landed just under 52% of votes, to

DENNIS K. JOHNSON

become the new French president. Parliamentary elections a month later sealed his grip on power, with the Socialists winning a comfortable majority (273 seats) in France's 577-seat National Assembly, and thus paving the way for Hollande to govern France during Europe's biggest economic crisis in decades.

Cultural Highs

Within the cultural arena, France is savouring something of a high. Art lovers are bursting with excitement over the reopening in Paris, after months of painstaking renovation, of both the Musée Picasso and the country's most prestigious theatre, the Comédie Française, where Molière trod the boardwalks. Construction work on Paris' new €336 million philharmonic concert hall, to open in 2014, is back on track after being stalled in 2010 for lack of national funding; while world-renowned Frank Gehry is the architect behind dazzling projects in the capital (a glass crystal-shaped contemporary art gallery in Paris' Bois de Boulogne) and French provinces (a shimmering cultural centre in Arles, southern France). At the 2012 Academy Awards, the French-made silent film *The Artist,* starring the quintessentially French-sexy Jean Dujardin, stole the show by scooping five Oscars. Enter the much-heralded renaissance of French cinema.

Then there is the Louvre-Lens that will see priceless works of art from the original Louvre whisked up north to a striking new gallery space in former coal-mining town Lens. Innovative, daring and decidedly bold, it promises to inject new creativity into the conventional French museum experience.

Environmental Lows

The protection of France's lyrical landscapes has never been straightforward, as demonstrated by recent developments at one of the country's most iconic sights, the stunning abbey-crowned mount of Mont St-Michel. A €200 million project is designed to stop the mythical bay silting up by building a dam, ridding the mount of cars and motorised vehicles from its traffic-congested foot, and replacing the original tidal causeway trodden by pilgrims since 1879 with an ultra-lightweight bridge (by 2014). This would allow the 15m-high tidal waters for which this part of Normandy is famed to swirl without environmental consequence. Yet, just as the motorised vehicles go and the 2.5 million annual visitors embrace the final leg of one of France's top tourist pilgrimages on foot or by shuttle, Mont St-Michel risks losing its Unesco World Heritage status. The reason: the proposed construction of offshore turbine farms some 20km out to sea from the priceless mount.

History

Louis XIV's bed chamber, Château de Versailles (p101)

DENNIS K. JOHNS

Few nations have a history as rich and rewarding as France. With everything from ancient artworks to Gothic cathedrals and regal châteaux, France often feels like one long history textbook. Even the tiniest towns and villages are littered with reminders of the nation's often turbulent past. Encompassing everything from courtly intrigue to intellectual enlightenment, artistic endeavour and bloody revolution, one thing's for sure – French history certainly isn't dull.

Prehistory

The first people to settle in France in significant numbers were small tribes of hunter-gatherers, who arrived around 35,000 to 50,000 years ago. These nomadic tribes lived seasonally from the land while pursuing game such as mammoth, aurochs, bison and deer. They often used natural caves as temporary shelters, leaving behind many sophisticated artworks, such as those in the Vézère Valley.

c 30,000 BC

Cro-Magnon people arrive in the Vézère Valley and create many cave paintings.

The next great wave of settlers arrived after the end of the last Ice Age, from around 7500 BC to 2500 BC. These Neolithic people were responsible for the construction of France's many megalithic monuments, including dolmens, burial tombs, stone circles and the massive stone alignments of Carnac. During this era, warmer weather allowed the development of farming and animal domestication, and humans increasingly established themselves in settled communities, often protected by defensive forts.

Gauls & Romans

Many of these communities were further developed from around 1500 BC to 500 BC by the Gauls, a Celtic people who migrated westwards from present-day Germany and Eastern Europe. But the Gauls' reign was shortlived; over the next few centuries their territories were gradually conquered or subjugated by the Romans. After decades of sporadic warfare, the Gauls were finally defeated in 52 BC when Caesar's legions crushed a revolt led by the Celtic chief Vercingetorix.

France flourished under Roman rule. With typical industriousness, the Romans set about constructing roads, temples, forts and other civic infrastructure, laying the foundations for many modern French cities (including Paris) and (more importantly in the opinion of many) planting the country's first vineyards, notably around Burgundy and Bordeaux.

The Rise of the Kings

Following the collapse of the Roman Empire, control of France passed to the Frankish dynasties, who ruled from the 5th to the 10th century, and effectively founded France's first royal dynasty. Charlemagne (742–814) was crowned Holy Roman Emperor in 800, around the same time that Scandinavian Vikings (also called Norsemen, thus Normans) began to raid France's western and northern coasts. Having plundered and pillaged to their hearts' content, the Normans eventually formed the independent duchy of Normandy in the early 11th century.

In 1066, the Normans launched a successful invasion of England, making William the Conqueror both Duke of Normandy and King of England. The tale of the invasion is graphically recounted in the embroidered cloth known as the Bayeux Tapestry.

During this time, Normandy was one of several independent duchies or provinces (including Brittany, Aquitaine, Burgundy, Anjou and Savoy) within the wider French kingdom. While each province superficially paid allegiance to the French crown, they were effectively self-governing and ruled by their own courts.

Intrigue and infighting were widespread. Matters came to a head in 1122 when Eleanor, Queen of Aquitaine, wed Henry, Duke of Anjou (who was also Duke of Normandy and, as William the Conqueror's great-grandson, heir to the English crown).

1500–500 BC

The Celtic Parisii tribe settle on what is now the Île de la Cité, Paris.

c AD 100–300

The heyday of Gallo-Roman France results in the construction of many splendid Roman buildings.

987

The Capetian dynasty comes to power and remains the French royal family for 800 years.

Henry's ascension to the English throne in 1124 effectively brought a third of France under England's control, with battles that collectively became known as the Hundred Years' War (1337–1453), sowing the seeds for several centuries of conflict.

Following particularly heavy defeats for the French at Crécy and Agincourt, John Plantagenet was made regent of France on behalf of Henry VI in 1422, and less than a decade later he was crowned king of France. The tide of the war seemed to have taken a decisive turn, but luckily for the French, a 17-year-old warrior by the name of Jeanne d'Arc (Joan of Arc) rallied the French forces and inspired the French king Charles VII to a series of victories, culminating in the recapture of Paris in 1437.

Unfortunately things didn't turn out well for Joan – she was subsequently betrayed to the English, accused of heresy and witchcraft, and burnt at the stake in Rouen in 1431.

The Best... Roman Sites

1 Pont du Gard (p324)

2 Les Arènes (p312) & Théâtre Antique (p313)

3 Theâtre Romain (p236)

4 MuséoParc Alésia (p209)

5 Trophée des Alpes (p343)

Renaissance to Revolution

During the reign of François I (r 1515–47), the Renaissance arrived from Italy, and prompted a great flowering of culture, art and architecture across France. Many lavish royal châteaux were built along the Loire Valley, showcasing the skills of French architects and artisans and projecting the might and majesty of the French monarchy. This great era of castle-building reached its zenith under the reign of Louis XIV (1643–1715), known as the Sun King, who emphasised the supposedly divine status of the French monarchy and constructed the ultimate playground palace at Versailles.

The pomp and profligacy of the ruling elite didn't go down well with everyone, however. Following a series of social and economic crises that rocked the country during the 18th century, and incensed by the corruption and bourgeois extravagance of the aristocracy, a Parisian mob took to the streets in 1789, storming the prison at Bastille and kickstarting the French Revolution.

Inspired by the lofty ideals of *liberté, fraternité, égalité* (freedom, brotherhood, equality), the Revolutionaries initially found favour with the French people. France was declared a constitutional monarchy, but order broke down when the hard-line Jacobins seized power. The monarchy was abolished and the nation was declared a republic on 21 September 1792. Three months later Louis XVI was publicly guillotined, as an example to the people, on Paris' place de la Concorde. His ill-fated queen, Marie-Antoinette, suffered the same fate a few months later.

1066
William the Conqueror invades England, making Normandy and England rivals of the kingdom of France.

1337–1453
The French and English battle for control of France during the Hundred Years' War.

1530s
The Reformation embraces France, leading to Protestant-Catholic conflict during the Wars of Religion (1562–98).

As the pillars of French society crumbled, chaos ensued. Violent retribution broke out across France. During the Reign of Terror (September 1793 to July 1794) churches were closed, religious monuments were desecrated, riots were suppressed and thousands of aristocrats were imprisoned or beheaded. The high ideals of the Revolution had turned to vicious bloodshed, and the nation was rapidly descending into anarchy. France desperately needed someone to re-establish order, give it new direction and rebuild its shattered sense of self. From amidst the smoke and thunder, a dashing (if diminutive) young Corsican general stepped out from the shadows – Napoléon Bonaparte.

The Napoléonic Era

Napoléon's military prowess quickly turned him into a powerful political force. In 1804 he was crowned emperor at Notre Dame Cathedral, and subsequently led the French armies to conquer much of Europe. His ill-fated campaign to invade Russia ended in disaster, however; in 1812, his armies were stopped outside Moscow and decimated by the brutal Russian winter. Two years later, Allied armies entered Paris and exiled Napoléon to Elba.

Off with His Head

Prior to the Revolution, public executions in France depended on rank: the nobility were generally beheaded with a sword or axe (with predictably messy consequences), while commoners were usually hanged (particularly nasty prisoners were also drawn and quartered, which involved being eviscerated while still alive and then pulled to pieces by four oxen).

In an effort to provide a more civilised end for the condemned, in the early 1790s a group of French physicians, scientists and engineers set about designing a clinical new execution machine involving a razor-sharp weighted blade, guaranteed to behead people with a minimum of fuss or mess. Named after one of its inventors, the anatomy professor Ignace Guillotin, the machine was first used on 25 April 1792, when the highwayman Nicolas Jacques Pelletie went down in history as the first man to lose his head to the guillotine.

During the Reign of Terror, at least 17,000 met their death beneath the machine's plunging blade. By the time the last was given the chop in 1977 (behind closed doors – the last public execution was in 1939), the contraption could slice off a head in 2/100 of a second.

1643–1715

Louis XIV assumes the French throne and shifts his royal court from Paris to Versailles.

HULTON ARCHIVE/STRINGER

1789–94

Revolutionaries storm the Bastille. Louis XVI and Marie-Antoinette are guillotined. Louis XVI threatened by revolutionaries, Tuileries, Paris

The Best... Historic Pilgrimages

1 Château de Versailles (p101)

2 Alignements de Carnac (p143)

3 Mont St-Michel (p128)

4 Grotte de Lascaux (p216)

5 Sanctuaires Notre Dame de Lourdes (p283)

But that wasn't the last of the Little General. In 1815 Napoléon escaped, re-entering Paris on 20 May. His glorious 'Hundred Days' ended with defeat by the English at the Battle of Waterloo. He was exiled again, this time to St Helena in the South Atlantic, where he died in 1821. His body was later reburied under the Hôtel des Invalides in Paris.

New Republics

Post-Napoléon, France was dogged by a string of ineffectual rulers until Napoléon's nephew, Louis Napoléon Bonaparte, came to power. He was initially elected president, but declared himself Emperor (Napoléon III) in 1851.

While the so-called Second Empire ran roughshod over many of the ideals set down during the Revolution, it actually proved to be a relatively prosperous time. France enjoyed significant economic growth and Paris was transformed by urban planner Baron Haussmann, who created the famous 12 boulevards radiating from the Arc de Triomphe (including the celebrated Champs-Élysées).

But like his uncle, Napoléon III's ambition was his undoing. A series of costly conflicts, including the Crimean War (1854–56), culminated in humiliating defeat by the Prussian forces in 1870. France was once again declared a republic – for the third time in less than a century.

The Belle Époque

The Third Republic got off to a shaky start: another war with the Prussians resulted in a huge war bill and the surrender of Alsace and Lorraine. But the period also ushered in a new era of culture and creativity that left an enduring mark on France's national character.

The belle époque ('beautiful age'), as it came to be known, was an era of unprecedented innovation. Architects built a host of exciting new buildings and transformed the faces of many French cities. Engineers laid the tracks of France's first railways and tunnelled out the metro system still used by millions of Parisians today. Designers experimented with new styles and materials, while young artists invented

1851
Louis Napoléon proclaims himself Emperor Napoléon III of the Second Empire (1851–70).

1914–18
WWI: 1.3 million French soldiers are killed and many historic cities destroyed.

1939–44
WWII: Nazi Germany divides France into a German-occupied zone and a puppet Vichy state.

a host of new 'isms' (including impressionism, which took its title from one of Claude Monet's seminal early paintings, *Impression, Soleil Levant*).

The era culminated in a lavish Exposition Universelle (World Fair) in Paris in 1889, an event that seemed to sum up the excitement and dynamism of the age, and also inspired the construction of one of the nation's most iconic landmarks – the Eiffel Tower.

The Great War

Sadly, the *joie de vivre* of the belle époque wasn't to last. Within months of the outbreak of WWI in 1914, the fields of northern France had been transformed into a sea of trenches and shell craters; by the time the armistice had been signed in November 1918, some 1.3 million French soldiers had been killed and almost one million crippled. A trip to the battlefields of the Somme or Verdun provides a chilling reminder of the unimaginable human cost of WWI.

Desperate to forget the ravages of the war, Paris sparkled as the centre of the avant-garde in the 1920s and '30s. The liberal atmosphere (not to mention the cheap booze and saucy nightlife) attracted a stream of foreign artists and writers

Orangerie (p104), Château de Versailles
PHOTOGRAPHER: CHICUREL ARNAUD/HEMIS.FR

1949
France joins North America and Western Europe in a mutual defence alliance (NATO).

1981
The high-speed TGV smashes speed records. Journey time from Paris to Lyon falls to under two hours.

1994
The 50km-long Channel Tunnel links mainland France with Britain.

The French Resistance

Despite the myth of '*la France résistante*' (the French Resistance), the underground movement never actually included more than 5% of the population. The other 95% either collaborated or did nothing. Resistance members engaged in railway sabotage, collected intelligence for the Allies, helped Allied airmen who had been shot down and published anti-German leaflets, among other activities. Though the impact of their actions was relatively slight, the Resistance served as an enormous boost to French morale – not to mention the inspiration for numerous literary and cinematic endeavours.

to the city, and helped establish Paris' enduring reputation for creativity and experimentation.

WWII

Unfortunately, the interwar party was short-lived. Two days after Germany invaded Poland in 1939, France joined Britain in declaring war on Germany. Within a year, Hitler's *blitzkrieg* had swept across Europe, and France was forced into humiliating capitulation in June the same year. Following the seaborne retreat of the British Expeditionary Force at Dunkirk, France – like much of Europe – found itself under Nazi occupation.

The Germans divided France into two zones: the west and north (including Paris), which was under direct German rule; and a puppet-state in the south based around the spa town of Vichy. The anti-semitic Vichy regime proved very helpful to the Nazis in rounding up Jews and other undesirables for deportation to the death camps.

After four years of occupation, on 6 June 1944 Allied forces returned to French soil during the D-Day landings. Over 100,000 Allied troops stormed the Normandy coastline and, after several months of fighting, liberated Paris on 25 August. But the cost of the war had been devastating for France: half a million buildings had been destroyed, many cities had been razed to the ground and millions of French people had lost their lives.

Poverty to Prosperity

Broken and battered from the war, France was forced to turn to the USA for loans as part of the Marshall Plan to rebuild Europe. Slowly, under the government of French war hero Charles de Gaulle, the economy began to recover and France began to rebuild its shattered infrastructure. The debilitating Algerian War of Independence (1954–62) and the subsequent loss of its colonies seriously weakened de Gaulle's government, however, and following widespread student protests in 1968 and a general strike by

2002

The French franc, first minted in 1360, is dumped when France adopts the euro. A €1 coin

PETER DAZELEY

2004

The National Assembly bans religious symbols such as the Islamic headscarf in state schools.

10 million workers, de Gaulle was forced to resign from office in 1969. He died the following year.

Subsequent French presidents Georges Pompidou (in power from 1969 to 1974) and Giscard d'Estaing (1974–81) were instrumental in the increasing political and economic integration of Europe, a process that had begun with the formation of the EEC (European Economic Community) in 1957, and continued under François Mitterrand with the enlarged EU (European Union) in 1991. During Mitterrand's time in office, France abolished the death penalty, legalised homosexuality, gave workers five weeks' holiday and annually guaranteed the right to retire at 60.

In 1995 Mitterrand was succeeded by the maverick Jacques Chirac, who was re-elected in 2002. Chirac's attempts at reform led to widespread strikes and social unrest, while his opposition to the Iraq war alienated the US administration (and famously led to the rebranding of French fries as Freedom fries).

The Best... History Museums

1 Musée National du Moyen Âge (p69)

2 Bayeux Tapestry (p124)

3 Musée de la Civilisation Gallo-Romaine (p236)

4 Mémorial – Un Musée pour la Paix (p126)

5 Musée des Civilisations de l'Europe et de la Méditerranée (p301)

Sarkozy's France

Following Chirac's retirement, the media-savvy Nicolas Sarkozy was elected president in 2007, bringing a more personality-driven, American-style approach to French politics. The centre-right politician wooed voters with policies about job creation, lower taxes, crime crackdown and help for France's substantial immigrant population – issues that had particular pulling power coming from the son of a Hungarian immigrant father and Greek Jewish-French mother. Yet his first few months in office were dominated by personal affairs as he divorced his wife Cecilia and wed Italian multimillionaire singer Carla Bruni a few months later. Sarkozy's popularity plummeted, and continued to do so during a presidential term that had the misfortune to be dogged by a global banking crisis (during which the French government injected €10.5 billion into France's six major banks) and a stubbornly persistent economic crisis in Europe.

2007

Pro-American pragmatist Nicolas Sarkozy beats Socialist candidate Ségolène Royal to become French president.

2011

French parliamentary ban on burkas in public comes into effect; Muslim women publicly wearing the face-covering veil are fined.

2012

Amid economic crisis, elections usher in France's first socialist president in 17 years.

Family Travel

Jardin des Tuileries (p65), Paris

CHRISTOPHER GROENHOUT

Dining, celebrating or travelling, the French are great believers in doing it en famille (as a family), making France a great place to travel with kids. Be it the kid-friendly extraordinaire capital of Paris, or the rural hinterland, this country spoils families with its rich mix of cultural sights, activities and entertainment – some paid for, many free. To get the most out of travelling en famille, plan ahead.

Trip Planning

Consider the season: teen travel is a year-round affair (always something to entertain, regardless of the weather), but parents travelling with younger kids will definitely find spring the easiest: the warmer, dry weather means more relaxed and casual dining alfresco; queues are shorter so less hanging around with impatient little ones; and museum gardens suddenly open up (for quick run-arounds between galleries).

With a little planning and creativity, kid appeal can be found in almost every sight in France, top sights included. Skip the formal guided tour of Mont St-Michel, for example, and hook up with a walking guide to take you and the kids barefoot across the sand to the abbey; trade the daytime queues at the Eiffel Tower for a tour all-a-twinkle after dark; don't dismiss wine tasting in

Provence or Burgundy outright – rent bicycles and turn it into a family bike ride instead.

Paris history and art museums can be a challenge but the Louvre, Musée d'Orsay and many others offer *ateliers* (workshops) for children and/or families. Outside the capital, consider which area is best suited to your children and their interests: the fairy-tale châteaux of the Loire Valley and the high-octane activities of the French Alps are always popular, while the Atlantic Coast and French Riviera guarantee endless seaside frolics. Older kids fascinated by history might enjoy the Dordogne (prehistory), Burgundy (Roman), the Loire Valley (Renaissance), northern France (WWI) and Normandy (WWII).

The Best... Family Days Out

1 Aiguille du Midi (p244) by gondola and across glaciers into Italy (kids over over four years)

2 Chantier Médiéval de Guédelon (p211)

3 Les Machines de l'Île de Nantes (p280)

4 Gouffre de Padirac (p212)

5 Musée Océanographique de Monaco (p345)

6 Canoeing beneath Pont du Gard (p324) (kids over seven years)

À table!

Make eating out in France a trip highlight. Classic French mains adored by most children include gratin *dauphinois* (sliced potatoes oven-baked in cream), *escalope de veau* (breaded pan-fried veal) and bœuf bourguignon (beef stew). Alpine cheese fondue and *raclette* (melted cheese served with potatoes and cold meats) and *moules frites* (mussels and fries) are favourites with local children.

Most French restaurants are accommodating of younger diners. Many offer a *menu enfant* (set children's menu) – usually *saucisse* (sausage) or *steak haché* (beef burger) and *frites* (fries) followed by ice cream – but don't be shy in asking for a half-portion of an adult main instead. s

A basket of bread, specifically crusty chunks of baguette, is brought to the table before or immediately after you've ordered. This is to the glee of children, who wolf it down while they wait. Watch for the fight to ensue over who gets the *quignon* (the knobbly end bit, an equal hit with teething babies!).

Dining *en famille* after dark is perfectly acceptable providing the kids don't run wild. Few restaurants open their doors, however, before 7.30pm or 8pm. This means that brasseries and cafes – many of which serve food continuously from 7am or 8am until midnight – are more appealing for families with younger children.

Snack Attack

France is fabulous snack-attack terrain. Parisian pavements are rife with crêpe stands and wintertime stalls selling hot chestnuts. Savoury *galettes* (pancakes) make for an easy light lunch, as does France's signature *croque monsieur* (toasted cheese and ham sandwich) served by most cafes and brasseries. *Goûter* (afternoon snack), devoured after school around 4.30pm, is golden for every French child and *salons de thé* (tea rooms) serve a mouth-watering array of cakes, pastries and biscuits. Or go local: buy a baguette, rip off a chunk and pop a slab of chocolate inside. Really!

Need to Know

- **Changing facilities** Generally only in women's toilets (dads, don't be shy...).
- **Cots** Most midrange and top-end hotels have them.
- **Health** No special inoculations required.
- **Highchairs** Hit or miss whether a place has one.
- **Kids' menus** Offered in most restaurants.
- **Nappies (diapers)** Purchase in supermarkets and pharmacies.
- **Strollers (pushchairs)** Steps and cobbles make pushchairs a challenge; bring a baby sling.
- **Transport** Reduced fares for kids on trains, buses and metros.

Accommodation

Parents with just one child and/or a baby in tow will have no problem finding hotel accommodation – most midrange hotels have baby cots/extra beds and will happily pop one in your room for minimal or no charge. Countrywide, hotels with family or four-person rooms are harder to find.

In rural France, B&Bs and farmstays, some of which cook up tasty evening meals, are the way to go. Or what about a hip baby-and-toddler house party in a Burgundy château or a chalet retreat in the French Alps? For older children, treehouses decked out with bunk beds and Mongolian yurts create a real family adventure.

Camping is wildly popular with families and for good reason: check into a self-catering mobile home, chalet or family tent; sit back on the verandah with wine in hand and watch as your kids – wonderfully oblivious to any barriers language might pose – run around with new-found friends.

Architecture

Paris (p64)

ALLAN BAXTER

Love it or hate it, French architecture nearly always makes a statement. From the illustrious châteaux of the Loire Valley to modern icons such as Paris' Centre Pompidou and Pyramide du Louvre, French architecture is always on a grand scale. French leaders have long recognised the importance of an iconic building or two to their own political legacy.

Ancient & Roman Architecture

France's oldest architecture can be found in Brittany, where megalithic builders left behind many impressive stone monuments, including the 3000-odd menhirs of the Alignements de Carnac. In contrast, the nation's Gallo-Roman legacy is mainly concentrated in the south, including the impressive amphitheatres in Nîmes and Arles, and the huge Pont du Gard aqueduct near Nîmes.

Gothic Architecture

During the Gothic period, France's architects really aimed for scale, as demonstrated by monumental Gothic buildings such as Avignon's pontifical palace and the massive cathedrals of Chartres, Reims, Metz and Paris' Notre Dame. Telltale signs of French Gothic buildings include flying buttresses,

The Best... Contemporary Creations

1 Musée du Quai Branly (p64)

2 Centre Pompidou-Metz (p171)

3 Louvre-Lens (p173)

4 Fondation Maeght (p334)

ribbed vaults, pointed arches and plenty of luminous stained glass.

The Renaissance

During the 15th and 16th centuries architects developed a taste for extravagance, epitomised by the lavish châteaux of the Loire Valley. Embellished with sweeping staircases, gabled windows, lacy turrets and decorative motifs, these castles were built to impress rather than to defend against attack. The era of architectural showiness reached its peak with the royal palace of Versailles near Paris.

Neoclassicism & the Belle Époque

The 18th and 19th centuries were about order and elegance. This was the era of the grand boulevard and the great public square, exemplified by Arras' Place des Héros, Nancy's Place Stanislas, Strasbourg's Place de la République, and Paris' most famous street, the Champs-Élysées. The era also inspired many of Paris' best-known buildings, including the Arc de Triomphe.

The late 19th century in France was a time of artistic experimentation and industrial innovation. Belle époque architects combined iron, brick, glass and ceramics in exciting new ways, and even the most mundane structures – from covered markets and town halls to swimming pools and metro stations – acquired a dash of class.

Modern Architecture

After the ravages of WWII, French architects were given free reign to reinvent the nation's shattered cities. Some favoured a brutally functional style of architecture, while others adopted a more playful approach. France's most celebrated architect, Le Corbusier (1887–1965), rewrote the architectural textbook during the 1950s with his sweeping lines and sinuous forms.

The French tendency for experimentation has continued throughout the modern era. The 1970s and 1980s witnessed the construction of many exciting buildings, including the Grande Arche in the Parisian skyscraper district of La Défense, the world's first ever 'inside-out' building aka Paris' Centre Pompidou, and IM Pei's glass pyramid at the hitherto sacrosanct Louvre – an architectural cause célébre that paved the way for Mario Bellini and Rudy Ricciotti's magnificent 'flying carpet' roof atop the Louvre's Cour Visconti in 2012.

France continues to be an exciting showroom and playground for the world's most renowned contemporary architects: Frank Gehry, Norman Foster and Jean Nouvel.

The Arts & Literature

Monet, Renoir...Chagall. Journeys around the Mediterranean multimedia show, Carrières de Lumières, Les Baux de Provence (p335) © Nuit de Chine

NUIT DE CHINE ©

In a country where style and panache count for so much, it comes as no surprise that culture still matters deeply to French people. France has a long and distinguished legacy in literature, painting, sculpture and cinema, and the arts continue to play a crucial role in the nation's collective culture.

Painting

From the dreamy landscapes of the impressionists to the radical experiments of cubism, France has been the crucible for a host of artistic movements.

Classical & Romantic

According to Voltaire, French painting began with Nicolas Poussin (1594–1665), whose dramatic paintings based on mythological and biblical scenes set the benchmark for classical French art. Later, romantic painters such as David (1748–1825), Géricault (1791–1824) and Délacroix (1798–1863) drew their inspiration from French history and political events, creating lifelike canvases packed with power and emotion. Key works by all these artists can be seen in the Louvre in Paris.

Other artists moved out of their studios in search of subjects from everyday life.

The Best... Iconic Art Museums

1 Musée d'Orsay (p71)

2 Musée du Louvre (p73)

3 Louvre-Lens (p173)

4 Centre Pompidou-Metz (p171)

5 Monet's garden (p123) and Musée des Impressionismes (p123)

Jean-François Millet (1814–75), the son of a Norman farmer, depicted peasant life in France's rural villages: his *L'Angélus* (The Angelus; 1857) is the best-known French painting after the *Mona Lisa* (the original *L'Angélus* is in Paris' Musée d'Orsay).

Impressionism & Post-Impressionism

During the late 19th century, artists experimented with capturing an 'impression' of a scene, emphasising colour, light and atmosphere above strictly realistic representation. This movement (dubbed 'impressionism' after an early painting by Claude Monet, 1840–1926) included artists such as Claude Pissarro, Alfred Sisley, Eugène Boudin, Edgar Degas and Auguste Renoir, but it's Monet's work that encapsulates the spirit of impressionism for many people – particularly his series of *Nymphéas* (Water Lilies) paintings, which he composed in the grounds of his own garden in Giverny, near Paris.

During the post-impressionist period, artists continued to push the boundaries of acceptability, both in terms of subject and technique. The intense light and lush landscapes of Provence and the Riviera attracted many artists, including Paul Cézanne (1839–1906) and the Dutch artist Vincent van Gogh (1853–90), while the hustle and bustle of *fin-de-siècle* (end of the century) Paris attracted others, such as Henri de Toulouse-Lautrec (1864–1901), best known for his paintings of Parisian brothels. Other artists travelled further afield: Paul Gauguin (1848–1903) emigrated to Tahiti, where he produced rich, sensual paintings inspired by his adopted tropical home.

Meanwhile in St-Tropez, pointillist painters applied paint in small dots to produce a colourful mosaic-like effect: the works of Georges Seurat (1859–91) and his pupil Paul Signac (1863–1935) are on display at St-Tropez's Musée de l'Annonciade.

Fauvism, Cubism & Surrealism

The dawn of the 20th century inspired a bewildering diversity of artistic movements, many of which inspired considerable controversy. Fauvist artists such as Henri Matisse (1869–1954) and André Dérain (1880–1954) moved even further from the confines of representational art, often using bold, brash colours that bore little relation to reality; the movement famously got its name from a shocked art critic who compared the artists with *fauves* (wild animals) after an exhibition in 1905.

Fauvism marked the start of an experimental century. Cubism completely threw out the artistic rule book, breaking subjects into component shapes and ignoring long-established rules of perspective and composition: among its key figures were the Spanish-born artist Pablo Picasso (1881–1973) and the French artist Georges Braque (1882–1963).

Meanwhile, surrealist artists delved into their subconscious in search of hidden dreams and desires, inspired by the theories of the psychoanalyst Sigmund Freud. Dadaism, an offshoot of surrealism, was shot through with a rebellious spirit and an anarchic sense of humour – one of its most famous exponents, Marcel Duchamp (1887–1968), famously made a sculpture from a men's urinal and painted a goatee on the *Mona Lisa*.

Modern Art

After WWII, the focus shifted from Paris to southern France in the 1960s with new realists such as Arman (1928–2005) and Yves Klein (1928–62), both from Nice. In 1960 Klein famously produced *Anthropométrie de l'Époque Bleue,* a series of imprints made by naked women covered from head to toe in blue paint rolling around on a white canvas.

More recent artists have increasingly moved towards conceptual art, using practically every medium other than paint to express their concerns. Among the best known are Daniel Buren (b 1938), the *enfant terrible* of 1980s French art, and Sophie Calle (b 1953), who brazenly exposes her private life with her eye-catching installations.

The Best... Unexpected Art Museums

1 Musée Picasso (p67) and Musée Rodin (p80)

2 La Piscine Musée d'Art et d'Industrie (p171)

3 Musée des Beaux Arts, Dijon (p204)

4 Mamac (p325)

5 Fondation Maeght (p334)

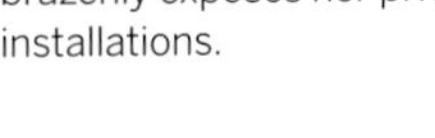

Cinema

France is the nation that invented cinema, so it's hardly surprising that film continues to be one of its most enduring art forms. The *septième art*, as cinema is often known, is a quintessential French passion, celebrated every May during the annual Cannes Film Festival. The festival attracts big-name stars to the French Riviera and hands out one of the world's most coveted film prizes, the Palme d'Or.

Early Cinema

The Lumière brothers (Auguste and Louis) shot the world's first motion picture, *La Sortie des Usines Lumières* (Exit of the Lumières Factories) in one of their family factories in Lyon on 19 March 1895. Today, the Lyonnais factory houses the Musée Lumière, a museum exploring cinema's beginnings and screening classic films.

Despite several early classics, French cinema only really hit its stride in the 1930s. The classic *La Grande Illusion* (The Great Illusion; 1937) is a devastating portrayal of the folly of war, based on the trench warfare experience of director Jean Renoir (1894–1979). Hot on its heels came Renoir's seminal *Les Règle du Jeu* (The Rules of the Game; 1939), a biting satire of the French upper classes, set in the years before WWII. French cinema's reputation for stylish photography, sharp dialogue and intellectual subject matter was confirmed.

A decade later, surrealist artist-writer-philosopher Jean Cocteau made two back-to-back masterpieces, *La Belle et la Bête* (Beauty and the Beast; 1945) and *Orphée* (Orpheus; 1950). But it was the directors of the *nouvelle vague* (new wave) who arguably made the greatest contribution to French cinema as an art form. With small budgets, no complex sets and no big stars, these young French directors made highly personal films, pioneering the use of fractured narratives, documentary-style camerawork and new editing techniques.

Key directors of the new wave include Claude Chabrol, Alain Resnais and François Truffaut, but the quintessential new wave director is Jean-Luc Godard (b 1930), who captured the essence of Parisian cool in *À Bout de Souffle* (Breathless; 1960) before later branching out into experimental films such as the apocalyptic black comedy *Le Weekend* (1969).

The Best... Art Trails

1 Cézanne in Aix-en-Provence (p314)

2 Van Gogh in Arles (p312)

3 Matisse in Nice (p328)

4 Picasso in Paris (p67) and Antibes (p332)

5 Artists galore in Montmartre (p62) and St-Tropez (p338)

1970s to 1990s

After the fireworks of the new wave, French cinema lost its experimental edge. Lesser-known directors such as Éric Rohmer (b 1920) made beautiful but uneventful films in which the characters endlessly analyse their feelings. Other directors retreated into nostalgia, characterised by Jacques Demy's *Les Parapluies de Cherbourg* (The Umbrellas of Cherbourg; 1964), a bittersweet love story set in Normandy.

The trend continued into the 1970s and '80s, as filmmakers switched to costume dramas and commercial comedies in an attempt to compete with growing competition from the USA. Claude Berri's sentimental portraits of pre-war Provence in *Jean de Florette* (1986) and *Manon des Sources* (1986) found big audiences both at home and abroad, as did Jean-Paul Rappeneau's glossy version of the classic French fable *Cyrano de Bergerac* (1990); all three films starred France's best-known actor, Gérard Depardieu. Other directors such as Luc Besson gave a Gallic spin to American genres.

The 1990s also saw French cinema acquire a grittier edge, epitomised by Mathieu Kassovitz's hard-hitting *La Haine* (1995), which explored the bleak lives of French youth in Parisian housing estates.

Contemporary Cinema

French cinema has produced some significant hits over the last decade, most notably big-budget versions of the Astérix comics. *La Môme* (known overseas as *La Vie en Rose*), a biopic of Édith Piaf, scooped the Best Actress Oscar for French actress Marion Cotillard at the 2008 Academy Awards and the same year a French film won the Palme d'Or at Cannes for the first time since 1987: Laurent Cantet's *Entre Les Murs* (The Class) used real pupils and teachers to portray a year in the life of a school in a rough Parisian neighbourhood.

French Cinema in 10 Films

- *La Règle du Jeu* (The Rules of the Game, 1939)
- *Les Enfants du Paradis* (Children of Paradise, 1945)
- *Et Dieu Créa la Femme* (And God Created Woman, 1956)
- *Les Quatre Cents Coups* (The 400 Blows, 1959)
- *À Bout de Souffle* (Breathless, 1960)
- *37.2°C du Matin* (Betty Blue, 1986)
- *Delicatessen* (1991)
- *Jeanne d'Arc* (Joan of Arc, 1999)
- *Le Fabuleux Destin d'Amélie Poulain* (Amélie, 2001)
- *Bienvenue chez les Ch'tis* (Welcome to the Sticks, 2008)

Some contemporary directors find an audience by employing shock tactics. *Enfant terrible* Gaspar Noé ruffled feathers with his violent films *Irréversible* (2002) and *Into the Void* (2009), while Jacque Audiard's tough 2009 prison drama, *Un Prophète*, narrowly missed out on an Oscar for Best Foreign Film at the 2010 Academy Awards. 'New French Extremity' is the tag given to the unforgivingly realistic, socially conscious, transgressive films of talented Paris-born, Africa-raised filmmaker Claire Denis. Watch her *Matériel Blanc* (White Material; 2009), scripted by Parisian novelist Marie NDiaye, to explore the legacy of French colonialism.

The true renaissance of French cinema came with *The Artist* (2011), a silent B&W, French-made romantic comedy set in 1920s Hollywood and starring the ever charismatic French actor Jean Dujardin. It scooped five Oscars at the 2012 ceremony, making it the most awarded French film in history.

Literature

Early Literature

The earliest surviving examples of French literature are the epic lyrical poems written during the early medieval period, most of which were based around allegorical tales and mythological legends (courtly love and King Arthur were particularly popular subjects in early French literature). Chrétien de Troyes (12th century), Pierre de Ronsard (1524–85) and the mischievous François Rabelais (1494–1553) were among the most important writers of the period, while the influential prose writer Michel de Montaigne (1533–92) penned essays on topics ranging from cannibals to public drunkenness.

The 18th century was dominated by one of France's greatest writers and philosophers, Voltaire (1694–1778), a key figure of the European Enlightenment. Through a prodigious output of novels, plays, poems, essays and political pamphlets, Voltaire tirelessly championed the values of freedom, equality and civil liberties for

Voltaire's tomb, Panthéon (p70)
PHOTOGRAPHER: HUW JONES

The Best... Books Set in France

1 *A Moveable Feast* (Ernest Hemingway)

2 *Birdsong* and *Charlotte Gray* (Sebastian Faulks)

3 *Perfume* (Patrick Suskind)

4 *A Year in Provence* (Peter Mayle)

5 *Chocolat* (Joanne Harris)

everyone, not solely for the ruling elite. His writings subsequently played an important role in the development of the fundamental principles of the French Revolution a century later.

The Age of the Novel

The 19th century was the great era of the novel in France. French writers took to the form with gusto. Victor Hugo (1802–85) penned historical epics such as *Les Misérables* and *Notre-Dame de Paris* (The Hunchback of Notre Dame), while Alexandre Dumas (1802–70) wrote swashbuckling tales of derring-do, such as *The Three Musketeers* and *The Count of Monte Cristo*, and Jules Verne (1828–1905) pioneered the sci-fi genre with his fanciful tales of moon rockets, submarines and round-the-world balloon flights.

Perhaps the greatest French novel writer of the period, however, was Gustave Flaubert (1821–80), whose 1857 tome *Madame Bovary* caused a storm of controversy due to its frank treatment of sex, adultery and the plight of women in French society.

The 19th century also witnessed the emergence of several important French poets, including Charles Baudelaire (known for his seminal collection *Les Fleurs du Mal*, 1857) and the symbolist poets Paul Verlaine (1844–96) and Arthur Rimbaud (1854–91).

Modern Literature

The early 20th century produced two great French writers: Colette (1873–1954), whose picaresque novels and short stories explored the amorous exploits of gutsy heroines such as Claudine and Gigi against the backdrop of bourgeois French society; and Marcel Proust (1871–1922), whose *À la recherche du temps perdu* (Remembrance of Things Past), published in seven volumes over 14 years, is the longest novel ever written.

After WWII, Paris' Left Bank became the centre for existentialist writers, who pondered cheery topics such as the meaningless of human existence: key figures include Jean-Paul Sartre (1905–80), Simone de Beauvoir (1908–86) and Albert Camus (1913–60), known for troubling novels including *The Outsider* and *The Plague*.

Marc Levy is France's best-selling writer. The film rights of his first novel were snapped up for the Stephen Spielberg box-office hit, *Just Like Heaven* (2005), and his novels have been translated into 42 languages. *L'étrange voyage de Monsieur Daldry* (The Strange Journey of Mr Daldry, 2011) is his latest.

No French writer better delves into the mind of France's ethnic population than Faïza Guène (b 1985), the French literary sensation who writes in a notable 'urban slang' style. She stunned critics with her debut novel, *Kiffe Kiffe Demain* (2004) and, like her first, her second novel, *Du Rêve pour les Oeufs* (2006), published in English as *Dreams from the Endz* (2008), was set on the ghetto housing estate outside Paris where she grew up.

Another French writer to address ethnic issues so engagingly is JMG Le Clézio. In 2008 he was the Nobel Prize in Literature winner, confirming France's ranking as the country with the most literary Nobel Prize winners.

French Cuisine

French cheese

DAG SUNDBERG

If there's one thing the French are famous for, it's food. In many ways this is the nation that taught the rest of the world how to dine, and if you approach food and wine here with half the zest les français do, you'll be welcomed, encouraged and exceedingly well fed indeed.

Food

Eating well is of prime importance to most French people, who spend an inordinate amount of time thinking about, discussing and enjoying food and wine. While there are many classic national dishes, each region has its own distinctive flavours, ingredients and cooking styles.

Two natural factors determine what you eat on your French travels. Season and geography see the hot south favour olive oil, garlic and tomatoes; the cooler, pastoral regions of northern France turn to cream and butter; and coastal areas are awash with mussels, oysters, saltwater fish and other seafood.

Meals in France

The classic French breakfast *(petit déjeuner)* consists of baguette, jam, coffee, and fruit juice (croissants and pastries are traditionally reserved as treats for the weekend,

French Cheese Etiquette

- Cut small, circular cheeses into pie wedges.
- Larger cheeses already sliced into a wedge must be cut tip to rind – don't slice off the tip.
- Chop semihard cheeses horizontally.
- Only serve cheese with fresh baguette, never crackers or butter.
- Bring out the cheese board *before* dessert, not after.

although they're normally always included in hotel breakfasts).

Lunch *(déjeuner)* is served from noon to around 2pm, and is often the main meal of the day for French people. There is usually a good value two- or three-course *menu du jour* (daily menu) consisting of a *plat du jour* (daily special) with an entrée (starter) and/or a dessert. Most restaurants only offer the *menu du jour* at lunchtime, which is why it's often easier to find a free table for dinner than for lunch.

Dinner *(diner)* usually starts around 6.30pm and continues till around 10pm. Two or three courses are the norm; fixed menus generally offer better value than *à la carte*, but you'll have fewer dishes to choose from.

Cheese

France is cheese land and the *fromagerie* (cheese shop) is the pongiest shop in town. With more than 500 varieties, buying cheese can be an overwhelming affair. Any self-respecting *fromager* (cheese merchant) will let you taste before you buy.

To treat your taste buds to the perfect balance of cheese, take at least one of each type from the cheeseboard:

- **Goat's cheese** *(fromage de chèvre)* French goat's cheese is creamy, sweet and faintly salty when fresh, but hardens and gets saltier as it matures. Key varieties include Ste-Maure de Touraine, Crottin de Chavignol and St-Marcellin, a runny white cheese.

- **Blue cheese** Everyone knows Roquefort, a powerful, veined, marbled, mature cheese with a strong flavour and fragrance.

- **Soft cheese** *(fromage à pâté molle)* The classic variety of French cheese, served soft, smelly and runny. Common types include Camembert and Brie (both from Normandy) and Munster (from Alsace).

- **Semihard cheese** *(fromage à pâté demi-dure)* These cheeses, especially common in the Alps, have a squishy, semi-firm texture, a thick rind and a fairly mild flavour. Try Tomme de Savoie or Cantal.

- **Hard cheese** *(fromage à pâté dure)* The hardest type of French cheese, typified by Beaufort, Comté, Emmental and Mimolette, an Edam-like bright-orange cheese from Lille.

Bread

Buying bread is a French daily ritual, it being served – *sans beurre* (without butter) – at breakfast, lunch and dinner. Plain old *pain* (bread) is a 400g, traditional-shaped loaf, soft inside and crusty out. The iconic classic is the baguette, a long thin crusty loaf weighing 250g and best eaten within four hours of baking (it is truly astonishing just how rock-hard a baguette becomes after 12 hours).

Meat & Charcuterie

Meat in France isn't simply a matter of steaks, chops and cutlets – French chefs make use of practically every part of the animal, including tongue, trotters and pretty much every type of offal you can imagine.

Charcuterie traditionally denotes meat products made from pork, but encompasses other things such as cold cuts, pâtés and terrines. The classic charcuterie is the *saucisson* (a cured sausage similar to salami). *Saucisse* denotes a fresh, uncooked sausage that's boiled, grilled or fried before eating.

When ordering steak, know how you like it cooked: *bleu* (almost raw), *saignant* (rare), *à point* (medium rare), *bien cuit* (with just a hint of pinkness) or *très bien cuit* (very well done).

The Best... Signature Dishes

1 Bouillabaisse, Marseille

2 Camembert, Normandy

3 Cheese fondue, French Alps

4 Oysters and shellfish, Brittany

5 Black truffles, Dordogne

Fish & Seafood

The coast is the obvious place to eat *poisson* (fish). In Brittany, Normandy and along the Mediterranean coastline, *moules-frites* (mussels and chips) is a menu staple alongside each region's own seafood specialities: Brittany and the Atlantic Coast are known for their shellfish and oysters; Provence and the Riviera are the best places to try *bouillabaisse* (a rich seafood stew) and *soupe de poissons* (fish soup), both traditionally accompanied by *rouille* (a spicy mayonnaise of oil, chillis and garlic).

Truffles

The Dordogne's most celebrated delicacy is the *diamant noir* (black diamond or black truffle), a subterranean fungus that grows in chalky soils (often around the roots of oak and hazelnut trees) and is notoriously difficult to find; a good spot one year can be inexplicably bare the next, which has made farming them practically impossible. Serious truffle hunters use specially trained dogs (and sometimes pigs) to help them search. A vintage crop of truffles can fetch as much as €850 a kilo.

The truffle season runs December to March.

Poultry

When it comes to birds, the French don't just limit themselves to chicken and turkey – they eat other types of poultry with equal gusto, including *canard* (duck), *oie* (goose), *perdrix* (partridge), *faisan* (pheasant), pigeon and *caille* (quail).

Pâté de foie gras (a rich, smooth pâté of fattened duck or goose livers, sometimes flavoured with Cognac and truffles) is a particular delicacy, especially in southwest France. *Confit de canard* and *confit d'oie* are duck or goose joints cooked very slowly in their own fat, making them very tender and packed with flavour.

Price Ranges

Price indicators refer to the average cost of a two-course meal, be it an entrée (starter) and *plat* (main course) or main and dessert, or a *menu* (pre-set meal at a fixed price). Lunch menus can often yield a better deal.

€ budget < €20
€€ midrange €20–40
€€€ top end > €40

Dare to Try

- **Andouillette** Sausage made from pig intestine; try it in Lyon.
- **Oursins** (sea urchins) Caught and eaten west of Marseille.
- **Epoisses de Bourgogne** France's smelliest cheese.
- **Escargots de Bourgogne** (snails) Oven-baked shells stuffed with garlic and parsley butter.
- **Cuisses de grenouilles** (frogs' legs) Frog farming is outlawed in France, but frogs' legs are imported from Southeast Asia, ensuring this tradition remains alive and kicking.
- **Foie gras** Fattened duck or goose liver, raw and chilled, enjoyed with Monbazillac wine.
- **Pieds de cochon** (pig trotters) Or go for *mouton* (sheep) or *veau* (calf) trotters.
- **Tête de veau** (calf's head) Just that.

Cakes & Sweets

Enter any *boulangerie* (bakery) or patisserie and face an irresistible assortment of pastries, cakes and sweet treats, including the classics: the croissant (butter pastry), *pain au chocolat* (butter pastry with dark chocolate inside), meringues, *sablés* (shortbread biscuits), *tartes aux fruits* (fruit tarts) and colourful macarons.

Indulgent desserts include *tarte tatin* (upside-down apple cake), *tarte aux pommes* (apple tart) and various types of gateaux (cakes) and crêpes (thin pancakes served with a sweet filling of jam, chocolate, Nutella, or simply butter and sugar).

French Wine

French wines might not be the world's most venerated, but making them is an ancient art and tradition that bears its own unique trademark, and *dégustation* (tasting) is an essential part of the French travel experience.

The quality of French wine is governed by four factors: the grape type, the climate, the soil and the vigneron's skill.

Quality wines are designated Appellation d'Origine Contrôlée (AOC, label of inspected origin), equivalent to the European-wide Appellation d'Origine Protegée (AOP). French AOC can cover a wide region (eg Bordeaux), a sub-region (eg Haut-Médoc), or a commune or village (eg Pomerol). Some regions have a single AOC (eg Alsace), while Burgundy has dozens.

French wines are also divided by a complex grading system; the best are awarded the label of *grand cru* (great growth), and command a premium price.

Seven key areas produce the vast majority of French wine: Alsace, Bordeaux, Burgundy, Champagne, Languedoc, the Loire and the Rhône. Organic and biodynamic wines are increasingly popular.

Burgundy

During the reign of Charlemagne, monks began making the wine that gave Burgundy (Bourgogne in French) its sterling reputation for viticulture. Burgundy vineyards are small (rarely more than 10 hectares), hence produce small quantities of wine – reds with pinot noir grapes and whites with chardonnay. The most famed winegrowing areas are Côte d'Or, Chablis, Châtillon and Mâcon. Lesser-known Irancy is a charming, local wine-tasting favourite.

Bordeaux

Bordeaux has the perfect climate for producing wine; as a result its 1100 sq km of vineyards produce more fine wine than any other region in the world. Bordeaux reds are often described as well balanced, a quality achieved by blending several grape varieties. The grapes predominantly used are merlot, cabernet sauvignon and cabernet franc. The foremost winegrowing areas of Bordeaux are the Médoc, Pomerol, St Émilion and Graves. The nectar-like sweet whites of the Sauternes area are the world's finest dessert wines.

Côtes du Rhône

Dramatically different soil, climate, topography and grapes in the Rhône Valley region means very different wines in this vast appellation – France's second largest – covering 771 sq km. The most renowned is Châteauneuf du Pape, a full-bodied wine bequeathed to Provence by the Avignon popes who planted the distinctive stone-covered vineyards, 10km south of Orange.

Champagne

Champagne has been the centre for bubbly production since the 17th century, when the monk Dom Pierre Pérignon perfected a technique for making sparkling wine. It is made from the red pinot noir, black pinot meunier or white chardonnay grape; and is labelled *brut* (extra dry), *extra-sec* (dry, but not as dry as *brut*), *sec* (dry), *demi-sec* (slightly sweet) or *doux* (sweet). Famous Champagne houses include Dom Pérignon, Moët & Chandon, Veuve Clicquot, Mercier, Mumm, Krug, Laurent-Perrier, Piper-Heidsieck, Taittinger, De Castellane and Pommery.

Swaths of fresh-green vineyards in the Champagne region could be graced with Unesco protection if its 2013 bid to become a World Heritage Site proves successful. Meantime, such is the global demand for the 320 million bottles of fizz it sells each year that the body regulating where Champagne can be made has agreed to enlarge the production area for the first time since 1927. In 2017 the first new vines will be planted in 40 new Champagne-producing villages. *Santé*!

Picnic Perfect

- **Baguettes** from the *boulangerie* (bakery), stuffed with Camembert, pâté and *cornichons* (miniature gherkins), or *rosette de Lyon* (salami). *Voilà*, picnic perfection!
- **Macarons** from Ladurée (p85) in Paris. No sweeter way to end a picnic.
- **Kouign amann**, the world's most buttery, syrupy cake, aka Breton butter cake.
- Big juicy **black Apt cherries**, **peaches**, **apricots** and **tomatoes** from the Rhône Valley, Provence and the Riviera.
- **Provençal olives or peppers**, marinated and stuffed with edible sins from market stands.
- **Champagne** from Reims and *biscuits roses* (sweet, pink biscuit).
- Country **pâté**, **walnuts** and **foie gras** from the Dordogne.

The Best... Wine-Tasting Experiences

1 Champagne houses in Reims (p158) and Épernay (p162)

2 L'Imaginarium (p208)

3 Château de Pommard (p208)

4 Châteaux in and around Bordeaux (p264) and the Médoc (p267)

5 Self-drive Alsatian wine route, Route des Vins d'Alsace (p175)

6 Cognac houses (p271)

The Loire

The Loire's 700 sq km of vineyards rank it as France's third-largest area for the production of quality wines. The most common grapes are the muscadet, cabernet franc and chenin blanc varieties. Wines tend to be light and delicate. Be sure to sample wines from Pouilly-Fumé, Vouvray, Sancerre, Bourgueil, Chinon and Saumur.

Provence

Côtes de Provence is the region's largest appellation and France's sixth largest, producing 75% of Provençal wine. Few other appellations support such a variety of grapes – at least a dozen. Drunk young and served at 8°C to 10°C, its wines are among the world's oldest. Vines were planted by the Greeks in Massilia (Marseille) around 600 BC.

The star of Provence is deep-flavoured red Bandol, with its own AOC since 1941. West along the same coast is Cassis, known for its crisp whites.

Alsace

Alsace produces almost exclusively white wines – mostly varieties not produced elsewhere in France – that are known for their clean, fresh taste and compatibility with the often heavy local cuisine. Unusually, some of the fruity Alsatian whites also go well with red meat. Alsace's four most important varietal wines are riesling (known for its subtlety), gewürztraminer (pungent and highly regarded), pinot gris (robust and high in alcohol) and muscat d'Alsace (not as sweet as muscats from southern France).

Aperitifs & Digestifs

A meal in France is not a meal without an aperitif to kick-start it. *Kir* (white wine sweetened with a fruit syrup such as blackcurrant or chestnut) and *kir royale* (Champagne with blackcurrant syrup) are classics countrywide, while *pineau* (Cognac and grape juice) is popular in and around Bordeaux, and a glass of sweet, white, local Coteaux du Layon is favoured in the Loire Valley. In the hot south, aniseed-flavoured pastis (clear in the bottle, cloudy when mixed with water) is the aperitif to drink alfresco.

After-dinner drinks accompany coffee. France's most famous brandies are Cognac and Armagnac, both made from grapes in the regions of those names. *Eaux de vie,* literally 'waters of life', can be made with grape skins and the pulp left over after being pressed for wine (Marc de Champagne, Marc de Bourgogne), apples (*calvados*) and pears (Poire William). In the Loire Valley a shot of orange (aka a glass of local Cointreau liqueur) ends the meal well.

When in Normandy, do as the festive Normans do: refresh the palate between courses with a *trou normand* (literally 'Norman hole') – traditionally a shot of *calva* (calvados) or a contemporary scoop of apple sorbet doused in the local apple brandy.

The French

Latin Quarter (p68), Paris

KEVIN CLOGSTOUN

Arrogant, bureaucratic, chauvinistic and stylish... France is a country whose people has attracted more myths and stereotypes than any other in Europe, and over the centuries dozens of tags have been pinned on the garlic-eating, beret-wearing, sacre-bleu-swearing French. (The French, by the way, hardly ever wear berets or use old chestnuts such as 'sacre bleu' anymore.)

Being French

Most people are extremely proud to be French and are staunchly nationalistic, a result of the country's republican stance, which places nationality (rather than religion, for example) at the top of the self-identity list. This has created an overwhelmingly self-confident nation, both culturally and intellectually, that often comes across as one with a superiority complex.

Contrary to popular belief, many French speak a foreign language fairly well, travel and are happy to use their language skills if necessary. French men, incidentally, deem an English gal's heavily accented French as sexy as she might find a Frenchman speaking English.

Lifestyle

The French are full of contradictions: they drink and smoke more than anyone else, yet

Faux Pas

- **Forget the school-textbook French** *'S'il vous plaît'* – never *'garçon'* (meaning 'boy') – is the *only* way to summon a waiter.
- **Don't split the restaurant bill** The person who invites pays, although close friends often go Dutch.
- **Don't fondle fruit, veg, flowers or clothing in shops** Ask if you want to touch.
- **Get the name right** 'Monsieur' for men, 'Madame' for 'Mrs' and 'Mademoiselle' for unmarried women.
- **Take Champagne or flowers** Gifts are an important gesture when invited to someone's home. But don't take chrysanthemums, only for cemeteries.

live longer; they eat like kings, but have a lower rate of obesity than most European nations. But if there were such a thing as Monsieur et Madame Tout le Monde (Mr and Mrs Everyone), what might they be like?

They'd most likely work in one of France's big cities, and rent their apartment from a private landlord (home ownership in France is low, with only 57% of households owning their own home). They'd dunk croissants in bowls (yes, bowls) of fresh coffee for breakfast, buy a baguette every day from the bakery and recycle little bar a few glass bottles.

Madame would buy a stack of weekly gossip magazines, while Monsieur would regularly pop out to meet his mates for a game of boules and a glass of *eau de vie* (brandy). They'd put everything on the *carte bleue* (credit or debit card) when shopping, and only ever holiday in August.

They'd go to the flicks once a month, work precisely 35 hours a week, and have two kids who would have both been through university (France's state-run universities are free to anyone who passes the baccalaureat).

French Kissing

Kissing is still the traditional way for French people to greet each other (although the expression 'French kissing', as in with tongues, actually doesn't exist in French).

In Paris it is definitely two kisses: anything more is deemed affected, although trendy 20-somethings and teenagers often swap three or four cheek-skimming kisses just to be different. Travel south and the *bisous* (kisses) multiply, three being the norm in Provence, and four in the Loire Valley.

To avoid any embarrassing moments, do as the French do and always start with the right cheek.

Outdoor Activities

Parc Nacional de la Vanois (p248)

JACQUES PIERRE/HEMIS.FR

From the peaks, rivers and canyons of the French Alps to the sparkling beaches and craggy cliffs of the Riviera, France offers plenty of opportunity for exhilarating outdoor adventure. Match your interests with the best bit of France in which to do it: for surfing it is Biarritz on the Atlantic Coast; the French Alps are No 1 for snow sports; and Mont Ventoux in Provence is the cyclist's ultimate idyll.

Cycling

If there's one sport the French take seriously, it's cycling. Cycling is one of the country's most popular outdoor activities, and every year swaths of the country grind to a halt during the Tour de France. The country is criss-crossed by a network of *voies vertes* (literally, 'green ways') that have been developed specifically for cycling, often along the course of old bridleways or disused railway tracks.

Road-cycling is the most popular form in France, although VTT (*vélo tout-terrain*, or mountain-biking) is rapidly catching up, especially in the Alps, Pyrenees and Massif Central. Bikes are a great (and green) way of exploring flat regions such as the Dordogne, Burgundy, the Loire Valley and much of Provence. Tourist offices can supply route suggestions and information on bike rental.

The Best... Natural Wonders

1 Dune du Pilat (p273)

2 Mont St-Michel (p128)

3 Mont Blanc, Chamonix (p240)

4 Gouffre de Padirac (p212)

5 Gorges du Verdon (p382)

Skiing & Snowboarding

France has around 400 ski resorts, all of which offer a range of groomed runs suitable for both novice and experienced skiers and boarders; some also have snowparks where adventurous types can practise jumps and tricks. The ski season in France lasts from mid-December to late March or April. The slopes get very crowded at Christmas and during the February school holidays.

The biggest (and busiest) resorts are located in the Alps. Smaller resorts in the Pyrenees tend to be quieter, cheaper and substantially less glitzy – forget posing on piste or hobnobbing over an après-ski aperitif. The Jura is the centre for *ski de fond* (cross-country skiing). Usually, the cheapest way to ski is to travel on a package deal that includes flights, lift passes and accommodation.

Hiking

The French countryside is criss-crossed by a staggering 120,000km of *sentiers balisés* (marked walking paths), which pass through every imaginable terrain in every region of the country. No permit is needed to hike. Probably the best-known walking trails are the sentiers de Grande Randonnée (GR), long-distance paths marked by red-and-white-striped track indicators.

Water Sports

France's coastline is fantastic for all types of water sports. The best surfing is on France's west coast, especially around Biarritz. Windsurfing is especially popular in Brittany, Normandy and along the Atlantic Coast.

White-water rafting, canoeing and kayaking are practised on many French rivers, especially in the Alps, but also in the deep canyons of the Gorges de l'Ardèche, Gorges du Tarn and Gorges du Verdon, and along the Dordogne and Lot Rivers.

Web Resources

- **France Montagnes** (www.france-montagnes.com) Comprehensive information on skiing, snowboarding and other mountain pastimes.
- **Fédération Française de la Randonnée Pédestre** (www.ffrandonnee.fr) Hiking tips from the French Ramblers' Association.
- **Rando Velo** (http://randovelo.fr) Multilingual site offering cycling routes across France.
- **Voies Vertes** (www.voiesvertes.com) Map of and guide to France's green trails.
- **Club Alpin Français** (www.ffcam.fr) Mountain-activity advice from France's oldest alpine club.
- **ESF** (www.esf.net) Ski, hike and revel in mountain fun with the largest ski school in the world, aka France's École du Ski Français.

Survival Guide

Languedoc-Roussillon

PHOTOGRAPHER: GLENN BEANLAND

Directory

Accommodation

Be it a fairy-tale château, a boutique hideaway or floating pod on a lake, France has accommodation to suit every taste, mood and pocket.

CATEGORIES

As a rule of thumb, budget covers everything from basic hostels to small, simple, family-run places; midrange means a few extra creature comforts such as satellite TV and free wi-fi; while top-end places stretch from luxury five-star palaces with air- conditioning, swimming pools and restaurants to boutique-chic chalets in the Alps. Self-contained accommodation has its own kitchen and bathroom and, typically, a private entrance, such as a group of self-contained flats.

COSTS

Accommodation costs vary wildly between seasons and regions: what will buy you a night in a romantic *chambre d'hôte* (B&B) in the countryside may get a dorm bed in a major city or high-profile ski resort.

PRICE RANGES

The price indicators refer to the cost of a double room, including private bathroom (any combination of toilet, bathtub, shower and washbasin) and excluding breakfast unless otherwise noted. Breakfast is assumed to be included at a B&B. Where half-board (breakfast and dinner) and full board (breakfast, lunch and dinner) is included, this is mentioned in the price.

€ (budget) less than €80 (less than €110 in Paris)

€€ (midrange) €80 to €180 (€110-€200 in Paris)

€€€ (top end) more than €180 (more than €200 in Paris)

B&BS

For charm, a heartfelt *bienvenue* (welcome) and solid home cooking, it's hard to beat France's privately run *chambres d'hôte* – urban rarities but as common as muck in rural areas. By law a *chambre d'hôte* must have no more than five rooms and breakfast must be included in the price; some hosts prepare evening meals *(table d'hôte)* for an extra charge of €20 to €30. Pick up lists of *chambres d'hôte* at local tourist offices, or find one to suit your style online:

Bienvenue à la Ferme (www.bienvenue-a-la-ferme.com)

Fleurs de Soleil (www.fleursdesoleil.fr) Selective collection of 550 stylish *maisons d'hôte* (guesthouses), mainly in rural France.

Gîtes de France (www.gites-de-france.com) France's primary umbrella organisation for B&Bs and *gîtes* (rental holiday accommodation, with the owner residing nearby). Search for properties by region, theme (charm, with kids, by the sea, gourmet, great garden etc), activity (fishing, wine tasting etc) or facilities (pool, dishwasher, fireplace, baby equipment, computer etc). Tourist offices often stock local Gîtes de France catalogues.

iGuidehotels (Accommodation Services; www.iguide-hotels.com) This is the online spot to find all the properties listed in the *Guides de Charme* printed guides; some of France's most charming and often-times most upmarket B&Bs.

Samedi Midi Éditions (www.samedimidi.com) Country, mountain, seaside... choose your *chambre d'hôte* by location or theme (romance, golf, design, cooking courses).

Book Your Stay Online

For more accommodation reviews by Lonely Planet authors, check out http://hotels.lonelyplanet.com. You'll find independent reviews, as well as recommendations on the best places to stay. Best of all, you can book online.

HOTELS

We have tried to feature well-situated, independent hotels that offer good value, a warm welcome, at least a bit of charm and a palpable sense of place.

Hotels in France are rated with one to five stars, although the ratings are based on highly objective criteria (eg the size of the entry hall), not the quality of the service, the decor or cleanliness.

- French hotels almost never include breakfast in their rates. Unless specified otherwise, prices quoted don't include breakfast, which costs around €7/10/20 in a budget/midrange/top-end hotel.
- When you book, hotels usually ask for a credit card number; some require a deposit.
- A double room generally has one double bed (sometimes two singles pushed together!); a room with twin beds *(deux lits)* is usually more expensive, as is a room with a bathtub instead of a shower.
- Feather pillows are practically nonexistent in France, even in top-end hotels.
- All hotel restaurant terraces allow smoking; if you are sensitive to smoke sit inside or carry a respirator.

Business Hours

French business hours are regulated by a maze of government regulations, including the 35-hour working week.

- The midday break is uncommon in Paris, common elsewhere; in general, the break gets longer the further south you go.
- French law requires that most businesses close on Sunday; exceptions include grocery stores, *boulangeries*, florists and businesses catering to the tourist trade.
- In many places shops close on Monday.
- Many service stations open 24 hours a day and stock basic groceries.
- Restaurants generally close one or two days of the week, chosen according to the owner's whim.
- Most (but not all) national museums are closed on Tuesday; most local museums are closed on Monday, though in summer some open daily. Many museums close at lunchtime.
- For standard business hours, see p388.

Customs Regulations

Goods brought in and out of countries within the EU incur no additional taxes provided duty has been paid somewhere within the EU and the goods are for personal consumption. Duty-free shopping is available only if you are leaving the EU.

Duty-free allowances (for adults) coming from non-EU countries (including the Channel Islands):

- 200 cigarettes
- 50 cigars
- 1L spirits
- 2L wine
- 50ml perfume
- 250ml eau de toilette
- other goods up to the value of €175 (€90 for those under 15 years old)

Higher limits apply if you are coming from Andorra; anything over these limits must be declared. For further details, see www.douane.gouv.fr (partly in English).

Electricity

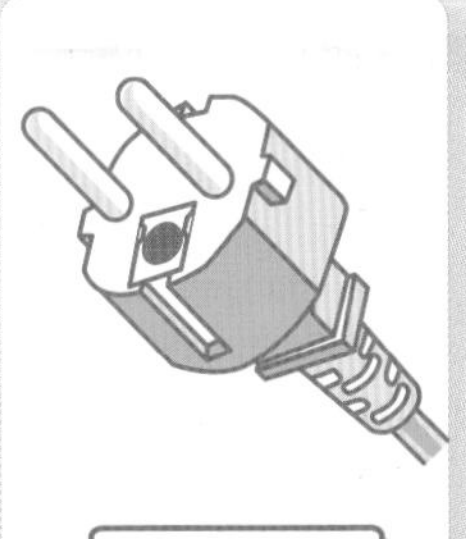

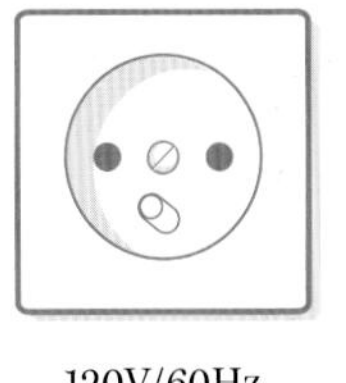

120V/60Hz

Gay & Lesbian Travellers

Gay mayors (including Paris' very own Bertrand Delanoë), artists and film directors, camper-than-camp fashion designers – the rainbow flag flies high in France, a country that left its closet long before many of its European

The Fine Art of Sleeping

A château, a country manor, Parisian opulence in the shade of the Eiffel Tower – whether you want to live like a lord, sleep like a log or blow the budget, there's a room with your name on it.

Alistair Sawday's (www.sawdays.co.uk) Boutique retreats and *chambres d'hôte* (B&Bs), placing the accent on originality and authentic hospitality.

Châteaux & Hôtels Collection (www.chateauxhotels.com) Châteaux and other historic properties, now boutique hotels, with a thousand tales to tell.

Grandes Étapes Françaises (www.grandesetapes.fr) Beautiful châteaux-hotels and multistar residences.

Hôtels de Charme (www.hotelsdecharme.com) Abbeys, manors, châteaux – this is a mixed bag of (as the name says) charming hotels.

Logis de France (www.logis-de-france.fr) Small, often family-run hotels with charm and a warm welcome.

Relais & Châteaux (www.relaischateaux.com) Seductive selection of villas, châteaux and historic hotels.

Relais du Silence (www.relaisdusilence.com) Fall asleep to complete silence in a gorgeous château, spa-clad *auberge* (country inn), vineyard hotel...

Small Luxury Hotels of the World (www.slh.com) Super-luxurious boutique hotels, chalets and resorts.

neighbours. *Laissez-faire* perfectly sums up France's liberal attitude towards homosexuality and people's private lives in general; in part because of a long tradition of public tolerance towards unconventional lifestyles.

- Paris has been a thriving gay and lesbian centre since the late 1970s, and most major organisations are based there today.
- Bordeaux, Lille, Lyon, Montpellier, Toulouse and many other towns also have an active queer scene.
- Attitudes towards homosexuality tend to be more conservative in the countryside and villages.
- France's lesbian scene is less public than its gay male counterpart and is centred mainly on women's cafes and bars.
- Introduced in 1999, PACS (civil solidarity pacts) afford same-sex couples most of the rights, legal protections and responsibilities as their married counterparts.
- Gay Pride marches are held in major French cities from mid-May to early July.

Health

France is a healthy place, so your main risks are likely to be sunburn, foot blisters, insect bites and mild stomach problems from eating and drinking with too much gusto.

BEFORE YOU GO

- Bring your medications in their original, clearly labelled, containers.
- A signed and dated letter from your physician describing your medical conditions and medications, including generic names (French medicine names are often completely different to those in other countries), is also a good idea.
- Dental care in France is usually good; however, it is sensible to have a dental check-up before a long trip.
- No vaccinations are required to travel to France but the World Health Organization (WHO) recommends that all travellers be covered for diphtheria, tetanus, measles, mumps, rubella and polio, regardless of their destination.

AVAILABILITY & COST OF HEALTH CARE

- Visitors to France can get excellent health care from hospital *(hôpital)* emergency rooms/casualty wards *(salles des urgences)* and at a doctors' office *(cabinet médical)*.
- For minor illnesses, trained staff in pharmacies – in every

village and town with a green-cross sign outside that flashes when open – give valuable advice, sell medications, can tell you when more specialised help is needed and will point you in the right direction.

- You will need to pay upfront for any health care you receive, be it at a doctor's surgery, pharmacy or hospital, unless your insurance plan makes payments directly to providers.
- The standard rate for a consultation with a GP/ specialist is €25 to €40.
- Emergency contraception is available with a doctor's prescription. Condoms *(les préservatifs)* are readily available.

Insurance

- Comprehensive travel insurance to cover theft, loss and medical problems is highly recommended.
- Some policies specifically exclude dangerous activities such as scuba diving, motorcycling, skiing and even trekking: read the fine print.
- Check that the policy covers ambulances or an emergency flight home.
- Find out in advance if your insurance plan will make payments directly to providers or reimburse you later for overseas health expenditures.
- If you have to claim later, make sure you keep all documentation.
- Paying for your airline ticket with a credit card often provides limited travel accident insurance – ask your credit card company what it is prepared to cover.
- Worldwide travel insurance is available at www.lonelyplanet.com/travel_services. You can buy, extend and claim online anytime – even if you are already on the road.

Internet Access

- Wireless (wi-fi) access points can be found at major airports, in many hotels and at some cafes.
- Some tourist offices and numerous cafes and bars tout wi-fi hot spots that let laptop owners hook up for free.
- To search for free wi-fi hot spots in France, visit www.hotspot-locations.co.uk or www.free-hotspot.com.

Which Floor?

In France, as elsewhere in Europe, 'ground floor' refers to the floor at street level; the 1st floor – what would be called the 2nd floor in the US – is the floor above that.

Climate

Bordeaux

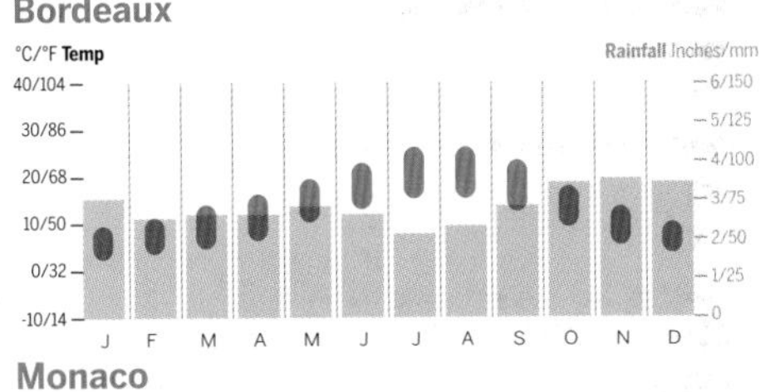

Monaco

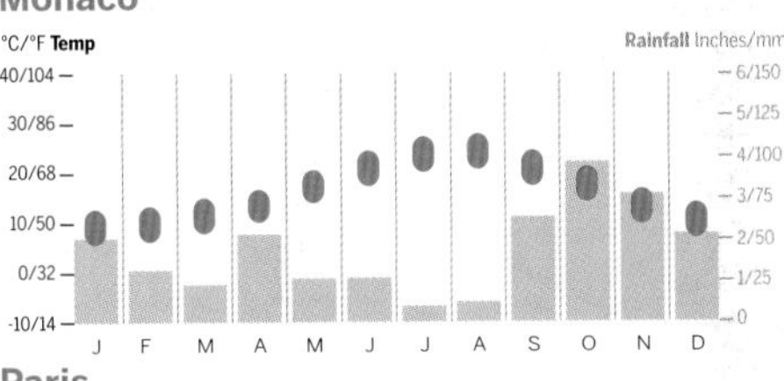

Paris

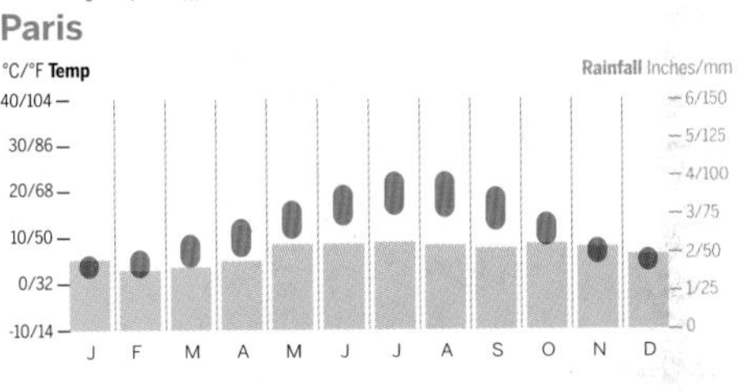

- Internet cafes are becoming less rife, but at least one can still be found in most large towns and cities. Prices range from €2 to €6 per hour.
- If you'll be accessing dial-up ISPs with your laptop, you will need a telephone-plug adaptor, available at large supermarkets.

Legal Matters

- French police have wide powers of search and seizure and can ask you to prove your identity at any time – whether or not there is 'probable cause'.
- Foreigners must be able to prove their legal status in France (eg passport, visa, residency permit) without delay.
- If the police stop you for any reason, be polite and remain calm. Verbally (and of course physically) abusing a police officer can lead to a hefty fine, and even imprisonment.
- You may refuse to sign a police statement, and have the right to ask for a copy.
- People who are arrested are considered innocent until proven guilty, but can be held in custody until trial.
- Because of the threat of terrorism, French police are very strict about security. Do not leave baggage unattended, especially at airports or train stations: suspicious objects may be summarily blown up.

Standard Hours

Business hours are generally as follows:

BUSINESS	OPENING HOURS
Banks	9am-noon & 2-5pm Mon-Fri or Tue-Sat
Bars	7pm-1am Mon-Sat
Cafes	7am or 8am-10pm or 11pm Mon-Sat
Nightclubs	10pm-3am, 4am or 5am Thu-Sat
Post offices	8.30am or 9am-5pm or 6pm Mon-Fri, 8am-noon Sat
Restaurants	lunch noon-2.30pm (or 3pm in Paris), dinner 7-11pm (until 10pm to midnight in Paris) six days a week
Shops	9am or 10am-7pm Mon-Sat (often with lunch break noon-1.30pm)
Supermarkets	8.30am-7pm Mon-Sat, 8.30am-12.30pm Sun

Money

ATMS

Automated Teller Machines (ATMs) – known as *distributeurs automatiques de billets* (DAB) or *points d'argent* in French – are the cheapest and most convenient way to get money. ATMs connected to international networks are situated in all cities and towns and usually offer an excellent exchange rate.

CASH

You always get a better exchange rate in-country but it is a good idea to arrive in France with enough euros to take a taxi to a hotel if you have to.

CREDIT & DEBIT CARDS

- Credit and debit cards, accepted almost everywhere in France, are convenient, relatively secure and usually offer a better exchange rate than travellers cheques or cash exchanges.
- Credit cards issued in France have embedded chips – you have to type in a PIN to make a purchase.
- Visa, MasterCard and Amex can be used in shops and supermarkets and for train travel, car hire and motorway tolls, though some places (eg 24-hour petrol stations, some autoroute toll machines) only take French-style credit cards with chips and PINs.
- Don't assume that you can pay for a meal or a budget hotel with a credit card – enquire first.

- Cash advances are a supremely convenient way to stay stocked up with euros but getting cash with a credit card involves both fees (sometimes US$10 or more) and interest – ask your credit card issuer for details. Debit-card fees are usually much less.

LOST CARDS

For lost cards, these numbers operate 24 hours:

Amex (☎ 01 47 77 72 00)

Diners Club (☎ 08 10 31 41 59)

MasterCard (☎ 08 00 90 13 87)

Visa (Carte Bleue; ☎ 08 00 90 11 79)

European Health Insurance Card

Citizens of the EU, Switzerland, Iceland, Norway and Liechtenstein receive free or reduced-cost state-provided health-care cover with the European Health Insurance Card (EHIC) for medical treatment that becomes necessary while in France. Each family member will need a separate card. UK residents can get application forms from post offices, or download them from the Department of Health website (www.dh.gov.uk), which has comprehensive information about the card's coverage.

The EHIC does not cover private health care, so make sure that you are treated by a state health-care provider *(conventionné)*. You will need to pay directly and fill in a treatment form *(feuille de soins);* keep the form to claim any refunds. In general, you can claim back around 70% of the standard treatment cost.

Citizens of other countries need to check if there is a reciprocal arrangement for free medical care between their country and France.

MONEYCHANGERS

- Commercial banks charge up to €5 per foreign-currency transaction – if they even bother to offer exchange services.
- In Paris and major cities, *bureaux de change* (exchange bureaux) are faster and easier, open longer hours and often give better rates than banks.
- Some post-office branches exchange travellers cheques and banknotes in a variety of currencies but charge a commission for cash; most won't take US$100 bills.

TIPPING

By law, restaurant and bar prices are *service compris* (include a 15% service charge), so there is no need to leave a *pourboire* (tip). If you were extremely satisfied with the service, however, you can – as many locals do – show your appreciation by leaving a small 'extra' tip for your waiter or waitress.

Public Holidays

The following *jours fériés* (public holidays) are observed:

New Year's Day (Jour de l'An) 1 January – parties in larger cities; fireworks are subdued by international standards

Easter Sunday & Monday (Pâques & Lundi de Pâques) Late March/April

May Day (Fête du Travail) 1 May – traditional parades

Victoire 1945 8 May – commemorates the Allied victory in Europe that ended WWII

Ascension Thursday (Ascension) May – celebrated on the 40th day after Easter

Pentecost/Whit Sunday & Whit Monday (Pentecôte & Lundi de Pentecôte) Mid-May to mid-June – celebrated on the seventh Sunday after Easter

Bastille Day/National Day (Fête Nationale) 14 July – *the* national holiday

Assumption Day (Assomption) 15 August

All Saints' Day (Toussaint) 1 November

Remembrance Day (L'onze Novembre) 11 November – marks the WWI armistice

Christmas (Noël) 25 December

Practicalities

- **Classifieds** Pick up the free **FUSAC** (France USA Contacts; www.fusac.fr) in Anglophone haunts in Paris for classified ads about housing, babysitting, jobs and language exchanges.
- **Laundry** Virtually all French cities and towns have at least one *laverie libre-service* (self-service laundrette). Machines run on coins.
- **Newspapers & Magazines** Locals read their news in centre-left **Le Monde** (www.lemonde.fr), right-leaning **Le Figaro** (www.lefigaro.fr) or left-leaning **Libération** (www.liberation.fr).
- **Radio** For news, tune in to the French-language France Info (105.5MHz), the multilanguage RFI (738kHz or 89MHz in Paris) or, in northern France, the BBC World Service (648kHz) and BBC Radio 4 (198kHz). Popular national FM music stations include **NRJ** (www.nrj.fr), **Skyrock** (www.skyrock.fm) and **Nostalgie** (www.nostalgie.fr).
- **Smoking** Smoking is illegal in all indoor public spaces, including restaurants and pubs (though, of course, smokers still light up on the terraces outside).
- **Travel Conditions** In many areas, Autoroute Info (107.7MHz) has round-the-clock traffic information.
- **TV & Video** TV is Secam; videos work on the PAL system.
- **Weights & Measures** France uses the metric system.

The following are *not* public holidays in France: Shrove Tuesday (Mardi Gras; the first day of Lent); Maundy (or Holy) Thursday and Good Friday, just before Easter; and Boxing Day (26 December).

Note: Good Friday and Boxing Day *are* public holidays in Alsace.

Safe Travel

France is generally a safe place in which to live and travel but crime has risen dramatically in the last few years.

Although property crime is a major problem, it is extremely unlikely that you will be physically assaulted while walking down the street. Always check your government's travel advisory warnings.

NATURAL DANGERS

- There are powerful tides and strong undertows at many places along the Atlantic Coast, from the Spanish border north to Brittany and Normandy.
- Only swim in *zones de baignade surveillée* (beaches monitored by life guards).
- Be aware of tide times and the high-tide mark if walking or sleeping on a beach.
- Thunderstorms in the mountains and the hot southern plains can be extremely sudden and violent.
- Check the weather report before setting out on a long walk and be prepared for sudden storms and temperature drops if you are heading into the high country of the Alps or Pyrenees.
- Avalanches pose a significant danger in the French Alps.

THEFT

Pickpocketing and bag snatching (eg in dense crowds and public places) are prevalent in big cities, particularly Paris, Marseille and Nice. There's no need whatsoever to travel in fear. A few simple precautions will minimise your chances of being ripped off.

- On trains, keep bags as close to you as possible: luggage racks at the ends of carriages are easy prey for thieves; in sleeping compartments, lock the door carefully at night.
- Be especially vigilant for bag snatchers at train stations, airports, fast-food outlets, outdoor cafes, beaches and on public transport.
- Break-ins to parked cars are a widespread problem. Never, ever leave anything valuable – or not valuable – inside your car, even in the boot (trunk).
- Aggressive theft from cars stopped at red lights is occasionally a problem, especially in Marseille and Nice. As a precaution, lock your car doors and roll up the windows.

Telephone

IMPORTANT NUMBERS

France country code ☎33

International access code ☎00

Europe-wide emergency ☎112

Ambulance (SAMU) ☎15

Police ☎17

MOBILE PHONES

- French mobile phone numbers begin with 06 or 07.
- France uses GSM 900/1800, which is compatible with the rest of Europe and Australia but not with the North American GSM 1900 or the totally different system in Japan (though some North Americans have tri-band phones that work here).
- Check with your service provider about roaming charges.
- If you have a compatible phone, you can buy a French SIM card (€20 to €30).
- Recharge cards are sold at most *tabacs* (tobacconists) and newsagents.
- SIM cards are available at the ubiquitous outlets run by France's three mobile phone companies, **Bouygues** (www.bouyguestelecom.fr), **Orange** (www.orange.com) and **SFR** (www.sfr.com).

PHONE CODES

- **Calling France from abroad** Dial your country's international access code, then 33 (France's country code), then the 10-digit local number *without* the initial zero.
- **Calling internationally from France** Dial 00 (the international access code), the *indicatif* (country code), the area code (without the initial zero if there is one) and the local number.
- **Directory inquiries** For national *service des renseignements* (directory inquiries) dial 11 87 12 or use the service for free online at www.118712.fr.
- **Emergency numbers** Can be dialled from public phones without a phonecard.
- **Hotel calls** Hotels, *gîtes*, hostels and *chambres d'hôte* are free to meter their calls as they like. The surcharge is usually around €0.30 per minute but can be higher.
- **International directory inquiries** For numbers outside France, dial 11 87 00.

Strikes

France is the only European country in which public workers enjoy an unlimited right to strike, and they avail themselves of it with carefree abandon. Getting caught in one of the 'social dialogues' that characterise labour relations in France can put a serious crimp in your travel plans. It is best to leave some wriggle room in your schedule, particularly around departure times.

What the Icon Means

Only accommodation providers that have an actual computer that guests can use to access the internet are flagged with a **computer icon** (@). The **wi-fi icon** (wi-fi) indicates anywhere with wi-fi access. Where this icon appears, assume the wi-fi is free unless otherwise specified.

Time

France uses the 24-hour clock and is on Central European Time, which is one hour ahead of GMT/UTC. During daylight saving time, which runs from the last Sunday in March to the last Sunday in October, France is two hours ahead of GMT/UTC.

The following times do not take daylight saving into account:

CITY	NOON IN PARIS
Auckland	11pm
Berlin	noon
Cape Town	noon
London	11am
New York	6am
San Francisco	3am
Sydney	9pm
Tokyo	8pm

Tourist Information

Almost every city, town, village and hamlet has an *office de tourisme* (a tourist office run by some unit of local government) or *syndicat d'initiative* (a tourist office run by an organisation of local merchants). Both are excellent resources and can easily provide you with local maps of the region you wish to visit as well as information on accommodation, restaurants and activities. If you have a special interest such as walking, cycling, skiing, food tours, architecture or wine sampling, ask about it.

Tourist office details appear under Information at the end of each city, town or area listing.

Many tourist offices are willing to make local hotel and B&B reservations, sometimes for a nominal fee. Some tourist offices have limited currency-exchange services.

Useful websites:

French Government Tourist Office (www.franceguide.com) This is the place to come for the low-down on sights, activities, transport and special-interest holidays in all of France's regions. Brochures can also be downloaded online. There are links to country-specific websites.

Réseau National des Destinations Départementales (www.fncdt.net) Listing of CRT (regional tourist board) websites.

Travellers with Disabilities

While France presents evident challenges for *handicapés* (people with disabilities) – namely cobblestone, cafe-lined streets that are a nightmare to navigate in a wheelchair, a lack of kerb ramps, older public facilities and many budget hotels without lifts – don't let that stop you from visiting. With a little careful planning, you can enjoy a hassle-free accessible stay.

The Paris metro, most of it built decades ago, is hopeless, but you will be pleased to know that taxi drivers are obliged by law to assist and accept passengers with disabilities (and their guide dogs, where relevant). Choose central accommodation to avoid spending a small fortune on taxi fares.

Whether you are looking for wheelchair-friendly accommodation, sights, attractions or restaurants, these associations and agencies should be able to point you in the right direction:

Infomobi.com (☎ 08 10 64 64 64; www.infomobi.com) Has comprehensive information on accessible travel in Paris.

Access Travel (☎ in UK 01942-888 844; www.access-travel.co.uk) Specialised UK-based agency for accessible travel.

Centre du Service Accès Plus (☎ 08 90 64 06 50; www.accessibilite.sncf.fr) Can advise on station accessibility and arrange a *fauteuil roulant* (wheelchair) or help getting on or off a train.

Mobile en Ville (☎ 09 52 29 60 51; www.mobile-en-ville.asso.fr; 8 rue des Mariniers, 14e, Paris) Association set up in 1998 by students and researchers with the aim of making independent travel within the city easier for people in wheelchairs.

Visas

For up-to-date details on visa requirements, see the website of the **Ministère des Affaires Étrangères** (Ministry of Foreign Affairs; 37 quai d'Orsay, 7e) and click 'Going to France'. Tourist visas *cannot* be extended except in emergencies (such as medical problems). When your visa expires you'll need to leave and reapply from outside France.

VISA REQUIREMENTS

- EU nationals and citizens of Iceland, Norway and Switzerland need only a passport or a national identity card in order to enter France and stay in the country, even for stays of over 90 days. However, citizens of new EU member states may be subject to various limitations on living and working in France.
- Citizens of Australia, the USA, Canada, Hong Kong, Israel, Japan, Malaysia, New Zealand, Singapore, South Korea and many Latin American countries do not need visas to visit France as tourists for up to 90 days. For long stays of over 90 days,

contact your nearest French embassy or consulate and begin your application well in advance as it can take months.

- Other people wishing to come to France as tourists have to apply for a **Schengen Visa**, named after the agreements that abolished passport controls between 15 European countries. It allows unlimited travel throughout the entire zone for a 90-day period. Apply to the consulate of the country you are entering first, or your main destination. Among other things, you need travel and repatriation insurance and be able to show that you have sufficient funds to support yourself.

Transport

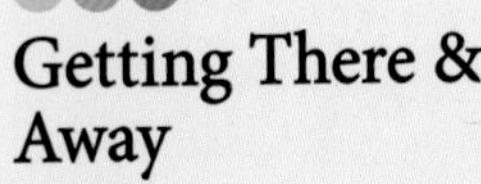

Getting There & Away

AIR

INTERNATIONAL AIRPORTS

Paris Charles de Gaulle (CDG; www.aeroportsdeparis.fr)

Paris Orly (ORY; www.aeroportsdeparis.fr)

Aéroport de Bordeaux (www.bordeaux.aeroport.fr)

Aéroport de Lille (www.lille.aeroport.fr)

Aéroport International Strasbourg (www.strasbourg.aeroport.fr)

Aéroport Lyon-Saint Exupéry (www.lyonaeroports.com)

Aéroport Marseille-Provence (www.marseille.aeroport.fr)

Aéroport Nantes Atlantique (www.nantes.aeroport.fr)

Aéroport Nice Côte d'Azur (http://societe.nice.aeroport.fr)

Aéroport Toulouse-Blagnac (www.toulouse.aeroport.fr)

LAND

CAR & MOTORCYCLE

A right-hand-drive vehicle brought to France from the UK or Ireland must have deflectors affixed to the headlights to avoid dazzling oncoming traffic. In the UK, information on driving in France is available from the **RAC** (www.rac.co.uk/driving-abroad/france) and the **AA** (www.theaa.com).

A foreign motor vehicle entering France must display a sticker or licence plate identifying its country of registration.

EUROTUNNEL

The Channel Tunnel (Chunnel), inaugurated in 1994, is the first dry-land link between England and France since the last ice age.

High-speed **Eurotunnel Le Shuttle** (www.eurotunnel.com) trains whisk bicycles, motorcycles, cars and coaches in 35 minutes from Folkestone through the Channel Tunnel to Coquelles, 5km southwest of Calais. Shuttles run 24 hours a day, with up to three departures an hour during peak periods. LPG and CNG tanks are not permitted, meaning gas-powered cars and many campers and caravans have to travel by ferry.

Eurotunnel sets its fares the way budget airlines do: the further in advance you book

Climate Change & Travel

Every form of transport that relies on carbon-based fuel generates CO_2, the main cause of human-induced climate change. Modern travel is dependent on aeroplanes, which might use less fuel per kilometre per person than most cars but travel much greater distances. The altitude at which aircraft emit gases (including CO_2) and particles also contributes to their climate change impact. Many websites offer 'carbon calculators' that allow people to estimate the carbon emissions generated by their journey and, for those who wish to do so, to offset the impact of the greenhouse gases emitted with contributions to portfolios of climate-friendly initiatives throughout the world. Lonely Planet offsets the carbon footprint of all staff and author travel.

Trains & Ferries

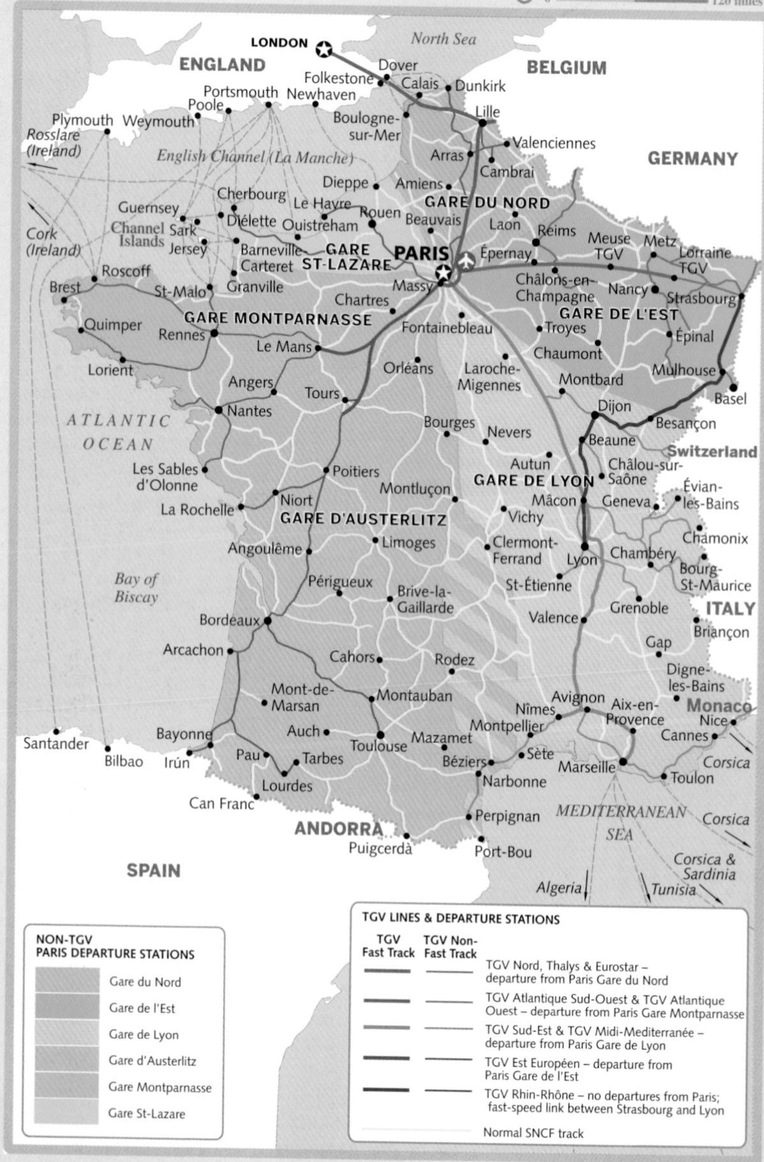

and the lower the demand for a particular crossing, the less you pay; same-day fares can cost a small fortune. Fares for a car, including up to nine passengers, start at UK£30.

TRAIN

Rail services – including a dwindling number of overnight services to/from Spain, Italy and Germany – link France with virtually every country in Europe. For details on train travel within France, see p400.

You can book tickets and get train information from **Rail Europe** (www.raileurope.

International Ferry Companies

COMPANY	CONNECTION	WEBSITE
Brittany Ferries	England–Normandy, England–Brittany, Ireland–Brittany	www.brittany-ferries.co.uk; www.brittanyferries.ie
Celtic Link Ferries	Ireland–Normandy	www.celticlinkferries.com
Condor Ferries	England–Normandy, England–Brittany, Channel Islands–Brittany	www.condorferries.com
CTN	Tunisia–France	www.ctn.com.tn
Irish Ferries	Ireland-Normandy, Ireland–Brittany	www.irishferries.ie; www.shamrock-irlande.com, in French
LD Lines	England–Channel Ports, England–Normandy	www.ldlines.co.uk
Manche Îles Express	Channel Islands–Normandy	www.manche-iles-express.com
Norfolk Line (DFDS Seaways)	England–Channel Ports	www.norfolkline.com
P&O Ferries	England–Channel Ports	www.poferries.com
SNCM	Algeria–France, Sardinia–France, Tunisia-France	www.sncm.fr
Transmanche Ferries	England–Normandy	www.transmancheferries.com

com). In France ticketing is handled by **SNCF** (Société Nationale des Chemins de Fer Français; French National Railway Corporation; ☎ from abroad +33 8 92 35 35 35, in France 36 35; www.sncf.com); internet bookings are possible but it won't post tickets outside France.

EUROSTAR

The **Eurostar** (☎ in France 08 92 35 35 39, in UK 08432-186 186; www.eurostar.com) whisks you from London to Paris in 2¼ hours.

Except late at night, trains link London (St Pancras International) with Paris (Gare du Nord; hourly), Calais (Calais-Fréthun; one hour, three daily), Lille (Gare Lille-Europe; 1½ hours, eight daily) and Disneyland Resort Paris (2½ hours, one direct daily), with less frequent services departing from Ebbsfleet and Ashford, both in Kent. Weekend ski trains connect England with the French Alps mid-December to mid-April.

For the best deals buy a return ticket, stay over a Saturday night, book up to 120 days in advance and don't mind nonexchangeability and nonrefundability. Discount fares are available for those under 26 or over 60.

SEA

Some ferry companies have started setting fares the way budget airlines do: the longer in advance you book and the lower the demand for a particular sailing, the less you pay. Seasonal demand is a crucial factor (Christmas, Easter, UK and French school holidays, July and August are especially busy), as is the time of day (an early evening ferry can cost much more than one at 4am). People under 25 and over 60 may qualify for discounts.

To get the best fares, check **Ferry Savers** (☎ in UK 0844-371 8021; www.ferrysavers.com).

Getting Around

Driving is the simplest way to get around France but a car is a liability in traffic-plagued, parking-starved city centres, and petrol bills and autoroute (dual carriageway/divided highway) tolls add up.

France is famous for its excellent public-transport

network, which serves everywhere bar some rural areas. The state-owned Société Nationale des Chemins de Fer Français (SNCF) takes care of almost all land transport between *départements*. Transport within *départements* is handled by a combination of short-haul trains, SNCF buses and local bus companies.

BICYCLE

France is great for cycling. Much of the countryside is drop-dead gorgeous and the country has a growing number of urban and rural *pistes cyclables* (bike paths and lanes; see Voies Vertes (www.voievertes.com) and an extensive network of secondary and tertiary roads with relatively light traffic.

French law requires that bicycles must have two functioning brakes, a bell, a red reflector on the back and yellow reflectors on the pedals. After sunset and when visibility is poor, cyclists must turn on a white headlamp and a red tail lamp. When being overtaken by a vehicle, cyclists must ride in single file. Towing children in a bike trailer is permitted.

Never leave your bicycle locked up outside overnight if you want to see it – or at least most of its parts – again. Some hotels offer enclosed bicycle parking.

TRANSPORTATION

The SNCF does its best to make travelling with a bicycle easy; see **velo.sncf.com** (www.velo.sncf.com) for full details.

Bicycles (not disassembled) can be taken along on virtually all intraregional TER trains and most long-distance intercity trains, subject to space availability. There's no charge on TER and Corail Intercité trains but TGV (*Train à Grande Vitesse*; French high-speed train), Téoz and Lunéa trains require a €10 reservation fee that must be made when you purchase your passenger ticket. Bike reservations can be made by phone (☎36 35) or at an SNCF ticket office but not via the internet.

Bicycles that have been partly disassembled and put in a box *(housse)*, with maximum dimensions of 120cm by 90cm, can be taken along for no charge in the baggage compartments of TGV, Téoz, Lunéa and Corail Intercité trains.

With precious few exceptions, bicycles are not allowed on metros, trams and local, intra-*département* and SNCF buses (the latter replace trains on some runs).

BIKE RENTAL

Most French cities and towns have at least one bike shop that rents out *vélos tout terrains* (mountain bikes; around €15 a day), known as VTTs, as well as more road-oriented *vélos tout chemin* (VTCs), or cheaper city bikes. You usually have to leave ID and/or a deposit (often a credit-card slip) that you forfeit if the bike is damaged or stolen.

A growing number of cities – most famously Paris and Lyon, but also Aix-en-Provence, Amiens, Besançon, Caen, Dijon, La Rochelle, Lille, Marseille, Montpellier, Mulhouse, Nancy, Nantes, Nice, Orléans, Rennes, Rouen, Toulouse and Strasbourg – have automatic bike-rental systems, intended to encourage cycling as a form of urban transport, with computerised pick-up and drop-off sites all over town. In general, you have to sign up either short term or long term, providing credit-card details, and can then use the bikes for no charge for the first half-hour; after that, hourly charges rise quickly.

BUS

Buses are widely used for short-distance travel within *départements*, especially in rural areas with relatively few train lines (eg Brittany and Normandy). Unfortunately, services in some regions are infrequent and slow, in part because they were designed to get children to their schools in the towns rather than transport visitors around the countryside.

CAR & MOTORCYCLE

Having your own wheels gives you exceptional freedom and makes it easy to visit more remote parts of France. Unfortunately driving can be expensive. For example, by autoroute, the 932km drive from Paris to Nice (nine hours of driving) in a small car costs about €75 for petrol and €85 in tolls – by comparison, a one-way, 2nd-class TGV ticket for the 5½-hour Paris to Nice run costs €70 to €150 per person. Also, in the cities, traffic and finding a place to park are a major headache. During holiday periods and over long weekends, roads throughout France also frequently get traffic jams *(bouchons)*.

Road Distances (Km)

	Bayonne	Bordeaux	Brest	Caen	Cahors	Calais	Chambéry	Cherbourg	Clermont-Ferrand	Dijon	Grenoble	Lille	Lyon	Marseille	Nantes	Nice	Paris	Perpignan	Strasbourg	Toulouse
Bordeaux	184																			
Brest	811	623																		
Caen	764	568	376																	
Cahors	307	218	788	661																
Calais	164	876	710	339	875															
Chambéry	860	651	120	800	523	834														
Cherbourg	835	647	399	124	743	461	923													
Clermont-Ferrand	564	358	805	566	269	717	295	689												
Dijon	807	619	867	548	378	572	273	671	279											
Grenoble	827	657	1126	806	501	863	56	929	300	302										
Lille	997	809	725	353	808	112	767	476	650	505	798									
Lyon	831	528	1018	698	439	755	103	820	171	194	110	687								
Marseille	700	651	1271	1010	521	1067	344	1132	477	506	273	999	314							
Nantes	513	326	298	292	491	593	780	317	462	656	787	609	618	975						
Nice	858	810	1429	1168	679	1225	410	1291	636	664	337	1157	473	190	1131					
Paris	771	583	596	232	582	289	565	355	424	313	571	222	462	775	384	932				
Perpignan	499	451	1070	998	320	1149	478	1094	441	640	445	1081	448	319	773	476	857			
Strasbourg	1254	1066	1079	730	847	621	496	853	584	335	551	522	488	803	867	804	490	935		
Toulouse	300	247	866	865	116	991	565	890	890	727	533	923	536	407	568	564	699	205	1022	
Tours	536	348	490	246	413	531	611	369	369	418	618	463	449	795	197	952	238	795	721	593

Motorcyclists will find France great for touring, with winding roads of good quality. Just make sure your wet-weather gear is up to scratch.

France (along with Belgium) has the densest highway network in Europe. There are four types of intercity roads:

Autoroutes (highway names beginning with A) Multilane divided highways, usually (except near Calais and Lille) with tolls *(péages)*. Generously outfitted with rest stops.

Routes Nationales (N, RN) National highways. Some sections have divider strips.

Routes Départementales (D) Local highways and roads.

Routes Communales (C, V) Minor rural roads.

For information on autoroute tolls, rest areas, traffic and weather, go to the **Sociétés d'Autoroutes** (www.autoroutes.fr) website.

Bison Futé (www.bison-fute.equipement.gouv.fr) is also a good source of information about traffic conditions. Plot itineraries between your departure and arrival points, and calculate toll costs with **Via Michelin** (www.viamichelin.com) or **Mappy** (www.mappy.fr).

Note that theft from cars is a major problem in France, especially in the south.

CAR HIRE

To hire a car in France, you'll need to be over 21 years old, have had a driving licence for at least a year, and have an international credit card. Drivers under 25 usually have to pay a surcharge *(frais jeune conducteur)* of €25 to €35 per day.

Car-hire companies provide mandatory third-party liability insurance but things such as collision-damage waivers (CDW, or *assurance tous risques*) vary greatly from company to company. When comparing rates and

Priority to the Right

Under the *priorité à droite* ('priority to the right') rule, any car entering an intersection (including a T-junction) from a road (including a tiny village backstreet) on your right has the right-of-way. Locals assume every driver knows this, so don't be surprised if they courteously cede the right-of-way when you're about to turn from an alley onto a highway – and boldly assert their rights when you're the one zipping down a main road.

Priorité à droite is suspended (eg on arterial roads) when you pass a sign showing an upended yellow square with a black square in the middle. The same sign with a horizontal bar through the square lozenge reinstates the *priorité à droite* rule.

When you arrive at a roundabout at which you do not have the right-of-way (ie the cars already in the roundabout do), you'll often see signs reading *vous n'avez pas la priorité* (you do not have right of way) or *cédez le passage* (give way).

conditions (ie the fine print), the most important thing to check is the *franchise* (deductible/excess), which for a small car is usually around €600 for damage and €800 for theft. With many companies, you can reduce the excess by half, and perhaps to zero, by paying a daily insurance supplement of €10 to €16. Your credit card may cover CDW if you use it to pay for the rental but the car-hire company won't know anything about this – verify conditions and details with your credit-card issuer to be sure.

Arranging your car hire or fly/drive package before you leave home is usually considerably cheaper than a walk-in rental, but beware of website offers that don't include a CDW or you may be liable for up to 100% of the car's value.

International car-hire companies:

Avis (☎ 08 21 23 07 60; www.avis.com)

Budget (☎ 08 25 00 35 64; www.budget.com)

Easycar (☎ in France 08 26 10 73 23, in the UK 08710-500 444; www.easycar.com)

Europcar (☎ 08 25 35 83 58; www.europcar.com)

Hertz (www.hertz.com)

National-Citer (www.nationalcar.com)

Sixt (☎ 08 20 00 74 98; www.sixt.fr)

Deals can be found on the internet and through companies such as the following:

Auto Europe (☎ in USA 1-888-223-5555; www.autoeurope.com)

DriveAway Holidays (☎ in Australia 1300 723 972; www.driveaway.com.au)

Holiday Autos (☎ in the UK 0871 472 5229; www.holidayautos.co.uk)

Note that rental cars with automatic transmission are very much the exception in France and will usually need to be ordered well in advance.

All rental cars registered in France have a distinctive number on the licence plate, making them easily identifiable – including to thieves, so *never* leave anything of value in a parked car, even in the boot.

DRIVING LICENCE & DOCUMENTS

An International Driving Permit (IDP), valid only if accompanied by your original licence, is good for a year and can be issued by your local automobile association before you leave home.

Drivers must carry the following at all times:

- passport or an EU national ID card
- valid driving licence (*permis de conduire;* most foreign licences can be used in France for up to a year)
- car-ownership papers, known as a *carte grise* (grey card)
- proof of third-party liability *assurance* (insurance)

FUEL

Essence (petrol), also known as *carburant* (fuel), costs around €1.45/L (US$6.80 per US gallon) for 95 unleaded (Sans Plomb 95 or SP95, usually available from a green pump) and €1.30 for diesel (*diesel, gazole* or *gasoil*, usually available from a yellow pump). Many small petrol stations close on Sunday afternoons and, even in cities, it can be hard to find a staffed station open late at night.

INSURANCE

Third-party liability insurance *(assurance au tiers)* is compulsory for all vehicles in France, including cars brought in from abroad. Normally, cars registered and insured in other European countries can circulate freely in France, but it's a good idea to contact your insurance company before you leave home to make sure you've got coverage – and to check whom to contact in case of a breakdown or accident.

If you get into a minor accident with no injuries, the easiest way for drivers to sort things out with their insurance companies is to fill out a Constat Aimable d'Accident Automobile (European Accident Statement), a standardised way of recording important details about what happened. In rental cars it's usually in the packet of documents in the glove compartment. Make sure the report includes any information that will help you prove that the accident was not your fault. Remember, if it *was* your fault you may be liable for a hefty insurance deductible/excess. Don't sign anything you don't fully understand. If problems crop up, call the police.

PARKING

In city centres, most on-the-street parking places are *payant* (metered) from about 9am to 7pm (sometimes with a break from noon to 2pm) Monday to Saturday, except bank holidays.

ROAD RULES

Enforcement of French traffic laws (see www.securiteroutiere.gouv.fr, in French) has been stepped up considerably in recent years. Speed cameras are becoming ever more common, as are radar traps, unmarked police vehicles and saliva drug tests. Fines for many infractions are given on the spot, and serious violations can lead to the confiscation of your driving licence and car.

Speed limits outside built-up areas (except where signposted otherwise):

Undivided N and D highways 90km/h (80km/h when raining)

Non-autoroute divided highways 110km/h (100km/h when raining)

Autoroutes 130km/h (110km/h when raining, 60km/h in icy conditions)

To reduce carbon emissions, autoroute speed limits have recently been reduced to 110km/h in some areas.

Unless otherwise signposted, a limit of 50km/h applies in *all* areas designated as built up, no matter how rural they may appear. You must slow to 50km/h the moment you come to a white sign with a red border and a place name written on it; the speed limit applies until you pass an identical sign with a horizontal bar through it.

Most of the speed-limit signs you'll see in cities, towns and villages merely remind you of something you're already supposed to know – that's why they begin with the word *rappel* ('remember'). You can be fined for going as little as 10km over the speed limit.

Other important driving rules:

- Blood-alcohol limit is 0.05% (0.5g per litre of blood) – the equivalent of two glasses of wine for a 75kg adult. Police often conduct random breathalyser tests and penalties can be severe, including imprisonment.
- All passengers, including those in the back seat, must wear seat belts.
- Mobile phones may be used only if they are equipped with a hands-free kit or speakerphone.
- Turning right on a red light is illegal.
- Cars from the UK and Ireland must have deflectors affixed to their headlights to avoid dazzling oncoming motorists.
- Radar detectors, even if they're switched off, are illegal; fines are hefty.

Child-seat rules:

- Children under 10 are not permitted to ride in the front seat (unless the back is already occupied by other children under 10).
- A child under 13kg must travel in a backward-facing child seat (permitted in the front seat only for babies under 9kg and if the airbag is deactivated).

- Up to age 10 and/or a minimum height of 140cm, children must use a size-appropriate type of front-facing child seat or booster.

All vehicles driven in France must carry a high-visibility reflective safety vest (stored inside the vehicle, not in the trunk/boot), a reflective triangle, and (as of 1 July 2012) a portable, single-use breathalyser kit. The fine for not carrying any of these items is €90.

If you'll be driving on snowy roads, make sure you've got snow chains *(chaînes neige)*, required by law whenever and wherever the police post signs.

Riders of any type of two-wheeled vehicle with a motor (except motor-assisted bicycles) must wear a helmet. No special licence is required to ride a motorbike whose engine is smaller than 50cc, which is why rental scooters are often rated at 49.9cc.

LOCAL TRANSPORT

France's cities and larger towns have world-class public-transport systems. There are *métros* (underground subway systems) in Paris, Lyon, Marseille, Lille and Toulouse, and ultramodern light-rail lines *(tramways)* in cities such as Bordeaux, Grenoble, Lille, Lyon, Nancy, Nantes, Nice, Reims, Rouen and Strasbourg, as well as parts of greater Paris.

In addition to a *billet à l'unité* (single ticket), you can purchase a *carnet* (booklet or bunch) of 10 tickets or a *pass journée* (all-day pass).

TAXI

All medium and large train stations – and many small ones – have a taxi stand out front. In small cities and towns, where taxi drivers are unlikely to find another fare anywhere near where they let you off, one-way and return trips often cost the same. Tariffs are about 30% higher at night and on Sundays and holidays. Having a cab wait for you while you visit something costs about €20 an hour (about €30 in Paris). There may be a surcharge to get picked up at a train station or airport and a small additional fee for a fourth passenger and/or for suitcases.

TRAIN

Travelling by train in France is a comfortable, classy and environmentally sustainable way to see the country. Since many train stations have car-hire agencies, it's easy to combine rail travel with rural exploration by car.

The jewel in the crown of France's public-transport system – alongside the Paris *métro* – is its extensive rail network, almost all of it run by the state-owned SNCF. Although it employs the most advanced rail technology, the network's layout reflects the country's centuries-old Paris-centric nature: most of the principal rail lines radiate out from Paris like the spokes of a wheel, the result being that services between provincial towns situated on different spokes can be infrequent and slow. Up-to-the-minute information on *perturbations* (service disruptions), eg because of strikes, can be found on www.infolignes.com (in French).

Since its inauguration in the 1980s, the pride and joy of SNCF – and the French – is the renowned **TGV (Train à Grande Vitesse; www.tgv.com)**, pronounced 'teh zheh veh', which zips passengers along at speeds of up to 320km/h (198mph).

The main TGV lines (or LGVs, short for *lignes à grande vitesse*, ie high-speed rail lines) head north, east, southeast and southwest from Paris (trains use slower local tracks to get to destinations off the main line):

TGV Nord, Thalys & Eurostar Link Paris Gare du Nord with Arras, Lille, Calais, Brussels (Bruxelles-Midi), Amsterdam, Cologne and, via the Channel Tunnel, Ashford, Ebbsfleet and London St Pancras.

TGV Est Européen Connects Paris Gare de l'Est with Reims, Nancy, Metz, Zurich and Germany, including Frankfurt and Stuttgart. At present, the super-high-speed track stretches only as far east as Lorraine but it's supposed to reach Strasbourg in 2016.

TGV Sud-Est & TGV Midi-Méditerranée Link Paris Gare de Lyon with the southeast, including Dijon, Lyon, Geneva, the Alps, Avignon, Marseille, Nice and Montpellier.

TGV Atlantique Sud-Ouest & TGV Atlantique Ouest Link Paris Gare Montparnasse with western and southwestern France, including Brittany (Rennes, Brest, Quimper), Tours, Nantes, Poitiers, La

Rochelle, Bordeaux, Biarritz and Toulouse.

TGV Rhin-Rhône France's most recent high-speed rail route – the first section of which opened in December 2011 – bypasses Paris altogether in its bid to better link the provinces. Six services a day speed between Strasbourg and Lyon, with most continuing south to Marseille or Montpellier on the Mediterranean.

The TGV tracks are interconnected, making it possible to go directly from, say, Lyon to Nantes or Bordeaux to Lille without having to switch trains in Paris or transfer from one of Paris' six main train stations to another. Stops on the link-up, which runs east and south of Paris, include Charles de Gaulle airport and Disneyland Resort Paris.

Long-distance trains sometimes split at a station – that is, each half of the train heads off for a different destination. Check the destination panel on your car as you board or you could wind up very far from where you intended to go.

Left-Luggage Facilities

Because of security concerns, few French train stations still have *consignes automatiques* (left-luggage lockers), but in some larger stations you can leave your bags in a *consigne manuelle* (staffed left-luggage facility) – usually in an out-of-the-way corner of the station – where items are handed over in person and x-rayed before being stowed. Charges are €5 for up to 10 hours and €8 for 24 hours; payment must be made in cash. To find out which stations let you leave your bags and when their *consignes* are open (they're often closed on Sunday and after 7pm or 8pm), go to www.gares-en-mouvement.com, select a station, click 'Practical Information' ('Services en gare') and then the 'Services' tab.

TICKETS & RESERVATIONS

Large stations often have separate ticket windows for international, *grandes lignes* (long-haul) and *banlieue* (suburban) lines, and for people whose train is about to leave *(départ immédiat* or *départ dans l'heure)*. Nearly every SNCF station has at least one *borne libre-service* (self-service terminal) or *billeterie automatique* (automatic ticket machine) that accepts both cash and PIN-chip credit cards. Select the Union Jack for instructions in English.

Using a credit card, you can buy a ticket by phone or via the SNCF internet booking, **Voyages SNCF** (www.voyages-sncf.com), and either have it sent to you by post (if you have an address in France) or collect it from any SNCF ticket office or from train-station ticket machines.

Before boarding the train, you must validate *(composter)* your ticket by time-stamping it in a *composteur*, one of those yellow posts located on the way to the platform. If you forget (or don't have a ticket for some other reason), find a conductor on the train before they find you – otherwise you can be fined.

SNCF FARES & DISCOUNTS

Full-fare tickets can be quite expensive. Fortunately, a dizzying array of discounts are available and station staff are very good about helping travellers find the very best fare. But first, the basics:

- 1st-class travel, where available, costs 20% to 30% extra.
- Ticket prices for some trains, including most TGVs, are pricier during peak periods.
- The further in advance you reserve, the lower the fares.
- Children under four travel for free (€8.50 to any destination if they need a seat).
- Children aged four to 11 travel for half price.

Discount Tickets

The SNCF's most heavily discounted tickets are known as **Prem's**. They can be booked on the internet, by phone, at ticket windows and from ticket machines a maximum of 90 days and a minimum of 14 days before your travel date. Once you buy a Prem's ticket, it's use it or lose it – getting your money back or changing the time is not allowed.

Bons Plans fares, a grab bag of really cheap options on a changing array of routes and dates, are advertised on www.voyages-sncf.com under the title 'Dernière Minute' (last minute).

In an effort to make train travel both affordable and hip for the iPod generation, the SNCF's youthful subsidiary **iDTGV** (www.idtgv.com) sells tickets (online only) for as little as €19 for advance-purchase TGV travel between about 30 cities.

On regional trains, discount fares requiring neither a discount card nor advance purchase:

Loisir Week-End rates Good for return travel that includes a Saturday night at your destination or involves travel on a Saturday or Sunday.

Découverte fares Available for low-demand 'blue-period' trains to people aged 12 to 25, seniors and the adult travel companions of children under 12.

Mini-Groupe tickets In some regions, these bring big savings for three to six people travelling together, provided you spend a Saturday night at your destination.

Certain French *régions* offer great deals on intraregional TER transport for day trips or weekend travel.

DISCOUNT CARDS

Reductions of at least 25% (for last-minute bookings), and of 40%, 50% or even 60% (if you reserve well ahead or travel during low-volume 'blue' periods), are available with several discount cards (valid for one year):

Carte 12-25 (www.12-25-sncf.com; €50) Available to travellers aged 12 to 25.

Carte Enfant Plus (www.enfantplus-sncf.com; €71) For one to four adults travelling with a child aged four to 11.

Carte Escapades (www.escapades-sncf.com; €76) For people aged 26 to 59. Discounts on return journeys of at least 200km that either include a Saturday night away or only involve travel on a Saturday or Sunday.

Carte Sénior (www.senior-sncf.com; €57) For travellers over 60.

RAIL PASSES

Residents of Europe who do not live in France can purchase an **InterRail One Country Pass** (www.interrailnet.com; 3/4/6/8 days €205/226/288/319, 12-25yr €139/149/190/211), which entitles its bearer to unlimited travel on SNCF trains for three to eight days over the course of a month.

For non-European residents, Rail Europe offers the **France Rail Pass** (www.francerailpass.com; 3/6/9 days over 1 month €242/349/443).

You need to really rack up the kilometres to make these passes worthwhile.

Language

The sounds used in spoken French can almost all be found in English. There are a couple of exceptions: nasal vowels (represented in our pronunciation guides by 'o' or 'u' followed by an almost inaudible nasal consonant sound 'm', 'n' or 'ng'), the 'funny' *u* sound ('ew' in our guides) and the deep-in-the-throat *r*. Bearing these few points in mind and reading our pronunciation guides below as if they were English, you'll be understood just fine.

To enhance your trip with a phrasebook, visit **lonelyplanet.com**. Lonely Planet iPhone phrasebooks are available through the Apple App store.

BASICS

Hello./Goodbye.
Bonjour./Au revoir. — bon·zhoor/o·rer·vwa

How are you?
Comment allez-vous? — ko·mon ta·lay·voo

I'm fine, thanks.
Bien, merci. — byun mair·see

Excuse me./Sorry.
Excusez-moi./Pardon. — ek·skew·zay·mwa/par·don

Yes./No.
Oui./Non. — wee/non

Please.
S'il vous plaît. — seel voo play

Thank you.
Merci. — mair·see

That's fine./You're welcome.
De rien. — der ree·en

Do you speak English?
Parlez-vous anglais? — par·lay·voo ong·glay

I don't understand.
Je ne comprends pas. — zher ner kom·pron pa

How much is this?
C'est combien? — say kom·byun

ACCOMMODATION

I'd like to book a room.
Je voudrais réserver une chambre. — zher voo·dray ray·zair·vay ewn shom·brer

How much is it per night?
Quel est le prix par nuit? — kel ay ler pree par nwee

EATING & DRINKING

I'd like ..., please.
Je voudrais ..., s'il vous plaît. — zher voo·dray ... seel voo play

That was delicious!
C'était délicieux! — say·tay day·lee·syer

Bring the bill/check, please.
Apportez-moi l'addition, s'il vous plaît. — a·por·tay·mwa la·dee·syon seel voo play

I'm allergic (to peanuts).
Je suis allergique (aux cacahuètes). — zher swee a·lair·zheek (o ka·ka·wet)

I don't eat ...
Je ne mange pas de ... — zher ner monzh pa de ...

fish	*poisson*	pwa·son
(red) meat	*viande (rouge)*	vyond (roozh)
poultry	*volaille*	vo·lai

EMERGENCIES

I'm ill.
Je suis malade. — zher swee ma·lad

Help!
Au secours! — o skoor

Call a doctor!
Appelez un médecin! — a·play un mayd·sun

Call the police!
Appelez la police! — a·play la po·lees

DIRECTIONS

I'm looking for (a/the) ...
Je cherche ... — zher shairsh ...

bank	*une banque*	ewn bongk
... embassy	*l'ambassade de ...*	lam·ba·sahd der ...
market	*le marché*	ler mar·shay
museum	*le musée*	ler mew·zay
restaurant	*un restaurant*	un res·to·ron
toilet	*les toilettes*	lay twa·let
tourist office	*l'office de tourisme*	lo·fees der too·rees·mer

Behind the Scenes

Our Readers

Many thanks to the travellers who used the last edition and wrote to us with helpful hints, useful advice and interesting anecdotes:

Suzan Farah, Tony Long, Michael Nowlan, Heather Sherwood, Nancy Sturgeon and Joel Walz

Author Thanks

NICOLA WILLIAMS

Merci mille fois to French experts Jane Anson, Michael Edwards, Elizabeth Lewis, Niko Salvatore Melissano, Silvain Postolle, Jack Lecoq, Elsa Sauvé, Eric Favret, Jean-Pierre Xiradaki and Patricia Wells for sharing their passion, expertise and insider secrets. Kudos to my *France* co-authors who resolutely persevered with an ambitious project that, at times, felt akin to scaling the Eiffel Tower on tiptoes in stilettos; and at home to Matthias, Niko, Mischa and Kaya for tolerating the domestic mayhem so graciously.

Acknowledgments

Climate map data adapted from Peel MC, Finlayson BL & McMahon TA (2007) 'Updated World Map of the Köppen-Geiger Climate Classification', *Hydrology and Earth System Sciences*, 11, 163344. Illustrations p74-5, p82-3, p102-3, p130-1, p306-7, p346-7 by Javier Zarracina.
Cover photographs: Front: Mont St-Michel, Marc Schlossman/Getty Images; Back: Cathédrale de Notre Dame de Paris, Rachel Lewis/LPI

This Book

This 3rd edition of Lonely Planet's *Discover France* guidebook was written and coordinated by Nicola Williams, and researched by Nicola Williams, Oliver Berry, Stuart Butler, Jean-Bernard Carillet, Gregor Clark, Kerry Christiani, Emilie Filou and Catherine Le Nevez. Alexis Averbuck and John Vlahides contributed to the Provence & the French Riviera chapter; Christopher Pitts contributed to the Paris chapter.

Commissioning Editors Joanna Cooke, James Smart, Dora Whitaker
Coordinating Editor Karyn Noble
Coordinating Cartographer Jacqueline Nguyen
Coordinating Layout Designer Joseph Spanti
Managing Editors Barbara Delissen, Annelies Mertens
Managing Cartographers Adrian Persoglia, Anthony Phelan
Managing Layout Designer Chris Girdler
Assisting Editors Carolyn Boicos, Kellie Langdon, Luna Soo
Assisting Cartographer Alex Leung
Cover Research Naomi Parker
Internal Image Research Aude Vauconsant
Language Content Branislava Vladisavljevic
Thanks to Ryan Evans, Larissa Frost, Genesis India, Jouve India, Catherine Naghten, Trent Paton, Raphael Richards, Jessica Rose, Amanda Sierp, Gerard Walker

SEND US YOUR FEEDBACK

We love to hear from travellers – your comments keep us on our toes and help make our books better. Our well-travelled team reads every word on what you loved or loathed about this book. Although we cannot reply individually to postal submissions, we always guarantee that your feedback goes straight to the appropriate authors, in time for the next edition. Each person who sends us information is thanked in the next edition, and the most useful submissions are rewarded with a free book.

Visit **lonelyplanet.com/contact** to submit your updates and suggestions or to ask for help. Our award-winning website also features inspirational travel stories, news and discussions.

Note: We may edit, reproduce and incorporate your comments in Lonely Planet products such as guidebooks, websites and digital products, so let us know if you don't want your comments reproduced or your name acknowledged. For a copy of our privacy policy visit lonelyplanet.com/privacy.

Index

A

000 Map pages

D

E

F

000 Map pages

M

000 Map pages

N

O

P

Q

R

S

T

000 Map pages

How to Use This Book

These symbols will help you find the listings you want:

- Sights
- Beaches
- Activities
- Courses
- Tours
- Festivals & Events
- Sleeping
- Eating
- Drinking
- Entertainment
- Shopping
- Information/ Transport

These symbols give you the vital information for each listing:

- Telephone Numbers
- Opening Hours
- Parking
- Nonsmoking
- Air-Conditioning
- Internet Access
- Wi-Fi Access
- Swimming Pool
- Vegetarian Selection
- English-Language Menu
- Family-Friendly
- Pet-Friendly
- Bus
- Ferry
- Metro
- Tram
- Train

Look out for these icons:

FREE No payment required

A green or sustainable option

Our authors have nominated these places as demonstrating a strong commitment to sustainability – for example by supporting local communities and producers, operating in an environmentally friendly way, or supporting conservation projects.

Reviews are organised by author preference.

Map Legend

Sights
- Beach
- Buddhist
- Castle
- Christian
- Hindu
- Islamic
- Jewish
- Monument
- Museum/Gallery
- Ruin
- Winery/Vineyard
- Zoo
- Other Sight

Activities, Courses & Tours
- Diving/Snorkelling
- Canoeing/Kayaking
- Skiing
- Surfing
- Swimming/Pool
- Walking
- Windsurfing
- Other Activity/ Course/Tour

Sleeping
- Sleeping
- Camping

Eating
- Eating

Drinking
- Drinking
- Cafe

Entertainment
- Entertainment

Shopping
- Shopping

Information
- Post Office
- Tourist Information

Transport
- Airport
- Border Crossing
- Bus
- Cable Car/ Funicular
- Cycling
- Ferry
- Metro
- Monorail
- Parking
- S-Bahn
- Taxi
- Train/Railway
- Tram
- Tube Station
- U-Bahn
- Other Transport

Routes
- Tollway
- Freeway
- Primary
- Secondary
- Tertiary
- Lane
- Unsealed Road
- Plaza/Mall
- Steps
- Tunnel
- Pedestrian Overpass
- Walking Tour
- Walking Tour Detour
- Path

Boundaries
- International
- State/Province
- Disputed
- Regional/Suburb
- Marine Park
- Cliff
- Wall

Population
- Capital (National)
- Capital (State/Province)
- City/Large Town
- Town/Village

Geographic
- Hut/Shelter
- Lighthouse
- Lookout
- Mountain/Volcano
- Oasis
- Park
- Pass
- Picnic Area
- Waterfall

Hydrography
- River/Creek
- Intermittent River
- Swamp/Mangrove
- Reef
- Canal
- Water
- Dry/Salt/ Intermittent Lake
- Glacier

Areas
- Beach/Desert
- Cemetery (Christian)
- Cemetery (Other)
- Park/Forest
- Sportsground
- Sight (Building)
- Top Sight (Building)

JEAN-BERNARD CARILLET

Normandy, Loire Valley & Central France Paris-based (and Metz-born) journalist and photographer Jean-Bernard was delighted to research his own turf. He has clocked up countless trips to all French regions and written extensively about Provence, the Basque Country, Brittany, Alsace, Corsica and, of course, Burgundy and Normandy. As a hopeless French gourmand, he confesses a pronounced penchant for *cuisine du terroir* and robust tipples (Pernand-Vergelesses and Gigondas being two of his favourites). Just after completing this project he set off to Beaujolais and Marais Poitevin.

KERRY CHRISTIANI

Champagne & Northern France, Lyon & the French Alps Kerry has been travelling to France since her school days to brush up her *français*, which she studied to MA level. The high-altitude pull of the Alps, Alsace's sweet eccentricities and Champagne's wineries draw her back time and again. Kerry has authored some 20 guidebooks and frequently contributes to magazines, including *Olive*, *Lonely Planet Magazine* and bbc.com/travel. She tweets at @kerrychristiani and lists her latest work at www.kerrychristiani.com.

Read more about Kerry at:
lonelyplanet.com/members/kerrychristiani

GREGOR CLARK

Champagne & Northern France, Loire Valley & Central France, Lyon & the French Alps Gregor's love affair with France started on the midnight streets of Paris at age 14, when, jetlagged and culture-shocked, he ordered a crêpe and discovered that his high school Franglais actually elicited a response. He's been feeding his France obsession ever since, picking fruit on summers off from university, leading bike tours, and writing for Lonely Planet since 2000. Highlights of this research trip include sharing his daughters' enthusiasm for their rented Loire Valley troglodyte house, and hiking the Massif Central.

Read more about Gregor at:
lonelyplanet.com/members/gregorclark

EMILIE FILOU

Provence & the French Riviera Emilie was born in Paris but spent most of her childhood holidays roaming the south of France. She left France when she was 18 to go travelling and never quite made it back. She now lives in London, where she works as a freelance journalist specialising in development issues in Africa. She still goes to the Côte d'Azur every summer. See more of Emilie's work on www.emiliefilou.com; she tweets at @emiliefilou.

Read more about Emilie at:
lonelyplanet.com/members/emiliefilou

CATHERINE LE NEVEZ

Paris & Around Catherine first lived in Paris aged four and she's been returning at every opportunity since, completing her Doctorate of Creative Arts in Writing, Masters in Professional Writing, and post-grad qualifications in Editing and Publishing along the way. Revisiting her favourite Parisian haunts and uncovering new ones is a highlight of this (and every) book. Catherine's writing on Paris includes numerous Lonely Planet guides to the city, country, continent and beyond. Wanderlust aside, Paris remains her favourite city on earth.

Our Story

A beat-up old car, a few dollars in the pocket and a sense of adventure. In 1972 that's all Tony and Maureen Wheeler needed for the trip of a lifetime – across Europe and Asia overland to Australia. It took several months, and at the end – broke but inspired – they sat at their kitchen table writing and stapling together their first travel guide, *Across Asia on the Cheap*. Within a week they'd sold 1500 copies. Lonely Planet was born.

Today, Lonely Planet has offices in Melbourne, London and Oakland, with more than 600 staff and writers. We share Tony's belief that 'a great guidebook should do three things: inform, educate and amuse'.

Our Writers

NICOLA WILLIAMS

Coordinating Author, Paris & Around Author, travel writer and editorial consultant, Nicola Williams has lived in France and written about it for more than a decade. From her hillside house on the southern shore of Lake Geneva, it's a quick and easy hop to the French Alps (call her a ski fiend...), Paris (art buff...), southern France (foodie...). She has worked on numerous titles for Lonely Planet, including *Food Lovers Guide to the World*, *France*, *Paris*, *Provence & the Côte d'Azur* and *The Loire*. She blogs at tripalong.wordpress.com, tweets @Tripalong.

Read more about Nicola at:
lonelyplanet.com/members/nicolawilliams

OLIVER BERRY

Loire Valley & Central France, Bordeaux & French Basque Country Oliver's French love affair began at the age of two, and he's since travelled right across L'Hexagone while contributing to several editions of Lonely Planet's *France* guide, amongst other books. Research highlights for this edition included hunting for truffles in the Dordogne, canoeing in the Gorges du Tarn and hiking to the Cirque de Gavarnie in the Pyrenees. He lives and works in Cornwall as a writer and photographer. You can see his latest work at www.oliverberry.com.

Read more about Oliver at:
lonelyplanet.com/members/oliverberry

STUART BUTLER

Brittany, Bordeaux & French Basque Country Stuart's first encounters with southwest France came on family holidays. When he was older he spent every summer surfing off the beaches of the southwest until one day he found himself so hooked on the region that he was unable to leave – he has been there ever since. When not writing for Lonely Planet he hunts for uncharted surf on remote coastlines. The results of these trips appear frequently in the world's surf media. His website is www.stuartbutlerjournalist.com.

Read more about Stuart at:
lonelyplanet.com/members/stuartbutler

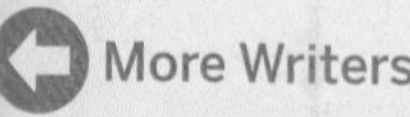

More Writers

Published by Lonely Planet Publications Pty Ltd
ABN 36 005 607 983
3rd edition – May 2013
ISBN 978 1 74220 564 9

10 9 8 7 6 5 4 3 2 1
Printed in China